THE INTERNATIONAL SURVEY OF FAMILY LAW

2001 EDITION

PUBLISHED ON BEHALF OF
THE INTERNATIONAL SOCIETY OF FAMILY LAW

THE INTERNATIONAL SURVEY OF FAMILY LAW

2001 EDITION

General Editor

Andrew Bainham

Fellow of Christ's College, Cambridge
Lecturer in Law, University of Cambridge, UK

Associate Editor (Africa)
Bart Rwezaura
Associate Professor of Law
University of Hong Kong
Hong Kong

Associate Editor (Asia)
Savitri Goonesekere
Vice-Chancellor
University of Colombo
Sri Lanka

Family Law

Published by Family Law
a publishing imprint of
Jordan Publishing Limited
21 St Thomas Street
Bristol
BS1 6JS

British Library Cataloguing-in-Publication Data

A catalogue record for this book is available from the British Library.

ISBN 0 85308 704 0

This volume is produced in-house by Jordans.
Printed in Great Britain by MPG Books Ltd, Bodmin, Cornwall

THE INTERNATIONAL SURVEY OF FAMILY LAW

PUBLISHED ON BEHALF OF
THE INTERNATIONAL SOCIETY OF FAMILY LAW

PRESIDENT
Professor Lynn D Wardle
School of Law, 518 JRCB
Brigham Young University
Provo, UT 84602
USA
Tel: +1(801) 378-2617
Fax: +1(801) 378-5893
e-mail: Wardlel@lawgate.byu.edu

SECRETARY-GENERAL
Professor Gillian Douglas
Cardiff Law School
PO Box 427
Cardiff CF10 3XJ
Wales, UK
Tel: +44 (0)29 2087 4704
Fax: +44 (0)29 2087 4097
e-mail: DouglasG@cardiff.ac.uk

TREASURER
Professor Paul Vlaardingerbroek
Tilburg University
Postbus 90153
5000 LE Tilburg
The Netherlands
Tel: +31-13-466 2032/466 2281
Fax: +31-13-466 2323
e-mail: P.Vlaardingerbroek@kub.nl

EDITOR OF THE INTERNATIONAL
SURVEY
Dr Andrew Bainham
Christ's College
Cambridge University
Cambridge CB2 3BU
England
Tel: +44 (0)1223 33 4978
Fax: +44 (0)1223 33 4967
e-mail: ab10030@cam.ac.uk

IMMEDIATE PAST PRESIDENT: Professor Petar Sarcevic, Croatia

VICE PRESIDENTS

Professor Michael Freeman, UK
Professor Peter Lodrup, Norway
Professor Bea Verschraegen, Austria/Germany

Professor Olivier Guillod, Switzerland
Professor Nigel Lowe, UK

EXECUTIVE COUNCIL 2000–2002

Margaret Brinig (USA), Ruth Deech (UK), John Dewar (Australia), William Duncan (Ireland and the Netherlands), Olga Dyuzheva (Russia), John Eekelaar (UK), Rainer Frank (Germany), Marsha Garrison (USA), Dominique Goubau (Canada), Maarit Jantera-Jareborg (Sweden), Sanford Katz (USA), Miroslava Gec-Korosec (Slovenia), Eduardo de Oliviera Leite (Brazil), Miguel Martin Casals (Spain), Marygold Melli (USA), Marie-Thérèse Meulders (Belgium), Thandabantu Nhlapo (South Africa), Linda Nielsen (Denmark), Koji Ono (Japan), Maria Donata Panforti (Italy), Stephen Parker (Australia), Patrick Parkinson (Australia), Bart Rwezaura (Hong Kong and China), Jacqueline Rubellin-Devichi (France), June Sinclair (South Africa), Barbara Bennett Woodhouse (USA)

Bank Account: Postbank, Amsterdam, The Netherlands 63.18.019

A   THE HISTORY OF THE SOCIETY

On the initiative of Professor Zeev Falk, the Society was launched at the University of Birmingham, UK in April 1973. The Society's first international conference was held in West Berlin in April 1975 on the theme *The Child and the Law*. There were over 200 participants, including representatives of governments and international organisations. The second international conference was held in Montreal in June 1977 on the subject *Violence in the Family*. There were over 300 participants from over 20 countries. A third world conference on the theme *Family Living in a Changing Society* was held in Uppsala, Sweden in June 1979. There were over 270 participants from 26 countries. The fourth world conference was held in June 1982 at Harvard Law School, USA. There were over 180 participants from 23 countries. The fifth world conference was held in July 1985 in Brussels, Belgium on the theme *The Family, The State and Individual Security*, under the patronage of Her Majesty Queen Fabiola of Belgium, the Director-General of UNESCO, the Secretary-General of the Council of Europe and the President of the Commission of the European Communities. The sixth world conference on *Issues of the Ageing in Modern Society* was held in 1988 in Tokyo, Japan, under the patronage of H.I.H. Takahito Mikasa. There were over 450 participants. The seventh world conference was held in May 1991 in Croatia on the theme, *Parenthood: The Legal Significance of Motherhood and Fatherhood in a Changing Society*. There were 187 participants from 37 countries. The eighth world conference took place in Cardiff, Wales in June/July 1994 on the theme *Families Across Frontiers*. The ninth world conference of the Society was held in July 1997 in Durban, South Africa on the theme *Changing Family Forms: World Themes and African Issues*. The Society's tenth world conference was held in July 2000 in Queensland, Australia on the theme *Family Law: Processes, Practices and Pressures*. The Society has also increasingly held regional conferences including those in Lyon, France (1995); Quebec City, Canada (1996); Seoul, South Korea (1996); Prague, Czech Republic (1998); Albuquerque, New Mexico, USA (June 1999); and Oxford, UK (August 1999). A North American regional conference will take place in Kingston, Ontario in June 2001.

B   ITS NATURE AND OBJECTIVES

The following principles were adopted at the first Annual General Meeting of the Society held in the Kongresshalle of West Berlin on the afternoon of Saturday 12 April 1975.

(1)   The Society's objectives are the study and discussion of problems of family law. To this end the Society sponsors and promotes:

   (a)   International co-operation in research on family law subjects of world-wide interest.

   (b)   Periodic international conferences on family law subjects of world-wide interest.

   (c)   Collection and dissemination of information in the field of family law by the publication of a survey concerning developments in family law throughout the world, and by publication of relevant materials in family law, including papers presented at conferences of the Society.

(d) Co-operation with other international, regional or national associations having the same or similar objectives.

(e) Interdisciplinary contact and research.

(f) The advancement of legal education in family law by all practical means including furtherance of exchanges of teachers, students, judges and practising lawyers.

(g) Other objectives in furtherance of or connected with the above objectives.

C   MEMBERSHIP AND DUES

In 2000 the Society had approximately 550 members in some 60 countries.

(a) Membership:

- Ordinary Membership, which is open to any member of the legal or a related profession. The Council may defer or decline any application for membership.
- Institutional Membership, which is open to interested organisations at the discretion of, and on terms approved by, the Council.
- Student Membership, which is open to interested students of law and related disciplines at the discretion of, and on terms approved by, the Council.
- Honorary Membership, which may be offered to distinguished persons by decision of the Executive Council.

(b) Each member shall pay such annual dues as may be established from time to time by the Council. At present, dues for ordinary membership are *Hfl.* 180 (or equivalent) for three years or *Hfl.* 75 (or equivalent) for one year, plus *Hfl.* 15 (or equivalent) if cheque is in another currency.

D   DIRECTORY OF MEMBERS

A Directory of Members of the Society is available to all members.

E   BOOKS

The proceedings of the first world conference were published as *The Child and the Law* (F. Bates, ed, Oceana, 1976); the proceedings of the second as *Family Violence* (J. Eekelaar and S. Katz, eds, Butterworths, Canada, 1978); the proceedings of the third as *Marriage and Cohabitation* (J. Eekelaar and S. Katz, eds, Butterworths, Canada, 1980); the fourth, *The Resolution of Family Conflict* (J. Eekelaar and S. Katz, eds, Butterworths, Canada, 1984); the fifth, *Family, State and Individual Economic Security (Vols I & II)* (M.T. Meulders-Klein and J. Eekelaar, eds, Story Scientia and Kluwer, 1988); the sixth, *An Ageing World: Dilemmas and Challenges for Law and Social Policy* (J. Eekelaar and D. Pearl, eds, Clarendon Press, 1989); the seventh *Parenthood in Modern Society*

(J. Eekelaar and P. Sarcevic, eds., Martinus Nijhoff, 1993); the eighth *Families Across Frontiers* (N. Lowe and G. Douglas, eds, Martinus Nijhoff, 1996) and the ninth *The Changing Family: Family Forms and Family Law* (J. Eekelaar and T. Nhlapo, eds, Hart Publishing, 1998). These are commercially marketed but are available to Society members at reduced prices.

F   THE SOCIETY'S PUBLICATIONS

The Society regularly publishes a newsletter, *The Family Letter*, which appears twice a year and which is circulated to the members of the Society and reports on its activities and other matters of interest. *The International Survey of Family Law* provides information on current developments in family law throughout the world and is received free of charge by members of the Society. The editor is currently Andrew Bainham, Christ's College, Cambridge, CB2 3BU, UK. The Survey is circulated to members or may be obtained on application to the Editor.

PREFACE

The International Survey of Family Law (2001 Edition) contains contributions from some 30 jurisdictions across the world. It is particularly pleasing that four of these – Costa Rica, Estonia, Jordan and Kenya – are appearing in the *Survey* for the first time. It is also worthy of note that the contribution from Costa Rica is the first which has ever been received from any of the countries of Central America which has hitherto perhaps been the single most difficult region of the world to cover.

This *Survey* follows the tenth world conference of the International Society of Family Law in Brisbane, Australia. At its meeting in Brisbane the newly constituted Executive Council of the Society approved the appointment of associate editors to assist with the commissioning and securing of articles. I am delighted that Bart Rwezaura, now of the University of Hong Kong and formerly of Tanzania, has agreed to become an Associate Editor to assist me particularly in obtaining articles from Africa, and that Savitri Goonesekere has agreed to perform a similar role in relation to Asia. I would like to welcome them both to the team and I hope that in due course it will also be possible to appoint an Associate Editor for the Americas.

Once again I have received the invaluable assistance of Peter Schofield with translation of the Spanish texts and of Carol Dowling with production of the manuscript. As always I am very grateful to both of them and, as usual, I would like to thank all those who have contributed to this volume.

ANDREW BAINHAM
Christ's College, Cambridge
May 2001

INTERNATIONAL SOCIETY OF FAMILY LAW
SUBSCRIPTION FORM

☐ I prefer to communicate in ☐ English ☐ French

☐ Please charge my credit card ☐ **MASTERCARD or EUROCARD** ☐ VISA

  ☐ for 3 years (NGL 180)

  ☐ for 1 year (NGL 75)

Name of Card Holder: _____

Card no. | | | | | | | | | | | | | | | | | | | | | | |

Expiry date: ——— / ———

Address of Card Holder: _____

           _____

           _____

           _____

☐ I pay *NGL 180*[1] (three years) or *NGL 75* (one year), plus *NGL 15* if cheque is in another currency, by *postgiro* to **63.18.019** from

   The International Society of Family Law,
   Den Hooiberg 17
   4891 NM Rijsbergen
   The Netherlands

 (We have a bank account at the Postbank, Amsterdam, The Netherlands.)

☐ Payment enclosed *by cheque* to the amount of *NGL 195* (three years) or *NGL 90* (one year)

Date: _____ Signature: _____

☐ *New member, or*

☐ *(Change of) name/address:* _____

           _____

       Tel: _____

       Fax: _____

       e-mail:

Comments: _____

_____

_____

To be sent to the treasurer of the ISFL:
Prof. Paul Vlaardingerbroek
International Society of Family Law
Den Hooiberg 17
4891 NM Rijsbergen
THE NETHERLANDS (or by fax: +31-13-466 2323;
e-mail address P.Vlaardingerbroek@kub.nl)

---

[1] Or its countervalue in US Dollars (in March 2000: 87 US$).

ASSOCIATION INTERNATIONALE DE DROIT DE LA FAMILLE
FORMULAIRE DE COTISATION

☐ Pour la communication avec ISFL je préfère la langue ☐ française ☐ anglaise

☐ Je vous prie de charger ma carte de crédit: ☐ **MASTERCARD/EUROCARD** ☐ VISA

☐ pour 3 ans

☐ pour 1 an

Le nom du possesseur de la carte de crédit: _____

Card no. | | | | | | | | | | | | | | | | | | | |

Date d'expiration: _____ / _____

L'adresse du possesseur de la carte de crédit: _____

_____

_____

_____

☐ Je payerai *Hfl. 180,-*[1] (trois ans) ou: ☐ *Hfl. 75,-* (un an), plus *Hfl. 15,-* surcharge si paiement est en autre cours, *par postgiro* à ***63.18.019***

(du)
The International Society of Family Law
Den Hooiberg 17
4891 NM Rijsbergen
The Netherlands
(Nous avons un crédit au Postbank, Amsterdam, les Pays-Bas)

☐ Paiement est inclus avec un chèque de ☐ *Hfl. 180,-* (trois ans) ou *Hfl. 75,-* (un an), plus *Hfl. 15,-* surcharge si paiement est en autre cours.

La date: _____ Souscription: _____

☐ *Nouveau membre, ou*

☐ *(Changement de) nom/adresse:* _____

_____

Tel: _____

Fax: _____

e-mail: _____

Remarques: _____

_____

_____

Veuillez envoyer ce formulaire au trésorier de l'Association:
Prof. Paul Vlaardingerbroek
International Society of Family Law
Den Hooiberg 17
4891 NM Rijsbergen
LES PAYS BAS (ou par fax: +31-13-466 2323; e-mail address P.Vlaardingerbroek@kub.nl)

---

[1] Ou la contrevaleur en francs français ou US dollars.

CONTENTS

CONTRIBUTORS

International   *Geraldine Van Bueren* and *Randini Wanduragala*
Queen Mary College
University of London
Faculty of Law
Mile End Road
London E1 4NS
England

Argentina   *Cecilia P. Grosman* and *Delia B. Iñigo*
C/o Corrientes 1515
PISO 60 'B'
1042 Buenos Aires
Argentina

Australia   *Frank Bates*
Faculty of Law
The University of Newcastle
University Drive
Callaghan
Newcastle 2308
Australia

Austria   *Bea Verschraegen*
Institute of Comparative Law
University of Vienna
Schottenbastei 10-16
A-1010 Wien
Austria

Canada   *Nicholas Bala*
Faculty of Law
Queen's University
Kingston
Canada

Costa Rica   *Sergio Alonso de Valverde y Alpizar*
Apartado 4814
Zona Postal 1000
San José
Costa Rica

England and Wales *Gillian Douglas*
Cardiff Law School
PO Box 427
Law Building
Museum Avenue
Cardiff CF1 1XD
Wales

Estonia *Kai Kullerkupp*
Pepleri 12-28
51003 Tartu
Estonia

Germany *Rainer Frank*
Direcktor des Institut für Ausländisches und Internationales
    Privatrecht – Abt. II
Europlatz I
D-7800 Freiburg 1
Germany

India *Anil Malhotra* and *Ranjit Malhotra*
Malhotra & Malhotra
Bungalow 584
Sector 16-D
Chandigarh 160015
India

Republic of Ireland *Paul Ward*
University College Dublin
Faculty of Law
Roebuck Castle
Belfield
Dublin 4
Republic of Ireland

Israel *Rhona Schuz*
Faculty of Law
Bar-Ilan University
Ramat-Gan
Israel 52900

Italy *Elena Urso*
Dipartmento di Diritto Comparato
Facoltà di Giurisprudenza
Università degli studi di Firenzi
Via Benedetto Vardi 2
50132 Firenze
Italy

Jamaica

Eileen Boxill
21 Ravinia Mews
Kingston 6
Jamaica

Japan

Kazuhiko Niijima
Cardiff Law School
PO Box 427
Law Building
Museum Avenue
Cardiff CF1 1XD
Wales

Jordan

Lynn Welchman
School of Oriental and African Studies
Department of Law
Thornaugh Street
Russell Square
London WC1H 0XG
England

Kenya

Michael Nyongesa Wabwile
1st Floor Wareng House
Ronald Ngala Street
PO Box 6928
Eldoret
Kenya

Malta

Ruth Farrugia
Faculty of Law
University of Malta
Valletta
Malta

The Netherlands

Caroline Forder
Rijksuniversiteit Limburg
Faculteit der Rechtsgeleerdheid
Vakgroep Privaatrecht
Postbus 616
Maastricht 6200 md
The Netherlands

New Zealand

Bill Atkin
Reader in Law
Faculty of Law
Victoria University
PO Box 600
Wellington
New Zealand

Northern Ireland   *Lisa Glennon*
                    The Queen's University of Belfast
                    Faculty of Law
                    Belfast BT7 1NN
                    Northern Ireland

Scotland   *Elaine E. Sutherland*
                    School of Law
                    University of Glasgow
                    Stair Building
                    Glasgow G12 8QQ

Slovenia   *Miroslava Geč-Korošec* and *Suzana Kraljić*
                    Institute for Civil, Comparative and Private International
                       Law
                    Law School
                    University of Maribor
                    Mladinska ul. 9
                    SLO 2000 Maribor
                    Slovenia

Spain   *Gabrial Garcia Cantero*
                    Catedratico de Derecho Civil
                    Facultad de Derecho
                    Pedro Cerbuna 12
                    50009 Zaragoza
                    Spain

Sweden   *Åke Saldeen*
                    Uppsala Universitet
                    Juridiska Institutionen
                    Box 512
                    Uppsala 75120
                    Sweden

Tanzania   *Bart Rwezaura*
                    The University of Hong Kong
                    Department of Law
                    Pokfulam Road
                    Hong Kong

The United States   *Marsha Garrison*
                    Brooklyn Law School
                    250 Joralemon Street
                    Brooklyn
                    New York 11201
                    United States of America

Yugoslavia

Gordana Kovacek Stanic
Faculty of Law
University of Novi Sad
Trg Dositeya Obradovicá 1
2100 Novi Sad
Serbia
Yugoslavia

Zambia

Chuma Himonga
University of Cape Town
Faculty of Law
Dept of Private Law
Private Bag
Rondebosch 7700
Cape Town

Zimbabwe

Fareda Banda
School of Oriental and African Studies
Department of Law
Thornaugh Street
Russell Square
London WC1H 0XG
England

ANNUAL REVIEW OF INTERNATIONAL FAMILY LAW

Geraldine Van Bueren * and *Randini Wanduragala* **

I GLOBAL TRENDS

This section looks at international developments and trends that have had an impact on family life. In particular it will focus on where responsibilities lie when the family unit breaks down and the role of women in the family. The UN General Assembly Special Session: Women 2000 (the Beijing Plus 5 Annual Summit for Women), looked at the critical role being played by women in the family unit. It acknowledged that the structure of the family did not always provide adequate support or protection for women and that this undermined efforts to achieve gender equality. The last year also saw the introduction of the Optional Protocol to the UN Convention on the Elimination of All Forms of Discrimination against Women[1] (CEDAW) which greatly strengthened the scope of the Convention.

II A FAMILY OF PROTOCOLS

On 16 May 2000 the General Assembly adopted two additional optional Protocols to the Convention on the Rights of the Child on, respectively, the involvement of children in armed conflict, and the sale of children, child prostitution and child pornography.[2]

The armed conflict Protocol raises to 18 the minimum age for compulsory recruitment of children and of children taking a direct part in hostilities.[3] Voluntary recruitment of those under 18 is permitted under specific conditions, including with the consent of the parents and the legal guardians. This is distinguished from 'armed groups' who are not permitted under any circumstances to recruit or use in hostilities those under 18. The standard set by the African Charter on the Rights and Welfare of the Child, to which South Africa is party, is higher, prohibiting all direct child participation and recruitment.[4]

The Optional Protocol on the sale and exploitation of children covers the same ground as Articles 32 to 36 of the Convention on the Rights of the Child prohibiting the sale of children, child prostitution and child pornography, but it does make significant improvements in the enforcement of law and in creating child-centred

---

* Professor of International Human Rights Law and Director of the Programme on International Rights of the Child, University of London, Queen Mary College.

** Child Rights Officer at World Vision UK and a Research Associate of the Programme on International Rights of the Child, University of London, Queen Mary College. The comment and observations made in this article are those of the author and do not in any way reflect the policy of World Vision UK.

1 E/CN.6/1999/WG/L.2.
2 UN Doc A/54/L.84.
3 Articles 1 and 2.
4 Article 22(2) of the African Charter on the Rights and Welfare of the Child 1990.

proceedings. The Protocol usefully clarifies that it may be necessary for a State to exercise extraterritorial jurisdiction – thus taking the issue of universal jurisdiction for such violations out of the backwoods realm of State sovereignty.[5] Offences concerning the sale of children, child prostitution and child pornography are deemed extraditable. Where a request for extradition is received from a State which has no extradition treaty, the requested State may usefully consider the Protocol as the legal basis for such extradition.[6]

The Protocol is particularly valuable in its focusing of government responsibilities on the creation of child-friendly proceedings. Article 8 seeks to protect the rights of child victims and witnesses without prejudicing the rights of the accused to a fair trial. States should inform child victims of their rights, role and scope, timing and progress of the proceedings and provide 'appropriate support services to child victims', including the protection of the children's privacy. Uncertainty as to the actual age of the victim should not prevent the initiation of criminal investigation.

Despite the positive aspects of these two Protocols, they raise serious issues about the expenditure of resources (time, money and personnel) so soon after the conclusion of the original treaty, in seeking to raise standards, when not only have many of the existing standards not yet been fully implemented but also the standards incorporated in the new instruments are not in places significantly higher. It would have been more effective had the opportunity also been taken to remedy the serious flaws in the implementation procedure, in particular the lack of a petitioning procedure for children to the UN Committee on the Rights of the Child.

In contrast, the UN Convention on the Elimination of All Forms of Discrimination Against Women does now have an Optional Protocol which creates a petitioning mechanism by which individuals or groups may petition in relation to a violation of their CEDAW rights. The Protocol was due to enter into force on 22 December 2000.

III   CRISES IN THE FAMILY UNIT AND THE ROLE OF THE STATE

When there is a break up of the family unit, the responsibility for the children of the family can often devolve on one or other member of the immediate or extended family. The response to such situations can include the State taking steps to regulate the position or itself stepping in and taking the place of the parents or guardians.

There is a great deal of case-law concerning the parameters of State power when taking on this role and the respect States must accord to the right to family life enshrined in various international human rights instruments.[7] In two recent cases before the European Court of Human Rights concerning Finland, the Court came to very different conclusions about the extent to which the State should preserve the right to family life when the family unit was in a state of crisis. In *K*

---

5   Article 4.

6   Article 5.

7   Articles 5, 9, 18 and 20 of the UN Convention on the Rights of the Child; Articles 17, 23 and 24 of the International Covenant on Civil and Political Rights.

& T v Finland,[8] the applicant mother, who suffered from schizophrenia, had two children by different fathers. She was hospitalised on several occasions. The children were placed in care as an interim measure due to allegations of behavioural problems. This was later confirmed as a final decision and K was denied access to the children. In the case of *L v Finland*,[9] the applicant father had two children who had been placed in interim care following suspected sexual abuse and, following further investigations, the care order was confirmed as final, with the applicant being denied further access to the children. In both cases the applicants alleged that the right to family life had been infringed. The Finnish government accepted the existence of the violations but alleged that the action taken by the State was in accordance with the law, pursuant to legitimate aims and necessary in a democratic society. The court affirmed in both cases that the mutual enjoyment by a parent and child of each other's company constituted a fundamental element of family life and any measures which hindered that amounted to a violation of the right to family life.

In *K & T v Finland*, the court concluded that whilst the domestic courts enjoyed a wide margin of appreciation when taking children into care, stricter scrutiny was called for when further restricting parental rights of access once the children were in care. Such limitations endangered family relations, especially between parents and young children. Whilst the mother did suffer from mental illness, she posed no threat to the children and consequently the State had acted in an arbitrary and unjust manner. In particular, when children were taken into care the overriding assumption was that any measures should be consistent with the aim of ultimate reunification with the natural parents. Balanced against this was the principle of the best interest of the child which the court affirmed may override that of the parents, particularly where harm to the health or development of the child was at stake. When balancing these competing rights, the court found that the serious absence of effort to consider termination of public care on the part of the State amounted to a violation of the right to family life.

This need to balance competing interests led to a different conclusion in *L v Finland* where the court did not find any violations of the right to family life because the primary consideration when considering termination of access was whether the development of the child was being hindered. Therefore, the refusal to terminate care did not amount to a violation. Crucially, the court noted that in this case the parents had separated and 'did not constitute a family any more'.

The State response to children facing family crisis situations can vary greatly. In some countries, the State plays little or no part in the lives of children experiencing exclusion and abandonment when the family unit breaks down. For example, the phenomenon of street children has been linked by some commentators not to poverty but to problems within the family structure and the existence of family violence.[10] The existence of street children in many parts of the world points to a situation where State responsibility is either minimal or non-existent. In extreme cases, the State not only fails to step into the shoes of parents

---

8   ECHR Application No 25702/94.

9   ECHR Application No 25651/94 27 April 2000.

10 D Ordonez Bustamente, *Family Structure Problems, Child Mistreatment, Street Children and Drug Use: A Community-Based Approach*, IPEC (Unpublished Material).

but can collude in, or be active perpetrators of, violence against children who have abandoned the family unit for various reasons. Children can be tortured or killed by agents of the State.

The decision of the Inter-American court in the case of *Villagren-Morales v Guatemala*,[11] provides an important benchmark as to the extent of State responsibility when children are abandoned or out of their family unit. The case, brought under the American Convention on Human Rights, concerned four street children in Guatemala who had been apprehended and beaten by armed men. Some days later their bodies were found tortured and mutilated. One week later a fifth street child was detained and found shot dead. In terms of specific violations, the court determined that the right to life imposed not only a negative duty but also a positive duty on the State, particularly in relation to children who did not have the protection of their families.

The court ruled that children are entitled to special measures of protection not just by virtue of being children but also where they are susceptible to special vulnerabilities – as when they are outside their family environment. Whilst the court determined that the primary protector of children's rights was the family, it also ruled that State measures were necessary in the case of children at risk, which is not dissimilar to the stance taken by the European Court of Human Rights in the Finnish cases. These obligations encompassed a wide range of social, economic, civil and political measures and, by applying or tolerating a system of violence against children who were outside their natural family environment, the State was in fact conducting a 'double aggression' against children in crisis. First, the State's failure to prevent children from living in misery deprived them of the minimum conditions necessary for a dignified, full and harmonious life.[12] Secondly, by being the actual perpetrators of violence, the state violated the physical, mental and moral integrity of the lives of the children. The court also concluded that in determining whether or not cruel, inhuman or degrading treatment had taken place, the violations extended not only to the immediate victims but also to their families. Thus, factors like the lack of State action in pursuing the prosecution of the offenders, the failure to identify the victims, the lack of adequate efforts to locate the next of kin and the lack of opportunity for the families to bury their children all led to pain and suffering for the family which amounted to cruel, inhuman and degrading treatment.[13]

A significant development in this case was the use by the court of a series of international instruments for the purposes of interpretation. The court determined that in interpreting the American Convention on Human Rights, in so far as it related to the protection of children, it was entitled to look at and consider other human rights instruments that the State had ratified. In particular it determined that the Convention on the Rights of the Child formed a '*corpus juris*' for the

---

11   Int. Am. Ct. H.R. (Judgment of 19 November 1999).

12   The court stated that 'every child has the right to harbour a project of life that should be tended and encouraged by the public authorities so that (he or she) may develop this for (their) personal benefit and that of the society to which (they) belong'.

13   See also *William Llaurente & Others v Peru*, Inter American Commission Inl. Report No 54/99, Inter-Am. ChR, OEA/Ser, L/V/II 95 Doc 7 rev at 917 (1998) referred to in *Villagren Morales v Guatemala*.

protection of children in Guatemala where the State had signed and ratified the treaty.

The Federal Court of Australia adopted a somewhat different approach in the 'Stolen Generation' cases. In the case of *Cubillo v Commonwealth of Australia*,[14] the State had been an active participant in breaking up the family unit. The applicants were members of the 'Stolen Generation' of part-Aboriginal Australians who were taken as children from their families and placed in missions or institutions. The Federal Court noted that the actions did result in the destruction of association with their aboriginal families and their culture and that this may well have been a regrettable consequence of the policy. Nevertheless the case was dismissed as these actions were thought 'at the time' to have been in the best interests of the children. By making a clear distinction as to what principles constituted the best of interests of children and the time frame for the application of those principles, this decision is likely to have implications for adults who were taken into care as children and who are now seeking redress against the State for the treatment they experienced as children.

At an international level, courts are beginning to take a robust view as to the responsibilities of States when family units break down and the *Villagren-Morales* case in particular has enormous implications for street children throughout the world.

IV WOMEN AND THE FAMILY

The Beijing Plus 5 Annual Summit for Women provided an opportunity for States to appraise critically the progress that had been made in addressing discrimination against women. The family is often considered to be the arena in which women and girls suffer the greatest discrimination and these attitudes go on to be reflected in the wider societal framework.[15] The report on recent trends for women compiled by the United Nations[16] gives some indications of women in the context of family life. Women, both in the developed world and in developing countries, are generally marrying later. The timing of marriage is changing and the composition of families continues to be diverse. Informal unions are common in most countries although the benefits of legal protection have not always been extended to women entering these unions. Birth rates have declined in all regions of the world as women are having fewer children, but there is a large pool of women of reproductive age, which leads to a continued growth in population.

More women are in the labour force and in many countries more than half of mothers with children under three are employed – although obstacles persist in combining family responsibilities with employment. Women still have to reconcile employment with family responsibilities, which often dictate the type of work they do. This tends to be in the informal sector, in household economic activities or as unpaid workers in family businesses. It translates into lower wages

---

14 2000 FCA 1084 (11 August 2000).

15 R Cook (ed), *Human Rights of Women, National and International Perspectives*, (1994) University of Pennsylvania Press.

16 *The World's Women 2000: Statistics and Trends*, United Nations Statistics Division 2000.

for women. The report makes an interesting link between the level of wages and the context of family life. It suggests that earnings differentials between men and women are influenced by the division of labour within the family, with women continuing to spend substantially more time on unpaid work like cleaning and caring for the family. The presence of small children is likely to require women to allocate more time to unpaid work.

Overall, life expectancy has increased for women globally except in parts of Africa. There it has decreased dramatically as a result of HIV/AIDS with women now accounting for almost half of all cases of HIV/AIDS. In the context of family units, more people are living alone in the developed regions – the majority of whom are women. Added to this is the factor that the ageing population is expected to grow, with many more older women than men. Although women outnumber men in most regions of the world, alarmingly men outnumber women in parts of Asia.

Following on from Beijing Plus 5, the UN General Assembly adopted the final summit report 'Women 2000: gender equality, development and peace for the twenty-first century' which concluded that women play a critical role in family life. However, inadequate support for women, both within and outside the family context, and insufficient protection to their families affected and undermined efforts to achieve gender equality. In particular, the issue of violence against women and girls in the family context and other issues such as marital rape and honour killings of women were given prominence. The report focused on the need for promoting an environment that does not tolerate violence. The need to make changes in legislation that removed discriminatory provisions by 2005 and to eliminate legislative gaps that leave women and girls without effective legal protection was seen as critical. The need to recognise and address gender-related persecution, in the international context of granting refugee status and asylum, was also seen as a critical factor.

Women's social and economic contribution to the welfare of the family was considered to be inadequately addressed, as was the social significance of maternity and paternity. It was noted that women continue to bear a disproportionate share of household responsibilities and the care of the sick, children and the elderly. Such imbalances need to be addressed through appropriate policies and programmes – in particular those geared towards education and through legislation.

Addressing the above issues and holding States more accountable for their actions or lack of progress have been strengthened immeasurably under international human rights law. The Convention on the Elimination of Discrimination Against Women (CEDAW) has been ratified by all but 26 countries, which makes it the second most widely ratified human rights treaty. The introduction of the Optional Protocol has brought it into line with other human rights treaties which have a mechanism for individual complaints, and both individuals or groups of individuals are empowered to seek redress for violations of the Convention by States. This is likely to prove a significant development in holding States accountable on issues affecting women in the context of families and in turning rhetoric into reality.

ARGENTINA

NON-PAYMENT OF A MAINTENANCE OBLIGATION: NEW RULES, JUDICIAL DECISIONS AND INITIATIVES IN ARGENTINA

*Cecilia Grosman** and Delia B. Iñigo***

I   INTRODUCTION

Failure to pay maintenance for children after divorce or separation represents a serious problem in Argentina. When a parent does not accept responsibility for support, the mother – as the parent usually looking after the children – has to meet the cost of the children's upkeep, alone or with the help of her family. If, by dint of much effort, some mothers do manage this, usually the mother is not in a position to provide for the children, whose fundamental rights to health, housing, education and recreation are adversely affected. This reduces to the level of an empty legal promise, practically devoid of effect, the joint responsibility for the children's upbringing and education, recognised in international treaties to which Argentina attributes constitutional status.[1] Consequently, the irresponsibility of fathers creates a situation of inequality detrimental to the interests of mothers and children alike, exposing them to a double abandonment. Deprived of what is necessary to ensure their development, they also lose the personal care of their mother, who is forced to work long hours outside the home to earn a living.

The causes of this failure to keep up payments are many. Fathers often unload onto the children their animosity towards a former partner. Often they are unwilling to pay, thinking that the woman may waste or misuse the money. Others manipulate money as a means of wielding power or as an expression of their immaturity or selfishness. Equally, it is sometimes the woman who rejects relations between the children and their father, who is reduced to a mere economic provider. To sum up, in such situations, the treatment of children or provision for their support plays out the relationship between their parents, converting children into objects through which each parent expresses his or her feelings of bitterness, contempt or apathy towards the other.

However, there are other parents who, through low income, unemployment or the undertaking of new family relationships, simply cannot meet these obligations.

---

*   Titular Consultant Professor of Family Law and Succession, Faculty of Law, University of Buenos Aires.

**   Professor of Family Law in the Faculty of Legal and Social Sciences of the Universidad Nacional del Litoral.

     Translated by Peter Schofield.

1   Convention on the Elimination of all Discrimination against Women, Articles 5b and 16d, and Convention on the Rights of the Child, Article 18.

This combination of circumstances necessarily calls for an adequate holistic family policy which can tackle the causes of non-performance: actions at a social level allowing families to give their children the support they need. It is worthy of note that Argentina undertook to guarantee the basic minimum wage necessary for parents to enable them to rear their children, in adopting the Convention on the Rights of the Child.[2]

II   LEGAL SOLUTIONS

A variety of legislative measures have been adopted to speed up proceedings and to apply a degree of pressure to encourage voluntary payment of support.

(1)   Mediation

In the area of the City of Buenos Aires, requests for fixing the quantum of maintenance, and for its increase or reduction, must be submitted to mediation as a necessary preliminary step in the judicial process, under Law No 24.573. This does not delay justice, since the hearing is held within a very brief period after the petition; if one party refuses to co-operate, the other receives a certificate enabling him or her to go ahead with the judicial process. This is similar to the interpretation adopted by the European Court of Human Rights under Article 6.1 of the European Convention on the Protection of Human Rights and Fundamental Freedoms 1950.

Mediation produces a favourable environment for clarifying the real underlying basis of the maintenance debtor's failure to pay and, since it is a very flexible procedure, it allows alternative arrangements to be sought to ensure that economic support is forthcoming. Similarly, the involvement of the parties in resolving their conflict themselves makes it more likely that they will comply with the result, in contrast to the situation where a solution is imposed by the judge, where the debtor often delays, or refuses outright to co-operate.

(2)   *Registro de Deudores Morosos*

Nonetheless, parents who are economically capable very often show no interest in their child's welfare and fail, wholly or in part, to discharge their support obligation. For such cases, there has been established, in the territory of the City of Buenos Aires, a Recalcitrant Maintenance Debtors Register.[3] The irresponsibility of certain parents, which defeated the normal measures available to the courts to ensure the payment of maintenance, was the driving force behind the introduction of this instrument. The creation of the Maintenance Debtors Register was the result of a serious social preoccupation, apparent in various initiatives presented in various legislative bodies in the country, and in numerous proposals discussed at scholarly conferences, with the aim of providing the means

---

2   Article 18.2.
3   *Registro de Deudores Morosos*, Law No 269.

of giving effect to responsibility for support, particularly as it falls on biological parents, in relation to their children, in cases of divorce and separation.

The principal function of the Maintenance Debtors Register is to single out the persons whose maintenance payments are in arrears;[4] the second is to issue the certificates required by the public institutions and organisations established by law. A judicial decision is needed for a person to be placed on the register or removed from it. It covers all maintenance debt, that owed to a spouse, relatives in line of ascent or descent, siblings and half siblings, and relatives by affinity within the first degree.[5] The law provides that a debtor should be placed on the register if three successive payments or five alternate payments are overdue. Under Article 4 of the law, public institutions and organisations of the City of Buenos Aires are not to open current accounts or issue credit cards to anyone on the Register, and a certificate is required before credit can be granted or renewed in such a bank.

As a condition of obtaining licences, concessions or authorisations which are subject to the government of Buenos Aires, it must be certified that the applicant is not listed in the Register.[6] In this way, for instance, a registered debtor cannot obtain a driving licence, a concession, or authorisation for commerce or industry. In relation to a driving licence, there is a possibility of granting one provisionally for up to 45 days if the vehicle is required for work. Under the law, in order to be registered as a supplier in the relevant part of the government of the city, the person concerned must provide a certificate that he has no maintenance debt. Likewise, in the case of a corporate body, all the directors must meet this requirement.[7]

No business, industry or site can be authorised to anyone who is included in the Register.[8] In a similar way, both transferor and transferee must produce a certificate when a change of ownership is to be registered. Where the existence of a maintenance debt appears, the transfer cannot be completed until the situation is regularised. This means that the transaction can go forward, but the matter is not finalised until the register is cleared.[9] In case of corporate persons, the certificate required must cover those principally responsible, whether for the initial authorisation of a business, industry or site, or for its transfer. We understand that when the law refers to those 'principally responsible' – this means the directors of the company, foundation or institution.

Persons aspiring to elected office in the city must not be on the register of maintenance debtors, which makes such a certificate an essential condition for candidature to be authorised.[10] A similar requirement applies to anyone wishing to act as a magistrate or official of the Judicial Power. If the existence of a maintenance debt is established, the person concerned cannot take part in the appropriate competition or be appointed to a post in the judicial sector until it is

---

4   Law No 69, Article 2.
5   Article 368 of the Civil Code.
6   Law No 69, Article 4.
7   Law No 269, Article 7.
8   Article 4 of Law No 269.
9   Article 8.
10   Article 9.

confirmed that the debt is cancelled.[11] Nor can a person be appointed to a senior public service position (*funcionario jerárquico*) if he is included in the Register. '*Jerárquico*' refers to anyone exercising managerial responsibility at any level.

The restrictions and incapacities contained in the law under reference are based on international undertakings and on the internal order taken on by the Argentine State in adopting the measures required to ensure payment of support obligations.[12] Some may say that public registration and the publicity given to the information on the Register, on the application of any natural or corporate person, is an encroachment on the right to privacy of the person registered. We believe that the legal data inscribed in the Register do not relate to the family life, the privacy of which a person is entitled to have protected. This is not a question of matters in respect of which a party is entitled to secrecy, because they affect family members, any more than secrecy can be claimed in relation to incidents of domestic violence. Family life is confidential, but this does not extend to favouring or promoting the violation of family obligations.

The setting up of the Register is an important step contributing to a change in social awareness and affirming the principle of responsible parenthood. Parental desertion shows that the support of children, the natural response of a parent living with them, is resented if there is no community of life between the parents. They become unable to reach agreement among themselves, and the responsibility for child support is unloaded onto the parent living with the child. Failure to pay maintenance is not seen as a legitimate response. The law is aimed at affirming the importance of the support obligation and the recognition that failure to perform it is a serious moral fault.

(3) Calculation of liability

Regarding children, ensuring that parents perform the support obligations that their status imposes on them is an undertaking that goes beyond the limit of strictly private law. The community at large has an interest in due performance. Consistent with Article 3.2 of the Convention on the Rights of the Child, the State has taken on the responsibility for ensuring children receive the protection and care necessary to their welfare. Hence the State has to take extreme measures to get parents to provide sufficient economic resources for the children to enjoy suitable living conditions.[13]

To achieve this aim, judges have insisted that the respondent to a maintenance claim should co-operate so that his true income may be determined as the basis on which to calculate the appropriate level of maintenance.[14] That is to say that, even if it is up to the applicant for maintenance, in principle, to prove her needs and the respondent's ability to meet them, in practice the burden of proving his inability to pay falls on the respondent. In a way it is presumed that he is in a position to pay maintenance unless he proves the contrary. Judicial decisions have always taken a narrow view of the justifications advanced by debtors seeking to avoid paying the

---

11   Article 10.
12   Article 27 of the Convention on the Rights of the Child.
13   Article 27.2 of the Convention.
14   *La Ley*,1998-C-802.

amount assessed, since it is considered that: 'It is an inescapable duty of the father to contribute in large measure to the support of his children, whatever efforts he may have to make so to do'.[15]

Inability to find work, usually put forward as a reason to avoid paying maintenance, has to be proved in certain form, so a mere general assertion is not enough. The aim is to discourage attitudes of lack of concern, of idleness, dissipation or vice, as well as dissimulation of the facts behind false appearances created deliberately by the debtor. The basic principle is that he who fathers children must exhaust all possibilities to find remunerative work to enable him properly to support them.[16] So it has been judicially held not to be a valid excuse 'to invoke the insufficiency of income, unless this is the consequence of impossibility or of difficulties that are, in practice insurmountable'.[17]

It is thus clearly established that anyone subject to an obligation of support is obliged to work. Only by pleading and proving specifically that it is impossible to find paid work can one be relieved of this duty.[18] This rule is so clearly laid down that a claim can be made only against other relatives subject to a support liability – those in line of ascent, siblings and half siblings[19] – once all means of enforcing a support claim against the two parents have been exhausted. Their obligation is treated as subsidiary.[20]

In Argentine practice, although legally the support obligation falls on both parents[21] even in cases of divorce, nullity or de facto separation, and regardless of the manner of affiliation (in or out of wedlock or adoptive), judges place the greater part of the economic burden on the parent who is not living with the child.

The usual argument cited by judges is that the parent living with the child is supporting the child by personal involvement in care and giving up time to his physical, mental and emotional development. As a result, 'The mother's contribution is always looked at in relation to her contribution in kind in the form of the children's upbringing to the extent that they are in her care'.[22] In line with this principle, the amount of maintenance to be paid has been reduced to recognise the time the child resides with the maintaining parent, setting off the contribution in the work of looking after the child and providing support and other necessaries.[23]

Having to meet new obligations arising out of a subsequent marriage is no obstacle to keeping the maintenance at the same level, since this does not inevitably mean a reduction in the living standard of the paying parent, bearing in

---

15 Cámara Nacional Civil, Sala A, 21 March 1997, M.S.R. y otros c/ T.L.A., *La Ley* 1998-B-916, Caso 12.463.

16 Juzgado de Primera Instancia de Menores No 1, de Córdoba, 22 February 1999, *La Ley* Córdoba, 1999-748.

17 Cámara Nacional Civil, Sala H, 13 August 1997, O.S.A. c/ M.G.W.L., *La Ley*, 1998-B-709.

18 Cámara Nacional Civil, Sala F, 16 September 1997, G.A.L.M. c/ A.F.L., *La Ley*, 1998-C-548.

19 Article 367 of the Civil Code.

20 Cámara Nacional Civil, Sala G, 24 September 1997, S.S. c/ D.N.A., *La Ley*, 1998-B-916, caso 12.463.

21 Article 271 of the Civil Code.

22 Cámara Nacional Civil, Sala A, 21 March 1997 MS.R. y otros c/ T.L.A., *La Ley*, 1998-B-916 caso 12.463.

23 Cámara Nacional Civil, Sala B, 24 April 1997, D.L.S. c/ P.R.A., *La Ley*, 1998-D-274.

mind that both partners contribute to the household.[24] Nor can discrimination be made between children of earlier and later marriages. It has been judicially held that the parent must see to it that the needs of all beneficiaries are met on an equal basis.[25]

III   MEASURES TO ENSURE COMPLIANCE

Taking account of the fact that fixing the amount of maintenance, by its nature, involves continuing support, judges have found it essential to ensure that payments based on the same cause will continue in future. With this aim, if when the amount to be paid is assessed, circumstances indicate that there are likely to be difficulties in the future, judges have looked favourably at requests for an embargo, or similar measures – even in the absence of any law obliging them to do so.[26]

Among other situations where precautionary measures are taken before non-payment begins are: when there have been other defaults in the past; where there is a risk that the debtor will dispose of assets; or where there has been abuse of process with the aim of delaying the judgment.[27] Another way in which future maintenance is guaranteed is to order that funds deposited with a bank are blocked for a specified cause – for instance to secure payment of compensation ordered against the depositor. This does not increase his burden, but merely anticipates a future payment and protects the creditor against the uncertainty as to whether funds will be available to meet the expenses of her support or that of their common issue. The court has held that 'This is not to be seen as a precautionary seizure (*medida cautelar*), but merely as a step which makes it more certain that the amount assessed will be received'.[28]

It has even been held that related lawsuits can be stayed as a means of overcoming a maintenance debtor's unjustified resistance, where this is detrimental to the rights of the creditor. Naturally, such a stay is a measure restrictively applied, so as not to infringe the party's fundamental rights under the constitution, such as the right to defend before the court.[29]

With the same objective, some authors call for the introduction of economic sanctions, described as '*astreintes*' (default fines) in face of unjustified non-performance or of undue delay in paying the maintenance. Perhaps the fear of suffering a loss of property may persuade the debtor to pay on time, where judicial constraint or social pressure are not enough. Usually, *astreintes* are fixed at a daily rate set by the judge at his discretion, in proportion to the amount of maintenance

---

24   Cámara Nacional Civil y Comercial, Sam Isidro, 8 September 1998M.J. S. c/ R.I.S /cessation of maintenance award, *El Derecho*, 182-20.

25   Juzgado de Familia No 1, Córdoba, 5 June 1998, Caso 41.813, *La Ley*, 1999-D-796.

26   Cámara Nacional Civil, Sala K, de la Capital Federal, 7 May 1997, *La Ley*, 1998-S-934, Caso 13.071.

27   Cámara Nacional Civil, Sala B, 2 April 1997, C.M.C. c/ F.G.R., *La Ley* 1998-D-934, Caso 13.073.

28   Cámara Civil y Comercial, Junin, Provincia de Buenos Aires, 2 October 1997, M.A.M c/ M.B., *La Ley Buenos Aires* 1997-1387.

29   Cámara Nacional Civil, Sala I, 19 June 1997, C.A. c/ M.B., *La Ley* 1998-D-934.

that has been ordered. The basis of this is the harm the creditor suffers through not being able to receive the correct amount on time so as to meet the unavoidable expenses of child support. Clearly, what the creditor needs is for the debt to be discharged on the due date, but this is at least some redress for the damage inflicted on the creditor.

IV INITIATIVES FOR REFORM

There are various legislative proposals in addition to the laws we have considered, aimed at giving greater effect to the support obligation. Among them are the following:

(a) A person who 'fails to comply with a court order (garnishee order) to retain the sum equivalent to what is due from his dependant or creditor under a maintenance order shall be jointly liable for the maintenance debt'.[30]

(b) The judge shall have the power of prohibiting a person who has been held liable to pay maintenance from leaving the country until he has given sufficient security for the future performance of his obligation.[31]

(c) Constitution of real and personal guarantees for the payment of provisional, definitive and agreed maintenance.[32]

(d) Any maintenance debtor who defaults on two successive or on four alternate payments, fixed by a firm judgment for provisional maintenance, or agreed maintenance sanctioned by a court, must take a course of not less than two months' duration on the father's obligations to children, and on the effect on children of deprivation of the necessary support. Failure to attend such a course, or continuing to default on payments having completed it, will give rise to one or more of the following sanctions at the discretion of the judge:

(1) refusal of a passport and prohibition on leaving the country;

(2) prohibition on authorisation of a business;

(3) prohibition on opening a bank current account, deposit account, savings account or on applying for a credit card;

(4) ban on applying for or renewing a driving licence;

(5) notifying the Professional Colleges or organisations to which the debtor belongs.[33]

(e) The Project for Reforming the Civil Code, drawn up by the commission set up under Decree 685/95, currently being debated in the National Congress, provides measures for the protection of the right to maintenance in articles 628 to 630. To ensure payment, the usual precautionary measures will be available (embargo, general prohibition on assets, etc). Faced with actual default of payment, the judge will be able to apply punitive sanctions, which will also be applicable to future defaults. If a person ordered to retain

---

30 Project for Reforms of the Civil Code of 1993, article 324.

31 Project for Reforms of the Civil Code of 1993, article 328.

32 Article 328 of above-mentioned Project.

33 Ponencia XVI Jornadas de Derecho Civil.

a sum equivalent to the maintenance obligation of his dependant or creditor fails to comply with the order, he will be jointly liable up to the limit of the retention ordered against him.

The measures thought up by the authors of the reform are calculated to persuade the maintenance debtor to pay up, faced with the threat of coercion to make him pay. However, it is certain that compulsion is not sufficient. What is vitally needed is to bring in a system of justice closer to the people, a legal aid service which guarantees effective access to justice, and an efficient procedure.

As we have already pointed out elsewhere, the right way to reinforce the maintenance obligation is to strengthen the principle that, divorced or separated, spouses remain jointly parents of their children, since it is above all the parent's regular contact and communication with his children that will induce him to try to fulfil his obligation.

AUSTRALIA

'THE GLAMOUR OF CHILDISH DAYS'[1]: AUSTRALIAN FAMILY LAW IN 1999

Frank Bates[*]

I   INTRODUCTION

A major change in law and policy was made to Australian family law by the insertion of a new Part VII into the Family Law Act 1975. Those novel provisions wholly reorganised and recreated the private law relating to children[2] but, with the very significant exception of the decision of the Full Court of the Family Court of Australia in *B and B: Family Law Reform Act 1995*,[3] these provisions had not attracted much in the way of curial comment. This may be a consequence of the much publicised delays[4] in the processes of the Family Court of Australia; however, in 1999, there were a number of very significant decisions at an appellate level involving children. Hence, it is only appropriate to begin this account of Australian family law in 1999 with a consideration of those cases. This, though, is not to say that other areas of activity have not been represented, especially in the field of evidence and procedure, even though those areas have also involved children.

II   CHILDREN

The landmark decision in *B*[5] was immediately concerned with the issue of the topographical relocation of parents with residence orders and its effect on contact parents. That matter came before the Full Court of the Family Court of Australia once again in *H v E*.[6] In that case, the mother of a four-year-old child appealed against a decision at first instance which had the effect of requiring her and the child to return from Brisbane to Melbourne so as to enable the child's father to have regular and frequent contact with the child. The facts were unusual in that,

---

1   DH Lawrence, *Piano* (1916) st 3.

*   LLM, Professor of Law, The University of Newcastle (NSW).

2   For comment on the new Part, see PE Nygh, 'The New Part VII – An Overview' (1996) 10 Aust J Fam L 4; R Chisholm, 'Assessing the Impact of the Family Law Reform Act 1995' (1996) 10 Aust J Fam L 177; RJ Bailey Harris, 'The Family Law Reform Act 1995 (Cth): A New Approach to the Parent/Child Relationship' (1996) 18 Adelaide LR 83.

3   (1997) FLC 92-755. For comment on this case, see F Bates, 'Something Old, Something New ...! Australian Family Law in 1997' in *The International Survey of Family Law 1997*, ed A Bainham (Martinus Nijhoff Publishers, 1999) at 23.

4   See L Star, *Counsel of Perfection: The Family Court of Australia* (1996) especially at 114–115.

5   Above, note 3.

6   (1999) FLC 92-845 at 85, 891.

apart from three weeks after the child's birth, the parties had never lived together. In 1996, the father sought defined contact and, in consequence, consent orders provided for regular contact and prohibited the mother from moving the child from the State of Victoria.

In 1996, the mother married one H and there was evidence that the mother regarded contact between the child and his father as a nuisance. H then applied for a transfer in his employment from Melbourne to Brisbane on the grounds that it was necessary to alleviate the child's asthmatic condition. It was unclear whether the mother was aware that H had initiated the transfer. Without informing the father, and in breach of court orders, H relocated the family to Brisbane. The child flew to Melbourne on alternate weekends for several months before the father discovered the reality of the situation. Thereafter, contact continued in monthly four-day blocks.

At first instance, the trial judge was critical of the mother for her deliberate breach of court orders and of H for applying for an employment transfer without notifying the father (and, possibly, the mother). It appeared that the various competing considerations requiring the child and his family, as opposed to permitting them, to remain in Brisbane were addressed and balanced. The restrictions on the mother's freedom, any expenses associated with returning to Melbourne, as well as the mother's genuine wish to remain in Brisbane were all acknowledged. The trial judge found that frequent and regular contact with his father was in the child's best interests and required that the mother live in Melbourne from a specified date onwards and that the mother be restrained from removing the child from Melbourne without consent, except for holidays within Australia or establishing a new contact regime.

The mother appealed, arguing that the orders requiring her to relocate with the child were against the weight of evidence, that undue weight had been placed on the issue of *bona fides* and that section 60B of the Family Law Act 1975 had been misapplied. The Full Court of the Family Court[7] dismissed her appeal.

On the first issue, the Court emphasised[8] that the so-called 'relocation cases' had little bearing on cases where the relocation had already been effected.[9] The Court also took the view that, although there might be cases where the effect of time might make a difference to the ultimate adjudication, the present case was not one of them. The trial judge, the Full Court considered, had predicated his decision on the relationship which presently existed between the child and his father. In the end, the Court regarded[10] that as being the central issue.

As regards the issue of *bona fides* raised by the mother, the Court noted[11] that a medical report on which she had sought to rely was, at best, equivocal. The Court were of the view that:

'It was open to the trial judge to find, as he did, that there was no real imperative for the mother or Mr H to go to Brisbane and that Mr H's planning, without consultation

---

7   Ellis, Kay and Steele JJ.

8   (1999) FLC 92-845 at 85, 891.

9   The Court were fortified in that conclusion by an unreported decision of the Full Court in *Rajahn v Butterfield* (unreported, 5 November 1998) at para 4.15 per Ellis, Lindenmayer and Warick JJ.

10   (1999) FLC 92-845 at 85, 893.

11   Ibid at 85, 892.

even of [the child's] parents, indicated that he was not acting in good faith. It was clearly open to the trial judge to retain doubts as to whether or not the wife knew that Mr H had engineered the move ...'

Similar consideration applied to the arguments relating to the application of section 60B of the Act, which sets out the objects and principles underlying Part VII.

Finally, the Court expressed the opinion[12] that the only submission which might have demonstrated appealable error was that the child and his father had been able to establish and maintain a good relationship on limited contact and, hence, it was not necessary for any further contact for the relationship to develop. Indeed, it had been said in *B*[13] that, 'Circumstances often arise where it becomes necessary or desirable for one or other parent to relocate'. However, the Court in *H v E* were at pains to point out[14] that the problem involved in the case was that the relocation took place in circumstances which were neither necessary nor desirable. More specifically, however, the Court stated that:

'If the Court ordered a return to Melbourne based significantly upon its dismay at the manner in which injunctions had been flouted, then the Court would be open to the criticism that the welfare of the child had been sacrificed on the altar of high principle, namely that people should not be able to get away with flouting court orders.'

The Court were particularly of the view that the trial judge had not elected to follow that path but rather had emphasised the quality and quantity of contact between the child and his father.

The magnitude of the problem presented by *H v E* is emphasised by the fact that the Court pointed out that the orders made at first instance might not have been made by any of the judges in the Full Court. Indeed, they stated that there were powerful reasons for reaching a conclusion different from that arrived at by the trial judge. Thus, there are three matters which arise out of *H v E*: first, it is clear that the case demonstrates that appellate courts in the family law area will regard themselves, as did the Court in *H v E*,[15] as being strictly bound by the principles laid down by the High Court of Australia in *Gronow v Gronow*[16] and *House v R*,[17] regarding the role of such courts in relation to appeals from an exercise of discretion. Secondly, the eventual adjudication might well help to still some of the criticism which the contrary adjudication in *B*[18] provided. Thirdly, the present writer cannot but feel some disquiet at the result: the relationship between the mother and the child's father was not, and never had been, successful and ongoing, whilst that between the mother and H, conduct apart, seems to have been. If the orders prejudice that relationship, the consequences may have been other than those sought by all the judges involved! Of course, those issues are far

---

12 Ibid at 85, 893.
13 (1997) FLC 92-755 at 84, 22 per Nicholson CJ, Fogarty and Lindenmayer JJ.
14 (1999) FLC 92-845 at 85, 894.
15 Ibid at 85, 893.
16 (1979) 144 CLR 513 at 505 per Stephen J.
17 (1936) 55 CLR 499 at 505 per Dixon, Evatt and McTiernan JJ.
18 Above, note 3.

from uncontradictory. There is little doubt but that the matters involved in *H v E* will be revisited by the Family Court of Australia.

The relevance of the *B* decision was considered by the Full Court in *Cooke v Stebhens*[19] which involved an appeal against interim contact orders under which the father of the two relevant children was to have overnight contact with the parties' two children each alternate weekend and for an extended period during the Christmas school holidays. The parents had never married, but lived together for two periods of time – between June and September 1987 and for three weeks in May 1988. There were two female children of the relationship, aged two and eight, who lived with their mother who had married in 1994. She lived with the two daughters, her husband and their son. The parties lived approximately 100 kilometres apart.

In 1991, the parties reached an informal agreement that the mother, who had been the girls' primary caregiver, was to have sole custody of them, with the father having access which was supervised by the mother. In outlining the history of the matter, the trial judge noted that the father, despite some periods of absence, had maintained regular contact with the children since 1994. However, the mother alleged that he had, on some contact occasions, abused her trust by taking the children into public houses, shoplifting in their company and telling them that if he was unable to afford something he stole it.

At first instance, it was found that there was no significant risk of harm to the children by their having overnight contact as they had had regular weekend contact with their father for some years. The trial judge found the mother's allegations about their father's conduct to be of limited relevance given the length of the contact period and the absence of complaints about the father. Accordingly, the trial judge made the orders which were the subject of the appeal.

On appeal, the mother argued, in essence, that the trial judge had failed to give sufficient weight to her having been the sole parent to the children and that an order for overnight contact was inconsistent with the orders for sole parental responsibility which had been made in her favour.[20] The Full Court of the Family Court of Australia[21] allowed the mother's appeal in part.

First, the Court took the view[22] that, in their own words:

> 'In the event that the court decides that a contact order should be made, in our view, the existence of a sole parenting order in favour of the residence parent should not be, and is not, an inhibiting factor. The sole parenting order must be read down to the extent necessary to enable the contact parent to make all necessary decisions with respect to day to day care of the child during contact. In most cases those decisions will probably be in quite narrow ambit but that would depend on the circumstances of each case.'

---

19   (1999) FLC 92-839.

20   In addition, as had been the case at first instance, the Full Court granted the mother's application for her mother to act on her behalf as an advocate on the basis, first, that there was no objection made by the father; secondly, that the mother was not in an emotionally fit condition to be able to represent herself effectively; and, thirdly, that the nature of the application necessitated its immediate hearing.

21   Ellis, Lindenmayer and Mushim JJ.

22   (1999) FLC 92-839 at 85, 822.

Secondly, the Court were of the opinion[23] that the trial judge had rightly based her decision on the objects and principles of Part VII of the Family Law Act: namely, the promotion of the continuing role of both parents in the lives of their children. Thirdly, however, the Court considered[24] that there were significant difficulties in relation to the extended contact order over the Christmas period, the reason being that the trial judge had given no reason for her decision. In the earlier case of *In the Marriage of Bennett*[25] the Full Court had stated that:

'... if adequate reasons are not given in a custody proceeding, it becomes impossible for an appellate court to properly examine the decision appealed from. In the absence of adequate reasons, the Full Court is not obliged to uphold a judgment merely because the result may be said to fall within the wide ambit of the Judge's discretion.'

The Court went on to emphasise that they were not suggesting that the reasons given need be extensive and that their adequacy had to be judged by reference to the issues which had been raised at the trial.

On the facts of the case, the Full Court found themselves unable to appreciate how the trial judge had arrived at her decision in respect of the extended access over the Christmas period. Thus, the Court elected[26] to exercise their discretion in the place of the trial judge and, hence, decided that there should be no additional contact beyond the alternate weekends originally prescribed.

Thus, the decision in *Crooke v Stebhens* emphasises the importance of the principles which the legislation sought to entrench in the 1995 amendments to the Family Law Act as well as pointing the need for trial judges to provide appropriate reasons for their decisions. Both of these outcomes are, in the context of the new Part VII, wholly to be applauded.

Another factor which was given considerable emphasis in the new Part VII was the relevance of domestic violence to residence, custody and related disputes. This matter was raised in the Full Court's decision in *Blanch v Blanch and Crawford*[27] which involved an appeal against an order at first instance that the three children of the marriage reside with the husband. The parties had begun cohabitation in 1997 and had married some three years later; the three children of the marriage were aged eight, six and three. In October 1990, the wife was raped by an unknown assailant and since that time she claimed that the husband had been violent towards her. The parties separated in early 1997 when the husband left the matrimonial home with the children. Immediately, the wife applied for residence but withdrew the application when the parties attempted a reconciliation. Apart from a short period in 1997, when the youngest child lived with the wife, the children had lived with the father at his mother's home since their original separation.

At about the same time as the initial separation, the wife began a relationship with T who, in addition to assaulting the husband on at least one occasion, had

---

23   Ibid at 85, 823.
24   Ibid at 85, 824.
25   (1991) FLC 92-191 at 78, 267 per Nicholson CJ, Simpson and Finn JJ.
26   (1999) FLC 92-839 at 85, 825.
27   (1999) FLC 92-837.

convictions for assault which dated back for well over ten years. In June 1997, the husband consented to an apprehended violence order made under State legislation[28] and cross-applied in respect of the wife's new application for residence. In November 1997, consent orders were made which provided that the husband have interim residence in respect of the children and that the wife have contact each alternate weekend.

At the time of the hearing at first instance, the wife and T had separated and the future of their relationship was uncertain. The wife was living with her mother, while T and his son from a previous relationship were living in the parties' former matrimonial home. In April 1998, orders were made that the children reside with the husband except for two consecutive weekends in every three, and a half of all school holidays when they were to reside with the wife. The reasons given by the trial judge were that, since the separation, the husband had been the children's primary caregiver, though the mother had also played a large part in the children's lives. The judge, with the assistance of a counsellor, regarded each party as being an adequate parent as well as finding that the children had an excellent relationship with both parents. Indeed, the trial judge queried the counsellor's finding that the children's primary attachment was to their mother.[29] The trial judge was also not satisfied that the violence demonstrated by the husband towards the wife was the product of inherent violence; rather, he felt that it was attributable to circumstances which had arisen during the marriage. However, he had expressed concern regarding the wife's relationship with T. In consequence, the trial judge concluded that the best interests of the children required that they remain with their father. In so doing, he found that he was not bound by the recommendations of the children's representative,[30] who had supported the mother's application, though he had been especially conscious of having departed from them. Thus, on appeal, there were two central issues: first, the trial judge's treatment of the various pieces of evidence regarding primary attachment and, secondly, his treatment of the issue of domestic violence.

The Full Court allowed the wife's appeal and remitted the matter for rehearing. It is quite apparent that the major issue was that of domestic violence: this is not surprising in view of the focus of the amendments to the Act[31] and the pre-existing cases of *In the Marriage of JG and BG*[32] and *In the Marriage of Patsalou*.[33] In the Full Court, Lindenmayer J was of the view[34] that the trial judge's findings on the issue were 'less than satisfactory'. Mullane J likewise felt[35] that there had been no consideration in any detail of extensive allegations of a pattern of abuse over a long period. Kay J noted[36] that the wife had left the home because of a pattern of violent conduct and had brought an immediate application;

28　Crimes Act 1900 (NSW) sections 562B–562R.

29　That view, (1999) FLC 92-837 at 85, 740, was based on the children's responses during a test known as 'The Island Game' and not on the observed interactions between children and parents.

30　See Family Law Act 1975, s 68L.

31　Ibid, s 68F(2)(g), (i), (j).

32　(1994) FLC 92-515.

33　(1995) FLC 92-580.

34　(1999) FLC 92-837 at 85, 745.

35　Ibid at 85, 747.

36　Ibid at 85, 749.

the only reason for the delay in hearing the mother was the congestion in the court lists. This last, it must be said, has been a comment made about the court since its inception.[37]

Lindenmayer J expressed the view[38] that in cases where:

'... a case of sustained and severe domestic violence by one party is advanced by the other, the Court is obliged to give a clear indication whether it accepts or rejects that case and, in either event, to explain why it has reached that conclusion.'

After noting the relevant statutory provisions and the case-law,[39] Lindenmayer J commented that *Blanch* was not a case where similar allegations were made by each party against the other, with little or no corroboration,[40] the issue depending on the relative credibility of the parties. Here, '... the wife's allegations were quite precise and detailed and her evidence was the subject of a good deal of corroboration ...'. Any apparent finding that any responsibility for the violence which may have occurred during the relationship was a matter of equal responsibility was not reasonably open to the trial judge on the evidence.

Similarly, Lindenmayer J was critical of any finding that the violence was a product of the relationship. The trial judge, Lindenmayer J emphasised,[41] had failed properly to address the risk to the children's emotional development arising from growing up in a violent household under the influence of a violent role model. Lindenmayer J continued by saying that a judicial attitude which represented:

'... an attribution of responsibility away from the perpetrators towards the victim is simply not acceptable, at least in the absence of any evidence of an expert nature to the effect that the sort of behaviour attributed to the victim by other evidence in the case was of such a nature as to provoke a violent response from *any* reasonable person and that the actual response of the perpetrator to that provocation was not disproportionate to the provocation offered.'

It followed that the trial judge's discretion had miscarried.

Mullane J was of the similarly expressed view[42] that the trial judge had failed, in any detail, to consider:

'... extensive allegations of abusive behaviour by the father over a prolonged period by way of assaults on the mother, damage to property as expressions of anger and verbal and emotional abuse of the mother. The evidence involved allegations that the children were exposed to all of these types of violence.'

---

37 See L Star, above, note 4 at 114–115.

38 (1999) FLC 92-837 at 85, 745.

39 Above text at notes 31–33.

40 By reason of the Evidence Act 1995 (Cth, NSW) ss 164, 165, the corroboration requirement, and the need for warning, has been abolished. This comment suggests, as this writer suspected, that corroboration is not thereby rendered defunct.

41 (1999) FLC 92-837 at 85, 746.

42 Ibid at 85, 747.

Mullane J concluded his judgment[43] by saying that any suggestion that the husband had behaved abusively and that this was not because of his personality but because of the nature of the parties' relationship, appeared to shift responsibility from the husband's behaviour and:

> '... run contrary to the fact that some people do use violence in their dealings with other people but most people don't.'

However, Kay J, though agreeing with Lindenmayer and Mullane JJ, was of the view[44] that it was impossible to substitute the Full Court's discretion for that of the trial judge. In particular he remarked that, while there were many issues to be resolved regarding the husband and his behaviour, there were 'very dark shadows indeed' which were raised in the wife's case and, especially her relationship with T and the violence which seemed to be involved in that relationship.

As regards the issue of the expert evidence, Lindenmayer J (the other judges did not consider the matter) was of the opinion[45] that the trial judge was in error in finding that the counsellor's opinion was based solely on the children's responses in the 'Island Game'.[46] Even though there was little evaluation of that test, there had been no challenge to that evidence and the trial judge had, therefore, erred in departing from it.

Blanch is an interesting and important case, particularly as regards its approach to domestic violence. It clearly, optimistically at least, suggests that the Family Court of Australia is taking the legislative provisions in the Act[47] very seriously and this is as it should be. It may also be that *Blanch* suggests that some judges, at any rate at the appellate level, are prepared to ascertain decisions at first instance on policy grounds.

Even more global issues were involved in the Full Court's decision in *Re Lynette*[48] which touched upon a wide variety of central considerations. This case was an appeal by the father against orders made in respect of a 12-year-old girl. The trial judge had made parenting orders in favour of a Ms L who had cared for the child's mother during her terminal illness and to whom the mother had entrusted care of the child since early 1996. The child had had no contact with the father since 1991. Ms L had instituted proceedings for final orders as to parenting responsibilities in October 1996 and there had been numerous interlocutory applications and appeals against orders made by judges prior to the matter coming to the final hearing.

At first instance, the judge rejected all of the arguments advanced by the father which had sought to impugn the motives of Ms L or her capacity to care for the child. He also found that the father had been insensitive to the needs of the child, that the child did not want contact with her father and, especially, that the father: '... could not advance the welfare of Lynette in any particular whatsoever'.

---

43   Ibid at 85, 749.
44   Ibid at 85, 749.
45   Ibid at 85, 742.
46   Above, note 29.
47   Above, note 31.
48   (1999) FLC 92-863.

In reaching that conclusion, the trial judge had been assisted by a psychologist who had been engaged by the child's separate representative.[49] The trial judge ordered that the child reside with Ms L and that she have sole responsibility for the child's long-term and day-to-day welfare and development. Further, he ordered that there be no contact with the father. In addition, he ordered that there be final orders under the Act[50] preventing the father from instituting further proceedings without the leave of the Court.[51] At his unsuccessful appeal, the father, who represented himself,[52] did not advance any oral argument but relied on his written arguments. He also sought to adduce fresh evidence regarding the mental health of the mother prior to her death.

First, the Full Court[53] refused[54] to permit the reception of fresh evidence[55] on the grounds that the alleged mental state of the deceased mother was irrelevant as to whether the order which was the subject of the appeal was in error. The Court were of the view that what may have been the mother's mental condition could not be relevant to the determination of the child's current and future interests. Similarly, how the child came into the care of Ms L was irrelevant and the trial judge had attempted to explain that to the father.

The father's second argument was that the trial judge had failed to take section 116 of the Australian Constitution into account. This provides that:

> 'The Commonwealth shall not make any law for establishing any religion, or for imposing any religious observance, or for prohibiting the free exercise of any religion and no religious test shall be required for any office or public trust under the Commonwealth.'

The reason why this provision came under scrutiny was that the father alleged that the grant of parental responsibility to Ms L, which involved the child's religious upbringing, infringed his constitutional rights. The Court properly regarded[56] the argument as being untenable: it had long been accepted that matters associated with religious upbringing were regarded as an incident of guardianship[57] and that translated into an incident of parental responsibility under the 1995 amendments.[58] In the constitutional area, the husband had also argued that the Constitution guaranteed the right of parents to bring up their children without unwarranted interference by third parties. This, again, was properly rejected; the Court saying[59] that the argument ignored the valid power of the Court to make orders regarding

---

49 See above, note 30.

50 Ibid, s 118.

51 Previous interim orders to the same effect had been made by another judge and an appeal against those orders had been dismissed. The trial judge also ordered that the father pay Ms L's costs.

52 For further comment on self-represented parties, see below text at note 96 *ff*.

53 Nicholson CJ, Kay and Holden JJ.

54 (1999) FLC 92-863 at 86, 198.

55 See *CDJ v VAJ* (1998) FLC 92-828.

56 (1999) FLC 92-863, at 86, 199.

57 See, for example, *In the Marriage of Morrison* (1995) FLC 92-639.

58 Above, note 1.

59 (1999) FLC 92-863, at 86, 200.

parental responsibility under legislation.[60] The Court also emphasised that the fact of biological parenthood did not place a party in a preferred position. Thus, in *Re Evelyn*,[61] the Full Court had said, that:

'... while the fact of parenthood is an important and significant factor in considering which of the proposals best advance a child's welfare, the fact of parenthood does not establish a presumption in favour of a natural parent ...'

The father's next argument was that the Family Law Act was in conflict with the United Nations Convention on the Rights of the Child. Australia's signature of the Convention, it should be said, has been the subject of strenuously critical comment, especially from male interest groups,[62] so that the argument, though inevitably unsuccessful, was unusual. The situation had been clearly articulated in *B and B: Family Law Reform Act 1995*[63] where it was said that:

'Unlike the United States and continental legal systems, where the entry into treaties or conventions creates self executing law, the English and Australian position is that treaties do not enter into automatic force unless and until there is a legislative act.'

In addition to that argument, the husband argued that section 43 of the Family Law Act 1975, as amended, was in conflict with sections 68D–68K. Section 43, something of a controversial provision,[64] deals with the principles which courts applying the legislation are required to apply. Sections 68D–68K concern the determination of the best interests of the child, especially section 68F which details the matters which courts must take into account in deciding what is in the child's best interests. The Court in *Lynette*, not unsurprisingly, rejected[65] that contention. There can be no doubt that, as the Full Court had earlier put the matter in the *B* decision,[66] the welfare of the children was the paramount consideration. In particular, the trial judge had properly spoken of the *right of the child*[67] to contact on a regular basis with both parents, not the right of the parents.

Yet more exotic claims were made by the father: he next argued that the trial judge was wrong in law when he had found that the case ought not to have been heard by the Family Court at all, but by a jury before the Equity jurisdiction of the Supreme Court of Victoria because the respondent had, in effect, 'stolen' the child and hence, this gave rise to the 'clean hands' doctrine.[68] The Full Court in *Lynette*

---

60   Family Law Act 1975, s 64B.

61   (1998) FLC 92-807 at 85, 106 per Nicholson CJ, Ellis and Lindenmayer JJ.

62   See M Tsamenyi and M Otlowski, 'Parental Authority and the United Nations Convention on the Rights of the Child: Are the Fears Justified?' (1992) 6 Aust J Fam L 137.

63   Above, note 3 at 84, 223 per Nicholson CJ, Fogarty and Lindenmayer JJ.

64   For a consideration of some of the issues arising out of section 43, see F Bates, 'Principle and The Family Law Act: The Uses and Abuses of s 43' (1981) 55 ALJ 181.

65   (1999) FLC 92-863 at 86, 201.

66   (1997) FLC 92-755 at 84, 214.

67   Author's emphasis.

68   The Court described, (1999) FLC 92-863 at 86, 201, the expression as meaning '... a principle adopted by courts of equity which, broadly expressed, calls upon those seeking equitable relief not to have acted unconscionably.'

described[69] that contention as being 'utterly misguided'. The Family Court of Australia was, the Court thought (and properly so), the creature of statute enacted by the Government of the Commonwealth of Australia which had been granted jurisdiction and power to deal with children who were covered by the provisions of the Family Law Act 1975. The trial judge had made no error in his assessment of the respondent's credit or motivations.

A further submission that the judgment at first instance was reduced to absurdity in the face of the criminal law was, once more, dismissed as 'fanciful'. The Court were of the view[70] that the father's case, regardless of his experience in this series of litigation, was based on his notion of what the law ought to be, rather than what it was.

The applicant also claimed to have been denied natural justice, an argument which seems to have been based on the degree of interruption and intervention by the trial judge. The basic principles are, of course, well known[71] and need not be rehearsed here. However, the Court considered[72] that the trial judge afforded the father:

'... the degree of latitude appropriate to a party representing themselves [*sic*] in these proceedings without permitting him to oppress the other party under cross-examination in person by him in person, or unduly prolong proceedings.'

The Court were also of the opinion[73] that the judge's interventions were directed towards ensuring that evidence and questions which the father had advanced were relevant to the disposition of the case. The Court commented that this had, apparently, been no easy task as the father had been: '... resistant to understanding that matters of personal significance to him were not, as a matter of law, relevant to a trial judge'.

Next, the applicant argued that he had been unable to keep pace with evidence and exhibits. Once again, the Court were of the view[74] that the ground was without substance. The Court noted that it was apparent that the trial judge had taken a relatively active role in conducting the trial; that, they said, was not uncommon in proceedings involving unrepresented parties and, in this particular case, was essential. They emphasised, in the context of this submission, that, it was:

'... imperative that trials not be unduly delayed by obstructive or time wasting conduct by litigants, whether unrepresented or otherwise and whether in the course of submissions or in the examination and cross examination of witnesses.'

---

69 Ibid at 86, 202.
70 Ibid.
71 See particularly, *Jones v National Coal Board* [1957] 2 QB 55.
72 (1999) FLC 92-863 at 86, 202.
73 Ibid at 86, 203.
74 Ibid at 86, 203.

Lastly, the Court totally rejected[75] a submission that the cross-examination of the applicant had been conducted in a manner discriminatory against Dutch people.

Re Lynette illustrates many of the problems which the Family Court faces in relation to unrepresented parties. Given the parlous situation regarding legal aid in Australia in relation to non-criminal matters,[76] unrepresented parties (in family law matters, presently estimated at one-third) are likely to increase[77] and present the kind of problems with which the Court was faced in that case.

III   PROPERTY

A useful starting point is provided by the Full Court's decision in *Carson v Carson*.[78] There, the husband sought to appeal against orders which adjourned property proceedings until his superannuation fell due which had the effect of requiring him to make mortgage payments on the former matrimonial home. The marriage had lasted for 15 years; the two children of the marriage, aged 14 and 11, lived with the wife in the former matrimonial home. The home was the parties' main asset, being valued at $205,000 but with $90,000 in outstanding mortgages. The husband been a member of a superannuation scheme and his immediate entitlement was $207,936, but the scheme would not vest for another 13 years at least. He also had leave entitlements with an after-tax value of $102,300.

The Full Court[79] held, first, that the trial judge was in error in finding that the husband was capable of making the mortgage payments. The Full Court found[80] that the husband was incapable of reasonable self-support while making those payments. At the same time, the Court noted that the husband conceded that the very least the wife could expect would be the entire equity in the former matrimonial home. It followed that an interim order ought to have been made,[81] to the effect that the home ought to have been transferred to the wife, subject to her being responsible for the outgoings and indemnifying the husband in respect of them. The reason for his view was that the equity in the home was a relatively modest amount and any attempt to provide the husband with an interest would have a far more deleterious effect on the wife's capacity to rehouse herself and the children. In other words, the balance of hardship favoured the wife.

Other broad issues were raised by the Full Court's subsequent decision in *In the Marriage of Dickson*[82] which involved an appeal that an asset pool of some

---

75   Ibid at 86, 204.

76   In criminal matters, the situation is less parlous because of the decisions of the High Court of Australia in *Dietrich v R* (1992) 109 ALR 385.

77   In the Australian State of Victoria both Supreme Courts and Courts of Appeal judges have issued a statement to the effect that litigants' lack of legal knowledge was creating a risk that important issues might be overlooked at trial and that justice might miscarry. See, 'Legal Aid Cuts Alarm State Judges: Unrepresented Litigants are Impeding Victoria's Legal System' *The Age* (Melbourne) 17 December 1999 at 9.

78   (1999) FLC 92-835.

79   Kaye, Holden and Dawe JJ.

80   (1999) FLC 92-835 at 85, 693.

81   See *In the Marriage of Harris* (993) FLC 92-378 at 79, 929.

82   (1999) FLC 92-843.

$6.6 million be distributed 75:25 in favour of the wife. The parties had been married for 26 years and, at the time of the trial, the husband was aged 68 and the wife 57. All their three children were self-supporting adults. The trial judge had found that the wife had made the 'overwhelming' financial and non-financial contributions to the family. She had entered the marriage with some $255,000 worth of assets, as they had been valued in the 1960s. She was also skilled in property investment and had supported the family in that way. The husband worked as an agent in the family's real estate franchise though, in the words of the trial judge:[83] 'It appears that a general picture of him at the office ... was with the racing form spread out in front of him.' Both parties had received legacies during the marriage: the wife had inherited the family home in 1982 (its present value being $1.9 million) and her earnings continued to be greater than those of her husband, although she agreed that her working life was effectively at an end. The parties had relatively modest superannuation entitlements.

The Full Court[84] upheld the husband's appeal in part. First, they accepted[85] the trial judge's findings regarding the amount of the asset pool and were of the view that he had been entitled to reject uncorroborated assertions by the husband[86] regarding assets to be excluded from the pool. As regards the issue of contribution, it was both open to the trial judge, and appropriate for him, to take a global approach, rather than an asset by asset approach.[87]

The Court then went on to consider the approach towards the relevant statutory provisions (sections 79(4) and 75(2) of the Family Law Act 1975). The Court considered[88] that a trial judge must take financial and non-financial contributions into account and, in the light of other relevant matters, arrive at a result which is just and equitable in the circumstances. However, the statutory requirement[89] that the order be just and equitable required an adjustment beyond contributions. The Court stated that this was a case:[90]

'... where the disparity of financial position of the parties once allocations had been made for contributions, considered together with prospective matters, including the age of the parties and standard of living that in all circumstances was reasonable, was such that it demanded a further adjustment.'

Accordingly, the Full Court re-exercised the discretion to order a settlement 70:30 to the wife.[91]

---

83 Quoted by the Full Court, ibid at 85, 864.
84 Lindenmayer, Kay and Warick JJ.
85 Ibid at 85, 869.
86 For comment on the matter of corroboration, see above text at note 40.
87 See *Mallet v Mallet* (1984) 156 CLR 605; *Norbis v Norbis* (1986) 161 CLR 513.
88 (1999) FLC 92-843 at 85, 869.
89 Family Law Act 1975 s 75(4)(e).
90 (1999) FLC 92-843 at 85, 872.
91 This 5% adjustment reduced the disparity between the parties by $660,000.

IV   EVIDENCE AND PROCEDURE

An especially interesting instance relating to evidence in relation to child abuse is provided by the judgment of Nicholson CJ in *DT v JT*.[92] The domestic history of the parties was very complex but, in the end, the father sought to rely on the evidence of two children (one aged seven and one aged nine) of the wife's prior marriage. This related to an allegation made by the father that the relevant three-year-old child had been taken to hospital suffering from injuries incurred whilst in the care of the mother and her *de facto* husband. It was argued by the mother that section 100A of the Family Law Act 1975 should not be applied for the purpose of admitting the evidence. Section 100A(1) provides that:

> 'Evidence of a representation made by a child about a matter that is relevant to the welfare of the child or another child, which would not otherwise be admissible as evidence because of the law against hearsay, is not inadmissible solely because of the law against hearsay in any proceedings under Part VII.'

Section 100A(2) goes on to specify that the court may give such weight to evidence admitted under the previous subsection as it thinks fit. Emphatically, section 100A(3) states that the section applies in spite of other legislation or rule of law.

The mother, in effect, argued that the evidence was so doubtful that the Court ought not to exercise its discretion to admit it. She found support in the shape of the decision of the Full Court of the Family Court of Australia in *VJ v CJ*[93] which suggested that the evidence of children made in the circumstances of the case ought not to be admitted without careful scrutiny. In *VJ v CJ*, the Full Court had pointed out[94] that section 100A was an enabling section but that it had not: '... been applied in such a manner as to enable lengthy and detailed statements of children to be introduced into evidence in lieu of the filing of an affidavit on behalf of the child'. In the present case, it had been argued that the expertise of the people making assessments of the case was inadequate. Nicholson CJ rejected[95] that submission, although he did suggest that the question might be relevant to the question of weight, though he did point out that the present case involved a situation: '... where a child has suffered unexplained injuries which neither the mother nor the other person living in the house was able to explain'. In those circumstances, the Chief Justice thought, it appeared that the evidence had considerable potential probative value.

There was also reliance placed on the earlier decision of the Full Court in *S v R*[96] where it had been said that: '... [the] utmost caution needs to be taken before such evidence can be relied on to establish such a serious allegation as sexual abuse'. Nicholson CJ sought factually to distinguish the cases on a rather

---

92   (1999) FLC 92-851.
93   (1997) FLC 92-772.
94   Ibid at 85, 524, per Lindenmayer, Kay and Maxwell JJ.
95   (1999) FLC 92-851, at 86, 013.
96   (1999) FLC 92-834 at 85, 683 per Kay, Holden and Mullane JJ.

minuscule ground[97] without dealing with the serious policy issues raised by section 100A. Nicholson CJ also refused to accept a submission that the relationship between the mother and her *de facto* husband had changed; however, he felt justified[98] in that conclusion by the fact that an apprehended violence order[99] had been taken out, which had not been disclosed to the Court, and which gave him considerable concern as to the real nature of the relationship.

Very important issues relating to evidence and, more particularly, procedure were raised in *S v R*, to which reference had been made in *DT v J*. *S v R* involved an appeal against orders that the two children of the marriage reside with the wife and that no contact be permitted to the husband. The parties had been married in 1991 and lived in Western Australia; they separated in 1995 when the wife moved with the children to New South Wales. Prior to that final separation, there had been various periods of separation, during which a shared parenting regime had been established. Since the final separation, the children had lived with the wife and had limited supervised contact with the husband. At trial, the wife sought to deny contact to the husband claiming that he had sexually abused the children. The husband made a counter application, denying that any abuse had taken place. At the hearing, the husband was unrepresented. The evidence which had been used by the trial judge to support a finding of abuse included an affidavit by the wife, to which was attached a transcript of a police interview with the children, made more than one year after the last possible opportunity for the abuse to have occurred. There was also an affidavit by a clergyman who had supervised contact on one occasion and two reports made by a clinical psychologist.[100]

Relying on the test which had been enunciated by the High Court of Australia in *M v M*,[101] the trial judge, in the absence of countervailing evidence, made a positive finding of abuse but did not particularise the abuse. Accordingly, orders were made which granted residence to the wife and denied contact to the husband (apart from telephone calls and gifts). The husband appealed to the Full Court, claiming that he had been denied procedural fairness as a self-represented litigant and that the positive finding of abuse was against the weight of the evidence. The Full Court[102] allowed the appeal and ordered an expedited retrial.

First, as regards the matter of procedural fairness, the Full Court found that the trial judge had failed to seek submissions regarding the circumstances, where there was great doubt as to their admissibility and there might be significant ground to exclude them. This brought the Court to consider[103] the application of the principles which had been laid down in the earlier case of *Johnson v*

---

97 In *S v R*, the interviewers were not called to give evidence at all and there was no evidence as to how the relevant interview was carried out. Conversely, in *DT v JT*, the interview had been called.

98 (1999) FLC 92-851, at 86, 013.

99 See Crimes Act 1900 (NSW), ss 562A–562R.

100 In addition, the trial judge had exercised his discretion to hear evidence from the clergyman and the clinical psychologist by telephone.

101 (1988) 166 CLE 69. For comment on this case, see F Bates, 'Evidence, Child Sexual Abuse and the High Court of Australia' (1990) 39 ICLQ 413. There has been something of a retreat from the *M* test, see F Bates 'New Developments in Child Sexual Abuse and the Fact-Finding Process' (1998) 5 Canberra LR 111.

102 Kay, Holden and Mullane JJ.

103 (1999) FLC 92-834.

Johnson.[104] In that case, the Full Court of the Family Court of Australia[105] set out seven obligations on trial judges when hearing cases involving unrepresented litigants. They were as follows: first, to inform the litigant in person of the manner in which the trial was to proceed, the order of the calling of witnesses and right which the litigant has to cross-examine the witnesses. Secondly, to explain to the litigant in person any procedures relevant to the situation. Thirdly, generally to assist the litigant by taking basic information from witnesses called, such as name, address and occupation. Fourthly, if a change in normal procedure is requested by other parties, such as the calling of witnesses out of turn, to explain to the unrepresented party the effect and, perhaps, the undesirability of the interposition of witnesses and his or her right to object to that course. Fifthly, if evidence is sought to be tendered in respect of which the litigant in person has a possible claim of privilege, to inform the litigant of her or his rights. Sixthly, to ensure that a level playing field is maintained at all times. Finally, the judge should attempt to clarify the substance of the submissions of unrepresented parties, especially in cases where, because of garrulous or misconceived advocacy, the substantive issues are ignored, given little attention or obfuscated.[106] At the same time, they considered it undesirable for legal advice to be given to a litigant in person because it might be unfair, or have an appearance of unfairness, to the other parties and the advice given might not be given with full knowledge of the facts.

In *S v R*, the trial judge had failed to seek submissions from the husband regarding the admissibility of various documents or of any discretion to exclude them, in circumstances where there was great doubt as to their admissibility and significant reason to exclude them. The Court were of the view[107] that the trial judge was in breach of the sixth guideline which had been laid down in *Johnson*. Further, they were of the view[108] that a particularly heavy onus lay on the trial judge to conform with guideline six because of the centrality of the evidence to the proceedings and the gravity of the outcome, in that the children would be most unlikely to be able to see their father again.

The Court also found[109] that the positive finding of abuse was against the weight of the evidence and that the trial judge had failed to take proper account of the appropriate standard of proof which emphasised the consequences of the finding. Having regard to the standard of proof, the positive finding of abuse was not, on the evidence, open to the trial judge, who had failed to exercise appropriate caution when the child who had made the relevant statements was not available for cross-examination. Further, an absence of countervailing evidence did not justify a positive finding of abuse and the trial judge had incorrectly overlooked the husband's denials in stating that there was no countervailing evidence.[110]

---

104 (1997) FLC 92-764 at 84, 421.

105 Ellis, Lindenmayer and Baker JJ.

106 See *Neil v Nott* (1994) 121 ALR 148.

107 (1999) FLC 92-834 at 85, 679.

108 Ibid at 85, 675.

109 Ibid at 85, 680.

110 As regards the evidence by telephone, the Court (ibid at 85, 677) found that the trial judge had failed to seek submissions from the husband regarding the desirability and consequences of obtaining evidence by telephone.

S v R is an interesting decision in that it demonstrates at least some of the problems regarding appropriate process which face judges at first instance. It is readily apparent both from *S v R* and *Re Lynette*[111] that unrepresented parties are going to present problems.

However, these are not the only problems presented to the courts by the present situation in which the Family Court of Australia finds itself, as is illustrated by the Full Court's decision in *KS v DS*,[112] which involved an appeal by a husband against orders made at first instance, in the words of the Court,[113] after a lengthy hearing: '... which was conducted by his Honour and with due consideration that the husband was appearing in person ...'. The hearing involved the four children of the parties, aged between four and 12 years. One of the principal issues involved allegations of violence perpetrated by the husband on the wife and children and the trial judge made findings on that issue. The incidents revealed a pattern of conduct on the part of the husband and, the wife having left the matrimonial home, she and the children had lived either in a refuge or in housing provided under the auspices of the refuge. In the course of his judgment, the trial judge had made findings that were largely supportive of the wife's evidence together with various witnesses who had been called by both sides. The effect of the orders made at first instance was that the wife should have residence of the children and the husband have supervised contact. An order was also made which prevented the husband from making further applications without the leave of the Court or a judge.

There were some 106 grounds set out in the husband's notice of appeal and neither the wife nor the children objected to a further four grounds being introduced at the hearing. The husband did not provide a summary of agreement as required by the Family Law Rules.[114] In the light of the material before it, the Full Court was prepared to grant the husband a total of approximately three hours to present oral argument on the matters. At the conclusion of that time, the husband indicated that he wished to continue to present argument, but the Court took the view that to permit him to do so would be a fruitless exercise. The Full Court dismissed the husband's appeal.

In so doing, Nicholson CJ stated[115] that the grounds of appeal appeared to him to be entirely without substance and: '... to permit the husband to have occupied himself with lecturing the Court would have ... been an abuse of process of the Court'. The Chief Justice also rejected[116] an argument that there had been a breach of natural justice because the trial judge had declined to interview the children in chambers and he commented, in accordance with prior case-law,[117] that it was always a matter for the trial judge as to whether to interview a child and many judges, for sound reasons, elected not to do so. The Chief Justice also found that the case was a wholly suitable one for the making of an order that no further

---

111 Above text at note 48 *ff*.
112 (1999) FLC 92-860.
113 Ibid at 86, 162 per Nicholson CJ. Coleman and Martin JJ agreed with the Chief Justice.
114 Family Law Rules O32, r 2(3)(c).
115 (1999) FLC 92-860 at 86, 163.
116 Ibid at 86, 165.
117 See, for example, *In the Marriage of Joannou* (1985) FLC 91-642.

application be made without the leave of the Court.[118] The case was, indeed, as Nicholson CJ described it, troublesome.

V   LEGISLATIVE DEVELOPMENTS

There have been a number of proposed and actual legislative developments at both Federal and State levels. At the Federal level, the Family Law Amendment Bill 1999 contains three Schedules which amend the Family Law Act 1975 as well as the Child Support (Registration and Collection) Act 1988 and the Child Support (Assessment) Act 1999. The first Schedule introduces a three-tier regime for the enforcement of parenting orders and a separate regime for the enforcing of money and property orders. Schedule 2 introduces a regime for the making of binding financial agreements and Schedule 3 makes amendments to implement a system of private arbitration.[119]

Again at Federal level, the Federal Magistrates Bill 1999 and the Federal Magistrates (Consequential Amendments) Bill 1999 seek to establish a new Court whose jurisdiction will include family law matters. This is likely to prove a controversial development as there is considerable friction between the Commonwealth Attorney-General and the Chief Justice of the Family Court regarding funding of the Court and it is very likely that the development will simply be perceived as an attempt by the present Commonwealth Government to administer family law at bargain basement levels.

The Attorney-General, in a speech to the National Press Club,[120] indicated that he would continue research into outcomes of matrimonial property proceedings, to be undertaken by the Australian Law Reform Commission and the Australian Institute of Family Studies. There would also be special reforms in relation to bankruptcy and superannuation, which have caused considerable difficulty over the last twenty or so years.

In addition, the Attorney-General also suggested that he was keen to pursue a reference of power from the States to the Commonwealth in relation to property of *de facto* couples. It is in the area of *de facto* relationships that the States have been most active. In New South Wales, the De Facto Relationships Act 1984 has become the Property (Relationships) Act 1984 and significant changes have been made to it. In particular, section 5(I)(b) of the Act extends the legislation to:

> '... a close personal relationship (other than a marriage or a de facto relationship) between two adult persons, whether or not related by family, who are living together, one or each of whom provides the other with domestic support and personal care.'

Thus, the legislation is applicable to gay and lesbian couples, siblings living together, or long-term personal friends. The legislation is thus congruent with the Domestic Relationships Act 1994 in the Australian Capital Territory.

---

118 See Family Law Act 1975, s 118.
119 The Bill also makes a number of miscellaneous amendments in Schedule 3.
120 27 October 1999.

Although these Acts are broader in scope than other legislation, it means that all Australian jurisdictions (the De Facto Relationships Act 1999 having been passed in Tasmania) with the exception of Western Australia, have laws which govern property relationships between informal partners.

VI CONCLUSIONS

1999 was a far from uneventful year in Australian family law and the process seems to be ongoing. The Court is now faced with a plethora of unrepresented litigants, who are likely to continue to challenge the judiciary's capacity to ensure that procedures can be devised which are capable of dealing with the phenomenon, as it can properly be called. The impact of the 1995 amendments in respect of children are beginning to have effect. Although prediction is a peculiarly hazardous business in this area of legal activity, it seems safe to say that next year's commentary is likely to be saying much the same.

AUSTRIA

FAMILY LAW REFORMS IN AUSTRIA FROM 1992 TO 1999

*Bea Verschraegen**

I   INTRODUCTION

From 1992 to 1999 the Austrian legislator enacted four important statutes in the field of family law: The Law on Medically Assisted Procreation,[1] the Law on the Name and the Conditions for Modification of the Name,[2] the Law on Protection against Violence by Family Members[3] and the Law amending Marriage Law.[4] An important reform of child law is under discussion, but not yet in force. This draft law provides for the lowering of the age of full capacity from 19 to 18 years of age, joint custody for both parents on divorce and other amendments. It will be discussed in the next *Survey*.

II   THE LAW ON ASSISTED PROCREATION

The Law on Assisted Procreation establishes the conditions for assisted procreation and introduces detailed provisions, especially in the field of parentage, on the consequences of medically assisted procreation. Modern techniques of medically assisted procreation must take into account human dignity, the welfare of the child and the right to procreate; the new law tries to protect these principles. Basically, no objections were expressed with regard to a homologous system – in other words where procreation without a donor is assisted. The reason for this is that parenthood is not split between genetic and social parents, the ability to procreate and fertility cannot be exploited, and, finally, the selection of the child according to certain questionable criteria is only possible to a limited extent. It would have been logical, then, to limit assisted procreation to the gametes of the parents or cohabitants concerned. Nonetheless it seemed wise to allow (at least) donor insemination, because it is an easy method of procreation, but very hard to control. The legislator therefore opted for a pragmatic approach in that only those methods of insemination where practical obstacles have to be surmounted should be subject to a legal prohibition. By contrast, in-vitro fertilisation requires professional medical training and an important technical standard. Therefore, this

---

*   Full Professor at the Law Faculty of the University of Vienna, Présidente de la Commission Internationale de l'État Civil.
1   'Fortpflanzungsmedizingesetz' (FMedG), Bundesgesetzblatt (BGBl., Federal Gazette) 275/1992.
2   'Namensrechtsänderungsgesetz', BGBl. 25/1995.
3   'Gewaltschutzgesetz', BGBl. 759/1996.
4   'Eherechts-Änderungsgesetz, BGBl. I 125/1999.

method can easily be subject to control. As the legislator basically prefers the homologous system, egg donation and transfer of gametes are prohibited.

Only married couples or (heterosexual) cohabitants have access to assisted procreation.[5] The purpose of the law is to remedy infertility of couples. Assisted procreation is, therefore, only available if all possible and reasonable medical treatments aimed at the inducement of a pregnancy by sexual intercourse have failed or probably will not lead to pregnancy.[6] This is why posthumous insemination is not allowed. As in-vitro fertilisation is limited to genetic parents, surrogate motherhood is prohibited. Whereas prenatal genetic diagnosis is allowed, pre-implantation genetic diagnosis is only permitted if inducement of pregnancy requires it. Genetic interference is explicitly prohibited by law.[7]

Medically assisted procreation may only be offered by specially licensed hospitals. Homologous insemination may, though, be carried out by hospitals and gynaecologists.[8] The intention to carry out such an insemination must be reported to the head of the government of the province.[9] Hospitals need a special licence, which will be granted when staff and equipment ensure a treatment according to actual standards of medical science and experience.[10]

Spouses must be informed about the medical implications of assisted procreation. Cohabitants and donors must, in addition, be informed about the legal implications.[11] The reason for this distinction is the following: spouses will usually quite correctly assume that they will be the parents of the child, therefore medical information is sufficient. Cohabitants and donors, however, may be less aware of the legal consequences, hence they must be fully informed. The woman giving birth to the child will be regarded as the mother of the child,[12] whereas the father is the man who recognised fatherhood or was determined as father in a judicial proceeding; a donor cannot become the (legal) father of a child,[13] but his identity may be disclosed; he does not enjoy anonymity. Any child of 14 years or older has the right to know the donor's identity, but this remains without consequences as to parentage, because no donor can be established as the father of the child.[14]

Spouses must give their consent to medically assisted procreation in a written form; cohabitants must consent in a qualified form (eg a notary deed). A qualified consent will always be required when the semen of a donor is used.[15] A person lacking capacity cannot consent to medically assisted procreation, whereas a person having partial capacity can give personal consent but also needs the agreement of his/her legal representative.[16]

---

5   Article 2 para 1 FMedG.
6   Article 2 para 2 FMedG.
7   Article 9 para 2 FMedG.
8   Article 4 para 1 and 2 FMedG.
9   Article 5 para 1 FMedG.
10   Article 5 para 2 FMedG.
11   Article 7 para 1 and 3 FMedG.
12   Article 137b Allgemeines Bürgerliches Gesetzbuch (ABGB, Austrian Civil Code).
13   Article 163 para 4 ABGB.
14   Article 20 para 2 FMedG.
15   Article 8 para 1 FMedG.
16   Article 8 para 2 FMedG.

Only the semen of one donor may be used.[17] The donor and his semen must be examined closely in order to prevent health risks for the woman or the child.[18] Further, the semen may only be used for three (married or unmarried) couples;[19] the hospital is obliged to make an inventory of the marriages or cohabitations for which the semen was used.[20] Finally, the donor will not be paid for his contribution.[21] Semen, ova and viable cells may be stored for no longer than one year.[22] Providers of semen and cells cannot claim any right to their 'product'.[23]

Any violation of the Law on Assisted Procreation may lead to administrative sanctions (fines of up to 500,000 Schilling), unless the Penal Code provides for a criminal sanction.[24]

By and large, the Austrian Law on Assisted Procreation[25] pursues a restrictive policy. Medically assisted procreation is regarded as a mere remedy, ie treatment of difficulties in the process of procreation of couples of different sex. Therefore, surrogacy, cloning and the creation of hybrids and chimeras are necessarily prohibited by law. Storage of embryos and gametes is limited to one year. Clearly, embryos must be destroyed upon expiration of that time-limit, although the law does not say so expressly. In line with the policy to treat insufficiencies of nature, genetic interference is absolutely forbidden. It seems, however, that practice shows some inclination to use modern scientific methods in order to ensure physical resemblance and to take into consideration comparable socio-cultural conditions. Although hospitals and specialists must keep records of the data mentioned above, this duty is limited to thirty years; after this period the data will be transferred to the head of the government of the province. It may, in practice, not be so easy for a child of 14 years of age or older to discover the identity of the donor.

III THE LAW ON THE NAME AND THE CONDITIONS FOR MODIFICATION OF THE NAME

The Law on the Name and the Conditions for Modification of the Name was a reaction to several developments. First, the Austrian Constitutional Court[26]

---

17 Article 9 para 3 FMedG.
18 Article 12 FMedG.
19 Article 14 FMedG.
20 Article 15 para 2 FMedG.
21 Article 16 FMedG.
22 Article 17 para 1 FMedG.
23 Article 17 para 2 FMedG.
24 Articles 22–25 FMedG.
25 For more details, see, eg Memmer, 'Rechtsfragen im Gefolge medizinisch assistierter Fortpflanzung post mortem vel divortium', *Juristische Blätter (JBl.)* 1992, 361; idem, 'Eheähnliche Lebensgemeinschaften und Reproduktionsmedizin', JBl. 1993, 297; Bernat, 'Die rechtliche Regelung von Fortpflanzungsmedizin und Embryonenforschung in Deutschland, Österreich und der Schweiz', *Österreichischer Amtsvormund (ÖA)* 1993, 47; idem, 'Neue Aufgaben für das Notariat', *Notariats-Zeitung (NZ)* 1992, 244; Pichler, 'Probleme der medizinisch unterstützten Fortpflanzung', ÖA 1993, 53; Schwimann, 'Neues Fortpflanzungsrecht in Österreich', *Das Standesamt (StAZ)* 1993, 169.
26 VfSlg. (Collection of the decisions of the Constitutional Court) 10384/1985.

rendered a decision declaring unconstitutional the provision according to which spouses must use a common family name. This common name was the name of the husband unless the spouses, before they got married, chose the name of the wife as the common name. Where the common name was the name of the husband, the wife had the personal right to add her name with a hyphen. The Constitutional Court was of the opinion that the Constitution was violated by this provision, because the husband did not have the right to add his name with a hyphen where the wife's name was chosen as the common family name. The legislator amended the law in 1986 to allow, *inter alia*, the husband the right to hyphenate his name with that of the wife as the common family name. In the meantime, the German legislator enabled spouses to use a double name and a spouse was given the possibility of putting his/her name, as used hitherto, ahead of the name of the other spouse. The German Constitutional Court rendered a decision in 1991, declaring unconstitutional the provision of the German Civil Code by which spouses could not keep their family name, as used hitherto; they should, in other words, each have the right to keep their own family name upon marriage. The German legislator enacted a law in line with this decision and also provided that if spouses prefer to use a different name they should agree upon the name of one of them for any (future) child. In default of such an agreement, the court should appoint one of the spouses to take a decision on the family name of the child. Again, legislative reforms, taking into consideration the developments in Germany, were discussed in Austria but the topic remained highly controversial.

Some of the provisions of the Law on the Name and the Conditions for Modification of the Name will now be considered.[27] According to this law, spouses should basically carry a common family name. This can be the name of the husband or that of the wife. In the absence of an agreement before or on the occasion of the marriage, the common family name is the name of the husband.[28] The wife can declare that she wants to keep her own name.[29] If the spouses opt for a common family name, they must declare this before or on the occasion of their marriage, in which case each of them can add or put ahead his/her family name, as used hitherto.[30] This can, eventually, also be the family name carried in a former marriage. Legitimate children carry the common family name of their parents; if the spouses kept their own name, they can agree upon one of the two names as a family name for all their children. In default of such an agreement, the children will carry the name of their father.[31] Illegitimate children carry the family name of their mother.[32]

The Law on the Name and the Conditions for Modification of the Name simplified the conditions under which a name can be modified, in that an important reason is no longer required. Modification of a name is possible when a

---

27   For further details see, eg Hintermüller, 'Namensrechtsänderungsgesetz – Kurzinformation über die wichtigsten Neuerungen für den Praktiker', in: *Österreichisches Standesamt (ÖStA)* 5/95, 46; Zeyringer, 'Zweifelsfragen im Zusammenhang mit dem Namensrechtsänderungsgesetz', in: *ÖStA* 7-8/95, 63.

28   Article 93 para 1 phrase 3 ABGB.

29   Article 93 para 3 phrase 1 ABGB.

30   Article 93 para 2 ABGB.

31   Article 139 paras 2 and 3 ABGB.

32   Article 165 ABGB.

person simply applies to have his/her name modified.[33] This administrative procedure is free of charge if the person concerned has an important reason to have his/her name modified; otherwise there is a charge. The modification of the name by the competent administrative authority remains without influence on the name of the spouse.[34]

IV THE LAW ON PROTECTION AGAINST VIOLENCE IN THE FAMILY

Growing concern about violence within the family led to the Law on Protection against Violence in the Family.[35] This law protects close relatives against one another. Any person who renders family life of a close relative unacceptable due to a physical attack, the threat of such an attack or any behaviour that severely interferes with the psychical health of that close relative, can be forced to leave the family home and its immediate vicinity. He/she can also be forbidden to return to the family home or its immediate vicinity, if the petitioner needs the family home. The court makes such an order upon petition of the close relative concerned. Close relatives are spouses and cohabitants, brothers and sisters, lineal descendants and ascendants, adopted children and foster children as well as adoptive parents and foster parents, their spouses and cohabitants. A close relative can also (to prevent the behaviour mentioned above) file a petition to forbid the other person to reside at specified places and to force him/her to avoid any contact with the petitioner, unless such an order is contrary to substantial interests of the other person. Only lineal descendants and ascendants, adopted children and foster children, adoptive parents and foster parents, spouses and cohabitants, as well as brothers and sisters of spouses or cohabitants, are regarded as close relatives for the purpose of the last-mentioned petition. Interim injunctions may also be granted without any connection to a procedure to dissolve the marriage or to distribute the marital articles of daily use and the marital savings, or, as the case may be, to decide upon the right to use the family home, but then, their binding effect will not exceed three months.[36] A second interim injunction is not admissible. Damages can be awarded to the person whose sexual integrity, negligently and in breach of the law, has been violated.[37]

The purpose of the law is to calm down close relatives living in a family home and to prevent (further) violence by separating them for a certain period of time. The range of protected persons is quite large. An example may highlight the extent. The cohabitant of the homeowner's daughter can file a petition for expulsion of his cohabitant's father, if family life is unacceptable for the reasons set out above.[38] He may also be successful with a petition aimed at prohibiting the

---

33 Article 2 para 1 no 8 NÄG (Namensänderungsgesetz, Law on the Modification of the Name).
34 Article 1 para 3 NÄG.
35 Bundesgesetz zum Schutz vor Gewalt in der Familie (GeSchG), BGBl. 759/1996.
36 See Article 382b EO (Exekutionsordnung, Statute on Enforcement of decisions).
37 Article 1328 ABGB.
38 For further examples see Sykora, 'Das Gesetz zum Schutz vor Gewalt in der Familie' (BGBl. 1996/759). 'Die Änderungen im Bereich der EO' (§§ 382b–382d), in: *Anwaltsblatt (AnwBl.)* 1998, 292 (293).

father's return to the family home. The prohibition on returning to the home may lead to an extremely difficult situation for the opponent of the petition himself. He may be liable to pay spousal support (including the costs for the family home), child support and debts and may lack sufficient means to finance a second (provisional) home. This, however, is necessary in order to enable the person concerned to live adequately and go to work. In any case, the authorities may expel the opponent from the home or prohibit him from returning if they reasonably suppose that there is a serious threat to life, health or freedom and the person in need of protection is in one way or the other in danger. The law in question[39] does not require the relationship to be between close relatives nor the living together in a family home.

V   THE LAW AMENDING MARRIAGE LAW

Finally, the Law amending Marriage Law deserves some attention. In the Reform Commission set up to discuss amendments of, *inter alia*, the divorce law, opinions proved to be extremely controversial. The abolition of the grounds for divorce based on fault elicited no approval. By and large, the reform remained a minor one. The main amendments relate to the following topics.[40] Marriage law was amended in that spouses can agree that one spouse is not obliged to help the other in his/her business undertaking.[41] Further, the spouse gainfully employed is obliged to help the other spouse in the household;[42] if a spouse chooses to change the arrangements of family life the couple must try to find a compromise.[43] The spouse working in the household is, under certain conditions, entitled to maintenance in money instead of in kind.[44] The grounds for divorce were simplified[45] but divorce based on fault was not abolished as such. However, spousal support on divorce, independent of fault, can be granted under limited conditions.[46] Support on divorce may be temporary and the amount restricted. Investments in a business undertaking may be considered, in terms of value, at the time of the division of property where there is a dissolution of marriage. The business undertaking should, however, not be put at risk;[47] finally, provision is made for mediation in divorce proceedings.[48]

The legal duty of each spouse to help the other in his/her business undertaking was (notwithstanding some political will to do so) not deleted, mainly because of

---

39   Article 38a SPG (Sicherheitspolizeigesetz, Law on the police force).

40   For further details see, eg Hopf/Stabentheiner, 'Das Eherechts-Änderungsgesetz 1999', in: *Österreichische Juristen-Zeitung (ÖJZ)* 1999, 821, 861; Grünberger, 'Die Regelung der Mediation im EheRÄG 1999', in: *ÖJZ* 2000, 50.

41   Article 90 para 2 ABGB.

42   Article 95 ABGB.

43   Article 91 para 2 ABGB.

44   Article 94 para 3 ABGB.

45   Article 47 EheG (adultery) and Article 48 EheG (denial of procreation) were abolished, but as severe matrimonial offences, adultery and causing physical violence or psychic harm were introduced in Article 49 EheG (Ehegesetz, Marriage Law).

46   Article 68a EheG.

47   Article 91 para 2 EheG.

48   Article 99 EheG.

its importance in agriculture and related social security provisions. Spouses may, however, agree to deviate from the law. The duty to help the other spouse in the household was set up to ensure that the contributions of each spouse to family life are largely balanced. The parties do have autonomy to determine the extent of their contributions, but severe violations of the principle to contribute equally are prohibited. Of course, the options and wishes of each party may change in the course of the marriage; therefore there must be some scope to respond to new developments. Conflicting interests of the parties and the children must also here be balanced. Until the law reform, the housekeeping spouse (as such, contributing to family life) had a right to maintenance *in natura*, and a claim to 'pocket-money' (about 5% of the net income of the other spouse). The law improved the situation of the housekeeping spouse by the introduction of a claim to maintenance in money, unless the assertion of such a claim would be inequitable. As to the grounds for divorce, adultery and denial of procreation as absolute grounds for divorce (ie a petition for divorce based on one of these grounds used to lead automatically to the dissolution of marriage, although they did not necessarily cause the breakdown of that marriage) were abolished as such. They can, as relative grounds for divorce, be considered as severe matrimonial offences leading to a divorce, if the offence caused the breakdown of the marriage.

Among severe matrimonial offences the legislator also included the causing of physical violence and severe psychic harm. Frustration, for example, does not constitute severe psychic harm. The judge has to take into account the intention of the party causing the harm, its duration and intensity. The most important amendment relates to support following divorce independent of culpable behaviour. First, support may be due if one spouse was not able to provide for his/her own support by gainful employment due to the care and education of a common child. That it is unreasonable to expect gainful employment is presumed when the child is under five years of age; this presumption can be rebutted. Further, support on divorce may be temporary.[49] This means that spousal support on divorce may be limited in time until the child reaches the age of five years. If the child is older than five years of age, spousal support may not exceed three years. It is possible to file a petition for prolongation of spousal support upon divorce; however, only under specific circumstances will the time limitation not apply – for example, if it is not foreseeable when the impediment to taking up gainful employment will cease (eg the child is disabled or the couple have several common minor children).[50] Support on divorce independent of fault may also be due when the housekeeping spouse gave up his/her training or profession in order to do the housekeeping and to assume care and education of the children, or even the nursing of a close relative, in agreement with the other spouse. Gainful employment may, therefore, have become unreasonable with regard to the tasks assumed during marriage. Factors such as lacking opportunity for gainful employment, the duration of the marriage, age and physical condition may render gainful employment unreasonable. These factors must be carefully balanced.[51] This claim for support can also be limited in time, but only if the court is of the

---

49   Article 68a para 1 EheG.
50   Article 68a para 1 EheG.
51   Article 68a para 3 EheG.

opinion that the ex-spouse will then be able to earn his/her own living. The time limitation in this case may not exceed three months. The extent of the support due was extremely controversial in the Reform Commission. Finally, agreement was reached that support upon divorce should cover adequately the necessities of life. Therefore, all depends on what the petitioner would have achieved if he/she had not married and had not invested in the marriage that broke down, taking into consideration the above-mentioned criteria that may render gainful employment unreasonable.

A marital home which was owned by one spouse before marriage, which he/she inherited or was given as a gift, can form part of the property to divide on divorce. Originally, the need of the other spouse was a valid reason for this. After the reform, the need of a common child may also be a valid reason to consider such property in the division procedure.[52] The welfare of the child must not necessarily be endangered; the transfer of the child to a new location could be considered a burden for the child. By and large, marital articles of daily use (including the home used by the couple and their child) and marital savings are divided according to the principle of equity. The contribution of each spouse to marital life as well as to debts and the needs of each party, including the needs of the common child, are factors to consider. Investments in a business undertaking will also be considered in a procedure to divide the marital property, ie the marital articles of daily use and the marital savings,[53] if they were financed by means of such marital property. In fact, many scholars have criticised the fact that business undertakings should be exempt from property division upon divorce and advocated the abolition of this exception. This new provision, therefore, constitutes a compromise. At the end of the day, the judge must consider whether the success of the business undertaking was not an economic advantage to the family, whether the economic means used for the business undertaking were not financed with its capital, and last but not least, whether the business undertaking would be endangered by considering the investments.

The last important amendment of the marriage law deals with the introduction of mediation in the divorce procedure.[54] Mediation provides for alternative dispute resolution. The mediator has an obligation of secrecy. Violations of this duty lead to criminal sanctions, if the legitimate interests of one of the spouses are violated. At present, the Austrian Ministry of Justice is working on a draft Bill concerning the profession of mediators. It remains to be seen what the conditions for the exercise of this profession will be.

---

52   Article 82 para 2 EheG.
53   Article 91 para 2 EheG.
54   Article 99 EheG.

CANADA

COURT DECISIONS ON SAME-SEX AND UNMARRIED PARTNERS, SPOUSAL RIGHTS AND CHILDREN

*Nicholas Bala**

I INTRODUCTION: THE SUPREME COURT AND FAMILY LAW

Led by the Supreme Court, Canadian courts have recently rendered a number of important family law decisions. These decisions are reshaping the legal regulation of non-marital relationships, using the Canadian Charter of Rights and Freedoms to grant greater legal recognition to same-sex partners and unmarried heterosexual cohabitants, and to move towards equating with marriage, the rights and obligations arising out of these long-term, non-marital intimate relationships.

The Supreme Court of Canada has clarified some of the complex issues surrounding division of pensions on spousal separation. The Court also dealt with a couple of spousal support cases, though it continued to emphasise that this is a discretionary exercise without clear rules for trial judges. In a custody dispute over an aboriginal child the Supreme Court emphasised the importance of the discretionary 'best interests' decision of the trial judge, and failed to articulate a clear preference for placement with aboriginal relatives. Canada now has Child Support Guidelines to determine the level of child support. The Supreme Court has also ruled that there is a strong presumption that the Guidelines amounts are to apply to very high-income parents.

The Supreme Court invoked the Charter of Rights to grant indigent parents the right to State-appointed counsel in a child-protection case, recognising that these proceedings pose a threat to the constitutionally protected rights of children and their parents to 'security of the person'. The Court also used the United Nations Convention on the Rights of the Child to afford substantive rights to parents and children in an immigration case, requiring consideration of the 'best interests of a child' before a parent of a child who is a citizen can be deported.

II LEGAL RECOGNITION OF SAME-SEX PARTNERSHIPS: THE SUPREME COURT IN *M v H*

Largely led by the courts, the Canadian legal system is moving towards the recognition of the 'familial' status of same-sex relationships, but the granting of 'spousal' rights to gays and lesbians remains contentious in Canada.

* Professor of Law, Faculty of Law, Queen's University, Kingston, Ontario. The author wishes to acknowledge the support of the Social Sciences and Humanities Research Council of Canada and the editorial assistance of Ms Erin McNamara (Queen's Law 01). Some portions of this paper are revised versions of earlier works by this author.

Starting with Quebec in 1976, most jurisdictions in Canada enacted legislation prohibiting discrimination based on sexual orientation in regard to such matters as employment. While a few jurisdictions did not enact this type of legislation, in 1998 the Supreme Court of Canada[1] ruled that Alberta's failure to include 'sexual orientation' as a prohibited ground of discrimination in its human rights statute was contrary to Canada's Charter of Rights and Freedoms.[2]

Despite a growing consensus that overt discrimination against gays and lesbians should not be tolerated in Canadian society, legislatures and courts have been reluctant to accord fully 'familial' status to same-sex partners.[3] In 1993 an Ontario appeal court dismissed a challenge by a same-sex couple who said their constitutional rights had been violated when they had been refused a marriage licence. In *Egan v Canada* in 1995, a narrow majority of the Supreme Court of Canada dismissed a constitutionally based claim by long-term, same-sex partners to 'spousal' benefits under the Old Age Security Act, even though unmarried opposite-sex partners in the same situation have the benefit of the Act.[4]

In 1996, the courts began to change their approach to the legal recognition of familial rights in same-sex relationships. An Ontario trial judge in *M v H* held that the failure of Ontario's spousal support statute to allow same-sex partners to seek support was unconstitutional.[5] The decision was affirmed by the Ontario Court of Appeal.[6] These decisions ruled unconstitutional Ontario's Family Law Act, section 29, which defined 'spouse' to include two unmarried opposite-sex partners who 'cohabit' for three years or cohabited in a relationship of 'some permanence' and are the parents of a child. The Ontario courts ruled that the Charter, required inclusion of same-sex partners in this statutory definition; the 1996 Supreme Court of Canada decision in *Egan* was distinguished on the basis that in *M v H* only 'private' rights were at stake, and no expenditure of public funds was required to redress the claim.

In May 1999, the Supreme Court of Canada upheld the lower court rulings in *M v H* and held that section 29 of the Family Law Act violates section 15 of the Charter, though the remedy the Supreme Court imposed was to declare the provision of no force and give the Ontario legislature six months to enact a constitutionally valid law.[7] The Supreme Court accepted that excluding individuals who had been partners in long-term, same-sex relationships from the opportunity to seek support at the end of the relationship constitutes

---

1   *Vriend v Alberta* [1998] 1 SCR 493. The Supreme Court of Canada has a free website with access to the Supreme Court Reports (SCR) as well as postings of recent decisions: <http://www.scc-csc.gc.ca/>.

2   Canadian Charter of Rights and Freedoms, Part I of the Constitution Act 1982, being Schedule B of the Canada Act 1982 (UK, 1982, c. 11), section 15 ('the Charter').

3   In general, judges have been more willing than legislators to extend legal recognition to same-sex couples. However, in 1997 the legislature of British Columbia significantly expanded the rights and obligations of same-sex couples, amending its family law legislation that deals with child custody and access, child support and spousal support, and included same-sex partners in the definitions of 'spouse' and 'parent' for these purposes. Family Relations Amendment Act 1997, S.B.C. 1997, c. 20.

4   *Egan v Canada* [1995] 2 SCR 513, 12 RFL (4th) 201, 124 DLR (4th) 609 (SCC).

5   (1996), 17 RFL (4th) 365 (Ont. Gen. Div.).

6   [1996] OJ 4419 (Ont CA).

7   [1999] 2 SCR 3, [1999] SCJ 23.

discrimination on the basis of sexual orientation. The majority of the Court emphasised the social importance of recognising same-sex relationships, with Cory J writing:[8]

'The societal significance of the benefit conferred by the statute cannot be overemphasized. The exclusion of same-sex partners from the benefits of s.29 of the *FLA* promotes the view that M., and individuals in same-sex relationships generally, are less worthy of recognition and protection. It implies that they are judged to be incapable of forming intimate relationships of economic interdependence as compared to opposite-sex couples, without regard to their actual circumstances. ... such exclusion perpetuates the disadvantages suffered by individuals in same-sex relationships and contributes to the erasure of their existence. ... the human dignity of individuals in same-sex relationships is violated by the impugned legislation.'

The Court was careful to note that the basis of the claim in *M v H* was that it is discriminatory to fail to give same-sex partners the same rights as unmarried opposite-sex partners, and did not directly compare same-sex partners to married opposite-sex couples. However, this type of rhetoric would suggest that the Court will be sympathetic in future cases to an argument that the failure to allow same-sex partners to marry is an affront to their 'human dignity'.

The majority decision of the Supreme Court recognised that 'there is evidence to suggest that same-sex relationships are not typically characterised by the same economic and other inequalities which affect opposite-sex relationships'.[9] Nevertheless, the Court accepted that:[10]

'... same-sex couples will often form long, lasting, loving and intimate relationships. The choices they make in the context of those relationships may give rise to the financial dependence of one partner on the other. ... While it is true that there may not be any consensus as to the societal perception of same-sex couples, there is agreement that same-sex couples share many ... "conjugal" characteristics. In order to come within the definition, neither opposite-sex couples nor same-sex couples are required to fit precisely the traditional marital model to demonstrate that the relationship is "conjugal".'

As the Supreme Court noted, it was only ruling that opposite-sex partners in long-term relationships may be eligible to seek support. In determining whether there will actually be entitlement in a specific case, a judge will have to consider the degree of interdependence and contribution in that particular relationship; in many same-sex relationships the limited nature of economic interdependence will result in no support actually being awarded.

In seeking to uphold the legislation, the government of Ontario attempted to invoke section 1 of the Charter to justify the legislation, as either necessary to

---

8　At paras 73–74.

9　Para 110, per Iacobucci J: Same-sex couples are much less likely to have children, and it would appear that *on average* gays and lesbians are less likely than heterosexuals to enter long-term monogamous relationships with significant degrees of economic interdependence, though this does not mean that same-sex partners should have different rights and obligations from opposite-sex partners; see 'The Price of Equality', *Globe & Mail,* 18 March 2000, p R9.

10　Para 55, per Cory J.

protect the interests of women, who are usually the dependent partners, or to support family units in which there are children. The Court rejected these arguments, noting that the FLA allows either a male or a female 'spouse' to seek support, and that it is not necessary for opposite-sex partners to have children to be eligible for support under the FLA. Further, some same-sex partners have joint responsibility for the care of children, whether the children are adopted, from a previous relationship, or born to one person in the same-sex relationship with the expectation that both will parent the child. The Court also noted that imposing a support obligation on same-sex partners at the end of a relationship may save the Government from making welfare payments.

Technically, Ontario was the only province directly affected by *M v H*. However, it is clear that the other territorial and provincial governments must also respond to the decision, or they will quickly be forced to do so by the courts. The government of Ontario responded begrudgingly to the Supreme Court decision, with Conservative politicians emphasising that they only acted because they had been forced to do so by the Court. This attitude was reflected in the formal name of Ontario's legislative response: An Act to Amend Certain Statutes Because of the Supreme Court of Canada Decision in *M v H* (Bill 5).[11] There was a clear effort by Conservative politicians to reserve the traditional definition of 'spouse' for heterosexual 'conjugal' relationships (married or unmarried). Ontario Premier Harris commented disparagingly on same-sex unions: 'It is not my definition of the family'.[12] Rather than changing the definition of 'spouse,' Ontario's Bill 5 adds the new concept of the 'same-sex partner', preserving the term 'spouse' for heterosexuals who are married or have long-term relationships. However, 'same-sex partners' are given all the rights and obligations of unmarried heterosexual cohabitants in the 67 Ontario statutes that already recognise unmarried heterosexual partnerships, for example for such purposes as support and dependants' claims against estates. Although there is a new concept added, the 'same-sex partner', the requirements for acquiring this status are the same as for opposite-sex unmarried partners: a period of three years continuous cohabitation, or cohabitation in a relationship of some permanence if they are the adoptive parents of a child.[13]

The rhetoric of the Liberal politicians who have introduced the federal government's response to *M v H* was a little more supportive of gays and lesbians than that of the Ontario politicians responsible for Bill 5, but the legal effect of the response was quite similar.[14] Bill C-23 amended 68 Federal statutes to recognise

---

11   Ontario, Bill 5, 1st Session, 37th Parliament, Third Reading, 27 October 1999.

12   'Ontario gets "on message"' *Globe & Mail*, 25 October 1999, p A15.

13   The legislation actually stipulates that one can be a 'same-sex partner' if one has 'cohabited' with another person of the same sex 'in a relationship of some permanence, if they are the *natural* or adoptive parents of a child.' This uses exactly the same language as for opposite-sex partners, though it is biologically impossible for two same-sex partners to be the natural parents of a child. It is clear that under legislation like Ontario's Family Law Act, section 1, a person may assume the rights and obligations of a 'parent' towards the biological child of a same-sex partner, even without adoption or three years cohabitation, if that person has 'demonstrated an intention to treat the child as a child of his or her family.' Family Relations Amendment Act 1997, SBC 1997, c.20.

14   See eg 'Gay-rights Bill Stirring Up Liberal caucus' *Globe & Mail*, 10 February 2000. Some backbench MPs in the Liberal government and many members of the opposition Reform Party oppose the recognition of same-sex relationships. One Reform MP, Philip Mayfield said: 'I am

as 'common law partners ... two persons who are cohabiting in a conjugal relationship, having so cohabited for a period of at least one year'.[15] The slightly more sympathetic Federal attitude was reflected in the fact that there is no attempt to have different names for same-sex and opposite-sex partners – both are referred to as 'common law partners,' and in the name of the new law, the Modernisation of Benefits and Obligations Act. This Bill extended to same-sex partners most of the rights and obligations already afforded to heterosexual unmarried partners, for example, for purposes of Federal income tax law and Federal pension plan eligibility.[16] Federal law already used a definition of one year's cohabitation in contrast to Ontario's three years for acquiring ascribed status.

After a contentious set of hearings, the Liberal government felt obliged to 'reassure the public' that it did not intend to undermine the institution of marriage, and amended the law to specify that 'for greater certainty, the amendments made by this Act do not affect the meaning of the word "marriage", that is, the lawful union of one man and one woman to the exclusion of all others'.[17] The hope of the proponents of this amendment is that it might be used against a future Charter challenge by gays and lesbians seeking 'same-sex marriage'.

The rights (and obligations) for same-sex couples that are imposed by the recently enacted legislation, like Ontario's Bill 5 and the Federal Bill C-23, appears to provide a satisfactory response to the immediate constitutional challenge posed by *M v H*.[18] However, there remain some very important differences between the rights that may arise by 'ascription' (rights and obligations that are imposed after a period of cohabitation) and those that arise out of marriage; as well, there is not yet full legal recognition of same-sex relationships. There is a profound psychological and social difference that results from gays and lesbians being treated unequally and not having the option to have formal legal recognition for their relationship at any time they wish. A major legal difference is that until the parties have cohabited for the prescribed period, they do not do not have the rights and obligations towards each other or other parties that spouses have. There may also be a lack of clarity for the partners and others as exactly when the ascribed status is (or is not) attained.

Charter-based challenges have been launched seeking to give gays and lesbians the right to marry.[19] It may be difficult for Canadian courts to distinguish *M v H* in a challenge that raises the claim to the right to marry. Although historically same-sex partners (and unmarried opposite-sex partners) were denied

---

one of those ... who believes that families are made up of a man and a woman and the children in between.' 'Reform Questions Timing of Bill', *Globe & Mail*, 9 February 2000.

15 Bill C-23, 36th Parliament, 2nd Session, as passed by the House of Commons, 11 April 2000.

16 The Federal Government still has to address some issues such as immigration sponsorship rights for same-sex partners.

17 Section 1.1: see 'Amendment to Same-Sex Benefits Law Sparks Ruckus', *National Post*, 23 March 2000.

18 However, the applicant in *M v H* is planning to bring a motion in the Supreme Court of Canada challenging the failure of the Ontario government to respond adequately to the decision and continuing to discriminate by failing to include same-sex partners within the definition of 'spouse' and using the different 'same-sex partner' terminology. *Globe & Mail*, 25 November 1999.

19 Challenges have been launched in Ontario, Quebec and New Brunswick. See 'Toronto Seeks Ruling on Gay Marriage Licence', *National Post*, 20 May 2000 on a case in Ontario; also 'Group Hopes Lawsuit Spurs Legislative Action on Gay Rights', *Globe & Mail*, 8 January 1999.

the rights and obligations of marriage, the denial of the psychological, social, economic and legal benefits of marriage seems to be a clear violation of the 'human dignity' of same-sex partners, and discrimination under section 15 of the Charter.[20] Although there may be some differences between the 'typical' same-sex relationship and the 'typical' opposite-sex relationship, same-sex relationships serve profoundly important social and economic functions, and merit legal recognition as equivalent to opposite-sex familial relationships.[21]

III   UNMARRIED OPPOSITE-SEX COHABITATION

Since the 1970s there has been a steady rise in unmarried cohabitation in Canada, accompanied by dramatic changes in the law. In 1996, 14% of all Canadian couples residing together were unmarried, up from 6% in 1981.[22] As a result of the growing incidence of unmarried heterosexual cohabitation, this has been accepted as a social institution and has received growing legislative recognition.

Many Canadian statutes which give rights and obligations to 'spouses' now also include unmarried heterosexual partners who have 'cohabited in a conjugal relationship' or 'lived together as husband and wife'. Spousal status is generally acquired under these legislative schemes if there has been cohabitation for a specified period (generally one to three years) or the cohabiting couple has a child. Most, but not all provinces included such definitions for such purposes as being able to claim 'spousal' support or rights to claim against the estate of a deceased partner.

The 1995 decision of the Supreme Court of Canada in *Miron v Trudel*,[23] extended the statutory definition of 'spouse' for the purposes of an automobile insurance policy to include an unmarried opposite-sex partner, ruling that excluding long-term unmarried cohabitants from the statutory definition of 'spouse' was discriminatory and contrary to section 15 of the Charter of Rights.

Alberta, one of Canada's more conservative provinces, gave relatively little statutory recognition to unmarried cohabitants. The 1998 decision of the Alberta Court of Appeal in *Taylor v Rossu* dealt with a support claim by a woman who cohabited with a man for 30 years.[24] Citing the Supreme Court decision in *Miron v Trudel*, the Alberta Court ruled it was a violation of section 15 of the Charter to exclude a person in this position from the definition of 'spouse' in that province's

---

20   Of course given the Charter's guarantee of freedom of religion, no government can enact a law to require any religion to perform such marriage services. Conversely, the religious same-sex 'marriage ceremonies' that some religious figures in Canada now perform have no legal significance.

21   For a fuller discussion of issues related to same-sex marriage and alternatives for legislative reform in Canada, see generally Volume 17(1) of the *Canadian Journal of Family Law*; Kathleen Lahey, *Are We 'Persons' Yet? Law and Sexuality in Canada* (Toronto: University of Toronto Press, 1999); and Law Commission of Canada, *Recognising and Supporting Close Personal Relationships Between Adults: Discussion Paper* (Ottawa, May 2000) Catalogue No. JL2-10/2000; <http://www.lcc.gc.ca/en/forum/cpra/paper.html.>

22   Statistics Canada, 1996 Census. See 'More People are Giving Marriage a Try', *National Post*, 22 May 2000.

23   [1995] 2 SCR 418.

24   *Taylor v Rossu* (1998), 39 RFL (4th) 242 (Alta.C.A.).

Domestic Relations Act, giving the legislature a year to respond. The Alberta legislature amended the law to include within the definition of 'spouse' for the purposes of the Act an opposite-sex partner if there has been a 'marriage-like' relationship where the partners have had a child or cohabited for three years.[25]

Division of property is one area where Canadian legislation still makes a distinction between married and cohabiting couples. No province has enacted legislation to allow an unmarried cohabitant to claim statutory 'marital' property rights or to enjoy the possessory rights of a married spouse to the family home,[26] though the courts may use equitable remedies to compensate one partner for a contribution to the acquisition or maintenance of property by the other.[27]

There have recently been a number of reported decisions that have relied on the Charter to recognise claims to the statutory rights of married spouses by women at the end of long-term, unmarried relationships. The effect of these decisions has been to eliminate any significant legal distinction between married persons and those in long-term, opposite-sex relationships (and the courts have also recognised that same-sex partners are entitled to the same rights as those who are unmarried opposite-sex partners).

In its April 2000 decision in *Walsh v Bona*, the Nova Scotia Court of Appeal ruled in favour of the constitutional challenge of a woman who lived with a man for 10 years in a common-law relationship[28] in which two children were born. The Court noted the practical and procedural burdens placed on unmarried partners forced to rely on such equitable remedies as the constructive trust, and held that the failure to include an unmarried cohabitant within the definition of 'spouse' in the province's marital property law violates section 15 of the Charter. Citing the 1995 Supreme Court of Canada decision in *Miron*, Flinn JA ruled that, by excluding same-sex partners, the Matrimonial Property Act 'perpetuates the view that unmarried partners are less worthy of recognition, or value, as human beings or as members of Canadian society, equally deserving of concern, respect and consideration.'[29]

The Government tried to defend the differential treatment, but the Court concluded that it failed to provide 'any satisfactory explanation as to why it is pressing to exclude persons in common law relationships from the provisions of MPA while including them on the same basis as married persons in other provincial legislation'.[30] The Court rejected the argument that a common-law partner could have had the benefit of the legislation by entering into a cohabitation agreement. Having an agreement is not a matter in her 'sole control', but rather would have required the active co-operation of her partner. The Court also

---

25 S.A. 1999, c. 20, section 2.

26 Only the Northwest Territories and Nunavut Territory have property statutes that include in the definition of 'spouse' a person of the opposite sex who has cohabited outside of marriage for two years or in a relationship in which the couple are the natural or adoptive parents of a child; Family Law Act SNWT 1997, c. 18 section 1.

27 See *Peter v Beblow*, [1993] 1 SCR 980 where the Supreme Court used constructive trust concepts to recognise a woman's domestic contributions as the basis for awarding her a house owned by her partner before the relationship began.

28 In Canada the term 'common law marriage' is often used to describe an opposite-sex couple who reside together without being legally married.

29 [2000] NSJ 117, at para 50, Glube CJNS and Roscoe JA concurring.

30 Para 76.

rejected the claim that it was interfering with the individual autonomy of those who do not wish to marry: 'providing those in a common law relationship with the ability to contract out of the MPA is of far less consequence than denying all others in a common law relationship the benefits of the MPA'.[31]

The Nova Scotia Court of Appeal in *Walsh v Bona* gave the legislature 12 months to remedy this defect, recognising that there would be some practical issues to address, and that the legislature might choose to exclude those in 'transitory relationships'. The Court also invited the female applicant in this particular case to return to court to make submissions for immediate relief.

While a number of law reform agencies in Canada have written reports that have advocated equating long-term, opposite-sex cohabitation with marriage, politicians have been reluctant to deal with such controversial political issues.[32] The courts, however, cannot avoid dealing with these issues. The recent decisions establish a clear trend towards granting unmarried heterosexual cohabitants the same statutory rights (and obligations) as the married, though there is some variation in the remedies afforded.

While in comparison to marriage, non-marital relationships tend to be shorter in duration, have fewer children and involve less economic integration, the courts are sending a clear message that the contributions and functions of individual relationships are to be assessed. Although those in non-marital opposite-sex relationships may be *eligible* for treatment as spouses, the nature of roles, contributions and expectations will affect how courts deal with specific cases. It is not a coincidence that those bringing Charter challenges have been women in long-term relationships, with a high degree of economic interdependence, usually with children. These relationships are functionally identical to marriage. Whatever the expectations of the parties may have been at the beginning of the relationship, it would be unfair to ignore the interdependencies and vulnerabilities that have in fact arisen.

The message from the courts is that if a party to a long-term, non-marital relationship wishes to argue that there was a lack of consent to the imposition of marital rights and obligations, there is an onus on that party to have a domestic contract opting out of the imposition of marital rights. In most long-term unmarried relationships there is likely to be some ambiguity of expectations, and expectations may change over time, or not be consistent between the two parties. If a party to such a long-term relationship, invariably the man, wishes to argue that there should not be equitable treatment, he has an obligation to ensure that this truly was the expectation of both parties. In the absence of an explicit agreement, a significant period of having the benefits and pleasures of cohabitation in a marriage-like relationship will be deemed to be consent to the imposition of marital obligation.

---

31 Para 73.

32 See, eg Law Reform Commission of Nova Scotia, *Final Report on Reform of the Law Dealing with Matrimonial Property in Nova Scotia* (Halifax: 1997); and Ontario Law Reform Commission, *Report on the Rights and Responsibilities of Cohabitants Under the Family Law Act* (Toronto, 1993). Both of these reports were cited by the Nova Scotia Court of Appeal in *Walsh v Bona*.

IV SPOUSAL RIGHTS AND OBLIGATIONS: SPOUSAL SUPPORT AND PENSIONS

In 1999 the Supreme Court of Canada decided three cases in which spousal support was an issue without providing any real guidance to lower courts or lawyers. In one of these cases the Court also dealt with issues related to the division of pensions, providing significant guidance to practitioners on pension valuation problems.

In 1992 the Supreme Court of Canada in *Moge v Moge* articulated an approach to spousal support that focussed on its 'compensatory' nature, with spousal support being aimed at providing compensation to those who assume roles in marriage that may affect their ability to earn income long after separation.[33] This decision was expressly intended to address the issue of the feminisation of poverty and resulted in more women receiving spousal support, often on an indefinite basis.[34] This approach led some judges to conclude that spousal support could only be awarded to compensate a spouse for roles assumed during marriage. In 1995, the trial judge in *Bracklow v Bracklow* ruled that a woman who became sick and unable to work during the course of marriage and cohabitation of a seven-year period was not entitled to spousal support, though the judge endorsed the husband's agreement to pay $400 a month for 18 months as transitional support. As both parties worked during most of the marriage, the trial judge concluded that *Moge* required the court to 'look upon marriage in the same manner as a tort claim ... [Since in this case] no economic consequences flowed to her disadvantage as a result of the marriage' no support should be awarded.[35] The trial judge also rejected the woman's argument that it was possible to rely on their marriage vow, in which each spouse had pledged to care for the other 'in sickness and in health', as the basis for a spousal support claim. The trial decision was upheld by the British Columbia Court of Appeal.

The Supreme Court of Canada allowed an appeal by the woman but remitted the issue of support back to the trial court, with a very general set of instructions. Writing for the Supreme Court, McLaughlin J acknowledged that it is 'not the bare fact of marriage, so much as the relationship that is established and the expectations that may reasonably flow from it that give rise to the obligation of support under the statutes'.[36] While compensation for roles assumed during marriage is usually the dominant purpose for awarding support it is not the only basis for doing so:[37]

'the statutes and the case law suggest three conceptual bases for entitlement to spousal support: (1) compensatory, (2) contractual, and (3) non-compensatory. Marriage ... is a "joint endeavour", a socio-economic partnership ... a review of cases suggests that in most circumstances compensation now serves as the main reason for support.

---

33 [1992] 3 SCR 813.

34 See, eg Rogerson, 'Spousal Support After Moge' (1996–97), 14 Can. Fam. L.Q. 281.

35 (1995), 13 RFL (4th) 184 (BCSC), at paras 24 and 25.

36 [1999] 1 SCR 420, 44 RFL (4th) 1, at para 44. See commentary JG McLeod, 'Annotation to *Bracklow v Bracklow*' (1999), 44 RFL (4th) 5–9; and DAR Thompson, 'Rules and Rulelessness In Family Law: Recent Developments, Judicial and Legislative' (2000), 17(4) Can. Fam. L.Q.

37 At para 49.

However, contract and compensation are not the only sources of a support obligation. The obligation may alternatively arise out of the marriage relationship itself. Where a spouse achieves economic self-sufficiency on the basis of his or her own efforts, or on an award of compensatory support, the obligation founded on the marriage relationship itself lies dormant. But where need is established that is not met on a compensatory or contractual basis, the fundamental marital obligation may play a vital role. Absent negating factors, it is available, in appropriate circumstances, to provide just support.'

While the Court recognised that illness and need *might* justify an award of spousal support, the decision was frustratingly vague and the case was remitted to the trial court without clear directions as to how the various factors should be balanced. Justice McLaughlin concluded that Mrs Bracklow was not disentitled to support merely because her need arose out of illness, but that she *might* not be entitled to any further support:[38]

'... While the combined cohabitation and marriage of seven years were not long, neither were they (by today's standards) very short. Mrs. Bracklow contributed, when possible, as a self-sufficient member of the family, at times shouldering the brunt of the financial obligations. These factors establish that it would be unjust and contrary to the objectives of the statutes for Mrs. Bracklow to be cast aside as ineligible for support, and for Mr. Bracklow to assume none of the state's burden to care for his ex-wife.

... I leave the determination of the quantum of support to the trial judge, who is in a better position to address the facts of this case than our appellate tribunal. My only comment on the issue is ... that all the relevant statutory factors, including the length of the marital relationship and the relative independence of the parties throughout that marital relationship, must be considered, together with the amount of support Mr. Bracklow has already paid to Mrs. Bracklow. I therefore do not exclude the possibility that no further support will be required, i.e., that Mr. Bracklow's contributions to date have discharged the just and appropriate quantum.'

The parties were thus put to the expense of a rehearing without a clear direction from the Supreme Court. The case was dealt with by another trial judge, who concluded that spousal support should be awarded for a time-limited period, so that the total period of receiving support was roughly equal to the seven years of cohabitation; the amount of support, $400 a month, supplemented her disability pension of about $800 a month, but clearly did not maintain her at the marital standard of living. The trial judge observed[39] that cases that:

'involve entitlement based on non-compensatory grounds, with an ongoing need by the recipient and an ability to pay by the payer, are the most difficult to determine, particularly where the relationship and/or marriage is relatively short. Unless a time limit is imposed on an award for spousal support in a relatively short marriage, the redistributive paradigm could develop into an entitlement flowing from the relationship/marriage per se.'

---

38   Paras 60 and 61.
39   [1999] BCJ 3028 (SC) per D Smith J.

A few months after *Bracklow*, the Supreme Court rendered another decision emphasizing the discretion of the trial judge to resolve issues of spousal support. In *Hickey v Hickey*,[40] the parties had entered into a separation agreement in 1986, providing for spousal support of $1,000 per month and child support of $750 for each of the two children, ie total support of $2,500 per month payable to the custodial mother. The agreement had a clause permitting either party to seek variation for a 'material change in circumstances.' By 1996, one of the children had reached adulthood.[41] The mother agreed to end support for this child, but applied for an increase in support. The trial judge, recognising that inflation had eroded the value of the original order and that there are greater costs for older children,[42] increased the child support for the remaining child from $750 per month to $1,500, and increased spousal support from $1,000 to $1,300. The Manitoba Court of Appeal reduced child support to $900 per month, and restored the original amount of spousal support at $1,000.

In restoring the decision of the trial judge, the Supreme Court of Canada recognised that, even without specific evidence, trial judges could consider the effects of inflation and use this as a basis for increasing spousal support. The Supreme Court also emphasised the discretionary nature of support awards and limited scope for appeals in spousal support cases.[43]

> 'There are strong reasons for the significant deference that must be given to trial judges in relation to support orders. This standard of appellate review recognises that the discretion involved in making a support order is best exercised by the judge who has heard the parties directly. It avoids giving parties an incentive to appeal judgments and incur added expenses in the hope that the appeal court will have a different appreciation of the relevant factors and evidence. This approach promotes finality in family law litigation and recognises the importance of the appreciation of the facts by the trial judge. Though an appeal court must intervene when there is a material error, a serious misapprehension of the evidence, or an error in law, it is not entitled to overturn a support order simply because it would have made a different decision or balanced the factors differently.'

The Supreme Court was also recently confronted with a case that raised interrelated spousal support and pension issues. While all Canadian jurisdictions allow for some form of division of pensions, there is significant variation in the extent to which legislation provides for valuation and division of pensions.[44] In

---

40 [1999] 2 SCR 519, 46 RFL (4th) 1; see commentary JG McLeod, 'Annotation to *Hickey v Hickey* (1999)', 46 RFL (4th) 5–8; and DAR Thompson, 'Rules and Rulelessness In Family Law: Recent Developments, Judicial and Legislative' (2000), 17(4) Can. Fam. L.Q.

41 In Canada, child support can be ordered for an adult child who is pursuing an education, is disabled or otherwise unable to support him or herself; see Divorce Act RSC 1985, c. 3 (2nd Supp.), s 2(1) and *Bragg v Bragg* (2000), 2 RFL (5th) 344 (Nfld UFC)

42 The trial in this case occurred before the *Child Support Guidelines* were in effect; these *Guidelines* do not allow an increase in the amounts of child support because a child is older, but increased costs for extracurricular activities or post-secondary education may be the basis for an increased award of child support.

43 Para 12.

44 See, eg E Diane Pask, *Division of Pensions* (Toronto: Carswell, 1990) (loose-leaf); Ontario Law Reform Commission, *Report on Pensions as Family Property: Valuation and Division* (Toronto, 1995).

and several other jurisdictions, there is little legislation to guide and
late the courts in dealing with the valuation of private employment pensions,
.. .n though these are the most valuable asset for many families.

In *Best v Best*[45] the spouses separated after 12 years of marriage. It was a
second marriage for both. The husband worked as a teacher for more than 20 years
before the marriage, and continued this employment during and after the marriage.
He had a defined benefit pension, with the amount of pension payments reflecting
his years of service and his highest five years of salary. A central issue in the
Supreme Court was the valuation of the portion of the pension acquired during the
marriage, with this sum to be divisible between the spouses. The majority of the
Supreme Court, reversing the lower courts, held that it was 'fairer' to use the *pro
rata* method. The *pro rata* method of valuation divides the discounted present
value as of the date of separation of the future pension payments, in proportion to
the number of years of employment during and before the marriage. In this case, it
meant that about 12/32 of the discounted present value of the pension was
divisible. Madam Justice L'Heureux-Dubé, in dissent, preferred the value-added
method, which deducted the discounted present value of the pension stream
acquired as of marriage from the discounted value of the pension at separation. As
she noted, the value-added approach would provide more benefit to the vulnerable
non-employee spouse (typically the woman) if a couple separates close to
retirement. The *Best* decision has provoked considerable adverse comment since
the *pro rata* approach of the majority of the Supreme Court treats the valuation of
pension differently from other assets, and seems inconsistent with the general
approach of the legislation to the valuation of property.[46] Like most
commentators, the Court advocated legislative action to facilitate valuation and
division of pensions, but politicians seem reluctant to take further action on the
complex and contentious issues involved.

In *Best*, the trial judge ordered that the man was to satisfy the equalisation
claim by making cash payments spread over a ten-year period and also ordered the
man to pay $2,500 as spousal support. The Supreme Court rejected the husband's
appeal on the remedy question; he argued that the court should have ordered a
division of the pension at source. While the Supreme Court accepted that this is a
possible remedy, it held that appeal courts should give 'deference' to the 'highly
contextual and fact-based determination'.[47] Given the fact that a very substantial

---

45 [1999] 2 SCR 868, 49 RFL (4th) 1.

46 For commentaries see JG McLeod, 'Annotation to *Best v Best*' (1999), 49 RFL (4th) 1–22;
Burrows and Hebert, 'The Supreme Court of Canada and *Best v Best*' (2000), 17 Can. Fam. L.Q.
263–276; and DAR Thompson, 'Rules and Rulelessness In Family Law: Recent Developments,
Judicial and Legislative' (2000), 17(4) Can. Fam. L.Q.

47 At para 109. Justice Major also thought that the trial judge was justified in making this decision
since division of the pension at source would 'require … a continued financial association
between the ex-spouses that obviates a "clean-break" after the divorce' [para 111]. However,
since 1988 Ontario legislation has allowed for an order to be made that when the employee
spouse retires (or terminates employment for death or other reasons), there can be a division of
the pension at source. The order can require payments by the plan administrator directly to non-
employee spouse, with the payments not affected by the length of the employee's life.
Alternatively the non-employee spouse may have the value of her portion of the plan transferred
to her own pension. *Pension Benefits Act*, RSO 1990, c. P. 8, section 51. Ontario Law Reform
Commission, *Report on Pensions as Family Property: Valuation and Division* (Toronto, 1995),
33–42.

portion of the property award reflected the value of the pension and that the husband was already close to retirement age at the time of trial, this would have seemed to be an appropriate case in which to make a division of the pension at source, so the Court's ruling on the remedy issue is puzzling.

By the time that *Best* was decided by the Supreme Court, the man had already retired and he also argued that spousal support should be eliminated, or at least reduced. He argued that since the woman was already receiving property payments that reflected her share in the pension, he should not also be obliged to pay support out of the pension, which was by that time the primary source of his income. While the Supreme Court recognised 'double-dipping' as a 'serious problem when spousal support orders are based on an equalised pension', the Court declined to resolve this issue since the man was still employed at the time of the trial. His retirement before the Supreme Court hearing 'might' be a ground for variation of the amount of spousal support, but he was expected to bring another court application to decide this question. The lack of clear direction from the Supreme Court about how to deal with the 'double dipping' issue doubtless caused the parties in *Best* additional expense to resolve it, as well as being a missed opportunity for the Supreme Court to provide guidance on a subject which the Court acknowledged has divided judges and commentators.[48]

V CHILD SUPPORT AND CHILD CUSTODY

In 1997 Canada adopted Guidelines to help determine amounts of child support in a fairer and more efficient manner.[49] The Guidelines have tables which determine the amount of child support by reference to the payer's income. Although in some situations courts have discretion to order greater or lesser amounts, it is a limited and structured discretion. As in most jurisdictions with child support guidelines, there is some flexibility for dealing with high-income cases, in Canada those cases where the payer's annual income is over $150,000. The tables provide that for a high-income payer the amount of child support is roughly 8% of pre-tax income for one child, and 12% if there are two children. Section 4 of the Guidelines provides that if the payer's income is over $150,000 per year and the table amount is 'inappropriate', the court may award an amount that it considers 'appropriate' having regard to the needs of the children and the means of both of the parents. Given the amounts involved and the costs of litigation, it is not surprising that the first, and thus far, the only case dealing with the Guidelines to reach the Supreme Court of Canada has involved a very high-income payer and section 4.

Though relatively rare, cases involving payers with high incomes understandably receive considerable attention from the media and in the legal profession.

In *Francis v Baker*[50] the parties signed a separation agreement soon after the separation in 1985. After the agreement was signed the father's economic position improved dramatically, while the mother's situation had changed little. By 1997

---

48 Paras 119 and 120.

49 For the Guidelines and explanatory materials, see http://canada.justice.gc.ca/en/ps/sup/index.html

50 28 RFL (4th) 437, [1997] OJ 2196 (Q.L.) (Ont. Gen. Div).

r had an annual income of $945,000 while the mother's income was
_0. In 1997 the trial judge refused an application to set aside the entire
separation agreement on the ground of duress, but invoked the court's statutory
jurisdiction to vary the support provisions of the agreement. The mother received
a $500,000 lump sum as spousal support and, according to the Guidelines, the
judge ordered $10,000 per month to be paid in addition, as child support for the
two children. The child support was set according to the percentage for payers
earning over $150,000 per year. The mother had prepared a budget for the
children's expenses, including private school tuition, a part-time nanny, summer
camps, vacations and so on, which totalled about $9,000 per month. The trial
judge considered it 'appropriate' to apply the table percentage and order a higher
amount than the budget to allow for 'discretionary spending'. The judge noted that
the father 'spares no expense for himself and probably when the children are with
him. Mr Baker's financial wealth is such that it is appropriate that the children
have the benefit of that wealth' when they are with their mother. The trial decision
was upheld by the Ontario Court of Appeal in a strongly worded judgment in
which Abella JA ruled that the table amounts set a floor for child support when
there is a high-income payer.[51] She concluded that 'inappropriate' in section 4
means 'inadequate', and accordingly that the table amount could be increased but
not lowered. Since almost all high-income payers are fathers, this was widely
regarded as a pro-mother approach, with Abella JA dismissing the argument of the
father that the court was in effect increasing the standard of living of the custodial
mother through the child support payments:

'By and large, the *Guidelines* render irrelevant the debate about the point at which a
child support order is, by virtue of its largesse, thereby transformed into spousal
support masquerading as child support. That debate represents an academic
conversation from an era when the prevailing pretence was that one could separate the
economic well-being of children from that of the parent with whom they lived.'

The Supreme Court of Canada upheld the lower court decisions. While the
Court rejected the argument that the Guideline amount is a 'floor' for high income
payers and accepted that the table amount could be reduced, the Court accepted
that there is a 'presumption' in favour of the table amount.[52] In rejecting the
argument that the table amount could not be reduced, the Supreme Court followed
some British Columbia cases[53] in which both parents had high incomes and the
courts concluded that there should be a division in proportion to income of all
'reasonable' expenses associated with the care of a child.

While in most child support cases there is no requirement for an applicant to
prepare a budget of child-related expenses, the Court appeared to accept that such
budgets would be an ordinary part of litigation involving high income payers.
Justice Bastarche stated:[54]

---

51 [1998] OJ 924, 34 RFL (4th) 317 (CA).
52 [1999] 3 SCR 250, 50 RFL (4th) 228; see accompanying critical annotation by JG McLeod, 50 RFL (4th) 232–236.
53 See, eg *Plester v Plester* (1998), 56 BCLR (3d) 352 (SC).
54 At paras 48 and 49.

'It is clear that "preparation of a budget is not an exact science" ... and that the custodial parent is prone to overestimating or underestimating the amounts ... Nevertheless, there is nothing objectionable ... about recognising that trial judges have the discretion to require custodial parents to produce child expense budgets in cases in which s 4 of the *Guidelines* is invoked. Along with other factors, these budgets speak to the reasonable needs of the children ... What is objectionable, however, is that in the pre-*Guidelines* jurisprudence, custodial parents often had the burden of proving the reasonableness of each budgeted expense on a balance of probabilities ... under the *Guidelines*, custodial parents are entitled to the Table amount unless that amount is shown to be inappropriate. It follows that, while child expense budgets may be required under s 4 in order to allow for a proper assessment of the children's needs, custodial parents need not justify each and every budgeted expense. Courts should be wary of discarding the figures included in their budgets too quickly ... While child expense budgets constitute evidence on which custodial parents can be cross-examined, their inherent imprecision must be kept in mind. Where one figure is over-estimated, it is possible that another is under-estimated. Furthermore ... the unique economic situation of high income earners must be acknowledged. Child expenses which may well be reasonable for the wealthy may too quickly be deemed unreasonable by the courts. Of course, at some point, estimated child expenses can become unreasonable ... a proper balance is struck by requiring paying parents to demonstrate that budgeted child expenses are so high as to "exceed the generous ambit within which reasonable disagreement is possible".'

It is apparent from the fact that the trial judgment was affirmed in *Francis v Baker* that in cases where there is a substantial disparity in the income of the parents, there is a strong presumption in favour of the table amount.[55] However, in cases where both parents have high incomes or the amounts of monthly child support become astronomical, the courts may award less than the table amount, while in the 'moderate high' income range (eg well-paid professional payers with incomes of $150,000 to $350,000) it may be possible to persuade a court to increase the table amount, for example for private schooling.

Unlike with child support, where clear presumptive rules are developing to help resolve most disputes, in custody disputes the courts use a highly discretionary 'best interests' of the child approach. The 1999 Supreme Court decision in *H(D) v M(H)* illustrates that each custody case is decided on its unique facts, without presumptive rules, and raises issues about the relative importance of economic wealth as opposed to placement of an aboriginal child with biological relatives of aboriginal heritage. The child involved was almost four years old by

---

55   In *Simon v Simon* (1999), 1 RFL (5th) 119, 46 OR (3d) 349 (CA), the father was a professional hockey player who had married the mother but left her before the birth of their child. By the time of trial the boy was three years of age and the father's income had risen dramatically to about $1.4 million, with a table amount of child support of $9,215 per month. The trial judge ordered $5,000 per month in child support, reflecting the modest lifestyle of the father both when living with the mother and at time of trial; the $5,000 per month included $1,000 to be placed in trust for future expenses, in the expectation that the father's income would decline dramatically after he retired from professional sports and that child support would be substantially reduced. The Ontario Court of Appeal, citing the Supreme Court decision in *Francis v Baker*, ordered the full table amount, and set aside any trust requirement. The Court of Appeal held that the father failed to show that the proposed budget was 'unreasonable' or that the mother would 'misuse' the funds, although the Court accepted that the mother could use some of the support to acquire a 'modest' home and might well decide to save some of the present support payments to cover future expenses when child support would be lower.

.ne case got to the Supreme Court of Canada. He was born in the United
to a mother who was born in Canada as an aboriginal child. The mother,
.ther with her sister, had been adopted at the age of six by a financially secure
Caucasian couple who moved to the United States.

For the first eight months of the boy's life, he was primarily cared for by the
adoptive parents of his mother in the United States. The mother had been out of
contact with her biological family for many years, but after the boy's birth she
located her own biological father, the boy's grandfather, in Vancouver where he
cohabited with a woman who was the mother of one of his other children. On a
pretext of taking the child to visit her sister, the mother took the child from her
adoptive parents and went to Vancouver.

Soon after the child came to British Columbia with the mother, the child was
apprehended by the child welfare authorities as the mother had numerous
problems, since she herself was a victim of fetal alcohol syndrome. The mother's
adoptive parents came to British Columbia and began litigation to regain care of
the child, but the child was placed in the interim custody of the biological
grandfather. The putative father was known, but had expressed no interest in the
child. The mother was not seeking custody, but she supported the claim of the
biological grandfather, who shared aboriginal ancestry with the mother and child.
By the time of trial the child had spent over a year living with the biological
grandfather. The trial judge recognised the blood tie and 'obvious love and
affection' that the grandfather had for the child and that he had 'a demonstrated
ability to provide a home and care for his family'. However, the trial judge was
concerned about the grandfather's 'lack of employment' and the possibility that he
might move with his family back to their reserve which might be 'unsettling' to
the child. The trial judge concluded that it was in the child's best interests to be
placed in the custody of the mother's adoptive parents, based on 'the economic
stability of their home and their apparent economic ability to provide ... [the
child] with many advantages'.[56] Pending appeal the child remained with the
grandfather, and the British Columbia Court of Appeal reversed the trial judgment
and awarded custody to the grandfather, observing that the trial judge 'placed
undue emphasis on economic matters and underemphasised ties of blood and
[aboriginal] culture'.[57] The appeal court also expressed concern about disrupting
the child from his home, and noted that the mother was supporting the position of
her father.

In a very short judgment, the Supreme Court of Canada concluded that there
had been no error made by the trial judge, and awarded custody to the mother's
adoptive parents.[58] The decision in *H(D) v M(H)* might be justified as a case that
recognises the importance in a custody case of the findings of a trial judge, who
has the opportunity to meet and assess the parties. However, in other cases, the
Supreme Court has been willing to reverse 'best interests findings' of trial judges
in custody cases[59] and this decision has been criticised as a 'decision ... infected
by class bias, neatly hidden from view by the "neutral appearance" of the best

---

56   [1997] BCJ 2144 (QL) (BCSC).
57   (1998), 40 RFL (4th) 370 (BCCA), at 375.
58   [1999] 1 SCR 328 and 761, 45 RFL 270 and 273.
59   *Catholic CAS of Metro Toronto v M(C)* (1994), 2 RFL (4th) 313 (SCC).

interests test'.[60] This brief Supreme Court decision offers little guidance to lawyers or trial judges, seemingly emphasising the individualised and discretionary nature of 'best interests decisions'. It is disappointing that the Supreme Court did not clearly address fundamental issues raised in the case about the weight to be placed on such factors as biological ties, continuity of care and social class. The failure to consider adequately the issue of the child's aboriginal status was especially controversial in the light of the unique constitutional status of Canada's aboriginal peoples. There is a growing body of research revealing that while in general interracial adoption is often successful, there are frequently serious adjustment problems with aboriginal children adopted by Caucasian parents, even as infants, when they reach adolescence.[61]

VI PROTECTING PARENT–CHILD RELATIONSHIPS: THE CHARTER AND THE CONVENTION

In two important decisions the Supreme Court of Canada has afforded protection to the parent-child relationship. In one case the Court has used the Charter of Rights to recognise the right of indigent parents in a child protection proceeding to state paid counsel, while in the other the Court invoked the United Nations Convention on the Rights of the Child in an immigration case.

There are few instances of more dramatic State interference with individual and familial autonomy than in child protection proceedings, in which agents of the State have broad powers to enter premises, apprehend children from their homes and terminate profoundly important relationships. However, in the decade after the Charter of Rights came into effect in 1982, Canadian appeal courts were unwilling to subject this type of State action to constitutional scrutiny, focusing on the fact that this type of proceeding is *intended* to protect children and promote their welfare, and refused to find that constitutional issues are engaged.[62] In its 1995 decision in *RB v Children's Aid Society of Metropolitan Toronto*[63] the Supreme Court of Canada was deeply split over whether, in principle, parents (or children) should enjoy constitutional rights in litigation with a child protection agency. Four of the nine justices adopted a constitutional analysis which was originally developed in the United States[64] and recognised that parents have a constitutionally protected interest in their relationship with their children.

---

60 DA Rollie Thompson, 'The Rap on the Supreme Court, or What About the Interests of All Children', in Law Society of Upper Canada, *Best Interests of the Child* (Toronto, 1999), 7-7 and DAR Thompson, 'Rules and Rulelessness In Family Law: Recent Developments, Judicial and Legislative' (2000), 17(4) Can. Fam. L.Q.

61 See, eg 'The Battle Over Native Adoption,' *Globe & Mail*, 23 February 1999; and 'A Reprehensible Ruling on Native Adoption,' *Globe & Mail*, 25 February 1999.

62 See, eg *Catholic CAS v TS* (1989), 20 RFL (3d) 337 (Ont. CA) dismissing claims to parental rights in child protection proceedings.

63 [1995] 1 SCR 315, 9 RFL (4th) 157.

64 See, eg *Meyer v Nebraska*, 262 US 390 (1923); *Stanley v Illinois* 405 US 645 (1972). This analysis was long advocated by Canadian legal scholars; see, eg Bala and Redfearn, 'Family Law and the "Liberty Interest": Section 7 of the Canadian Charter of Rights' (1983), 15 Ottawa L. Rev. 274, quoted by La Forest J in *R.B.*

However, the majority of the Court was not prepared to adopt this view. Chief Justice Lamer stated that:

> 'the liberty interest protected by section 7 [of the Charter] ... includes neither the right of parents to choose (or refuse) medical treatment for their children, nor more generally the right to bring up or educate their children without undue interference by the state ... the autonomy or integrity of the of the family unit ... does not fall within the ambit of section 7.'

However, in its 1999 decision in *New Brunswick (Minister of Health) v G(J)*, the Supreme Court of Canada sent a strong and clear message that parents do have a vital interest in their relationship with their children, an interest that is entitled to protection under section 7 of the Charter as an aspect of 'security of the person'.[65] The Court concluded that an indigent mother whose children had been apprehended by a child welfare agency had the constitutional right to be represented by counsel paid by the Government, pursuant to section 7 of the Charter, to ensure that the temporary wardship proceedings are 'in accordance with the principles of fundamental justice'.

Writing for the majority of the Court,[66] Lamer CJC focused on the argument that a child-protection proceeding represents a threat to the 'security of the person' of both parent and child, thereby purporting to distinguish his own decision in *RB v CAS of Metropolitan Toronto*, in which he dismissed the notion that section 7, and in particular the 'liberty interest' could be engaged in child protection proceedings.[67] While the cases are clearly factually distinguishable, the rhetoric and approach of Lamer CJC in the two cases is very different. It is now clear that when faced with a concrete situation in which parents or children are being subjected to treatment in a child protection proceeding that does not accord with the 'principles of fundamental justice,' the courts will respond.

In *G(J)* Chief Justice Lamer wrote:[68]

> 'The interests at stake in the custody [child protection] hearing are unquestionably of the highest order. Few state actions can have a more profound effect on the lives of both parent and child. Not only is the parent's right to security of the person at stake, the child's is as well. Since the best interests of the child are presumed to lie with the parent, the child's psychological integrity and well-being may be seriously affected by the interference with the parent–child relationship.'

The Court recognised that in the specific circumstances of the case it was dealing with a permanent termination of the parent–child relationship, but only a

---

65 [1999] 3 SCR 46, 50 RFL (4th) 63; see accompanying annotation by DAR Thompson at RFL 74–78.

66 L'Heureux-Dubé J gave an opinion concurring with Lamer CJC arguing that 'liberty' as well as security of the person were involved (an academic distinction only) and that section 15 issues were also raised in this situation, since the vast majority of parents affected by child protection proceedings are low income, single mothers.

67 Section 7 of the Charter provides: 'Everyone has the right to life, liberty and security of the person and the right not to be deprived thereof except in accordance with the principles of fundamental justice'.

68 At para 76.

review of temporary wardship, but nevertheless concluded that the parent's constitutional rights were engaged. Although some of the analysis considered the rights and welfare of the children, it is clear that the final decision protected the constitutional rights of parents. While this decision emphasises that an indigent parent does not have an absolute right to state-paid counsel in a protection proceeding, the complexity and importance of any contested wardship application, and the limited education and sophistication of most parents involved in these cases, means that there will be few cases in which a trial judge will refuse to direct that representation be provided. In practice, it seems likely that Legal Aid plans will ensure that indigent parents have representation in any case where a child may be removed or kept from parental custody. The analysis in *New Brunswick (Minister of Health) v G(J)* may be relevant for a range of other issues that may arise in child protection, adoption and other child-related proceedings.[69]

Canada ratified the United Nations Convention on the Rights of the Child in 1989.[70] While it has been used as a political advocacy tool and analytical framework, until 1999 it did not have a significant legal impact.[71] Although Canada signed and ratified the Convention, indicating its intention to be bound by the Convention as a matter of international law, no steps were taken to enact legislation that would give the Convention legal effect in Canada. The traditional approach in Canada was to view an international treaty that was not enacted in domestic legislation as having no direct legal effect, although it might be considered as an aid to the interpretation of the Charter of Rights.[72] However, in its 1999 decision in *Baker v Canada (Minister of Citizenship and Immigration)*[73] a majority of the Supreme Court of Canada held that the Convention and its best interests principle should be used to interpret and apply Canadian legislation. The case involved the threatened deportation of a woman without landed immigrant status who lived in Canada for 18 years and had children who were born in Canada and hence were Canadian citizens. Two of the children were in the mother's care, and the other two resided with their father but regularly saw the mother. The Supreme Court ruled that the immigration officer considering the woman's application to be permitted to apply from within Canada for permanent resident status based upon 'humanitarian and compassionate' grounds was obliged to give some consideration to the best interests of the children, though this was

---

69 In February 2000 the Supreme Court of Canada heard argument in *Winnipeg Child & Family Services (Central Area) v W(KL)* (1998), 41 RFL (4th) 291 (Man. CA) a child protection case from Manitoba that challenges the constitutional validity of warrantless apprehensions in non-emergency situations. As in several other provinces, in Manitoba agency workers may seek a warrant from a justice of the peace to search for and apprehend a child believed to be in need of protection, but they may also enter premises and apprehend a child without a warrant if they have reasonable grounds to believe that a child is in need of protection. Given the highly intrusive nature and disruptive effect for both parents and children of an apprehension by child welfare workers, the Supreme Court is likely to give this issue careful consideration.

70 T.S. 1992, No 3.

71 See, eg Canadian Coalition on the Rights of the Child, *Canada and the UN Convention on the Rights of the Child: Developing A Monitoring Framework* (Ottawa: 1997); and Bailey and Bala, *Does Federal and Ontario Legislation Comply With the United Nations Convention on the Rights of the Child?* (Ottawa: Child Welfare League of Canada, 1999).

72 *Capital Cities Communications v CRTC* [1978] 2 SCR 141; *Slaight Communications v Davidson* [1989] 1 SCR 1038.

73 [1999] 2 SCR 817, 174 DLR (4th) 193 (SCC).

only one factor and not necessarily determinative. Justice L'Heureux-Dubé wrote:[74]

> 'Children's rights, and attention to their interests, are central humanitarian and
> compassionate values in Canadian society ... [An] indicator of the importance of
> considering the interests of children when making a compassionate and humanitarian
> decision is the ratification by Canada of the *Convention on the Rights of the Child*, and
> the recognition of the importance of children's rights and the best interests of children
> in other international instruments ratified by Canada ... the ... important role of
> international human rights law as an aid in interpreting domestic law has ... been
> emphasized in other common law countries ... . The values and principles of the
> *Convention* recognise the importance of being attentive to the rights and best interests
> of children when decisions are made that relate to and affect their future. In addition,
> the preamble ... recognises that "childhood is entitled to special care and assistance".
> ... The principles of the *Convention* and other international instruments place special
> importance on protections for children and childhood, and on particular consideration
> of their interests, needs, and rights.'

Baker was relatively easy for the Supreme Court to decide since the immigration officer gave *no* consideration to the interests of the children when deciding about the immigration status of the mother. The Convention only states that the best interests of the child are to be '*a* primary consideration'. While the decision in *Baker* is important, it does not give any indication of how much weight is to be given to the interests of the child in making the decision about the parent.[75]

VII CONCLUSION

There has already been significant criticism of the judiciary, especially the Supreme Court of Canada, for being too activist, and usurping the role of politicians when dealing with contentious familial issues like abortion, same-sex relationships and unmarried heterosexual cohabitation. However, Canadian politicians have been reluctant to deal with these controversial issues, and some politicians have been quietly content to let the courts take the lead in dealing with difficult issues. Public attitudes among the Canadian public towards many of family law issues have been changing, in part influenced by the discourse and decisions of the courts. For example, public attitudes towards same-sex relationships have been influenced by the rights-based discourse inherent in the judicial process, and there may be more support among members of the Canadian

---

74   At paras 67–71.

75   *Francis (Litigation guardian of) v Canada (Minister of Citizenship and Immigration)*, [1999]
      SCCA No 558, seeking leave to appeal [1999] OJ 3853 (CA) (QL) is a case that raises other
      issues related to the deportation of parents of children who are citizens. If the Supreme Court of
      Canada grants leave to appeal, this case may help clarify the rights of children at the deportation
      hearings of their parents.

public than among politicians for using the Charter to recognise the equality of gay and lesbian relationships.[76]

On a broader policy level, there are concerns that Canada lacks clear and supportive policies towards families and children.[77] Advocates are arguing for more 'family friendly' policies such as longer parental leaves, increases in financial support and more breaks for families with children, improved services for children and greater government support for the care of pre-school children. While some progress is being made, for example to increase the length of parental leaves and government support for child care,[78] there are concerns about government priorities and resource commitments, as well as controversy over the extent to which governments should support programmes like day care, as opposed to providing support for child-care arrangements provided by stay-at-home parents.[79]

---

76 See 'Top Court Inspires Highest Confidence', *Globe & Mail,* 31 May 2000 reporting on a study of public attitudes to courts and the *Charter* by Joseph Fletcher and Paul Howe, *Public Opinion and the Courts,* Vol 6(3) of *Choices* (Institute for Research on Public Policy, Montreal, May 2000). See <http://www.irpp.org>.

77 See, eg 'An MP's Passion for Families', *Globe & Mail,* 18 September 1999; Jenson and Stroick, *A Policy Blueprint for Canada's Children* (Ottawa: Canadian Policy Research Networks, October 1999). See <http://www.cprn.org/back_press/bpbc_e.htm>.

78 See, eg 'New Parents to Get More Paid Leave', *Globe & Mail,* 13 October 1999; and 'Women Driving State Funding for Child Care', *National Post,* 7 June 2000.

79 See, eg 'Tax Fracas: Martin Tries to Limit Damage – Minister Asks How System Can be Made Fairer for At-home Parents', *National Post,* 9 March 1999; and 'Profiting from the Taxing Issue of Family Values', *Globe & Mail,* 12 March 1999.

public than among politicians for using the Charter to recognize the equality of gay and lesbian relationships.

One area for policy ... both there are concerns that Canada needs clearer and more supportive policies towards families and children. Advocates are arguing for more 'family-friendly' policies such as longer parental leaves, increases in financial support and ... breaks for families with children, improved services for children and greater government support for the care of pre-school children. While some progress is being made, for example to increase the length of parental leaves and government support for child care, there are concerns about government priorities and resource commitments, as well as controversy over the extent to which governments should support programmes like day care, as opposed to providing support for child-care arrangements provided by stay-at-home parents.

76. See "Court Ordin: Highest Confidence," Globe & Mail, ...
...

COSTA RICA

FAMILY LAW DEVELOPMENTS IN COSTA RICA: THE CHILDHOOD AND ADOLESCENCE CODE 1998

Sergio Alonso de Valverde y Alpízar[*]

I   INTRODUCTION

Although Christopher Columbus himself gave the name of Costa Rica (Rich Coast) to this small country, paradoxically it was ancient and proverbial poverty which had the magical effect of generating a pluralist, tolerant and democratic society there. 'Coast' certainly, bordered by two oceans, but 'Rich?' – well, not in economic terms. These conditions, and the growing independence of the judiciary (above all from the second half of the nineteenth century, in which the principle was explicitly set out in the Political Constitution) have favoured the creation of a particular legislative culture; this is reflected both in the diverse legal institutions which have been created and in the wisdom and dynamism shown in the progress of judicial decisions. These are the conditions that have allowed the introduction, at very early dates, of important legal developments such as the abolition of the death penalty, divorce (from the nineteenth century), or direct and informal access to the Constitutional Court for all citizens. Today we have laws guaranteeing even the rights of minors to participate in the taking of decisions affecting them. The law of Costa Rica shows its individuality clearly in laws which often appear paradoxical, for, while the majority of the people are Roman Catholic, the dissolution of marriage was quickly and calmly accepted, although the law has always firmly protected human life from the moment of conception.

The final decade of the twentieth century saw an important legal revolution in Costa Rica, as the result of the work of a modernising (*vanguardista*) Constitutional Court. There has also been an important legislative output relating to the family, enabling account to be taken of scientific advances (for example, genetic markers and DNA) in court procedures; recognising the priority of the fact of a family rather than marriage (law regulating stable *de facto* couples); and enacting an important codification placing children and adolescents (minors in general) in a special position among groups specially protected by the law.

In this first article on the family law of Costa Rica to be published in *The International Survey of Family Law*, we propose to give a short introduction to the country as well as to its law. Thus, we shall give a short account of the history of family law in Costa Rica, the origins and main characteristics of the Code of the Family, and lastly concentrate our attention on the Code of Childhood and Adolescence, which marks the final step in the process of democratising the

---

[*]   Judicatory Member, Costa Rican Supreme Court of Justice, Master of Public Law (Costa Rica), Master of Constitutional Law and Political Sciences (Spain), Chair member of the Costa Rican Academy of Genealogical Sciences. Translated by Peter Schofield.

family: the full and effective recognition of the minor as the possessor of rights and obligations (in numerous instruments).

II   COSTA RICA: GENERAL INFORMATION

Costa Rica is a Central American republic, bordering Nicaragua, the Caribbean, Panama and the Pacific. A mere 51,060 square kilometers in area, the capital is San José. The majority of the (approximately 3.5 million) population is of European (mainly Spanish) descent. Whites and persons of mixed race (of Spanish and indigenous descent) form over 90 per cent of the population; the small black community is entirely of Jamaican origin. About half the population lives in rural areas. Spanish is the official language, but English is also spoken in social groups with higher levels of education and among the Jamaican population. Catholicism is the official State religion (professed by 85 per cent of the population), but the Constitution guarantees religious freedom. Life expectancy is 73 years for men, 76 for women (according to United Nations figures for 1986 to 1987). *Per capita* income is about 1,636 dollars a year (figures from the World Bank for 1988 to 1990). The level of literacy in Costa Rica is among the highest in Latin America at about 93 per cent. Primary and secondary education are free, and attendance compulsory, from 6 to 13 years of age. The University of Costa Rica in San José, established in 1843, has some 30,000 students. The Government is presidential, with a single legislative chamber and, since 1948, the country has had no armed forces. Costa Rica has remained traditionally neutral in regional and international conflicts. President Oscar Arias Sanchéz was awarded the Nobel Peace Prize for having negotiated a peaceful settlement with guerillas operating in the Central American region.

Legislation is the primary source of law; nonetheless, the ninth Article of the Civil Code establishes that precedents created by a consistent line of judicial decisions shall *contribute* to informing the judiciary as to the doctrine regularly accepted in the courts. Despite this, Article 13 of the Law of the Constitutional Court (1989) provides that the decisions and precedents of that Court are binding (*vinculantes*) on all apart from the Court itself. This means that the Constitutional Court has become one of the primary sources of law in Costa Rica; and it is also worth noting that, once ratified, international treaties have constitutional force in matters of fundamental rights.

The classical modes of interpretation of norms – literal, historical, teleological, systematic and logical – apply to legislation in Costa Rica. Article 10 of the Civil Code provides that norms must be interpreted in conformity with the meaning of their words, in relation to their context, their historical and legislative antecedents, as well as with the social reality of the time when they come to be applied, taking account of the spirit and objective of the norms themselves. Likewise, Articles 11, 12 and 13 of the Civil Code allow the court to consider the merits of a case and to apply by analogy when the law makes no specific provision for the facts of a particular case, but does set out rules for other similar cases where the basis and grounds are the same and where there is no rule forbidding this (as there is in the case of temporal and penal laws, and also in the field of exceptional laws).

III HISTORY OF FAMILY LAW IN COSTA RICA

In the colonial period, the family law of Costa Rica was that of the Kingdom of Spain, set out in the *Siete Partidas*,[1] and later, between 1805 and 1821, was governed by the *Novísima Recopilación*, which even of its kind was a work of poor quality (Tomás y Valiente, 1997). The so-called 'Indian law' (*derecho indiano*) had no particular relevance in family law matters. The study of family law in Costa Rica in the republican period leads us into that of the codification of civil law. This is because the country inherited the Romanist legal tradition of the European continent. Like all the other Latin American civil codes that were enacted in the nineteenth century, that of Costa Rica is based on the French Civil Code of 1801. In addition, the Code of 1888 in Costa Rica is much more closely linked to the project for the Spanish Civil Code which was promulgated later in 1889.

An interesting fact is that Costa Rica was the first country to legislate for the family in the Political Constitution (of 23 December 1859)[2] itself, though we must allow that the nature of this legislation was more closely related to criminal law. Article 53 provided for suspension of citizenship in case of 'ingratitude to one's parents, or notorious and scandalous abandonment of the duties of a head of family'. A somewhat timid protection, for sure. It is in the Weimar Constitution of 11 August 1919 that we see the fullest development of social rights and the protection of the family. Emulating the Weimar Constitution, many European constitutions of the 1920s and 1930s introduced provisions protecting the family, eg Danzig (11 May 1922), Poland (17 May 1921), Yugoslavia (28 May 1921), the Spanish Second Republic (9 December 1931), etc.

Returning to Costa Rica, we have to say that it was very advanced for a late nineteenth century code promulgated in a Latin American state. It recognised the married woman's full legal capacity (eschewing the so-called 'marital authority'), and gave her the free administration of her assets. Further, it allowed divorce *a vinculo*; both of which institutions took many years to reach the statute book in other American, and even European countries. Nonetheless, faithful to hierarchical and antidemocratic standards and to macho bias, this Civil Code imposed restrictions on the action to determine paternity of children conceived in adultery; allowed the guilt of a spouse that had resulted in separation or divorce to determine the retention or loss of parental authority (paying no attention to the 'best interests of the child'); provided grounds for divorce for the husband which were not the same as those for the wife; relegated children born out of wedlock to second class status, and prevented women from exercising tutorship. The virtues of many of its provisions notwithstanding, the archaisms of the family law system provided in the Civil Code made its demise inevitable.

The Civil Code of Costa Rica remained – and continues – in force, but its field of application becomes ever narrower as new laws are promulgated. The

---

1   Literally 'Seven Parts' by which name the *Libro del Fuero de las Leyes* is usually known, because it is divided between the seven basic areas of law: the Church, the kingdom and war, things, judicial procedure and 'organisation, family and relations of vassal to lord, obligations, succession, penal'. This is attributed to Alfonso X 'el Sabio' ('the wise') and is regarded as the foremost early mediaeval legislative compilation in the world.

2   Calle de la Artillería, No 5, Imprenta del Album, 1859.

attack on its model for family law began in 1949. The political constitution approved in this year contained important innovations in family law, despite the conservatism of many of the members of the Constituent Assembly. We should note that it established:

-     the principle of equality of the spouses in marriage (Article 52);
-     everyone's right to know who are his parents (Article 53);
-     that there must be no classes of filiation (Article 54); and
-     that the State has a special duty to protect the family and in particular the mother and minors (Articles 51 and 55).

The principal Articles of relevance in the 1949 Constitution are set out below.

Social Rights and Guarantees

ARTICLE 50

'The State shall ensure the greatest welfare of all residents of the country, organising and encouraging the production of wealth and its proper distribution.

Everyone has the right to a healthy and ecologically balanced environment.

To this end anyone has standing to bring proceedings against acts infringing this right and to claim redress for any damage caused.

The State shall fix the relevant duties and sanctions.'[3]

ARTICLE 51

'The family as the basic natural unit of society has the right to be protected by the State. Likewise entitled to such protection are mothers, children, the elderly and the disabled.'

ARTICLE 52

'Marriage is the essential basis of the family and rests on the equality of rights for both spouses.'

ARTICLE 53

'The obligations owed by parents to their children born out of wedlock are the same as those owed to children of their marriage.

Every person has the right to know who are his parents in accordance with the law.'

---

3   As amended by Article 1 of Law No 7412, of 3 June 1994.

ARTICLE 54

'Discrimination based on the nature of filiation is prohibited.'

ARTICLE 55

'The special protection of mothers and of minors shall be the responsibility of an autonomous institution called the *Patronato Nacional de la Infancia* (National Foundation for Childhood), assisted by other institutions of the State.'

Important reforms of the constitutional text called for a complete revision of Book I of the Civil Code, and of the other laws related in one way or another with the said reform. Law No 1443 of 21 May 1952 made some of the changes, but these were only cosmetic alterations at root. The full and detailed revision of family legislation was put off. This change in legislation took another 21 years to come about.

IV THE FAMILY CODE

The work of preparing the project of the Family Code was undertaken between November 1968 and April 1970 – 18 months' labour – at the end of which only the substantive rules of the Code were complete. Of Part II – administrative procedures – and Part III – judicial procedures – there were only brief sketches in the discussions of the Commission. Recognising that family law was a discrete subject, and deciding to draw up a new Code, rather than to reform the Civil Code, was a defining moment in the work of the Commission. Family law was at last recognised as an independent discipline, in which economic benefits played a minor role, and child protection was the main consideration, together with the support of the family and the development of good relations between family members, on a basis of equality and mutual respect.[4]

The legislative working out of the project for a Family Code was a convoluted process. But there was the involvement of an important feminist pressure group to be reckoned with. This movement was started by two professors of the Law School, Señoras Sonia Picado and Elizabeth Odio. We could say that the development of the project represents the first example of the influence of a feminist pressure group on the legislature. Despite a failed attempt by the 'Legal Section of the Spiritual League of Catholic Professionals' to oppose it, the project was approved and received the President's signature on 21 December 1973. Among the main achievements of the feminist pressure group was the equalisation of the grounds for divorce. Before, the husband's adultery was not a sufficient ground, whereas that of the wife was.

Thus, Costa Rica became the second western country to acquire a Family Code. The first was Bolivia, with its 1972 Code, and they were followed by Cuba which enacted its Code on 4 January 1975. However, this choice to codify family

---

4   Guttierréz, 1976.

law outside the Civil Code had already been taken in East European countries (Czechoslovakia, Romania, Poland, Hungary, East Germany) and in the Union of Soviet Socialist Republics.[5]

There are some 228 Articles constituting the Code – quite a small number for a law setting out to cover all of family law. In general, the Code follows the principle of homogeneity in separating articles: for each idea a separate rule, save where it is intended to group together a rule and an exception, the basic rule and the manner of implementing it, and cases which need to be enumerated. It is not a new family law system, for it does not reform it totally, rather it draws on past experience, past decided cases, doctrine and comparative law.

It is left to the courts to develop the contents of the law. So the Code sets out guidelines (general principles), and a certain 'regulatory power'. The interpreter must first turn to those provisions of the Code which are 'programmatic' in character, that is to say, the rules which are marked out as providing basic rules for its application and construction. These are:

– the unity of the family;
– the interests of the children;
– the interests of minors;
– equality of the rights and duties of the spouses; and
– not discriminating and the equality of rights and duties of children born in and out of wedlock.

As a rule, the Family Code avoids embarking on legal concepts. Rather, it indicates directions and aims and does not tie the judge to the letter of the law. The vigorous development of decided cases shows how the judges have taken up this facility.[6]

The Family Code has tried out some important innovations, such as the Law to Regulate Stable *de Facto* Unions.[7]

Thus, Article 242 (as renumbered) provides: A public, notorious, exclusive and stable union of a man and a woman having capacity to marry each other, which has lasted for more than three years, shall, if it comes to an end for whatever reason, give rise to the same property rights as would flow from lawful wedlock.

Either partner or his or her heirs have standing to bring the action to recognise a *de facto* union. However, a very short period – only two years from the separation or from the death of either partner – suffices to bar the claim.[8] The property rights referred to go back to the beginning of the cohabitation, and permit claims for periodical maintenance payments in appropriate cases. Should one or other partner lack capacity to marry (say, on account of a prior existing marriage), recognition is given to the *de facto* union once it has lasted for more than four years, but only, as regards property rights, to the extent of sharing acquests from the period of cohabitation, and no provision is made for alimony.

---

5   Moisset de Espanés, 1994.
6   Trejos, 1982.
7   Law No 7532 of 1995 on stable *de facto* couples.
8   Article 243.

We should note again the paradox of Costa Rican society which, for all its strong catholicism and concern for protecting human life from the moment of conception, yet has no hesitation in giving legal protection to the 'effective family', taking this as the *de facto* reality and not as a fiction based on marriage.[9] Article 52 of the Political Constitution unambiguously holds marriage to be the 'essential basis of the family', yet we must add that it is not the sole possible basis. So the *de facto* family is entitled to the full protection of the judicial order and the law of Costa Rica so provides.

Legislation and judicial decisions in Costa Rica clearly favour the protection of the 'effective family' as we have seen and, as we are about to see, the paramount interest of the child must be even more strongly maintained. In this situation it will be of interest to see the reasoning of the courts faced with a joint application to adopt, made by a homosexual couple. Elsewhere, such an adoption has been allowed on the ground of the paramount interest of the child, pointing out that adoption is not just a right exercised by adults. Paradoxically, the courts of some States in the USA allow it, since it is not forbidden, while other, more conservative States, prohibit it. In contrast, the courts of the Netherlands refuse to authorise such adoptions, there being no legislation to support it, although such legislation is currently being promoted by the influential homosexual lobby.

Moving on to other matters, the reform introduced by Law No 7689 of 21 August 1997, on evidence admissible in proceedings to establish or to deny paternity, is also interesting. The high degree of reliability of genetic markers has practically allowed a reversal of the normal burden of proof[10] as can be seen from the terms of the law:

'**Article 98.**   *Investigation and proof of paternity and non-paternity. Evidence.*

In any proceedings to investigate or to impugn [a claim of] paternity, scientific evidence directed at establishing the relation of parenthood is admissible. Such evidence may be provided by the Forensic Investigation Service (*Organismo de Investigación Judicial*) of the Supreme Court or by a service duly accredited by the Supreme Court following the report of the Forensic Investigation Service, and is conclusive, reasonably, one way or the other. In all cases, the evidence will be weighed in accordance with the scientific conclusions and other relevant material. If a party refuses, without good reason, to submit to tests required by the court, this may be held to be malicious. Further, this may be relied on to raise a presumption of the truth of the fact the test was directed to establishing.'

This rule was challenged before the Constitutional Court, which in Judgment No 384-94 held in favour of its validity, relying on its consistency with the 'principle of proportionality', and out of respect for the paramount interest of the child. The following is extracted from the judgment of the court:

'**VII** [...] In the matter to which this case relates, falling within family law, there are important governing principles, such as the interest of the minor, now contained in the Convention on the Rights of the Child, duly approved by our country by Law No 7184 of 18 July 1990, and thereby incorporated at the highest normative level into the legal

---

9   Serrano Moreno, 1987.
10   Valverde Alpízar, 1990.

order as a result of Article 24 of the Political Constitution. This being so, various interests come into play: the minor's right to know who is his father; that of the putative father to be exculpated in a fair hearing; and that of the administration of justice to reach a conclusion which corresponds as closely as possible to actual truth. We do not find that the norm of Article 98 of the Family Code overvalues the first of these interests at the expense of the second; rather, in pursuit of the third, it opens a reasonable way for a critical and reasoned judicial analysis of all the evidence laid before the court, including whether that of the genetic markers justifies the claim ...'

As to questions of 'gender', while these do not fall properly within the ambit of family law, we should note, as an important indication of progress towards democratisation of relations in the family, Law No 7142 of 2 March 1990 on Promoting the Social Equality of Women (*Ley de Promoción de la igualdad social de la mujer*). This law was necessary to give effect to the United Nations Convention on the Elimination of All Forms of Discrimination against Women, ratified by Costa Rica in Law No 6968 of 2 October 1984. It contains a chapter with specific measures for sexual protection, against violence, including a duty of the Ministry of Justice to set in train adequate programmes, coordinated with the Centre for Women and the Family (*Centro para la Mujer y la Familia*), for protection, training and prevention and the obligation of the Judicial Authority to make sure all judges are able to deal with cases in which there has been aggression against a woman.[11] There has been fierce criticism of some of these provisions as 'positive discrimination against men', because, for instance, percentages of women are set both for functions subject to public election and for the appointment of public office holders. We think these are fair arguments particularly in the light of the precedent set by the *Sala Constitucional*, which is generally binding, holding that any normative provisions in which 'man' is mentioned should be taken to include males and females.

Another body of law, of enormous social impact, is Law No 7586 of 10 April 1996, the Law against Domestic Violence (*Ley contra la violencia doméstica*). This contains basic measures of protection to guarantee the life, personal integrity and dignity of victims of intra-family violence. It defines the following forms of violence: psychological, physical, sexual or patrimonial. These forms are not to be applied restrictively; thus the measures can apply to other forms of violence not mentioned specifically in the law. Further, the judge *proprio motu/ex officio* may order protective measures other than those applied for at his discretion.

Among interesting innovations in this law are the following measures: persons affected who are over the age of 12 years are given capacity to apply for protective measures, and public and private institutions are enabled to carry out programmes for the protection of human rights and of the family when the injured party so requests. Among other protective measures established we find reparation in money for harm suffered by the injured party, or for assets which are indispensable to continue normal life (including relocation expenses, property repairs, lodging and medical costs). The victim also has the right to petition the court and, in exceptional circumstances, to hold the hearing in the absence of the alleged aggressor. It upholds the principle of favouring the injured party, in case

---

11   Costa Rica. *Centro Nacional para el Desarrollo de la Mujer y la Familia*, 1998.

of doubt, in the assessment of evidence. It places on the police authority the duty of intervening in situations of domestic violence *de officio* or on the request of the victim or a third party, together with the duty to help the injured party even if s/he is within the home, to arrest aggressors and bring them to court, to draw up formal documents, to seize weapons and objects, etc. The police can act without judicial order in pursuance of these duties.

Despite this wide panorama, after thirty years in force, academic production in Costa Rica relating to the Family Code, and to the various legal institutions created under it, has been minimal. Barely 299 pieces of work are listed by the US Library of Congress (out of a bibliographical base of some 90 million works). Among these 299, sadly, we find the successive editions of the Family Code, further extending the available bibliography. Despite this, in various universities in Costa Rica, it is necessary to write and defend a thesis in order to complete one's legal studies. Many of these are on family law, but are not commercially published, so access to them is very limited. Therefore, to study family law in Costa Rica it is essential to examine the licenciate theses compulsorily deposited in the National Library of Costa Rica.

V   CHILDHOOD AND ADOLESCENCE CODE (CÓDIGO DE LA NIÑEZ Y LA ADOLESCENCIA)

The increasing recognition of the rights of minors at the international level has given the minor the status of a subject of preferential rights (*sujeto preferente de derecho*), which implies that, in any case of conflict, his interests must prevail. In this matter, we also see the trend to codification, with the example of Ecuador (1976), Bolivia (1975), El Salvador (1974), etc.[12]

Following the worldwide development of the 'child's best interest' test, Costa Rica has continued its policy of codification, promulgating, in 1998, the Childhood and Adolescence Code. This new Code is set up along with the new general status of minors in Costa Rica. It marks the second, perhaps the final, stage in the process of internal democratisation of the family: the first being the equalising of the position of the woman with that of the man; now defining the place of the child and of the adolescent in the home, as much as outside in society. The Childhood and Adolescence Code (hereafter ChAC) [*Código de la Niñez y la Adolescencia*] of 1998 draws in a special way on the American Human Rights Convention (*Convención Americana sobre Derechos Humanos*, also known as the *Pacto de San José de Costa Rica*), which declared in Article 19 that every child has the right to the measures of protection that his situation as a minor requires on the part of his family, of society and of the State; on the Convention on the Rights of the Child, of 1989, duly approved by Costa Rica under Law No 7184 of 18 July 1990, and many other international public law texts going back to the Geneva Declaration (*Declaración de Ginebra* or *Tabla de los Derechos del Niño*), of the early twentieth century; and not forgetting the Convention on the Protection of the Child and on Co-operation in Relation to Adoption. We must not overlook the

---

12   Pérez Vargas, 1978.

constitutional provisions which ensure, in a programmatic way, the advancement of the condition of minors.

This Code sets the legal benchmark for the integrated protection of the rights of minors. It sets out the basic principles for participation both in society and in the community and in any administrative or judicial proceedings involving the rights and duties of minors. As to administrative or judicial interpretation, norms of whatever level offering greater protection or benefits to minors will outrank the provisions of the Code.

In contrast to the Family Code which, as we have seen, is characterised by its narrow extent and desire to avoid conceptualising the various legal institutions, the ChAC does go in for definitions. Thus, it divides minors into (a) children and (b) adolescents. Children are considered to be persons between the moment of conception and the age of 12 years; adolescents from 12 to 18. In case of doubt, adolescent status is assumed rather than that of an adult, and the status of child rather than adolescent. In addition, Article 9 provides for the preferential application of the 'child's best interest' test in case of doubt.

It is very important to note that in Costa Rica abortion is totally prohibited, except where the mother is in danger of death, since the interest of the child prevails from the moment of conception. This results from the American Convention on Human Rights (*Convención Americana sobre Derechos Humanos*) and is formally enacted in ChAC Article 2. Although this expresses well the humanitarian character of Costa Ricans, we have to remember that, despite being subject to heavy criminal penalties, illegal abortions are widely practised.

As to its applicability, the ChAC applies to all minors, regardless of their parents' ethnicity, culture, gender, language, religion, ideology, nationality or any other particular condition of the minors or of their guardians or legal representatives. The rights and guarantees it provides for minors are 'of public interest' (*de interés público*) and thus are superior to ordinary laws and cannot be renounced or bargained away. Article 5, which elaborates on Article 51 of the Political Constitution, which we have set out above, provides that any public or private activity which relates to a person aged under 18 must take account of his paramount interest. This is a guarantee of respect for his rights in a healthy physical and mental environment, and scope for full personal development. Consequently the consideration of the best interests of a minor must take account of:

–   his position as the possessor of rights and liabilities;
–   his age, maturity, understanding and other personal conditions;
–   his socio-economic background; and
–   the relation of individual to social interests.

So we see, specifically recognised, the possession of rights and interests of children and adolescents, within the limits of their particular stage of development and the standard of protection set out in the Political Constitution.

Parental authority means:

'the lawful power exercised by adults, be it mother, father, legal representatives, masters, or public authorities, for the purpose of ensuring the protection and care necessary for the welfare of any child or adolescent. Hence, it is understood that the authority exercised over minors assumes a basic standard of intervention, the sole meaning and purpose of which is to protect this social group, seeing that its particular condition of "developing persons" marks it out as needing special protection to enable its members to attain, gradually, greater responsibility, the level of authority, meanwhile, progressively reducing and the degree of freedom increasing.'

Article 58 is very demanding since, in setting out national educational policies, it imposes a duty on the State to provide high quality education and equal opportunities for minors; to encourage the highest levels of science and technology, of artistic and cultural expression and of ethical and moral values; to facilitate early access to technical training on the completion of general, basic secondary education; to promote and extend awareness of the rights of minors; to stimulate at all levels the development of independent, critical and creative thought, showing repect for the individual characteristics of the student; and to further the inclusion in educational programmes of themes related to sexual education, reproduction, teenage pregnancy, drugs, sexual violence, sexually transmitted diseases, AIDS and other serious problems.

The law incorporates general norms for the total protection of children and adolescents in relation to the fundamental principles of participation both in society and in the community and in administrative or judicial procedures involving the rights and duties of social groups. It establishes basic rights and freedoms, rights of personality, the right to family life and support, to health, to education, to culture, to recreation and to sport. It sets up a special regime to protect adolescent workers. It ensures access to justice by means of judicial and administrative guarantees.

It also sets up the Integrated Welfare System for Childhood and Adolescence ('*sistema de protección integral de los derechos de la niñez y la adolescencia*') formed by governmental institutions, organisations of the civil society represented before the National Council for Childhood and Adolescence (*Consejo Nacional de la Niñez y la Adolescencia*) and the Children's and Adolescents' Protection Boards (*Juntas de Protección de la Niñez y la Adolescencia*) and the Tutelary Committees for the Rights of Childhood and Adolescence (*Comités Tutelares de los Derechos de la Niñez y la Adolescencia*). The National Council for Childhood and Adolescence was set up under the aegis of the Executive Power as a forum for deliberation, cooperation and coordination between the Executive Power, the decentralised institutions of the State and organisations representing the community which are involved in this field. Its remit consists of ensuring that the formulation and execution of official policies comply with the requirement to give total protection to the rights of children and adolescents within the scope of the relevant code and with established principles. The Children's and Adolescents' Protection Boards are subject to the National Foundation for Childhood (*Patronato Nacional de la Infancia*), so as to form part of the national system and act as local bodies to coordinate and develop suitable policies in this field. It sets up the Tutelary Committees for the Rights of Childhood and Adolescence, as organs of the Communal Development Associations (*Asociaciones de Desarrollo Comunal*), to work in the field of the Law on Community Development, as a resource for childhood and adolescence with the aim of financing the development of actions for integrated protection at a community level and working co-operatively between institutions.

Article 4 of the ChAC marks a step forward in the protection of minors, since in relaton to the national strategy, the State has the general obligation of adopting all necessary administrative, legislative and other measures of whatever nature to give full effect to the fundamental rights of persons under the age of majority. What makes this Article particularly remarkable is its third paragraph which provides that, in accordance with the regime of special protection guaranteed to minors by the Political Constitution, the Convention on the Rights of the Child, the ChAC and other relevant laws, the State cannot rely on budgetary limitations to restrict the duties thereby imposed. Although this ranks as an ordinary, not a constitutional law, the legal system of Costa Rica will allow a budgetary (economic) law which would disadvantage the interests of minors to be challenged before the constitutional court. This is because such interests, as relating to fundamental rights, have a constitutional dimension.

Participation by minors in decision-taking already exists, though to a very limited extent and with the means of selection subject to executive regulation. Minors have representation, by voice and by vote, in the Children's and Adolescents' Protection Boards set up under the Organic Law of the National Foundation for Childhood, but this only applies to the second level of minors – adolescents aged from 15 to 18 years.

The ChAC continues to develop the procedural aspects of the system for the protection of minors, establishing administrative as well as judicial procedures. These are typically initiated *ex officio* (*proprio motu*), without formality (or ritual), oral, direct, with the emphasis on speed, the search for truth, admitting all relevant evidence, etc. Moreover, in any proceeding or procedure which might affect the interests of a minor, the latter has the right to be heard in his own language and to have his opinions and statements taken into consideration in the judgment; he is entitled to a translator or interpreter of his choice when necessary and may attend hearings accompanied by a social worker, a psychologist or other similar professional or person whom he trusts. He also has the right to have a clear and precise explanation from the judge of the significance of all that takes place in the hearing, as well as of the reasoning and the import of any decision; he is also entitled to protection of and discretion regarding his image in connection with the proceedings, and finally to appeal against judicial or administrative decisions. Further, from the procedural point of view, the 'paramount interest of the child' counts as an '*interés difuso*' making it actionable at the suit of anybody.

A profound change in the criminal law on the sexual exploitation of minors was brought about by a law of 29 June 1999, in two ways; bringing up to date the definition of the crimes and increasing the penalties. This facilitates prosecution of paedophilia, the abuse of the internet, etc.

We shall not embark on a merely descriptive approach to the family law and the law of minors in Costa Rica. A detailed consideration of the legislative technique adopted in the ChAC and in the procedural regulations which it introduces deserve separate studies which will be better undertaken once judicial interpretation of the recent Code has taken place. Many other themes remain open to investigation and analysis. In the family, the pre-eminence of the man has been replaced by the equality of the woman. There is no doubt that minors have been given a stronger position. Is it right that the family should be thus changed? Should homosexual couples be allowed to adopt in Costa Rica? What should be the position of the law of Costa Rica faced with the phenomenon of multiple parenthood made possible by medically assisted fertilisation?

VI STATISTICAL CHARTS

The number of decisions reached in family cases in Costa Rica, listed by the type of claim, and the duration of the proceedings is set out in the chart below. The period covered is from January to May 1998. During this time, a total of 2,557 judgments in 25 separate procedures took altogether 26,633 months' work. There follows a tabulation which is based on figures collected by Licenciado Emilio Solana Río, Head of the Statistical Section of the Supreme Court of Justice of Costa Rica:

Procedure Type	*Quantity*	*Average Duration*
Divorce	314	16 months
Adoption	92	12 months 3 weeks
Paternity investigation	96	17 months 2 weeks
Challenging paternity	76	17 months
Child access regulation – visitation	59	13 months 3 weeks
Recognition of a child	38	9 months 3 weeks
Appointment of tutor	6	10 months 1 week
Stable *de facto* couple in fact	21	11 months 3 weeks
Parental authority modification	14	24 months 1 week
Child access demand	4	8 months 3 weeks
Paternity declaration	7	10 months

VII FURTHER REFERENCES

Armijo, G. (1999). *La tutela constitucional del Interés Difuso.* (Prólogo del Dr. Luis Paulino Mora Mora, Presidente de la Sala Constitucional de la Corte Suprema de Justicia de Costa Rica). San José: Investigaciones Jurídicas S.A. 289 folios.

Avendaño-Solano, Carlos Manuel. (1997). *Derecho de los padres a determinar la educación de sus hijos en el derecho internacional y en el ordenamiento jurídico costarricense.* (tesis inédita). San José: Universidad de Costa Rica. 254 folios.

Benavides-Santos, Diego (ed.). (1999). *Código de Familia [de Costa Rica]*. Actualizado, concordado y comentado con jurisprudencia constitucional y de casación. San José: Editorial Juritexto. 405 folios.

Costa Rica. Centro Nacional para el Desarrollo de la Mujer y la Familia (eds.). (1998). *Avances Legales hacia la equidad de género*. (Leyes, proyectos de ley y decretos ejecutivos sobre derechos de las mujeres, equidad de género y familia: período 1994–1998, Centro Nacional para el Desarrollo de la Mujer y la Familia; Asamblea Legislativa). San José: Centro nacional para el desarrollo de la Mujer y la Familia. 285 folios.

Costa Rica. (1999). *Código de la Niñez y la Adolescencia*. (con índice alfabético, resolución de la Corte Plena sobre reglas prácticas para la aplicación del Código de la Niñez, Convención sobre los Derechos del niño, Ley Orgánica del Patronato Nacional de la Infancia). San José: Investigaciones Jurídicas S.A. 158 folios.

Chávez-Arroyo, Iliana. (1988). *Tutela de los derechos del menor*. (tesis inédita). San José: Universidad de Costa Rica.

González-Lépiz, Juan José. (1987). *Autoridad parental con relación a los hijos extramatrimoniales*. (tesis inédita). San José: Universidad de Costa Rica. 116 folios.

Gutiérrez, Carlos José (1976). La legislación de Familia, antes, ahora y lo que falta. *Revista de Ciencias Jurídicas*, San José, No 28 enero abril, Universidad de Costa Rica, folio 51 y ss.

Jiménez-Rivas, Carmen Leticia y Quirós Vargas, Rolando Alberto. (1983). *Abuso de la patria potestad en materia penal*. (tesis inédita). San José: Universidad de Costa Rica. 214 folios.

Medaglia-Gómez, María de los Angeles. (1988). *Abandono de los menores de edad como causal de suspensión de la patria potestad: tratamiento institucional*. (tesis inédita). San José: Universidad de Costa Rica. 219 folios.

Miranda-Fonseca, Jorge Hugo. (1998). *Implicación de las nuevas regulaciones en materia de autoridad parental*. (tesis inédita). San José: Universidad de Costa Rica. 397 folios.

Moisset de Espanés, Luis. (1994). *Codificación civil y derecho comparado*. Buenos Aires: Zavalia Editor. 364 folios.

Morales Hernández, Mérida. (1976). *Contenido de la autoridad parental según el Código de Familia de Costa Rica y la jurisprudencia nacional*. (tesis inédita). San José: Universidad de Costa Rica. 145 folios.

Pérez-Vargas, Víctor. (1978). La dimensión personalista-comunitaria en materia de relaciones entre padres e hijos en el sistema jurídico latinoamericano. *Revista de Ciencias Jurídicas*. No 35, mayo–agosto. San José. Folios 237 a 256.

Pérez-Vargas, Víctor. (1984). Las consecuencias jurídicas de la filiación y el interés del menor: el contenido de la patria potestad. *Revista Judicial*. No 30, setiembre. San José: Corte Suprema de Justicia. Folios 127 a 134.

Pérez-Vargas, Víctor. (1976). *Nuevo derecho de familia en Costa Rica*. San José: Editorial de la Universidad de Costa Rica. 69 folios.

Rodríguez-Rojas, Marjorie. (1983). *Responsabilidad parental con relación a los hijos extramatrimoniales*. (tesis inédita). San José: Universidad de Costa Rica. 305 folios.

Serrano-Moreno, José Luis. (1987). *El efecto familia, veinticuatro tesis sobre derecho constitucional de la familia*. Granada, Ediciones Tat. 147 folios.

Solano-Pacheco, Grettel. (1988). *Suspensión o pérdida de la patria potestad*. (tesis inédita). San José: Universidad de Costa Rica. 136 folios.

Soler-Aira, Esteban. (1989). La intervención del Patronato [Nacional de la Infancia] en los conflictos de patria potestad. *Revista Judicial*. Año XIV, No 48, diciembre. San José: Corte Suprema de Justicia. Folio 185.

Tomás y Valiente, Francisco. (1997). *Manual de Historia del Derecho Español*. 4a edición, 8a reimpresión. Madrid: Tecnos. 630 folios.

Trejos, G. (1982). *Derecho de Familia Costarricense*. (con la colaboración de Marina Ramírez Altamirano, Directora del Digesto de Jurisprudencia de la Corte Suprema de Justicia). San José: Editorial Juricentro. 496 folios.

Umaña-Rojas, Ana Lorena. (1982). *Representación en el derecho privado*. (tesis inédita). San José: Universidad de Costa Rica. 596 folios.

Valverde y Alpízar, Sergio Alonso. (1990). *El fallo en conciencia del consejo de disciplina del Colegio de Abogados*. (tesis inédita). San José: Universidad de Costa Rica. 220 folios.

Valverde y Alpízar, Sergio Alonso. (1999). *El ejercicio de potestades públicas en las relaciones paterno filiales*. Tesina dirigida por el Dr. Agustín de Asis Roig. Madrid: Centro de Estudios Políticos y Constitucionales. 109 folios.

Varela-Quirós, Luis Alberto. (1971). *Concepto y alcances de la patria potestad en el proyecto de Código de Familia*. (tesis inédita). San José: Universidad de Costa Rica. 145 folios.

ENGLAND AND WALES

BALANCING RIGHTS

Gillian Douglas[*]

1999 saw a continuation of the limbo into which much of family law has been cast by the Government's hesitation in implementing the major divorce reforms enacted in the Family Law Act 1996.[1] Uncertainty as to the wisdom of introducing such a profound change, and nervousness about the political consequences should this prove unpopular, led to the Lord Chancellor announcing that the legislation would not be brought into force before the end of 2000. Further piloting and evaluation of the proposals were to be carried out before a final decision would be taken.[2] Meanwhile, family lawyers began to prepare for implementation of the Human Rights Act 1998[3] and to consider the implications of viewing family law through the prism of fundamental human rights. Indeed, examination of the developments in the law during 1999 reveals an underlying theme of judicial attempts to balance the competing rights of family members, across a wide range of issues. To illustrate this theme, this chapter begins with consideration of the parent/child relationship, then child protection, and then examines some developments in ancillary relief and property rights.

I   THE PARENT–CHILD RELATIONSHIP[4]

A   The 'natural parent presumption'

Some years ago, Lord Templeman, in the House of Lords' decision *Re KD (A Minor) (Ward: Termination of Access)*,[5] stated that:

> 'The best person to bring up a child is the natural parent. It matters not whether the parent is wise or foolish, rich or poor, educated or illiterate, provided the child's moral and physical health are not endangered. Public authorities cannot improve on nature.'

---

[*]   Professor of Law, Cardiff University.

1   Discussed in *The International Survey of Family Law 1996*, ed A Bainham (Martinus Nijhoff Publishers, 1998) at 160–169.

2   HL Weekly Hansard, vol 602, WA 39, June 17, 1999.

3   Discussed in *The International Survey of Family Law (2000 Edition)*, ed A Bainham (Family Law, 2000) at 131–132. See also J Herring, 'The Human Rights Act and the welfare principle in family law – conflicting or complementary?' [1999] CFLQ 223 and J Fortin, 'The HRA's impact on litigation involving children and their families' [1999] CFLQ 237.

4   For an excellent socio-legal analysis of issues relating to parenthood, see A Bainham et al (eds) *What is a Parent? A Socio-Legal Analysis* (Hart Publishing, 1999).

5   [1988] AC 806.

In that case, their Lordships had to decide whether a local authority should be permitted to terminate a parent's contact with her child, preparatory to the child being placed for adoption. However, the dictum has been used since as an illustration of a legal presumption in favour of the natural parent as the carer of a child, including in disputes with other private individuals. Thus, in *Re D (Care: Natural Parent Presumption)*[6] the Court of Appeal relied on it to overturn a ruling at first instance that a child whose two half-siblings were in the care of their grandparents should be placed with them rather than with his father. The children were to be made subject to care orders in favour of the local authority, the mother being unable to care for them, and the 'care plan' was for the two elder children to live with the grandparents and the youngest to be with the father. The trial judge considered that the welfare of this child would be best served by placement with the grandparents so that he could be with his half-siblings. The Court of Appeal, however, rejected the judge's attempt to 'balance' the merits of placement with the father on the one hand and the grandparents on the other. Rather, it held that he should have asked first, whether there were good grounds to reject the presumption in favour of the father and only then to have considered other matters. This decision provides a valuable template for courts dealing with conflicting claims based on the Human Rights Act 1998, since it sets out clearly and correctly the approach required by Convention jurisprudence which emphasises the rights of birth parents under Article 8.

B   Asserting the genetic relationship with the child[7]

In recent years, often relying on Article 7 of the UN Convention on the Rights of the Child, courts have generally asserted the view that a child has the right to know the truth about the identity of his genetic father. They will direct that a blood test to establish paternity should be carried out, unless it can be shown that this is against the child's interests.[8] However, in *Re K (Specific Issue Order)*[9] a more cautious approach was adopted. The father had ill-treated the mother during their relationship. Although the child had been registered with the father's surname at birth, after the mother left him, she changed the child's name by statutory declaration. She vehemently refused to have anything to do with him and told the child that the father was dead. The High Court rejected an application by the father that the child, now aged 12, should be told the truth about his paternity and the existence of the father. The judge held that, due to the mother's hatred of the father, informing the child of the truth at this stage would cause the child emotional disruption which would be seriously detrimental to his welfare.

In a less extreme case, *Re J (Parental Responsibility)*[10] Stuart-White J upheld the decision of a family proceedings court to refuse an unmarried father a parental

---

6   [1999] 1 FLR 134. See J Fortin, '*Re D (Care: Natural Parent Presumption)* Is blood really thicker than water?' [1999] CFLQ 435.

7   See A Bainham, 'Parentage, Parenthood and Parental Responsibility: Subtle, Elusive Yet Important Distinctions' in A Bainham et al (eds), op cit.

8   *S v McC (Otherwise S), W v W* [1972] AC 24.

9   [1999] 2 FLR 280.

10   [1999] 1 FLR 784.

responsibility order (which would vest him with the same rights and duties as all mothers and married fathers). There is no presumption in favour of fathers obtaining such orders but courts are generally 'disposed to grant orders to deserving fathers' because 'it is desirable for the sake of a child's self-esteem to grow up, wherever possible, having a favourable and positive image of an absent parent'.[11] Here, however, his Lordship agreed that contact between father and child on probably little more than five occasions over the course of eleven years did not demonstrate sufficient commitment or attachment on the part of the father to justify the making of the order. The Government intends to legislate to grant all fathers automatic parental responsibility if they are named on the birth register and so this particular issue will disappear from the courts. However, the broader question of balancing the parent's right to respect for – and recognition of – his family life against the equally strong right of the child to be secure within her own *de facto* family unit will assume even greater significance once the Human Rights Act 1998 is in force.

The prospect of a father seeking to claim a relationship with a child against the mother's (and child's) will is perhaps a modern development flowing from the growth in social acceptability of birth outside marriage and the strength of the 'fathers' rights' lobby. Traditionally, it might have been more common to see men resisting the attribution of fatherhood, often in order to avoid claims for maintenance for the child. The high level of child support payments produced under the formula assessment of the Child Support Act 1991 seems to have triggered a revival of such resistance, at least in the reported case-law. Notwithstanding the trend indicated above towards regarding the importance of discovering the genetic truth, the presumption that the mother's husband is the father of her child has remained enshrined in law. However, in *F v Child Support Agency*,[12] the High Court held that, even where this could apply, another man alleged to be the father may be fixed with paternity if he declines to undergo a blood test which could exclude him. The case might be seen as undermining the marital presumption; however, the mother had presented evidence that her husband had been excluded by DNA testing from being the child's father. It remains to be seen how a court would deal with a situation where both the husband and the other man refused to be tested. The court's approach to such a dilemma would shed light on how far modern law is prepared to go behind legal forms to establish another kind of 'truth'.

C   The child's surname

The question of what surname a child should bear continues to cause the courts difficulty.[13] In *Dawson v Wearmouth*,[14] the child's mother was divorced but had kept her married surname. She cohabited with the child's father for a while but

11   NV Lowe and G Douglas, *Bromley's Family Law* 9th ed (1998) at p 381.

12   [1999] 2 FLR 244.

13   This issue was discussed in *The International Survey of Family Law 1997*, ed A Bainham (Martinus Nijhoff Publishers, 1999) at 145–146.

14   [1999] 2 All ER 353. See M Hayes, '*Dawson v Wearmouth* "What's in a name? A child by any other name is surely just as sweet?"' [1999] CFLQ 423.

registered the child with her surname rather than his at the time of birth and her relationship with the father ended soon afterwards. The father sought an order that the child be known by the father's surname. Since the child had no relationship of any kind with the man whose surname he actually bore, one might think the courts would be sympathetic to this claim and the father succeeded at trial. However, the House of Lords upheld the view of the Court of Appeal that a change of surname must be justified on the basis of the child's welfare and there was no evidence to support this on the facts. The House also considered that wherever there is a dispute over a child's surname, the matter should be referred to the court for determination. They rejected the view that Article 8 of the European Convention was relevant to the issue, but with respect, this must be open to doubt. The European Court has accepted that a person's surname is a matter covered by Article 8.[15] Since parents will have to resort to the courts to resolve their disputes over surnames, the courts will have to engage with the arguments raised under the Convention at some point. This will inevitably involve them once again balancing the competing rights and interests of those concerned. Research suggests that children whose parents have divorced and re-partnered are most concerned to be 'the same' as the rest of those in their family unit.[16] Where such children live with the mother and her new husband, and where she takes his surname, they may wish to change theirs in order not to seem different. The Court of Appeal, however, has considered that this argument does not carry much weight.[17] Perhaps a way of reconciling the Court's view with what children themselves say would be to take careful account of their own expressed wishes. In *Re S (Change of Surname)*[18] the same Court in fact did precisely this in permitting a change of surname for a child in local authority care. Allegations were made that the father had sexually abused an elder sibling, but he was acquitted of criminal charges. The child and her sister wished to change their surname to that of their dead mother. The Court accepted that the child was of an age (15) to make up her own mind what name she should bear and that this must carry weight in determining her best interests.

D   The child's religious and cultural heritage

Two interesting cases were dealt with in 1999 concerning how far parental religious or cultural adherence should influence decisions over a child's future upbringing. In *Re P (Section 91(14) (Guidelines) (Residence and Religious Heritage)*[19] the child, who had Down's Syndrome, was born in 1990 into a very large Orthodox Jewish family. They could not care for her and, the local authority having failed to find a Jewish family to foster her, she was placed with a non-practising Roman Catholic family. These carers were granted a residence order, giving them parental responsibility for the child, in 1994. In 1998, the parents

---

15   *Burghartz v Switzerland* (1994) 18 EHRR 101.
16   I Butler et al, *Children's Perspectives and Experience of the Divorce Process*, report to the ESRC (2000).
17   *Re W; Re A; Re B (Change of Name)* [1999] 2 FLR 930. Cf *A v Y (Child's Surname)* [1999] 2 FLR 5.
18   [1999] 1 FLR 672.
19   [1999] 2 FLR 573.

sought the return of the child to their care. The Court of Appeal upheld the first instance judge's refusal to vary the residence order. In contrast to the application of the 'natural parent presumption' discussed above, the Court held that no such presumption applies in variation proceedings. Thus, the question to ask was why, if it had been right to make the original residence order in 1994, should the child be moved now? They recognised the significance of a child's religious and cultural heritage in determining her best interests.[20] However, they considered that her loss of this heritage had occurred because of the initial need to accommodate her away from her birth family and it could not take precedence over the risks of moving her from the foster carers now. As Ward LJ put it, having considered the relevant European Convention case-law, 'in the jurisprudence of human rights, the right to practise one's religion is subservient to the need in a democratic society to put welfare first'.[21]

A similar, but much less tragic, example of the same dilemma arose in *Re J (Specific Issue Orders: Muslim Upbringing and Circumcision).*[22] There, the five-year-old child had a non-practising Christian mother and a non-practising Muslim father. The marriage had ended and the child lived with the mother and had staying contact with the father. The father wished the child to be brought up as a Muslim and to be circumcised. Wall J refused to order the mother to bring up the child in the Muslim religion. He considered that it would be unusual to require a parent with whom the child resides to bring up a child in a religion other than her own and that there was no justification for such a course, given the father's own lack of observance. As to the question of circumcision, his Lordship concluded that this would not be in the child's best interests. While for a boy born into a Muslim (or Jewish) family, circumcision is a matter of family celebration and affirmation, for this particular child, it would be regarded by the mother as a stressful and traumatic experience, and this would be communicated to him. Furthermore, not only did the judge refuse to order the circumcision to take place, but he proceeded to prohibit the father from having it carried out, either in England and Wales or abroad. While he accepted the lawfulness of ritual circumcision for boys,[23] he concluded that, given that the child's upbringing was going to be essentially a secular one in England, the irreversible nature of the procedure was not justified by any strengthening of his identity as a Muslim which it might produce.

These decisions reflect a jurisdiction which is overwhelmingly secular and liberal and in which religious convictions and motivations are ultimately accorded relatively little weight. A sad and unusual twist to this theme was presented by a case concerning the disposal of the remains of a previously adopted child. In *Buchanan v Milton*,[24] an Australian Aboriginal child was adopted by an immigrant English family. They subsequently returned to England. The birth mother made

---

20 This is an aspect of the factor of the child's background to which a court must pay attention under section 1(3)(d) of the Children Act 1989 when deciding a disputed application for a residence (or other order) under section 8 of the Act.

21 At 598G–H, having considered *Hoffmann v Austria* (1994) 17 EHRR 293.

22 [1999] 2 FLR 678, subsequently upheld on appeal (reported at [2000] Fam Law 246).

23 Female circumcision is a criminal offence in the United Kingdom: Prohibition of Female Circumcision Act 1985.

24 [1999] 2 FLR 844.

contact with the family when the child was an adult, and he visited her in Australia and met her family. He himself had a daughter. He died at the age of 26 in a road accident. The birth mother wished his remains to be returned to Australia for burial; the adoptive family and his daughter's mother wished for cremation, which is unacceptable in Aboriginal culture. The case received media interest because the child had been regarded by his birth family as one of those 'stolen' from Aboriginal families as part of the prevailing white assimilationist policies of Australian administrations from the mid-nineteenth century to the late twentieth. However, Hale J, while recognising the inadequacies and inequities of the adoption law prevailing at the time of the child's birth, refused to 'establish a hierarchy in which one sort of feeling [that of the birth mother] is accorded more respect than other equally deep and sincere feelings'.[25] Accordingly, she declined to exercise the court's jurisdiction to displace the personal representatives of the deceased as having the right to dispose of his body.

E   Contact between a violent parent and the child

In the 1997 *Survey*,[26] attention was drawn to the extent to which the courts appeared to favour contact between the absent parent and the child, almost regardless, at times, of the concerns of the mother or the past violent history of the parents. It was noted that the courts had begun to distinguish between legitimate and illegitimate fears or hostility as a means of determining whether contact should be refused.[27] The current legislation does not refer directly to violence as a factor to consider when determining whether it is in the child's welfare to direct contact. In 1999, the Children Act Sub-Committee of the Lord Chancellor's Advisory Board on Family Law (ABFLA) issued a Consultation Paper[28] tentatively rejecting the need for a change. Instead, they proposed practice guidelines for the court to follow to require it to be more cautious before ordering contact in such cases. Meanwhile, reported cases suggest that there is a concerted attempt at the higher court level to get the message across of the need to think carefully before ordering contact where there is a history of domestic violence. An example is *Re M (Contact: Violent Parent)*.[29] There, Wall J (who chairs the ABFLA sub-committee) upheld the decision of magistrates to refuse direct contact with the father. There was evidence of violence witnessed by the children, of harassment of the mother and her new partner and of a resulting vulnerable emotional state in the eldest child. All were held to provide an ample basis for the refusal. His Lordship commented:

'Often in these cases where domestic violence has been found, too little weight in my judgment is given to the need for the father to change. It is often said that,

25   At p 855E–F.

26   Op cit at pp 147–148.

27   For a valuable consideration of the courts' practice, and an argument that they are shifting towards a more overt 'rights' approach, see R Bailey-Harris et al, 'From Utility to Rights? The Presumption of Contact in Practice' (1999) 13 *Int J of Law, Policy and the Family* 111.

28   ABFLA Children Act Sub-Committee, *Contact between Children and Violent Parents: The Question of Parental Contact in Cases where there is Domestic Violence.*

29   [1999] 2 FLR 321.

notwithstanding the violence, the mother must none the less bring up the children with full knowledge and a positive image of their natural father and arrange for the children to be available for contact. Too often it seems to me the courts neglect the other side of that equation, which is that a father, like this father, must demonstrate that he is a fit person to exercise contact.'[30]

In that case, indirect contact (through letters etc) was regarded as a suitable substitute for face-to-face contact. In *Re K (Contact: Mother's Anxiety)*[31] the mother herself was prepared to accept such indirect communication, even though she had undergone an extremely traumatic experience at the hands of the father. He had kidnapped the child, then aged under two, from the mother in the early hours of the morning and the child had been rescued by the police. The father was imprisoned, but on his release, pursued his application for contact. The same judge as in *Re M*, Wall J, ruled that the mother's hostility to the father was based on her justified fears about him and that her extreme distress was apparent to the child and making him feel guilty about enjoying the contact. If direct contact were to continue, the child was likely to suffer severe emotional harm from the mother's reaction; accordingly, indirect contact would be directed instead. Since the father and child had in fact met and had enjoyed their contact with each other, the grant of indirect contact is perhaps unsurprising, though one wonders if this concession by the mother had not been rather too generous, given the extreme circumstances as found by the judge. Another example of indirect contact being awarded as a compromise (or consolation prize) where direct contact is ruled out, can be seen in *M v M (Parental Responsibility)*.[32] There, the father had sustained brain injuries in a motor cycle accident, which had led to violent outbursts against the mother. The father's unstable mental condition was held by Wilson J to justify a refusal of both direct contact and a parental responsibility order.

II CHILD PROTECTION

All the issues considered above have concerned the balance of rights between parents, or between parents and the child, or between parents and other individuals. Where child protection procedures and policy are concerned, the role of the State becomes more directly manifested and there is a further need to balance family members' rights against those of the wider community. However, there is an increasing lack of confidence in the efficacy of the mechanisms presently available to deal with abuse and neglect. There has been a series of revelations of failures of the care system to protect children from abusers actually employed as care workers. There is continuing evidence of inefficiency and incompetence in the handling of child protection cases by social services departments and there is now long-standing evidence of the extent to which children leaving care are disadvantaged by a history of inadequate education,

---

30 At p 333B–C.
31 [1999] 2 FLR 703.
32 [1999] 2 FLR 737.

supervision and attention.[33] Three legislative measures were accordingly introduced in the 1999–2000 session of Parliament to attempt to address some of these problems. The Protection of Children Act 1999 was the only one to reach the statute book by the end of the year.[34]

A   The Protection of Children Act 1999

This Act, which, as is now usual with British legislation, was not brought into force immediately, places on a statutory footing the 'Consultancy Index List' maintained for a number of years by the Department of Health. This List contains the names of people deemed unsuitable for work with children in child care roles, based on information volunteered to the Department by employers. A person's inclusion on the list has been subject to no controls but nor has it been mandatory for employers, other than local authorities, to alert the Department to the existence of unsuitable care-workers. The Act will require child care organisations to refer eligible names for inclusion, and other organisations will be permitted to do so. Eligibility will be established where a person has been dismissed, transferred or suspended on the grounds of misconduct (whether or not in the course of their employment) which harmed a child or placed a child at risk of harm, or where a person *would* have been dismissed if they had not resigned or retired first. Where information which would have justified such action comes to the organisation's attention after the person has left their employment, referral will also be required or permissible.[35] Those named on the list will have a right of appeal to a tribunal. The Act also enables access to be given to other such lists, maintained by the Department for Education and Employment in relation to teachers, and by the Criminal Records Bureau of the police. This will enable a 'one stop shop' to be provided where an employer wishes to check on the suitability of a prospective child care worker. Under section 7 of the Act, child care organisations will be obliged to carry out such a check and, if the person is included on any of the lists, will not be permitted to offer them employment. Although it has been held that the current extra-statutory arrangements are lawful,[36] the new arrangements are clearly intended to ensure that this vetting system is not vulnerable to challenge under the European Convention on Human Rights. Providing a right of appeal will ensure compatibility with the right of access to a court under Article 6 and placing the List on a statutory footing will ensure that its operation is 'in accordance with law' under Article 8.

---

33   Sir William Utting, *People Like Us: The Report of the Review of Safeguards for Children Living Away From Home* (1997).

34   The others were the Care Standards Bill and the Children (Leaving Care) Bill, expected to be passed in 2000.

35   Section 2(2), (3).

36   An attempt to challenge their legality failed in *R v Secretary of State for Health ex parte C* [1999] 1 FLR 1073; appeal subsequently dismissed [2000] Fam Law 311.

B Disclosure of information about alleged abusers

While the 1999 Act is intended to deal with those employed in child care and related activities, there is the related problem of disclosing concerns about family members alleged or found to have abused their children, as a result of care proceedings under the Children Act 1989. Section 98(2) of the Children Act 1989 provides that a person cannot rely on the privilege against self-incrimination when giving evidence or answering questions in care and protection proceedings under the Act. However, any statement or admission made shall not be admissible in evidence against the person making it or his spouse in subsequent criminal proceedings. In 1996 in *Re C (A Minor) (Care Proceedings: Disclosure)*[37] the Court of Appeal held that this did not preclude the court granting disclosure to the *police* of such evidence, for the purposes of *investigation*.

In *Re V (Sexual Abuse: Disclosure); Re L (Sexual Abuse: Disclosure)*[38] by contrast, the Court held that disclosure should not be permitted where one local authority wished to pass on information held by the trial court to others to alert them to the identity of an abuser. In *Re V*, the court found that a man who coached junior football teams posed a risk of significant harm to the children of his girlfriend and although a care or supervision order was not made, a prohibited steps order was made to prevent his having contact with them. The judge wished the local authority to notify the relevant footballing authorities of the proceedings and the risk. In *Re L*, a father was found in care proceedings to have sexually abused his children, although he was acquitted of criminal charges. The father informed the judge of his new address but this was kept confidential from the other parties to the proceedings. The local authority asked the judge to disclose the address to them so that they could inform the authority of the area to which he had moved of the risk, as found by the judge, that he posed to the children of single female adults with whom he might cohabit. In each case, orders for disclosure were granted and the man appealed. The Court of Appeal held that the balance was firmly against disclosure, given that the men had not been convicted of any criminal offence and that the children who were the subjects of the proceedings were not in any danger. As one commentator pointed out,[39] however, this missed the point that the need for disclosure was in order to protect *other* children from harm. Moreover, the Court accepted that, if a local authority *asked* another for information about a person in their area, the authority could respond. But such enquiries are unlikely to be made if there is nothing to put the authority on notice of the potential risk. The Court noted that, where an abuser has been convicted of or cautioned for certain sexual offences, then the Sex Offenders Act 1997 requires that their name and address be kept on a national register and that the Index discussed above covers those in employment. It considered that if a broad disclosure mechanism was felt to be necessary to protect children, this was a matter for Parliament rather than the courts. The Court of Appeal's judgment may be supported from a human rights perspective as upholding a person's right to

---

37 [1997] Fam 76. The compatibility of s 98(2) with the requirements of Article 6 of the European Convention has been queried by Johnson J in *Re L (Care: Confidentiality)* [1999] 1 FLR 165.

38 [1999] 1 FLR 267.

39 V Smith, 'Passing on Child Abuse Findings – *Re V and Re L*' [1999] Fam Law 249.

respect for his private life under Article 8. It may also serve to counter some of the moral panic which has begun to colour this issue, but whether the result was correct on the particular facts in the two cases may be open to query.

C   Liability of local authorities for child protection decisions and actions

Probably the most significant development in the legal approach to child protection would be the attribution of legal liability for negligence on the part of local authority social workers, in the same way that other professional groups may be held liable for their failings. But in 1995, in *X (Minors) v Bedfordshire County Council; M v Newham London Borough Council*[40] the House of Lords ruled that a duty of care did not lie for such negligence. In the *Bedfordshire* case, social workers had failed to act to protect and remove children from the abusive and neglectful care of their parents. In *Newham*, they had removed a child from her mother on suspicion of sexual abuse, having wrongly identified her partner as the abuser, and kept the child away from home for a year before the error was rectified.

The House held that a common law duty of care should not be imposed where it relates to the exercise of discretionary powers or duties conferred by Parliament for social welfare purposes. Their Lordships considered that imposing such a duty would cut across the whole child protection scheme. This, after all, involves many professionals representing a number of organisations including the health service, police and education acting in an inter-disciplinary way. It would be wrong to impose liability only on one of the bodies participating in the system – the local authority social services department. Further, the decisions that must be taken about whether and how to intervene when a child is potentially at risk are enormously delicate and to face those taking them with the possibility of future legal action might prompt a defensive approach, to the detriment of the children concerned. The conclusion of the House was that no action, either for breach of statutory duty or negligence, could lie in such cases. However, the ruling has been challenged before the European Court of Human Rights and has been whittled down by the House itself in subsequent cases.

In *Barrett v Enfield London Borough Council*[41] for example, the plaintiff had been taken into care when aged ten months and remained there for the rest of his childhood. He claimed damages for negligence in the way the authority had handled his case, arguing that the result had been that he left care without family or attachments, suffering from psychiatric illness leading to alcohol abuse and self-harm. The House was faced with a ruling of the European Court of Human Rights, in *Osman v UK*.[42] There, the European Court held that a similar rule excluding the police from liability for negligence in the prevention or investigation of crime was a breach of Article 6, since those alleging negligence were not permitted to bring their claim to court for assessment on its merits. This was a clear message that blanket immunity from liability would be difficult to

---

40   [1995] 2 AC 633. See the commentary by Michael Freeman in *The International Survey of Family Law 1995*, ed A Bainham (Martinus Nijhoff Publishers, 1997) at pp 157–158.

41   [1999] 3 All ER 193.

42   [1999] 1 FLR 193.

justify and, in its ruling in *Barrett*, the House may be said therefore to have striven to limit the *ratio in Bedfordshire* while stopping short of actually overruling itself. It distinguished its earlier decision on the basis that there, the decision characterised as negligent was whether or not to take a child into care. By contrast, where a child *is* in the care of a local authority, then the way that the authority exercises its statutory powers in relation to the child *may*, depending on the extent to which this involves issues of policy, be justiciable. The greater the element of policy involved (such as in the allocation of public funds), the less likely the decision is to be found to be justiciable. However, it will be undesirable to strike out a claim at the outset, because it is necessary to examine its factual basis to determine whether it is indeed amenable to judicial scrutiny.

Whether this approach provides a tenable distinction that can be drawn by future courts will no doubt be established in further case-law or settled by the eventual ruling in the *Bedfordshire* case before the Strasbourg court.[43] At heart, as Lord Slynn explained,[44] the issue once more concerns a balance of rights and interests:

'there is a real conflict between on the one hand the need to allow social welfare services exercising statutory powers to do their work in what they as experts consider is the best way in the interests first of the child, but also of the parents and of society, without an unduly inhibiting fear of litigation if something goes wrong, and on the other hand the desirability of providing a remedy in appropriate cases for harm done to a child through the acts or failure to act of such services.'

III FINANCIAL PROVISION AND PROPERTY ON DIVORCE

The conduct and the outcome of finance and property disputes arising from divorce remain major concerns for the majority of family practitioners. An attempt[45] to streamline the court process to encourage settlement of these disputes will become generally operational in 2000. A device to minimise public expenditure on divorce litigation was also introduced at the end of 1998, originally on a pilot area basis, requiring litigants seeking legal aid to undergo an assessment for suitability for mediation before being granted support to bring their case.[46] If the case is deemed suitable for mediation, legal aid is directed to meet the costs of that mediation rather than pursuit of litigation. The dangers of allowing divorce litigation to spiral out of control were graphically illustrated by a case before the House of Lords, *Piglowska v Piglowski*.[47] There, the parties' litigation over assets worth £127,400 ran up costs to the Legal Aid Fund of some £128,000. The reason for this excess lay in the appeals system, under which five differently constituted

---

43 A case concerning whether foster carers could sue a local authority for placing a known child abuser with them, who then allegedly abused their own children, resulted in another decision by the House of Lords not to strike out the action: *W v Essex CC* [2000] 2 All ER 237.

44 [1999] 3 All ER 193 at p 209f.

45 The 'Ancillary Relief Pilot Scheme' was discussed in the 1997 *Survey* (fn 13 above) at pp 138–139.

46 Family Law Act 1996, s 29. See G Davis, 'Monitoring Publicly Funded Mediation' [1999] Fam Law 625.

47 [1999] 3 All ER 632.

courts had dealt with the case. As Lord Hoffmann commented, 'To allow successive appeals in the hope of producing an answer which accords with perfect justice is to kill the parties with kindness.'[48]

Their Lordships considered that the appeal raised no point of principle and hence should never have been brought. The problem, however, is that the court is granted a very wide discretion by the Matrimonial Causes Act 1973 to assess the merits of an application. Although the court is required to consider a number of factors (such as the resources and needs of the parties, their contributions to the welfare of the family, etc)[49] and to give first consideration to the welfare of any children of the family, there is no statutory guidance on what outcome is to be regarded as desirable in any given case. It is therefore hardly surprising when different judges – and different advisers – take different views on what is an appropriate outcome in any given case. A wish to find some way of balancing the needs and interests of the two parties is understandable. It could, of course, be argued that if they had been funding the litigation themselves, the issue would probably never have been allowed to run on for so long and to such excess.[50]

Strangely, however, although judges do their best to encourage parties to negotiate and settle their finances without resort to adjudication, an important ruling of the Court of Appeal made clear that ordinary contractual principles do not apply to ancillary relief applications. In *Xydhias v Xydhias*,[51] the spouses negotiated long and hard to reach an agreement. Eventually, a settlement was agreed and drafted for approval by the court, but shortly before the hearing the husband withdrew his offer. The wife sought to enforce the agreement on the basis that it was a concluded contract. The Court of Appeal held that the only way of rendering a settlement of an ancillary relief claim enforceable is to convert it into an order of the court (known as a consent order). This is because the court is required to review the terms of the settlement to ensure that it regards them as appropriate in the light of the factors contained in section 25 of the Matrimonial Causes Act 1973.

> '[T]he purpose of negotiation is not finally to determine the liability (that can only be done by the court) but to reduce the length and expense of the process by which the court carries out its function ... in every case the court must exercise its independent discretionary review applying the s 25 criteria to the circumstances of the case and to the terms of the accord.'[52]

As Dr Cretney has pointed out, English law reflects a tension between two conflicting principles. On the one hand, it is accepted that private ordering is preferable to adversarial litigation in the family sphere; on the other, 'the consequences of dissolving a marriage are a matter of public concern, much too

---

48   At p 644j.

49   See Matrimonial Causes Act 1973, s 25.

50   But even matrimonial lawyers appear to do silly things when their own affairs are concerned – see *Tee v Tee and Hillman* [1999] 2 FLR 613, CA, where the fact that the wife's lover was a family solicitor did not save her from engaging in 'furious adversarial litigation' resulting in costs of over £100,000.

51   [1999] 1 FLR 683. See S Bridge, 'Judicial Paternalism and Private Ordering on Divorce' [1999] CLJ 495.

52   Per Thorpe LJ at pp 692–693.

important to be left to the uncontrolled wishes of the parties'.[53] (In fact, it is doubtful how far the courts do, or can, effectively scrutinise the detail of consent orders to ensure that they meet the requirements of section 25.[54]) It is surprising to see the Court of Appeal producing a ruling that will inevitably lead to more caution in the search for a bargain which couples engage in on divorce, because of the need to obtain a binding court order before they can be confident of its enforceability. It is also worrying, because statistics and research suggest that only a minority of couples in fact proceed to obtain such orders.[55] In a number of cases, it seems that they rely on each other's word to carry out the terms of their settlement, usually to save the money that would otherwise be incurred in using the courts. Furthermore, if the new divorce regime were to be introduced, under section 9(2) of the Family Law Act 1996, it is envisaged that couples would have to present to the court a court order, negotiated agreement, or declaration that financial arrangements have been made or are unnecessary, before they could obtain their divorce order. As Dr Cretney also noted, there is nothing in the statute to suggest that any *scrutiny* of such documents is intended to be carried out. One is left puzzled as to where the balance between private ordering and state regulation should – or indeed, after *Xydhias*, currently does – lie.

IV HOMOSEXUAL PARTNERSHIPS

Finally, it is necessary to discuss a ruling by the House of Lords which is arguably the most significant of all in 1999. In *Fitzpatrick v Sterling Housing Association*[56] a majority of their Lordships ruled that a homosexual partner could be described as a member of the family of his deceased lover, for the purposes of succeeding to a rented tenancy. The ruling turned on the particular provisions of the legislation governing such tenancies,[57] which relates to where 'a person who was a member of the original tenant's family was residing with him in the dwelling-house at the time of and for the period of two years immediately before his death'. It does not, therefore, have general application to the question of homosexual rights. Nonetheless, it is important because the House discussed in depth what might be understood by the term 'family', an issue surprisingly rarely considered in family jurisprudence. This is no doubt because, until recently, the focus of family law has been upon determining the ambit of formal relationships created by law, such as marriage. With greater diversity in family forms an increasing characteristic of modern society, this approach can no longer suffice. Furthermore, the case is significant because the majority were prepared to go *beyond* the current ambit of

---

53 Address to the UK Family Law Conference organised for the judiciary, Inner Temple, London, June 1999.

54 G Davis et al, 'Ancillary relief schemes' [2000] CFLQ 43.

55 C Barton and A Bissett-Johnson, 'The Declining Number of Ancillary Financial Relief Orders' [2000] Fam Law 94; Perry et al, *How parents cope financially on marriage breakdown* (Family Policy Studies Centre/Joseph Rowntree Foundation, 2000).

56 [1999] 4 All ER 705. The Court of Appeal decision was discussed in the 1997 *Survey* (fn 13 above) at pp 143–144. All the judges in the House of Lords agreed that a homosexual partner could not be regarded as a 'spouse' of the tenant. Cf the opposite view taken by the Supreme Court of Canada in *M v H* [1999] 171 DLR (4th) 577.

57 Rent Act 1977, Sch 1, para 3.

European Convention jurisprudence in recognising that homosexuals, specifically, may share a *family* life.[58]

According to Lord Slynn:[59]

> 'the hallmarks of the relationship were essentially that there should be a degree of mutual inter-dependence, of the sharing of lives, of caring and love, of commitment and support. In respect of legal relationships these are presumed, though evidently they are not always present ... In de facto relationships these are capable, if proved, of creating membership of the tenant's family ... for the purposes of this Act, two people of the same sex can be regarded as having established membership of a family, one of the most significant of human relationships which both gives benefits and imposes obligations.'

Even if subsequent courts construe other legislation more restrictively than this, such dicta open up new avenues for argument and debate about where the boundaries of legal family relationships are to be drawn. *Fitzpatrick* demonstrates that the courts in England and Wales are capable of developing domestic jurisprudence without waiting passively for the European Court of Human Rights at Strasbourg to pronounce definitively upon an issue.

V   CONCLUSION

With a clear recognition of this kind that family relationships can be constituted outside traditional forms yet still be accorded recognition and protection, English law can be said to have left the twentieth century well prepared to face the challenges of the future. As this survey has suggested, the courts have long been experienced in balancing the interests of different family members and the wider community. Prediction is always dangerous, but it seems reasonably certain that one of the first of the challenges in a new century will be to articulate these interests in human rights terms.

---

58   Up to now the European Commission has regarded homosexual conduct as an aspect of *private* but not *family* life: *S v UK* (1986) 47 DR 274.

59   At pp 714h and 717b.

ESTONIA

FAMILY LAW IN ESTONIA

*Kai Kullerkupp**

I   INTRODUCTION

This article attempts to provide an overview of the present-day Estonian family legislation as well as give a hint on some possible future developments. As the Survey has not covered Estonian law before, the content of this article will not be confined to specific issues to be discussed in detail. Instead, it will provide a general introduction. Thereby it is hoped that the possibility will remain open for further contributions to the Survey in the future, addressing the newest developments and the Estonian experience in family law drafting.

During the past decade, the Estonian legislator has had, in effect, to renew the whole legal system. Drafting new legislation has been carried out to a remarkable degree with the support of foreign experts. Several of the laws of the 1990s have received international acknowledgement for their modernity and also their conformity to the *acquis*. Reforming family law has proved to be a different matter. Where any international standards exist,[1] they are of rather general nature and thus insufficient as a basis for a complete national family code. Moreover, family law is considered a field of law so tightly connected to a particular society, its traditions and life patterns, that an attempt to 'import' certain family law models from other jurisdictions would seem to many to be a renunciation of the historically developed system of values and cultural creeds.[2] Outside advisers will probably be less inclined to express their positions on different alternative solutions in family law – they might perceive this as an impertinent intervention in an 'intimate' sphere of national jurisprudence, a subject far more sensitive than, for example, commercial law or insolvency law.

However, it is characteristic of the Estonian family law system that, so far, the greater part of it has been 'imported'. Throughout the period of the First Estonian Republic (1918–1940), the private law for the Baltic Provinces of the Russian Empire remained in force in the Estonian territory. Although the law drafters of the time had completed a Bill for a Civil Code containing a chapter on Family Law by 1940, it never became law due to the outbreak of World War II. Following the annexation to the USSR, Soviet law was brought into force. In 1969 the

---

*   Ministry of Justice of Estonia, University of Tartu Law Faculty (Department of Private Law).

1   Eg the International Conventions (the European Human Rights Convention, other Conventions adopted under the aegis of the Council of Europe or the UN, the treaties of the *Commission International d'Etat Civil* and the Hague Conference on Private International Law) or recommendations of the Council of Europe.

2   See for example: D Martiny, 'Die Möglichkeit der Vereinheitlichung des Familienrechts innerhalb der Europäischen Union', in: D Martiny, N Witzleb (Hrsg.), 'Auf dem Wege zu einem Europäischen Zivilgesetzbuch', Frankfurt/Oder, 1999, pp 178–179.

Marriage and Family Code of the Estonian SSR (ESSR)[3] was adopted, which remained in existence until 1995. On 1 January 1995 the present Family Law Act[4] entered into force. As the urgent need for reforms did not allow for proper research to be carried out, to consider thoroughly each aspect of the new law in light of the legal tradition of Continental Europe, the Family Law Act bears a substantial resemblance to its predecessor, the Marriage and Family Code of the ESSR, in its basic concepts and the scope of the regulations.

Five years later, the time seems to be ripe for a reconsideration of the somewhat vague principles and ideals contained in the Family Law Act. Already in 1996, a working group was established by the Estonian Ministry of Justice, whose final goal is to submit a draft for a new Family Law Act. The new draft is expected to reflect the general family law structures and settings known in the Continental European legal tradition, of which the Estonian legal system is a part both culturally and historically. In preparing the new draft, the working group is expected to analyse existing experiences, as well as current tendencies in family law in other jurisdictions, primarily in those that have influenced the development of Estonian law to the largest degree. The results of such comparisons will then be taken into account in composing the best suited set of regulations to form the future Estonian family legislation. Thus, the situation of family law at the end of the first decade of the re-gained Estonian statehood may be described as a 'second round'.[5]

II   OVERVIEW OF ESTONIAN FAMILY LEGISLATION AND SOME CRITICAL REMARKS

A   Marriage

1   THE CONTRACT OF MARRIAGE

According to ss 1 and 3 of the Family Law Act, a marriage is to be contracted between a man and a woman of full age (18 years) on the mutual desire of the

---

3   The Estonian SSR Marriage and Family Code (*ENSV Teataja /The ESSR Official Gazette/* 1969, 31, Appendix; with later amendments; last amendment: *Riigi Teataja /State Gazette/* 1992, 11, 168).

4   Family Law Act, passed on 12 October 1994 (*Riigi Teataja /State Gazette/* I 1994, 75, 1326 with later amendments; latest amendment: *Riigi Teataja /State Gazette/* I 1997/35/538); entered into force 1 January 1995. An English translation of all major Estonian legal acts, including the Family Law Act, is available on the webpage of the Estonian Translation and Legislative Support Centre: <http:www.legaltext.ee>.

5   It should be noted that, although the present Family Law Act entered into force over five years ago, almost no scholarly materials have since then been published in this field. (In 1995, an introductory overview was published in the legal journal of the Tartu University Law Faculty, 'Juridica' (No. 1, 1995) by E Salumaa, M Seppik and J Odar who had also participated in elaborating the text of the present Family Law Act. However, this overview concentrated on the few changes the 1995 law brought in comparison with the earlier ESSR Marriage and Family Code.) No theses have been written by master or doctoral students of the Tartu University Law Faculty. There are still themes in family law in which no Supreme Court practice exists. On the one hand, this makes it difficult to outline comprehensively the present legislation. On the other hand, it will probably simplify the introduction of new concepts and changes since the existing ones are not very deeply entrenched.

prospective spouses. A marriage enters into force when the marriage registration is signed by the prospective spouses. Only a marriage registered at a vital statistics office upon celebration of the marriage has legal effect.

Obstacles to the conclusion of marriage include: (a) a subsisting previous marriage of one of the prospective spouses (prohibition of bigamy); (b) close kinship (prohibition of marriages between direct ascendants and descendants, brothers and sisters, half-brothers and half-sisters, adoptive parents and adopted children, or between children adopted by the same person) and (c) absence of active legal capacity of one of the prospective spouses.

An exception with regard to the age for marriage may be made for a minor between 15 and 18 years of age – they may marry with the written consent of their parents or guardian. In the absence of such consent, a court may grant permission to marry. Such permission can only be granted when the court finds the intended marriage to be in the interests of the minor.

A marriage may only be annulled by a court if the provisions prescribing the marriageable age or the obstacles to the capacity to marry have been violated, if an ostensible marriage was contracted, or if consent for marriage was obtained against the will of a prospective spouse by fraud or duress.

Estonian law does not attach any specific legal consequences to non-marital (heterosexual) cohabitation whereby concubinage would be legally approximated to the institution of marriage. However, court practice has for quite some time been applying the concept of the private law partnership to cohabiting couples, as a result of which the cohabitees may obtain common rights (shared ownership) to property falling within their common sphere of interest (such as the common home).[6]

As regards the registration of partnerships of same-sex couples, no initiative has so far been taken to regulate this matter.

2   PERSONAL RIGHTS OF SPOUSES (THE LEGAL CONSEQUENCES OF MARRIAGE IN GENERAL)

The personal rights of the spouses under the current Family Law Act cover the choice of surname and there is a general clause prohibiting the illegal restriction of the personal rights and freedoms of spouses by agreement (ss 5 and 6).[7]

The choice of surname is a matter for the free decision of the spouses. They may take the surname of one spouse as the common surname, whether either spouse will retain his or her pre-marital surname or whether the surname of one spouse will be added to the other spouse's pre-marital surname. There is no legal obligation or even a directive that the spouses should bear a common surname. While this freedom of choice has a rather long history in contemporary Estonian

---

6   For example, the decision of the Supreme Court (*Riigikohus*) No. 3-2-1-5-98 from 28.01.1998 (*Riigi Teataja /State Gazette/* III 1998, 5, 47). An unmarried couple had built a dwelling house in which they intended to live together with their two common children. The woman, who had mainly been taking care of the children, claimed the acknowledgement of her right to shared ownership of the house in the proportion of 50%. The court established that there was an agreement between the parties on continuing co-existence as a family, but also that they both participated in building the house with their work and financial contributions. Pursuant to these facts, the court applied the provisions of the Civil Code on private law partnership and acknowledged her ownership of 1/2 of the house.

7   The sections referred to are those of the Family Law Act unless otherwise specified.

family law, the majority of couples still continue to take the surname of the husband as the common family name according to the old tradition.

The present law allows for a considerable 'wandering' of surnames as the choice is not confined to the birthname of either spouse and in cases of (multiple) re-marriages a name acquired through marriage may be chosen as the common surname.

As regards other personal rights of the spouses to be secured and safeguarded under family law, s 6 barely states that 'agreements which restrict the personal rights and freedoms of spouses are void'.

The Family Law Act contains no provisions on the 'moral' rights and duties of spouses – eg guiding the harmonious and consensual building up of family life, requiring from the spouses mutual respect, support and assistance as well as fidelity or obligating the spouses to live together. Even though such provisions, known in a number of European legal orders,[8] may be merely of a declarative and symbolic nature, they may still have the effect of shaping a more abiding attitude towards the family within society and thus strengthening the family as an institution.

3   PROPERTY RIGHTS OF SPOUSES

The property relations of the spouses can be based on the statutory property regime or a marital property contract. The statutory marital property regime is of particular importance as it affects the great majority of marriages – most marrying couples in Estonia do not have a clear perception of the proprietary consequences of marriage and think little of making specific arrangements with regard to their assets. This is also one of the most complex issues to be reconsidered in the framework of the planned family law reform.

The statutory basis for the proprietary relations between spouses according to the 1995 Family Law Act (ss 14–20) is the joint property regime (also known as 'limited community of property'). In the absence of a marital property contract to provide for a different arrangement of the proprietary rights of the spouses, property acquired by the spouses during the marriage is considered to be their joint property. Property which was in the ownership of either spouse before the marriage, property acquired by the spouse during the marriage as a gift or by succession, and property acquired by the spouse after termination of conjugal relations, as well as personal effects acquired during a marriage, remain the separate property of the spouse concerned. However, a court may declare the separate property of a spouse, the value of which has significantly increased as a result of the work or monetary expenses of both spouses during the marriage, to be partly or wholly the joint property of the spouses.

Each spouse has an equal right to possess, use and dispose of joint property. Spouses are expected to agree mutually on the possession, usage and disposal of joint property. Failing agreement, a court must, at the request of a spouse, settle disputes regarding possession and use of joint property (s 17).

In relation to transactions concerning assets in the joint ownership of the spouses, different rules of consent apply based on the categorisation of assets into

---

8   Eg s 1353 of the German BGB, Articles 81 and 83 of the Dutch *Burgerlijk Wetboek*, s 90 of the Austrian ABGB.

(ordinary) movables, movables subject to entry in a register, and immovables. If one spouse enters into a transaction to transfer a movable, the consent of the other spouse is presumed – meaning that there is no obligation to certify specifically that the other spouse actually consents to the transaction. In the case of movables subject to entry in a register,[9] the written consent of the other spouse is required in order to transfer or pledge the item, regardless of in which spouse's name the movable is entered in the register. Although the law explicitly makes use of the term 'movables' (things) with no reference to intangibles, the regulation should in my opinion also cover proprietary rights subject to entry in a register (such as industrial property).

Rights concerning immovables (rights *in rem*) are generally to be entered in the Land Registry which also provides the basis of entitlement to undertake transactions. Therefore, no consent of the other spouse is necessary when the spouse entered in the Land Registry undertakes a transaction concerning that property. However, if an immovable may be deemed to be the joint property of spouses,[10] the other spouse may file a request aimed at the declaration of himself or herself as joint owner and amendment of the Land Registry entry (s 17). In that case, the provisions on shared ownership will apply, according to which either spouse would be entitled to an abstract fractionary portion of the immovable. A fractionary portion of an asset in shared ownership can be separately transferred by either co-owner, whereby the other co-owner will have a privileged buying right.[11]

The solution contained in the present Family Law Act, sorting assets of joint property according to their qualification in the law of property (*ius in rem*), is rather mechanical. Intangible property (such as claims against third persons or intellectual property rights etc) is not covered. The present regulation takes no account of the notion of regular economic activity (eg running a business) or a 'customary' volume of transactions, in which situations the requirement of a spouse's consent would seem rather unnecessary. On the other hand, there are no objective provisions to secure the preservation of the so-called 'family assets' belonging to the common sphere of interest of the spouses, such as the household commodities, or even the common home. The Act does not require the other spouse's consent where one of them intends to assume obligations.

The law prescribes joint liability of spouses for proprietary obligations assumed in the interests of the family with the joint property and the separate property of both spouses.

As regards the (personal) proprietary obligations of the spouses, each is liable for his or her debts incurred in relation to his or her separate property and in relation to the share of the joint property which would belong to the spouse upon division of joint property. This means that if the separate property of a spouse proves to be insufficient to satisfy the claims of the creditors, the joint property will be caught – an actual division of the joint property may have to be carried out.

9　Such movables include motor vehicles and aeroplanes.

10　Eg, the immovable was acquired during the marriage and no marital property contract declaring the immovable to be the separate property of one spouse has been signed.

11　Sections 71–79 on shared property of the Property Law Act (*Riigi Teataja /State Gazette/* I, 1993, 39, 590; 1999, 44, 509) are applicable for spouses insofar as the Family Law Act does not provide otherwise.

The statutory joint property regime of the present Family Law Act does not provide for protective mechanisms in the interest of the other spouse to cover the situation where one of the spouses runs into economic hardships, is overdebted or acts in a way that risks the property of the spouses. Considering that in the case of a marital property contract a spouse has the right to request the termination of the contract where the other spouse's conduct endangers the joint property, the logic of the statutory regime seems to be rather out-of-balance.[12] The freedom to sign a marital property contract at any time cannot be expected to provide a solution for cases of dispute.

4　DIVISION OF JOINT PROPERTY

Joint property of spouses may be divided during marriage, upon divorce or after divorce (s 18). The division is to be carried out by agreement of the spouses. Thereby, the shares of the spouses will be deemed to be equal, even if one spouse did not earn an income owing to the raising of a child or for other good reasons. A court may, however, depart from this principle of equality if the particular interests of a child or the other spouse so require; if without good reason one spouse did not participate in the acquisition of joint property with his or her income or work; if the joint property was acquired out of the separate property of one spouse; or if the value of the separate property of a spouse has significantly increased during the marriage as a result of the work or monetary expenses of the other spouse or out of the joint property of the spouses.

Upon division of the joint property of spouses, the property remaining with each spouse will be designated as a share in common ownership of things or proprietary rights and obligations.

Taking into account the shortcomings of the present marital property law system under Estonian law, some of which have been indicated above, it would seem reasonable to reconsider the whole system as such. A better balance between the proprietary interests of the spouses, confining the portion of property to be divided to that belonging to the common sphere of responsibility (and interest) pertaining to family life, is required. There is also a need for more effective protection for either spouse against the economic risks or lifestyle of the other.

Due to the complexity of the matter it would not suffice to make mere amendments to the present law. Instead, it might be desirable to replace the present marital property regime with a statutory system based on a greater separation of the assets of the spouses, such as a variation of the so-called community of surplus: during marriage the property of either spouse would be legally separated from that of the other spouse; upon winding up of the regime, the surplus acquired by the spouses (subtracting the opening value of their estate from the closing value) would be divided. This would, in its turn, also strengthen the independent responsibility of the individual as a subject of private law.

12　There is some court practice concerning the bankruptcy of one spouse. In its decision No. 3-2-1-104-96 from 3 October 1996 (published: *Riigi Teataja /State Gazette/* III 1996, 26, 350) the Supreme Court (*Riigikohus*) found that assets belonging to the joint property of the spouses cannot be excluded from the bankruptcy estate and may be seized if no division of the joint property has been carried out.

5   MARITAL PROPERTY CONTRACTS

The notion of the marital property contract is comparatively new to the Estonian legal order as the pre-1995 legislation did not provide for the possibility to deviate by a contract from the statutorily fixed regime.

A marital property contract is any agreement between spouses by which the mutual proprietary rights and obligations are specified in a way which deviates from the provisions of the statutory marital property regime. A marital property contract may be entered into before or during a marriage, it may later be amended by agreement of the parties. The only restriction in concluding a marital property contract is the prohibition of interference with imperative provisions of law. The law prescribes a compulsory notarised form for marital property contracts. They may, at the request of a spouse, be entered in the marital property contract register. An entry in the register will guarantee the validity of the marital property contract with respect to third persons, provided the entry concerning the marital property contract is made before the claim of the third person arises (s 10).

In a marital property contract, the spouses may regulate the following questions: (a) which goods (property) are to be considered the separate property of a spouse and what property is to be regarded as joint property; (b) administration of joint property; (c) division of joint property; (d) mutual maintenance duties of the spouses during the marriage and upon termination of the marriage. This is a non-exhaustive list: other mutual proprietary rights and obligations of the spouses may likewise be regulated in a marital property contract, provided this would not infringe the mandatory aspects of the law (s 9).

The law (s 9) expressly lists stipulations which may not be inserted in a marital property contract. Such a settlement may not deny a spouse or divorced spouse the right to receive maintenance on the bases provided for in the Family Law Act, waive the right to divide joint property of the spouses upon termination of the marriage or, in the case where one of the spouses has acquired property as a gift or by succession with the condition that it belong to the spouse as separate property, deem that property to be joint property of the spouses.

During marriage, a marital property contract can be terminated by a notarised agreement of the parties or by a court at the request of a spouse on the following grounds: (a) the other spouse is declared to be missing; (b) a court declares the bankruptcy of one spouse; (c) the other spouse significantly damages the property of the spouses or performs acts which may substantially damage the property of spouses. A marital property contract also terminates upon the termination of marriage due to the death of a spouse or upon divorce (ss 11–12).

According to the present regulation of marital property contracts, the (future) spouses have at their disposal extensive possibilities to tailor their proprietary relations by way of a notarised agreement in almost any way they wish. This might result in unbalanced circumstances and even manipulation to the disadvantage of the economically weaker spouse, as the law contains insufficient mechanisms in the shape of generally applicable norms to guarantee a mutually balanced marital property regime.[13] Therefore, it might be desirable to introduce a *numerus clausus* system of marital property regimes, where the spouses could

---

13   There is, however, no case-law of the Supreme Court (*Riigikohus*) pertaining to marital property contracts.

pick one of the several 'ready-made' alternative regimes. This would also increase clarity for the creditors of the spouses. Of course, an adequate degree of flexibility would have to be ensured.

6   MAINTENANCE OF SPOUSE

According to the present law, the mutual obligation of the spouses to provide (to) each other the necessary means of subsistence is to be seen as rather limited. It is the general understanding, not even explicitly set forth in law, that either spouse should personally participate in making a livelihood for himself/herself as well as for the overall needs of the family. The roots of this ideology can be seen in the Soviet family model which knew no 'housewife-marriages'. On the other hand, such an approach seems to correspond to the current trends towards a partnership-based marriage of equal and independent spouses. However, the nature of marriage, embodying a shared responsibility for the well-being of the family, might be perceived as being rather neglected in the light of the operative norms of the Estonian Family Law Act.

During marriage a spouse is only required to maintain the other spouse in the event that he/she needs assistance and is incapacitated for work. A husband must also maintain the wife during her pregnancy and child-care until the child attains three years of age. In both cases, the maintenance obligation arises only if the financial situation of the obligated spouse allows for provision of maintenance (s 21).

This regulation takes no account of the shared responsibility of the spouses for the maintenance of the family as such. In my opinion, the relevant provisions should be reformulated in the future legislation to the effect that both spouses are declared responsible for providing for the needs and covering the (*necessary*) living expenses of the whole family in proportion to their income and property and according to the mutually agreed arrangements governing their family life. These expenses would also include the subsistence of either spouse inasmuch as this corresponds to their living arrangements.

In the event of divorce, the Family Law Act prescribes the duty of maintenance towards the other (former) spouse in an equally restrictive way. The instances in which the current Act sets forth obligatory maintenance of a divorced spouse can rather be viewed as exceptional cases since, as a general rule, there is no obligation on either side to maintain a divorced spouse.

A right to receive maintenance would only be granted to a divorced spouse if he/she needs assistance and is incapacitated for work, ie does not have a sufficient and stable source of income, nor the prospect of obtaining one. The law goes further in restricting the right to receive maintenance after the termination of marriage by enumerating the occasions on which such a right may arise. A divorced spouse would have a right to receive maintenance from his or her former spouse only if he or she has – during the marriage – become disabled or attained pensionable age, is expecting a child conceived during the marriage or is taking care of a common child under three years of age. A further condition to found a right to maintenance is the sufficiently stable financial situation of the obligated divorced spouse to allow for the provision of maintenance (s 22).

Again, these provisions generally correspond to the principle of a partnership-based marriage of two independent individuals in which either side is responsible for providing the necessary means for his or her own personal needs. However, such a narrow concept of the mutual maintenance of spouses might evade the current economic reality and lead to hardship, eg when the spouses had agreed to shape their marital cohabitation to the effect that only one of them would have a substantial source of income outside the home and the other spouse would keep the house or assist the first one in running his/her business etc. Such mutual arrangements might result in one of the spouses being unqualified in terms of later obtaining an independent source of income, even if he/she stayed physically fit during the marriage and there were no small children to raise. The law does provide for the possibility of specifying the mutual maintenance duties of the spouses during the marriage as well as upon termination of the marriage through a marital property contract which differs from the statutorily fixed rules, but it is questionable whether the possibility of signing a marital property contract is a sufficient tool to solve the difficulties in maintenance matters. In my view, the possibility of receiving maintenance from the other spouse should be widened in the future legislation to include a broader range of cases where one side is factually incapable of supporting himself/herself due to circumstances pertaining to the marriage. On the other hand, the duration of such a right should be restricted to a reasonable period after which the 'beneficiary' spouse can be expected to obtain a sufficient income. The responsibility of earning sufficient for one's own subsistence after the dissolution of marriage should still remain the prevailing principle.

7   TERMINATION OF MARRIAGE

According to s 26 of the Family Law Act, a marriage terminates upon the death of a spouse or upon divorce.

As in a number of other 'Eastern Block' jurisdictions, Estonian law provides for both a 'judicial' and an 'administrative' divorce: it can be granted either by a court or by a vital statistics office. A vital statistics office grants a divorce upon agreement of the spouses on the basis of a joint written petition. The petition of one spouse will be sufficient if the other spouse is declared to be missing or without active legal capacity. The pre-requisite for granting a divorce by a vital statistics office is that there is no controversy between the spouses regarding child custody, the division of joint property or a support order. If the spouses disagree about the divorce or if, together with the divorce, a spouse desires to resolve a dispute concerning a child or concerning the division of joint property or desires support to be ordered, the divorce petition is to be heard by a court.

In cases of 'administrative' divorce, the spouses simply have to express their consensus that they wish their marriage to be terminated. A vital statistics office will conduct no examination of the actual failure of the marriage. Conversely, a court may only grant a divorce if it is shown that the continuation of the marriage is impossible. This implies dissimilar treatment of cases where both spouses agree on the divorce itself, but may or may not have controversies regarding, for example, the division of property (going to court because of a dispute pertaining to the marital property, they would automatically have to demonstrate the breakdown of their marriage).

The large number of divorces[14] has given rise to some discussion about whether the easy procedure of consensual (administrative) divorce might have contributed to the spread of an irresponsible attitude towards marriage and the family. It is therefore likely that in the future a clearer emphasis will be placed on the so-called 'breakdown principle' according to which an irretrievable failure of the marriage would constitute an obligatory prerequisite of a divorce. However, this will call for reconsideration of the present system of 'administrative divorces' since a vital statistics office would not be qualified to examine questions such as whether a marriage has irretrievably broken down. In parallel, the introduction of additional tools to help preserve families (perhaps a conciliation or mediation procedure, or even a waiting period) should be contemplated in elaborating the new draft. The present law contains no provisions on procedures intended to save marriages and families.

Moreover, the one-sided divorce (where one of the spouses is declared to be missing or without active legal capacity) should disappear from the future law.

B   The family

1   FILIATION OF CHILDREN

The mutual rights and obligations of parents and children arise from the filiation of children which is proven pursuant to the procedure provided by law. Thus, filiation is the only ground upon which familial relations between parents and children are based. Section 38 of the Family Law Act provides that: (a) a child descends from the mother who gives birth to the child; and (b) a child descends from the father by whom the child is conceived.

There are, however, certain legal presumptions with respect to filiation, intended to preserve the integrity of the family. In general, a child born or conceived during the marriage of the parents will be deemed to be descended from the man who is married to the mother of the child. In the birth registration of a child, the person who gives birth to the child is entered as the mother and the person who is married to the mother of the child is entered as the father on the basis of an application of either person. Where a child born or conceived during a marriage does not descend from the man who is married to the mother of the child, the spouses may submit a joint application, based on which the man will not be entered as the father in the birth registration of the child.

A child who is born after the death of the man who was married to the mother of the child, or after a divorce or annulment of marriage, will be deemed to be conceived during the marriage if not more than ten months pass from the date of death of the man or, respectively, from the date of divorce or annulment of marriage, to the birth of the child.

---

14   In 1998, 5,430 new marriages were concluded; at the same time 4,491 divorces took place. Ten
      years earlier, in 1988, 12,973 marriages were concluded and 5,924 marriages ended in divorce
      (source: the official webpage of the Statistical Office of Estonia, http://www.stat.ee).

If a man has given written consent to the artificial insemination of his spouse, the child will be deemed to descend from him.

The filiation of a child to the father who is not married to the mother of the child is ascertained on the basis of the joint written application of the father and mother which is submitted in person to a vital statistics office. In certain cases, paternity may be ascertained on the basis of an application by the father alone (ie if the mother of the child is deceased; the mother of the child is declared to be missing or without active legal capacity; the location of the mother of the child cannot be ascertained or the mother of the child has been deprived of parental rights).

If filiation of the child cannot be ascertained by way of recognition, paternity may be established in court at the request of the mother, the guardian of the child, a supervisory guardian or a person who considers himself to be the father of the child. Where the child has become an adult, he or she alone may request establishment of filiation to a father.

Estonian law does not differentiate between 'legitimate' and 'illegitimate' children. According to s 45 of the Family Law Act, a child descending from parents who are not married to each other has the same rights and duties with respect to his or her parents and their relatives as a child who descends from parents who are married to each other.

A child is given the common surname of the parents. If the parents have different surnames, the child is given the surname of the father or the mother by agreement of the parents. In the absence of an agreement, the supervisory guardian will decide which surname is given to the child.

A child will be given the surname of the mother if the mother is not married, or if the child born or conceived during marriage does not descend from the man married to the mother and filiation of the child from the father is not ascertained or established (s 47).

2 RIGHTS AND DUTIES OF PARENTS

Pursuant to s 50 of the Family Law Act, parents have the right and duty to raise a child and to care for a child. In the framework of parental rights, a parent is required to protect the rights and interests of his or her child. A parent is the legal representative of a child. As a legal representative, the parent has the mandate of a guardian.

In the exercise of parental rights the interests of the child are of decisive significance – a parent is not allowed to exercise his or her rights contrary to the welfare of the child. A parent has the right to demand his or her child back from any person who has control of the child without legal basis. However, the parent does not have the right to the return of the child if the return of the child would clearly be contrary to the interests of the child.

Generally, the right of access to the child is guaranteed to either parent. This also means that, in the case of breakdown of the family (eg dissolution of the marriage of the parents) the rights and duties of the parents remain the same and sole custody to one parent will not automatically be ordered.[15] Where the parents do not live together, the parent with whom the child resides is not authorised to obstruct the other parent's access to the child. If the parents disagree on the manner in which the parent not residing together with the child may participate in the raising of the child or how the right of access to the child is to be carried out, a supervisory guardian or, at the request of a parent, a court will settle the dispute.[16]

Two types of measures are available for those cases where the conduct or the pattern of life of one or both of the parents jeopardises the safety or the development of the child: a child may be temporarily removed from one or both parents, whereby the parental rights will be retained, or a parent may be deprived of parental rights by way of court procedure.

Removal of a child from one or both parents without deprivation of parental rights may be ordered by a court at the request of a parent, guardian or supervisory guardian, if it is dangerous to leave the child with the parents (s 53). If leaving a child with a parent threatens the health or life of the child, a supervisory guardian may remove the child from the parent prior to obtaining a court order. In such case the supervisory guardian must file a claim with a court within ten days for removal of the child or for deprivation of parental rights. When the reasons for removal of a child cease to exist, a court may order return of the child at the request of a parent.

At the request of a parent, guardian or supervisory guardian, a court may deprive a parent of parental rights if the parent: (a) does not fulfil his or her duties in raising or caring for a child due to abuse of alcoholic beverages, narcotic or other substances, or other reason which the court does not deem to be persuasive; (b) abuses parental rights; (c) is cruel to a child; (d) has a negative influence on a child in some other manner; or (e) without good reason, has not during one year participated in raising a child who resides in a child care institution (s 54). Upon depriving a parent of parental rights, a court shall order removal of a child from the parent.

A person who has been deprived of parental rights loses all rights with respect to a child. A supervisory guardian may, however, permit a person who has been deprived of parental rights to visit the child if this does not have a negative influence on the child. It should also be noted that the deprivation of parental rights does not release a parent from the duty to provide maintenance for the child. A court may restore parental rights with respect to a child if the person has improved his or her conduct, and desires and is capable of exercising parental rights as required. In any instance of restriction of parental rights, a supervisory guardian is responsible for arrangement of the care of the child where necessary.

The present law contains no milder measures to guarantee the welfare of the child and at the same time to keep the family together. In other words, it does not expressly prioritise the raising of the child in the family. This could be changed by

---

15   In fact, the Family Law Act does not contain any provisions on sole custody at all. The law does not explicitly authorise the court to restrict the parental rights (eg the right of access) of one parent in any other way than removal of the child or deprivation of parental rights – see below.

16   Whether any other measures besides removal and deprivation of parental rights are available, is not clear. This issue will need to be solved in a much clearer way in the future legislation.

introducing a system of 'family assistance' or supervision where the parents would get professional advice or even binding guidelines on raising a child.[17]

3   DUTY OF MAINTENANCE IN THE FAMILY

The Family Law Act sets out a variety of maintenance obligations within the family, primarily concerning maintenance between immediate ascendants and descendants (ss 60–69).

A parent is required to maintain his or her minor child and an adult child who needs assistance and is incapacitated for work. The obligation of a parent to maintain a child extends for the whole duration of secondary education (basic school, secondary school or vocational school) of the child, whereas support during higher education is not provided for explicitly.

If a parent fails to discharge the duty to provide maintenance for a child, a court will, at the request of the other parent, guardian or supervisory guardian, order monetary support to be paid for the child. Support for a child is to be specified as a monthly support payment based on the financial situation of each parent and the needs of the child. A court may refuse to order support or may reduce the amount thereof, or terminate payment of support, if the obligated parent is incapacitated for work, the child has sufficient income or there are other 'good reasons'.

A child who has become an adult is conversely required to maintain his or her parent who needs assistance and is incapacitated for work. Maintenance duties can also arise between other family members (grandparents, brothers and sisters, foster-parents and step-parents) inasmuch as the immediate family cannot be expected to provide for the subsistence of the needy persons (eg a grandparent would be obligated to maintain a grandchild where the grandchild does not have parents, a spouse or an adult child, or if it is not possible to obtain maintenance from these persons). If, after ordering support, the financial situation of the payer or recipient of the support changes or the recipient's need for assistance changes, a court may, at the request of either, change the amount of support or terminate payment of support.

4   ADOPTION (ss 73–91)

Adoption constitutes a basis for familial relations – the rights and duties between parent and child – between an adoptive parent and an adopted child. These rights and duties are the same as those based on the filiation of a child. Adoption may not be tied to a specified term or duration or some other condition.

A child may be adopted only in the interests of the child. In the case of adoption of a child over ten years of age, the consent of the child is required. The present Estonian Family Law Act explicitly forbids the adoption of an adult.

A child may be adopted by one person alone or by two persons jointly. The same child may be adopted only by persons who are married to each other. This provision precludes a joint adoption by two persons of the same sex, but in effect also adoption by a heterosexual unmarried couple.

---

17   Such a system already exists, for example, under Dutch law, see Articles 254–265 of the *Burgerlijk Wetboek*.

The requirements for a prospective adoptive parent include the following: he or she must be at least 25 years of age and capable of raising the adoptive child, caring for the child and maintaining the child. A court may also permit a younger adult to be an adoptive parent. Persons who have been deprived of parental rights or from whom a child has been removed; persons who have been relieved of the duty of guardian due to inadequate performance of duties; or those who have been declared to be without active legal capacity or whose active legal capacity has been restricted, may not be adoptive parents.

An adopted child and his or her descendants are deemed to be equal with respect to his or her adoptive parents and their relatives, and the adoptive parents and their relatives are deemed to be equal with respect to the adopted child and his or her descendants, with regard to personal and proprietary rights and obligations. An adopted child loses personal and proprietary rights and is released from duties with respect to his or her parent and relatives of the parent. Conversely, a parent loses personal and proprietary rights and is released from duties with respect to his or her child who is adopted and with respect to descendants of the adopted child. However, if a child is adopted by a man and the child has a mother who remains the mother of the child, or if a child is adopted by a woman and the child has a father who remains the father of the child, the rights and duties between the child and such parent and the relatives of the parent are preserved.

C   Guardianship and curatorship

There are two forms of guaranteeing adequate assistance and protection of the interests of persons unable independently to realise their rights and interests (ie children under age, adults without active legal capacity and the mentally or physically handicapped): (a) guardianship and (b) curatorship. Whereas guardianship must be established by a court, curatorship is an institution effected by a supervisory guardian, ie a non-judicial body.

Guardianship may be established both for children left without parental care or incapable adults, ie persons who are legally restricted in their actions (s 92). Therefore, the guardian appointed by a court will act as the legal representative of the person under guardianship. As the legal representative, he or she carries out legal transactions in the name of the ward or, where the ward has restricted legal capacity, supervises the transactions entered into by the ward (in most cases, consent of the guardian is required to effect a transaction). The activities of the guardian are inspected by the supervisory guardian whose approval is required before entering into certain transactions in the name of the ward.

A guardian is required to attend to the raising and maintenance of a child or, respectively, to care for and maintain a person without active legal capacity.

Curatorship is meant to assist an adult with active legal capacity who needs assistance in the exercise of his or her rights and duties due to a mental or physical disability. It is established for the performance of a certain legal act or a number of acts (s 105). A curator is not the legal representative of the person under curatorship. Thus, curatorship brings with it no restrictions on the freedom of the affected person to undertake legal acts.

Wardship issues are another area in which substantive changes are likely to take place in the future. A draft of a new Act on General Principles of the Civil Code was submitted to the Estonian Parliament in autumn 1999, in which it was proposed to abolish the present system allowing adult persons to be declared completely without active legal capacity. This has been reasoned with the consideration that the constitutional right of free self-realisation is inalienable and the restriction of this right by law should be balanced with the protection of similar constitutional rights. According to the Bill, minors regardless of their age and adults who are incapable due to mental illness or imbecility will have restricted legal capacity.[18] Above all, this will enable them to undertake transactions with approval of their custodian, thus allowing for a larger degree of independent acting. The turning into law of this new concept will make it necessary to reconsider the very functions of the custodian – these would probably range between those of the guardian and the curator under the present law. Finally, the roles of the court and supervisory guardian as a non-judicial institution will have to be reconsidered. On the one hand, relieving the court system of some of its traditional supervisory functions may correspond to modern trends in state organisation; on the other hand an adequate and unbiased protection of those with restricted legal capacity must be guaranteed.

III CONCLUSION

The fact that the Estonian family law system has so far been determined by outside influences to a very large degree without the consequence of completely ruining the Estonians' perception of family life could in my view be interpreted as confirmation of the belief that family law, like most other areas of law, can very well be the subject of international co-operation. The experiences of other family law systems can successfully be used as examples or models, and even 'imports' may prove to be helpful. It is evident that if and when family law reform takes place in Estonia, the new law will likewise be based on the experiences and models known in the Continental European tradition – meaning that there will be no 're-invention of the wheel'. As further efforts towards greater unification or harmonisation of family legislation on an international level have already been declared desirable by some scholars,[19] I hope that the way Estonia has chosen to draft its new family law will be perceived as an effort aimed in that very direction. This view could be supported with the perception that some of the problems still present in the Western family law systems today were already regulated in a rather modern way in the Eastern Block legislations, even if the ideological grounds may have been different. The equality of the spouses in all spheres, the no-fault based and/or consensual divorce; and the equality of children born in or outside of wedlock are some of the examples which constituted an integral part of the

---

18 According to the present law, minors under 7 years of age are incapable and minors aged 7–18 have restricted legal capacity.

19 K Boele-Woelki, *The road towards a European family law*, vol 1.1 *Electronic Journal of Comparative Law*, (November 1997), D Martiny, 'Die Möglichkeit der Vereinheitlichung des Familienrechts innerhalb der Europäischen Union', in: D Martiny, N Witzleb (Hrsg.), *Auf dem Wege zu einem Europäischen Zivilgesetzbuch*, Frankfurt/Oder, 1999, pp 177–189.

Estonian family law during the entire second half of the twentieth century. In this respect it is hoped that reforming societies like Estonia will have a helpful contribution to make to international efforts in the field of family law.

GERMANY

CIVIL LAW MARRIAGES WITHOUT LEGAL CONSEQUENCES

Rainer Frank[*]

While 1998 saw the passing of a number of family law reform Acts, particularly the Parentage Law Reform Act,[1] 1999 has been spared from the reforms of past years. The subsequent report is therefore not concerned with issues regarding legislation, but rather judicial decisions.

I   THE CONTRACTUAL EXCLUSION OF CLAIMS IN THE EVENT OF DIVORCE

German law, in the instance of a divorce, allows for three possible claims for one divorced spouse against the other: (1) a maintenance claim, the legal requirements of which are regulated in detail in § 1569 ff. of the German Civil Code (BGB); (2) a matrimonial property claim, where the spouses had been subject to the statutory matrimonial property regime of community of surplus (§§ 1363 ff. BGB); and (3) a claim to pension rights adjustment, which incorporates the equal division on divorce of all pension rights of the spouses accrued during the period of their marriage (§§ 1587 ff. BGB). It is provided by law, however, that the spouses may waive these post-nuptial claims. Regarding matrimonial property law, this option is provided for in § 1414 BGB, which stipulates that the spouses may, in place of the statutory property regime of community of surplus, choose to live under a marital property regime of separation of goods. Regarding the pension rights adjustment, the waiver is also regulated by statute: according to § 1409 section 2 p 1 BGB, the spouses may exclude the pension rights adjustment in a marriage contract by means of an explicit agreement. It is disputed, however, whether the spouses may, by means of an agreement, also waive their rights to post-nuptial maintenance. § 1585c BGB states, that the spouses may stipulate agreements regarding the issue of maintenance following divorce. This regulation is generally interpreted to mean that spouses may, in principle, make such an agreement at any time, including at the time of entering into the marriage. This again means that either one spouse alone or both may, on entering the marriage, waive their corresponding rights to post-nuptial maintenance.[2]

---

[*]   Professor of Law, Albert-Ludwigs-University, Freiburg.

1   Statute for the Reformation of Parentage Law, Bundesgesetzblatt I, 1997, p 2942; compare especially my report in *The International Survey of Family Law 1997*, ed A Bainham (Martinus Nijhoff Publishers, 1999).

2   For more detail see Büttner, 'Grenzen ehevertraglicher Gestaltungsmöglichkeiten', *FamRZ* 1998, 1.

It should not be questioned that spouses, in view of a forthcoming divorce, may arrange for post-nuptial maintenance claims. It is questionable, however, that they should be able to do so when entering into a marriage which from the outset has no legal consequences. A waiver of maintenance under these circumstances is expressed at a point in time when the spouses do not know and cannot know yet how long the marriage will last, whether and how many children they will have together, who will make personal and financial sacrifices, how the property rights will be arranged, and so on. In Germany today, these kinds of contracts stipulating a waiver of maintenance claims in the event of divorce are no longer a rare exception. The judiciary allows for the pre-arranged complete exclusion of post-nuptial maintenance claims. The courts regularly do not consider the waiver of a maintenance claim as contrary to public policy, even if it is a condition, on the part of the man, for marriage to the already pregnant woman.[3] The argument in favour of this practice, namely that the man might just as well distance himself from marriage altogether, sounds almost cynical. According to this argument, the woman therefore does not dispense of anything that would be due to her without marriage.[4] This is mitigated in part by the German Civil Code which, in cases of hardship, aims to help the spouse in need of protection by allowing the defence of malice (§ 242 BGB); however, it is only possible to rely on the defence provided for in § 242 BGB if the divorced spouse is looking after their common children and if it is in the child's best interest that the obligation to pay maintenance should not only arise in favour of the child, but also in favour of the divorced spouse. The maintenance claim can only secure the minimum standard of living for the divorced spouse.[5] It is questionable whether such adjudication is in compliance with Article 6 section 1 of the Constitution, which stipulates that marriage is under special protection of the State. A marriage which has no legal consequences and which can be dissolved with ease at any stage, can hardly be described as an institution which is meant to be for life (according to the wording in § 1353 section 1 sentence 1 BGB) and which is under special protection of the State (Article 6 section 1 of the Constitution). For this reason, the Constitutional Court has, in recent obiter dicta, indicated that former precedents are unconstitutional.[6]

II   JOINT CUSTODY AFTER DIVORCE

Joint custody for divorced parents has for a long time been a foreign concept to the Civil Code of 1900. For the first time in 1982, the German Constitutional Court allowed, against the wording of the law, joint custody in favour of divorced spouses. This was allowed on the condition that the parents have to make an application in this regard and that there exist no reasons why, in the best interest of the child, custody should be conferred on only one parent.[7] Since the passing of

---

3   Bundesgerichtshof *(BGH) FamRZ* 1992, 1403; *BGH FamRZ* 1991, 306; *BGH FamRZ* 1996, 1536
     = JZ 1997, 411 with critical commentary by Dethloff; *OLG Hamm FamRZ* 1998, 1299.
4   *OLG Hamm FamRZ* 1998, 1299.
5   *BGH FamRZ* 1992, 1403.
6   *FamRZ* 1999, 285, 288.
7   *BVerfGE* 61, 385.

the Parentage Law Reform Act on 1 July 1998, joint custody in favour of unmarried couples has become commonplace in law. A custody order by a court, in the event of divorce, is now only permissible if at least one of the spouses makes an application for it. If neither mother nor father make an application for custody, then they will have joint custody. Whether the parents live together, are separated, or get divorced, in principle does not change the fact that they have joint custody for their children. Since 1 July 1998 it has become a matter of dispute under what circumstances a court may on application, against the automatic legal position, rule for custody in favour of only one spouse. According to the wording of § 1671 section 2 BGB, custody in favour of only one parent is permissible only if the other parent agrees or if it is foreseeable that sole custody is 'in the best interest of the child'. If the parents both apply for sole custody, according to the new law, the court may still opt for joint custody if it is of the opinion that this solution is in the best interest of the child. The fact that the parents both apply for sole custody may be regarded as indication that joint custody would not be in the child's best interest, but this nevertheless only remains an indication. If the judge is convinced that the parents are both willing to co-operate, even though their applications for sole custody have been denied, then he may confer custody on both parents jointly. In fact, he is obliged to do so if this would be 'in the child's best interest'. Recently, there have been more judgments which confer joint custody on the parents, even though this is not in accordance with their wishes.[8] This reflects the conviction that the joint raising of a child is not only a right, but also an obligation of the parents. In accordance with this, the legislator chose to reverse the formulation in § 1626 section 1 BGB of the Parentage Law Reform Act of 1997, from 'the right and obligation' by the parents, to their 'obligations and rights'. This principle has in the meantime lead to a decision by the OLG Karlsruhe[9] in which sole custody of a problematic child had been conferred upon the father, even though he had willingly distanced himself from his daughter.

III HAGUE CONVENTION ON THE CIVIL ASPECTS OF INTERNATIONAL CHILD ABDUCTION

A spectacular case of child abduction between Germany and France was not only of particular interest to the press and the media. It also came twice before the highest German court, the Bundesverfassungsgericht (German Constitutional Court). The facts were as follows.

A German–French couple living in Germany had two children, aged three and seven. The French mother, in pending divorce proceedings, had bound herself not to leave Germany with her children until a ruling had been given with regard to custody. She nevertheless left for Paris in 1997 without informing her husband. Attempts by the German father to achieve a repatriation according to the Hague Convention on Child Abduction were unsuccessful. However, before a final judgment had been given in

---

8   *OLG Hamm FamRZ* 1999, 38; *OLG Hamm FamRZ* 1999, 1600; *OLG Bamberg FamRZ* 1999, 1005; *OLG Stuttgart FamRZ* 1999, 39; *AG Chemnitz FamRZ* 1999, 321.

9   *FamRZ* 1999, 801.

France, the father had, nine months later, kidnapped his children with the help of two accomplices. The two accomplices had forced the mother off the road and out of the car in darkness. They then took her car and drove it back to Germany with her children in it. The mother consequently made an application for the children's immediate repatriation relying on the Hague Convention on Child Abduction.

The Hague Convention on Child Abduction is based on the principle that the child's best interest is best protected in those cases where a child is wrongfully removed by a parent who is not entitled to custody of the child, or does not have sole custody, if the child is immediately returned to the place from where it was taken. This is meant to prevent the abducting parent benefiting from the fact that the court of the country to where the child has been taken will decide on the custody issue.

Particular problems are raised by a double 'reversed' child abduction. It is undisputed that the Hague Convention applies also in the case of reversed child abductions. The only condition in this type of case had been that the children had already, after the first abduction, established their habitual residence (Article 3 of the Convention). This was confirmed by the competent German Oberlandesgericht (Higher Regional Court), which therefore ordered the children's immediate return to France. An inquiry as to whether the children's return might cause 'psychological harm' to the children, which according to Article 13 section 1b might have caused the rejection of the application by the mother, had not been considered.

The Bundesverfassungsgericht (German Constitutional Court), before which the father had argued the matter on the basis of unconstitutionality, was of the opinion that the constitutionally safeguarded personal right of a child made it necessary to examine with special care whether, in the case of contra-applications for repatriation, an immediate return of the child would endanger the child's welfare. The case at issue might especially pose the risk that the French courts might sustain the application by the mother after all, so that the children would once more have to be ordered out of the country. The Constitutional Court further held that, in the instance of wrongful child abduction by both parents, those parents were not allowed to represent the child's interest in the proceedings, because they will have demonstrated an obvious self-interest. Instead, a curator should be appointed in order to guarantee that the interests of the child were safeguarded. For this reason, the Constitutional Court set aside the decision by the Higher Regional Court and referred the case back to the Higher Regional Court for further examination.[10] The Higher Regional Court appointed a curator and re-examined the matter as ordered by the Constitutional Court. The decision by the Higher Regional Court was, however, upheld. After a further constitutional complaint had been rejected by the Constitutional Court,[11] the children were returned to France. It is interesting to note that the repatriation of the children to France required five court decisions in Germany (Local Court – Higher Regional Court – Constitutional Court – Higher Regional Court – Constitutional Court). It is also interesting that, nevertheless, from the time of their forceful abduction by the father and the return of the children to France only 12 months had passed.

---

10   *BVerfG* = NJW 1999, 631 = *FamRZ* 1999, 85.
11   *FamRZ* 1999, 777.

INDIA

SOME PERSPECTIVES ON INDIAN FAMILY LAW

Anil Malhotra and Ranjit Malhotra***

The present India chapter analyses three areas of Indian family law: validity of marriages in the context of unmarried cohabitation under Hindu law; recent developments in international child abduction law; and the law of guardianship and inter-country adoption in India. The reason for focus on these select branches of law is because these areas are of immense interest to an international legal readership given the large size of the Indian population residing overseas.

I   HINDU LAW OF MARRIAGE

The principal law of marriage and divorce relating to Hindus is contained in the Hindu Marriage Act 1955 (hereafter HMA 1955), which came into force on 18 May 1955. The HMA 1955 also governs validity of marriages of those Indian spouses who are permanently resident overseas. It is an Act to amend and codify the law relating to marriage among Hindus. After outlining the main provisions of the HMA 1955 they will be discussed in appropriate detail.

A   Main provisions of the HMA 1955

Section 1 states the territorial application of the HMA 1955. In terms of section 2, the Act is applicable only to Hindus. Section 5 of the HMA 1955 stipulates the conditions for a valid Hindu marriage. Essential ceremonies for a Hindu marriage are laid down in section 7 of the Act. Registration of marriages is dealt with in section 8 of the Act. Sections 9 and 10 of the Act provide for restitution of conjugal rights and judicial separation.

Nullity of marriage and divorce are dealt with in detail in Chapter IV of the HMA 1955. The grounds for divorce are detailed in section 13 of the Act. Divorce by mutual consent is recognised under section 13-B of the Act.

The issue of jurisdiction and the procedure for obtaining divorce is provided in Chapter V of this Act. Provisions for maintenance pendente lite and permanent alimony are made in sections 24 and 25 of the Act, respectively. It is important to mention that section 29(2) of the Act recognises dissolution of marriage by

*   Advocate at the Punjab and Haryana High Court and the Supreme Court of India, New Delhi. Formerly part-time lecturer at the Faculty of Laws, Punjab University, Chandigarh.

**   Advocate at the Punjab and Haryana High Court and Supreme Court of India. Regional representative for India of the migration and nationality law committee of the International Bar Association.

custom, pleaded by parties to the marriage. The main provisions of the HMA 1955 are discussed below.

B   Extent and jurisdiction of the HMA 1955

Section 1 of the HMA 1955 states that the Act extends to the whole of India, except the State of Jammu and Kashmir, and applies also to Hindus domiciled in the territories to which this Act extends who are outside the said territories. In effect, the Act has extra-territorial application, because a Hindu carries with him the personal law of marriage.

C   Application of the HMA 1955

In terms of section 2 of the HMA 1955, Hindu law applies to the following three categories:

(a)   any person who is a Hindu, Jain, Sikh or Buddhist by religion;
(b)   any person who is born of Hindu parents; and
(c)   any other person domiciled in the territories to which this act extends who is not a Muslim, Christian, Parsi or Jew.

The Calcutta High Court in *Prem Singh v Dulari Bai*,[1] while interpreting sections 1 and 2 of the HMA 1955 held in para 5 of the judgment at p 426:

> 'This section read with Section 2(1)(a)(b) makes it equally clear that as regards the intra-territorial operation of the Act it applies to all Hindus, Buddhists, Jains or Sikhs irrespective of the question whether they are domiciled in India or not. The provisions of Clause (c) of the same section contemplates extra-territorial operation in the sense that the persons domiciled in other territory to which this Act may extend, if governed by Hindu Law, even though, residing outside the territory, would come within the purview of this Act.'

The court further held that the question of domicile assumes importance only when the marriage between the parties is prohibited by the domestic rule or law of the land to which one of the parties to the marriage, a foreigner, may belong.

D   Validity of marriages in the context of unmarried cohabitation under Hindu law

The specific area of focus in this analysis is situations where a Hindu couple, in the country of their origin, have been cohabiting as husband and wife without performance of any religious ceremonies and without the registration of the marriage and, subsequently, the male Indian spouse has migrated and married abroad.

---

1   *All India Reporter* 1973, Calcutta 425.

Cohabitation in this context would mean that the couple have initially been living under one roof, with family approval and public recognition. Some sort of token customary ceremony may also have been performed of which there exists no evidence at all. They are not ceremonies as envisaged in section 7 of the HMA 1955.

This is a common phenomenon with a certain category of non-resident Indians residing overseas, especially in England, Canada and Australia. Quite often, the male migrant Hindu spouse gets married abroad with the prime agenda of securing overseas citizenship. Once this purpose has been achieved, the earlier Indian spouse and the children may very conveniently be dumped and deserted. In the event of any litigation during the process of acquiring overseas citizenship, foreign immigration and family lawyers are confronted with the problem of addressing the validity of the alleged initial marriage on the home soil. Problems also arise with regard to alimony payable to the previous deserted Indian spouse. Quite often the couple may have been living in a joint family before the husband migrated abroad. The bitter battle starts when the Indian spouse demands her share of the family property or from any agricultural land holdings or any other assets owned by the husband, as the case may be.

The core issue in such a situation is the legal status of the previous unmarried cohabitation in the country of origin of the male migrated spouse under the main Indian law of marriage, ie the HMA 1955. If this previous relationship is a valid marriage, then the male migrant Indian spouse is a bigamist. Bigamy is a criminal offence under the Indian Penal Code and invites very serious consequences. The marriage performed overseas, in such a situation, would then stand nullified under the HMA 1955. The end result is that the prospects of acquiring overseas citizenship will be devastated.

The current debate on this situation has been triggered on account of a recent decision of the Supreme Court of India in *Surjit Kaur v Gajra Singh*,[2] which has substantially altered and rather reversed the tide of earlier judicial dicta. The Supreme Court of India held therein that, even if the parties hold themselves out before society as husband and wife and society treats them as such, without the proof of proper ceremonies of marriage they could not be considered as husband and wife. Long cohabitation creates no presumption of a valid marriage in such a situation. This decision contemplates the situation where the marriage has not been registered in terms of section 8 of the HMA 1955. It is pertinent to mention that registration of marriages is not compulsory under the HMA 1955.

On the other hand, there is ample earlier case law, contrary to this recent ruling, giving explicit legal recognition to a presumption of a valid marriage in such circumstances. The reverse proposition is discussed in the subsequent portion of this chapter.

The validity of such a purported marriage, as described above, will be governed by the provisions of the HMA 1955 (Act XXV of 1955 as amended by the Act in force on 18 May 1955. No. 73 of 1956, 58 of 1960, 44 of 1964 and 68 of 1976).

---

2   *All India Reporter* 1994 SC 135.

E   Requirements of a valid Hindu marriage

The legal validity of such an alleged marriage has to be scrutinised in terms of sections 5 and 7 of the HMA 1955. Section 5 provides as follows:

> '5: Conditions for a Hindu Marriage – A marriage may be solemnised between any two Hindus, if the following conditions are fulfilled, namely:
>
> (i)   neither party has a spouse living at the time of the marriage;
> (ii) at the time of the marriage, neither party –
>   (a) is incapable of giving a valid consent to it in consequence of unsoundness of mind; or
>   (b) though capable of giving a valid consent, has been suffering from mental disorder of such a kind or to such an extent as to be unfit for marriage and the procreation of children: or
>   (c) has been subject to recurrent attacks of insanity or epilepsy;
> (iii) the bridegroom has completed the age of twenty one years and the bride the age of eighteen years at the time of the marriage;
> (iv) the parties are not within the degrees of prohibited relationship unless the custom or usage governing each of them permits of a marriage between the two;
> (v)   the parties are not sapindas of each other, unless the custom or usage governing each of them permits of a marriage between the two ...'

Section 7 deals with ceremonial aspects:

> '7.   Ceremonies for a Hindu Marriage.
>
> (1)   A Hindu marriage may be solemnized in accordance with the customary rites and ceremonies of either party thereto.
> (2)   Where such rites and ceremonies include the Saptapadi (that is, the taking of seven steps by the bridegroom and the bride jointly before the sacred fire), the marriage becomes complete and binding when the seventh step is taken.'

Where the requisite ceremonies of marriage as envisaged in section 7 of the HMA 1955 are not performed, nor any custom is invoked by the couple rendering the performance of such ceremonies unnecessary, neither of the spouses in such a situation can claim the status of marriage in terms of section 7 of the HMA 1955.

Some of the relevant case-law on sections 5 and 7 of the HMA 1955 coupled with the issue of bigamy is discussed below.

F   Marriage registration under Hindu law not compulsory

Section 8 of the HMA 1955 deals with registration of marriages. The Act does not make the registration of marriages compulsory. This is primarily because Hindu marriages and most marriages in India have been always performed in public with wide publicity. Section 8(2) of the HMA 1955 provides that any State Government may make rules for compulsory registration of Hindu marriages. Furthermore, section 8(5) specifically lays down that failure to register a Hindu marriage shall in no way affect its validity. Even where compulsory registration of marriage is laid down under the rules, non registration does not affect the validity of the marriage. It merely entails a nominal fine. Unlike the entry of marriage pursuant to the English Marriage Act 1949, mere registration under section 8 of the HMA 1955 will not *ipso facto* make the marriage valid.

G Proof of marriages solemnised outside England and Wales

In England, rule 10.14 of the Family Proceedings Rules 1991 (subject to certain exceptions) stipulates requirements to prove the validity of a marriage celebrated outside England and Wales. Rule 10.14 provides that the validity of such a marriage under the law of the country where it was celebrated may, in any family proceedings in which the existence and the validity of the marriage is not disputed, be proved by the evidence of one of the parties to the marriage and the furnishing of a document purporting to be a marriage certificate or a similar document issued under the law in force in that country. Additionally, the evidence of a local expert in law is necessary to prove that such a certificate would be accepted in the country of origin as prima facie evidence that a valid marriage has taken place.[3]

H Case-law analysis – validity of marriages

1 CASE-LAW NOT SUPPORTING A PRESUMPTION IN FAVOUR OF A VALID MARRIAGE

Coming to the recent Supreme Court of India decision in the matter of *Surjit Kaur v Garja Singh*,[4] the operative part of which is found in para 13 at p 137.

> 'Prima facie, the expression "whoever ... marries" must mean "whoever ... marries validly" or "whoever ... marries and whose marriage is a valid one". If the marriage is not a valid one, according to the law applicable to the parties, no question of its being void by reason of its taking place during the life of the husband or wife of the person marrying arises. If the marriage is not a valid marriage, it is no marriage in the eye of law. The bare fact of a man and a woman living as husband and wife does not, at any rate, normally give them the status of husband and wife even though they may hold themselves out before society as husband and wife and the society treats them as husband and wife.'

Saptapadi, being an essential ceremony, establishes the fact of marriage. Saptapadi is the taking of seven steps by the bridegroom and the bride jointly before the sacred fire. Without proof of such a ceremony, the first 'marriage', does not exist and a case for bigamy cannot arise. This was the mandate of law laid down by the Supreme Court of India in *Smt. Laxmi Devi v Satya Narayan and Others*.[5]

Where the parties are governed by the customary law of marriage and divorce, there has to be a specific averment in support of the same. In the instant case it

---

3   See: Rayden and Jackson's *Law and Practice in Divorce and Family Matters*, volume 1 (Butterworths, London, 1997) at pp 122 and 127.

4   *Supra*, note 2.

5   1994 (30) *Hindu Law Reporter* 449.

was also held that, where the parties to the marriage had not proved that they were governed by any custom under which the essential ceremonies stipulated in section 7 of the HMA 1955 were not required to be performed, the fact of marriage could not be established.

The High Court of Punjab and Haryana has held in the matter of *Ashok Kumar Chopra v Krishna Kumari*:[6]

'In view of the above mentioned authorities it is very well made out that in order to make out a prima facie case for the commission of bigamy it is necessary to allege form of marriage as well as essential ceremonies required for solemnisation of a valid marriage and then to lead some evidence in support thereof. Even the admission of second marriage by the petitioner is of no avail to the complainant. This inherent infirmity exists in the pleadings as well as in pre-charge evidence which cannot be cured at the stage of trial and under these circumstances continuance of proceedings will amount to abuse of process of Court.'

As stated above, a typical situation is that no religious rights or ceremonies may have been performed between the cohabiting couple during the currency of their stay in the country of origin. Also relevant to the status of such an alleged marriage is the decision of the Supreme Court of India in the case of *Santi Deb Berma v Kanchan Prava Devi*.[7] In this case the performance of 'saptapadi' was not proved, neither was the accused's marriage performed by any custom which dispensed with saptapadi. The accused and his alleged second wife were living as husband and wife, but there was no specific evidence regarding the performance of the essential rites, namely Saptapadi. The Supreme Court categorically held in paras 6 and 7 of the judgment (at p 817) that, in the absence of any reliable and acceptable evidence, it was not sustainable to draw an inference as to the performance of ceremonies essential for a valid marriage. Accordingly, the accused was acquitted of the alleged offence of bigamy.

The Supreme Court of India held in *Lingari Obulamma v Venkata Reddy and Others*[8] that while assailing the second marriage where there was absolutely no evidence to prove Saptapadi or performance of prevailing customs in the community, which was neither mentioned in the complaint nor proved in the evidence, the conviction under section 494 of the Indian Penal Code for the offence of bigamy could not be sustained.

As early as 1966 the Supreme Court of India held in *Kanwal Ram and Others v The Himachal Pradesh Administration*[9] that, in a bigamy case, the essential ceremonies constituting an alleged second marriage must be proved. Admission of marriage by the accused is not sufficient for the purpose of proving marriage in an adultery or bigamy case. This ruling in *Kanwal Ram* has been recently reiterated in the above-mentioned case of *Smt. Laxmi*.[10]

Merely because the parties to the marriage have lived as husband and wife, the status of wife is not conferred as laid down by the Supreme Court of India in

---

6   1993 (27) *Hindu Law Reporter* 111 at 114.
7   *All India Reporter* 1991, SC 816.
8   *All India Reporter* 1979, SC 848.
9   *All India Reporter* 1966 SC 614 at 615.
10   *Supra*, note 5.

B.S. Lokhande v State of Maharashtra.[11] It was further held that merely going through certain ceremonies with the intention that the parties be considered married will not constitute the ceremonies prescribed by law or approved by any established custom. This Supreme Court ruling has been very recently reiterated by the Supreme Court of India itself in the above-mentioned case of *Surjit Kaur*.

In *Brij Lal Bishnoi v State and another*[12] the Delhi High Court held as follows:

'11. I have already noticed above the law and it is that in a case like the one in hand the complainant has to provide strict proof of the marriage. The mere fact that they had been living together as husband and wife giving birth to their progeny would not do in a prosecution for matrimonial offences. And, as for section 50 of the Evidence Act, the fact that the man and woman spoke of each other as husband and wife, that others coming into their life in the passing or to endure also took them as husband and wife, proves nothing more than conduct, and conduct alone is no substitute of strict proof.'

The Supreme Court of India in a very recent case *P. Satyanarayana and another v P. Mallaiah and others*,[13] held that legal evidence is necessary to prove the fact of marriage on the basis of the tests laid down by this Court in *Bhaurao Shankar Lokhande and Another v State of Maharashtr and Another*,[14] *Kanwal Ram and Others v The Himachal Pradesh Administration*[15] and *Priya Bala Ghosh v Suresh Chandra Ghosh*.[16] The two earlier Supreme Court rulings, ie *Kanwal Ram* and *B.S. Lokhande*, reiterated by the Supreme Court in this ruling have already been elaborated upon above.

Furthermore, the Supreme Court of India has also held in the matter of *Valsamma Paul v Cochin University*[17] that: '[R]ecognition by family or community is not a pre-condition for married status'.

2   CASE-LAW TO THE CONTRARY: RAISING A PRESUMPTION IN FAVOUR OF A VALID MARRIAGE

There is also ample case-law contrary to the above-mentioned proposition of law. Some of the decisions of the Supreme Court of India and various of the High Courts on the reverse proposition are discussed below.

In *S.P.S. Balasubramanyam v Suruttayan alias Andali Padayachi and others*[18] the Supreme Court of India further held:

'What has been settled by this court is that if a man and woman live together for long years as husband and wife then a presumption arises in law of legality of marriage existing between the two. But the presumption is rebuttable ... In the Hindu society no father would normally tolerate behaviour of his son having a concubine ...'

---

11   *All India Reporter* 1965 SC 1564.
12   1996 (3) *Recent Criminal Reports* 299 at 302.
13   *Judgements Today* 1996 (8) SC 203.
14   *All India Reporter* 1965 SC 1564.
15   *Supra*, note 9.
16   (1971) 1 *Supreme Court Cases* 864.
17   *All India Reporter* 1996 SC 1011 at 1022.
18   *All India Reporter* 1994 SC 133 at 134.

In *Chalakuttiyil Mutteri Karthiyayani Amma v Padinhare Talasseri Veettil Narayanan Nair*[19] the Kerala High Court observed as follows:

'Unnikrishna Kurup, J in the decision reported in *Kunji Pillai Amma v Somanathan Pillai*, 1971 KLJ 105, held as follows:

"The law appears to be clear that when the factum of marriage has been proved, the conditions required for a valid marriage would be presumed to have been fulfilled. The long course of conduct, the fact that the husband had openly acknowledged the 1st plaintiff as his wife and the 2nd plaintiff as his son, the marriage certificate and the various other circumstances afford ample proof that there was a valid subsisting marriage." '

In that case, the contention was that there was no legal evidence to show the presentation of cloth by the bridegroom to the bride as required by the provisions of the Nair Act. His Lordship relied on the decision of the Supreme Court in *Veerappa v Michael*,[20] and held that in so far as there is proof to show that the marriage had taken place, the law will presume that all the necessary ingredients have been performed.

In para 15 of this judgment at p 398, the Court followed *Badri Prasad*, which is discussed in the subsequent portion of this chapter.

In *Subhash Popatlal Shah v Smt. Lata Subhash Shah*[21] it was held by the High Court of Bombay as follows:

'However, at the hearing of these appeals, Mr Abhyankar, learned advocate appearing on behalf of the appellant, very vehemently urged that as per section 7 of the Hindu Marriage Act 1955, it had to be proved that a religious rite of completing saptapadi was performed and since there is no such evidence on record, a conclusion could not be drawn that the appellant and the respondent were legally wedded husband and wife. We are unable to persuade ourselves to agree with the submission of Mr Abhyankar for the simple reason that it is only when the marriage rites and ceremonies include saptapadi that the marriage becomes complete and binding when the seventh step is taken. There is nothing on record that there was such custom or rites and ceremonies between the parties before us. Thus, saptapadi is not always a must to prove valid marriage between the parties ... Therefore, even if saptapadi was not one of the items of the marriage ceremony undertaken by the parties before us, we are of the opinion that the marriage between the appellant and the respondent cannot be held to be illegal and invalid. In fact, when some sort of marriage ceremony was undergone by and between the parties, there is always a presumption of validity of marriage unless the presumption is rebutted by quite cogent and satisfactory evidence.'

Subsequently, in para 8 of this judgment, the Bombay High Court reiterated quotes from *Ningu* and *Badri Prasad*, which have already been reproduced above.

In *S.P.S. Balasubramanyam v Suruttayan alias Andali Padayachi and others*[22] the Supreme Court of India has held that where a man and a woman were living under the same roof and cohabiting for a number of years, a presumption arises

19   1998 (1) *Hindu Law Reports* 393 at 397.
20   *All India Reporter* 1963 SC 23.
21   *All India Reporter* 1994 Bombay 43 at 45.
22   *Supra* note 18.

that they lived as husband and wife; and such presumption could not be destroyed by the circumstance and evidence proved in the instant case; and that the children were not illegitimate.

In *Smt. Nirmala and others v Smt. Rukminibai and others*,[23] the Karnataka High Court expressly reiterated *Badri Prasad* and *S.P.S. Balasubramanyam*.

In *Ningu Vithu Bamane and other v Sadashiv Ningu Bamane and others*[24] it was held in para 20 of the judgment as follows:

'I am of the opinion that in a well-organised, orderly and civilised society like ours which is not of loose and uncertain morals, the institution of marriage occupies an important place and plays a very vital role in the process of development of human personality. We have definite views and strong convictions about marital relations. The law as to presumption in favour of marriage under ss. 50 and 114, Evidence Act, is well crystallised. Thus when a man and woman, live together as husband and wife for sufficiently long time and were treated as husband and wife by friends, relatives and neighbours there is always a presumption in favour of their marriage. If children are born to such a couple, there is a further presumption in favour of their legitimacy. The presumption in favour of marriage does not get mitigated or weakened merely because there may not be positive evidence of any marriage having taken place. But if there is some evidence on record that the couple had gone through some form of marriage, the presumption gets strengthened. Therefore, though marriage ceremony said to have taken place may not be valid, the marriage can be held to be valid by force of habit and repute and the onus of rebutting such a marriage would be on the person who denies the marriage. It may also be stated here that this presumption of law in favour of marriage and legitimacy is not to be repelled lightly by mere balance of probability. The evidence for that should be strong, satisfactory and conclusive. If the presumption is permitted to be rebutted lightly, the weaker and vulnerable sections of the society, *viz*, the women and the children could be the victims of the vagaries of uncertainties as to their positions and status in life. This would be very much detrimental in the development of their human personality. They would be the worst sufferers in the society.'

Section 114 of the Indian Evidence Act 1872 reads as follows:

'114. The Court may presume the existence of any fact which it thinks likely to have happened, regard being had to the common course of natural events, human conduct and public and private business, in their relation to the facts of the particular case.'

In *Badri Prasad v Dy. Director of Consolidation and others*,[25] the relevant portion of the judgment reads as follows:

'A strong presumption arises in favour wedlock where the partners have lived together for a long spell as husband and wife. Although the presumption is rebuttable, a heavy burden lies on him who seeks to deprive the relationship of legal origin. Law leans in favour of legitimacy and frowns upon bastardy. In this view, the contention of Shri Garg for the petitioner, that long after the alleged marriage, evidence has not been produced to sustain its ceremonial process by examining the priest or other witnesses,

---

23 *All India Reporter* 1994 Karnataka 247.
24 *All India Reporter* 1987 Bombay 27.
25 *All India Reporter* 1978 SC 1557.

deserves no consideration. If a man and woman who live as husband and wife in society are compelled to prove, half a century later, by eye witness evidence that they were validly married, few will succeed.'

After analysing the law, it is clear that there is a conflict of law situation as far as presumption in favour of valid marriages is concerned, on the basis of cohabitation without cogent evidence of performance of ceremonies as envisaged in section 7 of the HMA 1955. This is a situation which needs to be remedied by the Apex Court. In an appropriate case this issue should be referred to a Supreme Court Constitution bench for finality.

Dr WF Menski, in one of his articles, has discussed the far-reaching implications of *Surjit Kaur*. He is of the opinion that this judgment particularly affects women who remarry after a divorce or after the death of their first husband. In such situations, it is customary not to have the full marriage rituals as done for a first marriage. Menski further states that in some instances it will be customary to have no marriage rituals at all. He further states that there are many cases in which a man and woman simply contract to marry, and whether or not it is done in writing is immaterial. However, it may be added by way of clarification that marriage is a sacramental union under Hindu law and the English concept of contract to marry is alien to the Indian system. Under the HMA 1955, no form of writing is necessary to solemnise a marriage.

In *Surjit Kaur's* case gur (jaggery) was distributed to friends of the newly married couple. There was public recognition in addition to a document purporting to be registration of the customary marriage. Menski's interpretation of section 7 of the HMA 1955 is that it is perfectly possible to enter a legally valid Hindu marriage without going through elaborate Sanskrit rituals. He opines that *Surjit Kaur's* case looks even more out of line, especially in comparison to *S.P.S. Balasubramanyam*, a judgment delivered by the Supreme Court of India at the same time as *Surjit Kaur*. *Balasubramanyam's* case relaxes the burden of proof and is exactly opposite to the law laid down in *Surjit Kaur*. Menski concludes: 'Bad decisions of this kind no doubt contribute to keeping women in subordination.'[26]

I   Presumption of valid marriage – recent English law decision

As far as the position in English law is concerned, the Court of Appeal very recently held in *Chief Adjudication Officer v Bath* that where there was an irregular marriage ceremony followed by a period of long cohabitation, it would be contrary to the general policy of the law to refuse to extend to the parties the benefit of a presumption of marriage, which would apply to them if there were no evidence of any ceremony at all.

The Court of Appeal so held in a reserved judgment when it dismissed the appeal of the Chief Adjudication Officer challenging the decision of a social security commissioner, who on 7 May 1998, allowed the appeal of the claimant, Mrs Kirpal Kaur Bath, for benefits due to her as a widow. Initially, the social security appeal tribunal dismissed her appeal on 12 August 1994. The tribunal

---

26   See number 89 (July–August 1995) *Manushi*, pp 15–16.

held that it was not established and it could not be presumed that there was a valid marriage, because there was no evidence of a valid ceremony in accordance with the English Marriage Act 1949.

The claimant, aged 59, went through a Sikh marriage in 1956, when aged 16, with Zora Singh Bath, then aged 19, at the Sikh temple, the Central Gurdwara, 79 Sinclair Road, West Kensington, London, at a marriage ceremony administered by a Sikh priest in accordance with Sikh custom and religion.

They lived together as man and wife for 37 years until his death in January 1994. The temple moved to a new address some time between 1956 and 1983, at which latter date it was registered for marriages. There was some evidence that it was not a registered building for performing marriages in 1956.[27]

The facts of the above-mentioned case are a typical situation common to British Asians of Indian origin who migrated from the state of Punjab in the early sixties and seventies. The English ruling above will be of immense help to spouses of immigrants, in the event of any litigation, who had migrated at that point of time. From England itself, there are numerous instances where this class of early migrants altogether denied existence of their marriages to their Indian spouses, in divorce proceedings. This is with the ultimate agenda of avoiding paying any maintenance or stalling the distribution of assets. It is easy for the husband to deny the existence of the marriage, as registration of marriages in India is not compulsory under section 8 of the HMA 1955.

J Right to marry is not absolute

In a first of its kind judgment on the right of a patient suffering from contagious venereal disease to marry, the Supreme Court of India has ruled that, so long as the person is not cured of the disease or impotency, his right to marry cannot be enforced through a court of law. The judgment is reported as *Mr 'X' v Hospital 'Z'*.[28]

The Apex Court firmly held that if the man's marriage has been cancelled owing to his being an AIDS patient, his right to marry will remain a *suspended right*. Furthermore, he is not entitled to claim any compensation from the hospital which has disclosed his medical condition to the would-be bride's family.

The judgment came in the wake of a doctor's petition seeking compensation from the Apollo Hospital in Chennai. The hospital had detected that he was an HIV-positive patient. This fact was also disclosed to his would-be bride's family. The marriage was called off immediately. The doctor contended that the hospital had violated medical ethics by disclosing his medical condition to the bride's family. This led to his social ostracism.

The court dealt with yet another aspect of the matter in paras 40 and 41 of the judgment at p 503:

'Therefore, if a person suffering from the dreadful disease "AIDS," knowingly marries a woman and thereby transmits infection to that woman, he would be guilty of offences indicated in sections 269 and 270 of the Indian Penal Code.

---

27 For details see the legal page of *The Times*, London, 28 October 1999.
28 *All India Reporter* 1999 SC 495.

41. The above statutory provisions thus impose a duty upon the appellant not to marry as the marriage would have the effect of spreading the infection of his own disease, which obviously is dangerous to life, to the woman whom he marries apart from being an offence.'

Sections 269 and 270 of the Indian Penal Code read as follows:

'269   Negligent act likely to spread infection of disease dangerous to life – Whoever unlawfully or negligently does any act which is, and which he knows or has reason to believe to be, likely to spread the infection of any disease dangerous to life, shall be punished with imprisonment of either description for a term which may extend to six months, or with fine, or with both.

270   Malignant act likely to spread infection of disease dangerous to life – Whoever malignantly does any act which is, and which he knows or has reason to believe to be, likely to spread the infection of any disease dangerous to life, shall be punished with imprisonment of either description for a term which may extend to two years, or with fine, or with both.'

The issue in the above-mentioned case has gone a step further. A petition has been filed in the Supreme Court of India, seeking clarification of the above-mentioned judgment to facilitate marriage of an HIV-positive person after 'full, free and informed consent is taken for the marriage.'[29]

The same Supreme Court Bench comprising of Justice BN Kirpal and Justice S Saghir Ahmad, which had handed down the earlier above mentioned judgment has issued notices to the Union of India and the Medical Council of India to ascertain their views. The second petition on this subject has been filed by Sahara, a centre for residential care and rehabilitation of HIV-positive persons under the AIDS care project.

II   CHILD ABDUCTION AND GUARDIANSHIP

A   Child abduction principles

International child abduction law in India stands substantially modified in terms of a recent Supreme Court judgment in the matter of *Dhanwanti Joshi v Madhav Unde*.[30] This judgment was handed down on 4 November 1997. The said judgment deals with the provisions and case law analysis relating to the Hindu Minority and Guardianship Act 1980 read with the Guardian and Wards Act 1890. These two enactments principally govern the law relating to child custody under the Indian laws.

Under Indian law, ie the Guardian and Wards Act 1890 and Hindu Minority and Guardianship Act 1956, the prime consideration is the welfare of the child,

---

29   For details see: 'SC seeks opinion on AIDS patients' right to marry,' *The Times of India*, New Delhi, 8 February 2000.

30   *Judgements Today* 1997 (8) SC 720.

though section 6(a) of the latter Act says that the custody of a minor who has not attained the age of five shall ordinarily be with the mother.

It has been held in para 31 at pp 733–734 of the judgment, which is reproduced below for the purposes of ready reference :

'So far as non-Convention countries are concerned, or where the removal related to a period before adopting the Convention, the law is that the Court to which the child is removed will consider the question on merits bearing the welfare of the child as of paramount importance and consider the order of the foreign court as only a factor to be taken into consideration as stated in *McKee v McKee* (1951 AC 352), unless the Court thinks it fit to exercise summary jurisdiction in the interests of the child and its prompt return is for its welfare, as explained in *Re L* [1974] 1 All ER 913 (CA). As recently as 1996–1997, it has been held in *P (A Minor) (Child Abduction: Non Convention Country), Re:* (1996) 3 FCR 233 (CA) by Ward LJ 1996 (Current Law) (Year Book) (pp 165–166) that in deciding whether to order the return of a child who has been abducted from his or her country of habitual residence – which was not a party to the Hague Convention 1980 – the Courts' overriding consideration must be the child's welfare. There is no need for the judge to attempt to apply the provisions of Article 13 of the Convention by ordering the child's return unless a grave risk of harm was established.'

From the above mandate of law, it is clear that the Courts in India would not now exercise a summary jurisdiction to return children to the foreign country of habitual residence.

It has also been held, in para 21 of the above judgment, that orders relating to the custody of children are by their very nature not final, but are interlocutory in nature and subject to modification at any future time upon proof of change of circumstances requiring change of custody, but such change in custody must be proved to be in the paramount interests of the child. This was the position of law laid down by the Supreme Court of India in *Rosy Jacob v Jacob A. Chakramakkal.*[31] The law laid down in *Rosy Jacob*'s case has been explicitly reiterated in the above mentioned 1997 ruling.

It has been further held in this judgment that the custody order of a foreign court is only one of the factors which will be taken into consideration by a court of law in India. The Court in India will form an independent judgment on the merits of the matter with regard to the welfare of the children. Lastly, superior financial capacity cannot be a sole ground for disturbing the children from their mother's custody.

The tenor of law laid down in the above-mentioned judgment of *Dhanwanti Joshi* has very recently been reiterated by the Supreme Court of India in *Sarita Sharma v Sushil Sharma.*[32] The brief facts of this case are mentioned below.

The parents of the children were living in the USA. The children were put in the custody of the father, while the mother was given visiting rights. In exercise of visiting rights on 7 May 1997, the mother picked up the children from the father's residence. She was to leave the children next morning. The father got the information that the children were not brought back to the school. Eventually, the

---

31   1973 1 *Supreme Court Cases* 840.
32   *Judgements Today* 2000 (2) SC 158.

mother without obtaining any order from the American Court, flew to India with the children.

The father filed a habeas corpus writ petition in the Delhi High Court on 9 September 1997. The wife's contention was that by virtue of the orders dated 5 February 1996 and 2 April 1997 made by the courts in America, both of them were appointed as possessory conservators. Hence, both the children were in her lawful custody.

The Delhi High Court held that in view of the interim orders made by the American Court, the wife had committed a wrong in not informing that Court and obtaining its permission to remove the children from the jurisdiction of that Court. The Delhi High Court took note of the fact that a competent court having territorial jurisdiction had granted a decree of divorce and had ordered that only the father should have the custody of the children. The Delhi High Court allowed the petition and directed the wife to restore the custody of the two children to the father. It was also declared that it was open to the husband to take the children to the USA without any hindrance. The wife appealed to the Supreme Court of India.

The Supreme Court, in para 4 of the judgment at p 263, noticed from the record that there were serious differences between the two. The husband was an alcoholic and had indulged in violence against the wife. The conduct of the wife was also not very satisfactory.

In para 4 of the judgment itself, the court framed the following issues:

'The question is whether the custody became illegal as she had committed a breach of the order of the American Court directing her not to remove the children from the jurisdiction of that Court without its permission. After she came to India a decree of divorce and the order for the custody of the children have been passed. Therefore, it is also required to be considered whether the mother's custody became illegal thereafter.'

The Supreme Court of India held, in para 6 of the judgment at pp 264 and 265, as follows:

'6. Therefore, it will not be proper to be guided entirely by the fact that the appellant Sarita had removed the children from USA despite the order of the Court of that country. So also, in view of the facts and circumstances of the case, the decree passed by the American Court though a relevant factor, cannot override the consideration of welfare of the minor children. We have already stated earlier that in USA respondent Sushil is staying along with his mother aged about 80 years. There is no one else in the family. The respondent appears to be in the habit of taking excessive alcohol. Though it is true that both the children have the American citizenship and there is a possibility that in USA they may be able to get better education, it is doubtful if the respondent will be in a position to take proper care of the children when they are so young. Out of them one is a female child. She is aged about 5 years. Ordinarily, a female child should be allowed to remain with the mother so that she can be properly looked after. It is also not desirable that two children are separated from each other. If a female child has to stay with the mother, it will be in the interest of both the children that they both stay with the mother. Here in India also proper care of the children is taken and they are at present studying in good schools. We have not found the appellant wanting in taking proper care of the children. Both the children have a desire to stay with the mother. At the same time it must be said that the son, who is elder than the daughter, has good feelings for his father also. Considering all the aspects relating to the welfare of the children, we are of the opinion that in spite of the order passed by the Court in USA it was not proper for the High Court to have allowed the Habeas Corpus writ petition and directed the appellant to hand over custody of the children to the respondent and permit him to take them away to USA. What would be in the interest of the children requires a full and thorough inquiry and, therefore, the High Court should have directed the respondent to initiate appropriate proceedings in which such an inquiry can be held.'

Furthermore, para 31 of the judgment in *Dhanwanti Joshi*'s case, which has been already reproduced above was expressly reiterated by the Supreme Court of India in para 5 of the judgment in *Sarita Sharma*'s case. *Sarita Sharma*'s case is second in line ruling of its kind handed down by the Supreme Court of India, altering the earlier dicta of child abduction law.

Before the above-mentioned 1997 and 1999 rulings were handed down by the Supreme Court of India, there was case-law to the contrary, allowing enforcement of foreign court custody orders on the principle of comity on a case-by-case basis. Such orders were normally enforced by initiating habeas corpus petitions under Article 226 of the Constitution of India in the High Court of the region where the child was situated, or directly in the Supreme Court of India under Article 32 of the Constitution of India.

It is pertinent to mention that Article 137 of the Constitution of India provides for review of judgments or orders made by the Supreme Court of India. Article 141 of the Constitution of India mandates that the law declared by the Supreme Court of India shall be binding on all courts within the territory of India.

There is ample earlier case-law contrary to the law recently laid down in *Dhanwanti Joshi* and *Sarita Sharma*. One such Supreme Court of India ruling – *Surinder Kaur Sandhu v Harbax Singh Sandhu*[33] has been noticed in para 5 at p 262 in *Sarita Sharma*'s case. Para 10 of the judgment in *Sandhu*'s case has been reproduced in para 5 of *Sarita Sharma*'s case, which is reproduced hereunder for ready reference:

'We may add that the spouses had set up their matrimonial home in England where the wife was working as a clerk and the husband as a bus driver. The boy is a British citizen, having been born in England, and he holds a British passport. It cannot be controverted that, in these circumstances, the English Court had jurisdiction to decide the question of his custody. The modern theory of conflict of Laws recognises and, in any event, prefers the jurisdiction of the State which has the most intimate contact with the issues arising in the case. Jurisdiction is not attracted by the operation or creation of fortuitous circumstances such as the circumstance as to where the child, whose custody is in issue, is brought or for the time being lodged. To allow the assumption of jurisdiction by another State in such circumstances will only result in encouraging forum-shopping. Ordinarily, jurisdiction must follow upon functional lines. That is to say, for example, that in matters relating to matrimony and custody, the law of that place must govern which has the closest concern with the well-being of the spouses and the welfare of the offsprings of marriage. The spouses in this case had made England their home where this boy was born to them. The father cannot deprive the English Court of its jurisdiction to decide upon his custody by removing him to India, not in the normal movement of the matrimonial home but, by an act which was gravely

33   *All India Reporter* 1984 SC 1224.

detrimental to the peace of that home. The fact that the matrimonial home of the spouses was in England, establishes sufficient contacts or ties with that State in order to make it reasonable and just for the courts of that State to assume jurisdiction to enforce obligations which were incurred therein by the spouses. (See *International Shoe Company v State of Washington* [90 L Ed 95 (1945): 326 US 310], which was not a matrimonial case but which is regarded as the fountainhead of the subsequent developments of jurisdictional issues like the one involved in the instant case). It is our duty and function to protect the wife against the burden of litigating in an inconvenient forum which she and her husband had left voluntarily in order to make their living in England, where they gave birth to this unfortunate boy.'

The earlier mandate of law as laid down in *Sandhu*'s case elaborated above has not been followed by the Supreme Court of India in *Sarita Sharma*'s case.

In *Sarita Sharma*'s case, the Supreme Court has also noticed the earlier law laid down in *Elizabeth Dinshaw v Arvand M. Dinshaw.*[34] In this ruling the Apex Court had exercised summary jurisdiction regarding the return of the minor child. In *Dinshaw*'s case it was also stressed that the interest and the welfare of the minor child is the predominant criterion in child custody matters.

The earlier law laid down in *Sandhu* and *Dinshaw* stands substantially modified with the recent mandate of law in *Dhanwanti Joshi* and *Sarita Sharma*.

B   Forum for custody proceedings

As far as the forum for securing the return of children is concerned, it is important to mention that India is not a signatory to the Hague Convention on the Civil Aspects of International Child Abduction 1980. Under Article 226 of the Constitution of India, a parent whose child has been abducted can petition the State High Court to issue a writ of habeas corpus against the abducting spouse for the return of the child. Alternatively, a habeas corpus petition seeking recovery of the abducted child can also be directly filed in the Supreme Court of India under Article 32 of the Constitution of India.

C   Visiting rights cannot be denied

The Supreme Court of India, in a recent ruling reported as *N. Nirmala v Nelson Jeyakumar*,[35] held that deprivation of visiting rights is not justified. The question involved in this appeal concerned the custody of a minor daughter. The respondent-father was permitted to continue the custody as legal guardian. The learned single judge of the High Court confirmed the custody of the minor daughter with the father but gave visiting rights to the appellant-mother. Against the order passed by the learned single judge, the appellant-mother in search of an actual order of custody, appealed. The Division Bench of the High Court while dismissing the appeal held that the impugned judgment had deprived the appellant of her visiting rights for which there was no cross-objection on the part of the respondent.

---

34   *All India Reporter* 1987 SC 3.
35   *Judgements Today* 1999(5) SC 223.

The Apex Court held in para 3 at p 223 of the judgment:

'In our opinion, such a further adverse order against the appellant was not justified. The interest of justice will be served if the order of the learned Single Judge continuing the custody of the minor child with the respondent and as confirmed by the Division Bench is maintained subject to the modification that visiting right which was denied to the appellant by the Division Bench be continued.'

D   Welfare of the minor child is the paramount consideration

In *Om Prakash Bharuka v Shakuntala Modi*,[36] a custody dispute between the mother and father of the three minor children, custody had been granted to the mother. The wishes of the children were ascertained. They flatly refused to go and stay with their father. The court held, in para 17, at p 42 of the judgment:

'17. Merely because the father loves his children and is not shown to be otherwise undesirable cannot necessarily lead to the conclusion that the welfare of the children would be better promoted by granting their custody to him as against the wife who may also be equally affectionate towards her children and otherwise equally free from blemish, and, who, in addition because of her profession and financial resources, may be in a position to guarantee better health, education and maintenance for them. Thus therefore, the Court in case of a dispute between the father and mother is expected to strike a just and proper balance between the requirements of welfare of the minor children and the rights of their respective parents over them. In short, while giving custody of the children, the welfare of the children should be regarded as a paramount consideration.'

E   Foreign orders

The principles governing the validity of foreign court orders are laid down in section 13 of the CPC. This has already been discussed under the sub-heading, guidelines laid down by the Supreme Court of India on recognition of foreign matrimonial judgments.

It is reiterated, as elaborated above, that the Indian Courts would not exercise summary jurisdiction to return children to the country of habitual residence. The Courts in India would consider the question on its merits bearing in mind the welfare of the children as of paramount importance.

Section 14 of the CPC talks of a presumption as to foreign judgments. It provides that the court shall presume, upon the production of any document purporting to be a certified copy of a foreign judgment, that such judgment was pronounced by a court of competent jurisdiction, unless the contrary appears on the record; but such presumption may be displaced by proving want of jurisdiction.

---

36   *All India Reporter* 1993 Gauhati 38.

F   No provision for mirror orders in India

In light of the prevailing child abduction law in India as elaborated above, it is not possible to obtain mirror orders – a concept known to the English legal system – as there exists no provision for the same in the Indian legal mechanisms. Since foreign court custody orders cannot now be mechanically enforced, it is suggested that in the event of any litigation in the foreign country of habitual residence, a Letter of Request be obtained by the foreign court in which litigation is pending, incorporating safeguards and conditions to ensure the return of the minor child to the country of normal residence.

This Letter of Request should be addressed by the foreign court to the Registrar General of the High Court within whose jurisdiction the estranged spouse is residing with the minor child. It should also be categorically mentioned that the passports of the parent and the child should be deposited with the Registrar General of the State High Court.

G   Habeas corpus can also be issued by a person who is not a citizen of India

It is well established that a writ of habeas corpus can be issued to secure the custody of a minor child. This can also be sought even by a person who is not a citizen of this country as recently held in *Miss Atya Shamim v Deputy Commissioner/Collector, Delhi (Prescribed Authority under Citizenship Act) and others*.[37] The Jammu and Kashmir High Court in this ruling reiterated *Elizabeth Dinshaw's* case (AIR 1987 SC 3) where the Supreme Court of India had issued a writ at the instance of a person who was not a citizen of this country.

H   Child abduction and forced marriages

In a somewhat extreme and unusual set of circumstances, Mr Justice Singer of the High Court of London ruled that parents who take their children abroad to marry them off against their wishes were guilty of child abduction. This judgment was handed down by the Family Division, Principal Registry on 18 May 1999 and was reported as *Re KR (Abduction: Forcible Removal by Parents)*.[38]

The judge, in the opening paragraph of the judgment, highlights the extent to which courts and other agencies concerned need to be alert to safeguard the individual integrity of children from attack, even from their own family. This case has also highlighted the risk which adolescents, particularly girls of a marriageable age, encounter when they seek to depart from the traditional norms of their religious, cultural or ethnic group.

The ruling pertains to a 17-year-old British Sikh girl who had been taken by her parents to a remote village in India to be married to one of the suitors they had chosen for her. The judge employed the services of the British Foreign Office,

---

37   *All India Reporter* 1999 J and K 140.
38   [1999] 2 FLR 542.

Interpol, British High Commission, New Delhi and the Indian police to help the girl return to Britain.

The girl had left her home in April 1998 to avoid being married. She went to live with her 19-year-old sister, who had also left home to escape being forced into a marriage against her wishes.

In June 1998, the girl was taken to India where she stayed with her aunt in Punjab. Her passport was confiscated by the family. She was kept under a close watch. She managed to smuggle a letter to her sister in England pleading for help.

Her sister contacted Reunite, a renowned London-based international charity organisation, whose purpose is to give impartial and expert advice and support to the parents of children abducted or believed to be at risk of abduction. With Reunite's assistance, legal proceedings were initiated to make the girl a ward of the court and remove her from her parents' control.

Reunite had to act quickly because once the abducted girl was 18, she could no longer be a ward of the court. The English court wanted to be sure as to what were the intentions of the girl before it took any judicial steps. Her parents insisted that she wanted to stay in India and even provided taped telephone conversations and fax communications from her as proof. The court insisted that officials from the British High Commission should interview the girl. It was discovered that the girl was being moved from place to place to evade them.

Eventually, the girl convinced her parents that she should be taken to the British High Commission at New Delhi. She told the officials that she wanted to return to London.

During the course of the proceedings, Mr Justice Singer had drawn up an order which would have some extra-territorial effect, in the sense that it might encourage relevant authorities in India to give assistance. The judge rightly pointed out in the judgment that the order might be of assistance in comparable situations and it is reproduced hereunder:

'UPON hearing ...

AND UPON the application of all parties herein and by consent of all parties herein and upon reading ... and upon hearing ...

AND WHEREAS KR is a Ward of this Honourable Court and is a British citizen; born in and domiciled in the United Kingdom; and currently travelling with a United Kingdom passport

AND WHEREAS in consequence of the fact that this Court has ordered that KR remain a Ward of this Court while (until she attains the age of 18 years on [date]) she remains a minor, this Court is empowered and required to exercise its custodial jurisdiction over her and to ascertain her best interests and to facilitate and protect those best interests

AND WHEREAS this Honourable Court is anxious to protect and secure her well-being and best interests and to ensure that she may freely express her wishes concerning her country and place of residence

AND WHEREAS this Honourable Court is anxious to ensure that she is not induced or coerced into contracting any marriage or betrothal against her will

AND WHEREAS this Honourable Court is satisfied that all interested parties are before the Court including the Official Solicitor appointed by the Court to represent the Ward

AND WHEREAS this Honourable Court having heard limited oral evidence from [F and M] is of the view that serious grounds exist in the present circumstances to question whether this Honourable Court's Ward KR is able freely to express her views and wishes and in particular with regard to her country of residence

IT IS ORDERED that every person in a position to do so shall co-operate in assisting and securing the immediate return to England of KR, a Ward of this Honourable Court

AND NOW THEREFORE this Court invites all judicial and administrative bodies in the State of India to render assistance in establishing the whereabouts of the Ward of this Honourable Court and in arranging for her to be placed in contact with the British High Commission in New Delhi (Reference: [a named individual]) and to facilitate her travel to the British High Commission with a view to her immediate return to the United Kingdom.'

Indeed, the order was of assistance. The girl flew back to England on 5 March 1999. The court issued a protection order preventing her family from abducting her or trying forcibly to take her back to India.

The judge held at p 10 in the concluding portion of the judgment:

'Sensitivity to these traditional and/or religious influences is however likely, in English courts, usually to give way to the integrity of the individual child or young person concerned. In the courts of this country the voice of the young person will be heard and, in so personal a context as opposition to an arranged or enforced marriage, will prevail. The courts will not permit what is at best the exploitation of an individual and may in the worst case amount to outright trafficking for financial consideration.'

I   The Hindu Minority and Guardianship Act 1956 (hereafter HMGA 1956)

It is important to advert to the provisions of the HMGA 1956, which is an act to amend and codify certain parts of the law relating to minority and guardianship among Hindus. The provisions of the HMGA 1956 are supplemental to the earlier Guardians and Wards Act 1890. The HMGA 1956, like the HMA 1955, has extra-territorial application. It extends to the whole of India except the States of Jammu and Kashmir.

In terms of section 4(a) of the 1956 Act 'minor' means a person who has not completed the age of 18 years. A 'guardian' in section 4(b) is defined as the natural guardian or one appointed by will or a court of law.

Section 6 of the HMGA 1956 defines the natural guardians of a Hindu minor, which recently came up for interpretation by the Supreme Court of India in the matter of *Githa Hariharan (Ms) and another v Reserve Bank of India and another*.[39] Two cases involving a similar point of law were decided by the Apex court. In this landmark judgement the Supreme Court has given the mother her due place in the HMGA 1956 by ruling that both the mother and father would be treated as the natural guardians of their minor children.

In Writ Petition number 489 of 1995, the first petitioner and her husband, the second petitioner, jointly applied to the Reserve Bank of India, the first respondent, for the issue of Relief Bonds in the name of their son. They stated expressly that both of them agreed that the mother of the child, ie the first petitioner would act as the guardian of the minor for the purpose of investments made with the money held by their minor son. Accordingly, in the prescribed form of application, the first petitioner signed as the guardian of the minor. RBI replied to the petitioners advising them either to produce the application form signed by the father of the minor or a certificate of guardianship from a competent authority in favour of the mother. The bank contended that the mother was not the natural guardian of a minor in terms of section 6(a) of the HMGA 1956. Ultimately, the petitioners filed a writ petition under Article 32 of the Constitution of India seeking to strike down section 6(a) of the HMGA 1956 and section 19(b) of the GWA 1890 as a violation of Articles 14 and 15 of the Constitution of India. The petitioners also sought to quash and set aside RBI's decision not to accept the deposit from them and to issue a mandamus directing the acceptance of the same after declaring the first petitioner as the natural guardian of the minor. Article 14 mandates that the State shall not deny to any person equality before the law or the equal protection of laws within the territory of India, while Article 15 prohibits discrimination on grounds of religion, race, caste, sex or place of birth. Section 19 of the GWA 1890 contemplates three contingencies in which the Court has no authority to appoint or declare a guardian of a minor at all. By virtue of section 19(b), no order declaring a guardian can be made during the lifetime of a minor's father, unless in the opinion of the court he is unfit to be the guardian of the minor.

Section 6 of the HMGA 1956 is reproduced hereunder for ready reference:

'6. The natural guardians of a Hindu minor, in respect of the minor's person as well as in respect of the minor's property (excluding his or her undivided interest in joint family property), are –

(a) in the case of a boy or an unmarried girl – the father, and after him, the mother: Provided that the custody of a minor who has not completed the age of five years shall ordinarily be with the mother;
(b) in the case of an illegitimate boy or an illegitimate unmarried girl – the mother, and after her, the father;
(c) in the case of a married girl – the husband:

Provided that no person shall be entitled to act as the natural guardian of a minor under the provisions of this section –

(a) if he has ceased to be a Hindu, or
(b) if he has completely and finally renounced the world by becoming a hermit (vanaprastha) or an ascetic (yati or sanyasi).'

---

39   (1999) 2 *Supreme Court Cases* 228.

The judgment of the Chief Justice of India Dr AS Anand assumes significance as he ruled, in para 7 of the judgment at p 234:

'The expression "natural guardian" is defined in Section 4(c) of the HMG Act as any of the guardians mentioned in Section 6 (supra). The term "guardian" is defined in Section 4(b) of the HMG Act as a person having the care of the person of a minor or of his property or of both, his person and property, and includes a natural guardian among others. Thus, it is seen that the definitions of "guardian" and "natural guardian" do not make any discrimination against mother and she being one of the guardians mentioned in Section 6 would undoubtedly be a natural guardian as defined in Section 4(c). The only provision to which exception is taken is found in Section 6(a) which reads "the father, and *after* him, the mother". (emphasis ours) That phrase, on a cursory reading, does give an impression that the mother can be considered to be the natural guardian of the minor only after the lifetime of the father. In fact, that appears to be the basis of the stand taken by the Reserve Bank of India also. It is not in dispute and is otherwise well settled also that the welfare of the minor in the widest sense is the paramount consideration and even during the lifetime of the father, if necessary, he can be replaced by the mother or any other suitable person by an order of the court, where to do so would be in the interest of the welfare of the minor.'

Both the authors of the judgment, Justices Dr Anand and Srinivasan, interpreting section 6(a) of the HMGA 1956 in a manner to keep it in the ambit of constitutional validity held that the word 'after' need not necessarily mean 'after the lifetime.' It means 'in the absence of', the word 'absence' referring to the father's absence from the care of the minor's property or person for any reasons whatever.

The court held, in para 10 of the judgment at p 235, that on the following grounds the father would be treated as absent and the mother being the recognised natural guardian, can act validly on behalf of a minor as the guardian:

(a)   If the father is wholly indifferent to the matters of the minor even if he is living with the mother.
(b)   If by virtue of mutual understanding between the father and the mother, the latter is put exclusively in charge of the minor.
(c)   If the father is physically unable to take care of the minor either because of his staying away from the place where the mother and the minor are living or because of his physical or mental incapacity.

This progressive ruling also has a beneficial aspect for private international law. Paragraph 14 of the judgment at p 238 recites:

'The message of international instruments – the Convention on the Elimination of All Forms of Discrimination Against Women, 1979 ("CEDAW") and the Beijing Declaration, which directs all State parties to take appropriate measures to prevent discrimination of all forms against women is quite clear. India is a signatory to CEDAW having accepted and ratified it in June 1993. The interpretation that we have placed on Section 6(a) (supra) gives effect to the principles contained in these instruments. The domestic courts are under an obligation to give due regard to international conventions and norms for construing domestic laws when there is no inconsistency between them.'

Furthermore, Justice Banerjee, in para 35 of the judgment at pp 242 to 243, has drawn a parallel between English law and Indian law on the subject. It will be noticed from the English rulings below that the welfare of the child is the common denominator in both the jurisdictions. In *Re McGrath*,[40] Lindley LJ observed:

'The dominant matter for the consideration of the court is the welfare of the child. But the welfare of a child is not to be measured by money only, nor by physical comfort only. The word 'welfare' must be taken in its widest sense. The moral and religious welfare of the child must be considered as well as its physical well-being. Nor can the ties of affection be disregarded.'

Lord Esher MR in *Re Gyngall*,[41] stated:

'The court has to consider, therefore, the whole of the circumstances of the case, the position of the parent, the position of the child, the age of the child, the religion of the child, so far as it can be said to have any religion and the happiness of the child. Prima facie, it would not be for the welfare of the child to be taken away from its natural parent and given over to other people who have not that natural relation to it. Every wise man would say that, generally speaking, the best place for a child is with its parent. If a child is brought up, as one may say from its mother's lap in one form of religion, it would not, I should say be for its happiness and welfare that a stranger should take it away in order to alter its religious views. Again, it cannot be merely because the parent is poor and the person who seeks to have the possession of the child as against the parent is rich, that, wihout regard to any other consideration, to the natural rights and feelings of the parent, or the feelings and views that have been introduced into the heart and mind of the child, the child ought not to be taken away from its parent merely because its pecuniary position will be thereby bettered. No wise man would entertain such suggestions as these.'

Justice Banerjee has observed that English law has been consistent with the concept of welfare of the child. Likewise, Indian law also does not make any departure therefrom.

III   INTER-COUNTRY ADOPTION IN INDIA

This section briefly discusses the inter-country adoption procedure coupled with the relevant legislation to be complied with by foreigners seeking to adopt children from India. At the outset, it is important to clarify that at present there exists no general law on adoption of children governing non-Hindus and foreigners. Adoption is permitted by statute among Hindus and by custom among some other communities.

At present, non-Hindus and foreigners can only be guardians of children under the Guardianship and Wards Act 1890. In actual practice, foreign nationals desirous of adopting children from India first obtain guardianship orders from the District Court or the High Court, as the case may be, within whose jurisdiction the

---

40   (1893) 1 Ch 143: 62 LJ Ch 208.
41   (1893) 2 QB 232.

child is residing. This is with a view to formal adoption in accordance with the legal system of the country of their habitual residence.

The Ministry of Welfare pursuant to certain guidelines issued by the Supreme Court of India, in a public interest litigation petition reported as *Lakshmi Kanta Pandey v Union of India*,[42] framed guidelines governing inter-country adoption. This case was monitored by the Supreme Court from time to time until the year 1991. The court scrupulously reviewed the existing procedure and practices followed in inter-country adoptions. The objective was to prevent trafficking of children and to protect the welfare of adopted children.

After the implementation of the initial guidelines in 1989 it was felt necessary to revise them. Accordingly, a task force comprising a cross-section of representatives of adoption agencies under the chairmanship of former Chief Justice of India Mr Justice PN Bhagwati was constituted on 12 August 1992. The Chairman of the Task Force submitted its report on 28 August 1993. The Indian Government accepted the recommendations of the above mentioned task force, and accordingly, circulated revised guidelines to regulate matters relating to adoption of Indian children (1994). These guidelines were published by the Government in the *Gazette of India* on 20 June 1995. These guidelines are discussed below.

A   Procedure to be followed in inter-country adoption

In the first place, para 2.14 of the guidelines stipulates that every application from a foreigner desiring to adopt a child must be sponsored by a social or child welfare agency recognised or licensed by the Government of that country in which the foreigner is resident. Furthermore, the agency should be recognised by the Central Adoption Resource Agency (hereafter CARA) set up under the aegis of the Ministry of Welfare, Union of India. CARA is the principal monitoring agency of the Government handling all affairs connected with in-country and inter-country adoptions.

No application by a foreigner to adopt a child should be entertained directly by any social or child welfare agency in India working in the areas of inter-country adoption or by any institution or centre to which the children are committed by the Juvenile Court. The reasons behind this directive have been very appropriately summed up by MN Das in his recent book[43] at pp 80–81 and reproduced below:

'Firstly, it will help to reduce, if not eliminate altogether, the possibility of profiteering and trafficking in children, because if a foreigner were allowed to contact directly agencies or individuals in India for the purpose of obtaining a child in adoption, he might, in his anxiety to secure a child for adoption, be induced or persuaded to pay any unconscionable or unreasonable amount which might be demanded by the agency or individual procuring the child. Secondly, it would be almost impossible for the court to satisfy itself that the foreigner who wishes to take the child in adoption would be suitable as a parent for the child and whether he would be able to provide a stable and

---

42   *All India Reporter* 1984 SC 469.

43   MN Das, *Guardians and Wards Act*, 14th ed (Eastern Law House, 1995).

secure family life to the child and would be able to handle trans-racial, trans-cultural and trans-national problems likely to arise from such adoption, because, where the application for adopting a child has not been sponsored by a social or child welfare agency in the country of the foreigner, there would be no proper and satisfactory home study report on which the court can rely. Thirdly, in such a case, where the application of a foreigner for taking a child in adoption is made directly without the intervention of social or child welfare agency, there would be no authority or agency in the country of the foreigner who could be made responsible for supervising the progress of the child and ensuring that the child is adopted at the earliest in accordance with law and grows up in an atmosphere of warmth and affection with moral and material security assured to it.'

Regulation 2.15 of the new guidelines provides that where there is no recognised foreign agency in a particular country, then the concerned Government Department or Ministry of that country may forward the applications and related documents of the prospective adoptive parents to CARA. CARA will in turn examine and send those papers to the recognised Indian placement agencies indicated in the application.

It is also mandatory for the enlisted foreign agency to send a copy of the application, as well as the prescribed documents, including the home study report, to CARA. These documents have to be duly notarised by a Notary Public whose signature is additionally duly attested either by an officer of the Ministry of External Affairs or Justice or Social Welfare of the country of the foreigner or by an officer of the Indian Embassy or High Commission or consulate in that foreign country.

B   Home study report

Regulation 2.14 of these new guidelines categorically and emphatically enumerates the contents of the home study report. Since the home study report is a crucial document, it is mandatory that it should include the following information:

(1)   social status and family background;
(2)   description of the home;
(3)   standard of living as it appears in the home;
(4)   current relationship between the husband and wife;
(5)   current relationship between the parents and children (if there are any children);
(6)   development of the already adopted children (if any);
(7)   current relationship between the couple and the members of each other's family;
(8)   employment status of the couple;
(9)   health details such as clinical test, hearing condition, past illness etc (medical certificate etc);
(10)   economic status of the couple;
(11)   accommodation for the child;
(12)   schooling facilities;
(13)   amenities in the home;
(14)   reasons for wanting to adopt an Indian child;

(15) attitude of grandparent/s and relatives towards the adoption;
(16) anticipated plans for the adoptive child;
(17) legal status of the prospective adoptive parents.

Mere receipt of the application as well as other original documents will not entitle the Indian placement agency to proceed with the case. The Indian placement agency can proceed only after obtaining a 'no objection certificate' from CARA.

Regulation 2.14 further states that CARA should endeavour, as far as possible, to see that this no objection certificate should be issued within a reasonable period of time, say five weeks from the date of the receipt of the certified copies of the application and other relevant documents.

After the receipt of the original application and the original documents from the enlisted foreign agency by the Indian placement agency, the concerned placement agency will then register the name of the prospective foreign parents in the appropriate register.

The recognised Indian placement agency will then proceed to examine carefully the home study report of the prospective foreign adoptive parents and start the exercise in matching the home study report with the child study report. When it arrives at the conclusion that a child can be placed with that particular family then they will have to ensure that the concerned child is cleared by the Voluntary Coordinating Agency (hereafter VCA) for inter-country adoption. It is pertinent to mention that there exist separate VCAs in every state for that particular jurisdiction.

Thereafter, the recognised placement agency will send the child study report, the photograph of the child and the medical report to the sponsoring foreign agency for the approval of the prospective adoptive parents. After obtaining the approval of the child by the prospective adoptive parents, the recognised placement agency concerned will apply to CARA to get a clearance for the child.

It is at this stage that CARA will have to ensure that the recognised placement agency has put in adequate efforts to find an Indian family for the said child. CARA, after going through the information furnished by the recognised placement agency and the VCA, will immediately give the clearance to the agency. The VCA clearance is mandatory.

C   Guardianship order

The recognised placement agency will then process the case with the local court with jurisdiction to award the guardianship of the child to the foreign prospective adoptive parents.

Once again, the scrutinising agency must, at this stage, inspect all the documents and advise the competent court that the inter-country adoption is in the best interest of the child. The court will award the guardianship of the child to the foreign parents within the stipulated time as laid down by the Supreme Court of India.

On the basis of the court guardianship order the recognised placement agency must apply to the regional passport office for an Indian passport for the child.

Thereafter, the entry clearance/visa is to be obtained from the Embassy/High Commission of the country where the child is to live. After this rigorous drill has been carried out, the child leaves the country along with the prospective adoptive parents or with the escort, as the case may be, to go to the country of the prospective adoptive parents.

The Supreme Court of India in *Karnataka State Council for Child Welfare and another v Society of Sisters of Charity St. Gerosa Convent and others*[44] held that the rationale behind finding Indian parents or parents of Indian origin is to ensure that the children should grow up in Indian surroundings so that they retain their culture and heritage. This is definitely an issue which has a bearing on the question of the welfare of the children. The welfare of the children is the main and prime consideration.

The Gujarat High Court, in a progressive judgment, upheld the validity of guardianship orders in favour of two Norwegian couples who were appointed as guardians of Hindu children. In this particular matter, reported as *Jayantilal and another v Asha*,[45] the court tersely held in para 12 of the judgment at p 156:

> '... if the biological parents have died rendering the child an orphan then the society owes a duty to the child that at least a semblence of comfort and care which the biological parents could have provided will be provided to the child, if some people from howsoever distant a corner of this planet, come forth to do so. In such a case a petty contention like the change of religion or culture of the child can hardly stand in the way of the court in sanctioning inter-country adoption. Unfounded and imaginary apprehensions also are of little consequence and once the court is assured that there is no possibility of the child being abused, which assurance can flow from the independent agencies which are ordained for the purpose, then nothing can and need prevent the court from sanctioning an inter-country adoption.'

Experience of counsel while dealing with the Ministry of Welfare suggests that the documentation should be compiled meticulously. This is in order to avoid bureaucratic delays. In addition to the home study report, the following additional documents (see annex A of the Regulations) are required to be submitted by the foreign adoptive parents. Here, it will be noticed that the Indian requirements are quite similar to the stipulations prescribed in various appendices of RON 117 issued by the Home Office in Britain.

(1) recent photographs of the adoptive family;
(2) marriage certificate;
(3) declaration concerning health of adoptive parents;
(4) certificate of medical fitness duly certified by a medical doctor;
(5) declaration regarding financial status with supporting documents, including employer's certificate, wherever applicable;
(6) employment certificate, if applicable;
(7) income tax assessment order;
(8) bank references;
(9) particulars of properties owned;

---

44 *All India Reporter* 1994 SC 658.
45 *All India Reporter* 1989 Gujarat 152.

(10) joint declaration stating willingness to be appointed guardian of the child;

(11) undertaking from the social or child welfare enlisted agency sponsoring the foreigner to the effect that the child would be legally adopted by the foreign adoptive parents, according to the law of the country, within a period not exceeding two years from the time of arrival of the child;

(12) undertaking to the effect that the child would be provided necessary education and upbringing according to status of the adoptive parents;

(13) undertaking from the recognised foreign social or child welfare agency that the report relating to the progress of the child along with his/her recent photograph would be sent quarterly during first two years and half yearly for the next three years in the prescribed proforma through the Indian Diplomatic post in the country of the adoptive parents;

(14) power of attorney conferred by the intending parents in favour of the social or the child welfare agency in India which will be required to process the case and such power of attorney should also authorise the lawyer in India to handle the case on behalf of the foreign adoptee parents, if they are not in a position to come to India;

(15) certificate from the foreign enlisted social or child welfare agency sponsoring the application to the effect that they are permitted to adopt a child according to the laws of their country;

(16) undertaking from the overseas social or child welfare agency to the effect that in case of disruption of the adoptive family, before the legal adoption has been effected, it will take care of child and find a suitable alternative placement for the child with prior approval of CARA;

(17) undertaking from the overseas social or child welfare enlisted agency that it will reimburse all expenses to the concerned Indian social or child welfare agency as fixed by the competent court towards maintenance of the child and the processing charge fees.

It is important to reiterate that all the above certificates/declarations/documents in support of the application have to be notarised, as already explained in the preceding paragraphs.

D   Domestic law

The principal law relating to adoption in India by Hindus only is contained in the Hindu Adoptions and Maintenance Act 1956 (hereafter the HAMA 1956).

Having elaborated the law and procedure relating to inter-country adoptions, brief reference is made to the domestic law governing adoptions by Hindus.

E   Requisites of a valid adoption

Section 6 stipulates four conditions for a valid adoption which are reproduced hereunder:

(1) the person adopting has the capacity, and also the right, to adopt;

(2) the person consenting to adoption has the capacity to do so;

(3) the person adopted is capable of being adopted; and

(4)   the adoption is made in compliance with the other conditions mentioned in chapter 2 of HAMA 1956.

Section 6(iv) requires that the adoption should be made in compliance with other conditions mentioned in chapter 2 of HAMA 1956. In other words, in order that the adoption should be valid the provisions of section 7 to section 11 must be satisfied. Section 7 deals with capacity of a male Hindu to adopt; while section 8 talks of capacity of a female Hindu to adopt; section 9 qualifies persons capable of giving up children for adoption; section 10 categorises persons who may be adopted; section 11 enumerates other conditions for valid adoption. Thereafter, section 12 elaborates the effects of a valid adoption.

F   Effects of a valid adoption

Section 12 categorically deals with the legal effects of an adoption made in accordance with the provisions of HAMA 1956. Here it can be pointed out that section 12 of HAMA 1956 satisfies the requirements of clause (ix) of para 310 of H.C. 395 of the current British Immigration Rules governing adoption. This clause (ix) of para 310 in very harsh terms states that the adopted child 'has lost or broken his ties with his family of origin'.

Insofar as relating to the legal effects of a valid adoption, it is important to cite certain decisions of the Supreme Court of India. It was held by the Supreme Court of India in *Smt. Sitabai and another v Ramchandra*,[46] reported as A.I.R. 1970 S.C. 343, in para 6 at p 348:

'The true effect and interpretation of Sections 11 and 12 of Act No. 78 of 1956 therefore is that when either of the spouses adopts a child, all the ties of the child in the family of his or her birth become completely severed and these are all replaced by those created by the adoption in the adoptive family.'

Similarly, it was held by the Supreme Court in the matter of *Kartar Singh v Surjan Singh*,[47] that the wording in section 11(vi) 'with intent to transfer the child from the family of its birth to the family of its adoption' is merely indicative of the result of the actual giving and taking by the parents or guardians concerned referred to in the earlier part of the clause. Where an adoption ceremony is gone through and the giving and taking takes place, there cannot be any other intention. Much more recently, the Supreme Court of India, in the matter of *Chandan Bilasini v Aftabuddin Khan*,[48] held in para 6 of the judgment at p 81:

'Section 12 of the Hindu Adoptions and Maintenance Act clearly provides that an adopted child shall be deemed to be the child of his adoptive father or mother for all purposes with effect from the date of the adoption and from such date all ties of the child in the family of his or her birth shall be deemed to be severed and replaced by those created by the adoption in the adoptive family.'

---

46   *All India Reporter* 1970 SC 343.

47   *All India Reporter* 1974 SC 216.

48   1996 (1) *Hindu Law Reporter* 79 (SC).

Finally, section 15 of the 1956 Act underlines the irrevocability of the validly performed adoption.

G   Problems faced in inter-country adoption

At present non-Hindus and foreign nationals can only be guardians of children under the Guardianship and Wards Act 1890. They cannot adopt children. The child is a loser by being deprived of the benefits that are available in course of a valid adoption. There have been disturbing press reports about greedy social activists.[49] It has been pointed out that at the root of the problem is certain placement agencies' love for lucre and their propensity to extort money from childless foreigners. Secondly, it has been observed in this report that the paper work in practice is complex. The system is not working, on account of long delays at different levels of scrutiny. Thirdly, India has not ratified the Hague Convention on the Protection of Children and Co-operation in Respect of Inter-country Adoption (29 May 1993). As pointed out by the *Bhagwati* Panel, the political and legal rights of the Indian child with foreign adoptive parents can be best assured through bilateral pacts under the Convention.

H   Conflict of laws

As counsel dealing with adoption applications at the British High Commission, New Delhi, we have encountered a conflict of laws situation. Quite often non-resident Indians, who have been residing abroad for several decades, adopt children within the family itself. The preference is for immediate blood relatives. This is a common South Asian phenomenon.

The unsuspecting adoptive parents duly comply with the above-mentioned requirements of HAMA 1956 while taking the child in adoption. The adoption deed is flashed with pride and authority before the immigration authorities, and this is where the trouble begins. The UK immigration authorities completely disregard the Indian adoption deed. They are legally justified in doing so in terms of the Adoption (Designation of Overseas Adoptions) Order 1973 (SI 1973/19).

In terms of the 1973 Order, if a child has been legally adopted from a country whose adoption orders are recognised as valid for UK law (a 'designated' country), then the parents may apply for the child to join them in the United Kingdom as their adopted child.

If the child has not been legally adopted from a 'designated' country or the adoption is from a country whose adoption orders are not recognised as valid in UK law (a 'non-designated' country), entry clearance will have to be obtained for the child to travel to the UK for adoption through the English Courts. India is specified as a 'non-designated' country in terms of the 1973 Order.

The adoptive parents, then, are confronted with a refusal by the immigration authorities on the ground that the adoption deed is not valid under the above-mentioned 1973 Order although there has been due compliance of the provisions

---

49   See Sharma Vinod, 'Indian child losing out in adoption mart', *Hindustan Times*, New Delhi, 9 September, 1997.

of HAMA 1956. The only avenue then available to the parents is to challenge the refusal by way of appeal or lodge a fresh application.

The real dilemma in such a situation is to set back the clock to satisfy the requirements of British immigration law. How can a non-resident Indian adoptee couple obtain a guardianship order from a local court once a formal irrevocable adoption process has taken place? Certainly, a guardianship order is not on a better footing than a valid adoption under HAMA 1956. This is a proposition, which sooner or later will have to be tested by the British courts.

There has been a growing demand for a general law of adoption enabling any person irrespective of his religion, race or caste to adopt a child. There is now a clear case for overhauling the existing adoption law in India.

IV CONCLUSION

From the above analysis, it is clear that there is a conflict of law situation as far as the presumption in favour of valid marriages is concerned, on the basis of cohabitation without clear evidence of performance of ceremonies as envisaged in section 7 of the HMA 1955 and the marriage not having been registered. This is a situation which needs to be remedied by a larger bench of the Supreme Court of India. As far as foreign court child custody orders are concerned, they cannot be mechanically enforced in the Indian courts. The courts would come to an independent judgment, the prime consideration being the welfare of the minor children. The law of adoption also needs to be overhauled, to permit formal adoption by non-Hindus and foreigners rather than limiting them to mere custody orders.

REPUBLIC OF IRELAND

FAMILY LAW IN IRELAND: FAMILY LAW ISSUES IN THE SUPERIOR COURTS

Paul Ward[*]

I INTRODUCTION

This year again the developments in Irish family law have been varied and diverse, to the extent that there is no single major development warranting separate and exclusive treatment. The developments that have taken place are, however, quite interesting and important.

II CHILD CARE

For the 1997 edition of this publication, I wrote on the topic of 'Children: Detention and Abortion'[1] and I was last obliged again to air[2] the plight of severely disturbed children and, more so, the State's failure to vindicate and protect the rights of these children.

It is necessary to inform the readership that the status quo of State inactivity remains. Indeed, the whole system of providing State care for disturbed children is in utter disrepute. This position is evidenced by the latest cases decided by Kelly J and the extreme to which he has been prepared to go to ensure that the rights of these children are vindicated.

In *T.D. v the Minister for Education and others*,[3] Kelly J had to consider whether he should grant an injunction to each of the nine plaintiffs to compel the Minister to implement his plans for the provision of high support units within the time scale outlined by the Minister. The Minister, in an unexpected move, formally resisted the application. The Minister claimed that the plaintiff, T.D., had no *locus standi* in that, by the time a place became available for him, he would reach the age of majority and the State would have no obligation towards him. It was further argued on behalf of the Minister that an injunctive order would not be sufficiently specific to enable the Minister to comply with it and that this was a reason for not granting the relief sought. Finally, it was argued that an order of this nature could not be made as it trespassed upon the role of the executive in determining policy. Kelly J was taken aback by this response and by the

---

[*] College Lecturer in Family Law and Tort, University College, Dublin.

[1] *The International Survey of Family Law 1997*, ed A Bainham (Martinus Nijhoff Publishers, 1999) at 355–377.

[2] Ward, 'Judicial and Legislative Family Law Developments', in *The International Survey of Family Law (2000 Edition)*, ed A Bainham (Family Law, 2000) at 207.

[3] [2000] 2 ILRM 321.

Ministerial attitude. He considered the arguments in turn and concluded that he had the necessary jurisdiction to grant injunctive relief.

In relation to the *locus standi* argument, Kelly J was satisfied that there was ample evidence before the court that the various plaintiffs would be adversely affected by the Minister's inaction.[4] In relation to the lack of specificity of the order, Kelly J simply stated that he was merely compelling the Minister to abide by his own sworn evidence to the Court that the high support units would available within the time frame stated.[5] In relation to trespassing upon the executive's role, Kelly J referred to the Supreme Court decision in *D.G. v The Eastern Health Board*[6] where Hamilton CJ stated that:

> 'If the courts are under an obligation to defend and vindicate the personal rights of the citizen, it inevitably follows that the courts have the jurisdiction to do all things necessary to vindicate such rights.'[7]

Kelly J rejected the view that he was, in any event, making policy. He stated that he was merely ensuring that the policy framed by the Minister would be implemented. He accepted that if he was called upon to make policy in this regard, that he had the necessary jurisdiction to grant the relief sought in such exceptional and absolutely necessary circumstances to vindicate the rights of the citizen which the courts were constitutionally obliged to do.[8]

Kelly J then considered whether it was appropriate to grant the relief sought. In this regard there was considerable culpable delay on the Minister's behalf that amounted to a 'scandalous situation'.[9] The reasons for the delay are laughable. In relation to one of the premises, a former army barracks was to be transferred to the relevant health board. There was an interdepartmental dispute as to how much would be paid. Further, the Department of Defence, for fiscal reasons, wanted the transfer to take place in 2000 rather than 1999 and, in the meantime, no planning application was made for the conversion of the barracks, nor was an architect's report requisitioned. The effect of this conduct would be to delay the opening of the unit by some 18 months to 2002 when the Minister's officials had stated in evidence that the project would be completed by mid-2000. Kelly J concluded that the courts had declared such children entitled to high support unit care[10] and that to be effective in caring for such children such facilities had to be expeditiously provided. Any failure to provide such facilities, or a delay in providing for such, would have a profound effect on these children. In light of the inactivity, Kelly J felt that he had no alternative but to injunct the Minister, particularly as he had expressly declined to give an undertaking to the court to comply with his own schedule for the provision of these places. Had such an undertaking been given, Kelly J indicated that he would have adopted a flexible approach in the event that

---

4   Ibid, at 335–339 citing the expert witness evidence of the divisional inspector at the Minister's department.

5   Ibid, at 334.

6   [1997] 3 IR 511.

7   Ibid, at 522.

8   [2000] ILRM 321 at 341.

9   Ibid, at 333.

10   *F.N. v Minister for Education* [1995] 1 IR 409.

unforeseen obstacles arose in delaying the completion of these projects.[11] Kelly J was also influenced by the effectiveness of the order made in *D.B. v Minister for Justice*[12] which resulted in adherence to the schedule to provide high support units.

The *D.B., D.G. and T.D.* cases primarily concern the State's failure to assist a child where assistance will be of benefit to the child's welfare. The legal proceedings are long and complex and commence with a declaration by the High Court that the child in question be civilly detained to safeguard his welfare. As explained in the 1997 edition,[13] the primary legislation, the Child Care Act 1991, contains no provision to authorise the courts civilly to detain children in need of secure placement.[14] This mechanism is used only in rare circumstances and the detention can only be ordered for a limited period until appropriate accommodation for the child's needs is provided. It is the failure to provide appropriate alternative accommodation that results in government ministers being injuncted. The most recent case highlights the grave difficulties facing child care professionals in dealing with such children even with the backing of a High Court order.

D.H. v Ireland and others[15] was described by Kelly J as the 'most difficult' of these types of case that has come before him. Indeed, the facts are tragic, to say the least. *D.H.* is a 16-year-old girl and was born to a 15-year-old mother. She has no relationship with either her father or mother and her half-siblings are all in care. She was fostered until the age of ten during which time she was physically abused by her foster mother and thereafter placed in various residential placements. She was sexually abused at the age of seven and raped at the age of eleven. She abuses alcohol, lighter fuel and ecstasy which she funds from prostitution. She miscarried a pregnancy, self-mutilated herself and attempted suicide by setting fire to herself. In 1996 it was medically recommended that she be provided with a secure place. That never materialised.

The application before Mr Justice Kelly was whether *D.H.* should be committed to the Central Mental Hospital (the CMH).[16] It was accepted without question that *D.H.* required secure placement. Kelly J refused to make an order detaining *D.H.* in the CMH. This was mainly on the medical evidence given to the Court which objected to such detention on medical, ethical and moral grounds. The order would have been unprecedented, as *D.H.* was not suffering from a psychiatric illness. The CMH was full and, if she had been detained there, she would have deprived nine prisoners on a waiting list of a place and treatment. Further, *D.H.* would have to share accommodation with mentally ill patient prisoners who were guilty of gruesome murders and arson. She would be locked up for 12 hours a day and with no proper sanitation facilities. Further and most importantly, there would be no access to child or adolescence services. Kelly J

---

11 [2000] ILRM 321 at 333.

12 [1999] 1 IR 29.

13 Ward, 'Children: Detention and Abortion', in *The International Survey of Family Law 1997*, ed A Bainham (Martinus Nijhoff Publishers, 1999) at 355–377.

14 This deficiency in the Child Care Act 1991 is to be remedied when the Children Bill 1999 is brought into force. When this will happen remains to be seen.

15 Unreported, High Court, 23 May 2000, Kelly J.

16 The CMH is a secure psychiatric hospital for the criminally insane.

was reluctant to make.an order that would force the doctors to act against their clinical judgment and ethics to the extent that they ran the risk of being in contempt of court. In this regard, Kelly J was guided by Balcombe LJ in *Re J (A Minor (Medical Treatment)*.[17]

The alternative approach was to order the detention of *D.H.* in a psychiatric hospital along with 29 mentally ill patients. She would be subjected to 24-hour indoor detention under the supervision of a nurse and childcare worker. Owing to her violent behaviour, it would require up to eight nurses to restrain her so that a sedative could be administered to her. This, Kelly J noted, was the regime that the Minister urged upon the court as the appropriate course of action and was something that the Minister should 'not merely be embarrassed but ashamed' to ask the court to do.[18] Kelly J refused to make a mandatory order in these terms, but did make a permissive order enabling the health board to detain *D.H.* at any facility that the doctors approve and to allow the doctors to treat her as they consider appropriate. He injuncted the health board and the Minister, the former to carry out the necessary refurbishment of premises to accommodate *D.H.* by 23 August 2000. The latter was ordered to provide all necessary funding and support to enable the former to comply with the order.

T.D. and *D.H.* are merely the tip of the iceberg. The newspapers are littered with the review of cases concerning such children.[19] The matter has reached crisis point and such a situation demands an appropriate judicial response. On 19 October 2000, Kelly J injuncted three Ministers to provide immediately a secure place for a 17-year-old girl. The Ministers for Health, Justice and Education were threatened with contempt of court and would be subject to a fine, imprisonment or sequestration of departmental assets.[20] The Ministers attempted to have the order varied to make Ireland responsible for failure to abide by the injunction. This application was refused and Kelly J reiterated his threat to hold the Ministers in contempt.

Over the weekend, the situation had dramatically changed whereby a place had been found for the girl in question. In those circumstances, the order of 19 October was varied. The course of action adopted by Kelly J only highlights the extremely difficult problems facing the courts in their attempt to safeguard the

---

17   [1992] 2 FLR 165 at 175 he stated: 'I find it difficult to conceive of a situation where it would be a proper exercise of the jurisdiction to make an Order positively requiring a doctor to adopt a particular course of treatment in relation to a child unless the doctor himself or herself was asking the Court to make such an Order. Usually all the Court is asked to do is to authorise a particular course of treatment where the person or body whose consent is requisite is unable or unwilling to do so'.

18   Unreported, High Court, 23 May 2000, Kelly J at 16.

19   See *Irish Times*, 26 and 27 April 1999 where the detention was ordered of a 17-year-old boy in a child penal institution for a detoxification programme. It was submitted that the boy would die if released. *Irish Times*, 11 May 1999 where Kelly J considered sending a 15-year-old boy to the CMH when a penal institution for young offenders refused to accept him. *Irish Times* 12 October 2000 contained three reports on disturbed children. Two 15-year-old girls escaped from secure detention at the CMH and the other from a psychiatric hospital, who appears to be *D.H.* Warrants were issued for their arrest, detention and return to the respective units. Kelly J in a separate matter ordered the inquiry into the escape of a child who had been ordered to be detained. The child escaped on 31 July 2000 and was found dead on 24 August 2000. The third report concerned the detention of a 13-year-old boy at a Garda (police) station, as there was no place available for him in any institution, penal, mental or otherwise.

20   *Irish Times*, 20 October 2000.

welfare of such children. It is quite extraordinary that the only way of protecting and vindicating the rights of these children is to imprison, or at least to threaten to imprison, a government minister.

By contrast, the case of *Herron v Ireland*[21] demonstrates how the legal system can prove to be inflexible in deserving and urgent cases. *Herron* concerned judicial review proceedings dating from October 1993 where an order for mandamus was sought to compel Ireland to provide a secure residential placement in which the plaintiff's son, then aged 12, could receive psychological assessment, diagnosis and treatment. That application was granted by the High Court and, on appeal to the Supreme Court, a conditional order was made.[22] The condition related to the fact that the child was not in the jurisdiction at the time of the making of the Supreme Court order. The child had been taken to England and was the subject of Hague Convention proceedings for his return to Ireland.[23] The Supreme Court ordered that in the event that the English court ordered the return of the child to Ireland, then the child was to be brought before the High Court, where issues relating to his accommodation and welfare would be decided by that court. The English courts refused to return the child.[24]

In November 1998, the child had returned to Ireland and had presented himself to a local Garda Station. The child was now 18 years of age. The issue for the court was whether the conditional Supreme Court order was effective to detain the child so that he could receive treatment for his psychopathic characteristics and more particularly his sexual dysfunction of paedophile activity.[25] The child was an obvious danger to himself and to others and a mandatory order in the terms of the original judicial review proceedings would at least appear to have been essential. The High Court re-entered the proceedings and granted the relief sought.[26]

On appeal, the Supreme Court, however, held that the original Supreme Court order was ineffective as the condition precedent set therein had not been complied with, namely that the child be returned to this jurisdiction by order of the English court. Further, the Court held that the relief sought could not have been granted. The relief the plaintiff was seeking was by way of judicial review. The jurisdiction to grant that relief was primarily dependent upon the plaintiff's child being under the age of majority.[27] As he had now reached the age of majority, no order could be made civilly to detain him, even where to do so would be in his best interests. The High Court and the Supreme Court accepted that a court has jurisdiction under the Guardianship of Infants Act 1964 (the 1964 Act) to give any directions relating to the welfare of a child.[28] Such jurisdiction could be exercised in relation to a child who has exceeded the age of 18 where the child suffers from a mental or physical disability to the extent that it is not reasonably possible for the child to

---

21   Unreported, Supreme Court, 3 December 1999, Hamilton CJ (Nem. Diss.).

22   6 December 1993.

23   The child was abducted by his father on 19 October 1993.

24   *Re M (A Minor) (Abduction)* [1994] 2 FLR 127.

25   As averred to by the child's mother in her affidavit grounding the application for judicial review and cited by Hamilton CJ in his unreported judgment, 3 December 1999 at 18.

26   Unreported, High Court, 22 February 1999, Quirke J.

27   Unreported, Supreme Court, 3 December 1999, Hamilton CJ at 21.

28   Section 11 of the Guardianship of Infants Act 1964.

maintain himself.[29] Thus the relief sought by the plaintiff could be granted by a court, but the application would have to brought under the 1964 Act. In the present case, the plaintiff's claim for relief was brought by way of judicial review proceedings and not under the 1964 Act, and therefore the relief sought could not be granted.[30]

Herron is an important decision. It indicates a deficiency in child care law for individuals in the plaintiff's position. The orders that a court can make under the Child Care Act 1991 (the 1991 Act) relate only to persons under the age of 18 years. There is no disability provision whereby persons over the age of 18 who suffer from a mental or physical disability can be the subject of such orders. The State is not obliged to provide care facilities to children over the age of 18. The 1964 Act is primarily intended to provide the court with jurisdiction to resolve custody and access disputes between parents or guardians. Section 11 of the 1964 Act is sufficiently broad to allow the court to give directions concerning a child's welfare (whether such directions are enforceable against the State is not clear), but this may be the only practical option to safeguard the welfare of such individuals. The alternative would be to institute proceeding against the State seeking a declaration that they are entitled to the same status and rights, both legal and constitutional, as a child owing to their mental or physical disability. In that way they would be entitled to the care that has been ordered in *T.D.* and *D.H.*, which cases indicate clearly that the State's obligation to such individuals ceases when they reach the age of majority. Parents such as *Herron* can only resort to the Mental Health Act 1945 where an application for a reception order under section 162 may be sought to detain a person over the age of 18 in a psychiatric hospital.

This situation requires the balancing of potentially conflicting rights and begs answers to a number of difficult issues. Children and adults have the right to have their welfare safeguarded. Should this right cease on a child's eighteenth birthday in deference to a myriad of personal constitutional rights, and particularly the right to autonomy and self-determination, with the potential detriment to one's physical and mental welfare? Should ultimately, the State's obligation to its citizens terminate when children become adults at law? If this is to be position, then all necessary measures must be taken[31] while disadvantaged children remain minors, so that when the age of majority is reached such individuals are capable of leading a normal and purposeful life.

---

29   Section 6(b) of the Age of Majority Act 1985. The age extension period in the case of disability only relates to a parent's obligation to provide financial support for such children. See section 3(1)(b)(ii) of the Family Law (Maintenance of Spouses and Children) Act 1976, section 2(1)(b)(ii) of the Family Law Act 1995 and of the Family Law (Divorce) Act 1996.

30   Unreported, Supreme Court, 3 December 1999, Hamilton CJ at 21. The Court noted that the plaintiff's child was being treated in a psychiatric hospital that averted, in practical terms, the urgency of the matter.

31   See *The Eastern Health Board v McDonnell and C.K. (Notice Party), N.W. (Notice Party) and C.K. (A Minor)*, unreported, High Court, 5 March, McCracken J, which held that even where a care order is made in favour of a health board in relation to a child (which confers a status on the health board similar to that of a parent) the District Court retains a role in determining issues concerning a child's welfare whereby the court can make and enforce directions against a health board.

III RECOGNITION OF FOREIGN DIVORCES

The decision in *G.McG. v D.W. and A.R. (Notice Party)*[32] remains despite two further decisions in relation to this case.[33] McGuinness J adopted residency in the jurisdiction granting a divorce as a ground to recognise such a divorce as valid and effective in this jurisdiction. This ground is in addition to the domicile requirement provided for in the Domicile and Recognition of Foreign Divorces Act 1986 and the Supreme Court decision in *W. v W.*[34] In *G.McG. v D.W. (No 2)*[35] McGuinness J refused an application by the Attorney General to be joined as a notice party for the purpose of acting as a legitimus contradictor on the issues before the court in the original case. The issues in *G.McG. v D.W. (No 2)* are largely of a procedural nature and specifically whether the court had jurisdiction to re-open and vary a final decision made by the court. McGuinness J applied the Supreme Court decision in *Attorney General (SPUC) v Open Door Counselling Ltd (No 2)*[36] and was of the view that to do so would amount to a '... manifest and striking injustice to the parties to reopen a decision of such practical importance to their ordinary lives and in reliance upon which they have already acted'.[37]

That decision was appealed to the Supreme Court which unanimously upheld the High Court in dismissing the Attorney General's appeal.[38] A number of arguments were forwarded as to why the Attorney General should either be joined in the proceedings or that the court should alter the order made. The Supreme Court analysed section 29 of the Family Law Act 1995 (the 1995 Act). This section provides that a court may make a declaration as to the recognition of a foreign divorce, annulment or legal separation.[39] Notice of such proceedings may be given to the Attorney General[40] by application of either party or by the court of its own motion. Further, where the Attorney General applies to be joined as a party to the proceedings, the court must make an order joining the Attorney General.[41] It was argued, notwithstanding this statutory position, that the court has inherent jurisdiction to join the Attorney General. Denham J held that as the proceedings had resulted in a final decision of the court, there was no basis for the making of an order to join the Attorney General. In other words, there were no proceedings in being to which the Attorney General could be joined.[42] Murray J analysed the argument further and came to the view that the exercise of an inherent jurisdiction, in the fashion advocated by the Attorney General, could only

---

32   *G. McG. v D.W. (No 1)* [2000] ILRM 107.

33   Ward, 'Judicial and Legislative Family Law Developments', *The International Survey of Family Law (2000 Edition)*, ed A Bainham (Family Law, 2000) at 189–207.

34   [1993] 2 IR 467.

35   [2000] 1 ILRM 121.

36   [1994] 2 IR 333. At 340 Finlay CJ stated '... the court has not got, as a court of ultimate appeal, any such jurisdiction and that it must be obliged, as a matter of fundamental principle, to refuse to alter the order it previously made'.

37   [2000] 1 ILRM 121 at 136.

38   [2000] 2 ILRM 451.

39   Section 29(1)(d) and (e).

40   Section 29(4).

41   Section 29(5).

42   [2000] ILRM 451 at 464.

arise where there was no express statutory provision to join the Attorney General. Here there was express provision governing the circumstances in which the Attorney General could be joined and thus the court's jurisdiction in the matter was delineated to the exclusion of an inherent jurisdiction.[43] Murphy J also rejected the argument that there was a mandatory obligation to join the Attorney General. The 1995 Act provided the court with discretion to notify the Attorney General of proceedings and an obligation to join him or her once an application was made. Those were the stated circumstances in which the Attorney General could be joined in the proceedings and from them an obligation to join the Attorney General could not be inferred.[44] The Court did acknowledge that there may be circumstances of State and public interest that would make the joining of the Attorney General essential, of which the present case is a clear example. But even if that argument was presented to the court to justify joining the Attorney General, it would fail. The simple fact of the matter was that the proceedings were no longer in being and there were no proceedings to which the Attorney General could be joined.[45]

The Attorney General attempted to argue that the High Court decision was not final and thus he could be joined as a party. He argued that the order made was not binding on the State[46] and as there was no legitimus contradictor, the order of the High Court was not final. Further, he submitted that the court had an inherent jurisdiction to amend the order it had made in the proceedings. Murphy J noted that the 1995 Act authorised the court to make the declarations sought with or without the participation of the Attorney General and that such declarations were binding on the parties. As the Attorney General had not applied to be joined in the proceedings, that failure did not prevent the court making the declaration in accordance with the statutory provisions. Further, no issue remained outstanding between the parties to the proceedings and, in those circumstances, the order was final.[47]

The court also refused to alter the order made. There was no basis for this application, as such an alteration would only be made where it was necessary to correct an error so as to give true and final effect to the original order.[48]

Whilst the Attorney General failed to be joined in *G.McG. v D.W.*, he has been joined in another case, *M.E.C. v J.A.C.* and *J.D.C. v J.A.C.*[49] *M.E.C.* is the first wife of the respondent, from whom she was divorced in May 1980 in England. *J.D.C.* is the current wife of the respondent against whom he instituted judicial separation proceedings. *M.E.C.* instituted proceedings, seeking a declaration that the divorce granted by the English court in 1980 was not capable of recognition, in addition to seeking a number of financial ancillary reliefs under

---

43 Ibid, at 476.

44 Ibid, at 470.

45 Ibid, at 477 per Murray J.

46 Section 29(8) of the Family Law Act 1995 provides that a declaration made under the section binds the parties to the proceedings and the State where the Attorney General has been joined.

47 [2000] 2 ILRM 451 at 478 per Murray J.

48 Ibid, at 464 per Denham J and at 479 per Murray J citing *Belville Holdings Ltd v Revenue Commissioners* [1994] 1 ILRM 29 and *Attorney General (SPUC) v Open Door Counselling Ltd (No 2)*, [1994] 2 IR 333 relied upon by McGuinness J in the High Court.

49 Unreported, High Court, May 2000, Kinlen J (unapproved version).

the 1995 Act. Kinlen J held that the parties to the first marriage were resident but not domiciled in England at the date of the application for the divorce. The matter is currently awaiting a date for the hearing of the parties' submissions on whether the decision in *G.McG. v D.W. and A.R.*[50] is valid. Whatever decision the High Court reaches is certain to be appealed to the Supreme Court for a definitive view on this issue.

IV CHILD ABDUCTION

There have been a number of important decisions handed down by the Supreme Court on the interpretation of the Hague Convention on the Civil Aspects of International Child Abduction (the Convention), some of which are novel issues to be decided in this jurisdiction.

H.I. v M.G.[51] is of considerable importance to unmarried fathers. The Supreme Court, by a four to one majority,[52] held that where the law of a State does not confer legal rights of custody upon a parent, then such a parent is not exercising rights of custody which the Convention protects. The facts are unusual. The defendant mother is an Irish citizen who met the plaintiff father in New York. The plaintiff is of Egyptian extraction and the parties went through a Moslem marriage ceremony in March 1991. A son was born to the couple in July 1991. The Court accepted that the marriage ceremony was invalid according to New York law. The defendant acknowledged that the plaintiff was the father of her child and the child's birth certificate recorded this fact. The couple resided together with their son as a family from early 1990 until the defendant left the plaintiff in December 1996. In December 1996 she obtained a protection order against the plaintiff and temporary sole custody of the child. In January 1997, the plaintiff applied for a visitation, filiation and paternity acknowledgement order but before the court heard the application the defendant left New York on 3 February 1997. The defendant was an illegal alien in New York and would face deportation if detected. Further, it would be impossible for her to obtain legal status by her son applying on her behalf, as such an application could not be made by the son until he reached 21 years of age.

The issue for the court was whether the plaintiff was exercising rights of custody at the time of the removal of the child in February 1997. Of the three specified rights of custody adverted to in Article 3, the plaintiff had no rights of custody arising by operation of New York law. As an unmarried father, the only way in which such rights could arise would be by order of the court granting the father visitation or filiation rights, which were dependent upon proof of paternity. While the couple had resided together as a family, there was no agreement between them conferring enforceable rights of custody upon the plaintiff. While both parties had made applications to the New York courts, no order had been made by a court which either conferred upon the plaintiff rights of custody or precluded the defendant from removing the child from the jurisdiction of the New

---

50 [2000] 1 ILRM 81.

51 [1999] 2 ILRM 1.

52 Barron J, dissenting.

York courts.[53] Further, the removal of the child from New York was not in breach of rights of custody vested in a court. Keane J expressly refused to acknowledge that the Convention was intended to protect 'an undefined hinterland of inchoate rights of custody'.[54] He declined to follow the English Court of Appeal's decision in *Re B (A Minor) (Abduction)*.[55]

Barron J dissented. He argued for a flexible and practical interpretation of the Convention and adopted the views of Waite LJ in *Re B (A Minor) (Abduction)*[56] which was applied in *Re O (Child Abduction: Custody Rights)*.[57] Barron J emphasised the need to assess the nature of the rights as actually exercised by the parent in a practical day to day manner rather than in a formalistic legal fashion.[58] The issue was whether the duties and privileges enjoyed by the parent were of such a nature that a court would uphold their existence.[59] In this regard it was not necessary for a parent to establish a legal agreement, as this would rarely occur in reality. On the facts of this case, Barron J was satisfied that the rights exercised by the father, which were akin to those in a *de facto* family, would be recognised by a New York court. He drew a distinction between the existence of such rights, which were clearly evident in this case, and the enforcement of such rights which required the plaintiff to prove paternity, a matter that was not in dispute. The absence of proof of paternity did not nullify the practical reality that the father was exercising rights of custody at the time of the removal of the child by the defendant.[60] He further noted that the interference with the plaintiff's rights occurred not at the time of the removal of the child from New York to Ireland but rather when the defendant left the home the parties had established together.[61] Barron J noted that the primary function of the Convention was to safeguard children from the harmful affects of abduction. The Convention was child and not parent orientated in terms of rights. In this regard, the rights of the parent to custody should be viewed from the child's perspective in a qualitative and practical fashion. The Convention was intended to prevent occurring precisely what had occurred in this case.[62] The proper working of the Convention centres around universal application of its principles. In this regard, divergence amongst common law jurisdictions on the interpretation of such fundamental aspects of the Convention such as 'rights of custody' is unhelpful in the overall scheme of the Convention.

The case highlights the difficulties that unmarried fathers face in child abduction proceedings. It is essential that they either obtain court orders conferring upon them rights of custody or reach agreement with the mother of the child that they possess such rights. The need for custody as opposed to access

---

53   [1999] 2 ILRM 1 at 33–34.
54   Ibid, at 40.
55   [1994] 2 FLR 249.
56   [1994] 2 FLR 249.
57   [1997] 2 FLR 702, which held that a maternal grandmother was exercising joint rights of custody with the mother.
58   [1999] 2 ILRM 1 at 46.
59   Ibid.
60   [1999] 2 ILRM 1 at 48.
61   Ibid, at 51.
62   Ibid, at 52.

rights is important as the power to order a return under the Convention may only be invoked where the removal is in breach of custody rights as opposed to access rights. In this regard, Keane J speculated that where a court has made an order for access in favour of a parent, it may be construed by implication that child cannot be removed without the consent of the parent in whose favour the order has been made or until further order of the court. As that scenario had not arisen in the present case, he made no finding on the issue. Keane J did, however, note, that were such a scenario to arise, the appropriate mechanism for resolving the issue would not be by recourse to Article 3 but Article 21 which was the appropriate channel through which to resolve a violation of a parent's right to access.

This very issue arose in *W.P.P. v S.R.W.*[63] The defendant mother obtained an uncontested divorce from the plaintiff father in December 1994. The order of the court conferred sole custody upon the mother with the father having visitation rights every second weekend. There was also provision that the parties agree to discuss any out of State trips. The father was ordered to pay child support but defaulted, resulting in some $46,000 outstanding by March 1998. The plaintiff filed for bankruptcy in 1995 and on a number of occasions the defendant informed the plaintiff of her financial difficulties and of the necessity of returning to Ireland. On 3 September 1999, the plaintiff had access to the children and two days later the defendant removed the children to Ireland.

The issue for the Court was whether the plaintiff father was exercising rights of custody or access at the time of the removal. The Chief Justice was satisfied that the father was exercising rights of access. It was then necessary to examine whether California State law, by implication, prohibited the removal of the children without the prior consent of the father or order of the court. The affidavits of laws were inconclusive on this point. In relation to the provision to discuss out of State trips, Keane CJ was satisfied that the defendant had informed the plaintiff of her intention to return to Ireland on a number of occasions. With such information and his failure to seek an order restraining the removal of the children, Keane CJ was dubious as to whether the defendant was in breach of the divorce order.[64] Even if the plaintiff's right to access prevented the removal of the children without his or the court's consent, it had to be determined whether the plaintiff had invoked the correct procedure under the Convention. Keane CJ referred to the Canadian Supreme Court decision in *Thompson v Thompson.*[65] This identified the differing remedies under the Convention for a breach of custody rights which could result in a mandatory return, as opposed to a breach of access rights which does not amount to a breach of custody rights authorising mandatory return and for which Article 21 provides a mechanism for enforcement of access rights.[66]

The need for both the existence and exercise of rights of custody is best exemplified by another Supreme Court decision in *M.S.H. v L.H.*[67] The parties were a married couple when the defendant mother removed the two children from

---

63 Unreported, Supreme Court, 14 April 2000, Keane CJ (Nem. Diss.).

64 Ibid, at 15.

65 (1994) 3 SCR 551.

66 Unreported, Supreme Court, 14 April 2000, Keane CJ at 20.

67 Unreported, Supreme Court, 31 July 2000, McGuinness J.

England to Ireland in November 1999. At the time of the removal, the plaintiff father was serving a four-and-a-half-year prison sentence for dealing in heroin. Between September 1997 and December 1998, the defendant brought the two children to visit the plaintiff in prison once a week. Thereafter the paternal grandparents brought the children twice a month until their removal. The defendant mother unsuccessfully argued that the plaintiff was not exercising rights of custody but merely access rights at the time of the removal. McGuinness J held that the plaintiff possessed rights of custody[68] and those rights could not be nullified by his imprisonment.[69] There were many circumstances where a parent would have a low level of imput into the day-to-day physical care of a child. Such a fact alone could not deprive a parent of a legally established right nor could a court hold that a term of imprisonment could divest a parent of the right to custody.[70]

The Court also held that there was insufficient evidence to establish the 'grave risk' defence in Article 13(b).[71] McGuinness J noted that the decision to return children was discretionary[72] and indicated two particular facts of significance in this regard. Firstly, the defendant had removed the children in full knowledge of a court order precluding such and that the defendant had made an application, which she did not pursue, seeking leave to remove the children. Secondly, a hearing to determine the children's welfare had been listed in England for 24 July 2000, which was the appropriate venue for resolving in a timely fashion the immediate and long term welfare issues of the children.

T.M.M. v M.D.[73] provides an interesting example of how a trial judge can assess whether a grave risk exposes a child to physical or psychological harm or otherwise places the child in an intolerable situation. Here, the mother of the plaintiff mother removed the children from England to Ireland in October 1997, fearing that the plaintiff was incapable of caring for the children owing to her alcohol abuse. First, the Supreme Court accepted as valid the reading of social welfare reports by the trial judge. These reports, which had been prepared by a social worker employed by the local social services agency, indicated that the plaintiff mother had been in a physically abusive marital relationship and was currently in a similarly abusive relationship with her partner. Further, the reports revealed that the plaintiff had a ten-year history of alcohol abuse with which she was grappling at the time of these proceedings. It was accepted that these reports amounted to hearsay evidence but that under Article 13, the court could, although not obliged to, take such reports into consideration.[74] The evidence provided by these reports was substantiated by the plaintiff's conduct in court, which was a

---

68 Children Act 1989 confers upon a married parent the concept of 'parental responsibility' which is defined in section 3(1) of the 1989 Act as 'all the rights and duties, powers, responsibilities and authority which, by law, a parent of a child has in relation to a child and his property'.

69 Unreported, Supreme Court, 31 July 2000, McGuinness J, at 16.

70 Ibid, at 17.

71 Ibid, at 21.

72 Article 23.

73 Unreported, Supreme Court, 8 December 1999, Denham J.

74 Ibid, at 11. The relevant paragraph of Article 13 provides: 'In considering the circumstances referred to in this Article, the judicial and administrative authorities shall take into account the information relating to the social background of the child provided by the Central Authority or other competent authority of the child's habitual residence.'

matter that the trial judge was also entitled to consider,[75] and also the views expressed by the eldest child.[76]

The views expressed by the eldest child, aged 12, were also considered by the trial judge and were found to be a separate basis for refusing to return the children under Article 13.[77] In endorsing the approach adopted by the trial judge in conducting the interview, Denham J stressed the need for caution in the exercise of the discretion to interview children in abduction proceedings.[78] Here the approach of Balcombe LJ in *S. v S. (Child Abduction) (Child's Views)*[79] was approved. In this regard it was not first necessary for the parents to give their evidence in advance of the child's wishes being ascertained. The fact that the child's objection to being returned stemmed from a desire to remain with the abducting parent was of particular relevance. No minimum age limit should be set below which a child's views should not be ascertained and the exercise of the discretion to interview should revolve around the requirements the child objecting and whether the child is of a sufficient age and maturity at which it is appropriate to consider those views.

Denham J noted that a child who objects to the return is entitled to express those views and have them taken into consideration[80] but cautioned that the decision not to return should be that of the court and not that of the child.[81]

V   NULLITY OF MARRIAGE

The law of nullity in Ireland continues to provide a rich source of case law. This is no wonder as there is no provision for the granting of ancillary relief on the grant of a decree of nullity. There is thus a great financial incentive for the financially stronger spouse to attempt to obtain a decree of nullity on one of the numerous grounds recognised in Irish law.[82] It should be stated that the judiciary has never accepted this as a motive by a petitioner in seeking a decree of nullity but, nonetheless, the factual reality remains. A number of recent decisions are of interest in demonstrating how far the boundaries of the law nullity may be stretched.

For the 1996 edition of this Survey[83] I analysed the Supreme Court decision in *M.O'M. (orse O'C.) v B.O'C.*[84] (*M.O'M.*). Here the Supreme Court unanimously held that a failure by the respondent to disclose the fact that he had attended a psychiatrist during his laicisation amounted to preventing the petitioner from

---

75   Ibid, at 10.
76   Ibid, at 15.
77   Ibid.
78   Ibid, at 13.
79   [1992] 2 FLR 492 at 500–501.
80   Unreported, Supreme Court, 8 December 1999, at 15.
81   Ibid.
82   See Ward, 'Defective Knowledge: A New Ground for Nullity?', in *The International Survey of Family Law 1996*, ed A Bainham (Martinus Nijhoff Publishers, 1998) at 215–235.
83   Ibid.
84   [1996] 1 IR 208.

giving a full, free and informed consent. Similarly in *B.J.M. v C.M.*[85] (*B.J.M.*) the respondent's failure to disclose to the petitioner that she had a severely disfigured torso prior to their marriage prevented the petitioning husband from giving a full, free and informed consent to the marriage. In this author's opinion, these decisions amounted to a development of the existing law which was without foundation.

Recently the High Court has been asked to apply the Supreme Court decision in analogous circumstances. *P.F. v G.O'M. (orse G.F.)*[86] declined to apply *M.O'M.* The issue was a simple one. The petitioner claimed that he was unaware that the respondent had been conducting an affair with her employer prior to and during the marriage. In those circumstances he stated that had he known such to be the case, he would not have married the respondent. O'Higgins J rejected the respondent's denial of the affair and was satisfied that such had taken place.[87] He distinguished *B.J.M.* as concerning a case of physical disfigurement. *M.O'M.*, O'Higgins J held, could not have been intended to apply to anything but a disclosure relating to one's psychiatric condition.[88] A strict application of *M.O'M.* justifies this result. However, *M.O'M.* provided a broad test in relation to the issue of 'adequate knowledge'. Blayney J in *M.O'M.* clearly stated[89] that the test is a subjective one. Where the petitioner states that subsequent knowledge of a fact undisclosed at the time of the marriage ceremony would have resulted in the petitioner not consenting to the marriage, then no valid consent has been given, rendering the marriage void.

P.F. v G.O'M. (orse G.F.)[90] is an important decision. If this approach to the *M.O'M.* decision is followed, it will marginalise the potential of the Supreme Court decision as a precedent to be applied in analogous situations.

D.McC. v E.C.[91] (*D.McC.*) is another nullity decision of interest. The petitioner had been subjected to a sexually abusive childhood by his father and had witnessed his mother being physically abused by his father. He was an alcoholic at the time he met the respondent, who was also a recovering alcoholic. His petition was based upon the accepted ground of inability to enter into and sustain a normal marital relationship[92] owing to his 'extreme immaturity'.[93] This stemmed essentially from his childhood abuse and the fact that he had never

---

85   [1996] 2 IR 575.

86   Unreported, High Court, 26 March 1999, O'Higgins J.

87   The evidence of 17 witnesses was given over eight days.

88   Unreported, High Court, 26 March 1999, O'Higgins J, at 14.

89   [1996] 1 IR 208 at 217 he stated 'What has to be determined, accordingly, is whether the consent of the wife was an informed consent, a consent based upon adequate knowledge, and *the test is a subjective one,* that is to say, that the test is whether this spouse, marrying this particular man, could be said to have had adequate knowledge of *every circumstance relevant to the decision she was making,* so that her consent could be truly be said to be an informed one.' (my emphasis).

90   Unreported, High Court, 26 March 1999, O'Higgins J.

91   Unreported, High Court, 6 July 1998, McCracken J.

92   *H.S. v J.S.* [1992] 2 Fam LJ 33 accepted that immaturity arising from a psychiatric or personality disorder could affect the giving of a true consent or the capacity to enter into and sustain a normal marital relationship. Decrees have been granted in: *W. v P.,* unreported, High Court, 7 June 1984, Barrington J; *B. v M.,* unreported, High Court, March 1987, Barrington J; *P.C. v V.C.* [1990] 2 IR 91; *D. v E.,* unreported, High Court, 1 March 1989, Barr J; *G. v M.,* unreported, High Court, 22 November 1990, Lavan J.

93   Unreported, High Court, 6 July 1998, McCracken J at 7.

known or been in a home with a proper marriage relationship. These two factors were compounded by his alcoholism.[94] It is not explicitly stated in the judgment that these factors amounted to a recognised psychiatric illness manifesting itself in the form of extreme immaturity. The court was satisfied that the petitioner was incapable of both entering into and sustaining a normal marital relationship and that this essentially arose from the petitioner's dysfunctional childhood conditioning and upbringing. The court implicitly accepted that the petitioner re-enacted in his marriage that which he had been exposed to by his parents' marriage. Of further significance is the fact that the petitioner was relying upon his own incapacity in which case the general requirement is that the respondent must repudiate the marriage to enable a decree to be granted. In this case the respondent was opposing the grant of a decree. In this regard McCracken J followed O'Hanlon J in *P.C. v V.C.*[95] where the repudiation requirement was said to be not essential if both parties were incapable of entering into and sustaining a normal marital relationship or they did so innocently in that they were unaware of the incapacity. Kinlen J expressed similar views in *O'R. v B.*[96] In *D.McC.*, as the parties had innocently entered into the marriage, McCracken J held that repudiation was not a necessary proof for the grant of a decree. This approach is important as there is a division amongst the high judiciary[97] as to the absolute requirement of repudiation where the petitioner relies upon his or her own incapacity.[98] A Supreme Court decision is necessary to resolve this issue.

Such immaturity cases in nullity petitions are rare. *G.F. v J.B.(orse J.F.)*[99] provides another interesting factual basis for the petitioner's immaturity, which in this case was found to be gross rather than abnormal immaturity amounting to a personality disorder. The effect of the immaturity was twofold, both preventing the petitioner from entering into and sustaining a normal marital relationship and also making him unable to be fully free in his mind or fully informed to consent to the marriage.

The petitioner, according to the medical evidence accepted by the court, had an obsessive personality, he was insecure and suffered from depression and anxiety for which prescribed medication had no effect. A casual relationship with a student resulted in an unplanned pregnancy which was terminated. This severely distressed his mother, with whom he had a particularly close bond, and when the respondent became pregnant shortly after they met, he decided to marry the respondent rather than distress his mother. His decision to marry was made for the purpose of pleasing his parents. The marriage was a disaster and the evidence

---

94 Ibid.

95 [1990] 2 IR 91.

96 [1995] 2 ILRM 57.

97 *R.S.J. v J.S.J.* [1982] 2 ILRM 263 and *D.C. v D.W.* [1987] 7 ILRM 58.

98 The requirement stems from the voidable ground of impotence which requires repudiation by the potent spouse, see *R.(W.) v R.*, unreported, High Court, February 1980 and *E.C. v K.M.*, [1991] 2 IR 192. The ground of inability to enter into and sustain a normal marital relationship was developed in *R.S.J. v J.S.J.* [1982] 2 ILRM 263 and *D. v C.* [1984] 4 ILRM 173 by analogy with the impotence ground and extended it to a situation where the respondent suffered from a psychiatric illness.

99 Unreported, High Court, 28 March 2000, Murphy J.

indicated that the petitioner could only enter and sustain a normal marital relationship with a 'perfect person'.[100]

The medical evidence was highly supportive of establishing the immaturity ground as both the petitioner's psychiatrist and the court appointed psychiatrist concurred in their views on the petitioner's level of immaturity. In this regard, Murphy J acknowledged that the role of the medical inspector in giving evidence to the court was of pivotal effect but the ultimate decision as to whether the ground had been established was a matter for the court.[101]

These cases highlight the importance of the medical evidence in nullity petitions. The extent of the role and functions of the court appointed medical inspector has been explored in *P.McG. v A.F. (orse McG.)*[102] *(P.McG.)*.

P.McG. concerned how extensive the court appointed psychiatrist's examination could be in preparing a report for the court. Order 70 of the Rules of the Superior Courts enables the Master of the High Court to appoint a medical inspector to conduct a physical examination of the parties to a nullity petition and to provide a report to the court. With the development of the voidable ground of inability to enter into and sustain a normal marital relationship based upon psychiatric illness and gross immaturity, a psychiatrist is appointed rather than a gynaecologist or urologist. Appointment of the latter reflected the former state of the law, where impotence was acknowledged as the only voidable ground for a nullity decree. The petitioner wanted the psychiatrist to view the videotape of the wedding ceremony. As the respondent did not object to this, no issue arose.

The petitioner had come into possession of the respondent's personal diary, which the petitioner claimed contained important information relating to the respondent's state of mind at the time of the marriage. The respondent objected to the medical inspector having sight of the diary on the basis that it was illegally and unconstitutionally seized evidence.[103] The court accepted that there appeared to be a brazen and outrageous intrusion into the respondent's most personal and intimate privacy[104] but declined to decide the matter, holding that the diary should not for the present be made available to the medical inspector.[105] The matter should be reserved for a decision in the context of a discovery motion where the arguments for and against the production of the diary could be determined.[106] No view was expressed whether, even in the event that an order for discovery was made, the psychiatrist could have sight of it.

More contentious was the request that five third parties, the petitioner's brother and four other mutual friends of the parties, should be interviewed by the psychiatrist who indicated that such interviews would be of considerable benefit.

---

100 Unreported, High Court, 28 March 2000, Murphy J, at 6–8.

101 Ibid, at 10.

102 Unreported, High Court, 24 January 2000, Budd J.

103 Relying upon: *McGee v Ireland* [1974] IR 274 which established a constitutional right to privacy; *Kennedy v Ireland* [1987] IR 587, which established the constitutional right to private communication without third party interruption and surveillance; *O.C. v T.C.*, unreported, High Court, 9 December 1981 which held that illegally seized material was inadmissible in maintenance proceedings, and *The People (AG) v O'Brien* [1965] IR 142, on the constitutional inviolability of the dwelling.

104 Unreported, High Court, 24 January 2000, Budd J, at 8.

105 Ibid, at 9.

106 Following Waite J in *Hildebrand v Hildebrand* [1992] 1 FLR 244.

While Budd J was sympathetic to the psychiatrist's position, there were a number of reasons why no interview of third parties could be ordered. First, there was no provision in the Rules of Court for the medical examination of persons other than the parties to the proceedings.[107] Secondly, the respondent had agreed to attend the court-appointed psychiatrist on the understanding that only herself and the petitioner would be interviewed by the psychiatrist. She was not expecting that her examination would be based upon information provided to the psychiatrist by third parties which the respondent felt would be partisan as friends and family of the petitioner.[108] Thirdly, there were sound evidential reasons for precluding interviews with third parties. The opinion of the psychiatrist would be based upon the information provided by the third party. If the information of a particular third party was challenged, this would undermine the authenticity and fundamental value of the psychiatrist's opinion as it would be impossible to extrapolate the nature and effect of the information from the psychiatrist's overall opinion. Further, it would obviate the problem for the medical inspector in deciding which third parties to interview and remove the potential for interference with such informants by the parties with the ultimate result that the court remains in control of the inquiry that the court conducts into the validity of the marriage.[109] The court should adhere to the usual and preferred method of viva voce evidence untainted with hearsay.[110] Budd J did acknowledge, however, that interviews with third parties may occur where the parties agreed to such.[111] This is a curious view in the light of his opinion as to why third party interviews should not take place. Indeed, nowhere would it be more appropriate than in such a situation for the appointment of a legitimus contradictor, a matter Budd J expressly called for earlier in his judgment where he stated:[112]

'It is surprising, in a State in which the institution of marriage is noted with approval in the Constitution and where the marital status is accorded respect, that cases, in which a couple went through a marriage ceremony more than twenty years ago and from which liaison there may be a number of children, should now be coming before the court in nullity cases based upon psychological grounds without there being a legitimus contradictor to defend the marital status of the parties which might be thought to affect the entire community.'

---

107 Unreported, High Court, 24 January 2000, Budd J, at 14. Order 70 of the Rules of the Superior Courts provide for the physical examination of the reproductive organs of the parties. Whilst this has been adapted to the appointment of psychiatrists for the psychiatric and psychological examination of the parties to cater for the development in the law, it could not be extended to include an interview with a third party.

108 Ibid, at 15.

109 Ibid, at 19.

110 Ibid, at 21.

111 Ibid, at 22.

112 Ibid, at 18.

ISRAEL

CHILD PROTECTION IN THE ISRAELI SUPREME COURT: TORTIOUS PARENTING, PHYSICAL PUNISHMENT AND CRIMINAL CHILD ABUSE

Rhona Schuz[*]

I INTRODUCTION

In two recent precedent-creating decisions, the Israeli Supreme Court has championed children's rights by holding a parent liable for psychological damage caused to his children by breach of his parental duties;[1] declaring that reasonable parental punishment is no longer a defence to criminal assault and finding that regular use of hitting as a method of discipline constitutes the crime of child abuse. Whilst judicial recognition of children's rights is, of course, welcome and there is little doubt that the cases were decided correctly on their facts, the potentially far-reaching implications of the decisions are controversial. In particular, the cases raise fundamental questions about legal intervention in the family and the scope of judicial lawmaking.

II THE CASES

A *Amin v Amin* (hereinafter '*Amin*')[2]

1 THE FACTS

This is a tragic case in every respect. The plaintiffs, three siblings who were now adults, sued their father for the damage which had been caused to them by his cruelty and emotional abuse when they were children. Their mother had committed suicide when they were very young and shortly afterwards their father had remarried. He and his wife had agreed that the children would not be a part of their lives. Accordingly, the children spent the rest of their childhood either in foster care or in boarding schools and the father did not maintain contact with them or take any interest in them and rejected all efforts by them to have a

---

[*]   Bar-Ilan University, Ramat Gan.

[1]   In the judgment it was claimed that this was a world precedent and a recent article reveals that there have not been any such decisions in the US (see Steven G. Neeley, 'The psychological and emotional abuse of children: suing parents in tort for the infliction of emotional distress' 27 N.Ky.L.Rev 689). The author would be interested to hear from any readers of the *International Survey* who know of a similar decision in their jurisdictions (Schuz@mail.biu.ac.il).

[2]   C.A. 2034/98 *Amin v Amin* (not published).

relationship with him. The effect of this attitude was exacerbated by the love and attention shown to the children of the second marriage.[3]

The expert evidence, which was uncontradicted, showed that the emotional and psychological effect of the father's cruelty was devastating for the children, none of whom were able to lead normal adult lives.

The father's appeal to the Supreme Court from the decision of the District Court ordering him to pay damages to the children was dismissed for the reasons set out below.

2   THE SCOPE OF PARENTS' DUTY

The father did not deny that his behaviour had caused damage to the children, but claimed that there was no legal duty to love his children.

Justice Englard, giving the leading judgment, while agreeing that there can be no legal duty to feel the emotion of love, explains that there can be a legal duty to act in a way which is consistent with love. He brings the Biblical injunction 'and you shall love your neighbour as yourself'[4] as an example of where 'love' refers to external deeds rather than internal feelings.

The legal functions of parents are set out in section 15 of the Legal Competence and Guardianship Law 5752–1962,[5] which provides:

'The guardianship of the parents shall include the duty and the right to take care of the needs of the minor, including his education, studies, vocational and occupational training and work, and to preserve, manage and develop his property; it shall also include the right to the custody of the minor, to determine his place of residence and the authority to act on his behalf.'

The standard at which these duties must be performed is described in section 17 of the Law which provides: 'In the exercise of their guardianship, the parents shall act in the best interests of the minor in such a manner as devoted parents would act in the circumstances'.

Justice Englard held that the word 'education' in section 15 is wider than formal studies or training and includes 'shaping the complete personality of the child as a person by introducing him to values which constitute an end in themselves'. Furthermore, the reference to needs is not restricted to physical needs and includes emotional needs. In this case, the father's complete lack of contact with the children was in breach of the statutory duty[6] to educate both in the wider

---

3   In these circumstances, it is rather surprising that the judges do not comment on why the welfare authorities working with the children did not initiate proceedings to get the children freed for adoption.

4   *Leviticus* Chapter 19, v 18.

5   Laws of the State of Israel XVI, p 106.

6   Under section 63 of the Civil Wrongs Ordinance (New Version) Laws of the State of Israel NV II P.5 breach of a statutory duty gives rise to tortious liability where the duty was intended to be for the benefit or protection of another person and as a result of the failure to perform the duty that other person suffers damage of a kind or nature contemplated by such enactment.

and the narrower sense[7] and also in breach of the duty of care owed to the children by their father.[8]

Whilst recognising that, in principle, breach of a statutory criminal offence could give rise to civil liability, Justice Englard was not convinced that in this case there had been a breach of section 362 of the Penal Law,[9] which obliged parents to to provide the 'essential necessities of life' for their minor children. His inclination was that this referred only to material needs, such as food and clothing. It should be mentioned that it seems likely that the father's behaviour would amount to the crime of emotional child abuse within section 368(c) of the Penal Law, which was enacted in 1989, after the incidents in this case.[10]

3   THE 'SLIPPERY SLOPE ARGUMENT'

The father's argument that imposing such a wide duty on parents would open the floodgates of litigation to claims by disgruntled children[11] was answered by both Justices Englard and Orr.

The former emphasises that parents are only obliged to make an effort to take care of their child's physical and emotional educational needs. There is no duty to succeed. Furthermore, in determining the scope of parental duties, the interests of children have to be balanced with those of parents. Thus, despite the children's rights revolution and the fact that priority is generally accorded to children's interests, the law still recognises the autonomy of parents to fashion their own private life. Parents are not required to sacrifice their own interests to those of their children and thus, for example, a child could not claim for damage caused by the divorce of his parents, even though this is foreseeable.

Considerable guidance as to the appropriate balance can be found in the statutory immunity given to parents by section 22 of the Legal Competence and Guardianship Law[12] which provides:

'The parents shall not be liable for injury caused by them to the minor in exercise of their duties as guardians except where they acted otherwise than in good faith or without proper intent for the best interests of the minor; they shall not be liable for damage to the property of the minor caused by them in the exercise of their duties as guardians, provided they acted in good faith and with proper intent for the best interests of the minor.'

---

7   He had failed to respond to letters from the school informing him of the children's educational and behavioural problems and asking him to take an interest in the children.

8   Section 35 of The Civil Wrongs Ordinance (*supra* note 6) provides for liability in negligence where there is inter alia a failure to take such care as a reasonable prudent person would take in the circumstances 'in relation to another person to whom he owes a duty in the circumstances not to act as he did.' Under section 36 'every person owes a duty to all persons whom ... a reasonable person ought in the circumstances to have contemplated as likely in the usual course of things to be affected by an act of failure to do an act ...'.

9   Penal Law 1977, Laws of State of Israel Special Volume.

10   For discussion of the meaning of abuse in that section, see B3 *infra*.

11   This argument was expressed in the US case of *Burnette v Wahl* Or 588 P.2d 1105 (1978) in the words 'There are probably as many children who have been damaged in some manner by their parents' failure to meet completely their physical, emotional and psychological needs as there are people'.

12   *Supra* note 5.

In this case, even taking into account the father's desire for a new family life, his cruel, complete and utter rejection of children could not be justified. Moreover, the father could not rely on the statutory immunity since his actions were not motivated by a desire to promote the welfare of the children.

Justice Orr emphasises that there will only be tortious liability in respect of parental failure to care for their children's needs in exceptional cases. He refers to the tensions and frustrations of the child–parent relationship and warns that courts should be careful not to intrude into such relationships unless really necessary. He also explains the difficulty of judging parents' behaviour over a number of years *ex post facto*. Thus, it is necessary to draw a line, which allows children to sue their parents in appropriate cases and yet also recognises the autonomy given to the parents. While in this case it is not necessary to consider exactly where the line is to be drawn, because the case clearly falls on the children's side, the honourable judge has no doubt that the task is within the capacity of the courts.

B   *State of Israel v Plonit* (hereinafter '*Plonit*')[13]

1   THE FACTS

The appellant was a single mother of two children, aged five and seven. She was a strict disciplinarian and used smacking as a method of punishment on a regular basis. This included hitting the children on different parts of the body on an almost daily basis, sometimes with a slipper and occasionally with a household object. No serious injury was caused by these punishments, although their kindergarten teachers did testify that they had noticed marks on the children's bodies and one commented that the children recoiled in apparent fear from any attempt at physical contact by her.

In the District Court, the mother was convicted both of assaulting and abusing the children under sections 379 and 368C respectively of the Penal Law.[14] Justice Rotlevi held that the rule in the 44-year-old leading case of *Rasi*,[15] under which physical punishment of children was lawful provided that it was reasonable and moderate, was no longer good law. In her words, the decision:

'had passed from this world with the change in times and the change in norms, according to which children are no longer considered as the property of their parents, but as independent holders of rights including the right to respect and protection of their body' (my translation – RS).[16]

---

13   Cr. App. 456/98 *State of Israel v Plonit* (not published).

14   Enacted by the Penal Law (Amendment No 26) 1989, *Sefer Chukim* p 10.

15   Cr. App. 7/53 *Delael Rasi v The Attorney-General* PSD 7 790 (1953) (hereinafter referred to as *Rasi*). The case has been approved much more recently, for example, in 1992 in the case of *State of Israel v Asulin* (Cr.C. 570/91 District Court decisions 1992 vol 1431) where the father was acquitted on the basis that his kicking his unruly child had been a reasonable reaction to the child throwing a stone at his mother and baby sibling.

16   The judge also pointed out that the decision in the case of *Rasi (ibid.)* had been based on the English common law and that since the enactment of the Foundations of Law 1980, Laws of the State of Israel vol 34 p 181, the Israeli Courts were no longer bound to follow the common law. With respect, this misses the point that that Law expressly preserves the continued validity of common law rules which have already been absorbed into Israeli law.

The mother was sentenced to 12 months' imprisonment suspended and 18 months' probation.[17] Her appeal to the Supreme Court against the convictions was dismissed, but no decision was given in the appeal against sentence pending receipt of an up-to-date report from the probation officer.

2 THE REASONABLE EDUCATIONAL PUNISHMENT DEFENCE

Justice Englard dismissed the mother's appeal against conviction for assault in three lines. He simply held that the punishments were neither reasonable nor *de minimis*. This, it seems, is simply an application of the existing law and does not represent any change therein.

Of course it might be argued that there are previous cases in which more extreme physical punishments were considered as reasonable. However, this is not really relevant because the question of reasonableness is one of secondary fact, to be determined in the light of the specific circumstances of the case. Those circumstances can include changes in the attitude of society to the type and degree of physical punishment which is acceptable in particular situations.[18]

Justice Beinish, however, with whom the President of the Court agreed, took the opportunity to declare that the defence of reasonable physical punishment is no longer recognised at all. This conclusion is based on six main grounds:

(a)   It is the function of the Court to fix social norms. In doing so, it cannot ignore the social developments and the conclusions of educational and psychological research in relation to the legitimacy and utility of physical punishment.

Thus the approach of Anglo-American law,[19] under which reasonable physical punishment is still lawful, is inconsistent with the views of professionals in the fields of medicine, education and psychology[20] who consider that such punishments do no good[21] and can only cause harm.[22] Continued lawfulness of physical punishment is therefore a vestige of the outdated ideology that a child is his parent's property.

---

17   Under which the probation officer had to make a report to the Court on the defendant's progress every three months.

18   See per Justice Dorner in Crim. App 5224/97 *State of Israel v Sede Orr* (not published). Justice Beinish in the present case makes the same point in discussing the immunity from civil liability for reasonable punishment (at para 24).

19   For a very thorough analysis of the position in the USA, see K Johnson, 'Crime or Punishment: The Parental Corporal Punishment Defense — Reasonable and Necessary or Excused Abuse?' Univ. of Ill. LR [Vol 1998 no 2] 413.

20   See D Orentichler, 'Spanking and Other Corporal Punishment of Children by Parents, Overvaluing Pain, Undervaluing Children', 35 Houston LR 147 (1998).

21   Because they are an ineffective method of behaviour modification.

22   In the District Court, Justice Rotlevi refers to the research of Professor Murray Strauss in his book 'Beating the Devil Out of Them: Corporal Punishment in American Families' (Lexington Books, 1994) detailing the ill effects of physical punishment. It might be pointed out that most of this and other similar research involves children who were hit systematically and often severely. This tells us little about the effect of the occasional moderate smacks which are used by the majority of parents. See also the comment of Orentlicher *supra* note 20 at 160 that 'It is important to recognize that the empirical evidence on corporal punishment is not definitive' (Justice Beinish does not quote this part of the article!).

Accordingly, the approach adopted in countries such as Sweden, Finland, Denmark, Norway and Austria, in which physical punishment of children has been outlawed is to be preferred.

(b)   The approach taken in the earlier Supreme Court decision in *State of Israel v Sede-Orr*,[23] in which it was held that use of physical punishment by teachers for educational purposes 'defeated the very purpose of education in so far as education for a tolerant and violence-free society was concerned' (my translation – RS) was equally pertinent to education by parents, despite the differences between the status and rights of parents and teachers.

(c)   State intervention in the family unit is justified in order to fulfil the State's obligation of protecting children from harm, including harm caused by misuse of parental powers and failure to exercise parental duties properly.

(d)   The child's right to respect and freedom from violence is enshrined both in the Israeli Basic Law: Human Dignity and Freedom Law 1992[24] and the UN Convention on the Rights of the Child, which Israel ratified in 1991.[25]

(e)   Support for the view that criminal liability attaches even to 'reasonable' physical punishment can be found in the fact that a clause in the Proposed Penal Law (Introductory and General Part) 1992[26] which would have enacted a defence for reasonable physical punishment was deleted from the Bill in the course of its passage through the Knesset.[27]

(f)   Removal of the defence of reasonable punishment would not have the effect of criminalising the behaviour of large numbers of parents who occasionally resort to physical punishment because the criminal law contained sufficient 'filters' to prevent this. In particular the Penal Law provided a *de minimis* defence[28] and expressly conferred on the prosecution discretion not to prosecute cases where there was no public interest in so doing. Justice Beimish also clarified that there would be no criminal liability where a parent used reasonable force to protect the child or another from harm or in respect of light physical contact for the purpose of keeping order.

3   DEFINITION OF THE OFFENCE OF ABUSE

The Supreme Court was divided in relation to the conviction for abuse. Whilst the majority held that the appellant's behaviour did constitute abuse despite the fact that no individual event could be characterised as cruel or severe and no serious injury was caused, Justice England found that abuse required acts which could be described as 'especially severe' and that the facts of the present case did not come within this description. The are two main bases for this difference of opinion.

---

23   See *supra* note 18.

24   *Sefer Chukim* 150.

25   But has not yet been incorporated into municipal law.

26   *Hatzaot Chok 1992* p 138.

27   This provision was simply intended to codify the common law. Its exclusion was largely due to the successful lobbying of children's rights groups and in particular the Council for the Welfare of the Child.

28   Section 24Q of the Penal Law (introduced by Penal Law (Amendment 39)(Preliminary and General Part) 1994 (*Sefer Chukim* 348) provides 'A person will not be criminally liable for an action if in the light of the nature of the action, the circumstances thereof, the consequences thereof and the public interest, the action is of minor importance.' (my translation – RS) For further discussion of this defence, see below at III B4(b).

(a) The judicial function in interpreting criminal law statutes

Justice Beinish's only attempt to define abuse is negatively by declaring that the meaning of 'abuse' in this context is not necessarily the ordinary dictionary definition of 'hard, cruel behaviour'. Rather she considers that the phrase can be given content by the exercise of judicial discretion in the light of the purpose of the statute. Thus, she considers it sufficient to identify in a general and non-exhaustive way the foundations and characteristics of the offence of physical abuse.[29] These can be summarised as follows:

(1)   Any direct or indirect use of physical force against the child's body which 'had the potential to cause harm or suffering' could constitute abuse where 'conscience and emotion would not allow it to be treated as assault only'.

(2)   Whilst it would be easier to find that there was physical abuse where there was a series of assaults, even single occurrences could constitute abuse.

(3)   Conversely, acts which would not by themselves constitute abuse would, if repeated on a routine basis, become abuse.

(4)   'Physical abuse' is a behavioural and not a causal offence and thus it is not necessary that any actual harm was caused or that there was any intention to cause any harm.

In contrast, Justice Englard points out that the rule of law requires that criminal statutes should be construed in such a way that the factual element of the offence is certain so that citizens can know in advance what behaviour will attract criminal sanctions. This principle is given effect, *inter alia,* by section 34U of the Penal Law[30] which provides that where the law is open to two reasonable interpretations, which accord with its purpose, that which is more lenient towards the defendant should be adopted.

Accordingly, Justice Englard does not accept Justice Beinish's approach which, in his view, causes considerable uncertainty, but finds it necessary to define 'abuse' more precisely. After referring to a number of dictionary definitions and surveying case-law in which the meaning of 'abuse' is considered in various contexts, he concludes that there is no reason to deviate from the literal meaning, according to which abuse requires 'severe violence and cruelty towards the victim which involves some kind of humiliation'.

(b) The legislative purpose

Both judges support their conclusions by referring to the purpose behind the offence of abuse of a child which appears in chapter 11 of the Penal Law (entitled 'Harm to Minors and Those Who are Defenceless' and was enacted by the Penal Law (Amendment No 26) 1989).[31]

Justice Beinish learns from the explanation appended to the draft law that the amendment reflected the increasing awareness of the extent and severity of the phenomenon of violence against children and that the enactment of more severe

---

29   She does not discuss the scope of the offences of emotional and sexual abuse which appear in the same section of the Penal Law.

30   Introduced by Penal Law (Amendment 39)(Preliminary and General Part) 1994 (*Sefer Chukim* 348).

31   *Supra* note 14.

sentences for such violence was part of the campaign against this phenomenon. The facts in this case revealed that the children were 'battered children' as a result of the mother's consistent and prolonged use of violence as a method of discipline and thus it was within the category of cases at which the enactment of the offence of abuse was aimed.

Conversely, Justice Englard learns from the graduation of the maximum punishments proscribed in Chapter 11 of the Penal Law that the offence of abuse of a minor was envisaged as being of the same severity as the offence of a parent[32] causing serious physical injury to a minor.[33] Thus, abuse should be confined to actions which were particularly severe and analogous to causing serious physical injury.

Moreover, in the honourable judge's view, routinely characterising behaviour as abuse would devalue the moral significance of the offence and thus undermine the purpose of expressing the severity with which the legislature viewed the phenomenon of child abuse.

III ANALYSIS

A Increasing State intervention in the family

1 THE APPROPRIATE LIMITS OF THE NON-INTERVENTION PRINCIPLE

Whilst the Supreme Court's readiness to champion children's rights must be applauded, we cannot avoid asking whether they have gone too far in eroding the principle of non-intervention in family life. Indeed, the case of *Plonit* has provoked academic debate in Israel as to the appropriate level of intervention of the criminal law in the family. At a recent Conference on Criminal Law at Bar Ilan University, two diametrically opposed views were expressed. Dr Dana Pugach, relying on feminist writings, argued that criminal law should apply in the family exactly as between strangers, whereas Dr Lior Barshak, relying on theories of social structure, argued that the family (which is part of the wider concept of the 'familiarity zone') should be immune from interference by the law unless and until there occurs a gross breach of the fundamental legal duties which define the roles of the family members. With respect, general theories about the relevance of the public/private dichotomy are inadequate to explain either intervention or non-intervention in the child-parent relationship because they fail to address both the fundamental differences between that relationship and other domestic

---

32　Or other person responsible for a child.
33　Both of which attract a maximum sentence of nine years.

relationships[34] and the centrality of the child's welfare[35] and rights in formulating legal policy in respect of children.[36]

Clearly the judges in these cases assumed that intervention would promote both the welfare and rights of the children involved. However, they looked only at one side of the coin and they failed to consider whether their well-intentioned attempts to protect children might actually result in causing more harm not only to those children, but to many more children.[37] Criminalising and, *a fortiori* prosecuting, parents[38] may have a more adverse effect on children than the breach of their rights of which the parents are guilty. Similarly, children who sue their parents may gain financially, but the damage to the parent–child relationship may be irreversible. Moreover, it can even be argued that if parents feel that their every action may be subject to legal scrutiny (whether or not this is actually likely to happen), they will not be able to discipline their children effectively.[39] Also, there is a danger that children may be able to manipulate their parents by threatening to report or even fabricating parental infringements of the law. The main victims of the consequent destabilisation of the family are children. Similarly, if parents can no longer use simple smacks they are likely[40] to resort to means of punishment which are equally, if not more, harmful to the child[41] or not to discipline the child at all, which may have long-term negative effects on his personality.[42]

---

34   Thus, for example, whilst there may be substantial similarity between physical *abuse* of women and that of children, there is no equivalent of the parental duty to educate or to discipline in the relationship between adult partners (at least in the Western culture of the 21st century). Furthermore, the dependency of women is an artificial construct created by society, whereas that of children (at least young ones) is created by nature as a part of the human condition.

35   Whilst interventionists argue that breaking the patriarchal mould will free children from oppression and non-interventionists claim that treating the family as sacrosanct ensures stability which is essential for the healthy development of children, both claims are based on blanket unjustified assumptions and do not analyse carefully enough how children's interests can best be promoted. It would seem sensible to use the balance achieved in child protection legislation as a starting point for determining the level of intervention of the general law. Any greater intervention would have to be justified by reference to the specific purpose of the law in question. Clearly, the full implications of this approach need further consideration. In the case of *Amin*, there would clearly have been a basis on which to terminate parental rights. In the case of *Plonit*, although the children were not removed from the mother, it would have been appropriate to make a supervision order. However, in cases of occasional moderate physical punishment, it is very doubtful if even such an order would be justified.

36   Such rights will have to be balanced against any rights which the parents have in relation to the child (if they have any rights over and above those necessary for carrying out their responsibility: see discussion in Bainham, *Children: The Modern Law* (2nd edn) (Jordan Publishing, Bristol 1998) at pp 94–104), and in relation to their own lives.

37   The argument presented here is not that physical punishment is beneficial to children, but that outlawing it might be harmful to them.

38   Even in cases of clear abuse, the dictates of the welfare of the child is an important element in the decision to prosecute, see D Besharov, 'Child Abuse: Arrest and Prosecution Decision-Making', 24 *American Criminal Law Review* 315.

39   See, for example, O'Brien Steinfels in 'Children's Rights, Parental Rights, Family Privacy and Family Autonomy' in W Gaylin and R Macklin (eds) *Who Speaks for the Child* (1982, Plenum Press) at p 240.

40   Unless and until they learn more constructive methods of discipline – see B4(e) *infra*.

41   Who is to say whether severe verbal scoldings which destroy the child's self-esteem are less harmful than a light smack? Indeed, because a verbal scolding is perceived as a less severe punishment, parents may feel the need to use it more often and for longer periods of time than a smack.

42   And perhaps be in breach of his right to be educated!

The idea that the increased intervention in the family may not be in the interests of children may also provide an answer to the claim that Article 19(1) of the United Nations Convention on the Rights of the Child requires removal of all parental immunity for hitting their children or otherwise causing them harm. As is well known, Article 3 of the same Convention provides that 'in all actions concerning children ... the best interests of the child shall be a primary consideration'. Thus, for example, it can be argued that whilst the child's right not to be hit requires forbidding all forms of physical punishment this may be overridden by the fact that criminalising moderate physical punishment would breach his right to have his best interests treated as a primary consideration. In other words, it is not as clear as might be thought that even a children's rights perspective requires increased intervention of the type found in *Plonit*, and to a lesser extent in *Amin*.

Thus, whilst the Supreme Court judges are clearly correct in asserting and reiterating the duty of the State and the Courts to protect those who are unable to protect themselves and that the welfare of children should not be compromised, this rhetoric misses the point that the level of legal intervention in the family should not be increased without balancing very carefully the potential damage which might be caused to children thereby against the perhaps more obvious damage which intervention is designed to redress. No such balancing exercise can be found in either case.

2   WHAT IS THE EXTENT OF THE INCREASE IN INTERVENTION?

At first sight, it might seem that both cases take the same approach in increasing substantially the level of intervention in the parent-child relationship by making the parent's duty to educate and the method by which this duty is carried out respectively justiciable under the normal rules of civil and criminal liability. Thus, anti-interventionists might be expected to decry both equally. However, it is suggested that there are, in fact, significant differences between the two cases.

(a)   The scope of the decisions

The scope of the decision in *Plonit* is far-reaching: there is no longer any defence of reasonable chastisement.[43] Thus, the clear message is that smacking children is no longer lawful and attracts criminal sanctions. Neither the degree of uncertainty as to the real implications of the decision introduced by Justice Beinish's comments that the justification defence would still cover 'light contact to keep order' and that trivial cases will be covered by the *de minimis* defence,[44] nor the low probability that the new legal ruling will be enforced alter the significance of the change in normative regulation effected by the decision. This change, which is liable to turn thousands of respectable otherwise law-abiding citizens into

---

43   Justice Beinish's comment that the light contact to maintain order is permissible does not derogate from the fact that the effect of the decision is to abolish the defence of reasonable physical punishment. The permissible 'light contact' is not a punishment in the sense that it is not designed to 'teach the child a lesson' or to deter recurrence of the undesirable behaviour, but is a remedial measure necessary to restore the order at that time without any concern about future behaviour.

44   It is even arguable that the defence will not in fact have the effect envisaged. See B4(b) *infra*.

relatively frequent offenders in respect of acts performed within the family, represents a substantial increase in legal intervention in the family unit.

On the other hand, the scope of the decision in *Amin* is completely obscure.[45] The case opens up and fails to resolve numerous questions about the scope of liability in respect of tortious parenting and of the statutory immunity. Will only really extreme and unusual cases not be covered by the immunity? It would be unfortunate if the fact that a particular type of abusive behaviour is not exceptional means that it does not give rise to civil liability.[46] Will claims by children who are still minors be treated differently from those who have passed the age of majority?[47]

It is not difficult to think of examples of situations which could in theory constitute either breach of statutory duty or breach of the duty of care and that *prima facie* the conditions for immunity are not satisfied. Are parents who put their children into foster care or even put them up for adoption, for their own benefit, when they could have brought them up themselves liable if this results in damage? What about parents who are criminals and teach their children criminal values? Perhaps more common examples would be making a child leave school in order to contribute to the family's finances or arranged marriages for the parent's financial benefit.

However, it is likely to be very difficult to prove the lack of parental *bona fides* in these cases and the resulting damage. Moreover, given that most parents do act *bona fide* in the interests of their children and that the Court made clear that reasonable parents are allowed to take into account their own interests, it is likely that the sort of cases in which the immunity will not apply will be situations where the law already intervenes through child protection laws which allow parental rights to be judicially limited[48] and even terminated[49] on the basis of one of a number of specific grounds. Thus, it is not clear, bearing in mind the continued existence of the statutory immunity and the *obiter dicta*, that the decision does really represent any significant increase in the degree of legal intervention in the family.[50]

---

45 With respect, Justice England's statement that there exist clear limits on the intervention of the law in the family unit is incorrect. Even if the limits were clear before the decision in this case, they are certainly far from clear afterwards.

46 In the same way that the fact that domestic violence is not exceptional has prevented Courts from treating it as a reason not to return children under Article 13 of the Hague Convention on Child Abduction. See Miranda Kaye, 'The Hague Convention and the Flight from Domestic Violence: How Women and Children are being returned by Coach and Four' (1999) 13 *Int. J. Law, Policy and the Family* 191. The fact that there is an express statutory immunity from *civil* liability in respect of injury caused by reasonable chastisement (see below at B4(a)) does suggest that abuse which does not come within this defence should give rise to civil liability.

47 One of the main reasons why the majority in the US case of *Burnette v Wahl* Or. 588 P.2d 1105 (1978) refused to recognise civil liability for psychological harm caused by parental neglect and abandonment was because this prejudiced the chances of rehabilitating the family, which was the primary policy of the law. This point is not raised by the Israeli Supreme Court, presumably because the plaintiffs were no longer minors. Keeley (*supra* note 1) points out that the extent of the damage caused by emotional abuse is often only apparent after the child has reached adulthood.

48 The Youth (Supervision and Care) Law 5720 – 1960, LSI vol 14, p 44.

49 Adoption Act 5741 – 1981, Laws of the State of Israel vol 35, p 360.

50 Rather it may allow for damages to be claimed in cases where children are removed from their parents. See also Keeley (*supra* note 1 at 712).

(b)   Criminal law v civil law

An obvious difference between the two cases is that whilst *Plonit* deals with criminal law, *Amin* deals with civil law. It can be argued that intervention by the criminal law in the family unit is more problematic than intervention by the civil law[51] for a number of reasons:

(1)   The stigma of criminal liability is much greater and therefore the threat of intervention constitutes a greater threat to the autonomy of the family unit.

(2)   Civil cases will usually only be brought when the family unit has broken down. Where the family is still functioning, the child (even after (s)he is no longer a minor) may well gain little financially[52] from a successful suit unless the parent is insured.[53] Where this is not true, the 'child' (if he is now an adult) or his guardian ad litem can weigh up whether the financial gain will be worth the damage caused to the relationship with his parents. On the other hand, criminal prosecutions are brought by the State which may pay little if any regard to the child's wishes in the matter[54] or the consequential damage done to his relationship with his parents.

(3)   Widening the net of the criminal law 'too far' by criminalising behaviour which is widely seen as acceptable or at least not as criminal may adversely affect the criminal law system generally by reducing the stigma attached to crime.[55] Similarly, complete non-enforcement or symbolic arbitrary[56] enforcement will bring the law into disrepute. On the other hand, fixing civil law standards 'too high', particularly where they are unlikely to be invoked, does not damage the general perception of the whole system,[57] particularly as there will only be liability where it can be proven that actual damage has been caused by the parental behaviour.

---

51   Thus, some respondents to the Scottish Law Commission's discussion paper No 88 (*Parental Responsibilities and Rights; Guardianship and Administration of Property* – 1990) suggested that the right to administer corporal punishment be abolished for civil law, but not criminal law purposes. The Commission in their Report No 135 (*Family Law* – 1992) rejected this approach on the basis that it would create confusion.

52   Because the parents are likely to provide the child with as much financial assistance as they can and the child will inherit from them.

53   Where the damage was caused negligently, a home owner's insurance policy may cover it. Neeley (*supra* note 1 at p 714) reports two US decisions in which damages against a mother who failed to protect her daughters from sexual abuse by their father/step-father were recovered from the insurance company under such a policy.

54   Although he could refuse to give testimony. It might be argued that the child should be given the right to express his views on the matter under Article 12 of the United Nations Convention on the Rights of the Child, although bearing in mind his natural loyalty to the parent and that he is under the latter's influence it is doubtful if much weight can be placed on those views.

55   This is a reason sometimes given for suggesting that routine offences such as unlawful parking should be treated as regulatory offences and not criminal offences. In this context, however, the potential danger is much worse because the offence committed is one of violence. Therefore, the message transmitted, *inter alia*, to the child who sees his parents committing criminal offences is that transgressing the criminal law is not really so terrible.

56   Whether a parent's harsh disciplinary practices come to the attention of the authorities is likely to be purely fortuitous (or, even worse, to depend upon reports by malicious neighbours) and whether those authorities decide to take the matter further will depend to a large extent on the personal views of the officials involved.

57   Although it might result in potential tortfeasors (in this case parents) insuring against liability which they do not feel sure they can avoid.

B   Judicial lawmaking

1   INTRODUCTION

The decision of the majority in *Plonit*, abolishing the defence of reasonable punishment for educational purposes, is without doubt judicial legislation. Whilst, as we saw above a provision in a draft Law expressly providing for such a defence was withdrawn during the passage of the Law through the Knesset, this was clearly not sufficient to overrule the existing defence based on common law.[58] In contrast, the decision in *Amin*, whilst unprecedented, simply represents application of statutory provisions in a way in which the Courts have not previously had occasion to apply them.[59] Thus, this section will be confined to analysis of the judicial lawmaking in *Plonit*.

It will be argued below that even if in principle the parental right to punish their children physically ought to be abolished,[60] such a reform should only be made by legislation and that it is not an appropriate issue for judicial lawmaking.

Whilst Israeli law clearly does not adhere to the traditional common law declaratory theory, even supporters of judicial creativity recognise that the scope for such activity is not unlimited.[61] The discussion will focus on the main reasons why, in the author's view, the decision in *Plonit* oversteps the appropriate bounds of judicial legislation.[62]

2   'JUDICIAL BOLDNESS', LACK OF CONSENSUS AND PLURALISM

Professor Michael Freeman[63] argues that judicial lawmaking is inappropriate on issues about which there is no consensus in society[64] and that judges should not promote the interests of certain sections of society at the expense of others. The case which he brings to exemplify this undesirable 'judicial boldness' is the case of *Knuller v DPP*, in which the House of Lords created a new criminal offence of conspiracy to outrage public decency in a case brought against the publisher of

---

58   This was the view taken in the Magistrates Courts cases of Crim C. (Jerusalem) 2478/96 *State of Israel v Plonit* (takdin – Shalom vol 91(1) 1997 p 75) and Crim C. (Ashkelon) 1138/96 *State of Israel v Plonit* (takdin – Shalom vol 96(4) p 58).

59   In other words, the Court is simply interpreting the statute and not extending the law (see ATH Smith 'Judicial Law Making in the Criminal Law' (1984) 100 LQR 46 at p 76).

60   The arguments for and against abolishing the right of parents to punish their children physically have been widely debated recently, *inter alia*, in Anglo-American academic literature (see, for example *supra* notes 19 and 20), by the Scottish Law Commission Report (*supra* note 51) and by the UK Government in *Protecting Children, Supporting Parents* (The Stationery Office, 2000). However, all of the discussion assumed that any change in the law would be by statute.

61   See, for example, Professor A Barak, 'Judicial Discretion' (Yale University Press 1989 – translated from the original Hebrew) at p 152.

62   Reliance has been placed mainly on the following classic studies of judicial lawmaking: Barak *ibid*, MDA Freeman, 'Standards of Adjudication, Judicial Law Making and Prospective Overruling' (1973) 26 *Current Legal Problems* 166 and Cappelletti (1981–82) 8 *Monash U.L. Rev.* 14.

63   *Supra* note 62.

64   Barak's (*supra* note 61 at pp 213–215) approach is more flexible. Whilst recommending that judges should make not law which contradicts the public consensus (because it will damage the public's faith in the court system) he claims that there may be cases where there is an honest dispute about whether there is a consensus or where 'the case is so exceptional in its severity and that the values of the hour so acutely contradict the fundamental values that there is no alternative but to lead the pack.'

International Times in respect of small advertisements by homosexuals. Freeman denigrates the decision which 'injected uncertainty into the criminal law and its administration' and ignored the interests of homosexuals, as 'exemplifying judicial law-making at its worst'.

It might perhaps be added that the problem of judicial boldness is exacerbated by the fact that judicial legislation, unlike Parliamentary legislation, is retrospective. This is particularly unfortunate in relation to criminal law and means that people can be convicted of offences committed at a time when it was not known that the relevant behaviour constituted a criminal offence.[65]

While no doubt Professor Freeman, who has long been a staunch opponent of physical punishment of children, would applaud the decision in *Plonit* it is arguable that, at least in the Israeli context, the decision in *Plonit* can be considered to be an example of inappropriate judicial boldness for a number of reasons.

(a)   The judicial lawmaking was completely unnecessary

It was quite possible to come to the same result, as did Justice England, on the basis that physical punishments in this case were not reasonable. Indeed, Judge Strashnov contends that there is no relationship at all between the brutality of the mother in this case and the complex question of physical punishment of children.[66] The judge could have emphasised that changes in attitudes have considerably narrowed the scope of 'reasonable punishments' and could have even added a condemnation of all forms of physical punishment and a call to Parliament to legislate accordingly.

Thus, it seems that the Court went beyond the model of 'legislation as an incident to adjudication' advocated by Barak himself in his book and entered into the realms of the rejected policy model, according to which the judge's main task is to make policy.[67]

(b)   Uncertainty

The case injects considerable uncertainty into the criminal law and its administration. It is not clear when 'ordinary smacks' will come within the *de minimis* defence;[68] what degree of force will be considered to be 'light contact to keep order' and in what circumstances the prosecution authorities will decide that there is no public interest in prosecuting the case.

Whilst it is true that the exact limits of the reasonable chastisement defence were also uncertain, it was clear that the moderate punishment used by most parents came within it.

---

65   See ATH Smith *supra* note 59, but cf. Barak (*supra* note 61) at p 253 who argues that criminal law is no different from any other type of law.

66   Amnon Strashnov, 'Children and Youth in the Eyes of the Law' (The Israeli Bar Association, 2000) (Hebrew) at p 271.

67   Barak (*supra* note 61) at 231–233. It will be remembered that the President Barak concurred with the decision of Justice Beinish in the case of *Plonit*.

68   See *infra* at 4(b).

(c) Lack of consensus

There is no public consensus in Israel about parental physical punishment of children. The press reported a very mixed reaction to the decision in *Plonit*. Whilst recent surveys suggest that the level of support for physical punishment of children is less than previously thought,[69] it is still considerably higher than that recorded in Sweden before the reform of the law there.[70] This difference illustrates why it is likely that in Israel 'the political, social and legal[71] climate ... may be less receptive to an outright ban of corporal punishment'.[72]

Furthermore, contrary to the impression given by Justice Beinish, professional opinion is not unanimous. There is no consensus on three central issues: whether corporal punishment can ever be effective; whether mild corporal punishment which does not cause any physical injury causes emotional harm and whether there is any significant relationship between mild corporal punishment and child abuse.[73]

Thus, it was inappropriate[74] for the Court in *Plonit* to purport to adopt the Swedish approach[75] without further investigation.[76]

(d) Anti-pluralism

The decision could be said to flout the interests of those ethnic and religious groups who regard physical punishment as an indispensable educational tool. The issue of cultural pluralism with respect to children's rights generally has been

---

69 A survey conducted by the daily newspaper two days after the decision in *Plonit* found that 48% of those interviewed thought that it was permissible for parents to give light smacks in order to educate them. cf. Dr Hatav 'Psychological Aspects: The emotional harm caused by reasonable hitting of children' in The National Council for the Welfare of the Child, 'Education by Violence – Education to Violence' (1993) who assumed that the figure would be similar to the 90% recorded in England (and incidentally in the USA – see Johnson *supra* note 19 at 479).

70 35% – see Johnson *supra* note 19 at 478.

71 Before the ban in 1979, Swedish law had gradually curtailed the right to punish children physically; whereas, as we have seen, Israeli law was based on the common law approach which allows reasonable physical punishment. See Johnson *supra* note 19 at 479.

72 Johnson *supra* note 19 at p 479 who was referring to the USA. She goes on to argue that the process needs to be more gradual and suggests as a first step enacting a considerably tightened up statutory definition of forbidden physical force against children Interestingly, the Scottish Law Commission (*supra* note 51) and English Government (*supra* note 60) have taken a similar approach.

73 The Israeli educationalist Oren in his book 'Corporal Punishment of Children' Talpiot (1989) justifies the use of corporal punishment by comparing the results of traditional Jewish education with modern education, which in his view fails to impart any values. In particular, he comments that in modern schools there is no corporal punishment, but there is a lot of violence among the students; whereas in ultra-orthodox schools, where corporal punishment is still used, there is hardly any violence. However, many educationalists and psychologists take the view that physical punishment is ineffective at best and harmful at worst. See The National Council for the Welfare of the Child, 'Education by Violence – Education to Violence' (1993). To a large extent, however, they base themselves on research done abroad about which see *supra* note 22.

74 Given that it was not necessary to make any decision about mild physical punishment, Barak's 'exceptional severity' qualification (see *supra* note 64) cannot apply even if the judges believe that public support for such punishment does acutely contradict fundamental values.

75 In fact the decision in *Plonit* goes further than the Swedish reform because the Swedish ban on corporal punishment is not part of the Swedish Criminal Code and does not attract criminal sanctions. Also the accompanying education campaign (see 4(e) *infra*) was an integral part of the Swedish approach. See Olson, 'The Swedish Ban of Corporal Punishment' (1984) BYUL 447.

76 Indeed, it is well known that one of the dangers of comparative law is ignoring the social and cultural context of the law.

widely discussed in case-law and literature.[77] The prevailing view that traditions and cultural values can only be taken into account where they are not at odds with the basic child care standards of the society where the children live is relevant to the determination of whether particular parental behaviour comes within the reasonable punishment exception.[78]

However, this view does not deal with the question of the influence of those traditions and cultural values in formulating those basic norms in the first place. This issue is particularly pertinent in the Israeli context because a substantial proportion of the population belong to 'cultural groups' in which physical punishment is more acceptable and more widely practised than in the Israeli population as a whole: Arabs, immigrants[79] and ultra-orthodox Jews. It is therefore perhaps surprising that the Supreme Court decision in *Plonit* does not even refer to the issue of pluralism or even to Jewish law.[80]

In the District Court, however, Justice Rotlevi does discuss the Jewish law in some detail. She starts off by showing that the commonly cited phrase from the Biblical Book of Proverbs 'He who spares the rod, hates his child'[81] does not actually encourage or even permit parental violence. She brings the view that the word 'rod' does not refer to a stick but metaphorically to the rod of reproof [82] and cites other verses from Proverbs which are inconsistent with physical punishment.[83] She goes on to claim that Jewish sources from the time of the Talmud permitting physical punishment of children must be viewed in the light of the period in which they were made and are not relevant in the modern era of human rights, in particularly following the enactment in Israel of the Basic Law: Human Dignity and Freedom.[84] She adds various quotations from Jewish sources indicating that the Sages also regarded respect for human beings as an important value.

---

77   See, for example, A Bainham, 'Family Law in a Pluralistic Society' (1995) 22 *Journal of Law and Society* 234; MDA Freeman, 'The morality of cultural pluralism,' (1995) 3 *The Inter. J. of Children's Rights* and Abdullahi An-Na'im, 'Cultural transformation and normative consensus on the best interests of the child' (1994) 8 *Inter J. of Law and Family* 62.

78   The Israeli case of *Rasi* (supra note 15), which adopted the common law reasonable punishment defence, held that the excessive punishments in that case could not be justified by reference to the cultural norms of the Arab nuns who had punished girls in their orphanage. In subsequent cases, immigrant parents' defences that the harsh punishments inflicted on the children were in accordance with the normal practices of their community were rejected (see, for example, Cr.C. 39/92 *State of Israel v Garzi* (Iraq) and Cr. App. 5357/93 *State of Israeli v Ploni* (Ethiopia). See also the English case of *R v Deriviere* (1969) 53 Cr. App. Rep and *Re H* [1987] 2 FLR 12).

79   Particularly following the widescale immigration from Russia and Ethiopia during the last 15 years.

80   Apart from the issue of pluralism, there was arguably an obligation to refer to Jewish Law in respect of the lacuna which was created by rejection of the common law rule (under section 1 of The Foundations of Law 1980, *supra* note 16). Furthermore, the Basic Law: Human Dignity and Freedom (*supra* note 24) provides in section 1A that 'The purpose of this Basic Law is to protect the dignity and freedom of man, in order to anchor in a basic law the values of the State of Israel as a Jewish Democratic country' (my translation – RS).

81   Proverbs Chapter 23 v 14. The English saying 'Spare the rod and spoil the child' is in fact an inaccurate translation.

82   This view is based partly on the continuation of verse 14 which reads 'and he who loves his sons reprimands him' and on verse 16 of Chapter 22 which refers expressly to the 'rod of reproof'.

83   For example, Chapter 3 v 17 which reads: 'All her ways are ways of pleasantness and all her paths are of peace', referring to the Jewish Law.

84   *Supra* note 24.

However, this discussion fails to address the issue of pluralism. The prevailing view even among modern Rabbinical authorities is that moderate physical punishment of children for educational purposes is legitimate,[85] although the circumstances in which it may be used and the means for inflicting it are carefully limited.[86] Thus, many religious and particularly ultra-orthodox Jews in Israel[87] feel obliged to resort to physical punishment in their attempts to bring up their children as observant Jews. It is perhaps not surprising , therefore, that the reaction of one of the ultra-orthodox political parties to the decision in *Plonit* was to introduce into the Israeli Parliament a Proposed Law which would expressly declare reasonable chastisement for educational purposes lawful.[88]

Indeed, in a democratic society, surely it is the elected Parliament which is the correct forum for changing a prevalent legal norm, at least where the new norm is inconsistent with the cultural and religious practices and beliefs of significant sections of society; not the Courts, whose membership is not representative of society as a whole.[89]

3   LIMITED INFORMATION AVAILABLE TO JUDGES

The information available to judges upon which to base policy decisions is substantially more limited than that available to the legislature. Judges depend to a large extent on material submitted to them by the parties,[90] although they may do some independent research of their own. However, they are unable to commission empirical studies, call expert witnesses or engage in consultation.

In this case, Justice Beinish refers to a number of Anglo-American articles and books. However, this is by no means comprehensive coverage of the field. In

---

85   See for example, Rabbi Moshe Feinstein, 'Igeret Moshe' Choshen Mishpat, Para. 3 and A Sherman, 'Violence Of Parents and Teachers' Tchumin V. 16 160 (Hebrew). Chief Rabbi Bakshi Doron in reaction to the decision reaffirmed that educational smacks which did not cause any injury were definitely permissible (Newspaper Yediot Aharonot 26.1.00 (Hebrew). However some modern authorities consider that in the light of the change of children's attitudes, physical punishment is no longer an effective method of education. See, for example, Levi, Yitzchak 'Hitting Children (Reaction)', Tchumin V. 17, 157 (Hebrew).

86   In particular, physical punishment must not be inflicted in anger. This would, no doubt, delegitimise the majority of physical punishment administered by parents.

87   Statistics based on school enrolment suggest that around 23% of the population are religious and a further 6% can be categorised as ultra-orthodox.

88   The Proposed Law which was called 'He who Spares the Rod, Hates his Child' (from the verse in Proverbs *supra* note 81) was introduced by MK Avraham Ravitz on 20 July 2000 and provides 'A parent is obliged to educate his children; in special circumstances resulting from the duty to educate a parent is obliged to hit lightly in a way which does not harm the body or soul of his children provided that the hitting is reasonable and done with educational intent' – my translation (RS). There was no vote, but it was clear that there was a substantial majority against the Law. However, this does not necessarily mean that there would have been a majority for actively criminalising all corporal punishment. It should be noted that two other similar Proposed Laws were also laid before the Knesset, one of them by a non-religious MK.

89   None of the judges who heard the case belong to the 'cultural groups' mentioned earlier. It should perhaps be pointed out that for political reasons the legislative power of the religious parties is at times greater than their actual numbers. This is perhaps one reason why the secular Supreme Court is reluctant to leave law reform to Parliament on religiously sensitive issues.

90   ATH Smith (*supra* note 59) claims that allowing judicial lawmaking in criminal cases 'places on counsel a wide responsibility to consider reasons why the law should not be extended, when he is already concerned with the interests of his client'. He even suggests that the defendant might be reluctant to engage in policy arguments because this is recognising that the judicial extension of the criminal law is contemplated.

particular, it would have been appropriate to refer to the the discussion of the Scottish Law Commission Report[91] on the subject in which the opposing arguments are set out clearly and in which conflicting views of psychologists and other interested professionals and bodies is brought. Indeed, the Scottish Report illustrates how a law reform body has at its command a wider range of relevant information on which to formulate policy than the judiciary.

4   LIMITED RANGE OF OPTIONS AVAILABLE TO JUDGES

The options available to judges are considerably more limited than those available to the legislature since they can only consider the issue in front of them and cannot change the law concerning other related issues. Furthermore, they are only able to adopt solutions which do not involve invoking administrative machinery,[92] which is not at their disposal. The implications of these limitations can be seen in the decision in *Plonit* in a number of ways.

(a)   Anomalies caused by piecemeal reform

The Court was unable to repeal section 24(7) of the Torts Ordinance[93] which provides a statutory reasonable chastisement defence to the tort of assault for parents, guardians and teachers who cause harm to children, provided that the force used was reasonable and no more than was necessary for disciplining those children. The anomalous consequence is that a parent who causes a child actual harm when administering physical punishment may be convicted of a criminal offence, but is immune from civil suit.[94] Whilst this defence may be interpreted narrowly to reflect the changing attitude of society towards disciplining children, a finding that no physical punishment could ever be considered necessary would clearly render the section completely redundant.

It might be noted that even legislative repeal of section 24(7) of the Torts Ordinance[95] would not prevent a parent relying on the general immunity for damage caused in exercising parental duties found in section 22 of the Legal Capacity and Guardianship Law 1962.[96] The immunity given by this section would seem to be wider than that in the Torts Ordinance because the test is a subjective one depending on the good faith and intent of the parents, rather than the objective reasonableness criterion.

(b)   Lack of alternative methods of delegalising physical punishment and reliance on the de minimis defence

The law can remove its tolerance of physical punishment without actually criminalising such behaviour. Thus, it is possible simply to remove the immunity

---

91   *Supra* note 51.

92   See Freeman, *supra* note 62.

93   *Supra* note 6.

94   Analogously, Linde J in the case of *Burnette v Wahl* Or 588 P.2d 1105 (1978) states that it is incongruous to hold that the legislature provided criminal liability, but intended to exclude civil liability.

95   Justice Rotelevi in the case of *Cr.C. 22/98 State of Israel v Abu Chalatam* (not published) described the continued existence of the section in the Statute Book as an embarrassment and humiliation.

96   See II A 3 *supra*.

from civil suit or to declare that physical punishment is illegal, but is not subject to criminal sanction.[97] Similarly, of course, it is possible to limit the parental right to administer physical punishment by defining what forms of punishment are allowed and which are not. While these options are problematic,[98] the legislature is at least in the position to weigh their respective advantages and disadvantages against those of criminalisation. Justice Beinish, on the other hand, was faced with the option of criminalisation or simple declaration with no legal effect.

Having taken the criminal route, the only way out of the clearly undesirable consequence of turning thousands of citizens into criminals was to invoke the *de minimis* defence, the effect of which is to decriminalise trivial acts.[99] At first sight, this might seem to be an appropriate compromise between the conflicting views as to the desirability of criminalising simple smacks. However, in reality it is a compromise that pleases no-one and does not achieve its purpose.

On the one hand, since the *de minimis* defence will only apply where there is no public interest in the action which is alleged to be trivial, the very idea that this defence might prevent criminal liability arising suggests that there is no public interest in mild corporal punishment . Yet the cornerstone of the abolitionists is that there is a public interest in protecting children from so-called educational smacks.[100] On the other hand, the *de minimis* defence is designed to prevent prosecution of behaviour which, although criminal, is considered to be sufficiently anti-social as to justify activating the machinery of the criminal law. Yet the retentionists argue that reasonable physical punishment ought not to be condemned, but is justified and perhaps even to be approved.[101]

In practice, the fact that the person committing the assault is a parent who owes special duties to the child is likely to mean that even actions which might otherwise be considered trivial take on sufficient significance that the defence will not apply[102] and does not prevent the criminalisation of thousands of smacking parents.

---

97 It is interesting to note that in their submission to the Scottish Law Commission (*supra* note 51), EPOCH (End Physical Punishment of Children) which has lobbied vigorously against physical punishment of children did not recommend criminalising parents who use moderate and reasonable corporal punishment.

98 See Scottish Law Commission (*supra* note 51). However, the Commission's own recommended approach, to a large extent later adopted by the English Government, of criminalising punishment with an object or likely to cause harm can also be criticised cogently. See, for example, C Barton, 'Physical Punishment of Children — The Consultation Document' [2000] *Family Law* 257.

99 See *supra* note 28.

100 See Orly Sela, 'Discipline as a Justification for Corporal Punishment of Children' Master's Thesis, Bar Ilan University, Israel (in Hebrew) 1999, who claims therefore (at 144) that the use of the defence is 'an own goal for those who wish to draw attention to the public interest in the protection of the bodies and souls of children' (my translation — RS).

101 Ibid.

102 In the case of Cr.C.1360/97 *State of Israel v Aziz* (not published) the plea of a teacher, who had hit a six-year-old child who had failed to complete his punishment of writing a sentence one hundred times while standing in the corner with his satchel on his back, that the *de minimis* defence applied was rejected because there was a very clear public interest that the court should condemn such violent disciplinary behaviour by holding that the teacher was guilty of the criminal offence of assault. Of course, it might be argued that the public interest derived mainly from the fact that the case concerned a teacher who was teaching many pupils in a public educational institution.

(c)   Inability to formulate a rational prosecution policy

Criminalising acts which are routinely performed by many people must be accompanied by a clear prosecution policy.[103] Since prosecution is essentially an administrative function, although subject to judicial review, the judiciary are not in a position to formulate such policy. The undesirable result is that decisions in this sensitive area are left entirely to the discretion of the prosecution authorities.[104]

(d)   The need for publicity

Changes in the criminal law which affect the public should be publicised in such a way that most citizens are likely to be aware of the impact of the changes. This is particularly important where the change outlaws activities which were widely accepted by and enshrined in the culture of particular sections of society. Whilst the decision in *Plonit* did receive coverage in the national press, this was only for a few days and concentrated on the reaction to the decision rather than the exact implications for parents. In any event, journalists cannot be considered to be a reliable method for conveying such information to the public.

Where such a change in the law is made by Parliament, not only is the press coverage likely to be more extensive, but the Government will usually publish explanatory leaflets which are distributed to all parents.[105]

(e)   The need for a public education campaign

The emotional complexity of the parent–child relationship and parents' basic need to keep control over their children as well as the fact that they are naturally less 'on guard' in their own home means that the way in which parents treat their children is not easily susceptible to modification by the imposition of external deterrents. Just as the opponents of physical punishment argue that children's behaviour will not be modified by force, the same applies in relation to parents. The way to get them to change their approach to parenting is by methods which motivate them to want to change. Furthermore, even where parents are convinced that physical punishment is wrong, they may still find it difficult to stick to their decision unless they have alternative methods of discipline at their disposal. Thus, only by convincing parents that physical punishment is harmful and ineffective and by training them how to discipline their children in other ways will there be any significant reduction in smacking.

This requires a massive public education campaign involving advertisements in the media, distribution of literature and the widespread availability and promotion of parental guidance classes. Without such a campaign, which the Court is in no position to initiate, any change in the law is likely to have little effect. This point is of particular force in a society where physical punishment of children is part of the cultural traditions of many sections of the community.

---

103 It seems that the countries which have outlawed physical punishment by parents by legislation have adopted a non-enforcement policy.

104 See Strashnov, *supra* note 66 at 276.

105 As was done in Sweden, where the new law was advertised on milk cartons and explanatory literature distributed to all parents.

IV CONCLUSION

Whilst there is little doubt that rhetoric is important in the battle for increased recognition of children's rights,[106] taking an extreme and over-simplified approach may in fact backfire by antagonising reasonable parents. *Amin* and *Plonit* can be usefully compared in this respect. In the former, whilst Justice Englard asserts unequivocally the duty of the law to protect children in general and vulnerable orphans in particular, he is careful to explain that parents are not expected to sacrifice completely their own self-interest. Thus, although the law prefers the interests of children, parental freedoms are not totally abrogated. By contrast, in the latter, Justice Beinish castigates the reasonable chastisement defence as a remnant of the view that children are a parent's property. This statement simply does not do justice to the very many parents who smack their children, not for their own benefit and not because they do not respect their children's human rights, but out of love and concern for their proper development. Such inaccurate[107] polemics is what one expects from Members of Parliament and not judges.

Not surprisingly, children's rights advocates have applauded the decision in *Plonit* as placing Israel among the most advanced countries in the world.[108] However, they recognise that the decision is not enough and needs to be complemented by legislation banning corporal punishment and abolishing the statutory civil immunity and internalisation of the message by the public. Ironically, it is likely that the fact that the Supreme Court has already changed the law may reduce the chance of such legislation, which would have been likely to be much more effective in influencing public opinion than judicial declaration. Thus, it seems that the decision might have been a strategic error for the abolitionists and reflects yet another respect in which insufficient thought was paid to the wider consequences of the decision.

It is to be hoped that the prosecution authorities will not exacerbate this mistake by prosecuting borderline cases. Rather, as a matter of priority, all available resources should be put into persuading parents that there are preferable and more effective methods of discipline and helping them to master the use of more constructive parenting techniques.[109] Such a program is clearly long-term,

---

106 See, for example, Eekelaar, 'The Importance of Thinking that Children have Rights' (1992) 6 IJFL 221.

107 Because a property owner is motivated only by his own interest in deciding how to treat his property.

108 Dr Kadman, the head of the National Council for the welfare of the children compared this progress with the 'step backward' taken in England by the Government's Report which recommended defining what is reasonable physical punishment and which was published the week before the decision in *Plonit* (The newspaper, Ha'aretz 26.1.00) With respect, whilst it might be argued that the English proposal is too limited (see Barton, *supra* note 98), it is rather difficult to accept that it is a step backwards as it clarifies and narrows the scope of reasonable punishment and thus should reduce the incidence of discipline escalating into abuse. Indeed the US author Johnson (*supra* note 19 at p 479) regards her similar recommendations 'as a reasonable first step leading to a society that is less tolerant of child abuse'.

109 The author's personal impression is that parental guidance courses, mainly private, are considerably more widespread in Israel than in England. However, considerable long term public funding is required in order to provide the level of coverage required to produce noticeable results.

but if successful its benefits for children and society as a whole will be far wider than the reduced use of physical punishment.[110]

ITALY

DE FACTO FAMILIES AND THE LAW: DEALING WITH RULES AND FREEDOM OF CHOICE

*Elena Urso**

I   INTRODUCTION

In dealing with the much debated phenomenon of *de facto* families, it is necessary, at the outset, to underline the deep inter-relationship between legal and social issues and the continuous modifications that usually affect these families as a result of these reciprocal influences. This kind of analysis presupposes a wide and complex comparison, because the problems of society cannot be properly observed in a 'static' dimension. Thus, at first sight, the scope of this survey – which is, admittedly, limited to a specific national context – is likely to be seen as being in contradiction with the purpose of taking into account the multi-faceted and transnational character of the situations at stake. However, an effort will be made in this direction, even though the resulting perspective will probably appear too narrow. Furthermore, no definitive solution will be envisaged as 'the best one'. On the contrary, some comparative conclusions on these issues could hopefully be drawn from this brief description of the Italian experience in this area.[1]

Italy is, perhaps, the European country which represents one of the most interesting examples of the static situation that may stem from the deliberate decision not to modify a well-established system in which a central role has been exclusively conferred on the 'legitimate' family (ie the family based on marriage). This is so, both on a constitutional and on a legislative level, although there are good reasons to believe that the features of this model are not so universal today as they were in the past, given the clear recognition of the same legal position of married and unmarried parents – as far as the relationships of kinship are

---

*   Lecturer, Faculty of Law, University of Florence.

1   See Section VI below. For a legal comparison, see MA Glendon, *The Transformation of Family Law – State, Law and Family in the United States and Western Europe* (1989) Chicago–London. For the Italian social context, see, in English, DL Kertzer and RP Saller (eds), *The Family in Italy from Antiquity to the Present* (1991) New Haven; in Italian, see V Pocar and P Romnfani, *Forme delle famiglie, forme del diritto. Mutamenti della famiglia e delle istituzioni nell'Europa occidentale* (1991) Milan and, for recent attempts to trace the origins of some *contemporary* experiences back to Roman law, see Lise Arends Olsen, *La femme et l'enfant dans les unions illégitimes à Rome – L'évolution du droit jusqu'au début de l'Empire* (1999) Berne. However, for critical remarks on 'diachronic' analysis, in this field, because of the deep divergencies between the terms of the comparison, see L Peppe, 'La coppia in diritto romano; tra matrimoni formali ed unioni di tipo diverso, i figli legittimi ed altri figli' in F Brunetta and A D'Angelo (eds), *Matrimonio, matrimonii* (2000) Milan, 11 ff., at 15, footnote 19, with special reference to *Freie römische Ehe und nichteheliche Lebensgemeinschaft*, Grosse Ch. (1991) Bamberg.

concerned[2] – and because of the increasing social acceptance of these 'new' unions, regardless of the presence of children.[3]

The connection between the social and legal aspects of this issue might become clearer from a perspective that cuts through the strict boundaries of national systems, such as the one adopted from the first meetings of the International Society on Family Law in the second half of the 1970s.[4] In particular, it is worth mentioning the third Conference of the Society, which took place in Sweden in 1979. On this occasion, the 'representatives of the academic communities throughout the world [...] convened by Professor Agell of Uppsala'[5] created an outstanding example of the great variety of tones that can be assumed in the comparative dialogue devoted to this subject. A similar approach has been followed in more recent years in other contexts as well.[6] A wide number of legal

---

2   See S Rodotà, 'La riforma del diritto di famiglia alla prova', in (1975) *Politica del Diritto*, 661 ff.; *Il diritto di famiglia. Prospettiva storica, disciplina costituzionale, lineamenti della riforma* (1979) Turin; M Dogliotti, 'Sulla responsabilità del genitore per il fatto della procreazione', in (1978) *Giurisprudenza Italiana*, I, 2, 185; 'Sulla qualificazione giuridica della famiglia di fatto. Spunti, questioni, prospettive', in (1980) *Giurisprudenza Italiana*, I, 1, 346.

3   Naturally, stable cohabitation without marriage, characterised by a relationship of love and affection, is not a new phenomenon if seen from an historical point of view. It is a particular issue that has been studied in the more general context of the 'European' family which has been the subject of a lot of interesting socio-legal analysis. See, for example, among the works published in the last 20 years, J Eekelaar and S Katz, *Marriage and Cohabitation in Contemporary Societies* (1980) Toronto; M Mitterarur and S Sieder, *The European Family: Patriarchy to Partnership from Middle Ages to the Present* (1982) Oxford; J Goody, *The Development of the Family and Marriage in Europe* (1983) London, Chapter IV; M Freeman and C Lyon, *Cohabitation without Marriage* (1983) London; J Rubellin-Devichi, *Les concubinages en Europe- Aspects socio-juridiques* (1989) Paris; MT Meulders Klein, 'Mariage et concubinages, ou le sens et contresens de l'histoire', in *Des concubinages dans le monde* (1990) Paris, at 263; R Saller, 'European Family History and Roman Law', in 36 *Continuity and Change* (1991) 335 ff.; M Parry, *The Law relating to Cohabitation*, 3rd ed. (1993) London; M Gullestand and M Segalen (eds), *La Famille in Europe: parenté et perpetuation familiale* (1995) Paris; J Witte, Jr, *From Sacrament to Contract – Marriage, Religion and Law in the Western Tradition* (1997) Louisville; R Hausmann and G Hohloch, *Das Recht der nichtehelichen Lebensgemeinschaft* (1999) Berlin; MT Meulders-Klein, *La personne, la famille et le droit: trois décennies de mutations en occident, 1968–1998* (1999) Bruxelles; J Goody, *The European Family – An Historico-Anthropological Essay* (2000) Oxford.

4   Among the issues which were debated during the first meeting of the Society – held in Berlin, in April 1975, and devoted to 'The Child and the Law' – the condition of children born outside marriage was carefully dealt with. See F Bates (ed), *The Proceedings of the First World Conference of the International Society on Family Law* (1976), vol. I, part 5. In these years, a new trend started to emerge, in sociological studies. See, for example, M. Anderson (ed), *Sociology of the family. Selected Readings* (1971) Harmondsworth.

5   See JM Eekelaar and SN Katz (eds), *Marriage and Cohabitation in Contemporary Societies – Areas of Legal, Social and Ethical Change – An International and Interdisciplinary Study* (1980) Toronto. This book contains the collected papers presented at the Third World Conference of the International Society on Family Law, held on 5–9 June 1979, at Uppsala.

6   In European legal literature, see – among the contributions to initiatives organised by the Council of Europe – 'Les problèmes juridiques posés par les couples non mariés', in *Actes du Onzième Colloque de droit européen*, held at Messina on 8–10 July 1981 (1982) Strasbourg. More recently, the Fifth European Conference on Family Law – which was held at the Hague on 15–16 March 1999 – was devoted to 'Civil Aspects of Emerging Forms of Registered Partnerships: Legally Regulated Forms of Non-Marital Cohabitation and Registered Partnerships'. For a more up-to-date survey, see C Forder, 'Models of Domestic Partnership Laws: The Field of Choice' (paper presented at the conference on 'Domestic Partnerships' held at Queen's University, Kingston, Ontario in October 1999, forthcoming in *Transforming Family Relationships* (2001) The Hague).

writers have shown an increasing interest in this new field of family law with a view to greater understanding of current sociological developments and trends and have tried to find clearer answers to some complex – and partially unresolved – legal questions.[7]

Naturally, any attempt to draw sharp 'border-lines' between legal systems would inevitably reveal a very closed attitude, but it goes out without saying that a national survey cannot focus on all the general problems linked with *'Family Living in a Changing Society'*,[8] especially if its main purpose consists of listing the specific aspects of one (social and legal) experience only. Thus, as has already been said, this review will centre exclusively on the most relevant modifications of family life which characterise Italian society. Moreover, it will be limited to a 20-year time-span (1980–2000). In these decades, the emerging phenomenon of cohabitation without marriage became accepted and frequent social behaviour, the importance of which now calls for renewed attention to the real challenge: respecting the freedom of *de facto* couples on the one hand,[9] and protecting their fundamental rights, without eliminating the differences between such relationships and unions based on marriage, on the other.[10]

In Italian, see: 'Una legislazione per la famiglia di fatto?', *Atti del Convegno di Roma* (1988) Naples; A Corsi, G Saporito and F Tassinari (eds), 'La famiglia di fatto ed i rapporti patrimoniali tra conviventi', *Atti del XXXIII Congresso Nazionale del Notariato*, held at Naples on 29 September–2 October 1993 (1993) Rome. For information on legal developments in this field, it is now possible to consult some websites. Most of them have a transnational character, but, apart from the frequent presence of 'links', they contain also brief and up-to-date 'national legislative surveys' on-line. See, in Italian, for instance, <http://www.unionicivili.org>.

7   However, the most important modifications of this field of family law were made in the second half of the 1990s, when a growing number of States started to enact new Acts dealing with *de facto* couples. Articles and interesting up-to-date surveys also devoted to foreign legal systems have recently been published in Italy. See F Brunetta and A D'Angelo (eds), *Matrimonio, matrimonii* (2000), Milan; E Calò *Le convivenze registrate in Europa- Verso un secondo regime patrimoniale della famiglia (*2000) Milan; P Longo, 'Riflessi italici delle convivenze registrate europee', and E Calò, 'Le convivenze registrate nelle legislazioni dell'Unione Europea', in (2000) *Rivista del Notariato*, respectively at 186 ff. and at 1059 ff.; B Del Dotto, 'Sui rapporti patrimoniali tra conviventi *more uxorio*', and M. Astone, 'Ancora sulla famiglia di fatto: evoluzione e prospettive', in (1999) *Diritto di Famiglia e delle Persone*, respectively at 879 ff. and 1462 ff.; G Maccarrone, 'Sulla regolamentazione delle relazioni di coppie extralegali', in *Rivista del Notariato* (1997) 745 ff. However, a vast series of contributions have been published since the late 1970s. See: 'La famiglia di fatto', *Atti del Convegno Nazionale* (held at Pontremoli, in 1976) (1976) Montereggio; *La riforma del diritto di famiglia dieci anni dopo. Bilanci e prospettive,* Atti del Convegno di Verona, 14–15 giugno 1985' (1986) Padova.

8   This was the title of the Third World Conference of the International Society on Family Law, that was centred on cohabitation without marriage. See footnote 6 above. A clear and complete report was published in Italian the following year. See V Franceschelli, 'La famiglia di fatto da *deviant phenomenon* a istituzione sociale (a proposito di un recente Convegno)', in (1980) *Diritto di Famiglia e delle Persone,* 1256.

9   The title (and the contents) of one of the most famous essays which was devoted to this issue in the first half of the twentieth century point out this difficulty in a very clear way. See R Savatier, *Le droit, l'amour et la liberté* (1937) Paris. In Italian legal writings, see G Furgiuele, *Libertà e famiglia* (1979) Milan, at 277 ff.; L Mengoni, 'La famiglia in una società complessa', in (1990) *Iustitia* 3.

10   This is the reason why the problems linked to the proposals about the extending of marriage to lesbian and gay couples are not dealt with here. See, for some brief references, Section VI. On this issue, for different appraisals, see, in Italian, F Tommaseo, *Lezioni di diritto di famiglia* (2000) Padova, at 19–20 and E Calò, *Le convivenze registrate in Europa – Verso un secondo regime patrimoniale della famiglia* (2000) Milan, 72 ff. In a comparative perspective, see E Ceccherini, *Il principio di non discriminazione in base all'orientamento sessuale: un diritto degli omosessuali al matrimonio?*, in *Rivista di Diritto Pubblico Comparato ed Europeo*, no.1

Obviously, this implies constant activity which requires the balancing of opposing interests. In so doing, well-defined policy choices should be envisaged, but there are good reasons to believe that this has not happened in Italy, so far. As we shall see later on, when we look at the proposals presented in the last two decades, a lot of Bills were drafted, albeit in different styles, in order to regulate the principal aspects of unions not based on marriage, but there is still a complete lack of agreement as far as the existence and the scope of legislative intervention is concerned.[11]

At first glance, it seems that there has been a sufficient degree of attention to these problems if one emphasises the role that was played by some statutory provisions which dealt with certain aspects of the relationships of *de facto* couples.[12] However, these types of interventions were made on an *ad hoc* basis, so that it might be misleading to give them a wider importance.[13] Undoubtedly, in a growing number of cases, it is possible to observe an ongoing process of judicial modernisation of 'remedies and tools', which were applied to families based on marriage, and were extended to *de facto* families as well. [14] Generally speaking, it is possible to say that such developments do not form part of a deliberate project of reform in favour of *de facto* unions and families and, in the rare cases in which they produced (or are going to give rise to) legislative modifications, they represent the consequences of a set of free-standing innovations. They are, to a large extent, the final phase of a sort of preliminary work brought about by legal doctrine and by the case-law, in order to eliminate the worst aspects of unequal treatment leading to manifest inconsistency with the principles of social solidarity and of substantial equality enshrined, respectively, by Articles 2 and 3, para 2 of the Italian Constitution.[15]

(2001); A D'Angelo, *La difesa del matrimonio eterosessuale negli Stati Uniti*, in *Politica del Diritto* (2000) 295 ff. An up-to-date comparative overview is proposed by R Wintemute and M Andenæs (eds), *Legal Recognition of Same Sex Partnership – A Study of National, European and International Law* [forthcoming, (March 2001) Oxford]. This book is based on the papers from a Centre of European Law Conference organized by Dr Robert Wintemute at King's College, London, on 1–3 July 1999. On these issues, more generally, see R Wintemute, *Sexual Orientation and Human Rights* (1997) Oxford; S Balletti, 'Le coppie omosessuali, le istituzioni comunitarie e la Costituzione italiana', in (1996) *Rassegna di Diritto Civile*, 252.

11	Only the most recent Bills will be briefly examined. For further information on previous Bills (ie, no. 1647, presented on 9 October 1987 by the former Communist Party; no. 861, proposed by the former Christian Democrats and presented on 17 February 1988; and no. 2340, presented by the Socialist Party, together with the Social Democrats, the 'Liberali', the 'Radicali' and the Green Party, on 12 December 1988), see: A Segreto, 'Il convivente *more uxorio* nella giurisprudenza della Corte costituzionale', in (1989) *Diritto di Famiglia e delle Persone*, 823 ff., at 853–859; G Fuà 'Il legislatore e il giudice di fronte alla famiglia di fatto', in (1989) *Diritto di Famiglia e delle Persone*, 775 ff.; M Doglio, 'Due progetti di legge per la famiglia di fatto', in (1989) II, 328 ff.; M Astone, 'Ancora sulla famiglia di fatto', in (1999) *Diritto di Famiglia e delle Persone*, 1462 ff., at footnote 14, and at 1476 ff. See Section VI below.

12	On these issues, see E Roppo, 'Famiglia – III) Famiglia di fatto', in *Enciclopedia Giuridica Treccani* (1988) Rome; CM Bianca, 'La famiglia – Le successioni', in *Diritto Civile*, II (1992) 2nd ed, at 24-29.

13	Here, we are dealing mainly with rights conferred by the public law, or, rather, by statutory provisions which aimed at avoiding the most serious unjustified discrimination in *de facto* situations deserving special protection. See Section V below.

14	See Section V below.

15	Although the impact of the decisions of the Constitutional Court has been rather limited, a proactive role has been played by both First Instance and Appeal Courts, while the Court of Cassation has been more cautious, in this respect.

II THE CONSTITUTIONAL CONCEPT OF FAMILY

The first impression that one has, when following the long discussion concerning the various attempts to enact detailed or general statutory provisions in this context, is that an evident opposition has constantly blocked all of them. It is all the more clear that the mere fact that the most innovative ideas have been expressed almost exclusively by legal scholars and that the only concrete steps to date have been taken in case-law, does not, in itself, explain the lack of any ensuing legislative activity, or the spasmodic and very circumscribed character of the latter.[16] Not so, paradoxically, was the Constitution – and some of its 'core provisions' (ie the above-mentioned Articles 2 and 3) – which became the starting point of these deeply contrasting views.[17]

Both those who tried to confer a legal *status* on *de facto* unions and those who were firmly opposed to it have invoked the same constitutional guarantees to strengthen their own argument. On one hand, the promoters of a new concept of the family, which should be inclusive of *de facto* unions, recalled the

---

16 Given that the case-law has been decisive, in Italy, in this activity of widening private law protection in favour of the 'weaker member' of a *de facto* couple, one can argue from this that there is no need to make efforts to draft an Act, especially if private agreements can properly and legitimately adjust the *de facto* partners' interests. Moreover, lower jurisdictions tend to follow higher judges' decisions, and consequently it might be thought that legislative recognition of *de facto* relationships would only complicate the situation, in a useless way. It should, however, be remembered that, in a civil law system, precedents are followed only as far as they are considered persuasive, because they have no formal binding force. Thus, apart from any generic consideration about the higher level of certainty that can be reached by legislative provisions, the quest for a statutory reception of these judicial developments can be seen as due to the need to respect some general principles covering the interpretative criteria applicable throughout family law. In this area, there is no room for analogical interpretations – given the lack of an *'eadem legis ratio'* – and this may be deemed to be the most compelling reason for a formal transmission of the current (case-law) solutions into a legislative framework. As we shall see, although some proposals were also made with a view to expanding the scope of applicability of rules which were drafted for married couples, they are not convincing because of the absence of the fundamental foundations of any 'extensive interpretation' (*interpretazione estensiva*), which would be 'legislatively' imposed. Indeed, it is evident that the intention of *de facto* couples is contrary to the idea of being bound by a formal link analogous to that created by wedlock, and to accepting all the corresponding, reciprocal duties so that – in the event that their relationship should be compulsorily regulated (without any possibility of opting for an autonomous agreement) – the field of choice of cohabitants would be totally impaired.

Special legislation has been enacted mainly for this reason. For instance, this happened in the field of war-pension legislation (see later footnote 46) and in connection with the adoption of social measures (ie, for revenue purposes, in order to widen the number of the dependants not yet of age – t.u. no. 645 enacted in 1958; or with a view to defining a family, as far as its registration in the State Registry is concerned – d.P.R. no. 136, 31 January 1958, Article 2; and to allow some of the 'natural' relatives of a deceased beneficiary of an old age pension to enjoy it in reversibility – t.u. no. 1092 of 1973, Article 84), and to permit a person condemned to imprisonment to give assistence also to his or her cohabitants (L. no. 354, 29 July 1975), and to offer the information services on reproduction and contraception not only to 'single persons' and 'families', but also to 'couples' (L. no. 405, 7.29.1975, Article 1). Equal treatment between legitimate and *de facto* families for analogous social purposes has subsequently been achieved. For example, in Act no. 53, 8 March 2000 (implementation of the Directive of the European Union 96/34/EC), in the area of parental leave and in the general reform of the Italian system of social services and protection, recently approved by the Parliament (Act no. 328, 8 November 2000, 'Legge quadro per la realizzazione del sistema integrato di interventi e servizi sociali', in *Gazzetta Ufficiale*, no 265, 13 November 2000, supplemento ordinario).

See below in the text.

17 See Section V below.

constitutional approach *vis-à-vis* the recognition and protection of fundamental human rights – or, rather, the 'inviolable rights of man' (*'diritti inviolabili dell'uomo'*),[18] – which referred to the person 'both as an individual and as a member of the social groups (*"formazioni sociali"*) in which his personality finds expression'. At the same time, they stressed the affirmation – contained in the Constitutional Charter – of 'imperative political, economic and social duties' (Article 2). Furthermore, they observed a close connection between these general statements and the 'specification' contained in Article 29, which states that 'the [Italian] Republic recognises the rights of the family as a *natural association* founded on *marriage'*. In this way, they proposed the family as a 'natural association' relevant in itself, namely as a 'social group' (Article 2) which deserves constitutional protection *per se*, even in the absence of marriage.

On the other hand, this solution has been rejected openly by those who have followed a literal and historical interpretation of the Constitution, which is linked to the intention of its drafters. In brief, notwithstanding the importance of the changes in society and the objective relevance assumed by *de facto* unions in the long period of time which has elapsed since the Charter was enacted, the regulation of their relationships should continue to be only a 'matter of private law', and not a public law issue. Even if this is a substantive choice, after all, it is also based on a formal refusal to reach wide constructions of the constitutional text, whenever that text is sufficiently clear that it avoids any uncertainty.[19]

The greatest obstacles to a general, statutory modification of this field of family law are due to other difficulties as well, which depend on the need to respect another constitutional choice. In fact, beside the limitation that we have just seen, concerning the recognition of the rights of the family as a 'natural

---

18   This is the literal translation of the Constitutional provision embodied in Article 2. The English
      version of the Italian Constitution will be quoted, hereinafter, from the text provided by the
      Italian Embassy in London, in 1948, as reviewed and partially rewritten by C Fusaro, with the
      assistence of F Signorini.

19   It is interesting to remember the opinion expressed on this point by a great Italian
      constitutionalist, Paolo Barile. After stressing the disagreement which had arisen before the
      definitive approval, by the Constituent Assembly, of Article 29 (or, more precisely, of Article 23
      of the Tentative Draft of the Charter), he affirmed, on the one hand, that 'it is worthwhile
      underlining that the first paragraph and the second one of [this article] were voted separately [...,]
      so that the connection between the natural association and the marriage seemed even more
      evident – as can be said today as well'. On the other hand, he pointed out that, during the debate,
      severe criticism was shown of this choice, which was considered by Piero Calamandrei as a 'very
      serious mistake from a logical point of view [, because s]peaking of a natural association which
      springs from marriage – ie, from a legal institution based on an agreement [*negozio giuridico*] – is
      [...] a contradiction in terms': See P Barile, 'La famiglia di fatto – Osservazioni di un
      costituzionalista', in *La famiglia di fatto – Atti del Convegno Nazionale di Pontremoli*, 27–28
      maggio 1976 (1976) Montereggio, at 43–44.
          Given its link with marriage, the concept of 'natural association' appeared unclear, and its
      evocative meaning was criticized as a vague tribute to the theories of 'natural law'. However, if
      some criticism could be justified, the intent of the Drafters of the Constitution was easy to
      understand by interpreting their debate. Their opposing positions reinforce the idea that a
      compromise was reached. Indeed, the framers of the Constitution arrived at the composite
      'formula' of Article 29 only after a long discussion. In the preliminary Draft prepared by the sub-
      commission (the so-called *Commissione dei 75*), the provision devoted to the family, which
      remained unchanged in the final text, contained both the indications expressed by the main,
      opposing political groups. Thus, the more relevant modification, with respect to the previous
      version, was the elimination of any mention of the character of indissolubility of marriage (which
      was then present in the Civil Code).

association' on condition that it is 'founded on marriage', there is a further specification of the position of the legitimate family. According to Article 30, para 3 of the Constitution 'the law shall ensure the fullest legal and social protection for children born out of wedlock, consistent (*compatibile*) with the rights of the members of the legitimate family'. The priority conferred on the legitimate family is reflected by both the above-mentioned provisions, so that it is possible to say that no specific constitutional guarantee was given to *de facto* families.[20]

However, the meaning of these provisions cannot be correctly understood nowadays if a unique relevance is given to their wording only when and if they are read in isolation. In other words, when the Constitution was enacted, in 1948,[21] the system created by the Civil Code in 1942 was very different from the current one in this context, in the sense that the then so-called 'natural' children received very different treatment from that provided for 'legitimate' offspring. Indeed, amongst the most revealing instances of departures from the original code model it is worthwhile emphasising again the condition of children of unmarried parents, which has been almost completely equated to that of children born in a 'legitimate' family.[22]

---

20 In defining the family, another expression is commonly used, but always with reference to the constitutional 'model'. The family is also described as an 'intermediate' social group (*formazione sociale intermedia*), because of its position 'in the middle', between the individual and the State. However, this concept is a specification of the more general one contained in the Constitution (ie *formazioni sociali*), on which the entire fundamental guarantee framework is built up (Article 2). Family is specifically characterized by its 'voluntary origin and its consensual basis' and it is this feature that differentiates it from the social groups with a 'necessary and organic' character. See, for these remarks, recently, P Rescigno, 'Interessi e conflitti nella famiglia: l'istituto della "mediazione familiare"', in *Giurisprudenza Italiana* IV (1995) 73 ff.

21 During the previous period, the Italian Constitution was the *Statuto*, which had been granted by King Charles Albert of the Kingdom of Piedmont-Sardinia, on 8 February 1848. The *Statuto*, which became the Constitutional Charter of united Italy in 1861, was in force until the end of the Second World War. In the section devoted to 'The rights and duties of citizens' (Articles 24–32) there was no mention of the family or the institution of marriage. Article 1 of the *Satuto* proclaimed Roman Catholicism as the only state religion, but the other existing religious denominations were recognised. The Republican Constitution was drafted by a Constitutional Convention (*Assemblea costituente*) which was elected popularly. Its final text was approved by the *Assemblea costituente* on 22 December 1947 and the Charter entered into force on 1 January 1948. The enactment of the new Civil Code of the Kingdom of Italy – which substituted the 1865 Civil Code – dated back to 16 March 1942 (See R.d. 3.16.1942, XX, n. 262.) The lack of indications about the family, in the *Statuto*, which was a flexible Constitution, left enough room to the legislature, so that the 1942 Civil Code could make very conservative choices in this field.

22 This happened 25 years ago when the Act that reformed family law was enacted. The use of different expressions is not only a matter of choosing – as they say – the 'politically correct' ones, or some 'médications verbales', because there are 'painful words' ('des mots qui font mal'). It is a question of recognizing the need to avoid terms which have a real insulting character ('une connotation blessante'). See J Carbonnier, *Essais sur les loi* (1995) 2nd Paris, at 284. In Italy, '[e]ven if, for the current legislation, a "natural family" (*famiglia naturale*) does not, so far, exist, there is no doubt that the status of natural offspring has the nature of a status familiae, at least for the importance that this has with regard to the family of the natural parent. Furthermore, it is a contradiction to deny that the relationships of kinship and of parenthood, in the cases provided for by the law, have the nature of family relationships'. Cfr. 'Parentela naturale, famiglia e successione', Santoro Passarelli F, in (1981) *Rivista Trimestrale di Diritto e Procedura Civile*, 27 ff., at 30. See – on these issues – later in the text.

III   THE ABSENCE OF A PRIVATE LAW 'SYSTEM' FOR *DE FACTO* FAMILIES

As soon as the phenomenon of *de facto* unions started to become increasingly common – though not so widespread as today[23] – from the second half of the 1970s, some Italian legal writers engaged in a very interesting and lively debate on the issue and agreed on the need to draft *ad hoc* statutory provisions to regulate it.[24] Apart from certain unavoidable divergences about the details of this possible legislative intervention, there seemed to be a prevailing convergence towards the recognition of a special regime for these situations. Perhaps the reliance on public measures as the most useful instrument to protect family life reached its highest level in these years, so that the family could hardly be still considered as an autonomous private sphere,[25] or, rather, as an 'island' surrounded by the 'sea of the law', which could only lap on this 'rock in the wave'.[26]

---

23   The data collected by the Italian Institute of Statistics (ISTAT) confirm that the total number of *de facto* families is rather high today, but a new trend has been ascertained recently. According to these data, about three million persons have cohabitated or are cohabiting in Italy, outside marriage. Even if this is a general trend, it is more common in the North Eastern region of Italy, and in Emilia Romagna. The rate of cohabitant couples that decide to marry is increasing, but the partners do not necessarily decide to marry when they have a child, as happened more frequently in the past. The number of cohabitants was much lower (184,000) ten years ago, while it has risen to 344,000 in 1999, ie 2.3% of all Italian couples. While, in Southern Italy, the most pressing difficulty consists in finding a job, in other areas of the country housing problems are also very serious, especially for young couples. Thus, some of them (not only unmarried couples) have started to live in different towns. Cfr. Rapporto sull'Italia, ISTAT (1999) Bologna at 94 ff. On these issues, see also ML Sabbadini, 'Modelli di formazione e organizzazione della famiglia', contribution to the meeting 'Le famiglie interrogano le politiche sociali', held at Bologna, on 29–30 March 1999 (text available on the website: http://www.istat.it/Primapag/famiglia.html). More recently, see for a brief account of the outcomes of research made in 2000, in the media, 'Gli italiani si scoprono eterni fidanzati', in *Il Corriere della Sera*, 12.13.2000, at 17.

24   See N Lipari, 'La categoria giuridica della 'famiglia di fatto' e il problema dei rapporti personali al suo interno', and FD Busnelli, 'Sui criteri di determinazione della disciplina normativa della famiglia di fatto', in *La famiglia di fatto, Atti del Convegno Nazionale* (held at Pontremoli, in 1976) (1976) Montereggio, respectively at 53 ff. and 133 ff.

25   This is a well-known definition that is quoted often, and which was proposed for the first time in a famous essay, albeit in a more general context. See CA Jemolo, 'La famiglia e il diritto', in *Annali facoltà giur. di Catania*, II (1948) at 38 ff., also in L Scavo Lombardo (ed), *Pagine sparse di diritto e storiografia* (1957) Milan, 236. Jemolo observed that while 'economic values' can be satisfactorily protected by legal remedies, in contrast, in approaching the 'zone of immaterial values', the task for the legislator becomes more and more difficult, because the sphere of 'affection' (*'ambito affettivo'*) is at stake, and no legal rule can properly affirm duties or rights, in this field. In order to have a wider vision of this author's ideas, not only on these topics, see 'Jemolo, testimone di un secolo', in G Spadolini (ed), *Quaderni della Nuova Antologia*, 11 (1981) Florence.

26   Some of the new solutions adopted by the legislator gave a relevant role to the judge, whose intervention has been subordinated, however, to the possibility for the private parties to reach an agreement (see Article 316, paras 3 and 5, of the Civil Code). Experience will show how the reliance on this new judicial activity is too optimistic. After all, an excessive confidence in the resolutory function of an external subject may express a sort of renewed public dimension of family law, which can give rise to some undesired effects, linked to an idea of the family as an 'identity' differentiated from its single 'units' (ie from its components), so that its rights are put on a higher level, in comparison with those of its members. See, on this issue, before the 1975 Reform, P Barcellona, 'Famiglia (dir. civ.)' in XVI *Enciclopedia del diritto* (1967) Milan, 779 ff., at 782 ff.

   The 1975 Reform eliminated previous limitations to the acknowledgment and to the judicial ascertainment of paternity – contained in the Civil Code – except in a few enumerated cases (ie of incestuous offspring, whose relationship of kinship still cannot be recognised). A further, relevant

A completely new conception of ancient institutions conditioned deep changes in the family law field in this period, both from a substantive and a procedural point of view. Two fundamental developments influenced the entire system in a matter of years: the introduction of divorce in 1970,[27] and the enactment, in 1975, of the Act that reformed entire parts of the first book of the Civil Code, by inserting new Articles devoted to the personal and economic relationships between husband and wife, as well as with regard to the position of children.[28] This reforming trend has been unanimously considered to be the reaction to well known social changes, and

---

innovation deserves special attention, as it is connected with the new conception expressed by the Reform. A new provision was inserted into the Civil Code (Article 317-bis), in order to confer the parental powers ('*potestà*') on the parent who was the first to acknowledge the relationship of kinship. When the acknowledgement has been made by both parents, the law provides that they can exercise the '*potestà*' jointly, but on condition that they live together. The latter innovation has been correctly emphasised, because it represents an important and clear recognition of the 'constitutionalisation' of this area, but this does not mean that, in itself, it can found the basis of a system, in which *de facto* families receive an evident 'legislative *imprimatur*'. Naturally, this Article plays a central role, because it has produced a well balanced solution, that assumes different rules according to the special condition of the child. In fact, when the parents do not live together, the parental powers are exercised individually (ie, by the parent with whom the child lives or – in the event that the latter does not live with any parent – by the parent who was the first to make the acknowledgment). The parent who does not exercise the parental power can, however, supervise the education, the upbringing and the conditions of life of the child, but the Court (ie the Tribunal for Minors (*Tribunale per i Minorenni*) can decide differently, while taking into account the exclusive interest of the child. The competence of this Court was subsequently extended in later years (ie by the Adoption of Children Act, no. 183/1984). Originally, its role was more limited, more or less corresponding to the jurisdiction of juvenile courts. Moreover, these legislative interventions have not been well co-ordinated with the general reform of civil justice (which was gradually carried out in the 1990s). Thus, a (not so rational) separated competence still exists, together with a corresponding different procedure, in cases of proceedings which concern, respectively, the personal and the economic aspects of the relationship of kinship of children born out of wedlock. In the first hypothesis, the *Tribunale per i Minorenni* is competent, and 'in camera' procedural rules are applied, while latter cases are decided by the civil justices (*Tribunale ordinario*, whose members are professional judges, who no longer decide in panel and follow the ordinary procedure). Fundamental guarantees – constitutionally affirmed – may frequently be breached because of this illogical complication, which is even more unacceptable after the recent specification of the meaning of 'due process of law', thanks to the insertion of the principle that affirms the need that it lasts for a 'reasonable time' in the Constitution (see Article 111, as amended by the Constitutional Act no 2, enacted on 23 November 1999, in *Gazzetta Ufficiale*, 23 December 2000, n.300). For a brief and clear analysis see 'Servizi, magistratura e giusto processo', Pazé P, in *Minori-Giustizia* (1999), 7–10.

27   Act no. 898, 1 December 1970.

28   Act no. 151, 19 May 1975. The expression '*famiglia naturale*' – which has often been used in order to differentiate it from the 'legitimate' family- has started to be substituted by the term '*famiglia di fatto*', not only because of the complete absence of any, even indirect, discriminatory shade in its meaning, but also in order to underline the possibility that a *de facto* family may exist with or without children. It is worth repeating that almost complete equating has been statutorily recognised between the parental rights and duties of married and unmarried couples, thanks to the general reform which entered into force in 1975. First, no application to obtain a judicial order is necessary to confer parental rights, when the parent has recognised her motherhood or his paternity. The acknowledgment (or the judicial ascertainment) of the relationship of kinship is sufficient to give rise to a substantially identical position of all offspring – regardless of the so-called *status filiationis*. Some legal writers observed that it is the same fact of 'procreation' which determines both the legal relationship and the parental responsibilities. See M Dogliotti, 'Famiglia (dimensioni della)', in *Digesto delle Discipline Privatistiche, Sezione Civile*, Vol. VIII (1992) Turin, 174 ff., at 176, footnote 13. In a few words, the main difference concerns a peculiar inheritance right – or, rather, a preferred position – which is reserved to legitimate offspring only: they can decide whether to pay the 'natural' offspring's share of the parent's estate. They can give them a sum of money corresponding to the (identical) share of the assets of the deceased parent (the so-called '*diritto di commutazione*', embodied in Article 537, para 3 of the Civil Code).

expressed a very different way of thinking with respect to the original vision adopted by the drafters of the Code. It is beyond doubt that some indications could be inferred in this direction from the Republican Constitution, but both the principle of 'legal and moral equality of the spouses' (Article 29, 2°) and the right of equal treatment of all offspring (ie also 'those born out of wedlock' (Article 30, 1°)) had previously led to some decisive interventions by the Constitutional Court. The Court was called on to declare the unconstitutionality of some provisions which conflicted with the new principles affirmed by Constitutional Charter, especially in connection with the condition of so-called 'illegitimate' children.[29]

Other relevant modifications were made after the entry into force of the 1975 Reform, thanks to the 'constitutionalisation' of this field of family law, but in describing the influence of the Constitutional judges' intervention, it is possible to say that they have adopted a very cautious approach. Indeed, after the initial period of extreme lack of recognition – which ended in the late 1960s[30] – they displayed a more open attitude towards the 'cohabitations *more uxorio*'. In fact, after confirming – as a rule[31] – the constitutionality of the legislative choices, they

---

29   The Italian Constitutional Court started its activity in 1953. However, it was necessary to wait for the second half of the 1960s to see some developments in this context. See, for a clear survey, M Bessone and G Ferrando, 'Regime della filiazione, parentela naturale e famiglia di fatto', in (1979) *Diritto di Famiglia e delle Persone*, 1301 ff.; AG Danovi, 'Affidamento, potestà e conflitti nella famiglia di fatto', in (1989) *Diritto di Famiglia e delle Persone*, 780 ff.

30   In this first period, some provisions of the the Penal Code (enacted in 1930) were still in force. Indeed, both 'concubinage' (Article 560) and 'adultery' (Article 559) were criminally sanctioned. After two declarations of unconstitutionality, these crimes have been abrogated. The first decision declared the inconsistency between Article 559, 1° and 2° with the principle of equality of the spouses (Article 29, 2° Cost), because the law treated the wife differently, in comparison with the husband, and this discrimination was not deemed to be justified by the need to protect the 'unity' of the family. In fact, only the wife was considered criminally responsible for adultery or adulterous relationships. Thus, it was the new condition of women which called for completely equal treatment (Constitutional Court, no 126, 19 December 1968, in [1968] *Giurisprudenza Costituzionale*, 2191). The second decision was taken soon afterwards, in 1969. The Court underlined that further discrimination would continue to exist because of the applicability of Article 560, which punished exclusively the adulterous behaviour of the husband, but on condition that it gave rise to 'concubinage' (ie to a stable relationship) and that the mistress lived in the family home or in another place, provided that – in the latter case – this happened notoriously. Also the abrogation of this provision was motivated by the violation of the principle of equality (Constitutional Court, no 147, 3 December 1969, in (1969) *Giurisprudenza Costituzionale*, 2237).

31   An 'exception to the rule' is represented by a decision of unconstitutionality taken in 1988. After the tenant's death, the position of his or her unmarried partner towards the landlord is now identical to that previously affirmed only with respect to the tenant's spouse (or other relatives or persons who are 'stable cohabitants'), and treatment analogous to that provided for married partners is recognized for *de facto* couples also in the event of breakdown of the union, but on condition that they have children. This is one of the most important developments arising from the intervention of the Constitutional Court. However, this decision was not based on a comparison between legitimate and *de facto* families. In fact, there has been no declaration of unreasonableness of the statutory limitation (Article 6, 1° and 3°, L. no. 392/1978) for breach of the principle of substantial equality (Article 3, 2°, Constitution), or affirmation of the constitutional relevance of *de facto* unions. Indeed, the Court founded its reasoning on the assumption that the 'social right' to have a house has an unassailable nature, so that it falls under the protection of Article 2 of the Constitution. At the same time, it emphasised the corresponding social duty, to ensure that 'people' (*'delle persone'*) do not remain without a house, and reached the conclusion that the provision of the Rent Act – which had been subjected to judicial review – was partially unconstitutional as far as it did not allow the surviving partner of a *de facto* couple to succeed in the contractual position of the deceased partner and it did not equate the position of partner (in case of breakdown of the union, if there were children) to that of the spouse, after

show a certain concern about any clear legislative indication. All these considerations, which can be seen as 'subtle cracks' in the unitary 'structure' of the family described by the legislature, are contained, however, in *obiter dicta*, and this may justify the impression of the absence of formal and general recognition of the legal relevance of *de facto* unions. A third phase in the development of the constitutional case-law, has been characterised by more direct acknowledgment of the risks of unequal treatment, due to the persistence of clear divergencies in the statutory regulation of the position of married and unmarried couples, but no declaration of unconstitutionality has been made.[32] The extremely critical attitude often shown by a large number of legal writers towards these positions cannot be shared without any further elaboration. In fact, even if the present situation may appear unsatisfactory, because of the incomplete nature of the work performed by the Constitutional Court,[33] it cannot be 'accused' of a reactionary policy. In a civil law system, in which operates a centralised mechanism of judicial review of legislative activity, an eventual 'new structure' of

---

separation or divorce. See decision no 404, 7 April 1988, in (1990) *Diritto di Famiglia e delle Persone*, 766 ff., and for a comment, *ibidem*, M Dogliotti, 'La Corte Costituzionale attribuisce (ma solo a metà) rilevanza giuridica alla famiglia di fatto'.

The Constitutional Court has continued to follow this cautious approach in more recent years, in declaring the inadmissibility of further doubts about constitutionality. Apart from two decisions (no 341, 7.20.1990, in (1990) *Diritto di Famiglia e delle Persone*, 796 and no 203, 26 June 1997, in (1997) *Il Foro Italiano*, I, 2370), which declared, respectively, the unconstitutionality of the different legislative treatment of unmarried and married parents, as far as the requirements of the action for the judicial declaration of paternity and maternity is concerned, and in connection with the unjustified discrimination towards foreign parents, in comparison to the condition of married parents, as far as their right to reunion with their family is concerned (Article 4, para. 1, Act no. 943, 30 December 1986), all the other decisions were characterised by the denial of any possibility of equating the situations at stake.

See, for instance, Constitutional Court no.166, 13 May 1998 (on the impossibility of proposing an analogical interpretation – and an extension to *de facto* families – of the rules about the custody of children and the right to live in the family home after the separation of the married parents, Article 155 Civil Code), in (1998) *Giurisprudenza Italiana*, I, 1, 1782, annotated by C Cossu and in (1998) *Nuova Giurisprudenza Civile Commentata*, I, 678, annotated by G Ferrando; no 2, 29 January 1998 (on the inapplicability to *de facto* couples of the special régime of prescription embodied in Article 2941, para 1 Civil Code, in relation to husbands and wives), in (1998) *Il Foro Italiano*, I, 313; no. 8, 18 January 1997, in (1997) *Il Foro Italiano*, I, 2716, and no. 124, 23 July 1980, in (1980) *Diritto di Famiglia e delle Persone*, 1075 (both on the confirmation of the solution adopted by the Penal Code – Article 384 – in the sense of the justification of different treatment between members of *de facto* and legitimate families and the inadmissibility of the doubts of violation of Articles 3 and 20 of the Constitution); no 310, 26 June 1989 (on the constitutionality of the current exclusion of *de facto* partners from intestate succession rights – Articles 565, 582, 540, para 2, Civil Code, in (1989) *Diritto di Famiglia e delle Persone*, 474.

32   For instance, the choice to preclude unmarried couples from fully adopting a child (Article 6, Act no 184, 4 May 1983) has not been declared unconstitutional because it was considered a reflection of a specific statutory choice – an expression of the discretionary power of the legislature which cannot be subject to judicial review. However, the Court tried to indicate a different legislative solution, without contesting the foundation of the 'the first and indispensable requirement of marriage'. In fact, according to the current provision, a married couple can adopt a child only after a three-year period subsequent to the marriage. The Court affirmed that the suitability of the couple to adopt might be inferred from a different requirement in the sense that, in order to be adoptive parents, it might be sufficient that they had been living together for a long period, also before getting married, so that adoption could take place even before the expiration of three years of matrimonial life. See Constitutional Court, no. 281, 6 July 1994, in (1994) *Giustizia Civile*, 2706. For a brief analysis of some recent proposals made in order partially to modify this rule, see Section VII.

33   See for ample references S Patti, *Famiglia e responsabilità civile* (1984) Milan, 190 ff.

such a complex area of private law can be effected only by modifications of previous Acts. Thus, if one adopts a less partisan point of view, the judgment might be different. A realistic vision of the problem can justify, in some cases at least, the reluctance of Italian judges, who have never changed the scope of applicability of the set of rules that were 'built up' to regulate the (personal and economic) relationships of married partners. The Constitutional Court would unduly encroach on the area of pure political choices if it should engage in an open disavowal of the foundations of the current system. Whenever a question of equal protection needs to be solved, the 'reasonableness test' can be applied properly as far as a real similarity can be 'discovered' between situations only apparently differentiated, but which deserve identical legal protection. When, in contrast, the positions to be dealt with present relevant divergencies, any substantive enquiry may give rise to the risk of 'judicial legislation'. In the end, it is a matter of whether or not to accept the idea of the democratic foundations of the 'rule of law' and this necessarily implies, on one side, reliance on the balancing power produced by socio-political control, and, on the other, a certain degree of judicial self-restraint. Evidently, case-law modifications which are inevitably linked to single cases and their development – in the absence of clear statutory guidelines[34] – can be deemed to be an *'evolution'* or an *'involution'*, in connection with more general evaluations. In any case, they may correspond to a sort of *'devolution'* of power. If a lot of problems might have come to an end by following a substantive approach in the review of legislative choices, too great a tribute would have been paid, in this way, to an abstract dimension of the functions of constitutional justice. 'Hard choices' need to be supported by general consent, which has not been achieved so far. This is perhaps the principle which has resulted in the substantial abstinence from legislative activity.[35]

In continuing this brief description of the role of the judiciary, it is possible to observe that most of the decisions of the Court of Cassation and of lower jurisdictions offer another clear explanation of the complexity of the challenge at hand. Despite the persistence of some contradictions,[36] several general routes have

---

34   For a wider vision, see A Falzea, 'Problemi attuali della famiglia di fatto', in *Una legislazione per la famiglia di fatto?* (1988) Naples, 52 ff.; M Franzoni, 'I contratti tra conviventi "more uxorio"', in (1994) *Rivista Trimestrale di Diritto e Procedura Civile*, 737 ff.

For a very critical analysis of some judicial developments in this area, see A Trabucchi, 'Morte della famiglia o famiglie senza famiglia?', in (1988) I *Rivista di Diritto Civile*, 19 ff.; S Puleo, 'Famiglia – II) Disciplina privatistica: in generale', in *Enciclopedia Giuridica Treccani* (1988) Rome; S Puleo, 'Concetto di famiglia e rilevanza della famiglia naturale', in I (1979) *Rivista di Diritto Civile*, 381 ff.; A Trabucchi, 'Natura legge famiglia', in (1977) I, *Rivista di Diritto Civile*, 1 ff.; L Carraro, 'Riflessioni sulla nozione costituzionale di famiglia', in *Studi in memoria di Enrico Gucciardi* (1975) Padova.

35   The express mention of cohabitants in a recent piece of legislation (d.P.R. no 223, 30 May 1989, on the registration in the Registry Office of families which are resident in a municipal area) tries to solve only administrative problems. The 'cohabitants *more uxorio*' have been put in a position analogous to that of spouses in order to take the place of the deceased partner, so that they can obtain the same share of property in cases of co-operative societies which entail a joint ownership (Act 179/1992, Article 17, 2° and 3°). However, this is also an innovation which operates in a very striclty limited field.

36   For an up-to-date examination, see G Ferrando, 'Famiglia di fatto: gioielli e mobili antichi vanno restituiti alla fine della convivenza?', in (2000) *Famiglia e Diritto*, 284, at 286 ff. and, for a brief description of the current situation, D Morello Di Giovanni, 'Famiglia di fatto e dovere di contribuzione', in (2000) *Famiglia e Diritto*, 502–503. It is not possible to propose a complete list of cases which would be helpful in clarifying this trend. See, for instance, Court of Cassation,

been traced. Beginning with the area of 'external relations' (ie with third parties), a final solution has been recently found for some cases of tortious liability: *de facto* partners can claim and obtain compensation from the wrongdoer, for both the pecuniary and the non-pecuniary losses which they suffered as a consequence ·of the partner's wrongful death.[37]

Equal treatment has been recognised by the Constitutional Court also, as far as the possibility of succeeding to the tenancy rights of the partner is concerned, on condition that the partner has been living in the household, both in the case of the tenant's death and of the breakdown of the union when – in the latter case – there are children and the tenant left the family house.[38]

Similarly, if one thinks about the 'internal relationships' (ie the 'reciprocal relationships between the partners'), it is possible to find some clear signs of a certain legal recognition of the position of the 'economically weaker' member of the couple. In the case of spontaneous compliance with the 'social and moral' duty to contribute to his/her maintenance, there is no possibility of obtaining the restitution of the goods, or the money which formed part of these free transactions, which become personal acquisitions of the beneficiary (Article 2034, Civil Code).[39] Furthermore, apart from cases of professional co-operation or domestic activities (which are subject to a rebuttable presumption that they are not intended to affect legal relations), according to a well-established case-law trend, any other work activities done by one of the partners have to be regulated by common principles and the rules of labour law, which operate in the area of employment, provided that there is sufficient evidence to show the existence of this kind of relationship.[40] An analogous, high level of certainty is required in order to prove the participation of the partner in a commercial company or association.[41]

---

no. 4053, 24 April 1987, in (1987) *Diritto di Famiglia e delle Persone*, 582 (on the difference between valid and void agreements between the partners); no. 5410, 7 December 1989, in (1990) *Diritto di Famiglia e delle Persone*, 428 (on the contraposition between grants made by one partner with a view to marriage – Article 785 Civil Code – and economic contributions not linked to such a perspective); no 3505, 26 July 1989, in (1990) *Diritto di Famiglia e delle Persone*, 411 (on the applicability of Article 739 of the Code of civil procedure in cases of action for the judicial declaration of a 'natural' relationship of kinship). The number of decisions taken by First Instance Courts is so high that no complete references are possible here.

37   For a completely opposite solution, see Court of Cassation no 169/1958 and, for a comment on the previous situation, see G Sbisà, 'Risarcimento di danni in seguito a morte di un 'familiare di fatto', in (1965) *Rivista Trimestrale di Diritto e Procedura Civile*, 1254 ff.; G Gentili, 'Sul risarcimento del danno da morte del convivente, nella giurisprudenza francese e italiana', in (1985) *Diritto di Famiglia e delle Persone*, 1126 ff. The last decision, in favour of the equalisation of *de facto* partners, was taken in 1994, no. 2988.

        There has been no doubt that a *de facto* partner can take part (as *'parte civile'*) in criminal proceedings against a person accused of being the author of the homicide of his/her partner. Similarly, the compulsory insurance protection provided for the spouse, in cases of car accidents, by the Act no. 990, 24 December 1969 (Article 4) has been extended to the *'more uxorio* cohabitant'. See MG Cubeddu, 'Il rapporto di convivenza', in (1990) *Nuova Giurispridenza Civile Commentata*, 329 ff.

38   See Constitutional Court no. 404/1988. Subsequently, see Court of Cassation no. 9868/1997.

39   See, eg, Court of Cassation, nos. 69/1969, 2512/1973, 285/1989. In contrast, it is not so common that judges accept the hypothesis of 'unjust enrichment', given the absolute residuary nature of the corresponding claim (Article 2041, Civil Code) and the assumed 'justified' (and not 'unjust') character of the 'enrichment'. See Court of Cassation nos. 10271/1978, 2118/1967.

40   See Court of Cassation nos. 1024/1978, 3203/1971, 6083/1991.

41   See Court of Cassation nos. 1810/1980, 4221/1979, 1161/1977, 13261/1999.

Moreover, in the application of fundamental principles of contract law,[42] the agreements between the partners are not only considered valid, in the sense that they are no longer deemed to be in conflict with public policy, but they are judicially enforceable and a claim for restitution will be rejected by the Courts.[43]

A less convincing solution has been given to the problem of the applicability of a special provision on organised forms of productive activity within the family (the so-called '*impresa familiare*' regulated by Article 230-*bis*, Civil Code).[44] The justification for denying the possibility of extending this rule to the contribution of a *de facto* partner to productive activity organised in the family context is linked to the common refusal to use analogical interpretative criteria in the field of family law.[45]

In general, it is possible to observe that the situation has been gradually developed, thanks to these judicial interventions, which were made in the light of Constitutional principles (affirmed by Articles 2, 3 and 30, para 3). Now, that we have a wider vision of the scenario created by the reform of family law 25 years ago and of the main judicial trends, it is clear that further steps are necessary in order to ensure a real and complete correspondence between private law rules and these fundamental principles.[46] The 1975 reform was a good starting point, but its

---

42   Articles 1321, 1322, 1346, 1372, para 1, and 1418 of the Civil Code.

43   See for wide references, F Tommasini, 'La famiglia di fatto', I, *Trattato di diritto privato*, IV, Bessone (ed) (1997) Turin, 449 ff., at footnotes 45--49.

44   See, for a coherent refusal of the applicability of this rule, Court of Cassation no 4204, 5.2.1994, in *Il Foro Italiano* (1995) I, 1935. Article 230-bis Civil Code has introduced an exceptional regulation of this kind of work activity. In fact, 'except a different relationship can be envisaged', the member of the (legitimate) family who works in the family or in the '*impresa familiare*' has the right to be maintained, in proportion to the economic conditions of the family, and to share in the profits or in the properties acquired thereby and in the acquisitions. Less convincing reasons were given in other decisions. See Court of Cassation, no. 1701, 17 February 1988, in (1988) *Il Foro Italiano*, I, 2306.

45   See Court of Cassation nos 3012/1978, 1161/1977, 3012/1978, 1701/1988, 6083/1991, 4204/1994.

46   The role of the legislator has been generally characterised by extreme restraint. The very first piece of special legislation that conferred legal dignity on *de facto* relationships – by giving a legal protection corresponding to that provided for the wife to the unmarried partner – was an Act enacted soon after the First World War in order to deal with situations which are only of historical interest, today, but which are all the more relevant to understanding the outlines of the Italian 'legal framework'. This Act allowed the war pension (a) to a woman who had been engaged to an Italian soldier but who could not marry him because of his death, if he died more than one month after the date of the so-called 'pubblicazioni' (ie banns, or the formal publication of the promise of marriage) – Article 11 of d.L. 27 October 1918, n.1726 – or (b) whenever a soldier declared his intention to marry a woman, while he was in danger for his life – Article 12 – but provided that the couple had lived together in the past, and that both these situations could be demonstrated by a legal document (*atto giudiziale di notorietà*). In the latter case, the legislator attached clear importance to the fact of cohabitation *more uxorio*, while, in the former, the position of the soldier's fiancée was equated simply to that of a wife. This Act was subsequently incorporated, with a few amendments, into a new law, L. no. 313, 18 March 1968,which partially repealed the previous provisions and extended their applicability to all cases of war pensions.

      Then, the 1865 Civil Code was still in force, given that the new Civil Code became effective from 1942. For a deep analysis of this period of Italian family law history, which is comprehensive of the legal background prior to the unification of the Italian state (1861), see P Ungari, *Il diritto di famiglia in Italia – dalle Costituzioni 'giacobine' al Codice civile del 1942* (1970) Bologna. For a direct appraisal of the reasons underlying the legislative choice to give a strong protection to the 'legitimate family based on marriage', see the 'Relazione sul Progetto del Codice Civile', G Pisanelli, in *Codice Civile, preceduto dalle Relazioni Ministeriale e Senatoria,*

innovatory solutions are not sufficient for today. They were a decisive influence on the modernisation of the system of family law, but perhaps the fear of running counter to constitutional guidelines blocked a wider project. While the rights and duties of unmarried parents were expressly and totally equated with those of married parents [47] (in conformity with Article 30, para 1), the 'legitimate family' – which is the only one directly recognised by the Constitution and also protected by the general provisions of Article 2 – maintained its exclusive position, in the legislative context.[48]

Other aspects of the Italian constitutional system need to be briefly mentioned so as to describe the role ascribed to civil and religious marriage and to understand the reasons that might have influenced the social and legal rejection of several initiatives which tried to regulate the unions of unmarried couples.

---

dalle Discussioni Parlamentari e dai Verbali della Commissione coordinatrice (1887) Turin, at 20–28 and 88 ff.

47 See later in the text.

48 A certain relevance has been conferred on *de facto* unions in the criminal law, but there is still a clear difference between the position of the members of the legitimate family, in several respects. In addition to the legislative interventions already mentioned – see footnotes nos 13 and 45 above – others can be listed. All of them are characterised, however, for not representing 'systematic choices'. See, for example, the modification contained in the new code of criminal procedure (which entered into force in 1989, and changed the previous rule, embodied in Article 350 of the 1930 Code). According to Article 199, the close relatives ('*prossimi congiunti*') of a person charged with a crime are not obliged to testify in the proceedings. The judge – under penalty of nullity – gives them notice of this power of abstention and asks them if they want to exercise it. These provisions are applicable – although exclusively with regard to events that happened or are known, by the person accused, during the cohabitation – to a person who, albeit not married to the accused, lives (or has lived) with him/her as a husband or a wife (Article 199, 3, [a]).

However, no general equal treatment between the members of *de facto* and legitimate families has been achieved in the criminal law area. The Court of Cassation has denied that the position of *de facto* partners can be equated to that of the members of the legitimate family, as far as the application of Article 384 of the Penal Code is concerned. This provision excludes, *inter alia*, the possibility that a person can be punished when – notwithstanding the commission of facts which would otherwise be criminally sanctioned as public wrongs against the administration of justice – he/she was compelled to behave in this way because of the need to save a close relative from a serious and unavoidable harm to freedom or honour (see Court of Cassation no 181759/1989). Any extensive interpretation of the legal definition of close relatives (Article 307 Penal Code) has been rejected, so that the applicability of the provision at stake was excluded (see Court of Cassation no. 7684, 4 August 1982, no 6365, 27 May 1988; no 132, 20 March 1991).

Thus, there is no possibility of saying that the position of a *de facto* partner is equal to that of a spouse. The doubts of unconstitutionality, which were expressed with reference to the criminal sanctions applicable to *de facto* partners – and not to spouses and close relatives – in the case of abetting, were declared 'inadmissible' by the Court in an another decision (no. 237, 18 November 1986, in I (1986) *Giustizia Penale*, 353). See, for a detailed analysis of other decisions which have similarly declared unfounded (or inadmissible) further doubts of constitutionality, for instance, A Segreto, 'Il convivente *more uxorio* nella giurisprudenza della Corte costituzionale e della Corte di Cassazione' in (1995) *Diritto di Famiglia e delle Persone*, 1659 ff. For a critical appraisal, with regard to the applicability of the provision sanctioning the crime of ill-treatment of relatives (Article 572 Penal Code, which is considered applicable to *de facto* relatives), see F Mantovani, 'Riflessioni sul reato di maltrattamenti in famiglia', in (1965) *Studi in onore di F.Antolisei*, 393.

More generally, in the criminal law, see F Uccella, *La tutela penale della famiglia* (1984) Padova; G Pisapia, 'Famiglia (delitti contro la)', in Novissimo Digesto, III, Appendice (1982) Turin; G Ruggiero, *Riflessi penali del nuovo diritto di famiglia* (1979) Naples.

IV   FAMILIES WITHOUT MARRIAGE: A SOCIAL PHENOMENON AND A LEGAL CHALLENGE

The role of the Catholic Church has been – and is still today – very wide in Italy, not only in social life but also as far as its formal relationships with the State are concerned.[49] On the one hand, constitutional provisions affirm general principles of autonomy and equality. According to them, 'the State and the Catholic Church are, each within their own ambit, independent and sovereign' (Article 7, para 1). Beside this, '[a]ll religious denominations are equally free, before the law' (Article 8, para 1). On the other hand, specific provisions were devoted to the relationships between the Italian State and the Catholic Church, which are 'regulated' by special Agreements – signed in 1929[50] – whose modifications have to be accepted by both parties, although there is no need to follow a constitutional revision procedure for this purpose (Article 7, para 2). A further Agreement was reached in 1984, in conformity with the principle of equal treatment that is also expressly stated by the Constitutional Charter (Article 8, paras 2 and 3).[51]

Briefly, notwithstanding the respect for religious freedom, these provisions give rise to a peculiar mechanism of mutual recognition. This reciprocity implies a dual sovereignty: these autonomous powers can be justified in that they are not subject to any kind of unilateral, external limitation.[52] Such a situation may explain the reasons why deep tensions often arise, between lay and Catholic positions, whenever the idea of intervention by the Italian legislature is proposed, in order to confer legislative recognition on *de facto* unions.[53] A similar

---

49   See, on these issues, for an historical appraisal and a socio-legal analysis, F Margiotta Broglio, *Italia e Santa Sede: dalla grande guerra alla conciliazione: aspetti politici e giuridici* (1966) Bari; F Ruffini and F Margiotta Broglio, *Relazioni tra Stato e Chiesa: lineamenti storici e sistematici* (1974) Bologna; F Margiotta Broglio, *Cinquant'anni di concordato* (1979) Firenze; S Berlingò, V Scalisi and P Barile (eds), *Effetti civili delle sentenze ecclesiastiche in materia matrimoniale* (1983) Milan; P Barile, *Diritti dell'uomo e libertà fondamentali* (1984) Bologna; R Botta, *Matrimonio religioso e giurisdizione dello Stato* (1994) Bologna; 'Il matrimonio concordatario' in *Il diritto di famiglia*, in I vol., IV, *Trattato di diritto privato* directed by M Bessone (1999) Turin. For a comparative perspective in Italian legal literature, see recently F Margiotta Broglio, C Mirabelli and F Onida, *Religioni e sistemi giuridici: introduzione al diritto ecclesiastico comparato* (2000) Bologna. For essential references to some debated problems relating to the (exclusive or concurrent) jurisdiction of the ecclesiastical Courts, after the 1984 Agreement, see L Graziano, 'Nullità del matrimonio concordatario: ancora una sentenza sul difetto di giurisdizione del giudice italiano', note to Corte d'Appello di Firenze, 21 May 1999, in (2000) *Famiglia e Diritto*, 270 ff.

50   The so-called '*Patti Lateranensi*'.

51   'Religious denominations other than Catholic are entitled to organise themselves according to their own creed, provided that they are not in conflict with the Italian juridical organisation. Their relationships with the State are regulated by the law on the basis of agreements (*interse*) with their respective representatives'.

52   After the unification of the Italian State (1861) the so-called '*Questione Romana*' was not solved: the Pontifical State was not yet conquered. Rome – which was its capital – was annexed to Italy only in 1871. For historical references, see P Ungari, *Il diritto di famiglia in Italia* (1970), Bologna.

53   Very strong criticism was recently manifested towards the decision of the Italian government to postpone the debate on the proposal to approve a unitary Bill on *de facto* unions, without giving any indication of the reason underlying the delay, after the competent Ministry had announced the forthcoming discussion publicly. See 'Coppie di fatto, legge in panne – Barricate tra laici e cattolici', in *La Repubblica*, 29 September 2000, at 20. At the same time, the powerful dissent expressed to the contrary by the Pontifical Council for the Family – in a document issued just two months before, in July 2000, which is devoted to *Family, Marriage and 'De Facto' Unions*

innovation might be seen as an attempt to refuse to acknowledge the position assumed by both the parties to the Agreements, if a decisive value is conferred on the regulation of the so-called '*matrimonio concordatario*', that is celebrated in compliance with canon law but – in the presence of certain formal requirements – produces the effects of a civil marriage as well.[54] If the Italian State should decide to widen the concept of family, so that *de facto* unions receive public recognition, a sharp disagreement is likely to arise, as recently happened soon after the disclosure of the contents of a Unitary Bill – which was announced as a central point of the current Government agenda, but was suddenly eliminated the day before the date planned for the debate, without any explanation.[55] However, this is

---

(2000) Rome – should be emphasised. See, in particular, para II (9): '[...] In today's open democratic society, the State and the public authorities must not institutionalise *de facto* unions, thereby giving them a status similar to marriage and the family, nor much less make them equivalent to the family based on marriage. This would be an arbitrary use of power which does not contribute to the common good because the original nature of marriage and the family preceeds and exceeds, in an absolute and radical way, the sovereign power of the State'. Moreover, the Pontifical Council contested the common contraposition between a lay and a religious approach to these issues, in order to affirm a unitary concept of union (ie one based on marriage). However, in this Document it is possible to find a clear avowal of the need to distinguish the public perspective from the other ones. This can be interpreted as a confirmation of (instead of an opposition to) the need to adopt solutions which are not based on State imposition, but on the principle of separation between the Church and the State.

In Italian legal writings, see, for the thesis which denies a legal 'justification and legitimation' for the *de facto* family and for ample references in this sense, 'La famiglia 'di fatto' è giustificabile giuridicamente?', Palazzani L, in (2000) *Diritto di Famiglia e delle Persone*, 245 ff. – article previously published in (1999) *Iustitia*, 46 ff.

54   Clearly, the law also regulates the basis of the civil marriage, which is subject only to private law rules. Thus, the '*matrimonio concordatario*' is a distinct but 'parallel' figure, because, despite its different nature, it produces the same effect. It is regulated, respectively, by canon law – as far as its religious dimension is concerned – and by private law rules, with respect to its civil effects. This is a rather peculiar 'model' that was created by the above-mentioned Agreement signed in 1929. Indeed, the constitutional reference to this first Agreement (the so-called *Patti Lateranensi*) has to be extended to the *Concordato* (ie the Covenant that regulated this specific aspect of the relationships between the Catholic Church and the Italian State). Some modifications were made by another Agreement (the 1984 *Accordo di Villa Madama*). A religious marriage with civil effects is possible now not only in cases of 'catholic' marriages, but also in cases of religious marriages celebrated according to other creeds (eg the Baptist and Lutheran Churches, the Buddhist religion, Jehovah's Witnesses, the Assembly of God in Italy, etc). In any case of religious marriage, the effects are identical to those produced by a civil marriage (ie whose regulation is governed by the Italian State rules only), provided that there is registration (*trascrizione*) in the birth register of the Registry Office (*ufficio dello stato civile*). The Union of Italian Israelite Communities reached a special agreement with the Italian Republic (see Article 14, Act no. 101/1989). The 'Israelite marriage', celebrated in conformity with the Jewish rite, can be considered as a religious marriage with civil effects.

55   On this issue, it is worth mentioning an entire paragraph of the document issued by the Pontifical Council for the Family (see footnote 28 above) – para II (11) – in order to clarify the point better: '[I]t is good to keep in mind the distinction between public interest and private interest. Regarding the former, society and the public authorities must protect and encourage it; as to the latter the State must only guarantee freedom. Whenever a matter is of public interest, public law intervenes, and what, on the contrary, corresponds to private interests must be referred to the private sphere. Marriage and the family are of public interest; they are the fundamental nucleus of society and the State and should be recognised and protected as such. Two or more persons may decide to live together, with or without a sexual dimension, but this cohabitation is not for that reason of public interest. The public authorities can not get involved in this private choice. *De facto* unions are the results of private behaviour and should remain on the private level. Their public recognition or equivalency to marriage, and the resulting elevation of a private interest to a public interest, damages the family based on marriage [...] In marriage, different from *de facto*

not the only reason for the foreseeable imbalance which might result from such a modification. There is still no definitive agreement on all the contents of the proposed reform, between the political groups that have accepted the idea of regulating the so-called 'civil unions' (*unioni civili*), even within the same coalition.[56] Perhaps, even the decision to postpone the examination of the recent Government Bill was taken because of the persistence of unresolved conflicts, which re-emerge whenever a debate is planned, although – as happened in this case – a very limited 'project' is proposed. As we shall see, the main purpose of this Bill consisted in creating a sort of 'private law Charter for cohabitants' or, in other words, a 'Restatement' of existing (and never contested) rules and principles embodied in the Civil Code. No more direct evidence can be given to show how some opposing positions (and contradictions) are unavoidable, if there is no complete agreement on the idea that legislative regulation is necessary and appropriate.

V   SOME UNAVOIDABLE CONTRADICTIONS: THE 'PROS AND CONS' OF LEGISLATIVE INTERVENTION

No one can deny that – apart from some redefinitions of old statutory interventions that dated back to the war time legislation[57] and that expressed the almost exclusive need to give protection to the so-called 'quasi-widows' of Italian soldiers – all the subsequent attempts to regulate this field of family relationships can be seen as separate from a socio-political widely shared plan.[58] This is the reason why the different proposals contained both in the Government Bill and in some of the previous ones, which were presented during the Thirteenth Legislature in Italy, merit special interest.[59] For the first time, a relative convergence has been expressed, at least on some central issues. However, given that it is doubtful that these proposals will be turned into an Act in the near future, an explanation of this intense activity can be found in the pressure which has been exercised by the need to react to a clear 'European' trend.[60]

---

unions, commitments and responsibilities are taken publicly and formally that are relevant for society and exigible in the juridical context'.

56   See Section VI below.

57   See Section VI.

58   See later in the text.

59   See, for instance, on this subject, Lunardi, 'Progetti di riforma in Parlamento in materia di diritto di famiglia e di tutela del minore', in (1996) *Famiglia e Diritto*, 89 ff., at 93.

In order to widen the applicability of the current provisions, some parallels had been traced, in the past, with the provisions which are applicable – according to a constant judicial interpretation – to *de facto* unions in cases of foster care –'*affidamento familiare*' – and simple adoptions – '*adozione in casi particolari*' (Articles 2 and 44 of Act no. 184/1983). However, these constructions were not correct, being different, respectively, in the purposes and the effects of these institutions, in comparison with those of full adoption. In contrast, it is possible to appreciate one of the solutions envisaged by the Bill on the reform of adoption law which has been recently approved by the Senate, on 5 December 2000.

60   The most powerful opposition towards any proposal in favour of legislative intervention has been shown, in Italy, by parties which belong to the Christian Democratic tradition. In dealing with these problems, religious ideas usually play a decisive role, at a political level, also in other countries. However, while in Northern Europe there has been a more open attitude about the possibility of dealing with these issues by adopting a secular approach, as a result of the less

In Europe, the last two years (1998–2000) can be described as a period of most intense production of national studies,[61] of formal, 'supranational' documents,[62] of important judicial decisions[63], of new Acts,[64] and Bills[65]. All of

closed position of the Protestants, in Southern Europe – and particularly in Italy, where the influence of the Catholic Church is very strong – there has been a complete rejection, in this respect. This reluctance has not been limited to the refusal of legal recognition of homosexual unions. On this point, after all, a general reaction of rejection has unified almost all the Christian Democratic parties of both Northern and Southern European countries. The Italian criticism referred to any attempt to recognise and regulate *de facto* unions (both homosexual and heterosexual). A recent 'compromise' has only partially reduced these inner conflicts, within the European context. The final document approved at the meeting of the European parties of this area (PPE), which was held at Berlin on 13 January 2001, tried to take into consideration these different points of view. In a first draft of the document, there was the express recognition, beside the 'family as a place in which a man and a woman assume responsibility towards their children', of the existence of a 'new family model and of other forms of common life'. The Italian opposition entailed a different (and less innovative) definition of family. The definitive version of the document exclusively 'recognises the existence of other forms of common life which have developed'. No direct reference has been made to families not based on marriage. Thus, a cautious openness has been manifested only towards existing *de facto* unions. A sort of 'twin-level' approach (ie national and European) has been adopted in Italy, and this has amplified the tensions between the two opposing coalitions (ie the centre-left 'Olive tree' and the centre-right 'House of the freedoms'). The 'secular wings' of several parties that belong to the area of the centre (Christian Democratic) groups were opposed to the more traditional 'Catholic wings'. However, these 'wings' are present in both coalitions. It is not difficult to foresee that – at least in the near future – the Italian political debate will continue to show the absence of unanimity, inside and outside this area. See, for instance, for a first reaction in the Italian media, the article published on 14 January 2001, 'I popolari europei aprono alla famiglia di fatto', in *Il Corriere della Sera*, at 10 and on the front page.

61   See, for example, the *Lord Chancellor's Department Consultation Paper* on unwed fathers, '1. Court Procedures for the Determination of Paternity, 2. The Law on Parental Responsibility for Unmarried Fathers' (1998) London. 'Rénover le droit de la famille: Propositions pour un droit adapté aux réalités et aux aspirations de notre temps', *Rapport au Garde des Sceaux, Ministre de la Justice*, du groupe de travail présidé par Dekeuwer-F. Defossez, Lille, 1999.

62   These are without binding force. Their relevance is not, however, only symbolic, given the influence that they can have on future legal developments at a national level, as well as on the activity of some 'supranational subjects' – ie the European Parliament, the European Commission and the European Court of Justice. See, for instance, the Resolutions of the European Parliament, in this area. The first one – devoted to the equal rights of lesbian and gay people in the Community – dated back to 8 February 1994, the second one – about the equal rights of homosexuals – was taken on 17 September 1998, and the third one – which has wider scope, concerning the protection of human rights, and, *inter alia*, the recognition and regulation of *de facto* unions, the possibility of opening marriage for homosexual couples and their equal rights, in comparison with traditional couples and families, as far as treatment by the revenue, their economic régime and their social rights are concerned – was approved on 16 March 2000. More recently, the European Charter, which was approved on 6 December 2000, by the European Commission, the Parliament and the Council of the European Union, while confirming the autonomy of Member States (see Article 9, which leaves wide scope to State legislation – 'The right to marry and the right to found a family shall be guaranteed in accordance with the national laws governing the exercise of these rights') gave a very detailed definition to the meaning of the 'equal protection' guarantee (see Article 21, which affirms the principle of non-discrimination also with respect to 'sexual orientations').

63   See, for a clear survey, M Bell, 'Sexual orientation and discrimination in employment: an evolving role for the European Union', in R Wintemute and M Andenæs (eds), *Legal Recognition of Same-Sex Partnerships – A Study of National, European and International Law* (forthcoming (2001) Oxford).

64   See the French Act no 99-944, enacted on 15 November 1999, which introduced the XII Title in the first book of the Code Civil, devoted to the *Pacte Civil de solidarité* (PACS); the Spanish Ley de Parejas enacted in Aragona on 26 March 1999 and the Act enacted on 11 June 1998 in Catalunya; the Belgian Act enacted on 23 November 1998. The Danish Act on registered partnerships, no. 372, which dated back to 7 June 1989 (in force from 1 October 1989), was later amended by the Act no. 360, 2 June 1999, which entered into force on 1 July 1999. Registered

them are aimed at dealing with the problems of *de facto* unions by trying to abandon the cautious approach in order to adjust the conflicting interests at stake. At the same time, a lot of problems can arise, in some cases, because of the difficulty of finding practical solutions that can properly respect the positions of all the subjects concerned. Recognising a legal role for *de facto* unions is not a neutral choice, in many respects: it may be viewed as an undue interference with the partners' intention not to create a formal link between themselves, or as a thinly veiled token of favour towards situations that, for several reasons, are an expression of a more or less conscious refusal of the institution of marriage. However, the experience of the first countries, like Sweden, which have enacted statutes on *de facto* unions, has shown that the number of marriages has progressively decreased in the period subsequent to the entry into force of this legislation. Moreover, the heightened percentage of divorces and the increase of *de facto* unions in countries in which there has been no statutory regulation in this field are evidence of the fact that it is not legislative intervention which threatens to destroy the foundations of marriage. The phenomenon of breakdown of unions is widespread and can also be seen in the case of couples who married with a religious ceremony. At the same time, the decline in the number of marriages is not limited to couples without a religious commitment, because it is also related to unions of people who profess a religious faith. More generally, very complex questions need to be asked to understand the reasons underlying these kinds of 'social habits' (about the current influence of Christianity in social relationships and the correspondence between declared religious beliefs and personal choices reflecting their real incidence in everyday life). In brief, we are dealing with a trend which depends on 'variable' elements, so that the statutory recognition of certain legal guarantees, especially in favour of the most vulnerable partner, cannot represent a menace to an institution which is still facing a degree of uncertainty. While in some Northern European countries there has not been excessive concern about these developments by official representatives,[66] in Italy this is the central issue of the present debate in the political arena.

The historical reaction of rejection, which has been manifested by some parties in the centre (although in opposing coalitions) and by the Catholic Church, was founded mainly on these grounds. Therefore, it was easily foreseeable that the recent 'European' trends in favour of reforming the law relating to *de facto* couples (both heterosexual and homosexual ones) would have been followed by strong rejection by the official representatives of the Holy See, whose declarations had considerable impact in the Italian political debate recently, even if this can only be inferred. This reaction might have been decisive in stopping the advanced phase reached by the 'plans of the current executive' although the Bill was based on a 'minimum guarantee' perspective only. Even if the influence of the forthcoming election campaign might have been relevant, it played a secondary

---

partnerships were regulated in Sweden in 1994 (Act 23 June 1994), that entered into force on 1 January 1995; and in Iceland by the the Act enacted on 12 June 1996 (that came into force on 27 June 1996), in the Netherlands by the Act enacted on 5 July 1997, and in Norway by the Act enacted on 30 April 1993, in force on 1 August 1994.

65   For an overview of some Italian Bills, see later in the text.

66   See C Forder, 'Models of Domestic Partnership Laws: The Field of Choice' (see footnote 6 above), at footnote 24.

role. These issues always imply great difficulties, because of the dialectical character of the opposition between the parliamentary representatives.

The question at hand cannot be simply described as a typical Italian 'never ending story', or as an anachronistic 'crusade' in the name of an ideal concept of marriage. *De facto* unions are unanimously recognised as social phenomena which deserve deep interest.[67] After all, it is their contraposition to the family based on marriage that has made it possible to underline the fundamental differences between the corresponding relationships.[68] Some further references to the main features of the overall context in which this issue takes place may be useful now. Indeed, the purpose of this analysis is to deal with the Italian situation, but it is evident that to understand its development one cannot avoid looking at the surrounding context. In Italy, the peculiar solution adopted in order to regulate the relationships between the State and the Catholic Church – which have been much debated in recent times[69] – may have played a relevant role, but some of the

---

67   In this sense, see the Introduction to the document issued by the Pontifical Council for the family in July 2000, footnote 53 above.

68   Even if in different perspectives, Saint Augustine's ideas are often quoted, as the most revealing examples of a rigid rejection of out of wedlock relationships. See, for opposite views, L Peppe, 'Una lettera papale del 726 d.C.', in F Brunetta and A D'Angelo, *Matrimonio, matrimonii*, 21 ff., at 23, footnote 34, and the document of the Pontifical Council for the family, para 16, 'Recognition and equivalence of *de facto* unions discriminates against marriage' (2000) Rome, at footnote 19. However, it might be misleading to focus attention on well known positions only. The roots of the distinction between marriage and the *de facto* relationship can be found in Saint Augustine's autobiographical work, in his *Confessions*. Although the following quotation, if it is seen in isolation, might appear elusive or based on an over-simplified vision, if it is inserted in the wider context of his thought, it can be very interesting and helpful in understanding the reasons why there is no possibility of 'transplanting' criteria and experiences of an ancient past, in the evaluation of contemporary behaviour. The struggle between individualistic and social interests is mainly based, today, on a conflict between self-centred impulses and social openness. This contraposition could not even be imagined in a society in which the family was founded on a patriarchal basis. Thus, apart from any superficial comparison, and only with a view to emphasising the need to respect socio-historical differences, it is possible to quote an excerpt from the second Chapter, para 2, of the second Book of the *Confessions* of Saint Augustine: ' [...] In those years I had a mistress, to whom I was not joined in lawful marriage. She was a woman I had discovered in my wayward passion, void as it was of understanding, yet she was the only one; and I remained faithful to her and with her I discovered, by my own experience, what a great difference there is between the restraint of the marriage bond contracted with a view to having children and the compact of a lustful love, where children are born against the parents' will – although once they are born they compel our love' ('*In illis annis* unam habebam *non eo quod legitimum vocatur coniugio cognitam, sed quam indagaverat vagus ardor inops prudentiae*, sed una tamen, *ei quoque servans tori fidem; in qua sane experirer exemplo meo quid distaret inter coniugalis placiti modum, quod foederatum esset generandi gratia, et pactum libidinosi amoris*, ubi proles etiam contra votum nascitur, quamvis iam nata cogat se diligi' – emphasis added) .

69   See footnote 49 above. The debate about the persistence (or the absence) of renewed justifications for the solutions embodied in the *Concordato* has never ended, indeed. If the parties to the agreement (ie the Italian state and the Holy See) renounced their complete autonomy, with a view to recognising mutual privileges, it should be consistent with this choice to respect each separate ambit of intervention (ie of the 'secular' and the 'religious or spiritual' sphere, respectively). Anyway, such a (voluntary) limitation can influence the role of both parties and impair their freedom. If there is no longer the need to 'protect' the Church from the State, then the 'logic' underlying the *Concordato* seems to be very anachronistic. Perhaps, the principle 'a free Church in a free State' ('*libera Chiesa in libero Stato*') and the corresponding, real autonomy and freedom of both subjects, would better respect their roles in society. The Church might intervene in social discussions more freely and its position on the family as the basis of social life would not be seen as undue interference with a 'secular' debate. At the same time, the social vision of the state might be inserted in a wider context.

opposing forces are to be seen in a wider perspective, as they are based on legal objections as well.

A lot of Bills were presented in the last few years, while other European countries were enacting new legislation in this area. The description that follows deals only with the most recent ones. All of them deal with many aspects relating to the so-called '*unione civile*' or '*convivenza more uxorio*', apart from one Bill which only proposes to regulate inheritance rights of the partners,[70] with a view to allowing minimum protection for the surviving member of a *de facto* couple, on condition that evidence of the stability of the relationship is given, which has to be inferred from a four year period of cohabitation characterised by the presence of a 'common material and spiritual life'.

Furthermore, the surviving partner has to demonstrate that he/she is in need and incapable of providing for himself or herself. Intestate and testamentary succession rights were differently regulated, but there is a common element in this proposal: the clear inferiority of the position of *de facto* partners, if compared to those of spouses, because of the limitation of their part of the inheritance to one-sixth of the part attributed to the surviving married partner.[71]

The other Bills, on the contrary, as well as a very recent one – drafted by the Government but which has not been debated, so far[72] – have much wider scope.[73] They are aimed at creating a sort of parallel (albeit different) regulation for *de facto* unions, partially modelled on the rules operating for families based on marriage.

An overview of the Government Bill will precede a very brief description of the previous ones. Some of the innovative proposals contained in these latter 'projects' – which were introduced in the two Houses of the Parliament in the period 1997–1999 – have been inserted in the unitary document (on cohabitation agreements, '*accordi di convivenza*') drafted by the Department of the competent Ministry for equal opportunities. The Minister,[74] in her interviews, gave very detailed information on the contents and the purposes of this Bill, in the days preceding its planned discussion. She could not have foreseen that the Government would have opted for the removal of this issue from the list of the legislative measures which were planned in the field of social and family law and were due to be debated during the second half of September 2000. Leaving aside any further consideration of this (unexplained) decision, a brief analysis of the draft might be useful, not only in order to ascertain the reasons why it came to a halt, but also to realise what the prevailing perspective adopted by one of the coalitions is, and the eventual reasons set forth by the opposing coalition.

---

70 Ie no. 5933, presented on 20 April 1999 by Deputees De Luca and others.

71 See Articles 4–6 of the Bill.

72 The title of this draft is 'Disciplina degli accordi di convivenza'. However, this document – widely described and publicised – has not been examined by the Council of Ministries, so far.

73 See, for the Bills presented to the *Camera dei Deputati*: C.4657/1998 (Soda and others, 'Disciplina dell'unione affettiva'); C.2870/1998 (Buffo and others, 'Norme sulle unioni civili'); C.1020/1998 (Vendola and others, 'Disciplina delle unioni civili'); C.7297/2000 (Paissan and others); and, for those introduced in the Senate: S.935/1997 (Manconi and others); 2725/1997 (Cioni and others, 'Disposizioni in materia di unioni civili'); 1518/1997 (Salvato and others, 'Disciplina delle unoioni civili'). The texts of these Bills are available also in the official website of the Italian Parliament: <http://www.parlamento.it>.

74 The competent Minister is now Katia Belillo.

In the first place, the purposes of the Bill do not seem very wide. It aims only at regulating agreements between cohabitants concerning their mutual relationships during the cohabitation with a view to dealing with their reciprocal rights and duties after the breakdown of the union. Briefly, there is no trace of an intention to consider more general issues about the legal régime of *de facto* families and unions, or of their relationship with the law relating to legitimate families. Furthermore, a differentiation between these two types of family will be produced, if the Bill is approved, because there is no provision ensuring some unitary (even if minimum) public guarantees, given the private nature and voluntary basis of the cohabitation agreements at stake. The central choice consists of leaving the partners free and in emphasising – at the same time – their responsibilities, while favouring a social policy which should protect the partner who is economically weaker. Only six Articles have been drafted. The first ones (Articles 1–3) deal with the requirements and the scope of cohabitation agreements. The following provision regulates the conditions for their application, in cases of breakdown of the union (Article 4). The final Articles contain the formal and substantive criteria which are applicable to the so-called 'enduring power of attorney' (Article 5) and the rules concerning the part of the agreements relating to the exercise of parental rights (Article 6).

The first provision has a very symbolic character. It states that 'cohabiting persons who are of age can make agreements in order to regulate their relationship during and after their cohabitation'. Clearly, this is also possible today, in application of the general principles governing contract law (Article 1322, Civil Code), as interpreted by a constant flow of judicial decisions. Similarly, the Bill restates another fundamental principle, in the subsequent paragraph of its first Article, which confirms the general rule of the freedom of the parties to an agreement to give evidence of its existence – in the absence of any different requirements – due to the need for greater certainty in the field of property law (or, rather, in connection with rights concerning the so-called '*beni immobili*' (Article 1350, Civil Code). A completely open provision lists the criteria applicable to the contribution to 'common life', in the sense that the parties are free to decide (or not) to participate in the expenses necessary for this purpose. They can also follow a different approach (ie taking their own property and their professional or domestic working capacity into account). However, they are equally free to determine the extent and the conditions of these contributions differently.

While the innovative character of these proposals is very limited, a partially new solution has been inserted in Article 3. The Bill regulates even situations in which an *ad hoc* agreement is absent. In this event, economic contributions between the partners – whatever the formal position is, on condition that these contributions are proportional to the income and working capacity of each cohabitant partner – are deemed to be justified as social and moral obligations ('*obbligazioni natural*'). All in all, this is a marginal modification with respect to the current system: the same result is reached if the clear indications given by the case-law are followed.

In contrast, an examination of the concluding Articles of the Bill reveals some real changes. As far as the agreements on the consequences of the breakdown of the union are concerned, the freedom of the parties has been formally affirmed.

Article 4 enters into details, although it maintains the apparent 'neutral' approach of the Bill. Thus, the cohabiting partners are free to provide for a maintenance obligation, which can consist of either a lump sum or periodical payments. At the same time, the Article provides no compulsion in this respect for either partner. If the parties agree that one of them will continue to live – after the breakdown of the union – in the common household, they have to inform the owner of the house (or the person to whom this communication has to be addressed) of this agreement by sending a registered letter. In the event that the householder is one (or both) of them, they can decide which partner will leave the house, and the nature of the legal title of the partner who will continue to stay there (ie if he or she will have a 'personal' or an 'absolute' right of habitation – '*diritto relativo*' or '*diritto reale di abitazione*'). Moreover, in the absence of any different agreement, a three-year limitation period has been established in those cases in which the partners have signed a particular 'contract of tenancy' ('*comodato*'), which is – as a rule – not onerous and can be terminated at will. The possibility that third parties may be compelled to respect these rights of habitation will be regulated differently according to the corresponding rules embodied in the Civil Code.

Special formal requirements have been 'scheduled' for the 'designation' of one of the partners as the person responsible for taking the decisions concerning the health of the other partner (Article 5). A written 'agreement' is necessary, for this purpose, as well as the authentication of the signature. The fact that the Bill uses different expressions, in making reference to a designation (which may be unilateral) and to a 'written agreement', which is necessarily bilateral, may create great uncertainty. However, it seems clear that there is no need to obtain the designated partner's express acceptance and that the designation will directly produce its effects – in cases of ascertained and irreversible disability ('*incapacità naturale*') of the designating partner. The right to be informed about the health conditions of the disabled partner and the possibility of expressing or denying the consent to (already planned or necessary in the foreseeable future) medical treatment will be conferred on the designated partner. If a refusal of this treatment is opposed, doctors and medical personnel – who cannot intervene even if there is a danger to the health or the life of the person in question – will not be liable for the consequences of their legally 'authorised' lack of intervention.

Last but not least, the Bill contains a reformulation of a core provision of the Civil Code which is devoted to the parental rights of unwed fathers and mothers. A different version of Article 317-*bis* of the Code has been proposed. The present, general regulation of the scope and effects of judicial intervention has been modified. A further paragraph has been added to this Article, to deal with the breakdown of the union. Two hypotheses have been foreseen: the first is where there is a cohabitation agreement between the parents, which has also regulated the custody of the children and their maintenance. In this case, one or both parents can ask the judge (ie the *Tribunale per i Minorenni*) to verify whether the agreement is in the interests of the children. If, however, there is no agreement, for these purposes, the parents can jointly or separately ask the judge to decide who will have custody of the children, to determine the amount of money necessary by way of contribution for their maintenance, education and upbringing, and to take any further decisions in the 'moral' and economic interest of the children. The final provision of the Bill widens the scope of applicability of the rule which has just been mentioned by extending it to cases in which the parents do not live together and where there is no agreement between them.

Although the main features of the Bill are clear, some of the effects which it is likely to produce are less evident and – more importantly – they may be different from its objectives. One of its targets is represented by the increase in the number of cohabitation agreements and – for this reason – the drafters have opted for the express (even if not necessary) repetition of some central principles of contract law. This explanatory intention is probably linked to the fact that they aimed at eliminating the risk of formal rules that are too rigid and activities that are too expensive, which might discourage people who do not have deep knowledge of legal issues or significant economic means from entering into these agreements.

However, it is unlikely that an Act which, in great part, simply confirms the current possibilities will improve the awareness of the interested persons. If the members of a couple do not desire to be formally linked to one another, the fact that they will be able to give evidence of an eventual agreement without any formal evidence requirements may play a very secondary role. After all, even in countries in which legislation has been enacted to regulate registered partnerships, the practice has confirmed a well-known trend (ie the fact that, after a first period of 'enthusiastic' reaction towards the new possibility, unmarried partners do not express a clear preference to sign agreements). Moreover, whenever a (more or less extended) public law approach has been adopted, some aspects of *de facto* relationships will no longer be outside the legal sphere, notwithstanding the absence of agreements. On the contrary, if one thinks that there are only provisions for dealing with free agreements in the Italian unitary Bill, and that no regulation has been proposed for cases in which the parties have not found (or foreseen) any previous solution with a view to eliminating any future conflict between them, their relationships are likely to be regulated almost exclusively by the case-law.

It is not only a matter of accepting – in the abstract – the idea of legal regulation of these relationships and of informing the partners about this possibility. In evaluating the impact of private agreements in family life, it is also necessary to consider that a sense of distrust may arise, albeit unconsciously. This also happens in the case of married couples, in countries in which the scope for pre-nuptial agreements is very wide, as it is comprehensive not only of the economic, but also of the personal aspects of the relationships; such agreements, however, are void in Italy, as they are previous to the marriage and can undermine the freedom of the spouses). The partners in an unmarried couple – who often reject marriage because of their refusal to 'plan' their common life – can reveal an even more closed attitude towards any preventive regulation of their union.

Another critical remark is related to the statutory 'pre-definition' of the reciprocal, not binding and unenforceable duties of social solidarity between the partners as '*obbligazioni naturali*'. Given that no technical meaning can be attached to these duties, which – according to general principles of private law – are not subject to the rules operating in cases of legal obligations, a provision contained in a special statutory definition can create confusion, instead of more clarity, in people who are not 'legal experts'. Consequently, a judicial enquiry to ascertain the nature of the contributions and to verify the presence of this duty, in any specific situation, will always be necessary. A lack of co-ordination with the

Civil Code can also be assumed from Article 4 of the Bill. The drafters did not want to alter, even partially, the law of testate and intestate succession. Obviously, this is one of the most complex aspects of the regulation of *de facto* unions and the absence of any provisions in this field may be very dangerous, if one adopts a perspective in favour of legislative regulation.

Naturally, this problem cannot be solved through simple reference to the general duty to respect a fundamental principle of inheritance law, which forbids any kind of coercion of the free will of the testator (*'divieto dei patti successori'*). On the contrary, a revision of this field of private law will be necessary, if a coherent reform is approved in the future. The protection of the members of the legitimate family – the only ones that are contemplated, so far, by the Civil Code – may represent an insurmountable obstacle for the recognition of some inheritance rights for *de facto* partners.

In conclusion, if a positive reaction can be justified with respect to some provisions of the Bill (ie those regulating the agreements between parents – Article 317-*bis*), there are still some unconvincing aspects. As already observed, the references made to the co-ordination between the Civil Code system and some of the innovations proposed are too imprecise. For instance, the Bill affirms the applicability of the rules drafted for the separation of married couples (embodied in Article 155, paras 3, 5, 6 and 8, of the Civil Code) to the cases of breakdown of *de facto* unions, without any specification about the consistency of these provisions with the different situations at stake. However, a relevant difference exists: a mutual agreement (or a unilateral decision) is sufficient to terminate a *de facto* relationship, while a formal procedure has to be followed in cases of separation and divorce.

Thus, the main ground for criticism is the incomplete nature of the legal framework. Furthermore, the Bill does not define the characteristics of cohabitation (ie if a certain stability is necessary or not, if the partners have to be heterosexual or if they can be homosexual). It uses a very generic expression: 'cohabiting people' (*'le persone conviventi'*). In comparing this choice with the proposals contained in some previous Bills, it is particularly striking: all of them made reference to relationships or unions of 'two persons, of age' and – except for one Bill which was exclusively devoted to homosexual couples[75] – they extended their provisions 'also to' same-sex unions. Moreover, these Bills proposed a more detailed regulation of this area: they dealt with the requirements for the registration of the partnership, they contained the rules on certification, and considered several other relevant aspects (from the field of social rights to the area of non-discrimination).[76] Clearly, they expressed a different vision because a central role was given to the public law aspect of the issue, but if a *de facto* relationship assumes the features of a relationship which is legally recognised, it should acquire a certain level of certainty which can only be deduced from its stability. From this perspective, the 'private sphere' of the partners necessarily loses its original character. However, any legal recognition of a social group is always founded on a choice in favour of 'heteronomy': the total 'autonomy' of the parties is necessarily – albeit partially – sacrificed. There is regulation of a

---

75 C.4657/1998 (Soda and others).
76 See footnote 73 above, for a list of these Bills.

situation which originally had a *de facto* nature. A certain 'formalisation' of these unions is unavoidable when the legislator intervenes to regulate them. Naturally, this can be viewed as undue interference in the private life of two persons who have chosen not to be formally bound and not to be subject to duties and responsibilities imposed by the State, but the claim to respect for this freedom of choice can be considered founded only so far as there is no expectation of wide legal protection. Of course, *de facto* partners might be happy to accept that the State has become more sensitive towards their needs, but rights (of someone) always correspond to social or individual duties and obligations (of someone else).

Thus, the most convincing objections towards plans which try to draft legislative rules are those that underline the risks of an 'automatic' application of such rules, which may eliminate any field of choice.

Indeed, the central objective does not consist of reaching a perfect balance between the private and the public regulation of these relationships. If a certain degree of legal protection is deemed to be necessary (in the area of social security, of working regulations, of housing issues, and so on), a mixed approach needs to be followed. Consequently, a sort of '*auto/hetero-nomy*' will arise. The most difficult problem will consist of defining the scope of each field. However, this difficulty also arises in the absence of any structured, public law (authoritative) intervention, whenever judicial protection – based on private law instruments – is ensured in order to avoid 'unjust' treatment of *de facto* partners. The fundamental point is clearly linked to socio-political conceptions, because, in the end, it is a matter of defining the scope of State powers.

Instead of following extensive interpretative criteria or directly applying, by operation of law, rules which have been drafted for married couples, on the assumption that *de facto* unions can be considered as 'images' of 'legal' unions, an intermediate position might be wiser. It is possible to avoid both over-detailed new regulations and undue 'duplications' of old rules, whose expansion to *de facto* relationships would reflect the idea that they have a 'second order' relevance, as if they were partially resembling the legitimate ones. Of course, it is not easy to create a new régime, specifically tailored to these situations and more respectful of individual choices. The equilibrium between individual freedom and the social need to avoid unjustified discrimination has always been the most controversial aspect of the debate which has been carefully considered by Italian legal scholars.

VI THE NEED TO REGULATE AND THE DESIRE TO BE FREE

De facto unions have been carefully studied by Italian legal writers.[77] They have been usually defined as relationships between a man and a woman which have a

---

77 Naturally, it is not possible to give comprehensive and exhaustive references. A lot of studies have been made, from different perspectives. Besides the essays and articles quoted above, see also these books: F Prosperi, *La famiglia non 'fondata sul matrimonio'* (1980) Naples; F Gazzoni, *Dal concubinato alla famiglia di fatto* (1983) Milan; F D'Agostino, 'Un "diritto dei conviventi"?', in (1991) *Linee di una filosofia della famiglia nella prospettiva della filosofia del diritto* (1991) Milan; FD Busnelli and M Santilli, 'La famiglia di fatto', in G Cian, A Oppo and A Trabucchi (eds), *Commentario al diritto italiano della famiglia*, IV, 1 (eds) (1992) Padova, 757 ff.; F D'Angeli, *La famiglia di fatto* (1989), Milan; M Bernardini, *La convivenza fuori del*

tendency to be stable and are different from those based on marriage because of the absence of the intention to be bound by a formal, legal link – voluntarily and freely assumed – which gives rise to reciprocal rights and duties.[78] It has been a cliché not to speak about the 'positive' features of the first kind of unions. On the contrary, as a rule, the emphasis has been put on the absence of the elements that are present in the latter. This sort of 'negative' definition tends inevitably to reflect, albeit indirectly, a certain reprobatory attitude, which could be perceived initially by the words used to describe this social phenomenon. The unification element was seen in the contraposition to marriage: the terms 'concubinate' and '*more uxorio* cohabitation' underlined this point unambiguously.[79]

In the past, perhaps it might have been correct to say that *de facto* couples could be defined on a *contrario* basis only. All in all, these heterogeneous situations – apart from the presence of the cohabitation and of the sexual relationship between the partners – were unified by their rejection of marriage. However, the decision to reject or to postpone marriage and its commitments could be consistent with a variety of reasons, some of which are not so frequent (or even understandable) today. For instance, in some cases, in the past, civil marriage was refused by the spouses because of their religious beliefs, where they

---

matrimonio (1992) Padova; G Oberto, *I regimi patrimonionali della famiglia di fatto* (1991) Milan; *La convivenza fuori del matrimonio tra contratto e relazione sentimentale* (1992) Padova; V Pocar and P Ronfani (eds), *Coniugi senza matrimonio. La convivenza nella società contemporanea* (1992) Milan; *Rapporti patrimoniali tra coniugi e tra conviventi. Aspetti istituzionali e giurisprudenziali* (1994) Milan; D'Angeli, *La tutela della convivenza senza matrimonio* (1995) Turin; G De Luca, *La famiglia non coniugale – Gli orientamenti della giurisprudenza* (1996) Padova; B Mioli, *La famiglia di fatto* (1996) Rimini; E Quadri, *Famiglia e ordinamento civile* (1997) Turin; G Autorino Stanzione, *Diritto di famiglia* (1997) Turin, 417 ff.; R Tommasini, 'La famiglia di fatto', in Bessone (ed), *Il diritto di famiglia*, I, *Trattato di diritto privato*, IV (1997) Turin, 449 ff.; M Bessone (ed), 'La famiglia di fatto', G Ferrando, in II, *Giurisprudenza del diritto di famiglia. Casi e materiali* (1998) Milan.

78   As already stressed, the new proposal to take same-sex couples into consideration, with a view to allowing them to marry, needs a special and complex analysis which is outside the scope of this survey. We are dealing here with different-sex unions mainly because their position has been the object of a wider debate, so far, although it is necessary to clarify that the recent Bills on *de facto* unions refer to homosexual and heterosexual couples, even if their respective situations are not totally equated.

Some attempts to widen the scope of application of old statutory provisions (regulating the so-called *registri anagrafici*) in order to confer a formal *status* on *de facto* unions – both homosexual and heterosexual ones – were unsuccessful. Some Italian Municipalities tried to follow this path, which, however, was not confirmed by the competent judicial and administrative authorities. See R Romboli and E Rossi, *I registri comunali delle unioni civili ed i loro censori*, in *Foro Italiano* III (1996) 525; E Rossi, *Anagrafe della popolazione*, in *Enciclopedia Giuridica Treccani*, Aggiornamento (1996) Rome; E Quadri, *Rilevanza attuale della famiglia di fatto ed esigenze di regolamentazione*, in *Diritto di Famiglia e delle Persone* (1994) 292. More recently, see E Quadri, 'Problemi giuridici attuali della famiglia di fatto', in (1999) *Diritto di famiglia e delle Persone*, 502 ff.

79   This aspect was described very clearly in one of the most interesting works devoted to these issues. See F Gazzoni, *Dal concubinato alla famiglia di fatto* (1983) Milan at 5–8. The author denies that there is the possibility of saying that the legitimate and *de facto* families are 'parallel' phenomena. Both in the initial questions that he asked (at 8–14), and in the answer that he gave (20 ff.), one can find a clear contraposition between them: both the creation of a *de facto* union and its breakdown are not subjected to any formal procedure or legal requirement, so that no comparison might be proposed in order to apply the same provisions.

For a review, see R Tommasini, *Riflessioni in tema di famiglia fi fatto: limiti di compatibilità e affidamento per la convivenza*, in *Rivista di Diritto Civile*, II (1984) 256 ff.

were opposed to the idea of recognising the authority of the State in this field.[80] Of course, the institution of civil marriage was not ignored in Italy – as may still happen in other societies – so that this practice (which dated back to the late nineteenth century and the first decades of the twentieth century) can be viewed as a clear sign of the awareness of the different meaning of the religious sacrament and of the intent to respect the role of the Catholic Church.[81] Except for the difficulty of ensuring inheritance rights for the partners and their offspring, these situations – which are extremely rare today – did not create complex legal problems, although they could result in unequal treatment. All in all, these couples behaved and were socially considered as married, so that their different position could hardly be seen as justified. The need to afford them protection led to a peculiar solution, which was adopted in 1929, by a more general agreement between the Italian State and the Vatican. From its signature – as already pointed out – a religious marriage, in the presence of certain requirements, produces, in Italy, civil effects as well.[82]

Perhaps it is idle to say that the reasons why a couple decide not to be bound by a civil marriage are completely different nowadays. Apart from cases of 'trial unions',[83] which, however, are not inconsistent with the idea of getting married, the largest number of cases of cohabitation without marriage are clear expressions of completely different choices. Even if there are still some cases of impossibility of marriage (eg when divorce is pending), the most common situations are characterised by the refusal of marriage. The explanations for this phenomenon may vary, according to the different conceptions of family life that one can adopt. On the one hand, these unions have been described as based on relationships of 'love and freedom',[84] and as fully respecting the equality of the partners. This perspective, however, can lead to opposite conclusions. Indeed, it has been proposed to ensure them a certain level of legal protection, whenever it is necessary to react to the possible danger of abuses. In replying to this proposal, it was stressed that only 'the instrument of autonomy' can guarantee proper respect for the choice of the couple, which is freely renewed from day to day and 'cannot

---

80 Before the signature of the *Patti Lateranensi* (1929), a peculiar solution was followed by a large number of Italian couples, who only celebrated religious marriage, and did not perform the civil ceremony. This caused a great deal of serious difficulty, because the State did not confer any legal effects on these unions. This usage made it clear how, especially in some regions of Italy, the vision of marriage was profoundly rooted in the religious concept, so that it was seen as a sacrament, and not as a legal institution. See P Ungari, *Il diritto di famiglia in Italia* (1970) Bologna; G Vismara, *Il diritto di famiglia in Italia dalle riforme ai codici* (1978) Milan.

These unions were based on marriage, but only on the religious one. Therefore, no parallel can be traced with respect to the so-called 'common law marriage', which has never been known in the Italian experience, as well as that of other civil law countries. See in Italian, Franceschelli, *Diritto di Famiglia e delle Persone*, 502 ff.

81 Different solutions had been followed by the so-called '*legislazione preunitaria*' (ie the statutory provisions enacted before the unification of Italy, by different legislators, in the first half of the nineteenth century). In some States, marriage was regulated according to canon law and a special regime was applied to its effects. In others, in contrast, the legislation only dealt with the civil marriage so that in cases of celebration of religious marriage, the couple was not considered legally married.

82 See later in the text.

83 In Italian: *convivenze prematrimoniali* (ie when the members of a couple start cohabiting with a view to getting married in the future, but after living together for a 'probation period').

84 See footnote 9 above.

be punished by the imposition of imperative rules, with the declared purpose of protecting the weaker partner'.[85]

On the other hand, deep criticism has been made of the phenomenon of unions not based on marriage, which were defined as the outcomes of a mistaken vision of individualism.[86] From this point of view, *de facto* couples reject the idea of being united by the 'covenant of conjugal love', because they are opposed to the responsibilities that result from marriage (ie a 'bond that has been made or taken on publicly'). Their style of life is seen as influenced by 'pragmatism and hedonism', given the absence of any intention to comply with the reciprocal duties which are produced by a relationship based on marriage. These are unavoidable contrasts. They explain the reactions in Italy to some recent European Parliament Resolutions,[87] which are not examined here, as well as other relevant points that were hardly touched on, in this review.

VII CONCLUSION

If one takes a glance at the 'recent past', it is easy to understand that a very different critical approach towards the attempts to legislate in this field could be based not only on the same perplexities which are often still advanced today, but also in the absence of legislative examples in the Western legal tradition.[88] A clear

---

85   For these remarks, see F Gazzoni, in *Manuale di diritto privato*, 2nd ed. (1990) Naples, at 306.

     The author's criticism of the opposite position is not based on an 'old-fashioned' idea of the relationships between women and men. On the contrary, he says that it is the idea of protecting the 'weaker partner' which reflects an '[a]rchaic vision [...] which looks at the past and at the condition of the so-called *concubina* (mistress). [Such a vision] does not harmonise with the present moment, in which the cohabitation *more uxorio* represents a free choice also for the woman, and especially for her. She sees cohabitation outside marriage as a further reflection of sexual equality, in its substantial meaning, [in the sense that it] is not simply avowed, but [corresponding to] real life and daily choices' (F Gazzoni, *ibidem*).

86   Individualism has been examined from different perspectives. Of course, its meaning can change, being strictly connected with different social contexts, but the vision which prevailed in contemporary Western societies has been considered one of the 'reasons' underlying the choice to prefer unions without marriage. However, given the impossibility of detecting all the inner motivations of human behaviour, this reconstruction can be a matter for debate. On the 'old and new' concept of individualism, see (translations into Italian), J Dewey, *Individualismo vecchio e nuovo* (1948) Florence, and, for the analysis of the modern trends in family life, D Cooper, *La morte della famiglia* (1971) Turin.

     Even the idea that the radical modifications of social relationships necessarily lead to the 'death' of the family can be questioned. Although the 'model' of family which was created by industrial society (or, rather, that was influenced by its general innovations in the organisation of work) started a deep 'crisis', in the so-called post-industrial society, only a very superficial vision can explain the tension between these 'contrasting forces' (ie between individual freedom and openness towards social needs) as a struggle which inevitably destroys the family. The central question which still needs to be asked is: what does 'family' mean today?

87   See footnote 62 above.

88   See, for instance, E Calò, 'La giurisprudenza come scienza inesatta (in tema di prestazioni lavorative in seno alla famiglia di fatto', in (1988) *Il Foro Italiano*, I, 2306 ff., at 2312. The author, in concluding an interesting comment on a decision of the Court of Cassation (no. 1701, 19 February 1988) observed that any legislative intervention would give rise to a sort of authoritative marriage ('*matrimonio d'ufficio*'), in the absence of free will of the parties, so that such a solution would be contrary not only to constitutional principles – applicable to the legitimate family – but also to the freedom of the partners. Furthermore, he underlined that '*inter alia*, a lot of foreign Acts dealing with the *de facto* family [did] not belong to developed societies,

trend which favours a high level of proximity between the régimes applicable to different models of 'families' (ie based on marriage or not) has recently been followed by some Northern European countries which have adopted a solution consisting of an extension to *de facto* unions of the rules concerning married couples. The most common criticism of this kind of legislative development has been based on its evident contraposition to the free intention of the partners, but the reply was that these statutory interventions – which are supported by a very wide consensus – are legal reactions which are necessary to eliminate the previous situation of social uncertainty. In conferring equal rights on persons who are in a similar condition – through references to the existing regulation for unions based in wedlock – they do not impose any authoritative scheme, given the range of private agreements that can be reached by the parties. There is a great difference between these developments and the proposals made for recognising the institution of marriage for lesbian and gay couples. While heterosexual couples can decide to marry or not, single-sex partners have no choice, so far, because of the well known social and cultural meaning of marriage. This is not a question of 'ancient' traditions or religious influences. All in all, traditions can continue to exist as far as the repetitions of certain behaviours are constant, but – notwithstanding their frequent, powerful incidence in social life – they cannot, in themselves, furnish a sufficient ground for refusing to modify unjustified discrimination (no matter how deeply rooted they are). Moreover, marriage is a civil institution and, if there have been some connections in modern and contemporary Western societies with the religious sacrament, this cannot foreclose a totally 'secular' institution (which might be open to undifferentiated treatment for both heterosexual and homosexual couples). Thus, a vast social enquiry would be necessary to understand the reasons why the prospects of extending marriage to these completely new situations – ie same-sex couples – are not widely shared today. This proposal – which received the approval of the Lower Chamber of the Dutch Parliament[89] – has not been inserted in any piece of legislation so far. Its exclusion from the present analysis is due only to the decision to take into consideration *de facto* unions which, notwithstanding their (or the possibility of their being subjected to) statutory or judicial regulation, maintain a differentiation with respect to marriage. Marriage for same-sex couples was generally considered not even 'conceivable' some years ago, in Italy, independently of the position adopted here, mainly because of its unprecedented character,[90] but it might be unrealistic, today, not to 'see' what is happening in other countries, in this new area of family (law and) relationships.

---

but they [were linked to...] situations of underdevelopment, in which the lack of marriage [was] not depending on a free choice, being the result of the instability of the economic and cultural conditions'. For an analysis of the period prior to the more recent legal developments, see V Francheschelli, 'Il matrimonio di fatto: nozione, effetti e problemi nel diritto italiano e straniero', in *La famiglia di fatto* (1976) Pontremoli, 345 ff.; E Roppo, 'La famiglia senza matrimonio. Diritto e non-diritto nella fenomenologia delle libere unioni', in (1980) *Rivista Trimestrale di Diritto e Procedura Civile*, 697 ff., at 707 ff.; G Gazzoni, 'La famiglia di fatto tra legge e autonomia privata', in (1981) *Giustizia Civile*, II, 262 ff.

89 On 12 September 2000 (Parliamentary paper 26672, no 3, July 1999, 'Act on the Opening up of Marriage').

90 See P Barile, 'La famiglia di fatto – Osservazioni di un costituzionalista', in *La famiglia di fatto – Atti del Convegno nazionale* (1976) Montereggio, 41, at 46; A Trabucchi, 'Pas par cette voi s'il vous plait!', in *Rivista di Diritto Civile* I (1981) 329 ff. at 345. On these issues, see, recently,

A comparative vision, which does not aim at finding the 'better solution', or at proposing 'definitive answers' to legal questions, will certainly be helpful in order to realise the (positive and negative) effects of certain choices better. Naturally, even the decision not to enact statutory provisions is a choice, but even if a purely private law perspective should prevail in Italy – with or without legislation – there is always the need to follow a logical and coherent path.

A concluding example will probably clarify this point. As already mentioned,[91] a recent unitary Bill devoted to the reform of adoption law – which was approved by the Italian Senate on 5 December 2000 – proposes an interesting innovation. The pre-matrimonial stable 'cohabitation' of the spouses for at least three years will be equated to the elapse of the same period after marriage, which is provided for by the current legislation. Thus, cohabitation will receive legal recognition, although the requirement of marriage will not be eliminated.[92]

A more evident sign of the trend to treat equally the position of married and unmarried partners can be found in another Bill, on medically assisted reproduction, which was approved by the Senate on 2 June 1999,[93] and is still waiting for the definitive approval by the other Chamber of the Parliament (*Camera dei Deputati*). Article 5 proposes to confer the same position on all heterosexual 'adult couples', so that they are allowed to receive this medical treatment, on condition that they are 'of age'. Thus, it does not matter if they are married or cohabiting persons, provided that they have attained a 'potentially fertile age'.

The fact that these are mere projects inserted into two recent Bills cannot be undervalued, but wide agreement has been reached on both points in the Senate and it is possible to foresee that this position will be confirmed as soon as the debate arrives at its concluding phase, in the *Camera dei Deputati*. It is clear that the latter choice will eventually have a significant impact on the still unitary foundations of the notion of 'legal family', because 'legitimate' and *de facto* unions will receive completely equal treatment. Evidently, this modification will produce a wider effect, in comparison with any previous innovation.

The first proposal – which is not so 'new', as it was 'foreseen' by the Constitutional Court in 1994 – might become more far-reaching than one might expect.[94] First of all, this solution would hopefully accelerate the administrative activity which is necessary to enhance the level of certainty in the ascertainment of the existence of a stable *de facto* union (even if only for the period prior to the couple's marriage) and the criteria applicable for the evidence of the length of the cohabitation. Secondly, the decision whether to consider the prospective adopters

---

S Balletti, 'Le coppie omosessuali, le istituzioni comunitarie e la Costituzione italiana' (1996) *Rassegna di Diritto Civile*, 252. For various opinions on these issues, in the light of national, statutory regulation, see, for instance, for the French experience, D Borrillo, *Homosexualité en droit* (1999) 2nd ed. Paris; A Aoun, *Le PACS* (1999) Paris; JF Pillebout, *Le PACS, pacte civil de solidarité* (2000) Paris; C Mécary, *Droit et homosexualité* (2000) Paris.

91   See footnote 59 above.

92   See Article 6, para 1, of the Testo Unificato – ie of the unitary text that has been previously examined and approved by a Special Commission of the Senate (nos 130-*bis*, 160-*bis*;, 445-*bis*, 852, 1697-*bis*, 1895, 3128, 3228, 4648). If this innovation is finally approved by the other House of the Parliament (*Camera dei Deputati*), a relevant change will be made.

93   S. no. 4048.

94   See footnote 31 above.

as suitable (or not) will probably be taken after a wider comparative enquiry. The same investigations which are carried out today (on the psychological suitability and the economic capacity of the couple) will be extended from the post-marriage period to the whole duration of the cohabitation. The scope of this analysis will be expanded too because a greater number of situations will be taken into account.

This might influence the nature of the perspective too: the requirement of marriage will become (or felt) more 'formal' than it is now. Indeed, if one thinks about the first reactions to this innovation in the media and TV news, a clear sign of a modification of attitude can easily be 'discerned'. An extremely 'advanced' (albeit incorrect) interpretation was given to this provision of the Unitary Bill, soon after its approval by the Senate. Some authoritative Italian newspapers gave very wide information about the possibility of a future extension of full adoption to *de facto* couples. They put great emphasis on the fact that a three-year period of cohabitation prior to the application will be sufficient, on condition that the couple is married when the adoption takes place.[95]

Although the Bill does not contain such a radical innovation, the majority of voters are not accustomed to reading the parliamentary debates or to looking at the original text of a Bill.[96] Thus, one may wonder why this 'mistaken interpretation' – which evidently goes beyond the legislative intention and is contrary to the literal meaning of the provision at hand – has been proposed.

Perhaps, it was founded on a common understanding, which, however, deserves special mention. It is very likely that an amendment will be suggested, in

---

95 They spoke of an 'apertura alle coppie di fatto: se la legge attuale stabilisce che per fare domanda di adozione si debba essere sposati da almeno tre anni, la nuova considera 'validi' anche gli anni di convivenza purché al momento dell'adozione la coppia abbia contratto matrimonio' (see *La Repubblica*, 7 December 2000). Identical news could be read in the front-page of *Il Corriere della Sera*, 7 December 2000 : 'Adozioni, meno ostacoli per i genitori, ma le coppie di fatto dovranno impegnarsi al matrimonio [...data la] possibilità per le coppie conviventi, da almeno tre anni, di fare domanda di adozione, salvo poi sposarsi prima dell'adozione vera e propria'.

96 The social interest towards the reform of in-country adoption is currently very high, in Italy. However, it is rather difficult to have a complete vision of all the proposals made with a view to modifying the present Act (no. 184/1983). It is necessary to take into consideration not only the Bills expressly devoted to adoption law, but also those that concern registered partnership. Of course, after the drafting of the unitary Bills examined in the text, it is possible to envisage some points of agreement among different political groups. It is worth mentioning that only one Bill, devoted to the reform of adoption law, contained an express proposal in favour of the opening up of full adoption to single persons and to '*more uxorio* cohabitants, who have been living together for at least two years, according to the declaration (*dichiarazione anagrafica*) provided by article 13, d.p.r. 305.1989, n 223' (no. 1697 *bis*/ 1998, at Article 4). It is evident that there is a clear connection with the proposals concerning *de facto* unions. If we look at the most recent ones, the idea that there is no unanimity among political parties can be confirmed. Indeed, also in this field, there are still decisive divergencies. For instance, in some Bills there is a provision which expressly affirms that the parties of a civil union (*unione civile*) can become adoptive or foster parents, but 'according to the present legislation, and on equal conditions with respect to married couples' (C.no 2870/1998 – Buffo – Article 18). In contrast, in other Bills a similar solution is proposed in more 'uncertain' terms. For instance, there is only the specification that the 'condition' of the parties of a civil union cannot be an obstacle to adoption or foster care (see Bill S. no. 1518/1997 – Salvato – Article 15; and C. no 1020/1998 – Vendola – Article 15 and S. no. 2715/1997- Cioni- Article 16), or an even more generic indication (ie, a wide provision which aims at creating completely equal treatment between married and unmarried couples, as far as the rights of the family group are concerned – S.no 935/1997 – Manconi – Article 15). In another Bill – which has been presented by parliamentary representatives of the same (left) coalition – there is, on the contrary, a clear exclusion of the applicability of adoption law to the so-called '*unioni affettive*' (see C. no 4657/1998 – Soda and others – Article 3, para 5).

this direction. If this happens, the reform might come to a halt, in the final phase of the debate. Indeed, one of the most controversial and still unresolved questions is whether to maintain (or eliminate) the requirement of marriage in these (relatively new) fields of family law.

These examples show how the relationships of kinship (and also those 'not naturally' created) are still the starting points in the evolving trends in this area. However, the possibility of finding definitive answers which take the interests of all the subjects involved into consideration, and – among them – the best interests of the child, does not depend on the mere drafting of a legislative solution, at state level. In conclusion, it is worth emphasising again the need to consider not only the national, but also the supranational, the international and the private international law perspectives on this problem.

Some further examples, taken from the area of adoption law, might be useful to underline the need to foresee the results which can be caused by a specific (national) choice, and to evaluate them on different scales. For instance, a registered partner (both heterosexual and homosexual) can adopt the other partner's child (ie the so-called second parent adoption), according to the Danish Act no 360, enacted on 2 June 1999 (in force on 1 July of the same year). However, there is no possibility of adopting a child who is not resident in Denmark. Similarly, a recent Dutch Bill,[97] even if it will widen the possibilities for homosexual couples, so that they will also be able to adopt jointly a child who is not the child of one of the partners, contains a limitation, because the new provision will be applicable exclusively to children who are resident in the Netherlands. Inter-country adoptions will continue to be regulated by the current legislation. It is necessary to add that this Bill is strictly linked to the proposal for the extension of marriage to same-sex couples. All in all, from a purely national perspective, no difficulty is likely to arise, in the Netherlands, if both these proposals receive the final approval by the Higher Chamber of the Dutch Parliament.[98] However, some difficult problems will result abroad, in connection with these legislative solutions, given the difficulty of recognition, in any other foreign system, of both the marriage of same-sex couples and of this kind of adoption decision. It is not only a matter of principle. In fact, the nature of such problems is practical. In a few words, the risk of 'limping adoptions' is so high that the fear of jeopardising the interests of the child is not so unfounded. Of course, it is not sufficient to observe that a solution is radically innovative, to consider it irrational or unjustified. However, in dealing with family law issues (which are social issues) it is not possible to imagine that legal choices will be inserted into an empty space or that a purely abstract point of view can be adopted. Differences, in the scope of application of certain institutions, which give a legal dimension to human behaviour, are usually due to anthropological reasons, which cannot be 'explained' in rational terms. Thus, it is not possible to invoke an ideal concept of equality, without losing the sense of the real legal rules (and of the principles on which they are based).

---

97   See footnote 89 above.

98   Editorial note: Both proposals have now received the approval of the Dutch Parliament and the legislation came into force on 1 April 2001.

In continuing in this exemplificatory description, which is limited to the area of adoption law, it is possible to recall – apart from the provisions of the 1967 Council of Europe Convention on Adoption (Article 6) – the not so vague expressions used in the 1993 Hague Convention on the protection of children and co-operation in respect of inter-country adoption. To define the adopters, the Convention uses the words 'spouses' and 'a person', who are 'habitually resident in the receiving state' (Article 2, para 1). In contrast, in order to establish the concept of adoption, a decisive role has been conferred on it to the effect of creating a 'permanent parent-child relationship' (Article 2, para 2). However, the intentionally 'open' meaning of the latter provision cannot justify either strict preclusions or unforeseen extensions, even if the 1993 Convention does not aim at imposing any model, to national legislators, being aimed at creating an international system of protection for children, based on reciprocal collaboration between receiving and sending countries. Thus, if it does not expressly forbid joint adoptions by same sex partners, such a prohibition can be easily inferred, and not only from Article 2, para 1. In fact, apart from the results of a literal interpretation, it is possible to find clear indications in the preliminary works of the Convention. An evident rejection of this possibility has been manifested by almost all the Member States as well as by the other States which were invited to participate in the XVII Hague Conference Sessions. 'The question as to the persons who could be prospective adoptive parents was discussed at length in the Special Commission, in particular whether the Convention should cover adoptions applied for by non-married persons of different sex cohabiting together in a stable manner, or by homosexuals or lesbians, living as a couple or individually. [...T]he State of origin and the receiving State shall collaborate from the very beginning and they may refuse the agreement for the adoption to continue [...]'. Therefore, it is possible to conclude that – in cases of inter-country adoptions regulated by the 1993 Convention – problems of 'recognition' can arise, because the mechanism of automatic recognition presupposes the prior general acceptance of the fundamental principles regulating the procedural and substantive aspect of adoption law, even if different models can be affirmed, on a State level. Of course, other problems – which cannot be solved in the context of the Convention – deserve special attention, by national authorities. When a proposal was advanced in order to eliminate the word 'person' in the Article of the Convention which defines the adopters, the debate at the Hague Conference Sessions was focused on the pros and cons of this modification. In the end, it was thought that 'this elimination would not solve all the problems, because in that case the adoptions by homosexuals would be out of the scope of the Convention, and the children so adopted would not benefit from the Convention's rules. Besides, it may also be possible that a heterosexual couple adopt a child, and after being divorced one of them forms a couple with a person of the same sex. As a matter of fact, the only solution would be to prohibit the adoption by homosexuals, either as individuals or as a couple, and the revocation of the adoption, if such case occurs after a 'normal' adoption is granted. However, all those problems are not within the scope of the Convention and should be solved according to the internal law of each Contracting State'.[99]

---

99   See 'Explanatory report', Parra-Aranguren G, paras 79–85, at 79 and 82.

In the end, only a wide acceptance of totally new models of family institution – which is far from being likely today – might eliminate the serious dangers stemming from some innovations that, at present, may have only a 'symbolic' value. It is clear that, now that the Dutch Bill is definitively approved, the concrete impact of the modification at stake will be extremely limited: the number of joint in-country adoptions by same-sex couples will not be high and, moreover, the effects of these adoptions are not likely to be recognised in other countries. Evidently, we are not dealing here with the applicability of the rules embodied in the 1993 Hague Convention. In fact, even in the case of application of a traditional *exequatur* procedure, it is probable that recognition would be refused, in the near future at least, for being manifestly contrary to public policy (although the most compelling considerations should be linked to the protection of the best interests of the child). A good occasion to verify the actual scope of these innovative trends, in this field, is offered by the current situation in the USA. After the recent approval of the Federal law which has authorised the ratification of the 1993 Hague Convention on Inter-Country Adoption,[100] some clear steps will surely be taken, in State level legislation too.[101]

---

100 Public Law 106-279, signed by former President Bill Clinton on 6 October 2000.

101 See, for a first comment, WL Pierce, 'Hague Convention Becomes US Law. An Explanation of the New Law and Steps Required for Implementation' (2000), quoted in the bibliography of the Hague Conference (see Convention no 33, in the official website: http://www.hcch.net).

JAMAICA

FAMILY PROPERTY DIVISION AND DOMESTIC VIOLENCE

*Eileen Boxill**

I INTRODUCTION

This report provides an overview of proposed legislative reform in respect of family property and domestic violence.

The existing law governing the property rights of spouses is based on the separate property concept as modified by the principles of trust developed by the courts.[1] The reform of this area of law has been under consideration for a long time. Finally, last year a Bill entitled 'The Family Property (Rights of Spouses) Act' was introduced into the House of Representatives by the Minister of National Security and Justice. That Bill is currently being considered by a special parliamentary committee.[2]

The Domestic Violence Act was enacted in 1995 with the stated objective of providing speedy and effective remedies for victims of domestic violence. After four years of operation,[3] the Act is to be amended with a view to extending its scope and improving its effectiveness in the light of representations made by women's organisations[4] and the experience since its coming into force.

II FAMILY PROPERTY

The presentation of the Bill entitled 'The Family Property (Rights of Spouses) Act' marked the culmination of a lengthy process which began with the preliminary proposals put forward by the Family Law Committee (the FLC) in an Interim Report in 1976,[5] followed by the publication in 1984 of a Working Paper

---

* Director of Legal Reform, Legal Reform Department, Ministry of National Security and Justice.

1 The law governing the property rights of separated spouses was recently the focus of attention in a highly publicised case which was fought all the way to the Privy Council. This case involved a property dispute between a couple who had cohabited without marriage for over 30 years. See *Geddes v Stockert* – Privy Council Appeal No 66 of 1998.

2 The Bill was referred for the consideration of a Joint Select Committee of both Houses of Parliament. This allows members of the public an opportunity to comment on the Bill.

3 The Act came into force on 6 May 1996. The delay was to allow for the promulgation of Regulations to facilitate implementation of the Act.

4 Recommendations were made by the Association of Women's Organisations in Jamaica (AWOJA), which is an umbrella organisation.

5 This Interim Report was published in the form of a Green Paper and included also proposals for the reform of the law relating to divorce. The Committee's final recommendations on divorce reform were implemented by the Matrimonial Causes Act 1989 – see note in *Journal of Family Law* Vol 28, at 558.

which highlighted the deficiencies of the existing law, discussed various options for reform and solicited views on specific issues. In 1990 the FLC submitted a Report on Matrimonial Property Law Reform containing recommendations for the reform of the law relating to the division of property between separated and divorced spouses. Following upon consultations with women's organisations certain modifications were introduced. The Bill is based on the recommendations of the FLC as modified.

A   Modifications made to the recommendations of the FLC

The modifications which were made to the recommendations of the FLC relate to what are arguably the most significant features of the new property regime introduced by the Bill: the special status accorded the family home and the extension of the new statutory rules to couples cohabiting without marriage.

1   TREATMENT OF THE FAMILY HOME

Three possible approaches were considered by the FLC:

(1)   leaving property to be divided between the spouses by the court as it sees fit, subject to statutory guidelines – the discretionary approach;

(2)   giving each spouse a statutorily fixed entitlement to property – the fixed approach; and

(3)   giving each spouse a presumptive half share in the matrimonial home, and leaving the division of all other property to the discretion of the court – the composite approach.

The FLC in its Interim Report had expressed a preference for the composite approach, but in the final Report recommended instead the adoption of the discretionary approach as an initial phase of matrimonial property reform.[6]

The Government, however, after consultation with women's organisations, opted for the immediate introduction of the composite approach. It was felt that giving each spouse a fixed half share in the family home would not only be fair, but would also go a long way in mitigating disputes between spouses as to property rights, as in the majority of cases it is the most valuable item of property owned by the spouses and that which is most often the subject of dispute.

2   APPLICATION OF THE STATUTORY RULES TO COHABITANTS

The recommendations of the FLC related to the division of matrimonial property between a husband and wife upon the breakdown of marriage. They did not contemplate cohabitants or common law spouses as they are called. The Bill's Memorandum of Objects and Reasons states the justification for the extension of the application of the new rules to cohabitants.

---

6   This decision was largely influenced by a concern that the need to protect the interest of a non-title owning spouse against alienation of his/her interest in the matrimonial home without his/her consent would have certain administrative and financial implications which could delay the implementation of the proposed reform. See FLC Report on Matrimonial Property Reform, para 6.3.

'In enacting these new provisions the Government is also aware of the social reality of men and women living together in common law unions. They build families together, they work together and they accumulate possessions together. When the union breaks down, the parties experience the same kinds of financial dislocation as if they were married. In our society legal solutions for the problems of family breakdown must address not only married couples, but also common law spouses, if they are to be effective.'

The present policy is to recognise persons in stable and long-standing common law unions. The Bill adopts the criteria for eligibility which apply under other legislation which recognises a common law spouse.[7] 'Spouse' is defined to include 'a single woman who has cohabited with a single man as if she were in law his wife for a period of not less than five years'; and 'a single man who has cohabited with a single woman as if she were in law her husband for a period of not less than five years. A widow, widower or divorcee is regarded as having "single" status'.

B   The new statutory rules

The new rules introduced by the Bill will replace the rules and presumptions of common law and equity which now govern the determination of the property rights of spouses.[8] They recognise a distinction between the family home and other property owned by one or both of the spouses.

1   ENTITLEMENT TO THE FAMILY HOME

The new rules deal with entitlement to the family home in the event of marriage breakdown or cessation of cohabitation on the one hand, and in the event of the death of one spouse on the other hand.

On marriage breakdown or cessation of cohabitation each spouse will be entitled to a one-half share of the family home. Entitlement will arise, where the spouses are married, on the grant of a decree of nullity or dissolution of marriage or upon separation without the likelihood of reconciliation; and in the case of cohabitants, upon the termination of cohabitation.

The court will be empowered, on the application of a spouse, to vary the equal share rule where it is of the opinion that it would be unjust for each spouse to be entitled to a one-half share, taking into account such factors as it thinks relevant, including the fact that the family home was inherited by one spouse or was a gift to one spouse and the donor intended that spouse alone to benefit; that it was already owned by one spouse at the time of the marriage or beginning of cohabitation; or that the marriage or cohabitation was of a short duration.[9]

An agreement between spouses or prospective spouses as to how property is to be owned or divided in the event of the termination of their marriage or cohabitation will be permitted, but such an agreement must comply with stipulated

---

7   See eg the Intestates' Estates and Property Charges Act, section 2; the Inheritance (Provision for Family and Dependants) Act 1993, section 2.

8   Clause 4.

9   Clause 7.

requirements.[10] Moreover, any such agreement will be subject to judicial review, and liable to be set aside by the court if it is satisfied that to give effect to it would be unjust. An agreement between spouses will operate to displace not only the equal-share rule applicable to the family home, but also the discretionary power of the court to divide other property owned by the spouses.

Where the marriage or cohabitation is terminated by the death of one of the spouses the family home will be treated as having been held in joint tenancy, if it was not so held, with the result that the surviving spouse will be entitled to the entire interest in the family home. This provision will supersede the provisions of a will or the law relating to intestacy.[11]

While the reaction to the rules regarding entitlement to the family home has been generally supportive, certain aspects have been criticised. Issue has been taken with the application of the equal share rule to property which was owned wholly by one spouse at the time of the marriage or commencement of cohabitation. The view had been advanced that the owner spouse should not be put to the trouble and expense of applying to the court for a variation of the rule, but that the specific factors which the court is required to consider where an application for variation is made should be treated as grounds for excluding its application.[12] There is an argument for the exclusion of pre-nuptial property and property acquired by one spouse by way of inheritance or gift from shareable property, on the ground that such property does not represent the joint efforts of the parties and this is the approach taken under some matrimonial property legislation.

The provisions of the Bill follow the preliminary proposals in the Interim Report of the FLC. No recommendation was made in the final Report with regard to a family home to which these circumstances apply, as the FLC had recommended that the equal sharing of the matrimonial home should not be pursued at this time. The Report does, however, discuss the treatment of property which is not attributable to the marriage and the identification of shareable assets, and the observations made in this regard show a leaning towards the inclusive approach taken in the Bill. This is evident in the following statement regarding the restriction of the equal share rule to 'property acquired during marriage':[13]

'Where only property acquired during the marriage is to be shared, property acquired before the marriage will be excluded, and it is arguable that certain property, eg the matrimonial home and contents are inherently matrimonial property and should be the subject of sharing irrespective of when they were acquired.'

The approach taken in the Matrimonial Property Act 1976 of New Zealand presents a compromise which both the policy makers and the critics might find appealing. It provides that property which is acquired by way of gift or inheritance from a third person shall not be treated as matrimonial property (and therefore not liable to equal sharing) unless, with the consent of the spouse who received it, the

---

10   Clause 10.
11   Clause 6(2).
12   Submission by the St. Andrew Business & Professional Women's Club.
13   Ibid.

property or the proceeds thereof have been so intermingled with other matrimonial property that it is unreasonable or impracticable to regard that property or those proceeds as separate property.[14] However, this exemption does not apply with full force to the matrimonial home and family chattels. In respect of such property the equal share rule is limited but not excluded – it does not apply where the marriage has been of short duration. A marriage of short duration is defined as one which has lasted for less than three years or for such longer period as the court considers just.[15]

The entitlement of a surviving spouse to the entire interest in the family home upon the death of the other spouse is another aspect of the proposed new rules which has aroused some disquiet. The fear is that it will operate to the disadvantage of the children of the deceased spouse from a former marriage or union which, it is felt, would be particularly unfair in the case where the family home was acquired during the previous marriage and it is the only valuable asset which was owned by the deceased spouse. It has been suggested that the half share rule should apply also on the termination of the marriage or cohabitation by the death of one spouse.

The inheritance of the family home by a surviving spouse is intended to provide some economic security for that spouse. However, since the recommendation was made in 1976, certain developments have occurred which have the same objective. The entitlement of a surviving spouse was increased considerably by an amendment to the Intestates' Estates and Property Charges Act in 1988.[16] The Inheritance (Provision for Family and Dependants) Act was enacted in 1993, enabling certain family members, including a spouse, to apply to the court for maintenance provisions to be made out of a deceased person's estate, on the ground that adequate provisions have not been made for the applicant by will or the law relating to intestacy. It is arguable that in the light of these provisions a 50:50 division of the family home upon the death of one spouse would be reasonable. This would leave each spouse free to dispose of his or her half share of the family home as he or she sees fit.

The Bill provides two safeguards against an action by one spouse to defeat the interest of the other spouse where title to the family home is in the name of one spouse only. First, it authorises the taking by the other spouse of such steps as may be necessary to protect his or her interest, including the lodging of a caveat against the title. Protective action could also take the form of a transfer of the property to their joint names, to facilitate which a waiver of the payment of transfer tax is granted.[17]

Secondly, it requires the consent of both spouses to any transaction relating to the family home, unless such consent has been dispensed with by the court, and confers on the court power to set aside any transaction on the ground of non-compliance with this requirement. Where an interest was acquired by a bona fide

---

14 Matrimonial Property Act 1976 (NZ), section 10(1).
15 Matrimonial Property Act 1976 (NZ), section 13.
16 The Intestates' Estates and Property Charges (Amendment) Act 1988.
17 Clause 9.

purchaser for value without notice, the spouse whose interest is defeated will be entitled to claim the value of his share out of the proceeds of the transaction.[18]

2   ENTITLEMENT TO PROPERTY OTHER THAN THE FAMILY HOME

All other property (ie other than the family home) owned by one or both of the spouses will be subject to distribution by the court as it sees fit. The Bill provides guidelines for the exercise of this discretion, the objectives of which are to promote consistency in decisions, to ensure evenness in the weight attached to the various kinds of contribution, and generally to avoid the deficiencies to which the discretionary approach is prone. The provisions of the Bill are similar to those found in other legislation which follows a discretionary approach.[19]

One of the shortcomings of the present law is its focus on financial contribution and its failure to recognise services provided in the performance of the role of parent and homemaker in assessing a spouse's entitlement to property. Under the new rules the court is required to take into account 'the contribution, financial or otherwise, directly or indirectly made by or on behalf of a spouse to the acquisition, conservation or improvement of any property'. Contribution is widely defined and includes specifically caring for a child or an aged or infirm relative or dependant; the management of the household and the performance of household duties. It is also stated, for the avoidance of doubt, that there shall be no presumption that a monetary contribution is of greater value than a non-monetary contribution.

It should be noted that all property owned by one or both of the spouses, however and whenever acquired, will be subject to redistribution by the court. As the Report of the FLC points out, this does not mean that all the assets owned by a spouse will compulsorily be divided, but that it will be left to the court to decide what, if any, asset should be excluded.[20] The ability of the court to consider all property owned by the spouses is also intended to facilitate the consideration of maintenance provisions and property rights together, as was recommended by the FLC. The determination of appropriate financial provisions for a spouse and/or children will require an assessment of the overall economic position of the spouses, which necessarily involves a consideration of all the assets owned by them. A separate Bill on maintenance is being drafted, to be introduced as a companion measure to the Family Property (Rights of Spouses) Bill.

3   TIME FOR DIVISION OF PROPERTY

An application for property division may be made – by a married spouse on the grant of a decree of nullity or termination of marriage or upon separation where there is no reasonable likelihood of reconciliation; by a cohabitant, on the termination of cohabitation; and by spouses generally, where one spouse is endangering the property or seriously diminishing its value, by gross mismanagement or by wilful or reckless dissipation of property or earnings.

---

18   Clause 8.
19   The guidelines are actually based on the Family Law Act 1975 (Aus.) and the similarly entitled 1981 Act of Barbados.
20   The FLC Report on Matrimonial Property Law Reform, p 14, para 6.6.

The FLC had suggested, initially, that a spouse should be entitled to apply for division of property in the following circumstances – upon divorce; when the marriage is in serious difficulties; or upon actual separation. The feedback on this proposal indicated some unease with permitting the division of property during marriage, the view being that this would be inimical to the marriage. To meet this concern the separation ground was reformulated to indicate marriage breakdown, and the 'serious difficulties' ground was replaced by the more precise circumstance copied from the New Zealand Matrimonial Property Act 1976[21] to afford protection of property in a case where the relationship between the parties has not broken down irretrievably.

An application for division of property will normally have to be made within 12 months of the dissolution or annulment of marriage, separation or termination of cohabitation, but an out of time application will be possible with the leave of the court.

4   PROTECTION OF PROPERTY RIGHTS

Mention was made earlier of the mechanisms for the protection of a spouse's interest in the family home where that spouse is not a title-holder. The court's power to restrain a disposition which is about to be made, or to set aside a disposition which was made, will apply also to property which is subject to redistribution by the court.[22] Additionally, the disposal by one spouse of property which is the subject of proceedings will render that spouse liable to prosecution for a criminal offence.[23]

5   DECLARATION OF PROPERTY RIGHTS DURING MARRIAGE

Clause 11 of the Bill provides for the determination of the property rights of spouses during the marriage or cohabitation. The provisions of the Bill are essentially a re-enactment of the summary procedure provisions under the Married Women's Property Act which will be repealed when the new Act comes into force. The new procedure will differ from the existing one in two important respects. First, it will be available for the settlement of property disputes not only between a husband and wife, but also between cohabitants who meet the qualifying criteria. Secondly, the property rights of the spouses will be determined with reference to the new statutory rules.

This means, where the property in dispute is the family home, that each spouse will be entitled to a one-half share, subject to the displacement of this rule in one of the ways discussed earlier. A spouse's right in respect of other property is not as clear-cut, as this is determinable by the court. In this instance, the court is concerned with the ownership of the property in question, and not the division of property between the spouses. Both involve the exercise of the court's discretionary power but the focus is different. In the case of an application for division of property, the objective is to divide property equitably between the

---

21   Section 25(2)(c).

22   Clause 21. This power does not apply where property has passed to a bona fide purchaser for value without notice.

23   Clause 20.

spouses, which might require the alteration of ownership rights. In the case of an application for declaration of property rights, the court has to determine existing ownership rights. In this instance, the impact of the new statutory rules will lie mainly in the much wider definition of contribution and the treatment of financial and non-financial contributions as being of equal value.

6   DETERMINATION OF THE VALUE OF PROPERTY

The spouses' share in property will be determined as at the date of separation or, where they are still cohabiting, at the date of the application. In the absence of an agreement between the spouses, property will be valued as at the date of the hearing unless the court otherwise decides.[24] A valuer may be appointed jointly by the spouses or each spouse may appoint a valuer. In the latter case the value of the property will be the average of the two valuations.

7   PROTECTION OF CREDITORS

The rights of creditors will be unaffected by any right to property conferred on spouses by the proposed Act or an order of the court made under that Act.[25] The Bill specifically preserves the rights of a third party pursuant to a mortgage, charge or encumbrance which was registered or executed before the date of the making of the order.

The satisfaction of a spouse's interest in the family home, as also the determination of the value of shareable property, will be subject to the payment of debts secured on the property. Where property in which both spouses have an interest is liable for the payment of the debts of one spouse, the court may order an adjustment of their respective shares in the property or that the debtor-spouse pay compensation to the other spouse.

Any agreement, disposition or other transaction between spouses with respect to their family home or other property which is intended to defeat any creditor will be void.

III   THE DOMESTIC VIOLENCE ACT 1995[26]

Prior to the coming into effect of the Domestic Violence Act, the victims of domestic violence had to rely on the criminal sanctions and civil and matrimonial remedies, all of which had limited application and effect. The Domestic Violence Act addressed specifically the problem of domestic violence by providing two new remedies: (1) a protection order; and (2) an occupation order, which are available on application to a Family Court or a Resident Magistrate's Court. The protective coverage of the Act extends to a spouse, a parent, a child or dependant of the person against whom the order is sought (the respondent). For this purpose

---

24   Clause 12.

25   Clause 17.

26   The Act is based on a model Bill which was prepared for use by Commonwealth Caribbean countries. Similar legislation has been enacted in other Caribbean countries. For a review of such legislation, see 'Changing Concepts of Violence: The Impact of Domestic Violence Legislation in the Caribbean', *The Caribbean Law Review*, Tracy S Robinson, Vol 9 p 113.

'spouse' includes a cohabitant or common-law spouse and also a former spouse. 'Child' is widely defined to cover the biological child of either or both of the spouses, and any child who is or has been a member of the household, or of whom either spouse is guardian. 'Dependant' includes an adult member of the family who lives with the respondent on a regular basis.

A   Orders which may be made

1   PROTECTION ORDERS

A protection order is in the nature of an injunction. It may be invoked to prohibit the respondent from engaging in a number of specific types of conduct ranging from acts of physical violence to psychological abuse.[27]

A protection order may be made by the court if it is satisfied that the respondent has used or threatened to use violence against a prescribed person or has caused physical or mental injury to a prescribed person and is likely to do so again. The court may also grant a protection order where, having regard to all the circumstances, it considers it necessary for the protection of a prescribed person. The civil standard of proof on the balance of probabilities applies.

Breach of a protection order is a criminal offence which is punishable by a fine of up to ten thousand dollars, or to a period of imprisonment not exceeding six months, or to both such fine and imprisonment. Additionally, where a protection order is in force a constable may arrest without warrant a person whom he has reasonable cause to suspect of having committed a breach of the order, if he believes that this action is necessary for the protection of the person in whose favour the order was made.[28] The automatic attachment of a power of arrest to a protection order, instead of requiring an application to be made to the court, is intended to avoid the reported reluctance of the court to grant such an application. However, there is no evidence that this approach has afforded any significant advantage in practice.[29]

Either the complainant or the respondent may apply to the court for the discharge of a protection order. The court, in deciding whether to discharge the order, must have regard to the reasons for making the order in the first place. The main consideration will be whether the circumstances which influenced the making of the order no longer prevail, particularly where it is the respondent who is applying for the discharge of the order.[30]

2   OCCUPATION ORDERS

An occupation order entitles the person to whom it is granted to exclusive possession of the household residence. It may have effect notwithstanding that at the time of the order the parties were still living together and notwithstanding that

---

27   Section 4(1).

28   Section 5(2).

29   It is reported that the police continue to display an unwillingness to arrest a person for domestic violence, except where a serious prosecutable crime has been committed.

30   Section 6.

the excluded party has a legal interest in the home. Where the excluded party has been occupying the home, the order amounts to an eviction order.

The possibility of a person being evicted from a home of which he is the legal owner is the aspect of the Act which excited the strongest reaction, especially from men, at the time of its passage. Experience since has borne out the obsessive fear of men of being evicted from their own property. From information provided by the Family Court the larger number of applications under the Act are made by women seeking mainly protection orders. A relatively small number of applications are made by men and noticeably some of these are for occupation orders. The typical scenario is this. A man and a woman are cohabiting without marriage in a home of which the man is owner or tenant. At the first sign of breakdown of the relationship, the man applies for an occupation order to foil any attempt by the woman herself to make an application under the Act.

The court may make an occupation order only if it is satisfied that such an order is necessary for the protection of the prescribed person or would be in the best interest of a child.[31] The courts have heeded this directive and have been sparing in their use of this power. Where the applicant has no property rights in the home, especially if no child is involved, such an order is made only for such duration that would enable the non-owner spouse to find alternative accommodation.[32] An occupation order is normally made for a period not exceeding three months, although an extension may be permitted if the circumstances of the particular case warrant this.

An occupation order may be made on such terms and subject to such conditions as the court thinks fit. The court may also make ancillary orders granting to the applicant the use of any or all of the furniture, the household appliances and effects.[33] Such orders will normally last for three months or until the expiry date of the principal order, if earlier. Either party may apply to the court seeking a discharge or variation of an occupation order.[34]

An occupation order does not confer any rights as to ownership of property, nor does it affect the rights of a mortgagee or other charge holders whose interest in the property arose prior to the order.[35] For this reason the Act requires that all persons who have an interest in property to be affected by an occupation order must be notified before an order is made, and entitles them to appear and be heard in the matter of the application as a party to the proceedings.[36]

3   INTERIM ORDERS

The Act provides for the grant of both a protection order and an occupation order on an ex parte application.

The court may make a protection order on an ex parte application if it is satisfied that the delay that would result from proceeding in the usual way would or might

---

31   Section 7(3).
32   *Davis v Johnson* [1979] AC 264.
33   Section 12.
34   Section 10.
35   Section 20.
36   Section 11.

result either in risk to the personal safety of a prescribed person or serious or undue hardship.[37]

The conditions for the grant of an occupation order on an ex parte application are more restrictive. The court must be satisfied that: (1) the respondent has used violence against or caused physical injury to a prescribed person; and (2) the delay that would be caused by following the normal procedure could or might expose the prescribed person to physical injury.[38]

An order made on an ex parte application is an interim order which must specify a date for a hearing which shall be as soon thereafter as is reasonably practicable.[39]

B   Provisions relating to counselling, procedure and appeal

The court may, on making an order, recommend that either or both parties participate in counselling.[40]

Proceedings under the Act are held in camera. Only persons who are directly concerned with the case and persons permitted by the court are allowed to be present in court during hearings. Restrictions are imposed also on the publication of the reports of cases.[41]

An appeal against an order or the refusal to make an order lies to the Court of Appeal. Where an appeal is filed, the order will continue in force unless the court otherwise directs.[42]

C   Proposed amendments

Several amendments to the Domestic Violence Act are being considered. These are based on recommendations which have been made by women's organisations and other sources concerned with the implementation of the Act. Some of the proposed amendments go to the clarification of certain provisions and will therefore be in the nature of drafting refinements.[43] The substantive amendments will relate mainly to the categories of persons who are permitted to apply under the Act. These can be discussed only in terms of the broad issues to be addressed, as the precise form these amendments will take is not yet decided.

1   APPLICATION ON BEHALF OF SPOUSE, PARENT

Where the victim of domestic violence is a child or dependant, an application under the Act may be made on behalf of the child or dependant by any of the following persons – a person with whom the child or dependant normally resides, a parent or guardian, an approved social worker, or a constable. A spouse or

---

37   Section 4(3).

38   Section 8(1).

39   Section 13.

40   Section 18.

41   Section 16.

42   Section 19(5).

43   The recommendation made by AWOJA re the reformulation of the definition of 'child', to specify an age limit and to make it clear that a child in a non-spousal household is covered, is an example.

parent must apply on his or her own behalf. This is viewed as a limitation on the effectiveness of the Act as persons who are the victims of abuse are often so incapacitated that they cannot act on their own behalf.

Representations have been made for the amendment of the Act to permit an application to be made on behalf of a parent or spouse by specified persons, which include a medical practitioner, a nurse and a minister of religion. Persons specifically authorised to take such action are usually agents of the State who normally carry out this type of function, eg a constable.[44] Extending this to the other persons identified might not be practical, as they may be reluctant to assume this role. A more feasible approach would be to permit a person to act as the representative or agent of a parent or a spouse and to indicate the circumstances in which this may be done[45] or make this subject to the granting of leave by the court.[46]

2   PERSONS WITHIN THE PROTECTIVE COVERAGE OF THE ACT

The Act targets persons in a household; consequently a man and a woman who have an intimate relationship but who do not share a common residence – what is commonly known as a visiting relationship – are outside the coverage of the Act. The 'visiting union' is an established feature of family life in Jamaica. Although the parties do not live together, they spend a lot of time together, and in many cases have children together. The experience is that a number of women in visiting relationships are the victims of domestic violence, but are unable to access the remedies provided by the Act. This is one of the shortcomings of the Act.

The recognition of non-marital family unions has been confined so far to cohabitants. The criteria for recognition vary according to the purpose for which recognition is granted. In the case of domestic violence, the focus is on the exposure to risk, hence there is no stipulation as to duration or single status. The formulation for the identification of the visiting relationship presents an interesting challenge. Some guidance may be had from other legislation which recognise persons in a non-residential relationship. The Domestic Protection Act 1995 of New Zealand, for example, permits an application for a protection order by a person who is in a 'close personal relationship' with another, and it points to certain factors to assist the identification of such a relationship.[47] These include the nature and intensity of the relationship; the amount of time spent together; where and the manner in which that time is ordinarily spent; and the duration of the relationship. This approach could usefully be adopted with the necessary modifications to suit the Jamaican situation.[48] For example, whether the parties have a child together would be an appropriate addition to the identifying factors. There is no indication, at least at present, of any intention to extend the scope of

---

44   Eg the Domestic Violence Act 1991 of Trinidad and Tobago, section 7(3) permits an application to be made by a constable on behalf of an adult victim. The victim must be joined as a party to the proceedings.

45   See eg the Domestic Violence Act 1995 of NZ and the Domestic Violence (Protection Orders) Act 1997.

46   See Domestic Violence (Protection Orders) Act 1992, section 4(1)(d).

47   A similar approach is taken in the Bermudan Domestic Violence (Protection Orders) Act.

48   The category of relationships contemplated by the NZ Act is wider than that proposed in the Jamaican context.

the Act beyond a relationship between heterosexual couples; accordingly, a likely modification is the addition of a stipulation to this effect.

3   WHAT CONSTITUTES DOMESTIC VIOLENCE?

The Act does not define domestic violence, but lists the types of conduct which will ground an application for a protection order. Representation has been for the expansion of this list to include damage to property, destruction of personal property and deprivation of the use of personal property, on the ground that such acts are prevalent.

At present such conduct could qualify as an act of molestation under section 4(1)(e)(iv) which permits an application for a protection order to prohibit the respondent from molesting a prescribed person by 'using abusive language to or behaving towards the prescribed person in any other manner which is of such nature and degree as to cause annoyance to, or result in ill treatment of the prescribed person'.[49] The amendment sought would identify damage to property as a specific act of domestic violence. This would bring the Act in line with the approach taken in other domestic violence legislation.[50]

IV   CONCLUSION

After a long lull, it appears that family law reform is once again on the parliamentary agenda. Such legislation is usually not politically controversial, and should therefore have a relatively easy passage through Parliament. The proposed Family Property Act as well as the proposed amendments to the Domestic Violence Act will further the recognition of informal conjugal relationships. Having regard to the growing equation of a *de facto* marriage with a *de jure* marriage, the time might well be right for consideration to be given to the provision of a judicial mechanism for the establishment of the status of *de facto* spouse. This would certainly ease some of the complications that are likely to arise in relation to transactions involving a property which could qualify as the family home of a cohabiting couple.

---

49   Section 4(1)(e)(iv).

50   Eg Domestic Violence Act (Bermuda), section 2; Domestic Violence Act (Aus.), section 4A(1); Domestic Violence Act 1995 (NZ) section 3 (2).

JAPAN

GUARDIANSHIP FOR ADULTS

*Kazuhiko Niijima**

The year 2000 saw major changes in welfare legislation. First, the new 'Law on Public Care Insurance for the Elderly',[1] which was introduced in 1997, came into force on 1 April 2000. Secondly, the 'Law on Guardianship for Dependent Adults'[2] passed the National Diet on 1 December 1999 and was promulgated on 8 December 1999. It came into force on 1 April 2000.

In this paper I concentrate on the outline of the Law on Guardianship for Dependent Adults, as the background and the development of the legislative process of the new Law was introduced in detail by Professor Matsushima[3] and the Law on Public Care Insurance for Elderly has been examined very capably as well.[4]

I   AN AGEING SOCIETY IN JAPAN

As every industrialised country is faced with an ageing society, the welfare for the elderly is becoming a more important issue. Japan cannot be an exception since the county has a reputation for a long life expectancy.[5] The number of people living over the age of 65 has increased rapidly in recent years; in 1985 it was 10% of the population, it reached 15.7% in 1997 and it is expected to be 25% in 2020.

Today the elderly have greater economic independence and are much better off because of improvements in the social security system or company pension schemes. Many elderly people today own property. How to manage and protect their assets when they become unable to look after themselves due to ageing, suffering from ailments such as senile dementia, is a great concern.

---

*   Lecturer in Japanese Law, Cardiff Law School, Cardiff University.

1   Law No 123, 1997.

2   There are four Laws involved in this legislation: (1) Law on partial amendment of the Civil Code: Law No 149, 1999, (2) Law on Guardianship by Agreement: Law No 50, 1999, (3) Law on reform of laws concerned with the amendment of the Civil Code: Law No 151, 1999, and (4) Law on Registration of Guardianship: Law No 152, 1999.

3   Y Matsushima, 'What has made family law reform go astray?' in *The International Survey of Family Law 1997*, ed A Bainham (Martinus Nijhoff Publishers, 1999) at 193–206.

4   Ibid.

5   Average life expectancy of Japanese men was 77.01 years and 83.59 years for women in 1996.

II   PROBLEMS IN THE SYSTEM OF PROTECTION OF MENTALLY DISABLED PERSONS UNDER THE CIVIL CODE

Under the old law, two types of protection were provided for mentally disabled persons who did not have sufficient capacity to act on their own or had only limited capacity to act. These were incompetents and quasi-incompetents. An 'incompetent' denoted a person who was chronically mentally disturbed (former Article 7, Civil Code). A family court order was needed to declare a person incompetent. An incompetent person was not capable of acting on his own and could only act through a guardian (former Article 8). When he had acted on his own, that act was voidable (former Article 9). Quasi-incompetents were those who were mentally unstable but not totally disturbed, or spendthrifts (former Article 11). As with incompetence, quasi-incompetence was also a matter for the family court. A quasi-incompetent had limited capacity to act, and was required to obtain the consent of his/her curator when performing certain acts listed in the Civil Code. These acts included: borrowing money or becoming a guarantor, transactions concerning real property or movables of significance, receiving or investing funds, and initiating litigation (former Article 12, para 1). Any such act done without the consent of the curator was voidable and could be rescinded (former Article 12, para 2).

A number of problems existed under this old system. First, there were only two types of classification available; either incompetent or quasi-incompetent. It was only possible to be declared incompetent if all mental function ceased. It is obvious that the degree of loss of function varies from person to person, and once a person was declared incompetent he lost all power to deal with his own assets and they were taken out of his hands regardless of the degree of his remaining function. Therefore such an all-or-nothing test is often inadequate in protecting the interests and rights of the elderly. A person declared quasi-incompetent was placed under curatorship and consent was required to perform certain legal acts. Nevertheless, the curator did not have a right to rescind an act performed by the quasi-incompetent person without the consent of the curator,[6] and the curator was not regarded as an agent acting on behalf of the quasi-incompetent person. Thus, the protection was inadequate.

Moreover, the law provided that a spouse of the incompetent person should be first in line to be appointed as the guardian. If a husband or wife suffering from senile dementia was declared as incompetent, his/her spouse was automatically appointed as guardian. In most cases the guardian would be old as well and not suitable for providing adequate care and management of assets.

Secondly, only one guardian could be appointed. Thus the single guardian was given the responsibility both for care and for asset management. It was hard for the guardian to undertake these various responsibilities. Therefore a more flexible system in accordance with the different needs of the elderly has been sought.

Thirdly, the terms 'incompetent' or 'quasi-incompetent' (in Japanese '*Kin-chisan*' or '*Jun-Kin-chisan*') are regarded as discriminatory language in modern Japanese society and people adjudicated as incompetent or quasi-incompetent are

---

6   Article 120 (former), Civil Code of Japan.

recorded in the Family Register (*Koseki*). People are reluctant to use the system because of psychological resistance to it. For the above-mentioned reasons the system has been hardly used.[7]

III THE NEW LAW ON GUARDIANSHIP FOR DEPENDENT ADULTS

The new system has been introduced in response to the problems and criticisms levelled against the old one. The principle of the new system is based on the idea of 'normalisation' and is designed from the viewpoint of harmonising the principle of respect for self-determination and the principle of protection of the mentally disabled person.[8] Under the new system, guardianship is divided into two categories; 'statutory guardianship' and 'guardianship by agreement'. The latter is a new system specially introduced for the first time. The former is further divided into three categories.

A Statutory guardianship

There are three types of protection under this category:

(1) GUARDIANSHIP (*KOKEN*)

This classification corresponds to the incompetence adjudication under the old law, and is applicable to people who have lost their mental capacities. The Family Court may make an order to commence guardianship for a person in the habitual condition of lack of capacity owing to mental disorder. The order may be made on the application of that person, the spouse, any relative up to the fourth degree of relationship, the guardian for a minor, the supervisor of the guardian for a minor, the curator, the supervisor of a curator, the assistant, the supervisor of the assistant or of a public prosecutor (new Article 7, Civil Code). A medical test is required before making an order.[9] When the order is made a guardian is appointed by the Family Court (new Article 8). Under the new law more than one guardian can be appointed in cases where the court considers it necessary (new Article 843, para 3), so that different guardians can be appointed for different functions, ie one for the management of assets and another for physical care.[10] The spouse no longer automatically becomes a guardian as he/she did under the old system.[11] The Family Court has a discretion to appoint an appropriate guardian. The Court must take all the circumstances into consideration, such as the mental and physical condition of the person, the lifestyle and the assets of the person, the personal history, occupation and any interest between the person and the guardian. Under

---

7   There are about 1 million elderly people suffering from senile dementia and about 2 million people suffering from mental disability, but only 1,709 determinations of incompetence and 251 determinations of quasi-incompetence were made in 1998 (Judicial Statistics 1998).

8   Ministry of Justice, Civil Affairs Bureau, Counsellor's Office, *Outline of the Draft Proposal Relating to the Reform of the Adult Guardianship System*, published on 14 April 1998.

9   Article 24, Rules on Family Affairs Adjudication.

10   Physical care includes daily care, arrangement of hospital and nursing home.

11   (Former) Article 840.

the new system, a corporation can be appointed as a guardian.[12] A corporation likely to be appointed would be one which specialises in welfare business. If the guardian is a corporation, the court must consider the suitability of the corporation. In principle, the absolute right of rescission and power of attorney are granted to the guardian but, from the new point of view of respecting the person's remaining capacities, that person should be able to carry out independently actions limited to those required for everyday life (new Article 9). In response to the criticism against the terminology of 'incompetence', a new legal term 'guarded person' is employed.

(2)   CURATORSHIP (*HOSA*)

This type of protection corresponds to the former quasi-incompetence adjudication and is applicable to people who are feeble-minded. The Family Court may make an order to commence curatorship for a person whose capacity to make a reasonable judgment is gravely limited due to mental disorder. The order may be made on the application of that person, the spouse, any relative up to the fourth degree of relationship, the guardian, the supervisor of the guardian, the helper, the supervisor of the helper, or of a public prosecutor (new Article 11). The Family Court appoints a curator (new Article 11-2). The curator is granted the right to consent to important legal acts listed in the Civil Code. These acts include: borrowing money or becoming a guarantor, transactions concerning real property and movables of significance, receiving or investing funds, and initiating litigation (new Article 12, para 1). Any such act done without the consent of the curator is voidable and can be rescinded (new Article 12, para 4). The Court may grant leave in cases where the curator would not give a consent to the person performing the listed acts. Unlike the old system the curator may now have a power of attorney for specified legal acts if the court gives this power on application. To preserve respect for the self-determination of the person, the consent of the person is required if the application for the power of attorney is applied for by someone other than the person himself (new Article 876-4, para 2).

(3)   GENERAL AID (*HOJO*)

This is a new type of protection created by the legislation (new Article 14). It is applicable to people who are not feeble-minded but who do not possess sufficient capacity to make judgments and therefore require care: people with slight senile dementia, the intellectually or mentally disabled, autistic people and others requiring care. It is anticipated that this new type of protection would cover most mentally disabled people who were not covered by the old system because their degree of disability was not severe enough to be protected, and that it would give more flexibility to the system and be widely used in promoting welfare for the elderly. The Family Court may make an order to commence general aid for a person whose capacity to make a reasonable judgment is insufficient due to mental disorder. The order may be made on the application of that person, the spouse, any relative up to the fourth degree of relationship, the guardian, the

---

12   Article 843 (new), para 4 et al.

supervisor of the guardian, the curator, the supervisor of the curator, or a public prosecutor (new Article 14).

B   Introduction of a new system of 'guardianship by agreement'

A new method of protection of the elderly has been created by the new law[13] in response to the demand for a more flexible and easy-to-use system based on the principle of respect for self-determination of the elderly. The new system is called 'guardianship by agreement'. Under this system, a person chooses his guardian and a contract is concluded between the person and the agent before the person's capacity for judgment has deteriorated. The written contract should be concluded before a notary public to secure its authenticity.[14]

It was possible to use the law of agency to appoint an agent acting on behalf of the principal for management of assets and physical care. However, if the principal has lost capacity, the agency continues until the contract is terminated formally.[15] This means that if an agent does something contrary to the interest or the will of the principal, there is no way of checking each action of the agent.

Under the new system, the guardian appointed by the person is supervised by the supervisor of the guardian who checks the guardian's conduct. The Family Court appoints the supervisor on the application of the person himself/herself, the spouse, any relative up to the fourth degree of relationship or the guardian.[16] To avoid a conflict of interest between the guardian and his relatives, the spouse, the parents, the brothers and sisters of the guardian are not eligible to be a supervisor.[17] The supervisor has the duty to report the conduct of the affairs by the guardian to the Family Court regularly, and the Court has power to order the supervisor to review the conduct of the guardian and make a report to the Court if necessary. Also the Court has power to remove the guardian if any unjust act or gross misconduct has been performed by the guardian.[18]

C   Registration of guardianship

Under the old system, people adjudged be to be incompetent or quasi-incompetent were registered in the Family Register (*Koseki*). *Koseki* is a registration system under which every family is registered with the government. Birth, marriage, divorce, adoption and death as well as declarations of incompetence by the Court are recorded, as is the relationship between each person. The *Koseki* performs the identification function for Japanese people and carries great legal and social significance.[19] Japanese people are keen to keep their own *Koseki* as clean as

---

13   Law on Guardianship by Agreement, Law No 150, 1999.
14   Article 3, Law on Guardianship by Agreement.
15   Article 111, Civil Code.
16   Article 4, para 1, Law on Guardianship by Agreement.
17   Article 5, ibid
18   Article 8, ibid.
19   For detailed discussion concerning the significance of the *Koseki*, see Y Matsushima, 'The Development of Japanese Family Law from 1898 to 1997 and its Relationship to Social and

possible and this consciousness is one of the factors which contributes to the low divorce rate in Japan. As such, a record of incompetence in the *Koseki* would deter people using the system of guardianship for adults, as the recorded person would be the object of social prejudice. However, it is important to have a system which discloses a person's capacity to act for the protection of the other party in a legal transaction such as a contract, since an act performed by a ward without the consent of the guardian is voidable.[20] Under the new law, the record of the court order of the three kinds of statutory guardianship and guardianship by agreement is registered with the Register Office and not in the Family Register (*Koseki*).[21] The Register Office will issue a certificate to prove that a person is under guardianship and the name of the guardian.

IV   CONCLUSION

The new law has been introduced with the expectation that the system would be used widely and promote the welfare of the elderly consistent with the idea of respect for the dignity and self-determination of the elderly.[22] The three types of statutory guardianship and the guardianship by agreement will be used in accordance with the degree of a person's ability to make decisions. The new system seems to be more flexible and user friendly in its wider coverage of mentally disabled people and its ease of use, along with the changes to terminology and registration. However, we need to wait to see the results of the new system since it is at a very early stage.

Political Change' in *The Changing Family: Family Forms & Family Policy*, edited by John Eekelaar and Thandabantu Nhlapo, Oxford: Hart Publishing (1998) pp 85–101.

20   Article 9 (new), Civil Code.

21   Law on Registration of Guardianship, Law No 152, 1999.

22   For detailed discussion of the new system, see M Arai (ed.) *Seinen Koken* – Horitsu no kaisetsu to katsuyo no hoho (Adult Guardianship, Explanation of the law and its application), Yuhikaku publishing, Tokyo (2000), 'Special collection of articles on the new Adult Guardianship System' in *Jurist*, No 1172, 15 February 2000, pp 2–43.

JORDAN

CAPACITY, CONSENT, AND UNDER-AGE MARRIAGE IN MUSLIM FAMILY LAW

*Lynn Welchman**

I   INTRODUCTION

In Jordanian family law, the marriage of a girl under the legal age of capacity for marriage and failure to register a marriage through the proper channels are both criminal offences rendering those involved liable to a prison sentence, accompanied in the second case by a fine. An under-age marriage is irregular[1] at its conclusion, and in and of itself gives rise to no legal effects and is liable to be dissolved by the court. However, this irregularity does not permanently prejudice the contract, since the marriage may subsequently become valid, and a claim for its dissolution on grounds of its irregular conclusion be ruled out of the competence of the court, even if it is one of the spouses who is objecting to its continuation. The validity of an unregistered marriage is not affected by the failure to register it or by the imposition of criminal sanctions for the manner of its conclusion. Duress renders a marriage contract irregular, but legal remedy appears to be lacking in the event that the marriage has been duly documented and registered. These rules, in certain circumstances, can combine to deny an 'exit strategy' to parties married at young ages by their marriage guardians who would prefer not to remain in the marriage – more particularly, young women and girls, since a man can at least withdraw from the marriage if he wishes by pronouncing a unilateral divorce.[2] This article examines Jordanian law on these related areas, as elucidated by relevant *Shari'a* Appeal Court decisions, with a view to assessing proposals for changes to the law advanced variously by lawyers and non-governmental organisations (NGOs) – particularly women's groups – in Jordan.

II   CONTEXT: LAW AND LEGAL SYSTEM

The law most immediately under examination in this article is the Jordanian Law of Personal Status 1976 (JLPS) which replaced an earlier code, the Jordanian Law of Family Rights 1951 (1951) and governs marriage and family relations for the Muslim majority of the population, estimated by Government sources in 1994 at

---

*   Director, Centre of Islamic and Middle Eastern Law, Department of Law, School of Oriental and African Studies, University of London.

1   *Fasid*, as compared to void (*batil*). A void marriage may never become valid. See further below.

2   *Talaq*, or unilateral 'repudiation' of the wife by the husband. Jordanian law has incorporated in its rules on the traditional Sunni institution of *talaq* certain restraining reforms common to many codified laws of personal status in the Arab world.

around 97%.[3] Jordan maintains the system of separate jurisdictions for matters of personal status for recognised religious communities familiar in the region. Under this system, the majority Muslim population are governed by a codification of provisions drawn mostly from the rules of the four Sunni schools of law and legislated as State law for application by the *shari'a* courts (loosely and inadequately translated as Islamic law courts). Other recognised communities – in Jordan, certain Christian sects – apply their own family laws in separate communal courts. The *shari'a* courts comprise first instance courts and a *Shari'a* Court of Appeal sitting in Amman; the system is under the direction of the *Qadi al-Quda* (Chief Islamic Justice) who ranks as a Minister.[4] It runs parallel to the statute (*nizami*) legal system which administers civil and criminal law in all areas not under the limited jurisdiction of the *shari'a* courts.[5] The *shar'i* court system has separate rules for appointments, a distinct body of employees, and its own rules of procedure – notably, the Law of *Shar'i* Procedure 1959.[6]

As for the law that the *shari'a* courts apply, where there is no specific text on a matter under consideration, the JLPS requires the court to refer to the dominant opinion of the Hanafi school of law.[7] In matters of evidence and procedure, the default reference is to the Majalla, the Ottoman manual of rules of civil and contract law, some provisions of which remain in force where not replaced by the Jordanian Civil Code.[8] The rules referred to in the opening paragraph of this

---

3   UN Doc.HRI/CORE/1/Add.18/Rev.1: Core document forming part of the reports of the States Parties: Jordan, 3 January 1994: page 2 para 5. Jordanian Law of Personal Status, law no 61/1976, *Official Gazette* no 2668, 1 December 1976; Jordanian Law of Family Rights, law no 92/1951, *Official Gazette* no 1081, 16 August 1951. The JLPS is currently also applied in the West Bank to Palestinian Muslims.

4   In accordance with the Regulation on the Office of the *Qadi al-Quda*, 1993, *Official Gazette* no 891, 17 April 1993.

5   For a useful summary of mid-nineteenth developments in the Ottoman Empire to which various elements of Jordanian law and legal system can be traced, see F Ziadeh, 'Permanence and Change in Arab Legal Systems', 9/1 *Arab Studies Quarterly* 1987, 20–34, pages 23–25. On the operation of the millet court system in Ottoman times, see KS Abu Jabr, 'The Millet System in the Nineteenth-Century Ottoman Empire', 57 *Muslim World* 1967, 212–223. Article 99 of the Jordanian Constitution 1952 provides for three types of courts: regular (*nizami*), religious courts and special courts. For more detail on the Jordanian legal system, see L Welchman, 'The Development of Islamic Family Law in the Legal System of Jordan', 37 *International and Comparative Law Quarterly* 1988, 868–886, pages 869–870; and for an early overview, ET Mogannam, 'Developments in the Legal System of Jordan' 6 *Middle East Journal* 1952, 194–206.

6   Law of *Shar'i* Procedure, Law no 31/1959, *Official Gazette* no 1449, 1 November 1959. An early case from the *Shari'a* Court of Appeal illustrates the difference between the two systems. The first instance *shari'a* court had ruled to end a marriage through judicial dissolution (*faskh*) after the husband had been convicted in the regular (statute) court system of illegal intercourse with his wife's daughter (thus raising a legal impediment to the continuation of his marriage to his wife). The *Shari'a* Appeal Court held that the evidence on which the regular court had ruled would not have served in a *shari'a* court to establish the husband's guilt and that therefore his conviction could not in and of itself serve as a basis for ruling for dissolution of his existing marriage contract. Ruling 7967/1953. AMA Dawud, *al-qararat al-isti'nafiyya fi usul al-mahakimat al-shar'iyya* (*Appeal Decisions in Shar'i Procedural Law*), Amman: Dar al-Thiqafa li'l-Nashr wa'l-Tawzi', 1998, Volume I, 152.

7   Article 183 JLPS. The other three Sunni schools of law, from all of which certain provisions are taken in the JLPS, are the Shafi'i, Hanbali and Maliki schools.

8   The Majalla was promulgated in parts over the years 1869–1877; provisions quoted in this article are taken from the English translation in CA Hooper, *The Civil Law of Palestine and Transjordan*, Jeruslaem 1933. The Majalla remained in force in Jordan until its partial

article reflect principles from the vast discipline of Islamic jurisprudence now marshalled into legislated codifications for application in a territorially-defined State. They display varying degrees of resonance with the Muslim family laws of other Arab States.

III REGISTRATION

As a civil contract, marriage in Islamic law is constituted by the oral offer and acceptance of marriage by the two parties or their duly appointed representatives. The offer and acceptance are the 'two pillars' of the contract, and for most of the traditional schools of Islamic law had to be witnessed by two male Muslims or, in the case of the Hanafi school, one male and two females. Written documentation might of course be made of the oral contract, and historical research shows varying patterns of registration of marriage contracts at the *shari'a* courts in the area in Ottoman times.[9] Nevertheless, the fact of registration does not affect the validity of the offer and acceptance, nor is a marriage concluded without any documentation rendered invalid.

In the course of this century, different Arab States have sought to centralise control of populations and to affect custom and practice through, *inter alia*, instituting mandatory procedures of registration. Jordan is no exception. The JLPS maintains the classical position that marriage is contracted by the offer and acceptance, stipulates the requirement of witnesses, and then moves on to set out registration requirements.[10] According to these requirements, the contract must be registered in an official document by the court-appointed marriage notary, the *ma'dhun*, or in exceptional circumstances by the judge. In the event of a marriage contract being concluded without such official document, the person carrying it out, the two spouses and the witnesses are all liable to a fine of a maximum of one hundred dinars[11] and a prison sentence of one to six months.[12] The law also provides for the same penalties to apply to a *ma'dhun* who fails to document the contract in the official form after receiving the requisite fees, in addition to dismissal from post. In the section of the law dealing with void and irregular

---

replacement by the provisions of the Civil Code (Law no 43 of 1976, *Official Gazette* no 2645, 1 August 1976. See Ziadeh, *supra* note 5, 24 on the Majalla: and see S Onar, 'The Majalla,' 292 308 in: M Khadduri, and HJ Liebesny (eds.), *Law in the Middle East*, Washington 1955. By contrast to the terms of the JLPS, Article 2.2 of the Civil Code provides that recourse shall be had in the first place to 'the rulings of Islamic *fiqh* (jurisprudence) most suited to the terms of this law.' For a short (and early) comparative consideration of the place of *shari'a* in the civil codes of Arab states, see H Liebesny, *The Law of the Near and Middle East*, Albany: State University of New York Press, 1975, pages 93–101.

9   JE Tucker, *In the House of the Law: Gender and Islamic Law in Ottoman Syria and Palestine*, Berkeley: University of California Press 1998, 71. Imber states that 'it was customary, at least in cities, to register marriages with the judge', notes attempts in the sixteenth century to make registration compulsory, and observes that 'the effect of registration is to remove the marriage contract from the purely private to the public sphere, but without in any way affecting the essence of the contract itself.' C Imber, *Ebu's-su'ud: The Islamic Legal Tradition*, Edinburgh: Edinburgh University Press, 1997, 165–166.

10   Respectively, Articles 14, 16 and 17 of the JLPS.

11   Roughly the same in pounds sterling.

12   Article 279(1) of the Jordanian Penal Code 1960: Law no 16/1960, *Official Gazette* 1487 11 May 1960 as amended by Laws 9/1988 and 15/1991.

marriages, however, no mention is made of marriages concluded in violation of this provision, leaving intact their validity.[13] A decision from the *Shari'a* Court of Appeal in Amman in 1994 affirmed clearly that:

> 'The [involvement of] the *shar'i ma'dhun* is not a condition for the validity of the marriage contract, nor is it a condition that [the contract be] put down in writing, nor is the place [of its conclusion a condition]. It is established by *shar'i* evidence including the testimony of witnesses and establishing it is not confined to written documents.'[14]

Explaining the registration provisions, contemporary commentator Muhammad Samara emphasises that they are 'not part of the essence of the contract' and do not affect the question of whether the contract is lawful, but they are 'regulatory measures that bring a benefit' – particularly in affording protection against a later denial of the marriage by one of the parties, for example, with potential effects on the affiliation of children from the marriage.[15]

Samara's concern here is the extent to which the state legislature is allowed to effect changes to the traditional rules governing marriage found in the authoritative jurists' works. Since there was never a question of registration being instrumental in the conclusion of a marriage, a modern legislature such as Jordan would be vulnerable to criticism from at least some of the *shari'a*-trained scholars if they were to suggest that a marriage concluded entirely correctly from the point of view of the traditional rules was not to be recognised as valid under statute law. This applies equally to *talaq*, the form of divorce that takes effect through the unilateral 'repudiation' of the wife by the husband and which, under traditional Hanafi (and other Sunni) rules, can take place extra-judicially and without witnesses: in Jordan, extra-judicial *talaq* has been subjected to various constraints including registration procedures backed up by penal sanctions for failure to comply, but out-of-court, unregistered *talaq* remains valid.[16]

IV AGE OF MARRIAGE

Registration requirements are closely connected to the efforts to set and control a minimum age of capacity for marriage. The Ottomans issued registration requirements to accompany the 1917 Law of Family Rights which set specific ages of capacity for marriage for the first time in the area. The majority position of all classical schools of law held that minors could be contracted in marriage by their guardians, although consummation was not permitted until the minor was physically ready to enter a sexual relationship.[17] The differences between the schools of law centre on the role of the *wali* (marriage guardian), which depends

---

13 Articles 33 and 34 JLPS.

14 37682/1994, Dawud, *supra* note 7, 155.

15 M Samara, *sharh muqarin li-qanun al-ahwal ash-shakhsiyya* (Comparative Commentary on the Law of Personal Status) Jerusalem 1987, 146–147.

16 Article 101 JLPS sets out the registration requirements for *talaq*.

17 H Motzki, 'Child Marriage in Seventeenth Century Palestine', 129–140 in: K Masud, B Messick, and D Powers, (eds), *Islamic Legal Interpretation: Muftis and their Fatwas*, Cambridge, Mass.: Harvard University Press, 1996, 130.

upon the degree of relationship to the ward, the sex of the ward and the status of the female ward – that is, whether she has never been married and therefore has the status of *bikr* (virgin), or has been married and either divorced or widowed, in which case she is described as a *thayyib*. Furthermore, the schools distinguished a 'minor' from a 'major' through physical phenomena, rather than by a set age, with the onset of puberty signalling the end of legal minority.[18] Certain ages were, however, for the purposes of the law, identified as the minimum and maximum ages at which puberty was presumed to have been reached. The majority held the minimum age to be 12 for a boy and nine for a girl, with the maximum at 15 years for both; an influential opinion from the eighth century scholar after whom the Hanafi school is named held the maximum to be 17 for females and 18 for males.[19]

Because minority disqualifies a person from making a legally binding contract of marriage, the discussions focused on who was empowered to make the contract on their behalf. The rules on marriage guardianship in the traditional rules of Sunni jurisprudence are very complex and differentiate, *inter alia*, between guardianship with and without compulsion (*ijbar*). Although guardianship in marriage over minors affects both sexes, the jurists did focus more on the rules regarding women. Dawoud al-Alami explains this as follows:

'The basic reason for the guardian's acting on behalf of the woman is to protect her interests and her honour and that of her family, in that it is improper for a woman to mix in male society outside her immediate family; because the father's love and care for his daughter are usually taken for granted, he is the first to qualify as guardian provided that he meets the other requisites of guardianship.'[20]

The same perspective can be seen to underlie the perception of the majority of the jurists of guardianship over women in marriage as a 'duty rather than a right of the guardian, or at least a synthesis of both'.[21] This assumption may be glimpsed also behind the general Hanafi rule that the lawful marriage guardian – whatever his degree of relationship to the ward – was empowered to marry off a minor ward (guardianship with compulsion) but if he was other than the father or grandfather, the ward could refuse the marriage on reaching puberty and obtain a judicial decision terminating the contract (the so-called 'option of puberty'). Marriages contracted by the father or grandfather were not subject to dissolution in this way: by contrast, they were 'binding' (because, according to Samara, of the greater degree of affection to be relied on as informing the choices made on their wards' behalf by the two closer relatives).[22] The other Sunni schools, on the other hand,

---

18 Article 985 of the Majalla provides that: 'puberty is proved by the emission of seed during dreams, by the power to make pregnant, by menstruation, and by the capacity to conceive.'

19 M Sirtawi, *sharh qanun al-ahwal ash-shakhsiyya al-urduni* (Commentary on the Jordanian Law of Personal Status), Amman 1981, 65. For legal purposes the Hanafis also distinguished between 'discriminating' and 'non-discriminating' minors, the latter being under the age of seven and the former aged from seven to puberty.

20 D El-'Alami, 'Legal Capacity with Specific Reference to the Marriage Contract', 6/2 *Arab Law Quarterly*, 1991, 190–204, 193.

21 El-'Alami, *supra* note 20, 194.

22 Samara, *supra* note, 97. As Mona Siddiqui puts it, 'the law raises a presumption in their favour that they must have acted in the best interests of the minor.' M Siddiqui, 'The Concept of Wilaya

limit the authority of guardianship of compulsion to the father and in some cases the grandfather or the father's legally appointed agent (*wasi*), and do not recognise the 'option of puberty.' For the Hanafis, once the ward reaches puberty, he or she can legally contract their own marriage; the Hanafis were alone in the Sunni schools in allowing a woman to contract herself in marriage,[23] while allowing for the guardian to seek dissolution of such a marriage if she has married someone not her 'equal' according to certain specific criteria,[24] or for a dower less than that due someone of her status. This aspect of guardianship, which is concerned with the requirement of the guardian's consent to the marriage of an adult female woman, rather than her consent to her own marriage, is another very complex issue.[25] Suffice it to say that technically, since the marriage of minors is no longer lawful under Jordanian law, the institution of 'guardianship with compulsion' is no longer recognised; meanwhile, the law does not permit the judge to marry a woman aged under 18 if her father or grandfather, as her guardian, does not consent.[26] Further, the law implicitly requires the marriage guardian's consent to the marriage of a *bikr* – that is, any woman who has not previously been married, of any age.[27] The law is explicit only on the fact that an adult (18 or over) sane woman who has been previously married does not need her guardian's consent to her marriage.[28] This reflection in the law of society's expectation that the woman's marriage guardian shares in her choice of spouse is explained by legal commentators as a matter of family care and protection of the woman's interests in her marriage, as set out by el-'Alami above.[29]

---

in Hanafi Law: Authority versus Consent in al-Fatawa al-'Alamgiri,' 5 *Yearbook of Islamic and Middle Eastern Law* 1998–1999, 171–185, 176.

23 Although there were significant differences within the Hanafi school on this position.

24 See FJ Ziadeh, 'Equality in the Muslim Law of Marriage' 6 *American Journal of Comparative Law* 1957, 503–517; and M Siddiqui, 'Law and the Desire for Social Control: An Insight into the Hanafi Concept of Kafa'a with Reference to the Fatawa 'Alamgiri (1664–1672),' 49–68 in: M Yamani, (ed), *Feminism and Islam*, London: Ithaca Press, 1996.

25 It is a matter of some obscurity in Jordanian law: see L Welchman, *Beyond the Code: Muslim Family Law and the Shar'i Judiciary in the Palestinian West Bank*, Kluwer Law International 2000, 121–133. A thorough exposition of the rules of the different Sunni schools of marriage guardianship is to be found in el-'Alami, *supra* note 21. Another very useful source is the English translation of the relevant sections of a twelfth century text, the *Bidayat al-Mujtahid* by Ibn Rushd, known in English as Averroes: *The Distinguished Jurist's Primer*, translated by IAK Nyazee, and M Abdul Rauf, Garnet Publishing, Volume II, 1996, pages 1–16. The Hanafi rules are lucidly discussed in Siddiqui, 1998–1999, *supra* note 23.

26 Article 6 of the JLPS; if the guardian is other than these two relatives, the judge is empowered to marry the girl at her petition if the refusal by her (more distantly related) marriage guardian is 'without good reason'.

27 This seems to reflect the view of the majority of jurists and – it is argued – the expectations of society in general, rather than implementation of the Hanafi rules.

28 Article 13 JLPS.

29 Jordanian lawyer Ragheb al-Qasim, for example, explains that 'the guardian shares in the choice of spouse – this does not mean that he can marry [the woman] to the man of his choice, but that he gives consultation in her choice of partner so that she feels safe' and so that her family remains her security in the event that something goes wrong with the marriage; R al-Qasim, *qanun al-ahwal ash-shakhsiyya al-urduni bayn al-nazhariyya wa 'l-tatbiq* ('The Jordanian Law of Personal Status: Theory and Practice'), paper for Conference on Personal Status Laws in the Arab World: Theory, Practice, and Chances for Reform, convened by the Konrad Adenauer Stiftung and the Jordanian National Commission for Women, June 2000. A major social science survey in the early 1990s in neighbouring Palestinian society in the West Bank, Gaza Strip and East Jerusalem found that 80% of men and 76% of women surveyed felt that the choice of a girl's husband should be 'mainly the daughter's choice'. R Hammami, 'Women in Palestinian Society', 283–311

It seems likely that the marrying of minor wards was an established practice in the region, as elsewhere, before the twentieth century, although it is not possible to tell how broadly. Motzki, in his consideration of child marriage in neighbouring seventeenth century Palestine based on the work of the Ramla *mufti* Khayr ad-Din, concludes that marriages involving one or two minor parties were probably not uncommon, but similarly discerns, albeit tentatively, a comparatively high rate of breakdown of such marriages, and notes that the option of puberty was 'commonly invoked'.[30] It was upon the individual views of a few jurists, and citing various socio-economic factors, that the Ottomans relied in setting minimum ages of capacity for marriage, at 12 for the boy and nine for the girl, already recognised as the minimum age of puberty.[31] As well as the minimum age, an age of full competence for marriage was introduced: 18 years completed by the male and 17 by the female.[32] The setting of these ages drew upon the maximum ages of puberty according to Abu Hanifa and at these ages the parties attained full legal majority (*rushd*) (ie beyond puberty, *bulugh*) and were fully competent to marry. For an adolescent between the minimum ages of 12 or nine and legal majority (18 and 17) marriage could be authorised by the *qadi* provided the party concerned had reached puberty and the *qadi* held them to be able to sustain such an undertaking; the female also had to have her guardian's consent.[33] This 'discretion-of-the-*qadi*' age zone between the minimum age of marriage and full legal majority was taken over into the personal status codes of several Arab States that emerged later in the century, including Jordan. In the event of breach of the rules, the Ottoman law declared as irregular (*fasid*) a marriage where one of the parties did not fulfil the conditions of competence at the time of the contract; and stated that it was 'absolutely forbidden' for parties to remain in an irregular (or void) marriage. Later provisions modelled on the OLFR modified this position.

During the same period, in Egypt, a different approach was being taken towards preventing the marriage of minors. One of the first demands of the Egyptian Feminists' Union in 1923 was the establishment in law of a minimum age for marriage, at 16 for females and 18 for males; this was achieved the same year with a decree forbidding the registration of marriage where the parties were below these ages. By all accounts, this legislation was not particularly effective – in Margot Badran's words, it 'demonstrated the limits of legal reform',[34] even when followed by subsequent legislation denying judicial remedy in the case of unregistered marriages. A major weakness appears to have been the lack of reliable means of establishing ages.[35] Some decades after the Egyptian legislation, the Jordanians followed the Ottoman precedent of setting a substantive minimum

---

in M Heiberg, and G Ovensen, (eds), *Palestinian Society in Gaza, West Bank and Arab Jerusalem: A Survey of Living Conditions*, FAFO 1993, 293, table 10.6.

30   Motzki, *supra* note 18, 139; and see J Tucker, *supra* note 10, 46–47.

31   Samara, *supra* note 16, 105; Sirtawi, *supra* note 20, 64.

32   Article 4 Ottoman Law of Family Rights 1917.

33   Articles 5 (male) and 6 (female) OLFR.

34   M Badran, *Feminists, Islam and Nation: Gender and the Making of Modern Egypt*, Princeton: Princeton University Press, 1995, 128.

35   Badran, *supra* note 35, 128, notes that Egyptian feminists complained that some doctors falsified ages. See also Shaham, *Family and the Courts in Modern Egypt: A Study Based on Decisions by the Shari'a Courts 1900–1955*, Leiden: Brill, 1997, 58.

age, but used the procedural approach to add some flexibility into the provision. In the JLFR, full capacity for marriage was set at 18 for the male and 17 for the female, with the judge empowered to permit a marriage below this age provided the party (male or female) had reached the age of 15 and was 'capable of taking on marriage'; the female needed her guardian's consent. The Penal Code provided for a prison sentence of one to six months in prison for anyone who 'marries or carries out the ceremonies of marriage for a girl who has not completed her fifteenth year, or helps in carrying out these ceremonies in any capacity whatsoever' and a similar penalty for those involved in the marriage of a female under 18 without previously ascertaining that her marriage guardian had agreed to her marriage.[36]

With the introduction of the JLPS in 1976, the rules on the minimum age of spouses were changed in two ways. Firstly, the minimum age of marriage for males was raised to 16, while that for females remains 15.[37] Secondly, the JLPS effectively abolished the 'discretion-of-the-*qadi*' age zone, leaving assessment of the wisdom of a girl's marriage before the age of full legal majority (defined for this purpose as 18 by the lunar calendar)[38] to her guardian, and bringing in the *qadi* to give special consent only if the *wali* is refusing without good reason – and, as noted above, is a relative other than her father or grandfather. No special scrutiny is required by law of the marriage of a boy over 16 under the age of full legal majority (*rushd*).

Significantly, these ages are to be calculated according to the lunar calendar.[39] In effect, this makes the minimum age of marriage around 14 years and seven months for the female and 15 years and six months for the male by the solar calendar.[40] In the 1980s, amendments to the JLPS being drawn up for discussion proposed to replace the lunar with the solar calculation, with the intention of 'unifying these matters in Jordanian legislation'.[41] The Jordanian Civil Code, drawn up in the same year as the JLPS, sets the age of legal majority at 18 years by the solar calendar for both males and females.[42]

One further rule concerning the age of the parties to a contract of marriage was a Jordanian innovation in the JLFR, providing that:

> 'neither the *qadi* nor his deputy shall allow a marriage where there is a twenty year difference in age [between the spouses] before ascertaining the consent of the youngest party and the fact that they consent to [the marriage] without force or coercion, and that their interest is served thereby.'[43]

---

36 Article 279(2) and (3) of the Penal Code.

37 Article 5 JLPS.

38 Article 6(b) JLPS. On the varying references to the ages seventeen/eighteen in regard to the majority of females in the JLPS, see Welchman, *supra* note 26, 112.

39 Article 185 JLPS.

40 As specified by the Palestinian *Qadi al-Quda* when introducing these as the minimum ages of capacity for marriage in the Gaza Strip in 1995, to bring Gazan court practice into conformity with that in the West Bank courts applying the JLPS. Decision no 78/1995 of 25 December 1995.

41 Draft JLPS of 1987, Article 186. See Welchman, *supra* note 6, 885. The JLFR had also stipulated the lunar calendar: Article 127.

42 Civil Code 1976, Article 43(2).

43 Article 6 JLFR 1951.

This Article, an innovation in the JLFR, appears to address the social phenomenon of older men taking sometimes very young women in marriage, possibly in a polygamous union. Issues of consent may be complicated in many cases, but particularly so by such circumstances, and the introduction of this provision provided for the bride's consent to be given particular scrutiny, and gave room for the discretion of the *qadi* to be withheld. However, by 1957, cases in the Amman *Shari'a* Appeal Court had established that it was to be constrained by the ages of capacity, and that the *qadi*'s permission for the age difference was needed only where one of the spouses (clearly most usually the woman) was under the age of full competence (*rushd*) and so in any case needed the *qadi*'s permission to marry.[44] Variations on the theme of the Jordanian position were included in some subsequent Arab codifications of family law.[45] In the meantime, in the 1976 JLPS, the equivalent provision confirmed the Appeal Court's interpretation of the original article in the JLFR:

'The contract [of marriage] may not be concluded for a woman who has not completed her 18th year if her fiancé is more than twenty years her senior, unless the *qadi* has ascertained her consent and choice and made sure that this marriage is in her interest.' (Article 7)

The Explanatory Memorandum to the JLPS states explicitly that it was never intended that all marriages involving a 20-year age difference should be prevented, as might have been deduced from the terms of the JLFR, but that protection in this matter should be given to the woman under the age of legal majority (*rushd*). Under the JLPS, once the woman has completed her eighteenth (lunar) year, the *qadi* has no role to play in ascertaining whether in fact such a marriage is in her interest and is being concluded by her own free will. This position did not meet with unqualified approval, with some women's groups preferring the extension of what they considered the more protective pre-existing provision to all marriages involving an age difference of 20 years or more. A more recent (1996) comment on the more general issue of consent and the conclusion of marriage under the JLPS illustrates the kind of concern that may have provoked the original provision, noting that:

'there might be duress (*ikrah*) or pressure on the girl, especially if she is young and not fully empowered with giving her opinion; she could be forced to marry a man because there is a family interest in him, or he is an older, wealthy man, and in such circumstances what they think may be different from what she wants.'[46]

Right at the beginning of the operation of the JLPS, the Amman *Shari'a* Court of Appeal heard a case that illustrates a number of these issues while focusing, in the face of the lack of any registration of the marriage, on whether or not there

---

44 9661 and 9647/1957, MH Al-'Arabi, *al-mabadi' al-qada'iyya li-mahkamat al-isti'naf ash-shar'iyya* (Legal Principles of the *Shari'a* Court of Appeal), Volume I, Amman 1973, 77.

45 For example, the Syrian Law of Personal Status 1953, and the Law of the Family of the People's Democratic Republic of the Yemen 1974.

46 A Al-Ma'ayata (ed.), 'Overview of Laws affecting Women', 58–78 in *dalil al-mar'a al-urduniyya* (*Jordanian Women's Guide*) Amman: Konrad Adenauer Stiftung and al-Kutba Institute for Human Development Forum, 1996, 59.

was in fact a marriage to dissolve. The appeal was lodged by a man appealing the decision of the first instance court to dissolve his contract of marriage by reason of its irregularity. The mother of the wife who had sought the dissolution was charged by the court as acting for the petitioner in the case, as the wife herself was established to be a legal minor and under the age of puberty. The mother stated in court that her brother had carried out the contract of marriage of her daughter to the appellant 'in the Bedouin manner outside the court without her consent or even her knowledge, although the girl is a minor in her twelfth year, has not reached puberty, and there has been no consummation'. The first instance court (as it appears from the summarised appeal ruling) dissolved the contract on the basis of the difference in ages between the spouses, the husband being more than 20 years the girl's senior, since clearly no consent had been sought from or given by the *qadi*, rendering the contract irregular in its conclusion. The Appeal Court held the ruling for judicial dissolution to have been premature on procedural grounds, since there was no clarification as to the circumstances or formulation of the alleged 'contract of marriage' – indeed, nothing establishing that a contract of marriage had been in fact concluded.[47] Once the mother had established that there was a contract between the spouses and had claimed that it was irregular, the court should inquire of the respondent: if he acknowledged its irregularity, then the contract would be dissolved by the court. If he denied its irregularity, the mother would be charged with establishing that it was irregular. The file was returned to the first instance court with a note to the effect that it should not have considered from the beginning the question of the difference in age between the spouses 'since this comes after establishing whether the wife is of the age of capacity'.[48]

---

47   The court may have been taking into account here certain customary law practices amongst the Bedouin. Stewart refers to a relatively well-known customary betrothal ceremony among the tribes of southern Jordan involving the guardian of the female and the husband to be, or his representative, which 'has important legal consequences entirely distinct from those of marriage.' According to Stewart, the wedding may take place several years later, and the betrothal ritual is not legally recognised as 'marriage'. F Stewart, 'Tribal Law in the Arab World: A Review of the Literature,' 19 *International Journal of Middle Eastern Studies* 1987, 473–490, at 476. Tribal law courts were abolished in Jordan in 1976. In Islamic law, the 'engagement' (*khutba*) of the parties similarly gives rise to none of the rights and obligations arising from marriage. Often, however, the act of concluding the contract (*katab al-kitab*) may be socially a sort of formal 'engagement period' before the wedding celebration in which the bride is taken to her husband's house. However, in law, the rights and obligations arising from the contract are established (at least in so far as they are not dependent upon consummation), and a formal divorce will be needed if the couple decide to separate before the wedding. It appears that the Appeal Court was seeking to establish whether, in the case under consideration, the ceremony that the mother was objecting to did in fact constitute a *shar'i* contract or rather a customary agreement. A similar approach was taken by the Appeal Court in a 1987 case: 27352/1987, AMA Dawud, *al-qararat al-isti'nafiyya fi'l-ahwal ash-shakhsiyya* (Appeal Decisions in Personal Status), Amman: Dar al-Thiqafa li'l-Nashr wa't-Tawzi', 1999, 389. In this case, a man appealed the ruling for dissolution on the grounds of duress made by the first instance court, claiming that his wife actually wanted their marriage to continue but had been forced by her family to raise the action for dissolution. For her part, the woman denied this, and affirmed that she had been forced to marry the man and did not want the marriage to continue. The marriage had taken place out of court 'in the Islamic tribal manner' according to the woman, and had not been documented. The Appeal Court found the ruling of the first instance court to have been premature as there was no detail as to how the contract was actually carried out nor yet had the first instance court carried out a process of identification of the parties; the case was returned to the lower court for appropriate follow-up.

48   19541/1977; Dawud, *supra* note 48, 413–414.

An interesting gloss on the reference here to the 'Bedouin manner of marriage' mentioned in the above case comes in the regulation on court fees for the *shari'a* courts, which specifically empowers the *Qadi al-Quda* to waive the fees levied on registration of marriage contracts for 'individuals of the nomadic tribes'.[49] This may have been out of recognition of particular circumstances or in order to encourage a greater extent of marriage registration among the Bedouin, or a combination of both. In any case, the mother's action in challenging her brother's action is relatively unusual in the published case material, and was timely enough to secure her daughter's exit from the marriage provided that the existence of a 'contract' was established. The following section examines why the question of timing is so important.

V   EFFECTS AND IMPLICATIONS

Jordanian law classifies as irregular a contract of marriage concluded when one or both parties are not competent according to the conditions of capacity at the time of the contract.[50] The law distinguishes along broad Hanafi lines between void and irregular contracts. Void contracts give rise to no effects whatsoever. Irregular contracts give rise to no effects if they are not consummated, but once consummated give rise, *inter alia*, to the wife's right to dower from her husband, and to affiliation (the establishment of the husband as the father of any children from the marriage). Other rights such as maintenance and mutual inheritance rights are not established even in a consummated irregular marriage.[51]

This is equally the case for marriages that are irregular for other reasons: for example, if there were no witnesses or if the parties are found to be related in such a degree that they are not allowed to marry.[52] Duress (*ikrah*) also renders a marriage contract irregular. The law provides that spouses are prohibited from remaining in an irregular or a void marriage, and if they do not themselves separate, 'the judge shall separate them in the name of the public *shar'i* right'.[53] In the case of underage marriage, however, there is a rider:

'claims for irregularity of marriage for reason of young age shall not be heard if the wife has given birth or is pregnant, or if both parties fulfil the conditions of capacity at the time the claim is raised.'[54]

---

49   Regulation on Fees in *Shari'a* Courts, no 55/1983, article 20.

50   Article 34(1).

51   Article 42.

52   By relationship established by blood, marriage or breastfeeding. Article 34 JLPS.

53   That is, if neither spouse initiates a claim at court, the court itself must bring the action in order to 'protect the public welfare in general.' See B Messick, 'Prosecution in the Yemen: The Introduction of the Niyaba', 15 *International Journal of Middle East Studies* 1983, 507–518, 509, on the connection of this function to those of *hisba*, the general religious duty of Muslims to 'promote good and forbid evil'. Samara, *supra* note 16, 145–146, similarly describes this 'public' function of the court as *hisba*. The court's action to dissolve a marriage must be initiated by an official of the *shari'a* court appointed to the task by the *qadi*, who may not himself act in this capacity: 9076/1956 Dawud, *supra* note 48, 409.

54   Article 43.

These two conditions complicate the prospects for a woman illegally married under the legal age of capacity to terminate the marriage if that is – or becomes – her preferred choice. In effect, an action raised by the court or by a recognised party on behalf of the bride (usually the under-age party) has to be instituted before the girl has completed her fifteenth (lunar) year if the marriage is to be declared irregular and dissolved by the court. Collected principles from the Amman *Shari'a* Court of Appeal throw some light on the way courts have handled such claims. In 1980, for example, the Court heard a claim raised by a woman for the dissolution of her marriage on the grounds that she had been 'in her fifteenth year' at the time of the contract, rather than having completed it. The decision noted that previous to this she had also submitted in person a claim for maintenance against her husband; the court examined the papers and found her now to have completed her fifteenth year, and dismissed her petition. The case raises a number of points.

First, there is the issue of previous claims apparently recognising the validity of the marriage, and the capacity of the petitioner to litigate. The Jordanian courts here base their position on the Majalla and on traditional Hanafi rules to the effect that persons of the ages of 9–15 for a female and 12–15 for a male are in the age of adolescence (*murahiqa*) approaching puberty.[55] Before actual puberty is reached, a young person may not be a litigant in their own right at court; if they are an adolescent, they must be asked whether or not they have reached puberty.[56] A number of published case summaries show the Amman Appeal Court returning cases to the first instance courts because of mistakes in their investigation of whether or not the litigant had reached puberty; this may take the form of judging premature a decision made for dissolution on the grounds of the bride having been under-age because of queries as to whether or not the female litigant was competent to represent herself in litigation.[57]

Another potentially complicating factor is shown by a 1997 case, in which the Appeal Court returned a case to the first instance court after finding that the latter had summoned the wife's father to the hearing on the basis that she was under the age of capacity, 'but she is in the age of adolescence and therefore the court should have asked her whether she had reached puberty, and if she had, then her (status in the) litigation is correct, and if not, then she is to be represented by her father'.[58] The guardian, in most cases the father, who may be called in such cases,

---

55 Article 986 of the Majalla states that: 'The commencement of the age of puberty in the case of males is twelve years completed and in the case of females nine years completed. The termination of the age of puberty in both cases is fifteen years completed. If a male on reaching twelve years and a female on reaching nine years completed have not arrived at the age of puberty, they are said to be approaching puberty until such time as they do in fact arrive at the age of puberty.'

56 16306/1970, Dawud, *supra* note 48, 411–412.

57 Article 989 of the Majalla provides that: 'If a male or female approaching the age of puberty admit in Court that they have arrived at the age of puberty, and the condition of their bodies shows that their admission is false, such admission shall not be confirmed. If, however, the condition of their bodies shows that their admission is true, their admission shall be confirmed, and their contracts and admissions are executory and valid [...].' Appeal Court rulings 40276/1996, 40292/1996, 43866/1997, 29397/1988, and others: Dawud, *supra* note 48, 416–418.

58 Ruling 43866/1997 of 2 December 1997. The claim, for dissolution of a contract of marriage on the basis that the wife was underage, was brought by *shar'i* court officials in the name of the public *shar'i* interest. Dawud, *supra* note 48, 419. Similarly in an earlier claim where the Appeal Court questioned the validity of the female litigant's appointment (*tawkil*) of the person acting for

is also the person most likely to have represented the girl in the underage marriage.

Another factor to be taken into consideration is previous litigation between the spouses. This might establish the status of the complainant as a litigant, but might at the same time undermine a claim for dissolution for the irregularity of the contract, since previous litigation would be based upon the existence of a valid marriage giving rise to the established rights being claimed. In an early claim under the similar terms of the JLFR, the Appeal Court held that the fact that the wife, now seeking dissolution of her marriage by reason of her having been underage at its conclusion, had previously applied for a judicial divorce on the basis of 'discord and strife' between her and her husband: her acknowledgement in that claim that she was in a valid marriage to the man was held to prevent her from subsequently claiming the contract was irregular.[59] The same applies to a husband who may seek a dissolution on the grounds that his wife had been underage at the time of their marriage, although he retains the choice of divorcing her unilaterally. The latter course of action would render him liable to paying half of her dower if consummation had not occurred, while a judicial dissolution for irregularity would give rise to no financial rights in such circumstances. Early claims heard by the Appeal Court established that a man who has previously registered a divorce against his wife cannot subsequently sue for dissolution for irregularity of the contract.[60]

In 1980, the Appeal Court heard an appeal by a woman against the decision of the first instance court to reject her claim for maintenance against her husband. The woman had originally won a maintenance award from the first instance court which had been overturned on appeal because the documentation showed that she was 'in her fifteenth year' and the Appeal Court held that it should first be established whether her contract of marriage was valid or irregular (as a result of her age) before making a ruling for maintenance, since no maintenance is due in an irregular contract. The woman started her claim all over again at the first instance court and in the meantime obtained, through proper procedure from court officials in the regular court system, a correction to the year of her birth shown in the officially accredited documentation, establishing that she had been born a year earlier than originally shown. The first instance court rejected her claim for maintenance and she appealed. The Appeal Court noted that even with the correction to the year of her birth, she had still not completed her fifteenth year at the time of the original claim and was not at the age of capacity at the time of the marriage, rendering the contract irregular. However, by the time she raised the new claim for maintenance to the first instance court, she had completed her fifteenth year and had become of the age of capacity for marriage 'and in such cases claims for dissolution because of irregularity are not heard' in accordance with Article 43 of the JLPS, and 'this means that the contract between the

---

her in the claim, since she was under the age of 15 and the court had not questioned her as to whether or not she had reached puberty and was therefore competent to make such an appointment: 'if not, then her *wali* (guardian) shall act for her in the claim.' 11471/1961, Dawud, *supra* note 48, 411.

59   9810/1958 Dawud, *supra* note 48, 410.

60   9778/1958 Dawud, *supra* note 48, 409.

claimants has become valid.'[61] It is impossible to tell the circumstances of the claim from the summaries of the rulings of the Appeal Court but, in a case such as this, it might be that the spouses had not yet started to live together, and that the maintenance claim was a 'litigating strategy' by the wife (and her family) to encourage the man to prepare a suitable marital dwelling and move her to live with him. In these circumstances, if the contract was found to have been irregular and the wife was still underage at the time of litigation, the dissolution of the contract for its irregularity would have meant that the wife was not entitled to any rights against the husband.[62] As it was, the timing of the wife's subsequent claim in this case was such that the contract had become valid by the time she raised it, she was fully entitled to maintenance, and no case for dissolution for irregularity on the established fact that she had been under age at the time of its conclusion could henceforth be heard by the court.

While this provision may provide protection for women in the type of circumstances described, in cases where women wish to leave a marriage concluded when they were under age, the question of timing can prevent them seeking a divorce; and there is always a question as to what extent young girls married by their guardians when they are under age would be aware of the significance of this question.[63] These rules in current Jordanian law bear some resemblance to those governing the 'option of puberty' in traditional Hanafi law which, as noted above, governed the application for divorce by a person married as a minor by their marriage guardian. In that institution too, timing is critical: if the girl knows of the marriage then once she reaches puberty (by having her first period) she must do nothing to indicate acceptance of the contract and must have more or less immediate recourse to the court to exercise her 'option of puberty'. As Samara puts it, 'if she stays silent, this is consent, whether or not she knows that she has the right of choice'.[64] This goes also to the question of consent, considered further below.

Some effect of the traditional institution of the 'option of puberty' may also lie behind the other circumstance that may render valid a marriage concluded in violation of the rules on capacity – that is, pregnancy. The terms of the JLPS made a small but significant alteration to the previous JLFR on this point, prohibiting the hearing of claims for irregularity of marriage by reason of one or both parties being underage in cases where the woman is 'pregnant' as opposed to 'where pregnancy is apparent'. The significance of this is illustrated in a 1996 case when the *Shari'a* Appeal Court overturned a ruling by the first instance court dissolving the marriage of the woman appellant on the grounds of irregularity by reason of her being under age. The couple had been living in Iraq, and during the course of the court's investigation of her claim for dissolution, the woman produced a

---

61   21185/1980, Dawud, *supra* note 48, 414–415.

62   It is also interesting in this case that the summary includes the Appeal Court charging the husband, as the respondent, with paying all the related court fees and legal expenses including the lawyer's fees.

63   Government sources estimated female illiteracy among women aged fifteen and over at 20.6% in 1994 (compared to 48% in 1959). CEDAW/C/2000/1/CRP.3 2.

64   Samara, *supra* note 16, 98. If she does not know of the marriage, she must exercise the option immediately upon learning of it. See Siddiqui, *supra* note 23, 179–181.

document from the Ministry of Health in Iraq[65] establishing that she had miscarried there when she was around two months pregnant. The first instance court had ruled for dissolution because the foetus was not sufficiently formed as to permit distinction of its physiognomy; this was by analogy with the rules on the ending of '*idda* period after a divorce or the death of the husband, during which an ex-wife is not permitted to re-marry. If the woman is pregnant, the '*idda* period is terminated by childbirth; if she miscarries, it is ended if the foetus is partially or wholly distinguishable, but if not the woman has to continue for an '*idda* of three months.[66] The Appeal Court, however, held that the current law prevents the court from hearing such cases if the wife is to any degree pregnant, without regard to the period of pregnancy: 'because by her pregnancy, the woman is [shown to be] of capacity for marriage'.[67]

In a previous reported case under the JLFR, the Appeal Court had confirmed a similar though less detailed position, but this time in confirming a ruling on a case for dissolution brought by the *shari'a* court officials in the name of the public *shar'i* right (with the implication that neither of the spouses was seeking the dissolution of the marriage): that if the wife acknowledges that she has had a miscarriage and her husband acknowledges this, a claim in the name of the public *shar'i* right will be dismissed 'since the acknowledgement of a miscarriage establishes a prior pregnancy' and therefore prevents the court from hearing a claim for dissolution of the marriage.[68] In a more recent case, the Appeal Court reviewed a ruling made against the two spouses for the dissolution of their marriage (showing again that the case had been brought by an official of the court rather than by one of the spouses) and noted that the woman had been found to have reached puberty and that therefore the court should have investigated the claim made by her representative that she was showing the first signs of pregnancy.[69]

In the cases cited above, the wife was either seeking or at least not objecting to the continuation of her marriage and the establishment of her rights arising from therefrom. The connection between these rules and the more traditional 'option of puberty' lies in the fact that under the classical Hanafi rules, one of the ways a female married as a minor was taken to indicate her assent to her marriage was to consummate the marriage after reaching puberty: or, if it had been consummated before, to continue in the sexual relationship. In current Jordanian law, as noted above, claims for dissolution on grounds of one or both parties being underage shall not be heard if the wife has given birth or is pregnant. Pregnancy is proof of consummation and of puberty at the same time, thus under the classical rules closing the 'option of puberty' and, in current Jordanian law, preventing a wife from claiming dissolution for irregularity of the contract. While social reasons connected with the children from the marriage may be advanced in explanation also for this rule, it might also be remembered that in the event of consummation

---

65 Properly verified in accordance with the rules of procedure for acceptance by the Jordanian courts.

66 Article 140 JLPS. Commenting on this, Samara, *supra* note 16, 349, explains that the '*idda* is ended if the head or a hand or eye (for example) can be distinguished.

67 40092/1996, Dawud, *supra* note 48, 417.

68 17994/1974 Dawud, *supra* note 48, 412.

69 40276/1996 Dawud, *supra* note 48, 417.

of an irregular contract, paternity is established to the father and the children are therefore 'legitimate'. Another point to bear in mind is that such proof of consummation assumes consent to consummation, as in the traditional Hanafi rules.[70]

VI CONSENT AND DURESS

Contracts of marriage concluded under duress (*ikrah*) are irregular in Jordanian law, in a departure from the classical Hanafi rules which held certain types of disposals such as marriage and divorce as valid even in the circumstance of duress.[71] At the same time, such a contract can subsequently become valid through consent of the party who was under duress to its continuation. Duress is defined in the Jordanian Civil Code as 'unlawfully forcing (*ijbar*) someone to do something without their consent; it may be physical or mental'.[72] Hanafi law differentiates two forms of duress, variously translated as 'major/minor' and 'constraining/non-constraining'[73] with the first vitiating consent and invalidating choice, and the second vitiating consent but not invalidating choice, which may involve 'choosing between suffering what is threatened and making a contract which [the person] does not want'.[74] Most Hanafi jurists held that only 'major' duress had the impact of exempting the subject from tortious liability. Duress is described as a believable threat of grave and imminent danger to one's body or property and may also include threats to cause injury to one's parents, children, spouse or other close blood relative; a threat of imprisonment is recognised as a form of minor duress.[75] Dawud points out that since the JLPS does not specify which type of duress must be involved to render a contract of marriage irregular, this is confirmation that both types have the effect of making the contract invalid.[76]

In a few Appeal Court cases of which Dawud publishes extracts, however, the Court has instructed the lower courts to investigate which type of coercion is being claimed, including one where a man appealed the dismissal of his claim for dissolution of the marriage contract by reason of duress which he claimed had been exercised against him by the local Administrative Governor.[77] The circumstances of the case are not set out, but it is worth noting briefly the

---

70 See for example Siddiqui, *supra* note 23, 182. Beyond this assumption in family law, Jordanian criminal law does not recognise a crime of rape within marriage; Article 292 of the Penal Code provides that 'whosoever has sex with a woman (not his wife) without her consent, whether by duress (*ikrah*) or threat or deceit or duplicity shall be punished by hard labour for not less than ten years.'

71 Article 34(3) JLPS. See Dawud, *supra* note 48, 385–386.

72 Article 135 of the Civil Code.

73 In translating the Majalla, Hooper uses 'major'; AW El-Hassan, uses 'constraining' in 'The Doctrine of Duress (*Ikrah*) in Shari'a, Sudan and English Law', 1/2 *Arab Law Quarterly* 1986, 231–236.

74 El-Hassan, *supra* note 74, 231. Majalla, Articles 1003–1007. The same formula comes in the Jordanian Civil Code Article 138.

75 Jordanian Civil Code Article 137; Majalla Article 1007 with the example of threat of imprisonment. The Jordanian Civil Code also recognises that the assessment of duress will differ according to the position and status of the subject.

76 Dawud, *supra* note 48, 386.

77 31822/1990, Dawud 1999 389.

specification in law of what might otherwise arguably be construed as a form of 'minor duress' in the Jordanian Penal Code, in common with some others in the region. The section on 'assaults on honour' (*'ard*)[78] includes, for example, the crime of 'deflowering a *bikr* of 15 or over by deceit through the promise of marriage'; the process of prosecution for this crime or implementation of a penalty imposed after conviction may be suspended if a valid marriage is contracted between the perpetrator and his victim. The prosecution can resume, or the prison sentence be implemented, if the man divorces the woman 'for no legitimate reason' within three or five years, depending on the gravity of the offence.[79] It is not inconceivable that a man in such a situation might seek to argue at the *shari'a* court that the threat of imprisonment constituted duress, seeking a judicial dissolution that would not constitute 'divorce for no legitimate reason'.[80] If indeed such claims have been brought, the *Shari'a* Appeal Court certainly does not seem to have disputed the legitimacy of the Penal Code provisions in this regard, which are regarded by the legislature as being protective of the female victim of sexual violence and deception.[81]

Coming back to family law, in regard to relations between the spouses, the Jordanian Civil Code deals explicitly with the 'authority' exercised by a husband over his wife, stating that if the man were to abuse this authority 'by for example beating her or preventing her from seeing her family in order to induce her to waive something that is her right or to make him a gift of something', such action will render any such act on her part not executable.[82] The two examples of acts cited as constituting duress in this context are both unlawful. By contrast, in a 1995 case, the *Shari'a* Appeal Court considered the complaint of a woman who stated that she had signed a customary document (ie not an official document of waiver in court) handing her prompt dower over to her husband, under the threat

---

78 Asma Khadr, member of the Jordanian Bar Association but writing at the time about changes to Jordanian laws that might be sought from a future Palestinian legislature, made a compelling case for the re-categorisation of acts of sexual violence – including rape – currently included in the section as crimes against the person rather than against 'honour'. A Khadr, *al-qanun wa mustaqbil al-mar'a al-filastiniyyah*, Jerusalem: Women's Centre for Legal Aid and Counselling, 1998, 202.

79 Articles 304 and 308 of the Penal Code.

80 This was argued in a West Bank case under the same laws in the late 1980s, but the case was settled out of court after extensive procedures of customary dispute resolution. See Welchman, *supra* note 26, 317.

81 Such legal 'remedies' to these (and other) social situations are not modern innovations. Ziadeh, *supra* note 6, 22, reports a fourteenth century jurist criticising state officials 'for the practice of ordering a man guilty of defloration or of an intimacy leading to pregnancy to marry the woman in question lest the child be born without a name and lest a scandal arise'. The criticism was based on the fact that under *shar'i* rules such a marriage would not render the child the lawful offspring of the couple. Elsewhere in the region in more recent times, women's groups and other civil society actors have argued for the repeal of similar provisions suspending the penalty in the event that a man marries a woman he is accused (or convicted) of abducting and raping, from the perspective of this constituting a form of 'forced marriage' of the female victim. In Egypt in 1999, Article 291 of the Penal Code was repealed following a campaign by non-governmental organisations and support from various figures in the *shar'i* establishment, significantly a declaration by the Grand Mufti. See Steve Negus in *Middle East International* 21 May 1999. Mona el-Tahtawi in *The Guardian*, 6 May 1999, reports women's rights activists as arguing that 'the law acted as a reward to the rapist and placed pressure on the victim to accept marriage in order to salvage family honour.' Khadr, *supra* note 79, 202, called for the repeal of Article 308 of the Jordanian Penal Code by the Palestinian legislature in the West Bank and Gaza Strip.

82 Article 142 Civil Code and see Dawud, *supra* note 48, 384.

of divorce if she refused. The Appeal Court commented that duress is not realised solely by 'authority' and 'disciplinary action', and since the authority of a man over a woman includes the possibility that he will divorce her or marry another wife, this was not in and of itself considered duress.[83] The Jordanian Civil Code does not deal in similar fashion with the authority exercised by fathers over their children – for example, in the matter of marriage guardianship.

The legal assumption is clearly that any phenomenon of what might be understood as 'forced marriage' is covered by existing legislation in Jordan. The institution of 'guardianship with compulsion' – the word '*ijbar*', usually translatable as force – has, as explained above, been written out of Jordanian law and in any case was entirely distinct from 'duress' (*ikrah*) since guardianship was a recognised right/duty of the father and other close male agnates, to be exercised by law according to his assessment of his ward's best interest. It is now a criminal offence to marry off underage girls; and duress renders the contract irregular. On the other hand, the established authority of the father of the family, or other male guardian taking his place, in the particular matter of the marriage of young female wards may clearly still complicate the issue of 'consent' to marriage, as recognised in some of the changes being called for to the text of the law by women's groups.

While being explicit about duress and removing guardianship with compulsion by invalidating the marriage of minors, the JLPS is not explicit about the consent of parties to their marriage. The requirement of consent is assumed, rather than spelt out, except in the case of a woman under 18 marrying a man more than 20 years her senior, when the *qadi* has to ascertain her free consent to the marriage.[84] The same circumstances might of course apply in the marriage of a young woman even where the groom is not of such an age as to warrant the judge's particular and exceptional attention to the issue of consent.

In the traditional Hanafi rules, a man had to consent explicitly to his marriage, while for a woman it depended on whether she was a virgin (*bikr*) or had previously been married (*thayyib*). A woman who already had experience of men – through having been married and either divorced or widowed – was required to articulate explicit consent. On the other hand the consent of a *bikr*, a woman getting married for the first time, could be inferred implicitly from such actions as her silence. Samara, commenting on the JLPS, recalls the Hanafi rules in pointing out that while fully spoken consent is the most complete indication, actions such as crying could indicate consent 'unless this crying is accompanied by something that indicates refusal, such as screaming and striking her face', and that similarly smiling and laughing were to be taken as consent 'unless it is contemptuous laughter'.[85] Her refusal, on the other hand must be explicitly articulated 'since shyness may prevent a *bikr* from expressing her approval, while she will not be shy of [expressing her] refusal'.[86] Samara notes that the JLPS does not deal

---

83   38277/1995, Dawud, *supra* note 7, 178–179.

84   In its initial report to the Committee on the Elimination of Discrimination Against Women, Jordan stressed this provision as an example of its laws on consent to marriage. In a later paragraph it emphasised that 'Islam does give women the right to enter into marriage only with their full and free consent'. UN Doc CEDAW C/JOR/1 10 November 1997 paras 25 and 26.

85   Samara, *supra* note 16, 109. See on this Siddiqui, *supra* note 23, 182.

86   Samara, *supra* note 16, 109.

explicitly with the issue of consent to marriage or how it is to be given, but points out that since marriage under duress is held irregular, the consent of both parties is clearly required. He therefore deduces that the law does not deal with how consent is to be articulated 'because it provides that the court *ma'dhun* shall carry out the contract (and in special circumstances the judge himself) and the court would not carry out a contract if there was any duress involved, since mutual consent to the contract is a condition of capacity'.[87] Since marriages concluded according to the traditional *shar'i* rules but out of court and with no involvement of the *ma'dhun* are still entirely valid, this does not cover the whole issue; but the comment resonates with the positions taken on this issue by the Appeal Court in regard to the role of the *ma'dhun*.

For their part, the marriage notaries (*ma'dhuns*) are regulated by instructions which require that along with confirming the identity of all those involved, they must ascertain 'the capacity of the fiancés and their consent and the fact that they fulfil the conditions of the contract'.[88] No indication of how consent is to be ascertained is given in the instructions. Marriage notaries must be permanent residents of the jurisdiction to which they are appointed, and are selected by a committee headed by the *Qadi al-Quda* and including the judge of jurisdiction in which they are to work; there appears to be no explicit legal requirement that they be male, but in practice they are. They must take a qualifying examination in Hanafi jurisprudence, and the minimum requirement otherwise is that they hold a certificate of general secondary education.[89] The contract is drawn up by the *ma'dhun* of the area in which the fiancée is resident.[90] If there is ever a situation of potential (indeed imminent) 'forced marriage', in the sense of anything involving duress as defined in the law, the *ma'dhun* must immediately identify the risk and take appropriate action, specifically perhaps by seeking the greater authority and experience of the judge. This is, of course, also the case in the event of suspicion of a potential underage marriage, with the fiancée being presented as older than she actually is.[91]

In court, establishing duress that renders a marriage contract invalid appears to be complicated. Similar principles to those governing claims of irregularity on the basis of young age have been applied. Thus, the *Shari'a* Appeal Court ruled in a 1973 case that the fact that the woman had acknowledged the existence of a valid contract of marriage in a previous claim for maintenance and in defending an action for 'obedience' raised by her husband caused the dismissal of her subsequent claim that the marriage was irregular through having been concluded under duress.[92] In other cases, particular principles have been established. In 1976, the Appeal Court convened a special five-judge bench to decide a matter of interpretation. The Law of Procedure provides for such a panel to be convened

---

87 Samara, *supra* note 16, 111.

88 Instructions Regulating the Functions of *Shar'i Ma'dhuns*, no 1/1990, *Official Gazette* no 3672, 1 December 1990, as amended 1997; article 15(b).

89 Instructions Regulating the Functions of *Shar'i Ma'dhuns*, articles 3 and 6.

90 Instructions Regulating the Functions of *Shar'i Ma'dhuns*, article 17.

91 In the neighbouring West Bank, the Palestinian Deputy *Qadi al-Quda* has noted with concern the frequency with which the *shari'a* courts find fathers trying to marry off their daughters under the minimum age of marriage in the JLPS: as reported in *Al-Quds*, 8 March 1998.

92 17521/1973 Dawud, *supra* note 48, 387.

where there are contrasting Appeal Court rulings on the legal or jurisprudential matters before it, or where it sees it as appropriate to issue a ruling contrary to all previous rulings.[93] The matter under consideration in this case was the automatic review of certain first instance court rulings by the Appeal Court in the event that one or more of the litigants had not themselves appealed the lower court's decision within the requisite 30 days. The types of rulings to which this procedure of automatic review applies include those involving *haqq allah* (literally: the right of God) with the idea of public *shar'i* interest beyond the private interest of the parties: the examples given are rulings of judicial dissolution of marriage and judicial divorce.[94] A previous (1962) appeal decision had held that the provision for automatic review in the absence of an appeal by a litigant applied to the rejection by the lower court of a claim made for dissolution on grounds of duress rendering the contract invalid, just as it did to the granting of a judicial dissolution on such grounds. The later decision held that if the claimant did not appeal, this was to be considered a 'withdrawal' of her claim for dissolution by reason of duress, 'and in this case the public "right" is not concerned with the rejection of the claim'.[95]

In similar mode, in 1978, the Court held that lower courts were not to follow up on their own initiative allegations of duress not positively pursued by the claimant. In the case under consideration, the first instance court had heard a woman petitioner who had claimed that she had been forced under duress into appointing her father as her representative (*wakil*) in the marriage contract, but the parties had subsequently stopped attending court. The first instance court considered the petitioner's claim to have been dropped, but then renewed the case on its own initiative, on the basis that the public *shar'i* right was concerned with the claim of duress, and proceeded in the end to dissolve the contract as irregular. The Appeal Court overturned the ruling for dissolution, holding that the correct ruling was to drop the original claim, since 'a simple allegation of duress in the marriage is not among the matters which concern the public "right" if subsequently withdrawn; the contract is permitted in such circumstances'.[96] This is an indication also of the general principle that even if the contract had in fact been concluded under duress, this irregular conclusion does not permanently undermine its validity, provided it is subsequently accepted.[97]

Perhaps of more immediate significance is a further principle that seems to have been established by the Appeal Court involving the documentation drawn up for the conclusion of a marriage contract registered by the marriage notary. In 1980 the Appeal Court overturned a ruling by the first instance court which had dissolved the marriage of a woman on the grounds that her marriage had been carried out under duress and was therefore irregular. The Appeal Court held that the documentation (*mahdar*, or 'record') accompanying the contract of marriage included the statement that the woman had appointed her father as her representative in carrying out her marriage without force or duress. This

---

93   Article 150 Law of *Shar'i* Procedure.
94   Article 138 Law of *Shar'i* Procedure.
95   18903/1976 Dawud, *supra* note 48, 387–388. Reaffirmed in 22353/1981.
96   20266/1978 Dawud, *supra* note 48, 388.
97   See Article 141 of the Civil Code.

documentation is drawn up by the *ma'dhun* and signed by all involved including the two spouses and the wife's father. The Appeal Court referred to Article 75 of the Law of *Shar'i* Procedure, which provides that:

'Official documents which public employees draw up within the sphere of their competence – such as the marriage document, the birth certificate issued following childbirth, documents drawn up by the Clerk of Justice and registration documents are considered absolute proof for that for which they were drawn up. They may only be challenged on grounds of forgery.'

The Appeal Court held that the record drawn up by the *ma'dhun* came under the terms of this article and that therefore the statement in that record affirming the woman's willing appointment of her father in her marriage invalidated her subsequent claim of duress.[98] In effect this position appears to make it possible for claims for dissolution on the grounds of duress to be made only by those whose marriages have not been registered in accordance with the law.[99] It further emphasises the critical significance of the functions carried out by the *ma'dhun* in investigating the issue of consent under the current terms of Jordanian law.

VII PROPOSALS FOR CHANGE

A general overview of the *Shari'a* Appeal Court decisions considered above in applying the provisions of the JLPS on the matters under examination in this article might suggest the Court's tendency to look kindly upon defences by the married couple against a claim for dissolution by the *shari'a* court officials in the event that they both appear to wish the marriage to continue, while insisting on strong evidence from one spouse wishing to have the marriage dissolved against the wish of the other. Even as a generalisation, this would be in line with the general strongly pro-marriage (and anti-divorce) stand of Islamic law and Muslim jurists. However, there are clearly circumstances which would work against women seeking an exit from unwelcome marriages: in Jordanian law, while men always retain the power of unilateral divorce (as well as the option in law of polygynous marriage to another woman), women do not have equal access to divorce. And while a couple whose marriage is dissolved as irregular may, if they wish, remarry when they come of age and can legally do so, a young woman married underage may unwittingly be caught out by the passage of time, disallowing the courts from hearing her claim for dissolution on the grounds that it was irregular due to her lack of capacity. In this regard, the Jordanian National Commission for Women proposed, in a 1996 draft of suggested amendments to the JLPS, that a phrase be added to the existing article to the effect that the court shall not hear these claims if the spouses fulfil the criteria of capacity at the time 'and are content for marital life to continue'. This would seem a useful recourse,

---

98 21655/1980 Dawud, *supra* note 48, 388. A similar point was made in 21943/1981, Dawud, *supra* note 7, 149.

99 From other cases it seems that a similar acknowledgement of consent in 'customary documents' (not drawn up by public officials in the course of their duties) can be challenged on grounds of duress. 18732/1975 Dawud, *supra* note 7, 146.

at least in law, for girls illegally married before their fifteenth birthdays and unwilling to stay in the union.[100]

Similarly, given the social circumstances in which pressure amounting to duress might conceivably be brought to bear on young girls in the matter of their marriage, a position that effectively restricts the opportunity to complain of such duress to the time and place of the social occasion when her family and the groom's are gathered to conclude the contract is unlikely to be wholly effective in realising the objects of the law in protecting the principle of consent and the right of refusal. In a proposal clearly aimed at clarifying the role of the woman's marriage guardian in this regard, the JNCW suggested the addition of an explicit text to the effect that 'guardianship in marriage is shared between the *bikr* and the guardian, and the guardian must take her consent and is not allowed to force her (*ijbar*) into marriage'.[101] This indicates an acceptance that the law should reflect and accommodate the customary and social recognition of the role of the family (through the guardian) while weighting the daughter's choice through an explicit prohibition of compulsion (*ijbar*).

The JNCW's drafted proposals did not suggest a change in the age of capacity,[102] but among other groups in Jordan the establishment of the Civil Code's age of legal majority (at 18 for both sexes by the solar calendar) as the minimum age of capacity for marriage has been identified as a target for advocacy and campaigning. As an objective, this is justified both on the evidence of social science research into the effects of early marriage on young women and with reference to international instruments such as the Convention on the Rights of the Child.[103] Others suggest that while the age of capacity should be raised to 18, the *qadi* should retain the discretion to assess the girl's circumstances in particular cases where her guardian requests permission for her to be married below that age.[104] In effect, this would constitute a return to the sort of rules that applied under the previous JLFR, when the judge's approval as well as that of the marriage guardian was required for a marriage below the age of full capacity.[105] A legal question here would be whether directives would instruct the *shari'a* court judges as to what particular circumstances would justify a marriage below the minimum age of capacity, and whether specific attention would be directed to the scrutiny of consent in such exceptional circumstances. In 1999, non-governmental organisations participating in the submission of the NGO report on the

---

100 Article 39 of the draft produced by the JNCW: I am grateful to attorney Reem Abu Hassan for the text.

101 Article 12(b) of the draft amendments being proposed to the JLPS by the JNCW.

102 Article 353 of the JNCW draft sets the lunar year as the standard calculation unless specifically stated otherwise.

103 Noor El-Emam, 'Experience of the Jordanian Women's Movement in Amending the Personal Status Law,' paper for the regional conference on Personal Status Laws in the Arab World: Theory, Practice and Chances for Reform,' convened by the Konrad Adenauer Stiftung and the JNCW, June 2000, 7, and 9 on the campaign by the Jordanian Women's Union to raise the age of marriage to 18.

104 Ragheb al-Qassim, *supra* note 30, 15.

105 As for the official position, Jordan acceded to the Convention on the Minimum Age of Marriage in 1992 without reservation, and holds the age of capacity of 15 (lunar) years for females to be in accordance with the Convention on the Rights of the Child: CRC/C/8/Add.4 26 November 1993 para 1(d).

implementation of the Convention of the Rights of the Child in Jordan announced that they were:

> 'intensifying their endeavours to increase the age of marriage, for both men and women, to eighteen, since they are convinced that the physical, mental and emotional development on which eligibility for marriage is largely based cannot be found in persons under eighteen years of age.'[106]

The report then acknowledged 'fears that the incidence of offences against the code of morality might rise in hot and remote areas if the age of marriage were increased' and called for public awareness and education programmes to be carried out by NGOs 'in an attempt to avert such fears'. Different approaches and concerns thus mark, to some extent, the efforts being undertaken in Jordan to raise the age of marriage both in law and in practice, but there appears to be an emerging consensus on a shared objective.

---

106 CRC/C/70/Add.4 17 September 1999: Appendix, para 42.

KENYA

CHILD SUPPORT RIGHTS IN KENYA AND IN THE UN CONVENTION ON THE RIGHTS OF THE CHILD 1989

Michael Nyongesa Wabwile[*]

I   INTRODUCTION: CHILD POVERTY AND THE CASE FOR CHILD SUPPORT

The escalating number of destitute children on Kenyan streets is a constant pointer to the gravity of the problem of child poverty in this country.[1] Yet, poor children are not confined to streets. Many more are living rough with their families in slum areas and rural villages. More and more families, particularly polygamous ones, tend to have more children than their aggregate resources can support.[2] Poor young children deprived of bare necessaries cannot complete primary education and are given by their parents to labour as farm-hands in plantations and pastoral areas as well as in mines or quarries, and in homes as house-helps and child-minders, etc, to earn money to supplement the family income and make ends meet.[3] The declining economic performance and drop in real incomes are factors that have adversely affected Kenyan society.[4] Children, given their vulnerable position as dependants, have been the worst hit by these problems.

Indeed, child poverty is a serious social problem. It threatens the future of many children in our society and has grave implications for the destiny of this country in the long run. As the number of poor children continues to rise, it is

---

[*]   LLB (Hons), (Nairobi), LLM (Cantab), Dip Law, (KSL), F.C.C.S. Advocate, Assistant Lecturer in Law, Moi University Eldoret, Kenya.

1   A survey conducted in Eldoret municipality shows that of the 400 children committed to the Juvenile Remand home between February and April 2000, 350 had been apprehended in that town because they were vagrant and destitute.

2   Traditional customary law provides for polygamous marriages. Polygamy as a legal institution is a factor that may contribute to child poverty. Where a man acquires a second dependant wife and has children with both wives, all other factors remaining the same, the general standard of life of the children of the first marriage drops significantly. The money meant for the children of the first marriage is diverted to maintain a second wife and another set of dependants. The children of the second wife arrive into a family strained by stiff competition for limited financial resources of their father. Such a family structure is therefore not ideal for raising children. It is necessary to regulate the institution of marriage with a view to prohibiting family structures like polygamy that are clearly inconsistent with the ideals of a flourishing State.

3   These observations are based on a survey conducted by this writer in preparation for writing this paper. Moreover, the Government's *First Country Report on the Implementation of the UN Convention on the Rights of the Child* 1998 shows that 'cases of child labour have been increasing because of the rising levels of poverty in the country', p 99.

4   See Kenya Government, Ministry of Planning and National Development, *Economic Survey 2000 (Government Printer, Nairobi)* published on Friday 26 May 2000. See also *The Daily Nation* Nairobi on 26 May 2000. The *Survey* indicates that the rate of economic growth in 1999 dropped from the 1998 mark of 1.8% to 1.4%. As a result, the average monthly income per person dropped from Kshs 305 ($4.07) to Kshs 301 ($4.01).

necessary to turn to the legal system and public policy to assess what measures have been secured to address this problem. The object of this paper is to examine the provisions of the United Nations Convention on the Rights of the Child 1989 (hereinafter referred to as 'the Convention') relating to the financial support rights of children and assess to what extent Kenyan law and practice conform with these international norms. The study attempts to demonstrate that our national law and practice in this area has taken a course that is rather indifferent to the financial support rights of the child – a factor that exacerbates the current situation of child poverty. The paper argues that the Kenyan system of child support law falls short of the standards of the Convention and suggests measures that can be introduced to secure the financial support rights of the Kenyan child in a more comprehensive manner.

II   THE CHILD'S RIGHT TO FINANCIAL SUPPORT

What does the child's right to financial support entail? Starting from the premise that a right is a legally protected interest, the child's right to financial support is an interest of the child to have enough funds secured for him to meet his changing needs as he grows up and to secure an adequate standard of life. This interest becomes a legally enforceable right when the law imposes a duty on other persons to provide the required funds for the child, and can be asserted for all children generally as a class rather than for a particular child.[5]

The status of childhood entails many disabilities that render the child vulnerable and dependent on the adult community. For this reason, it is universally acknowledged that children are entitled to special care and assistance.[6] Therefore, there is a strong moral justification for the financial support of children since they are not yet mature enough to work and support themselves. It is not a question of whether child support is a right but rather how this right should be enforced. Typically, the law imposes a duty on a liable relative and the relevant State agency to secure for the child the requisite financial and material resources for the use of the child.

The United Nations Convention on the Rights of the Child 1989

The United Nations Convention on the Rights of the Child 1989 sets out a catalogue of legal rights which can be asserted for children and imposes duties on individuals and States to secure their implementation.[7] The focus of this study is on Article 27 of the Convention.[8]

---

5   A Bainham with S Cretney, *Children – The Modern Law* 1993 1st Edn (Jordan Publishing Ltd, Bristol), pp 92–93.

6   See the United Nations Convention on the Rights of the Child 1989, Preamble, and the Universal Declaration of Human Rights 1945, Article 25(2).

7   The Convention was ratified by this country in January 1990, but it is not directly enforceable since it has not been incorporated in municipal legislation. This country applies a monist system of law which requires international law to be incorporated in municipal law before it may be applied locally.

8   Article 27 provides as follows:

Article 27 recognises and declares four things: the child's right to financial support, the primary financial responsibility of parents, the parent–State partnership and the State obligation to provide for effective measures to recover child support payments. These are examined below in the context of the relevant law and practice.

III MEASURES TO ENFORCE PARENTS' CHILD SUPPORT OBLIGATIONS

Article 27(2) of the Convention emphasises the *primary responsibility of parents* to maintain their children. For this purpose Article 27(4) of the Convention requires: 'State Parties to take *all appropriate measures to secure recovery of maintenance for the child from the parents or other person having financial responsibility for the child,* both within the state party and from abroad'. There is clearly an obligation on the part of the Convention countries to establish and maintain robust procedures for recovering child support from absent parents.

A Provisions for matrimonial children

Kenyan family law provides a procedure for obtaining child maintenance payments from married parents when the family breaks down. The State may intervene in matrimonial proceedings, eg suits for separation, maintenance and divorce. The Matrimonial Causes Act (Cap. 152), the Subordinate Courts (Separation and Maintenance) Act (Cap. 153), the Mohammedan Marriage and Divorce Act (Cap. 155), the Hindu Marriage and Divorce Act (Cap. 157), the Judicature Act (Cap. 8) and the Magistrates' Courts Act (Cap. 10) empower courts having jurisdiction in matrimonial matters to make orders for the maintenance of the children of the parties whose marriage is the subject of the proceedings.

Moreover, persons with *de facto* care of children may obtain maintenance orders for matrimonial children against either of their parents.[9] And there are criminal sanctions for failing or neglecting to provide for the proper maintenance

---

'(1)   States parties shall recognise the right of every child to a standard of living adequate for the child's physical, mental, spiritual, moral and social development.

(2)   The parent(s) or others responsible for the child have the primary responsibility to secure, within their abilities and financial capacities the conditions of living necessary for the child's development.

(3)   States Parties, in accordance with national conditions and within their means shall take appropriate measures to assist parents and others responsible for the child to implement this right and shall in case of need provide material assistance and support programmes, particularly with regard to nutrition, clothing and housing.

(4)   States Parties shall take all appropriate measures to secure the recovery of maintenance for the child from the parents and other persons having financial responsibility for the child, both within the State party and from abroad. In particular, where the person having financial responsibility lives in a State different from that of the child, States Parties shall promote the accession to international agreements or the conclusion of such agreements as well as the making of other appropriate arrangements.'

See also Article 18(2) of the Convention.

9   The Children and Young Persons Act (Cap. 141), section 24(8).

of one's child.[10] The need to enforce extra-territorial maintenance orders is met by the Maintenance Orders Enforcement Act (Cap. 154). At least for children of the married family, the law seems satisfactory.

B   Provisions for children in the unmarried family

The problem arises however where the child's parents are not married. As Kenyan law now stands, the status of illegitimacy is still in our statute book[11] and there is no legal duty on the part of the unmarried father to maintain his illegitimate children. In 1959 the Affiliation Act (Cap 142) was enacted by the colonial legislature to provide a procedure for making and enforcing affiliation orders requiring putative fathers to make periodical payments for the maintenance of their illegitimate children. The affiliation orders were made on application by the mother of the illegitimate child and payments were remitted to her.

However, the Affiliation Act fell foul of the post-independence Parliament and was repealed in 1969.[12] The repeal of the Affiliation Act (Cap 142) in 1969, has prejudiced the financial support rights of the illegitimate child and excluded him from the legal process for recovery of maintenance payments due to him from his putative father. The illegitimate child has therefore been denied access to court to obtain maintenance provision from his putative father.

The first grave mistake we made was to repeal the Affiliation Act (Cap 142) without providing an alternative measure to implement the child's right to receive financial support from his parents. Consequently the whole concept of illegitimacy as applied in Kenyan child support law is discriminatory against children born out of wedlock and offends the anti-discrimination principle set out in Article 2 of the Convention.[13] The current law is unjust and manifestly hostile to the child born outside wedlock.

C   Judicial innovation? *Peter Hinga v Mary Wanjiku*

One dimension in this problem is the attempt by the High Court in *Peter Hinga v Mary Wanjiku*[14] to confer a quasi-marital status on a former cohabiting couple only for the limited purpose of securing financial support rights of the children of a relationship of an unmarried cohabitation. In that case the defendant cohabited

---

10   Ibid, section 23.

11   See the Legitimacy Act (Cap. 145).

12   It was argued that abuse of the Act by women was rampant and the entire process was encouraging immorality.

13   The Article provides:

'(1) States Parties shall respect and ensure the rights set forth in the present Convention to each child within their jurisdiction without discrimination of any kind, irrespective of the child's or his or her parents' or legal guardian's race, colour, sex, language, religion, political or other opinion, national, ethnic or social origin, property, disability, birth or other status.

(2) States Parties shall take all appropriate measures to ensure that the child is protected against all forms of discrimination or punishment on the basis of the status, activities, expressed opinions or beliefs of the child's parents, legal guardians, or family members.'

14   Nairobi H.C.C.A. No 94 of 1977 (unreported) published in Cotran, *Casebook of Kenya Customary Law* (1988) (Nairobi, Univ of Nairobi Press), pp 62–63.

with the plaintiff 'as man and wife' for 14 years during which time five children were born to them in their established home. No ceremony of marriage of any kind was ever performed by the parties. In 1976, the defendant unilaterally terminated the cohabitation, left the family home and married another woman in a Christian marriage ceremony and began a new family. The plaintiff brought an action for the maintenance of the six children of the family. The defendant argued that since there was no ceremony of marriage the plaintiff's children were illegitimate and therefore not entitled to maintenance from him. Miller J in upholding the decision of the magistrates' court held that there was a customary marriage between the parties and that the court would regard the children as matrimonial issue. He said:

'... This case poses a very serious state of affairs. *As this Court sees it, Mr Hinga, whether or not he has deliberately postponed the "ngurario ceremony, is relying on a mechanical point in Kikuyu customary law so as to take advantage of the repeal of the Affiliation Act.* I believe that the repeal of the Affiliation Act was to prevent women so inclined from freely collecting illegitimate children and then sit in legal receipt of custom. I am however quite certain that the Legislature by repeal never intended to grant men licenses to inflict unwanted and abandoned children upon our society ... *I endorse the findings of [the lower courts] that there is a recognizable Kikuyu customary law marriage between the parties ... I now legally pronounce Peter Hinga and Mary Wanjiku man and wife.*" ' (emphasis original)

While the result of this case was favourable to the plaintiff's children, the decision is liable to attack on three grounds. First, this case turned on whether the parties were married or not. In the absence of a ceremony of marriage, it was not lawful for the court to impose a marital status on the parties.

Secondly, it was unacceptable for the judge to purport to 'legally pronounce the parties man and wife', particularly where the defendant had vehemently denied that he ever consented to marry the plaintiff, but had only gone as far as cohabiting with her. What then was the effective date of commencement of the marriage, the date when the parties began their cohabitation or the date of the judgment? It could certainly not have been the former because at that point there was no marriage. Neither could it be the latter because, shortly before that litigation, the appellant had celebrated a Christian marriage with another woman and had no capacity to marry the respondent. In any event, courts have no executive powers under our marriage laws to celebrate marriages for this is a function of the marriage officers who preside over marriage ceremonies.

In fact, in a later case, the Court of Appeal has held that cohabitation and repute as such, alone and in the absence of a marriage ceremony, do not constitute a marriage and the legal status and consequences of marriage do not apply to cohabitees no matter what is the duration of the cohabitation.[15]

15　By a majority (Kneller and Nyarangi JJA, Madan JA dissenting): *Mary Njoki v John Kinyanjui and Others* [1982–88] I Kenya Appeal Reports 711. The parties had cohabited for six years and had no issue. It is submitted that the reasoning of the majority of the Court is correct and consistent with the conventional distinction between marriage and other family structures. The International Covenant on Civil and Political Rights provides that: 'No marriage should be entered into without the free and full consent of the intending spouses': Article 23(3). Note that

Thirdly, *Hinga v Wanjiku* does not lay down any general legal principle that would be applicable to any future claim for financial support by an illegitimate child. The decision fails to offer any guidance on what would have been the result if the court had found that the parties were in fact unmarried, especially where there has not been any family relationship, eg where the child has been conceived in a casual sexual relationship. Therefore, the decision should be confined to the particular facts of that case.

As the law was then and now, Kenyan courts have no jurisdiction to order payments to be made by putative fathers for the maintenance of their illegitimate children. The repeal of the Affiliation Act abolished the available procedure for the enforcement of this fundamental right of the child. It would have been more legally tenable for the Court to dismiss the suit for maintenance of the children so that the injustice of the law could be exposed to touch the conscience of this country's policy makers and probably trigger the campaign for reform. Unfortunately, the decision gives a false impression of the jurisdiction of the Court and clouds the real issues.

Therefore *Hinga v Wanjiku* is the second mistake we have made in that the judge erred in law in an attempt to give 'palm tree justice' to children without the due authority of law. The decision was *per incuriam* and should never be cited except for the limited purpose of showing the depths of error into which we have fallen.

D   An unconvincing explanation

It is possible to attempt one explanation, albeit an unconvincing one, for this state of affairs. It may be argued that under Kenyan law the unmarried father is not recognised as a parent and so does not have parental status, rights or even responsibility *vis-à-vis* his illegitimate child. He lacks a formal legal nexus with his illegitimate child. Therefore he is a stranger to the child, and does not come within the definition of 'persons responsible for the child' or 'persons having financial responsibility for the child' as described in the Convention. This position is evident in the restriction on the registration of unmarried fathers in the Register of Births.[16]

This view has been suggested by Barton and Douglas[17] in their analysis of the reluctance of English law to confer automatic parental rights on unmarried fathers. They argue that the test of parenthood seems to be the expressed intention to become a parent which, for men, is demonstrated by going through a ceremony of marriage and consummating it or obtaining an adoption order. But English law and practice is distinguishable because it imposes compulsory financial responsibility on genetic parents whilst denying the unmarried father automatic parental rights.[18]

Article 23(1) of the Covenant provides for the protection of the institution of the family which on a broad interpretation includes married and unmarried families.

16   Section 12 of the Births and Deaths Registration Act (Cap. 149) forbids the registration of an unmarried father in the child's record of birth unless both parents jointly apply to the Registrar.

17   Barton and Douglas, *Law and Parenthood* 1995 (London, Butterworths) chapter 5.

18   See the Child Support Act 1991, and the Children Act 1989 (England and Wales). I will return to this point later. For a full discussion of this point see Bainham, op cit Note 3.

By insisting that the unmarried father is not a parent because he did not intend to assume parental responsibility for his child, Kenyan law takes a position that is manifestly indifferent to the innocent child, callously labelled illegitimate. It is true that the unmarried father is not a parent in law because parenthood is a legal concept determined by the manner in which the legal system selects whom to recognise as such. But he is a father since fatherhood is a question of fact rather than law. This approach was taken in Article 81 of Children Bill 1995, which was however not passed by Parliament.

I maintain that the fact of fatherhood is constituted by a genetic link – the blood-tie between father and child. This is a sufficient basis for imposing compulsory financial responsibility for the child on all fathers regardless of their marital status. Money must follow blood.[19]

It must be emphasised that children do not just occur naturally like nitrogen in the atmosphere. The arrival of a baby in this world is a product of a series of conscious decisions made by the parents of that child, from the time before insemination through conception and throughout the pregnancy. The facts of life are well known to all. By choosing to have unprotected sexual intercourse whilst fully appreciating its consequences, the unmarried father must be presumed to have intended to bear all the logical consequences of his activity. Men who do not wish to sire children are, of course, at liberty to visit a clinic and receive free contraceptive advice and treatment to keep them away from the impact of parental responsibility.

Therefore, the primary financial responsibility for a child must lie with its parents, broadly defined to include all fathers. It is a sound principle that children should look to their natural parents for financial support. This principle of primary responsibility of parents is stressed in the Convention, particularly in Articles 18(1) and 27(2). Society must insist as a matter of principle that parents make adequate arrangements for the maintenance of their children when the family relationship breaks down.

In the cause of securing money for the child, we must insist on vigorous enforcement this parental obligation, particularly where the parent-child relationship has not been properly developed or has broken down. This will send a message to would-be parents to pause and plan their operations. In the result, the whole idea of having a child will become the subject of intensive calculation and careful economics by individuals so minded. We cannot allow parents to make foolish private decisions that prejudice the rights of their children for the long term result would be a break-down of the entire social order.

In a seminal paper, Eric Clive argues that the legal concept of marriage, together with its effects, should not be a relevant factor when considering the rights of children since it is unjust to discriminate against children because of their parents' non-compliance with the marriage laws.[20] By tying parental responsibility of fathers to the status of marriage, Kenyan law makes the serious mistake of

---

19 In Denmark this principle that all children are entitled to equal protection of law in securing financial support from their parents, regardless of their marital status, was recognised and effected by the Child Law Act of 1937, which removed all legal disabilities of illegitimacy.

20 EM Clive, 'Marriage: An Unnecessary Legal Concept?' in Eekelaar and Maclean (eds), *A Reader on Family Law: Oxford Readings in Socio-legal Studies 1994 (Oxford, Oxford University Press)*, pp 175–191, at 176.

mixing up the two distinct legal concepts of parenthood and marriage to the disadvantage of the child. The distinctions between categories of fathers based on marital status are artificial and must be discarded. It is unacceptable that the law should allow men of means to inflict unwanted and neglected children on our society and yet deny the child the right to benefit from his father's standard of living. This is the third mistake in our national thinking and practice that must now be corrected.

## E	Enforcing the parental obligation: the English approach[21]

The Child Support Act of 1991 broke new ground in English child support law. Responsibility for administration of the Act lies with the Secretary of State, and is exercised on his behalf by the Child Support Agency. This Act abolished the Affiliation Acts and removed the functions of assessing child support requirements in non-matrimonial proceedings from the judiciary to the Child Support Agency – a government agency. The Act imposes compulsory financial responsibility on all absent parents and establishes a Child Support Agency with powers to assess the financial needs of the child, trace absent parents and recover and collect this money for the use of the parent or other person having the care of the child.

An application for a maintenance assessment is made by the residential parent to the Child Support Agency. Liability attaches to a parent who, in relation to the child in issue, is an absent parent and the Act retains the traditional reluctance of English law to interfere with the financial arrangements of a functioning family unit. The concept of parenthood for the purposes of the Act is widely cast to mean 'any person who is in law the mother or father of the child'.[22] Where paternity is denied, the Agency is required to apply for a declaration of paternity by a court of law, which may order blood-tests to determine this fact. The Agency makes its assessment using a meticulous formula that is designed to balance the conflicting claims on the liable parent's money[23] and enforces its orders by attaching the income of the liable parent without recourse to any judicial process.

The English approach in the Child Support Act 1991 shows how the two concepts of marriage and parenthood can be kept separate, yet still have liability for child support resting evenly across the board for all parents.

## F	Lessons for Kenyan family law

From the above account it is evident that our law fails to implement even the modest provisions of Article 27(4) of the Convention. The First Country Report on the Implementation of the Convention 1998 acknowledges the fact that 'children whose mothers are not married lack adequate protection [of their

---

21	See, The Child Support Act 1991, *Children Come First*. The Government's proposals for the maintenance of Children (1990) (Cmnd 1263), Bainham, op cit n 3, pp 304–326, Cretney and Masson, *Principles of Family Law*, 6th edn, 1997 (London, Sweet & Maxwell), pp 501–553.

22	Section 54. However, step-parents and social parents are not liable.

23	There are provisions as to the absent parent's minimum protected income, below which the Child Support Agency must not by such assessments reduce: Schedule 1, para 6.

financial support rights]'.[24] But the Report does not disclose the mistakes we have made and avoids the history of the Affiliation Act altogether. Moreover, the Report does not have any concrete proposal on the implementation of Article 27(4) of the Convention.

There are indications that the preferred option on the way forward is to revive selected sections of the Affiliation Act as a part of the proposed new Children Bill.[25] It is submitted that the affiliation orders system entirely depends on the vagaries of the judicial process. This country does not as yet have any formal system of legal aid. So, in terms of costs to be borne by the applicant, the preferred reform would not be affordable to the wider majority of the carers of poor children. Secondly, the time constraints on ordinary courts mean that they would probably not cope with the work-load of disposing of applications for the grant, review or revocation of such orders, alongside other judicial business.

In this respect, it is submitted that the English Child Support Act model is undoubtedly more effective than the Affiliation Acts since administrative functionaries are better equipped to recover child support payments and personally supervise the finer details of child support than are the judicial procedures.[26] Compared to the court system, the Child Support Agency could be more efficient in terms of the cost to be borne by the parties and the time that the agency staff may have to assess and collect child support payments and oversee the application of those funds.

The foregoing English model approximates to the vision of Article 27(2) and (4) of the Convention[27] and, I suggest, should be considered as an option for law reform in this country. A section in the Department of Children's Services in the Ministry of Home Affairs could be re-structured into a Child Support Agency to carry out these functions without any additional cost to the State or the applicants.[28]

IV THE RIGHT TO AN ADEQUATE STANDARD OF LIFE

As already seen, the Convention requires States parties to recognise the right of every child to a standard of living adequate for the child's physical, mental, spiritual, moral and social development. It will be appreciated that setting a national standard of life might not be a simple task since there are considerable variations in the details of care given to children. However, it is possible to identify indicators of the standard of life applicable to children in a given society.

---

24 P 57.

25 See the Children Bill 1995, Article 81.

26 A survey conducted in the East Anglia region by this writer in June 1998 established that the Child Support Agency operatives regularly visit recipients of Child Support payments to assist, advise and generally supervise the application of those funds in the provision of the needs of the child.

27 For a similar view, see Bainham, op cit note 3, p 616.

28 In the course of my surveys I have frequently visited Children's Department Offices and my impression is that a considerable number of officers do not seem to have any clearly defined duties and while away the day, hardly creating any value. The proposed Child Support Agency would ensure that such officers have some cases to work on and thus enhance better staff rationalisation.

The most certain indicators of the standard of life are the social welfare and tax regimes that affect families with children.[29]

Presently, there is no official policy on child support standards and levels for the Kenyan child. Since this country does not have a universal (non-contributory) social security benefits system Kenyan families with children have to fend for themselves.

A   The State–parent partnership in child support law

Wider society has a public interest in developing the potential of its children to supply manpower resources – a healthy and educated population for the next generation. Children are the taxpayers of tomorrow whose income will in due course be taxed to pay pensions for today's taxpayers and meet the needs of general public investment and expenditure. Every progressive legal system must make provision for these long-term social needs.

The development of children's potential is achieved through the provision of adequate food and health and educational facilities for young people. These things cost lots of money. So, the entire society stands to benefit from the fruits of an educated, healthy and well adjusted working force. That is why child support is a public concern. Society, through the State agencies, has a legal duty to collaborate with parents to provide money for the purpose of raising the next generation of our country's working force.

This partnership principle is embodied in the Convention in Articles 18(2) and 27(3). Article 27(3) expresses the State–parent partnership in child support law. It imposes a legal duty on States to 'take appropriate measures to assist parents and others having responsibility for the child to implement the right of the child to financial support'. Here, the Convention lays down the framework for legal policies and programmes for social welfare schemes for children; known in that Article as 'material assistance, and support programs – particularly with regard to nutrition clothing and housing'.

Article 18(2) also declares the partnership principle: It states:

> 'For the purpose of guaranteeing and promoting the rights set forth in the present Convention, States Parties shall render appropriate assistance to parents and legal guardians in the performance of their child-rearing responsibilities and shall ensure the development of institutions, facilities and services for the care of children.'

Moreover, Article 26 declares the right of every child to benefit from social security.

In these Articles, the Convention declares rights of recipience for children, and corresponding positive duties of the State. How has Kenyan law tackled these issues? The Children and Young Persons Act (Cap 141) provides for State intervention in the family to remove children in need of care, protection and/or discipline, and put them in alternative care.[30] The Act also provides for the establishment, with State assistance of public and voluntary institutions and

---

29   See Section B below.
30   Sections 24, 25.

societies that are responsible for providing alternative care of children.[31] The Act authorises public funds to be applied to maintain and support such institutions of alternative care for children. In fact, a State-run rehabilitation centre for street children and other vagabonds and destitutes has been set up in Nairobi to cater for such children and the Minister for Home Affairs and National Heritage is authorised to give out money in the form of grants and aid to them. Indeed, public land and occasional grants have been allocated to such societies by the government from time to time to support charitable work.[32]

The thrust of Kenyan law and practice concentrates on intervention: to place poor and needy children in alternative care institutions, known as 'children's homes' (this is a euphemism since such baby farms cannot be homes in the strict sense of that word). What our law seems to be saying is that children are the private folly of their parents and that if they fail to secure enough funds to maintain them, the State will take the children away and commit them for rearing in 'children's homes'.

This approach to child support in Kenyan law is manifestly defective, and does not offer any sustainable solution to the problem of child poverty. This interventionist policy fails to tackle the problem of child poverty at its roots. Child poverty arises primarily because the child's parents are themselves deprived and cannot afford to give the child the basic support he requires for his development. Poor children are on the streets because their families have failed to provide material basics for them. To remove such children from their families and rear them in children's homes is only a short term measure because the space and other resources there cannot cope with increasing new arrivals on our streets.

The better policy would be to obviate the need to take children into alternative care in the first place – a preventionist policy, to create conditions that are more favourable to families to rear and retain their children. And children need families *not* 'institutional' care or 'children's homes'. The child needs the warmth, personal attention, sense of belonging and social identity of his family. These are social goods which are not available in institutional care where, the 'baby farm' syndrome of indifference to children's lack of social identity reigns. Rather than place children in 'children's farms', this country should attempt to address the problem by giving direct and indirect financial and material assistance to families with children.

While we insist that parents must maintain their children, we must also accept the social responsibility of the state to assist parents to maintain them. The Convention places a legal obligation on States to assist parents, to maintain their children, and to secure for them an adequate standard of living.

---

31 Section 78.
32 This statement is based on the writer's observation in Eldoret municipality where the Street Children's Rehabilitation Centre is located on land set aside for such humanitarian purposes in the town.

B   Modalities of implementing the State–parent partnership in child support

The realisation of the child's right to an adequate standard of living and financial security requires an outlay of sufficient funds, both from the private means of the child's parents and from the enlightened State. Many families are willing to care for both their own children as well as those of the extended family but lack financial resources to do so. Tackling child poverty must begin with State support of families with children, in the form of money and other material things required to maintain children, as a right and not as a charity to families.

The current Kenyan law does not have any benefit system for families with children. There is no provision in Kenyan law and policy for financial assistance to families with children. For too long now, the task of procuring money for raising the Kenyan child has been left to parents alone, yet the entire society stands to benefit from the contribution of healthy, educated and well adjusted individuals to the creation of national wealth. This is the fourth mistake we have made in our child care policy.

On the principle and modalities of the State–parent partnership in child support, Harry D Krause writes:[33]

'A [State–parent] partnership in child support is the appropriate goal. Child support is a public concern discharged primarily by parents but enforced and supplemented when necessary by the state through judicial enforcement, social welfare programmes tax subsidies and so forth. I have thought for some time that in a few decades our society may conclude that the enforcement of individual parental child support obligations at least at full support levels may no longer be good social policy ... In democratic Western European welfare states, society insists on but assists with, child support. Typically, those systems accept the two burdensome aspects of child support, health care, and higher education as primary social rather than private responsibilities yet even the duty of providing sustenance and personal care are tempered by children's allowances, subsidized day-care arrangements and subsidized housing.'

Even within the means of the current level of economic development, this country can implement the partnership principle in at least three ways, that is, income tax reductions, waiver of value-added tax on child supplies, and direct cash benefits.

1   INCOME TAX

Tax is a compulsory measure to exact money from individuals and institutions for general public purposes. Many enlightened States use income tax policies to lend their support to families with children. A person's ability to pay income tax must be assessed in light of the legitimate needs pressing on that income. The current Income Tax Act (cap 470) applies a flat rate of tax on all assessable persons,

---

33   'Child Support Re-Assessed: Limits Of Private Responsibility And The Public Interest' in Eekelaar and Maclean, (eds), *A Reader on Family Law: Oxford Readings in Socio-legal Studies 1994* (Oxford, Oxford University Press), pp 209–248 at 227–228. See also: M Minow, 'Rights For The Next Generation: A Feminist Approach To Children's Rights' 9 Harv. Women's Law Journal 1 (1996).

without any consideration of their financial obligations to society as rearers of children. A mother of eight is taxed at the same rate as a non-parent!

By taxing parents so indiscriminately, we are taking away a large portion of money which the parent would otherwise have to bring home for the maintenance of the child. This is the fifth mistake we have made, and it is hostile and cruel to the child. The principle that the State should lend financial assistance to parents in meeting the financial needs of the child must be accepted and reflected in income tax law.

The amounts of income tax chargeable to parents and other persons having the care of young children should be scaled down. This can be achieved in three ways. First, by adjusting the taxable income by a fixed allowance per child, by reducing the rate of tax for parents and increasing the tax relief by a certain amount per child. The net result of such measures would be that parents liable to pay income tax will be left with more money to bring home for the use of the child; an arrangement that is more likely to improve the standard of living for the Kenyan child.

2   WAIVING CONSUMPTION TAXES AND DUTY ON CHILDREN'S SUPPLIES

Consumption taxes should also be reviewed to take into account children's needs. Taxes on consumption have a bearing on the prices of those commodities comprising the tax base. They are indirect taxes that merchants pass on to the ultimate buyer. In Kenya, the main consumption tax is the Value Added Tax, hereinafter referred to as VAT. The VAT Act (Cap 476) does not recognise the need of the State to waive VAT on children's care supplies. VAT on childcare products should be reduced or abolished. Child care services and products such as nappies, clothes, shoes, food, blankets, drugs, and other medical supplies should be zero-rated for VAT purposes. That would make them more easily purchasable by the carers of the child.

Similarly, child care services must be subsidised to make them more affordable to children: medical services such as ante-natal and post-natal maternity care and childcare should be charged at lower rates to support families with children.

Moreover, where any childcare supplies have to be imported or manufactured, then all duties chargeable such as customs and excise duties should be charged. By these measures things required by those with the care of children would be made cheaper to buy.

3   DIRECT PAYMENTS AND BENEFIT

Not all parents will benefit from cuts in income tax. There is a need to provide direct financial and material assistance to families with children as a way of implementing the financial security rights of children. The main area of assistance should be nutrition. Presently, the Kenyan Government, in partnership with a number of NGOs, has school feeding programmes in arid and semi-arid areas (ASAL).[34] In the totally arid districts of the Moyale, Samburu, Turkana, Isiolo,

---

34   *The First Country Report on the Implementation of the UN Convention on the Rights of the Child 1998* p 27.

Mandera, Wajir, Garissa, Tana River and Marsabit, all school-going children in primary and pre-primary schools get lunch daily. While this is a good start, it can hardly be said to be adequate. Quite apart from the possibility that the food ration of one meal a day might not be enough, the food benefit is given directly to the child at school. This leaves out a large percentage of hungry children who are below pre-primary school age, for constant experience shows that from the time the new-born baby leaves the nursery to the time it is able to recite a chorus, it would have guzzled a considerable fortune in food and other care items.

It is submitted that this direct feeding initiative should be supplemented by a child support benefit to be dispensed as follows: families with children whose aggregate income falls below a certain level, say Kshs 10,000 per month should be entitled to 'food supplement' in the form of 'food stamps' or 'food vouchers' acceptable at suitable food stores. A food voucher of Kshs 3,000 per month for each child for parents whose aggregate income falls below Kshs 10,000 would certainly bring more food to the table for the Kenyan child. Alternatively, the benefit could be dispensed in cash, provided that the recipient signs an undertaking to apply it to the best interests of the child and to fully account for it.

C State assistance with child support: the German approach[35]

German law and practice on child care recognises that the upbringing and education of children entails a considerable financial burden on the family. The Federal Child Benefit Act 1986 was passed to ease that burden. Under this Act, parents or guardians are currently paid a child benefit for each child up to the age of 16, and for those children at school or undergoing vocational training, up to the age of 27.

The benefit, in 1995 was DM 70 per month for the first child, DM 130 for the second, DM 220 for the third, and DM 240 for each additional child. For parents in the higher income brackets, the child benefit is lower from the second child onwards.

Moreover, the Act provides for the payment of a child-raising benefit of DM 600 per month to every mother, for the first six months of each child's life, after which the benefit is varied, depending on the parents' income. German parents also enjoy tax relief in form of an annual Child Allowance of DM 4,104.

Such is the level of commitment of the German State and society to the financial support rights of the child. It is submitted that the German approach most closely approximates to the standards of the Convention and should be considered for adoption in this country.

D Expanding the States' capacities: a new child support levy?

The Convention recognises the practical limitations of some States and provides that the implementation of the right of the child to financial support by States shall be subject to their capacities. But this country cannot be heard to plead self-

---

35 The following account is taken from Peter Hoffmann (ed) *Facts About Germany* 1996 (Frankfurt/ Main, Societäts-Verlag), pp 351–352.

induced limitations of its capability to fulfil its financial support obligations to the child. At least, we can reduce tax on parents' income and also lower VAT on children's supplies. If we cannot pay cash benefits to families in need of income support for children, we can deposit money in food stores and pay it out in the form of food supplement vouchers. That can be the Kenyan way of taking a bold step towards better implementation of financial support rights.

Recently, it has been reported that 11,423 hungry primary school children in Kitui District in Eastern Province have deserted school because of famine.[36] If our children drop out of school because they have nothing to eat, then where are we heading? Unless urgent measures are taken to reverse this trend, we might be on the brink of a national catastrophe. The security of human resources of this country is a matter of paramount importance. While it may be appreciated that the proposed measures to secure financial support for children will demand a heavy financial allocation, I argue that such a venture is an absolutely necessary investment. It justifies measures to expand the national capacity to provide money for child support through the introduction of new taxes and levies.

For this reason, I suggest that a new tax to be known as 'the Child Support Levy' be introduced immediately to require every eligible person to contribute to the cost of raising the next generation of Kenya's workforce. The new child support levy could be imposed on certain luxuries like alcohol, cigarettes, casinos, cinema, sports goods etc and collected as a consumption tax. Also, the child support levy should be included in income tax for the upper income brackets. This would increase the tax revenue and allocation of this money would be administered by the proposed Child Support Agency which would disburse the child support benefit to qualifying families.

As to the argument that such benefits would undermine the current programmes for family planning and encourage people to have more children than they can afford to maintain and then become a burden to the welfare scheme, I would argue that there is an obligation to support families in raising children no matter how many children they might have.

It would be a mistake to imagine that the duty of parents to maintain children is entirely a private headache. Parents are only but trustees of the social investment in children and the entire society has a legal duty to assist them to perform the responsibility of raising children. Since there is a public interest in the well-being of children, parents in maintaining their children are discharging a public function, a service to the nation.[37] John Eekelaar is certainly right when he asserts that rather than parents only, the entire society is morally (and should therefore be legally) obliged to maintain its children.[38]

---

36 "Schools Deserted over Food" *Daily Nation*, Nairobi 27 May 2000, p 24.

37 John Eekelaar, 'What is Critical Family Law?' (1989) vol 105 *Law Quarterly Review* 244, at pp 254–258.

38 John Eekelaar, 'Are parents morally obliged to care for their children?' (1991) 6 *Oxford Journal of Legal Studies* 340.

V   THE OBLIGATION OF THE INTERNATIONAL COMMUNITY

While the Convention declares that responsibility for financial support of children is upon parents and States, that is only one side of the coin. There is the international dimension to this question in which the international community may have a moral and even legal obligation to support the world's children. Let me explain this point a bit further.

A   International security service

Chapter VII of the UN Charter of 1945 establishes rules and procedures to restore and maintain international peace and security. Article 43(1) provides that: 'all members of the United Nations, in order to contribute to international peace and security undertake to make available to the Security Council, on its call ... armed forces, assistance and facilities including rights of passage, necessary for the purpose of maintaining peace and security'.

Leaving aside the active combat military operations, the main concern of the UN is peace-keeping. At the moment, the UN has three major peace-keeping missions in the world: Kosovo (9,000 troops), East Timor (9,000 troops) and Sierra Leone (13,000 troops). In military logistics, numbers matter. Now, the UN Charter cannot work without men to move the tanks and launch and parry missiles. International peace and security and the success of the UN missions depend on the availability [on the right side of the political divide] of competent people – the international security staff to do these military jobs for the cause of the UN. Increasingly, developing countries (particularly India, South Africa, Kenya and Nigeria) have demonstrated ability and willingness to commit their troops for these UN missions. To leave the task of raising such international military staff to their families and nations alone would amount to abdication of a primary responsibility on the part of the international community, particularly the developed countries.

Similar arguments could also be made for the international civil service, which includes the regular staff of the international organisations as well as the emergency aid staff who handle humanitarian relief operations.

B   Creating a context for international co-operation

Now, the UN Convention envisages a role for the international community in the implementation of economic, social and cultural rights of children by making reference to 'the framework of international co-operation ...' However, it is the duty of the Convention countries to take the lead and start programmes and arrangements that establish a context for the international community to assist local initiatives to enhance the financial support rights of the child.

This understanding could provide a basis for bold steps to introduce a universal social welfare scheme for the Kenyan child, with a view to sourcing funds for the scheme from our own national endowment (which is by no means lean) and our collaborators abroad in the framework of international co-operation.[39]

VI CONCLUSION

In 1990, this country ratified the Convention and committed itself to observe the Convention's norms and standards.[40] Ten years on, we must ask what legal developments[41] have been achieved in this country, in response to the call of the Convention's international consensus on what the child should have in a progressive society. Leaving aside the hackneyed excuses of 'economic constraints of a developing country', it is submitted that the wide gap of difference between the national law and the letter of the Convention is evidence that things are not right. One of the main objectives of this paper is to point out the inadequacies in our law and advocate the cause for comprehensive reform of child support law in this country. Things cannot go on in this unsatisfactory manner for ever. There is need for urgent policy review and law reform in this area.

It is important to concede here that reform of the law alone without favourable developments in the material circumstances of this country will only at best deliver paper rights, without any tangible impact at all. However, law reform should be appreciated as an important and first step in the right direction, for four reasons. First, the package entailed in the proposed Child Support Act will help us trace absent parents and have them pay their part of child support. In addition, the proposed child support regime will create agencies, and establish measures, procedures and sanctions for better enforcement and implementation of child support rights in private law. That would deal with the glaring omissions in our current family law.

Secondly, its public law facet will source and allocate more money to families with children by increasing the State's financial capacity to provide for this need through the imposition of new fund raising tax regimes such as the child support levy. It will also effect major adjustments in fiscal policies to benefit children through reducing income tax chargeable on parents, and waiving VAT on children's supplies, giving 'food supplements', disbursing child benefits and allowances and so forth.

Thirdly, it will stake a new and major claim for children, on the national cake. This will put pressure on the State to explore means and ways of exploiting our untapped natural and human resources to produce more wealth to meet these formidable needs. For without such pressing claims on resources, they might continue to be underdeveloped as the nation idly waits for a donor miracle to

---

39 Article 45 of the UN Convention identifies specialised agencies such as the United Nations Children's fund as possible partners with Convention countries in these matters.

40 See the Government of Kenya, Ministry of Home Affairs and National Heritage, *First Country Report on the Implementation of United Nations Convention on the Rights of the Child 1998.*

41 Since 1989, there has not been any legislation on children's rights or generally affecting children. The old Neo-English colonial statutes such as the Legitimacy Act (Cap. 145) and the Children and Young Persons Act (Cap. 141) retained at independence are still law in force in this country. The traditional ideas have not been altered.

happen. All these are the tangible benefits we stand to gain by the proposed child care law.

Fourthly, the new child support law would of course play on educational role: it would express the norms and values of a progressive society and convey our moral philosophy of the rights of the child. It would reshape the way our society thinks about and treats children in the right direction.

In this paper, I have shown the mistakes we have made in failing to make provision for effective measures to enforce parents' financial responsibility towards their children and for the State's financial assistance to families with children. I have compared the approaches in other jurisdictions on these issues and suggested how these could be considered to inform our search for principles in child support law. It would be in the best interests of the Kenyan child and the social security rights of the inhabitants of this country that reform of our child support law and policy as suggested in this paper be considered a legislative project of high priority.

MALTA

IT'S ALL HAPPENING IN FAMILY LAW IN MALTA

*Ruth Farrugia**

After years of mulling over the utility of amending laws that seemed to be working quite happily, Malta has finally taken the plunge and decided to go for a comprehensive overhaul of the entire system relating to family law. Considering that, in the main, our law is based firmly in Roman principles dating back two thousand years with the odd amendment thanks to Napoleon, bated breath has turned into a strangled cry for fresh air!

I   FAMILY COURT ACT[1]

Perhaps the most fundamental change is expected through the enactment and enforcement of changes to the Family Court System.

At present all issues pertaining to family law are dealt with in the Second Hall of the Civil Court and in the First Hall of the Civil Court sitting as a Family Court. The Second Hall was set up under Roman Law principles as a court of voluntary jurisdiction and entrusted with the adjudication of applications regarding adoption, separation of community property, interdiction, tutorship and curatorship. Since that time, it has evolved into a court, which authorises separation[2] and gives decrees regarding provisional maintenance, allocation of the matrimonial home and care and custody of children as well as discharging its original tasks.

Once applicants to Second Hall move on the contentious arena of First Hall, cases grouped together because of their 'family law' content are adjudicated in the civil court. Over the years, it has become apparent that judges presiding in this court require considerable support from disciplines outside the legal system and considerable efforts from various groups have resulted in the appointment of psychologists, social workers, conciliators, mediators and a whole range of people qualified to lessen the trauma associated with the court process.[3]

However, appointment of such ancillary personnel remains discretionary and the procedure outlined by the law makes no reference to its existence. Although it

---

*   Advocate and Lecturer in Civil Law, University of Malta.

1   The author was a member of the first Commission to Set Up a Family Court whose report was concluded in 1997. Since that time, the present (new) Minister for Justice has included several amendments to the initial proposals and issued an additional Family Court brief in 1999.

2   Malta has still not introduced divorce legislation although it does recognise a divorce given by the judgement of a foreign court.

3   In an adoption case, the court will now automatically notify the Department of Family Welfare who will send a social worker to monitor the placement. This is pursuant to a Legal Notice containing such a regulation. In the case of determining custody allocation, the court is not bound by such regulation and is at liberty to decide whether to request help.

is up to the judge to decide whether or not to nominate an expert such as a psychologist or psychiatrist to assist in reaching a judgment, referring spouses and/or parents to conciliation and mediation is outside his remit.[4]

In fact one of the greatest points of debate centred on whether counselling services and conciliation should be mandatory prior to access to court proceedings. At first, the suggestion was to enforce a six-month cooling off period within which the spouses would be booked into marital therapy sessions. If the sessions failed, then the couple would be allocated a date for first hearing.

The objections to this were obvious and many. Although the principle of helping the spouses to iron out their differences was perceived as well intentioned it was not considered realistic. The majority of people who seek separation have thought long and hard about it and to consider their actions as being the result of a whim is insulting, to say the least. Some spouses may seek separation on the grounds of violence. In this case, the six-month period would not be sufficient for the offending spouse to follow a perpetrator's programme,[5] even taking for granted that he would wish to and that the injured spouse would be interested in continuing the relationship.[6]

Another objection came from the counsellors themselves who, while welcoming the weight given to their input, could not envisage working with people who were forced to attend sessions rather than spouses who came freely because of their interest in making their marriage work. The conclusion has been to encourage strongly spouses to seek marital therapy and to make access to such services and conciliation services far easier than before.[7] Time will tell whether this reaches the desired goals.[8]

Once in court, the proposal is to provide mediation where possible to enable spouses to agree where to disagree and only to refer the rest for court judgment. At present, where the spouses agree on two out of three bones of contention, proceedings are invariably instituted on all three grounds with substantial loss of time and effort all round. As studies have shown that agreements reached by the couple last longer and are honoured far more effectively than any decisions imposed by the court, mediation has reached an all time high in the court popularity ratings.[9]

---

4   The issue of who will foot the bill for these ancillary services is also unresolved. To date, the State picks up the greater part of the tab, but suggestions have been put forward to attempt recovery of dues where possible.

5   The Domestic Violence Act is proposing the mandatory pursuit of a perpetrator's programme, failing which penal sanctions should automatically apply.

6   Barbara Hart, 'Gentle Jeopardy: The Further Endangerment of Battered Women and Children in Custody Mediation', 7 *Mediation Quarterly*, 317, 1990; Douglas Knowlton and Tara Muhlhauser, 'Mediation in the presence of Domestic Violence: Is it the Light at the End of the Tunnel or Is it a Train on the Track?', *North Dakota Law Review*, Vol 70, 1994.

7   It has also been suggested that all professions involved be ethically obliged to make a strong suggestion for marital therapy where possible. As this attitude has long been practised, the implication that it was a new idea did not sit well in several quarters.

8   For the debate on mandatory and voluntary mediation see David Winston, 'Participation Standards in Mandatory Mediation Statutes: You Can Lead a Horse to Water ...', 11(1) *Ohio St. Journal on Dispute Resolution* 187, 1996; G Thomas Eisele, 'No To Mandatory Court-Annexed ADR, Litigation', Vol 18 No 1, Fall 1991.

9   Forrest Mosten, *The Complete Guide to Mediation: The Cutting Edge Approach to Family Law Practice*, American Bar Association, 1997, p 66 et seq; L Boulle, J Jones and V Goldblatt,

However, the family court does not only deal with spousal disagreement. It is responsible for a wide range of subjects principally focusing on children and must therefore make provision for this facet of its application. The proposed Family Court will be taking on responsibility for children placed under a care order and for the ongoing monitoring of all children removed from parental responsibility.[10] At present an administrative procedure in conjunction with the Juvenile Court deals with part of the issue[11] and it is felt that placing the burden on the Family Court will send a clear message that this is a family issue which should be resolved within one court setting.

However, this will mean that the Family Court will also exercise criminal as well as civil jurisdiction. Many lawyers have found a problem with this notion holding that the two should be kept distinct. In rejoinder, the Juvenile Court[12] has long functioned with concurrent jurisdiction and it can surely only be beneficial to have a court seized of all facets of the case rather than several courts dealing with the issues piecemeal.

Take the case of a couple who are requesting authorisation to separate in the Second Hall[13] while the husband has initiated proceedings for repudiation of a child in the First Hall[14] and the police are prosecuting the husband for violence in yet another court.[15] The conjoined Family Court will be able to deal with all these issues and save time and money all round while listening to the parties in one case. Again, only time will tell whether this will work well in practice.

Finally, another consideration of great importance within amendments to the Family Court concerns the hearing of children. Sadly, this aspect has been shelved pending further study,[16] so children will continue to be heard in conditions which are hardly conducive to their well-being. Whether the child is called as a witness or as a party to the proceedings, provision must be made to cause them the least possible trauma. The Children Act makes suggestions for the right of the child to

---

Mediation Principles, Process, Practice, New Zealand, Butterworths, 1998; Bennett Wolff, 'The Best Interest of the Divorcing Family – Mediation and Not Litigation', 29 *Loyola Law Review*, 55, 1993, *National Working Party on Mediation, Guidelines for Family Mediation – Developing Services in Aotearoa, New Zealand*, Butterworths, 1996, Joan Kelly, 'Is Mediation Less Expensive? Comparison of Mediated and Adversarial Divorce Costs', *Mediation Quarterly*, Vol 8 No 1 Fall 1990.

10　Also referred to in Parts VI and VII of the draft Children Act.

11　Laws of Malta, Chapter 285.

12　Laws of Malta, Chapter 287.

13　Malta still has no law on divorce although it recognises a divorce from a foreign court judgement. The separation process starts in the Court of Voluntary Jurisdiction, the Second Hall of the Civil Court where the spouses request authorisation to proceed to separation and the judge has a duty to determine whether there is any possibility of a reconciliation. Laws of Malta, Chapter 16, section 37.

14　The proceedings for repudiation signify that the father must bring proof according to law to show that the child registered as his, on the birth certificate, is not truly his child. All such cases are a matter for contentious jurisdiction and are heard before the First Hall of the Civil Court. Laws of Malta Chapter 16, sections 70–77.

15　This would be a matter for the criminal courts.

16　A Commission was set up in 1997 to study the possibility of amendments to the law in the taking of evidence from children. It would appear that the work of the Commission was suspended in 1998 and has not been resumed.

be represented[17] and to be enabled to make such representations in a way which does not impinge on his /her well-being, but the two Acts must work together.

II   THE CHILDREN ACT

What started out as a round-up of legislation relating to children resulted in a mammoth document containing all present legislation about children, amendments to laws which were not in keeping with the UN Convention on the Rights of the Child, fresh legislation to enable monitoring and implementation and the introduction of some ideas which might be deemed controversial in some quarters.[18]

A   Rights

The Act is based on the premise that children are persons in their own right[19], that a family is the preferred environment for the care and upbringing of children and that the state and entire community together have a responsibility to assist families in this objective.[20]

Substantial changes are put forward, with the definition of parental responsibility supplanting the Roman Law parental authority which is still in place in the year 2000, as this is being written.[21] Once the notion of responsibility is introduced, other amendments should follow as a matter of course, placing the emphasis on parents providing care and protection for their children rather than being endowed with power over them.[22]

---

17   An entire part of the proposed Act deals with the setting up of the office of the child advocate who would be responsible to represent the child in all court proceedings. Although this has been criticised as 'too much representation', it is felt that an impartial party should help the child decide on representation. Allowing the appointment as a discretionary measure on the pleas of one of the parents defeats the whole object of the exercise.

18   It totals 440 articles spread out under 12 headings. The author was commissioned to draft the Children Act by the Ministry for Social Policy and completed the task together with a small team of five in November 1999.

19   Malta, like most of the world, barring Somalia and the USA, has ratified the United Nations Convention on the Rights of the Child and the Convention was used as the basis for many of the provisions proposed in the Children Act. The author also defended the report of Malta to the United Nations Committee on the Convention of the Rights of the Child in Geneva in May 2000 where many provisions of the proposed Children Act were discussed.

20   Section 2(1), (2), (3) proposed.

21   Laws of Malta Chapter 16, sections 131–156.

22   This issue has been placed under the microscope in Malta with recent events in September/October 2000. The case of the conjoined twins born in England who were the subject of a highly controversial court case are the children of parents from Malta's small sister island, Gozo. The newspapers, radio and television have avidly sought anyone and everyone for an opinion with the general consensus indicating that the parents are the only persons capable of making a decision in the best interests of their children. The recourse to the courts and subsequent proceedings have been largely perceived as gross intervention and not as an attempt to serve the best interests of the children. The statements issued by the Roman Catholic Church in Gozo have strongly opposed separation of the babies on the grounds that such an act would be the wilful taking of a life and have also commented that parents know best. Throughout the proceedings, the parents were portrayed as hailing from some far-flung State with scant medical facilities and primitive support for the disabled as well as being the potential subjects of victimisation through

One section, which is sure to raise debate, is the proposal to protect the child from 'physical chastisement'. Smacking is still part of many a parent's reaction to the unco-operative child and, although many people feel quite strongly that physical retaliation does little to teach the child (other than that it is acceptable for adults to lash out in times of anger), many parents will have a problem with being told they can no longer administer a short, sharp slap.[23]

B   Care orders

Incorporated into the law are sections dealing with services for children and their families together with a responsibility on the State to make provision for a number of support structures.[24] If the aim is to ensure that children grow up in their family, all efforts must be made to assist those families rather than provide intervention when it is too late. At present, children are taken into care under a care order in cases where the parent/s are unable or unwilling to provide the care and protection essential to the child's development and well-being.[25] This service has been expanded and clarified in the draft Act but more emphasis has been placed on the variety of measures that should be taken before such a drastic measure is implemented.[26]

On the other side of the coin, the law is amended to include provision for termination of parental responsibility in a wider range of circumstances.[27] Although all efforts should be made to attempt reunification where families are experiencing difficulty, the law must proceed in favour of an alternative family for the child where such reunification is not forthcoming. To date, many children remain in residential care simply at the leisure of their parents. This is clearly unacceptable and while every help should be given to encourage and support parents to take care of their children, if this is not possible, children should not be subjected to watching their childhood pass them by.

To ensure that each person is clear about the responsibility the law imposes, the draft suggests clear guidelines with established dates for hearings before the court.[28] Once the case has started, time frames start to run for the convening of a case conference with the conclusion of a care plan for the child. Changes to the initial plan and subsequent case reviews are to be notified to the court and a date set for the termination of parental responsibility should the parents be unable or

---

superstition and/or religious opinion. Although I find popular opinion on parental rights questionable, I can understand its motivation. What is extremely objectionable is the slur cast on an island where the disabled are greatly supported and accorded their rights and where medical treatment has an excellent record and is even patronised by patients from the richer Middle Eastern countries seeking open heart surgery, for example.

23   At present the law permits 'reasonable chastisement' which has been interpreted restrictively. (The term is cited from Chapter 16, section 154 which deals with termination of parental authority on exceeding the bounds of reasonable chastisement.)

24   Part V, proposed.

25   Laws of Malta, Chapter 285, the Children and Young Persons (Care Orders) Act.

26   Part VI, proposed.

27   This is referred to in greater detail later in the paper.

28   The proposal is to ensure that at the very limit a final decision regarding a child is taken within one year. To many, this is still too long a time, but efforts to accommodate children's rights and parental rights resulted in this time frame.

unwilling to care for the child. The parents are to be notified of the consequence of their actions but the burden is now on them to prove interest rather than simply on the court which must still prove the contrary.[29]

To assist the court in this evaluation and monitoring, the present Children and Young Persons (Care Orders) Board will be transformed into a Children's Panel, taking on additional responsibility for juvenile offenders.[30] The proceedings of the Children's Panel are a cross between the New Zealand and Scottish counterparts, although they are based in the already long serving Care Orders Board.[31]

C   Foster care

Important additions are suggested in the advent of legislation to govern fostering and residential care.[32] These areas are largely unregulated at present with some incidental legal notices covering their application. The draft proposes their incorporation into a duly recognised area of alternative care. The setting up of foster care agencies and standards of selection for foster carers together with the responsibilities of all parties concerned are clearly enunciated in the draft.

The only issue, which may cause some debate, is that attached to payment for foster carers.[33] To date, foster carers receive no direct payment for the service they provide. Although the statutory children's allowance may be received by those carers whose salary falls below the maximum due for such allowance, in reality the greater part of those providing foster care have an income over this threshold.[34] The State exempts payment for examination fees due by children in foster care and has recently approved leave for public service employees to take parental leave when they are providing foster care, but otherwise no financial support has been forthcoming.

At a recent meeting held for foster carers,[35] the overwhelming majority of those present made it very clear that they disagreed with a salary for the care they provided but they did expect bills for health, education and transport to be settled by the State. The fear seems to be that foster care will be perceived as a business rather than the vocation it has always been assumed to be. However, in today's world, the sheer economic drawback of footing the bill for an extra child has made foster care the option only for those who can afford it. The draft suggests financial support for foster carers both in recognition of the service they provide and also in

---

29   It will be 'interesting' when the first case is contested on the grounds that the parent(s) did not receive adequate support to enable reunification.

30   The functions of the Children's Panel are clearly set out in Part VI and Part VII of the proposed Act.

31   Laws of Malta, Chapter 285. The Board sits every other week and hears cases relating to children placed under a care order. The recommendations of the Board are made following review of reports from all professionals involved and after hearing the children, parents, social worker(s) and all other interested parties.

32   Part VIII entitled Alternative Care.

33   Although the Children and Young Persons (Care Orders) Act does provide for some compensation to any family to whom a child under a care order is entrusted.

34   Reply to a recent Parliamentary Question.

35   The Care Orders Board held an extremely well-attended meeting open to all foster carers (including carers of children under a care order) in October 1999 and invited the Minister for Social Policy to address the meeting and listen to the opinion of the participants.

a bid to increase the number of people prepared to provide a home for children who would otherwise languish in residential care.

D   Residential care

Because of the situation in foster care and the reluctance of the prospective adopters to apply for adoption where no freeing process yet exists, residential care is a sad fact of life.[36] In the greater part it is provided by religious orders that have been a selfless contributor to child care over the past century. With dwindling numbers of vocations and escalating costs, many homes have closed down or resorted to the State for financial aid.

In the greater part, the State has recognised its responsibility to help both financially, as well as in kind, but in return it has imposed standards of care which were hitherto left to the discretion of the director of the residential care facility. As this is being written, a series of seminars and conferences are coming to their culmination with a national conference on standards of care in residential child care set for 31 October 2000. The hope is to produce the final draft of a document setting standards and providing support in the provision of services.[37] For the first time, due attention is paid to the voice of the child and the rights of children within the residential care setting. The draft Act includes many of the standards set out in the document and will make their observance a matter for the law and an inspectorate still to be appointed.

The situation at present consists of children being placed in residential care either voluntarily or as the subject of a care order. In the first case, the parent(s) may be in need of respite care in which circumstances they prefer to place their children temporarily with a religious order than ask for an alternative family to provide care. Alternatively, parents may simply leave their children to be cared for in a residential home pending the completion of their own agenda. Many children's homes now refuse direct admission and refer parents to their social work centre. In extreme cases, the principle remains that no child should ever be refused care, although there have been increasing numbers of children with behavioural problems who are denied admission.[38]

The reasons for resorting to residential care are mainly cultural, but also dependent on the scarcity of foster carers prepared to provide care on a short-term basis. Maltese people seem to have a genuine difficulty with caring for children and letting go. The notion of providing care is easily and almost universally accepted, but once contact is established the relationship becomes more difficult to break and, distances being as small as they are, the problem becomes compounded.

---

36   The author acknowledges the sincere and genuine support and loving environment residential homes continue to offer their children. However, the religious orders who run the homes are themselves the first to admit that they can be no real substitute for a family.

37   The first such draft document was discussed in a closed seminar in June 2000.

38   This resulted in the setting up of the only state run residential care facility called Fejda, which takes in female adolescents with behavioural difficulties. The programmes they offer have been largely successful and were chosen for their excellence in a pilot project of the Council of Europe earlier this year.

There is also the staunch religious tradition which influences many parents to trust the religious orders implicitly and to be clear that their children will be returned with no alternative parent having made any lasting impression on their mode of upbringing for the child. The Fostering Team[39] has been trying very hard to convince parents that foster care is not tantamount to adoption but the process is slow, even though many religious orders themselves encourage placement in a family as they are conscious of the effects of residential care on children.

Some residential care homes are small and friendly and really do resemble a family unit, except that where they are run by nuns there is no father figure and vice versa. Others, which are larger in size, have made genuine efforts to create artificially small units but old fashioned buildings, limited resources and the lack of uniform guidelines often made these attempts a haphazard affair. It is hoped that the outcome of the standards conference and the draft legislation will do much to ameliorate the situation.

E   Adoption

Amendments to adoption law[40] are dealt with within the draft mainly on two issues of concern, namely the freeing process and the elimination of private adoptions. Other sections set up a contact and counselling facility and regulate the adoption panels, which are to date functioning in an administrative limbo.[41]

The vast majority of adoptions in Malta are of children who come from overseas. In 1999, there were nine local babies given up for adoption and fourteen times that number adopted from abroad. Malta has adoption agreements with Romania and Albania, but couples also adopt from countries such as Pakistan and Brazil where Maltese missionaries help in making contact. Although adoptions finalised in the country of origin are screened by the courts and decreed applicable locally,[42] there do arise problems when the child has not been taken into adoption by persons who have been through the requisite screening process.

For instance, in the case of adoptions from Romania the child may only be placed after a home study report has been finalised by the Department of Family Welfare, together with a longer list of conditions.[43] In the case of the baby from

---

39   The Social Work Development Programme has recently upgraded its fostering service and doubled its complement of social workers in efforts to encourage more foster carers to undergo training.

40   The existing sections are found in the Civil Code: sections 113–130.

41   The Adoption panel is set up to make recommendation to the Director of Family Welfare following the appraisal of the home study report and presentation of the social worker. Although this is unlikely, the Director could refuse the recommendation and direct otherwise, as the Panel has no legal standing. Also objection to the recommendation of the Panel is not provided for except through direct objection to the Director of Family Welfare administratively.

42   Either by a fresh adoption application or by requesting the registration of the overseas adoption through the Ministry for Foreign Affairs. This latter alternative involves the publication of details relating to the adopters and the child in the *Government Gazette* and, mainly for this reason, is not popular.

43   These are detailed in the Bilateral agreement on inter-country adoption between Malta and Romania concluded in 1998. One such condition particular to the agreement provides for a visit by the Romanian Adoption Committee during the first year of the child's placement. One presumes that dissatisfaction with the conditions would result in termination of further adoption placements.

Pakistan, this is not essential and the private placement of the child may result in its being cared for by a person who would not otherwise be recommended to adopt.

The real problem arises when the prospective adopters choose to go to court to legalise the adoption and the court discovers that, although the legal requisites have not been adhered to, the child has been living in this new environment for a long period and his/her removal would cause additional trauma.[44]

Where the issue is age,[45] provisional placement pending adoption has been applied. But when the adopters are found to be undesirable to adopt the courts have to make the decision whether to place the child in residential care pending an alternative placement inevitably causing hardship for all concerned.

In the past couple of years, the police at immigration have also been instructed to exercise caution over the entry of children who have not been granted a visa. In the case of the Pakistani baby mentioned, the authorities would know nothing of the child's existence until s/he reaches the airport. But so far, no child has been returned to the country of origin, which would usually occur on humanitarian grounds. Until the law makes it clear that no child will be allowed entry unless the prospective adopters have authorisation and the application for screening is effected prior to taking a child into care with a view to adoption, potential catastrophes will continue to happen.

The notion of curtailing private adoption has already generated controversy with some lawyers arguing that a parent should have every right to entrust their child to whomever they wish. It is hard to follow the logic of this reasoning, particularly when it is common knowledge that babies can – and seem to be – traded for money in this way[46] and placed in homes where they are not always assured of a happy, healthy and safe family life.

The freeing process is linked to the issue of termination of parental rights. At present, children are often not given up for adoption on the pretext that their birth parents cannot bear to see them enter into another family and lose all legal ties.[47] The same birth parents are quite happy to let their children grow up in residential care with only the occasional phone call or visit to establish contact. While the Children Act is strongly in favour of keeping families together, it is equally strong in making alternative provision for children who do not have a family.

---

44 In a recent case of *Application of F* (Second Hall of the Civil Court), the adopter claimed to have been married to her partner for the requisite five years when requesting placement of a child through a Maltese missionary in Pakistan. The child was duly brought to Malta and an application for adoption was made two years later. Even at that late date, the adoption could not be decreed because the prospective adopters were not married and had been living together for three years, the prospective adoptive father was married but separated and had no consent from his wife and the prospective adoptive mother who could adopt on her own had not reached the age of 30. The case was finally decided in October 2000 by authorising the adoption, as this was the only solution in the child's best interests.

45 Civil Code: adoption is only permissible where at least one of a couple or the sole adopter has reached the age of 30 but not the age of 60.

46 It is a criminal offence to do so under Maltese law and the civil sanction may involve the child being entrusted to an alternative placement.

47 As chairperson of the Care Orders Board since February 1999, I have heard this argument vaunted on several occasions.

The proposal is therefore to make clear time frames for parents[48] to take over the care of their children and to provide all necessary support to assist this in happening. Where the parent remains unable and/or unwilling to take the steps necessary to care for the child and the time frame has elapsed, then the child should be declared by the court as free to be adopted. The courts are empowered, at present, to dispense with the consent of parents, which is otherwise usually vital in the granting of adoption.[49]

However, the process requires prospective adopters to take the risk that the courts will consider the parents' actions sufficient to justify the overriding of such lack of consent. Even though the powers of the judge are very wide in the dispensation of consent, it is far from the norm for judges to override parental consent and there have been cases where application has been made and the parent has been instrumental in halting the proceedings.[50] The freeing process would encourage many prospective adopters to take on the care of children without subjecting themselves to a most terrible trauma if things go wrong.

In addition to this suggestion is the amendment to include the concept of open adoption where this is of benefit to the child. Unofficially, social workers have been known to make available to birth parents periodic photos of children sent by their adopters and on the rare occasion, even contact has been sanctioned. In a country as small as Malta, the need for the imposition of confidentiality and the true severance of contact has always been perceived as essential. The birth parents could – and on occasion have – made life extremely unpleasant for the child and the adoptive parents. However, this should not be taken to mean that contact is contraindicated in all cases, particularly where the child to be adopted is older than the more usual baby.[51]

Measures are also proposed for the setting up of a tracing facility within the adoption service.[52] At present, social workers are very helpful in attempting to facilitate communication between children who have been adopted (once they

---

48   Referred to at footnote 29.

49   Civil Code, section 117: a. where the person required to give consent is incapable, cannot be found, has abandoned, neglected or persistently ill-treated or neglected or refused to contribute to the maintenance of the person to be adopted or has demanded or attempted to obtain payment for the granting of consent;

     - omissis -

     b. in view of special and exceptional reasons and taking into account the interests of all persons concerned, it is proper to dispense with any such hearing and consent.

50   In *re A* (Second Hall Civil Court), the child was placed with prospective adopters who were told that the boy was the child of an unwed mother and unknown father. Because of a series of mishaps, the proceedings took much longer than usual and a year later the 'unknown' father appeared to claim the child. The child was forcibly taken from the prospective adopters and placed with the man who had, by that time, acknowledged the child as his son.

51   Recent studies [as in the unpublished theses on Inter-country Adoption, by M Portelli (Social Work) and Legal Aspects of Cross Country Adoption by J Pace (Laws) both 2000] have shown that children who are aware of their background are more settled than their counterparts kept in the dark. Knowledge about birth parents and information as to health is now deemed of vital importance and the Malta/Romania agreement includes provision for a record book for the child relating ethnic background by means of photos, documents and notes taken by all persons who provided care.

52   Part IX proposed Act.

reach the age of 18)[53] and their birth parents or vice versa. The proposal is to make the provision of this service mandatory and to ensure that adequate counselling services are also made available in support.

F   Termination of parental rights

Perhaps one of the most controversial steps the law proposes is the termination of parental rights for a far wider range of reasons than ever before. At present, the parent(s) may have their authority removed when:[54]

(1)   the parent, exceeding the bounds of reasonable chastisement, ill-treats the child or neglects his education;
(2)   if the conduct of the parent is such as to endanger the education of the child;
(3)   if the parent is interdicted ...;
(4)   if the parent mismanages the property of the child;
(5)   if the parent fails to perform any of the obligations set out in section 3B in favour of the child [3B says: 'Marriage imposes on both spouses the obligation to look after, maintain, instruct and educate the children of the marriage taking into account the abilities, natural inclinations and aspirations of the children'].

The Act suggests the enlargement of the grounds[55] and includes:

(1)   abandonment of the child for a period of not less than three months;
(2)   inability of parental care through mental illness, substance abuse;
(3)   actual or attempted physical, sexual and/or mental abuse of the child or evidenced maltreatment to a sibling;
(4)   child exhibits severe emotional damage only protected by removal from physical custody of parents;
(5)   child has been cared for by alternative carer over long period of time and forced removal would cause child serious psychological harm which parent(s) have no capacity to cope with;
(6)   child left wilfully in foster care for period of more than 12 months with no progress made towards reunification;
(7)   reasonable efforts leading to rehabilitation with parents have failed.

The Act requires these factors to be taken into account by the court, together with considerations as to:

(a)   failure of parent(s) to provide maintenance, according to their means;
(b)   failure to maintain regular visits agreed to by parents;
(c)   failure to maintain consistent contact or communication with child;

---

53   According to law, any person may request access to personal original birth records on reaching the age of 18. However, no provision is made for the offer of counselling and/or support prior to this step.
54   Civil Code, section 154.
55   Section 31.

(d)   failure of parent(s) to attempt to meet the needs of child notwithstanding offer or receipt of services to achieve this goal.

After all the above factors are taken into account the court will then consider whether termination of parental responsibility is in fact in the child's best interests and so decree.

There are other conditions and variations dealt with under the proposals all aiming to ensure that children receive the parental care which the law considers their due right. In a culture which still deems children to be subject to their parents' authority, these amendments will undoubtedly raise the biggest popular outcry in many quarters.

G   Legitimacy

Finally the issue which consensus shows has become a non-issue should be resolved once and for all, with the Children Act removing illegitimacy from the Civil Code.[56]

Children born outside wedlock are still referred to as 'illegitimate' children, although the distinctions within the law are practically non-existent except in the case of succession. In this aspect of the law, the illegitimate child stands to inherit less than his/her legitimate counterpart for the only reason of being born on the other (so-called wrong) side of the blanket.

Back in 1997[57] the First Hall of the Civil Court gave a judgment on a constitutional case on this point and determined that the salient articles are null and void when read in conjunction with the Constitution of Malta, the European Convention on Human Rights and the First Protocol[58] and ordered a copy of the judgment to be served on Parliament. The case, which had been instituted against the Attorney General, was not appealed and the assumption has always been that amendments were only a matter of time. The outgoing President of the Republic of Malta made his final official act, in 1998, a plea to the Parliament to amend the relevant sections and public agreement seems to reign, requiring that the offending sections of the law be removed.

However in the year 2000, discriminatory succession rights are still there and should a person wish to make a will leaving equal shares of his inheritance to children born both outside as well as within wedlock, strictly speaking the notary drafting the will would be bound to inform the testator that this is not possible according to law.[59] Furthermore, as no doctrine of precedent exists in Maltese law,

---

56   I use the term consensus because numerous public debates, vox pops on TV and radio channels and numerous letters to the press agree on the unjust discriminatory treatment accorded to children born out of wedlock.

57   *Mario Buttigieg f'ismu proprju u bhala kuratur ad litem ta' ibnu minuri Keith Buttigieg versus L-Avukat Generali u jekk jidhirlu li ghandu interess l-Onorevoli Prim Ministru* decided on 17 January 1997 by Mr Justice Albert Magri (Rik Kost 544/96AJM). The judgment quoted extensively from decisions of the European Court.

58   Malta accorded the right of individual petition to the European Court of Human Rights in 1987.

59   The offending sections are to be found at sections 602, 640, 822 and overall sections 614–646 and 817–824, in contrast to Article 37 and 45 of the Constitution of Malta and Articles 8 and 14 of the European Convention and First Protocol.

the judge hearing any subsequent case would not be bound to decide in the same manner as his predecessor. What is sure is that if the case were taken to the European Court it would confirm the 1997 judgment and find that such discrimination is totally unacceptable. Legislation to remedy this quirk in the law is therefore obviously long overdue and forthcoming.

There are many other issues covered by the Act, but the most topical and the ones which will generate the most impassioned debate are the ones outlined above. The common practice in Malta for all such legislation is the gauging of public opinion through the publication of a White Paper. A full length version of the Act together with a concise and more accessible companion version are published with a time for feedback from all sectors of society and ample opportunity for anyone and everyone to air their views. The next few months will be a mixture of hot debate and cool logic but hopefully they will result in a much-needed overhaul of legislation for and about children.

III THE OMBUDSMAN FOR CHILDREN ACT

In the effort to make children's rights a reality, it has long been vaunted by the children's rights lobby and some pressure groups that a champion for children should be identified. The name given to this person has so far been the Ombudsman for Children, in keeping with the Scandinavian tradition.[60] Malta is no stranger to the office of the Ombudsman and has such an office responsible for administrative justice. We also have an Ombudsman for the University responsible to ensure that justice is done and seen to be done in all matters relating to Campus.

Some people have voiced their opinion that the term Ombudsman for Children may be a mouthful and have suggested Commissioner instead. However, in colloquial terms, the Commissioner means the Commissioner for Police and it is no one's wish to identify the children's representative as part of the police force. Attention is focused on the issue of the name largely because it is the only bone of contention.

The Ombudsman (Commissioner/Representative/Champion) will be responsible for a lengthy list of issues relating to the wellbeing of children and will be empowered to make investigation into alleged breaches of the rights of a child. The role will also include the provision of information and the making of reports regarding matters relevant to the rights of children. It is hoped that the person chosen will be a focal point for all matters relating to children and be positioned to bridge departmental and bureaucratic action in an attempt to speed up progress.

The Ombudsman will be directly responsible to Parliament and appointed by the President following a resolution indicating consensus in the choice. Many models were scrutinised before drafting an othoctonous law suited to our system and culture. The Ombudsman for Children Act is a separate draft from the

---

60   In drafting the Act, reference was made principally to the office of the
      Ombudsman/Commissioner in Sweden (Act to Establish the Office of the Children's
      Ombudsman), Canada (The Ombudsman and Children's Advocate Act), Iceland (Ombudsman for
      Children Act), New Zealand (New Zealand Commissioner for Children).

Children Act and its inception will hopefully put pressure on the adoption of many sections proposed in the best interests of children.

IV SOCIAL WORKERS WARRANT ACT

Another vital piece of the jigsaw enabling family law and child law to function better is the draft of an Act to ensure that social workers can only carry out duties subject to their being awarded a warrant. The growing recognition in the contribution of social workers and the important role they play in keeping families together, helping children and providing support for all family members has also led to the realisation that unless a social worker is qualified[61] there are instances when intervention may do more harm than good.[62]

Furthermore, because many associations are voluntary and rely on the good intentions of their volunteers, it had been the practice to make do with persons who had no formal qualifications but a good disposition towards helping those in need. This is clearly not acceptable and the great majority of non-governmental associations providing social work assistance increasingly do so by means of fully qualified social workers.[63]

The Act seeks to ensure that a person may only declare to be a social worker when so warranted. The warrant is awarded on attainment of stipulated criteria and falls under the jurisdiction of the Inspectorate set up to ensure the adequate provision of services to support families. The people happiest with the advent of the legislation are the social workers themselves who now feel that due recognition is being accorded to their profession.[64] Duties such as ongoing training and possible assessment have also been well received within the framework of professional education.

Other legislation pending in draft form includes the Domestic Violence Act, which contains some very interesting sections relating to: (i) the definition of who may qualify as a victim of domestic violence and (ii) proposed measures to curtail the perpetrator. In a seminar co-ordinated by the Commission for the Advancement of Women to discuss the proposed amendments, much of the debate centred on these definitions and on the introduction of civil jurisdiction to a hitherto strictly criminal arena. However, the hottest issue which remains unresolved is whether to continue to expect women to bring the action for

---

61 The term 'qualification' includes both academic requirements and expertise acquired through social work intervention as determined by the Board designated to determine criteria for fitness and eligibility.

62 Instances have been reported regarding persons posing as social workers offering counselling to the detriment of those seeking help.

63 Another (upcoming!) NGOs Act will crystallise the present State position on providing funding to voluntary organisations following presentation of a project document and projected costs. To date, the state is funding many NGO salaries where the work is in support of national needs. Glaring examples include the Hospice Movement, the Eden Foundation (work opportunities for persons with a disability) and Dar il-Kaptan (respite services for persons with disabilities).

64 Statement issued by the National Social Workers Association in 1999.

domestic violence themselves or enable the police to proceed without their consent and/or instigation.[65]

Forthcoming is another exciting piece of legislation to be entitled the Equal Opportunities Act. This is aimed at the removal of any remaining vestiges of discrimination on the grounds of gender and it proposes to introduce mechanisms to ensure the adherence to the law and provide a remedy when there has been a breach.[66]

With so many new items for discussion together with numerous other legislative amendments in view of Malta's upcoming inclusion in the European Union, it may be said that too much is happening too fast. But in reality, the law is simply evolving to keep in touch with social changes that took place ages ago. The only fear is that so much draft legislation will take overlong to be enacted. In the next contribution it will be interesting to assess the impact of legal change and evaluate its outcome.

---

65 Bringing the action by means of a *querela* means that it is liable to be dropped if the couple make up between the time of the offence and the date of the hearing. The suggestion is to render the offence liable to prosecution even where it is committed in the privacy of the home because of the public effect. There are also suggestions in the Children Act to terminate parental responsibility for the perpetrator and in those instances where the victim repeatedly refuses to seek help and continues to subject the child to domestic violence.

66 On signing CEDAW in 1991, Malta undertook a complete overhaul of the Civil Code and in 1993 produced amendments eliminating discrimination on the grounds of gender within the civil code and in the Constitution. (This formed the basis for my last contribution to *The International Survey of Family Law 1994*, ed A Bainham (Martinus Nijhoff Publishers, 1996).) Although the laws have been amended, there still remains no mechanism for enforcement and it has been felt that the issue requires an active rather than passive approach.

THE NETHERLANDS

TO MARRY OR NOT TO MARRY: THAT IS THE QUESTION

*Caroline Forder**

In this report I have decided to concentrate on the developments relating to marriage and the special arrangements relating to parenting by same-sex partners. These are the most distinctive features of Dutch law, when seen from a world perspective. However, it should not be forgotten that from a Dutch perspective these provisions do not deserve such a central position, but rather have to take their place in a busy legislative programme, which includes matters such as inheritance reform (which I will discuss in the next Survey), child protection and many innovative reforms in the field of health and biomedicine.

I   BILL TO OPEN UP MARRIAGE TO SAME-SEX COUPLES

The first round of parliamentary debates on this Bill, which was discussed in the last Survey,[1] was published on 10 January 2000.[2] The Labour Party – and VVD (Liberal-Left) – factions[3] and the Green Party faction[4] pronounced themselves in agreement with the Bill. The D66 faction responded to the Bill with a feeling of pride (since it was D66 Members of Parliament who had originally brought the issue into the Parliament).[5] The Christian Democratic Party faction had mixed feelings. It considered the reasons given by the Government for introduction of the right to marry to be inadequately motivated. Moreover, this faction would have liked to have first seen the review of the operation of registered partnership, which the Government is pledged to carry out in 2003, after registered partnership has been in operation for five years. The Christian Democratic party faction drew attention to the fact that in 1998 the Government had defended the view that the denial of marriage to same-sex couples was not discriminatory because the two situations were not similar.[6] Moreover, this party asked whether, if this reform could be made, there could be any reason to deny legal recognition to polygamous marriages.[7] The strict Protestant factions (*Gereformeerd Politiek Verbond-fractie*

---

*   Faculty of Law, Maastricht University, The Netherlands.

1   Dutch report, *The International Survey of Family Law (2000 Edition)*, ed A Bainham (Family Law, 2000) at 247–251.

2   Second Chamber 1999–2000, legislative proposal 26 672, no 4.

3   Ibid, pp 1–2.

4   Ibid, p 5.

5   Ibid, pp 4–5.

6   Ibid, pp 2–4.

7   Ibid, pp 21–22.

and the *Reformatorische Politieke Federatie-fractie*) asked the Government to provide motivation for the proposed reform. They asked for evidence to support the proposition that same-sex couples were discriminated against, and they wished to know upon which international law provisions the proposition was founded.[8] The *Staatkundig Gereformeerd Partij* faction (very strict Protestant) reacted with shock to the Bill. The opening up of marriage would conflict with their religious views.[9] The Government's response was that the Bill makes a distinction between marriage as a religious institution and marriage as a civil law institution, and only seeks to regulate the latter.[10]

Several factions commented on the distinction which would be made between marriage between partners of the same sex and marriage between partners of the opposite sex. The Bill insists that marriage between partners of the same sex cannot have the consequence that both partners to the marriage are automatically regarded as parent. Thus, there would be no extension of the presumption of paternity which currently applies in favour of a man married to the mother of a child born during the marriage. The D66 and Green Party factions considered that this distinction could be dropped, in the light of the fact that in many marriages between partners of opposite sex, the husband who is deemed to be the father is not, in fact, the biological father of the child.[11] The Government insists that, in the light of the fact that a child born into a relationship between two women can never be biologically related to both of them in the same way as is possible within an opposite-sex relationship, there should be no extension of the presumption of paternity.[12] The strict Protestant Party factions considered, contrariwise, that the Government had not paid enough attention to what, in its view, are essential differences between a marriage and a relationship between persons of the same sex. It also indicated that churches would most likely decide not to recognise a marriage concluded between persons of the same sex. These factions asked the Government to indicate whether, if the Bill became law, churches would be entitled to refuse to give a blessing or other celebration to same-sex marriages and whether testators would be entitled to make a distinction between marriages between same-sex and opposite-sex couples.[13] The Government confirmed that both the refusal and the making of such distinction would be possible.[14]

The VVD faction noted that the present prohibition on marriage or registered partnership between a brother and sister[15] should be extended to prohibit a same-sex marriage being concluded between two brothers. On 4 August, the Bill was amended to make it clear that a marriage cannot be concluded between two brothers or two sisters. This exclusion also applies between adoptive brothers or

---

8   Ibid, pp 5–7.
9   Ibid, p 7.
10   Second Chamber 1999–2000, 26 672, nr 5, p 6.
11   Second Chamber 1999–2000, 26 672, nr 4, p 9.
12   Second Chamber 1999–2000, 26 672, nr 5, p 9, 11.
13   Second Chamber 1999–2000, 26 672, nr 4, p 21.
14   Second Chamber 1999–2000, 26 672, nr 5, p 13.
15   Article 41, Book 1, Dutch Civil Code.

sisters. However, in the case of adoptive siblings of the same sex wishing to marry, it is possible to apply for dispensation from the prohibition.[16]

The strict Protestant party factions asked whether a civil status registrar could be excused from having to register a marriage between persons of the same sex on the grounds of conscience. The Government answered that there could be no reason for the civil status registrar to be entitled to refuse to do his job.[17] However, in debate in July 2000, the minister agreed to introduce an amendment to include a conscience clause for civil status registrars. This was the only concession which the minister made.

There was criticism for the Government's proposal to allow registered partnership to subsist alongside the possibility for same-sex couples to marry. The Christian Democratic Party faction and the strict Protestant parties pointed out that the quick scan carried out in the spring of 1999 (and discussed in the previous Survey),[18] which had given a rather buoyant picture of the level of use of registered partnership, was now outdated. In the first half of 1998, 2,700 partnerships were registered. This figure dropped to 1,900 in the second half of 1998, and 1,200 in the first half of 1999. In the view of these factions, this evidence suggests that interest in registering a partnership is much less than had first been estimated. The usefulness of continuing the institution must, in the view of this faction, be placed in doubt. Moreover, the Kortmann Commission had proposed abolition of registered partnership were marriage by same-sex couples to become possible.[19] The Government did not want to take a decision to abolish registered partnership yet; but will include this issue in the review which will be made after the Registered Partnership Act has been in force for five years. However, the D66 Party and the Green Party factions agreed that registered partnership should be retained as they considered it would be rather strange for those who had joined the institution to discover that they had joined a dying race.[20] The cabinet sees no particular problem in allowing the two institutions to co-exist, even though they closely resemble one another.[21]

The private international law questions received a lot of attention. This was the only point on which there was more-or-less agreement across the parties. The VVD and Christian Democratic Party factions asked why the matter had not been investigated before introducing the Bill. It was noted that this was also the view of the Council of State.[22] The D66 faction noted that the Government had so far failed to take action on the detailed proposal by the Permanent Committee on Private International Law regarding the private international law position of registered partnerships.[23] (This proposal is discussed in some detail in the previous Survey.)[24] The strict Protestant parties stressed the isolated position into which the

---

16   Second Chamber 1999–2000, 26 672, nr 7, p 2.
17   Second Chamber 1999–2000, 26 672, nr 5, p 27.
18   Loc cit note 1, at 240–242.
19   Second Chamber 1999–2000, 26 672, nr 4, pp 11–13.
20   Ibid, p 12.
21   Second Chamber 1999–2000, 26 672, nr 5, p 15.
22   Second Chamber 1999–2000, 26 672, nr 4, pp 14–16.
23   Ibid, p 17.
24   Loc cit note 1, at 243–247.

Netherlands would come.[25] Furthermore these factions considered that the Government made too light of the risk that a same-sex marriage would not be recognised abroad. They were critical of the failure of the Government not to ask the Permanent Committee on Private International Law to investigate the matter thoroughly before the Bill was presented to Parliament.[26] The Government agreed to put the question to the Committee on Private International Law.[27] It further acknowledged that, as far as the effects in foreign law were concerned, it could only hope for a constructive approach by the lawyers and civil status registrars in the countries which would be asked to recognise and give effect to a marriage concluded in the Netherlands between a couple of the same sex. The problems are very similar to those arising in relation to registered partnership and the Government considered that the proposals already made by the Committee on Private International Law regarding registered partnership could be equally pertinent to the case of marriage between two persons of the same sex.[28] Those proposals will not, as the Government had earlier suggested, be treated as mere policy rules, but will be enacted into legislation.[29]

On Tuesday 12 September the majority of the Second Chamber of Parliament voted in favour of the Bill (109 for: 33 against). Votes were individual. Three members of the Christian Democratic faction voted in favour of the Bill; the rest of the Christian Democratic faction was against. The strict Protestant factions voted against the Bill. The Labour Party, Liberal-Left Party, D66, Green-Left Party and the Socialist Party supported the Bill. Now the Bill will go to the First Chamber.

II   SHAM MARRIAGES

Following the report on the effectiveness of the Prevention of Sham Marriages Act at preventing sham marriages, discussed in the previous Survey,[30] the Government felt able to conclude: 'It appears from the report that the Act definitely has a preventative function'.[31] (For another view, see the previous Survey).[32] However, the Government considered a number of amendments to be desirable. These were introduced by a Bill on, *inter alia*, the prevention of sham marriages. The Bill was introduced into the Second Chamber on 28 October 1999. The Prevention of Sham Marriages Act operates by requiring, in the case of every marriage concluded in the Netherlands to which a foreigner is a party, a certificate to be handed to the civil status registrar from the immigration service specifying the residential status of the intending spouse. The civil status registrar must receive such certificate – known as a D79 declaration – before registering the depositions of intention to marry, or, if such has already happened, before preparing the marriage certificate. The same

---

25   Second Chamber 1999–2000, 26 672, nr 4, p 18.

26   Ibid, pp 10–11.

27   Second Chamber 1999–2000, 26 672, nr 5, p 14.

28   Second Chamber 1999–2000, 26 672, nr 5, p 17–18.

29   Second Chamber 1999–2000, 26 672, nr 5, p 22.

30   Loc cit note 1, at 252–253.

31   Second Chamber 1999–2000, 26 862, nr 3, p 3.

32   Loc cit note 1, at 252–253.

procedure applies to the registration of a marriage concluded abroad for which registration is sought in the municipal registers in The Hague or in the civil status registers. These will be marriages for which recognition is sought for a marriage when the parties have married outside the Netherlands but intend to settle within the Netherlands or otherwise claim effect of their marriage in accordance with Dutch law. The declaration is one part of the information which the civil status registrar relies upon to decide whether he is concerned with a so-called sham marriage for which, accordingly, registration should be refused. The requirement of a D79 declaration was imposed by the Prevention of Sham Marriages Act on all proposed marriages to which one party did not have Dutch nationality. The Government proposes in its new Bill to restrict the requirement of a D79 declaration to cases in which the foreigner concerned does not have an independent (ie independent from the intending spouse) right of residence without restriction. The exemption from the requirement of a D79 declaration will apply if both spouses have an unrestricted right of residence. This means that individuals from the European Union Member states and the European Economic Union will not have to have a D79 declaration. Furthermore, refugees with a recognised status, and holders of a settlement permit or a residence permit without limitation, will be exempted. However, the Government stressed that both partners to the marriage must have an unrestricted right of residence or Dutch nationality; if only one satisfies the requirements the proposed exemption from the D79 declaration does not apply.[33] Furthermore, the Bill proposes, in the case of marriages concluded abroad for which recognition in the Netherlands is requested, to exempt from the requirement of D79 declaration partners of marriages which have already been dissolved and parties to marriages which have already subsisted for a long time (at least ten years). If the marriage has already been dissolved, there can be no claim to any rights on the basis of it. The D79 declaration is in those circumstances a needless intrusion. If the marriage has subsisted for ten years, it is reasonable to conclude that the marriage has a certain durability and should not be subjected to the suspicion that it is a sham. All these provisions will be applied to registered partnerships too.[34]

Parliament's reaction to this proposed Bill was, in general, positive. The question was asked why the new provisions regarding the recognition of marriages of long standing and concluded outside the Netherlands will only apply to marriages of at least ten years. In the report on the evaluation of the Prevention of Sham Marriages Act, the committee recommended that the more favourable provisions should apply to marriages of five years' standing. The Labour Party faction asked why the Government had departed from the recommendation of the committee.[35] The same question was raised by the D-66 faction. Five years ought to be a long enough period for the immigration authorities to form an opinion as to whether there is evidence of a sham marriage or not. The Government responded that, because this provision is concerned with marriages concluded outside the Netherlands, there is little or no opportunity for the immigration service to check the authenticity of the marriage. The longer period of ten years has been chosen to discourage persons who might otherwise have thought that the conclusion of a sham marriage outside the

---

33 Second Chamber 1999–2000, 26 862, nr 6, p 4.
34 Second Chamber 1999–2000, 26 862, nr 3, p 5.
35 Second Chamber 1999–2000, 26 862, nr 5, p 3.

Netherlands would be an easy way of obtaining a right of residence. The effect in practice of the new provisions will be kept under review.[36] The D-66 faction also asked the Government to indicate how many people would be affected by the new provision. The Government replied that the Parliamentary research centre would investigate how many couples, where both partners were living outside the Netherlands at the time of marriage, have, since the coming into force of the Prevention of Sham Marriages Act, registered their marriage in the civil status registers in The Hague and subsequently started living in the Netherlands.[37] This faction further observed that the rules on immigration were in some circumstances too strict. For example, if a foreigner has acquired a right of residence in the Netherlands on the basis of a marriage with a Dutch citizen, it seems very harsh to remove all right of residence if the marriage is ended by the death of the Dutch partner after a period of three years. The faction suggested that a distinction could be made between marriages terminating as a result of divorce and those terminated by death.[38] The Government referred the faction to a recent note concerning dependent rights of residence.[39]

III BILL TO SIMPLIFY THE RIGHTS AND DUTIES OF SPOUSES

A The background

With all the discussion about legislative reform of access to marriage and alternative family forms, it is not surprising that there should also be some reflection on the content of the central institution itself. During parliamentary debate on registered partnership the question was raised whether the rights and obligations which apply to spouses during marriage, and which were to be applied by dint of the Registered Partnership Act to registered partners, were in need of reform. Moreover, the fact that a number of couples who could have married choose instead to register a partnership cannot be easily explained by any concrete difference between the two institutions. One theory is that these couples reject the symbolism attached to marriage.

The objective of this Bill is to modernise the law on the obligations arising between spouses. A particular problem with the provisions is that they were drafted at a time when it was commonly the case that one partner to the marriage (the woman) did not have any paid employment outside the home. A committee was appointed to investigate the matter. The committee published its report with its recommendations to the Second Chamber of Parliament on 23 December 1997.[40] The committee recommended simplification of the rights and duties of spouses laid down in Title 6 of Book 1 of the Civil Code. It recommended adjustments to the procedure to apply for judicial approval for the making or amending of marriage

---

36   Second Chamber 1999–2000, 26 862, nr 6, p 3.
37   Second Chamber 1999–2000, 26 862, nr 6, p 5.
38   Second Chamber 1999–2000, 26 862, nr 5, p 4.
39   Second Chamber 1999–2000, 26 862, nr 6, p 5: letter from the Secretary of State of Justice of April 25, 2000, kenmerk: 5020450/00DVB.
40   Second Chamber 1997–1998, 23 761, nr 18.

contracts concluded during the marriage. Furthermore, the committee recommended the preparation of a legislative proposal to make it possible for spouses-to-be to choose from one of two matrimonial property regimes: on the one hand, an amended community property regime, and, on the other hand, a system by which the debts and credits can be balanced. In order to explore the possibilities, it was recommended that a comparative investigation be carried out into the matrimonial property regimes in each of the neighbouring countries and that these should each be compared with the Dutch system. This research was published in November 1999.[41] The Government agreed in principle to introduce reforms along the lines suggested by the committee. The present legislative proposal is thus part of a wider scheme of reforms of matrimonial property. Two further legislative proposals are currently being prepared, to introduce the scheme of amended community of property and the system of balancing debts and credits between the spouses. These will be discussed in future Surveys.

The present reform concerns provisions which apply to spouses regardless of the matrimonial property scheme which applies to them. Most of the provisions cannot be excluded or modified by contract.

All references in this section to spouses should be read as including registered partners.

B   Basis of marriage

The basic provision, Article 81 of Book 1 of the Civil Code, will remain as it is. The Article prescribes that spouses owe one another loyalty, help and support. Furthermore, that what they have should be shared with each other. There is thus not only an obligation to help one another in need, but also to share in the general resources over which each spouse disposes. The subsequent provisions are based upon Article 81: in the case of a gap in one or other Article, reference can always be made to Article 81 to see whether the claim can be justified under the general principle in that Article. The general obligation to share does not, however, mean that the spouses are not entitled to contract to exclude all community of property.

C   Joint responsibility for upbringing of children

Article 82, Book 1 of the Dutch Civil Code provides that spouses are obliged to care for and bring up 'their children'. Already under the present law 'their children' is understood to include step-children. However, it is desirable also that foster children should be included. Therefore the phrase 'their children' will be amended to 'children of the family'.[42] According to the Government, the provision should only extend to minor children. But in a debate on this Bill published on 14 July 2000 the question was asked in Parliament whether this also applied if the children were developmentally challenged, so that even above the age of majority they are unable

---

41   B Braat, AE Oderkerk, GJW Steenhoff, *Huwelijksvermogensrecht in rechtsvergelijkend perspectief*, Molengraaff Instituut voor Privaatrecht, in opdracht van het Ministerie van Justitie, Utrecht, 1999.

42   Second Chamber 1999–2000, 27 084, nr 3, p 4.

to care for themselves. It may also be doubted whether the insertion of the word minor is at all necessary since the existing law is quite clear, including the special position of developmentally challenged children.[43]

D   Duty to live together

Article 83, Book 1 of the Civil Code lays down the obligation of the spouses to live together. The present Article allows the spouses not to live together if there are serious reasons for not doing so, if there is an interim order in force or there is a judicial separation. During the parliamentary debates on registered partnership it was questioned whether this one Article in particular is not very out-dated.[44] The committee on the rights and obligations of spouses recommended that the duty to live together should be amended into a presumption that they live together. However, the Government found this proposal too far-reaching. It would also affect the relationship to third parties. So the Government proposed to abolish the obligation between the parties *inter se*. The duty to live together would no longer be one of the legal characteristics of a marriage. The Government suggested that this proposal was less radical than appeared at first sight, as in many cases spouses did not seek to enforce the duty to live together, but simply breached the duty in mutual agreement. In any case there is almost no legal sanction against this breach of obligation. Only Article 84(6), Book 1 of the Civil Code provides a sanction: if the fact that the spouses are not living together is due to unreasonable behaviour on the part of one spouse, the obligation of the other spouse to support the spouse who is guilty of unreasonable behaviour is more restricted than would otherwise be the case. However, because this provision is really a vestige of the fault principle, the Government proposes that it should be abolished.[45]

The Government's proposal means that the requirement to live together can be imposed by legislation. For example, if one spouse wishes to claim the right to succeed to a tenancy held by his or her spouse, the relevant provisions insist that the residence in question is the spouse's main residence.[46] Furthermore, the provision that one spouse may not deal in any way with the house which is occupied by the spouses together or by the other spouse alone is left unaffected.[47] Moreover, the requirement that spouses live together in order to qualify for certain benefits in immigration law will remain in full force.

Since the main effect of a judicial separation is to excuse the spouses from the duty to live together, the abolition of the duty to live together *inter se* can be accompanied by an abolition of the judicial separation procedure.[48]

There were a number of reactions to this part of the proposal in the parliamentary debate published on 14 July 2000. In the first place, the committee on the rights and duties of spouses questioned the wisdom of the Government's decision to depart from the committee's recommendation to replace the duty to live

---

43   Second Chamber 1999–2000, 17 084, nr 4, p 3 (strict Protestant factions).
44   Second Chamber 1995–1996, 23 761, nr 6, p 17.
45   Second Chamber 1999–2000, 27 084, nr 3, p 8.
46   Article 7A:1623g Dutch Civil Code.
47   Article 88(1)(a) Dutch Civil Code.
48   Article 1:168 Dutch Civil Code.

together with a legal, rebuttable presumption that they live together. The Government's concern was that the presumption would also have effect in the public law sphere, thus presuming, for example, that a vital requirement for a residence permit was established. But the committee argued that it would also be possible to exclude the operation of the presumption from all contexts except the relationship between the spouses.[49] A different point is that there might be a discrimination problem if the requirement (or presumption) of cohabitation were to be applied for some purposes and not for others. When a distinction is made, the ground for distinction must be pursuant to a legitimate aim, and the means used must be proportionate to the goal pursued. The Labour Party faction asked the Government for clarification,[50] and the Christian Democratic faction and the Green-Left faction were also concerned. Why should the choice of a Dutch couple not to live together be respected, whereas the choice of two immigrants would not be? The latter might have very good reasons not to live together, such as for employment, or because they were deeply attached to one another but unable to get along together in one house.[51] The VVD faction was not convinced that the presence of the requirement of cohabitation had ever given rise to practical problems and asked why, in that case, it was necessary to abolish it.[52] The committee on rights and obligations of spouses furthermore advised the Government to investigate the fiscal consequences of abolishing the duty to live together.[53]

E   Liability of spouses inter se for the household costs

The present Article 84 of Book 1 of the Dutch Civil Code regulates the liability of the spouses *inter se* for the costs of running the household, including the costs of keeping the children. The Article provides that the costs are to be borne by the joint income of the spouses, and, insofar as this is insufficient, their private incomes. In the last event the costs should be divided in the proportion which the incomes bear to one another; if the husband's income is ten times that of the wife, then the wife should bear only one-tenth of the household costs. If the income is insufficient, the costs should be paid from the spouses' joint property, and, if that is also insufficient, the spouses' private property may be used, proportionately, as explained above in relation to the incomes, to defray the household costs. These complicated rules are of no relevance in practice. The only matter of concern to spouses is that there is enough money to defray the household costs and that the household debts are paid. There is generally little attention to the precise contributions of each spouse or for the contributions which each spouse is obliged by law to make. Moreover, according to Dutch Supreme Court case-law,[54] if the spouses do not work out those contributions and settle them at the end of each calendar year, the right to repayment by a spouse who has paid too much will readily be held to be estopped. This case

---

49   Second Chamber 1999–2000, 27 084, nr 4, p 4.

50   Second Chamber 1999–2000, 27 084, nr 4, pp 4–5.

51   Second Chamber 1999–2000, 27 084, nr 4, p 5.

52   Second Chamber 1999–2000, 27 084, nr 4, p 5.

53   Second Chamber 1999–2000, 27 084, nr 4, p 6.

54   Dutch Supreme Court, 22 May 1987, *Nederlandse Jurisprudentie* 1988, 231; Dutch Supreme Court, 29 April 1994, *Nederlandse Jurisprudentie* 1995, 561.

law is based on the experience that spouses do not keep very detailed accounts of household income and outgoings, which would make accounting of this kind quite impossible to achieve several years after the payments have been made.

For spouses who are aware of the legal rules and do live according to them, the rules provide an unfair advantage to a spouse who chooses to limit his or her income by, for example, purchasing shares which produce no income but which do increase in value. The other spouse is bound by the rules to spend his or her income on the household, whilst the property of the other can only be used to defray the costs if the income is insufficient. This particular difficulty has been tackled by Supreme Court case law, in which is established that the rules in Article 84 are characterised more as a guideline than a binding legal rule.[55] A further unsatisfactory feature of Article 84 is that it regulates the liability of the spouses *inter se* to pay for the household expenses. Their liability *vis-à-vis* third parties – for example, the family grocer – is regulated in Article 85(1). But Article 85(1) uses another phrase: 'the ordinary running of the household'. The difference between the concept of 'household expenses' in Article 84 and the 'ordinary running of the household' in Article 85 is artificial and obscure. In any event in an age in which payment is made with credit cards and other forms of plastic money there seems little reason for having a special provision regarding the liability *inter se* of the spouses for household costs.

In the light of all these arguments, the Government argues that a more flexible rule is needed, which takes account of the diversity in income and capital of the spouses.[56] According to the new provision, spouses will be liable in the light of their income, capital and the other circumstances. In a second paragraph it is provided that spouses are obliged to provide in advance the means of payment of the household costs. It will be possible to provide by written contract for a modification to the statutory scheme.

In the parliamentary debate published on 14 July 2000 attention was drawn to a number of other legal systems in which a provision like the one suggested by the Government appears. What emerges from these foreign provisions (Article 214 French Civil Code, Article 163 Swiss Civil Code, § 1360 German Civil Code, Articles 217 and 221 Belgian Civil Code) is that none of the legislators have attempted to define the liability of the spouses *inter se* in any detail (contrary to the present Dutch provision). Furthermore, in a number of ways, these provisions acknowledge the value of non-financial contributions to the cost of the household. The issue of recognition of unpaid housework should also be considered in the Dutch reforms. Despite several impressive studies of this problem by academics,[57] there has so far been little recognition of the problem in the legislative or judicial sphere.[58]

---

55   Dutch Supreme Court 16 October 1992, *Nederlandse Jurisprudentie* 1992, 791.

56   Second Chamber 1999–2000, 27 084, nr 3, p 7.

57   For example, J van Duijvendijk-Brand, 'Naar een nieuw huwelijksvermogensrecht?', *Verslag van de studiedag Vereniging FJR en KNB* 21 januari 1998, *Ars Notariatus XCIII*, Deventer, Kluwer, p 25.

58   Second Chamber 1999–2000, 27 084, nr 4, p 8.

F Joint liability vis-à-vis third parties for each other's debts

Article 85 of Book 1 of the Dutch Civil Code provides that if one spouse, Anne, incurs debts in the course of the 'ordinary running of the household' her creditor is entitled to seek repayment from Anne's spouse, Bert. The two questions raised in the explanatory notes relating to the Bill on rights and duties of spouses are:

(a) does the creditor who has supplied household items deserve to enjoy better legal protection than other creditors? and

(b) should creditors have this special advantage *vis-à-vis* married and registered couples whereas they do not have the advantage if the couple is unmarried?

Regarding the first question, the Government considers that the rationale behind Article 85 no longer applies. In modern-day conditions it does not often happen that the debts relating to the ordinary running of the household are not paid right away. Creditors may be expected to find their own method of ensuring payment, without relying on a special claim against the contracting party's spouse. Furthermore, Article 85 invites disputes as to which costs are covered by the term 'ordinary costs of running the household'.

Regarding the second question, there seems to the Government to be little justification for the discrepancy in treatment of married and unmarried couples. In general, the position of women is far more independent than it was at the time that Article 85 was drafted; this factor also justifies a new approach.[59]

In the parliamentary debate published on 14 July 2000 there were several critical comments. The VVD faction and the strict Protestant party factions were not persuaded that the creditor who supplied household goods should not be in a privileged position. These costs are the basis of the daily life of the couple; removal of the legal protection of creditors might make it more difficult for couples to maintain continuity of supplies and thus to maintain the stability of the family. The strict Protestant party-faction pointed to the link between Article 85 and Article 81 (explained above). In this view, the fact that the spouses were liable to support each other makes it logical that they could be liable for one another's debts.[60]

G Formalities for concluding and amending marriage contracts

In the same legislative proposal a number of amendments are proposed regarding the procedures to be followed by spouses wishing to conclude a marriage contract, or modify an existing marriage contract, during the marriage. I will not engage in a detailed treatment of these: the general trend is to reduce the number of limitations on the making or amending of such contracts. The present requirement that the spouses have been married for at least one year is recommended to be abolished. This recommendation acknowledges that there can be good reasons for making or amending a marriage contract in the year following the marriage. The requirement that, in addition to hiring a *notaris* to draft the contract, a *procureur*

---

59 Second Chamber 1999–2000, 27 084, nr 3, p 9.
60 Second Chamber 1999–2000, 27 084, nr 4, pp 11–12.

should also be hired, should, according to the Government, also be abolished. The hiring of a *procureur* provides an extra financial barrier, whereas it is not clear that it adds any extra safeguard than the involvement of the *notaris*. A further requirement that the parties should show that there are 'reasonable grounds' for making the contract or amending it should, according to the Government, also be abolished. There is no evidence that spouses frivolously enter marriage contracts or amend existing contracts. The cost of hiring a *notaris* surely provides enough safeguard. Moreover the requirement of 'reasonable grounds' is extremely vague in this context and does not lend itself to judicial interpretation. Accordingly it is proposed that this ground should be abolished. Instead, the making or amending of a marriage contract should be prohibited if there is a risk for creditors or one or more conditions violate binding legal provisions, good morals or public order.[61]

In the parliamentary debate reported on 14 July 2000 the committee on the rights and obligations of spouses questioned whether it was necessary to keep in any form the requirement of judicial consent to any making or amending of marriage contracts during the marriage. The committee's suggestion was that the requirement should not just be amended and made less onerous, as the Government proposes, but that it should simply be abolished.[62]

IV PARENTHOOD: THE THREE PROPOSALS ON SAME-SEX PARENTS

The reforms discussed in this section were all recommended by the Kortmann Commission in its report on opening up marriage to same-sex couples, discussed in the 1997 Survey.[63] The Commission recommended making it possible for same-sex couples to adopt children, the regulation of automatic custody rights in the event of a child being born to one of two registered partners, and the extension of inheritance rules to cover the relationship between a child and the child's mother's or father's same-sex partner. The proposal on adoption was introduced last year, and the provisions were discussed in last year's Survey.[64] In this survey an account of the parliamentary debate on that proposal is given. Furthermore, the proposal on automatic acquisition of custody by registered partners is now published and is discussed below. Although the inheritance provisions have not yet appeared, the general approach to the inheritance question has been set forth in a letter from the Minister to the Second Chamber; this is also discussed below.

A Bill to allow adoption by partners of the same sex

The first round of parliamentary debates on this Bill, which was discussed in the last Survey,[65] was published on 23 December 1999.[66] As may be expected the

---

61   Second Chamber 1999–2000, 27 084, nr 3, p 12.
62   Second Chamber 1999–2000, 27 084, nr 4, p 14.
63   *The International Survey of Family Law 1997*, ed A Bainham (Martinus Nijhoff Publishers, 1999) at 264–268.
64   *International Survey of Family Law (2000 Edition)*, loc cit note 1, at 261–264.
65   Ibid, at 261–264.

reaction was divided. The CDA (Christian Democratic) faction was impressed by the objections brought by the Council of State. This faction questioned the necessity for the reform in the light of the existing possibility of an application for joint custody. Moreover the CDA faction considered the proposal to be more motivated by a desire to improve the position of same-sex couples than a response to a real need on the part of the children concerned. Another concern of this faction was that the reform might have the tendency to stimulate surrogacy or sperm donation. Reference was made to the two Englishmen who in 1999 took charge of twins who were born to an American surrogate mother.[67] Any encouragement of children born to lesbian couples as a result of artificial insemination was regarded as equally undesirable by this faction.[68] However, the Government considered that there was no evidence that either of these practices would increase as a result of the Bill.[69] Nor was the Government impressed with arguments that it was not in a child's interests to be brought up by a same-sex couple. Such evidence as there was provided reason for cautious confidence about the quality of upbringing provided by same-sex couples. The Minister thought it unacceptable to continue to wait for research into the upbringing of children by same-sex couples which would provide an indisputable green light.[70] The strict Protestant factions *(Gereformeerd Politiek Verbond-fractie, Reformatorische Politieke Federatie-fractie)* were unable to appreciate the necessity of the reform. They used many of the arguments used by the CDA faction. Furthermore they emphasised the traditional role of marriage and the undesirability of departing from that pattern.[71]

However, there was a positive reaction from the factions left of centre, namely, the Socialist Party *(Socialistische Partij-fractie)*, D66 and the Green Party *(GroenLinks)*. For the D-66 faction the reform did not go far enough. It invited the Government to reform the law of descent so that the child born to a lesbian couple could become the child of the mother's partner simply by a recognition procedure. This procedure is already available to the male partner of the mother, and applies irrespective of whether he actually is the father. So why should this procedure not apply to the mother's female partner as well? Adoption was thought to be unduly cumbersome for the situation envisaged. In particular, the requirements of having to have lived together for three years and cared for the child for one year were considered to be excessive.[72] The Socialist Party faction also pointed to the allegedly unequal position of homosexual and lesbian parents in the law of descent when compared to a same-sex couple.[73] In the same line of thought, the

---

66 Second Chamber 1999–2000, legislative proposal 26 673, nr 4.

67 The children have been given a right of entry into the United Kingdom. No decision has yet been taken on whether the men will be entitled to a parental responsibility order or be allowed to adopt the children.

68 Second Chamber 1999–2000, 26 673, nr 4, pp 3–4, pp 13–14.

69 Second Chamber 1999–2000, 26 673, nr 5, p 5, 7–8.

70 Second Chamber 1999–2000, 26 673, nr 5, p 5: FC Verhulst and HJM Versluis-den Bieman, *Sociale en psychische aspecten van adoptie van een buitenlands pleegkind door één persoon en door twee personene van hetzelfde geslacht samen*.

71 Second Chamber 1999–2000, 26 673, nr 4, pp 6–7.

72 Ibid, pp 5–6, p 18 (D66); Second Chamber 1999–2000, 26 673, nr 5, p 33.

73 Second Chamber 1999–2000, 26 673, nr 4, p 6.

VVD faction asked why the proposal to make it possible for same-sex couples to marry[74] should not simply apply the presumption of paternity (parenthood) in respect of children born into the relationship.[75] The Government did not accept this argument, maintaining the position that the presumption of paternity and the possibility of recognition should only apply where there was a probability that the presumption of paternity or recognition reflected the biological reality.[76]

There was disagreement about the scope of the proposed reform. Some factions (VVD faction (*Volkspartij voor Vrijheid en Democratie*), D66-faction, Green-Left, Labour Party)[77] were anxious to discuss the possibility of extending the provisions on adoption by couples of the same sex to inter-country adoption.[78] Others (the CDA faction) stressed the lack of recognition which same-sex adoptions would find in other countries.[79] The strict Protestant parties perceived the objections of the countries of origin of children placed for inter-country adoption to be a reason for the Dutch Government to reconsider its position on the regulation of domestic adoptions. They doubted whether the separate treatment of domestic and international adoptions could be defended.[80] The Government's view on inter-country adoption by same-sex partners is that it is futile to take a principled stand and insist that inter-country adoption should be possible since such adoptions can always be blocked by the country of origin. To allow inter-country adoption would simply awaken hopes which could never be fulfilled.[81] Regarding the domestic scope of the new provisions, the Government does not expect any increase in adoptions. This is due to the limited number of children available for adoption in the Netherlands. Moreover, although an increase in adoption may be expected by lesbian couples who have conceived a child by artificial insemination, this is expected to be offset by a reduction in step-parent adoptions.[82]

The proposed new criterion to be applied in all adoptions, namely, that the child cannot expect anything from his biological (or birth) parents, was heavily criticised by all factions. Under this provision account has to be taken even of whether a sperm donor may have something to offer the child. Delay could be caused by the fact that he would have to be heard by a court before the adoption could take place. This was considered unreasonable since from the outset a sperm donor disclaims all interest in parenting.[83] The requirement of hearing the sperm donor was also considered to encourage would-be adoptive parents to make use of anonymous donors rather than an identified one. Yet this practice would cut across the policy expressed in the pending Bill on the Storage and Disclosure of Information Relating to Gamete Donors of promoting knowledge of biological

---

74 Discussed above.
75 Second Chamber 1999–2000, 26 673, nr 4, pp 19–20.
76 Second Chamber 1999–2000, 26 673, nr 5, pp 3, 6–7, 20, 33, 35.
77 Second Chamber 1999–2000, 26 673, nr 3, pp 20–23.
78 Ibid, p 10.
79 Ibid, p 9.
80 Ibid, pp 10–11.
81 Second Chamber 1999–2000, 26 673, nr 5, p 10.
82 Second Chamber 1999–2000, 26 673, nr 5, p 10.
83 Second Chamber 1999–2000, 26 673, nr 4, p 15, GroenLinks.

and genetic origins.[84] The Government considers that there is no reason to think that such is the case. Since the right of the sperm donor to be heard in adoption proceedings is based upon international law (Article 8, ECHR),[85] a court addressing the question whether the adoption is in the child's best interests is already obliged to hear a sperm donor who has a relationship to the child which attracts the protection of Article 8, ECHR. The introduction of the legislative proposal will not change this position at all.[86] The new criterion was also considered to be vague, difficult to apply, and to create uncertainty. How should the criterion be applied to a sperm-donor or surrogate mother who sought a declaration that she had nothing more to offer the child, but who in reality often had a demonstrated suitability to care for children and only did not wish to care for this particular child?[87] The possibility created by the legislative proposal that a biological (or birth) parent might continue to have a right of access even though it could be concluded that this parent had nothing more to offer this child *as a parent* did not add to the clarity of the proposal.[88] The Government's response to this concern was that the fact that access was being exercised could not be taken to indicate that the child could expect anything from that person as a parent, nor that he could not. Whether the child could expect anything from the person as a parent would depend on all the circumstances of the case. If adoption was granted, because the court determined that the person enjoying access to the child could not be expected to fulfil the role of parent in relation to the child, nevertheless the access could, in appropriate circumstances, be continued notwithstanding the adoption.[89]

In an amendment of 3 May 2000 the possibility of adoption by two persons of the same or of different sex who are within the prohibited degrees is explicitly excluded. Thus, it will not be possible for a mother and son, or a mother and daughter, to adopt a child together.[90]

On 12 September, this Bill was passed by a majority of the Second Chamber. It will now go to the First Chamber of Parliament.

B   Automatic acquisition of custody rights by dint of partnership registration

A Bill presented to the Second Chamber of the Dutch Parliament on 15 March 2000 introduces automatic shared custody when a child is born to one of two

---

84   Ibid, p 14 (CDA faction), p 15 (D-66 faction), pp 15–16 (GroenLinks faction), p 17 (strict Protestant factions), p 20 (VVD faction). A full account of this Bill is given in: C Forder, 'Opening Up Marriage to Same-sex partners and Providing For Adoption By Same-sex Couples, Managing Information on Sperm Donors and Lots of Private International Law', in *The International Survey of Family Law (2000 Edition)*, ed A Bainham (Family Law, 2000) at 256–261.

85   *Keegan v Ireland*, 26 May 1994, Series A Vol 290.

86   Second Chamber 1999–2000, 26 673, nr 5, p 19.

87   Second Chamber 1999–2000, 26 673, nr 4, pp 12–13.

88   Ibid, p 14 (CDA faction), p 17 (strict Protestant factions).

89   Second Chamber 1999–2000, 26 673, nr 5, p 19.

90   Second Chamber 1999–2000, 26 673, nr 6 (*Nota van wijziging*).

registered partners.[91] A similar provision is already in force in Iceland.[92] The proposal regulates two situations. The first is the case of opposite-sex partners. Anne and Bert are registered partners and a child is born to them. According to the law at present registered partnership has no consequences for parenthood or custody of the child, and Anne is the sole parent of the child. Bert has to recognise the child if he wishes to become a legal parent. Recognition is possible before birth. Under present law Anne and Bert can thereafter register themselves with the county court (*kantongerecht*) registrar as having joint custody.[93] According to the Automatic Shared Custody Bill, Bert will not become the legal father of the child by dint of the fact that he is the registered partner of the child's mother. However, if he recognises the child before it is born, he will share custody with the mother from the moment of birth and by dint of the registered partnership.[94] If he does not recognise the child before birth he will not be a 'parent' within the meaning of the proposed Article under which automatic joint custody is to be granted. In such case the mother will have sole custody.[95] The legal parenthood of the father is still thus a crucial difference when a married opposite-sex couple is compared with an opposite-sex couple in a registered partnership.

The second situation to which the Bill applies is when Alison has a child whilst she is in a registered partnership with Betty. By dint of birth Alison is the mother of the child and sole holder of custody rights.[96] Betty is not the biological parent of the child, but, according to the provisions of the bill, by dint of registered partnership she will automatically acquire shared custody. According to the present law registered partnership makes no difference to the relationship between Betty and the child. If Betty wishes to acquire shared custody, she and Alison must make an application to court.[97]

The Bill does not apply to two men, even if one of the men fathers a child while in a registered partnership. The Kortmann Commission had suggested providing for a procedure to allow the father of a child and his partner to register shared custody with the registrar of the county court (similar to the procedure now applicable to unmarried parents of opposite sex). This possibility would only apply if the child had no mother or if her custody rights had been terminated. It would have provided a possibility for two men to acquire custody without having to apply to the court. But the Government declined to introduce this mechanism. The most likely situation to which it could apply is that the mother has died whilst she had joint custody with the child's father. The child's father could thereafter, according to this proposal, share custody of the child with his partner by a simple registration procedure without having to apply to court. In these circumstances it seemed to the Government to be desirable that the court should make a decision,

---

91 Amendment to Book 1 of the Civil Code in connection with automatic shared custody in the event of a birth during a registered Partnership, Second Chamber 1999–2000, Bill 27 047 (15 March 2000).

92 Icelandic Children Act, Article 30, third paragraph.

93 Article 1:252 Dutch Civil Code.

94 Proposed Article 1:253aa Dutch Civil Code.

95 Second Chamber 1999–2000, 27 047, nr 5, p 23.

96 Article 1:198 Dutch Civil Code.

97 Article 1:253t Dutch Civil Code (or 1:282 Dutch Civil Code if Alison is also not the biological mother of the child).

and that custody should not pass to the father and his partner by a simple procedure. In particular the procedure safeguards that the child is asked what he or she would like regarding custody following the death of the mother and the safeguards for the mother should remain in place.[98] This argument applies with even greater force if the father does not have custody at the moment of the mother's death. Similar considerations apply if the mother loses her custody rights (for example because of neglect or mistreatment of the child, or because she has had to be placed under guardianship). It would be unsatisfactory to allow the father to acquire rights automatically without the intervention of a court.

The automatic shared custody can only apply regarding the child born to Alison whilst the registered partnership with Betty is subsisting if no man has recognised the child. Automatic shared custody can only apply if there is no other parent.[99] This is in accordance with the general concern in family law to prevent a child having more than two legal parents at any given time.

The most typical situation for which the Bill is intended is when a child is born to one of two women as a result of sperm donation. The donor has no rights in relation to the child, as long as he does not recognise it.

The first round of parliamentary discussions regarding this Bill were published on 24 May 2000.[100] The Bill met with the approval of the Labour Party faction, the VVD Party faction, D-66 faction and the Green Party faction.

The Christian Democratic Party faction was less satisfied. It regretted the departure, heralded by this bill, from the biological realities. In the view of this faction, a relationship between the child and the mother's partner should only be established by judicial decision.

The strict Protestant parties greeted the Bill with disappointment; the Bill brings registered partnership too close to marriage for the liking of these factions.

The failure to make provision for a simple registration procedure for two men was heavily criticised. This criticism is not surprising from the VVD Party faction, which supports the Bill but wishes it to be extended. The criticism of the Christian Democratic Party faction on this point[101] is more remarkable. That faction opposes the Bill, and seeks to show that the failure to make provision for two men who wish to share custody automatically reveals a fundamental inconsistency in the Bill. In my view the Government's arguments, explained above, that the restriction is needed in order to protect the rights of the mother and child are persuasive. The Government maintained its position on this issue in its response.[102]

Furthermore, the Christian Democratic Party faction ask why the Government is so concerned to provide two persons with custody in the situation of two lesbians, and not, for example, to provide automatic custody to the father – irrespective of his actual connection to the child or the mother – in the more common case of a lone mother.[103] The reaction of the Government was that, if a

---

98   Second Chamber 1999–2000, 27 047, nr 3, p 3.
99   Proposed Article 1:253sa Dutch Civil Code.
100 Second Chamber 1999–2000, 27 047, nr 4 (*Verslag*).
101 Second Chamber 1999–2000, 27 047, nr 4, pp 6–7.
102 Second Chamber 1999–2000, 27 047, nr 5, pp 9–10
103 Second Chamber 1999–2000, 27 047, nr 4, p 7; nr 5, p 23.

parent has no partner, there is nothing that legislation can do to change that, notwithstanding that it is generally better for a child to have two persons to bring him or her up. If that lone parent dies, or for some other reason ceases to be able to care for the child, there will be a 'custody vacuum'. This is unavoidable and should not be changed by legislation. This is quite different to the situation contemplated by the Bill, in which two persons, who have taken the step of consolidating their relationship in the form of a registered partnership, are able and willing to care for and bring up the child.[104] Moreover, the Government found the underlying suggestion by the Christian Democratic faction, namely, that a father should have joint custody in all circumstances, very far-reaching. It would mean that, if a child were born within a marriage, but was in fact conceived by another man, or was the result of sperm donation, the other man or sperm donor would be regarded as the father. It would also mean that a child, born to a mother who married Ben while she was pregnant with a child conceived by Bill, would be regarded as the child of Bill. It would also mean that if the child were conceived by Chris, but recognised by the mother's new partner Dave, the law would nevertheless accord custody to Chris. All these examples show that the suggestion of the Christian Democrats would not be a good road to go down.[105]

The question was raised concerning what consequences the termination of the registered partnership would have for the shared custody relationship between the parents. The Government replied that the termination of the partnership would have no consequences as such for the custody relationship. It would be open to the partners to apply to the court for some adjustment of the custody relationship (an award of sole custody or some other adjustment).[106]

The proposals have no special fiscal effects, either in succession tax or in relation to income tax. It has already been enacted in the General Taxation Act[107] that a 'child' includes all first degree relatives in the descendant line. And Article 1:3 of the Dutch Civil Code already provides that a child is a descendant in the first degree of the mother's registered partner. The effect of these provisions is that, for the purposes of succession taxation, the child of one registered partner is treated as a child of both partners. Moreover, a proposed reform of the General Taxation Act will include a foster child within the concept of child.[108]

Concerns were expressed about the possibility for the second biological parent (the father) to escape his liabilities if the mother's registered partner were to acquire joint custody automatically. However, joint custody by the mother and her partner will not prevent the begetter from recognising the child, or indeed, the mother bringing an action for judicial establishment of paternity of the child.[109] Nor is the mother prevented from suing the begetter for maintenance.[110] However, it will not be possible for the begetter to exercise joint custody with the mother by registration in the custody register, were custody already shared between the

---

104 Second Chamber 1999–2000, 27 047, nr 5, p 14.
105 Second Chamber 1999–2000, 27 047, nr 5, p 24.
106 Under Article 1:253n Dutch Civil Code, which will be made applicable by the proposed Article 1:253sa Dutch Civil Code; Second Chamber 1999–2000, 27 047, nr 5, pp 15, 21.
107 Article 2(3)(i).
108 Second Chamber 1999–2000, 27 047, nr 5, p 15.
109 Article 1:207 Dutch Civil Code.
110 Article 1:394 Dutch Civil Code.

mother and her registered partner.[111] The possibilities just mentioned in relation to the begetter do not apply to the sperm donor, who is deliberately excluded from the definition.

Concerns were expressed about the international recognition of joint custody held by partners of the same sex. The Government expressed the view that the Hague Convention on jurisdiction, applicable law, recognition, enforcement and co-operation with regard to parental responsibility and child protection measures (The Hague, October 1996) was favourable to the recognition in other countries of the proposed measures. The reason is that this Convention refers questions of jurisdiction and recognition to the place of the child's ordinary residence, whereas under the earlier convention (Hague Convention on the jurisdiction of authorities and the law applicable to child protection measures, 1961) these questions were referred to the law of the child's nationality.[112]

The mother's partner who acquires shared custody with the mother will also acquire the power to manage the child's property. If the child's father has died, leaving the child some property, and the mother subsequently registers a partnership with her new partner, the partner will acquire the power to manage the child's inherited property. However, even in the case of the child's parent managing the child's property, the parent's dealings are subject to the scrutiny of the county court (*kantonrechter*).[113]

C   Proposal on inheritance rights between a child and the child's mother's or father's same-sex partner

On 1 May 2000 the Ministry of Justice sent a letter to the Second Chamber of Parliament, explaining what the contents of the proposal on inheritance will be.[114] It is of course always possible for the co-parent to make provision by will for the child which is born to her or his partner. The debate is about whether provision should be made in intestate succession, such as providing that the child will be regarded as an heir of the co-parent. However it is, according to the Minister of Justice's letter, not as simple as was thought at first. Intestate provisions are based upon what the deceased would have done had he or she made a will. A provision of intestate law which departs from this principle would cause many testators to make wills in order to avoid the application of the provision. Furthermore, such provision might cause the parent and the co-parent to decide not to share custody, in order to avoid the application of the intestacy provision. So, in the view of the Minister, before legislation on this matter can be drafted, some certainty must be established regarding what parents and co-parents generally would want to do regarding inheritance *vis-à-vis* the child. In the Minister's view the following matters should be investigated:

---

111 Article 1:252 (2)(e) Dutch Civil Code; Second Chamber 1999–2000, 27 047, nr 5, p 16.

112 Second Chamber 1999–2000, 27 047, nr 5, p 19.

113 Article 1:253k Dutch Civil Code; Second Chamber 1999–2000, 27 047, nr 5, p 22.

114 Second Chamber 1999–2000, 22700 Leefvormen, nr 31 (*Brief van de Minister van Justitie aan de Tweede Kamer der Staten Generaal*).

(1)   Is shared custody between a parent and co-parent generally shared until
       the child attains majority, or is shared custody regularly terminated
       before such age of the child?

(2)   To what extent in practice is provision made by will by co-parents in
       respect of the children of their partner?

This investigation includes the practices of step-parents, who will shortly be
accorded the power to determine that a step-child will be treated as their own child
for the purposes of division of the estate.[115] Where this power is exercised, the
legal portions of the deceased's own children are necessarily reduced when a step-
child joins the group of children entitled to claim a legal portion. In general the
Minister thought that the effect of the new inheritance law should be studied
before making any change in the position of co-parents. The new law on
inheritance, which is expected to come into force in 2002, introduces a new
division between the spouse or registered partner and the children, by which the
spouse/registered partner is pushed into a greatly preferred position of taking the
entire estate, whilst the children have only the right to claim payment of their
share of the estate after the decease of the surviving spouse or registered partner.
If investigation into these matters reveals that shared custody is usually held until
the child attains majority and that use is regularly made of the power to dispose by
will of property in favour of the partner's children, this would, in the Minister's
view, be a strong indication that a provision regarding intestate succession should
be enacted. However, the Minister did consider that a provision could already be
considered which would place the children in a similar relationship to the partner
as step-children regarding the capacity of the person holding custody to pass
goods by will to the child. This means that a partner (A) should be able to leave
gifts to the child in respect of whom he or she shares custody with his or her
partner (B) by will without those gifts being defeated by claims to legal portion of
A's own children. Furthermore, the power under the new inheritance statute which
will allow a child to claim a sum from the estate of his or her parent insofar as
needed for his care and upbringing (until the age of 18) or for education and
maintenance (until the age of 21) could be extended to allow a claim against the
estate of a person sharing custody with the child's parent. Since the person sharing
custody is already subject to an obligation of maintenance, an extension of this
inheritance provision, which aims at protecting the child's maintenance needs, is
logical. Accordingly, a legislative proposal will be prepared to introduce these two
measures.[116]

---

115 *Boek 4* (in which the new inheritance law is laid down) is expected to come into force in 2002.
116 Second Chamber 1999–2000, 22 700, nr 31 (*Brief van de Minister van Justitie*).

NEW ZEALAND

PRIVATE LIVES AND PUBLIC PERSPECTIVES

*Bill Atkin**

I THE BABY LIAM SAGA – PUBLICITY v SUPPRESSION

A theme which surfaced in New Zealand family law in 1999 was the tension between the privacy often claimed for family life and the role of the State. Where to draw the boundary line between the two must be a difficult question in most jurisdictions, overlaid by religious, ideological and cultural factors. New Zealand is a typically pluralistic Western nation, with traditional religious affiliations on the wane, indigenous people's values and spirituality on the rise, and politics, although somewhat reversed by a centre-left government elected at the 1999 general election, driven mostly by new right and libertarian perspectives. The roles of the individual, family and State are less easy to define in this mix.

The question was most graphically illustrated in 1999 in a not so uncommon story involving a boy aged three, Liam Williams-Holloway. Liam suffered from cancer and had received chemotherapy at the hospital in the southern city of Dunedin. After two courses of treatment, however, the parents refused to allow this to continue and preferred to seek 'alternative' therapy. The hospital applied to have the boy made a ward of court, a procedure well tested in New Zealand in other medical cases.[1] In the face of medical evidence that the boy's condition was critical and that the parents and boy had disappeared, the Family Court judge had little option but to grant the order and consent to treatment.[2] At the same time, and somewhat unusually, the judge granted an application to release identifying information to the media in an endeavour to help efforts to locate the child.

Liam subsequently became the centre of much public debate and controversy. The media took full advantage of the situation to line up supporters of both sides. Public officers appeared to differ fundamentally on the appropriateness of judicial intervention. The Commissioner for Children fully supported the overriding of parental refusal to consent to treatment, but the Health and Disability Commissioner took the opposite view, strangely appearing to deny the court's power to intervene at all. Far from helping to track down the boy, the order allowing the release of information had a counter-effect. The family and their

---

* Reader in Law, Victoria University of Wellington.

1 Eg *Re J (an infant): B and B v Director-General of Social Welfare* [1996] 2 NZLR 134 (blood transfusions) and *Re Norma* [1992] NZFLR 445 (the use of native medicines instead of conventional treatment). The Family Court now has wardship jurisdiction, previously reserved to the High Court.

2 *Healthcare Otago Ltd v Williams-Holloway* [1999] NZFLR 804. A series of judgments of the same name are reported sequentially.

band of supporters took a more entrenched position. If anything, a culture of hostility developed between the parties.

Counsel for the child was concerned at the level of publicity which the case had provoked and, a month after the first proceedings, sought an order prohibiting further publication of information about the child once he had been located. In agreeing to this request, the judge said:[3]

> 'It is quite clear that the continuing media interest in the welfare of the child and his whereabouts are likely to have an adverse effect on the child's privacy and may be a contributing factor in the parents' decision to remain in hiding. As guardian of the child, the Court must be vigilant in requiring its agents to perform their designated functions. Constant and intrusive media coverage of their efforts to locate the child do not enhance these prospects.'

However, the effect of the Court's order went further than counsel for the child had sought. An immediate ban was placed on all media coverage of the story – preventing parties:

> 'from publishing or soliciting for publication any information identifying or relating to the location of the child, his parents or any person who is or has been involved in the child's custody, care, medical care or management, or publishing any photograph, film or video of the child, his parents or any person who has been involved in the child's care, custody, medical treatment or management.'

Counsel for the child would not have banned material already in the public domain but the order did not include any such qualification. The intention of the order was obviously to stop supporters of Liam's parents from pursuing the campaign in the public arena. The hope doubtless was that with the media coverage having gone quiet the parents would feel that they could front up to the hospital and that the boy's treatment could be continued with rather less public drama.

Litigation over the case did not cease. The news media challenged the suppression order but the Family Court judge, while accepting that the media had a right to be heard, dismissed the application to discharge or vary the order. He reiterated the view that the parents and their supporters were using the media to build up public support for their views, thus adding to the difficulties in locating and then treating the sick child. Counsel for the media had argued that the New Zealand Bill of Rights Act 1990, which includes the right to freedom of expression, should be the starting point in this situation. Judge Blaikie however said that he had 'not found the references to English authorities and competing rights when the protective jurisdiction of the Court has been exercised to be helpful ... The welfare of the child should not be subjugated to other considerations and the Court must ensure that his welfare is at the foremost of all determinations'.[4]

The judge's insistence on the welfare of the child is, perhaps, understandable. Section 23 of the Guardianship Act 1968, not unlike similar provisions in many

---

3   *Healthcare Otago Ltd v Williams-Holloway* [1999] NZFLR 794, 797.
4   Ibid at 798, 803.

other jurisdictions, makes the welfare of the child paramount and this notion is deeply ingrained in the culture of contemporary family law. Section 27A of the Guardianship Act 1968 prohibits the publication of proceedings under that Act unless leave of the court has been obtained and section 33(1) declares the Guardianship Act to be a code. The implications for family law however of more recently enacted human rights legislation are only slowly being unpacked. This process may be slower in New Zealand than in other jurisdictions, where, as in Europe, human rights jurisprudence has been leaving its mark for some time. Against this background, the media lodged a judicial review application against the decision to maintain the suppression order.

The judicial review proceedings came before two High Court judges, Panckhurst and Chisholm JJ.[5] The first issue was whether the welfare of the child was the paramount consideration in wardship cases. Counsel drew attention to an English rule which held that where the court was using its protective as opposed to its custodial jurisdiction the welfare of the child was not paramount.[6] The New Zealand judges, although accepting that the point was not free from doubt, held to the contrary. Section 23 of the New Zealand legislation refers both to custody and guardianship, and as the court's wardship powers relate to placing a child under the guardianship of the court, in the New Zealand statutory context it would have been a bold decision to hold that the welfare of the child was not paramount in wardship cases.

It might be thought that this would end the matter, but this was not so. The High Court held that the Family Court judge had materially misdirected himself in relation to the required approach. For while the welfare of the child remains the paramount consideration, other considerations can also be taken into account. One of these, according to the High Court, is freedom of expression, provided for in section 14 of the New Zealand Bill of Rights Act 1990. The judges saw no real inconsistency between freedom of expression and the child's welfare. They held that 'any suppression order should be tailored to intrude only to the extent necessary to ensure that Liam's welfare is protected as a first and paramount consideration'.[7] A balancing exercise was therefore necessary. A restriction on publication should be in clear terms 'but no wider than is necessary, to achieve the purpose for which it is imposed'. It appears that the welfare of the child trumps freedom of expression, but only just. While the High Court accepted on the evidence that a suppression order was properly based, the judges took a different view of the ambit of the order. They thought that it was not clear in its terms, that it should not suppress information already in the public domain and that careful consideration needed to be given to when the order should become operative and how long it should last.

Although the Family Court judge was required by the High Court to review his suppression order, this did not in fact take place, as it was overtaken by events. After a couple of months of failing to find Liam, the hospital decided that it was

5   *Newspapers Publishers Association of New Zealand Inc v Family Court* [1999] 2 NZLR 344, [1999] NZFLR 397.

6   *Re M and Another (wardship: freedom of publication)* [1990] 1 All ER 205.

7   *Newspapers Publishers Association of New Zealand Inc v Family Court* [1999] 2 NZLR 344, [1999] NZFLR 397, 405.

fruitless to continue and so it sought discharge of all orders, to which Judge Blaikie agreed.[8] At the time of writing, Liam is still alive but reported to be very sick. He has been to various parts of the world for both conventional and 'alternative' therapies.

What are the implications of the decision in *Newspapers Publishers Association of New Zealand Inc v Family Court*? Despite a legislative presumption that family law cases are to be private, it now appears that Family Court judges will have to engage in a careful assessment of whether privacy is justified. It will be so justified, it is suggested, only if some other principle such as the welfare of the child is at risk. This change in bias may not necessarily be a bad thing. A landmark case where a wife claimed a share of her wealthy husband's accountancy practice saw suppression of names and other details largely on commercial grounds.[9] This was controversial and may not survive the kind of reasoning in the latest decision. But it is surely very different where a child is involved or where there is a risk of violence.

Family Court judges are also going to have to be astute in the way in which they draft orders. The slightest impression that the terms of an order go too far may invite challenge.

Then, there may be wider implications. Family lawyers are going to have to be human rights lawyers as well. In custody and access cases, the court should surely be very vigilant not unnecessarily to infringe other rights in the New Zealand Bill of Rights Act 1990. Cases where one parent asks to shift with the children to another city or another country may have to be argued in the light of the right to freedom of movement, which should be breached no more than is 'demonstrably justified in a free and democratic society'.[10] Custody and access cases may also be affected by the right to freedom of association.[11] Prima facie, parents have a right of association with their children and the grounds for denying such association would need to be properly made out. Whether the results in these kinds of situations will be any different from what family lawyers have become used to is moot, but the mode of argument does appear to be shifting somewhat and when in doubt a court might favour the rights in the New Zealand Bill of Rights Act. In other words, the private lives of families and children are likely to be subject to public law principles in a way which was unknown until recently.

---

8   *Healthcare Otago Ltd v Williams-Holloway* [1999] NZFLR 812.

9   *Z v Z (No 2)* [1997] 2 NZLR 258 (Court of Appeal).

10   The right to freedom of movement is provided for in section 18 of the New Zealand Bill of Rights Act 1990. Under section 5, the rights and freedoms of the Act can be limited only where this is 'demonstrably justified in a free and democratic society'. The courts may however avoid resort to section 5 by defining the basic right narrowly. This occurred in *Re J (an infant): B and B v Director-General of Social Welfare* [1996] 2 NZLR 134 where the Court of Appeal, dealing with Jehovah's Witness parents who refused consent to blood transfusions for their son, faced a conflict between the child's right to life and the parents' right to freedom of religion. The Court resolved the issue by defining the right to freedom of religion sufficiently narrowly that it could not deprive the child of life.

11   Section 17, New Zealand Bill of Rights Act 1990.

II SUING CHILD PROTECTION AGENCIES

The tension between private lives and the public protective role of the State surfaces acutely when government agencies intervene in the interests of protecting a child supposedly at risk. In New Zealand in 1999, the responsible agency was restructured several times. What used to be the Children and Young Persons Service within the Department of Social Welfare became the Children, Young Persons and their Families Agency and then later in the year became the Department of Child, Youth and Family Services. The cost of this re-modelling was reported to be about $2.34 million.

Getting the balance right between intervention and non-intervention is extremely difficult. Over-intervention can cause as much damage as a failure to ensure a child's safety. When things go wrong, there is a growing tendency for individuals to sue the State but with mixed results. Three cases in 1999 are worth exploring.

In *W v Attorney-General*,[12] the Court of Appeal was faced with a woman claiming exemplary damages for breach of fiduciary duty and breach of statutory duty against the Department of Social Welfare. The claim related to sexual abuse allegedly occurring in the early 1970s by a foster father into whose care the woman had been placed as a child. Her complaints to departmental officers fell on deaf ears. Her subsequent life appears to have been miserable:

'serious and lasting psychological and emotional impairment, alcohol and drug abuse, criminal offending, psychiatric disorders, the presence of core symptoms such as anxiety, depression, and depersonalisation, and a marked inability to function or cope with the demands of daily life.'[13]

The claim was not based on vicarious liability but on the Department's own personal liability in breaching duties owed to the woman. The difficulty facing the plaintiff was the time which had elapsed between the alleged events and the commencement of proceedings. A High Court judge had thrown out her case on the basis that it was now out of time. This was reversed by the Court of Appeal which decided that, as the date when the plaintiff's cause of action accrued was a matter of considerable doubt, leave to bring the proceedings should be granted and any limitation issues determined subsequently at the trial.

The basic limitation rule in New Zealand with respect to claims for bodily injury is that the claim should be brought within two years from the date on which the cause of action 'accrued'. The court may, however, grant leave any time up to six years after the accrual of the action. The limitation period can also be frozen if the plaintiff was under a 'disability' preventing the filing of proceedings.

Most of the Court's discussion related to the question of when the cause of action accrued. Clearly if the cause of action accrued when the alleged events took place, there would be little hope for victims of childhood abuse who realise the impact of what happened to them only much later in life. A 'reasonable discoverability' test is therefore applied but the difficulty is knowing how

---

12 [1999] 2 NZLR 709.
13 Ibid at 709, 711.

objective and how subjective this test ought to be. The Court of Appeal decided that the test used in the High Court – 'an objective test based upon the reasonable person in the position of the intending plaintiff'[14] – was too objective. According to Tipping J, the correct test is that of 'this victim acting reasonably' or '[w]hether it was reasonable for this plaintiff, alleging sexual abuse and its various consequences, not to have made the link between the abuse and the harm any earlier'.[15] Salmon J took a similar approach and said that '[t]he Judge must not replace the victim with a construct of his or her own and then apply the objective test to that construct. When dealing with psychological damage one is necessarily dealing with a state of mind which must differ from that of the reasonable person who is so often the focus of assessment in arguments of this nature'.[16] Thomas J went further than this. He asked how sensible was the notion of 'a reasonable sexually-abused person ... I suspect that in the fullness of time the notion of the reasonable sexually-abused person will be perceived as a grotesque invention of the law'.[17] He took the view that the question as to when a woman might connect her abuse and her later behaviour was essentially subjective.

The plaintiff in this case won an important battle but not necessarily the war. Many hurdles still face her as she endeavours to get some redress from official authorities for what happened very privately to her as a child. The question of whether she did or should have made the link between the abuse and her later life at an earlier date is still at large, to be argued at a subsequent trial. Whether there was any fiduciary or statutory duty owed by the State and the exact nature of any such duty could be a matter of some controversy. Whether the actions or inactions of the State officials caused the damage in this case is debatable. Might the plaintiff not have suffered a miserable life even if the State had intervened when told of the alleged abuse? Further, the claim was for exemplary damages, compensatory damages being barred because of New Zealand's unique accident compensation system. As exemplary damages can be obtained only if there is outrageous and disgraceful conduct on the defendant's part, the question is whether there is such evidence here, ie by government officers as opposed to the abusing foster parent.

The second important case was *B v Attorney-General*.[18] This case illustrates the consequences of over-zealous intervention into the private lives of families. A five-year-old girl told a friend that her widowed father had been sexually abusing her. The friend told her mother, who then informed the authorities. The matter was investigated by Department of Social Welfare social workers and a clinical psychologist. During the course of these investigations, the five-year-old also claimed that her seven-year-old sister had been abused but the latter denied this. There was evidence that the five-year-old liked telling lies and, according to the plaintiffs, the psychologist undertook the task with a mindset that the reported abuse must be true. As a result of the investigations, a warrant to remove the children was obtained and lengthy care proceedings took place leading to a court

---

14   Ibid at 709, 735.
15   Ibid at 709, 735–736.
16   Ibid at 709, 739.
17   Ibid at 709, 725.
18   [1999] 2 NZLR 296.

order not on the basis of abuse but, with the father's consent, on the basis that the children were beyond his control. No criminal charges were laid against the father and eventually, 18 months after the sequence of events began, the girls were returned to the full-time custody of their father.

The father and the two daughters sued the Department of Social Welfare, a departmental social worker and the psychologist in negligence. By the time that the case reached the Court of Appeal, now over ten years after the beginning of the saga, the plaintiffs might have felt confident of success. The reason for this was an earlier decision of the Court of Appeal in *Attorney-General v Prince and Gardner*[19] where it had been held that a duty of care may be owed to a child where complaints of abuse had not been investigated or had been inadequately investigated. Surprisingly, however, in *B*, the Court of Appeal struck the action out and purported to distinguish *Prince*.

The Court of Appeal narrowed the rule in *Prince* so that a duty of care could arise only at the 'immediate triggering step' when a report of abuse had been made. The facts complained of in *B*, the Court said, occurred after that triggering step. At any later stage, the imposition of a common law duty of care would cut across the statutory scheme. The decisions to seek a removal warrant and to institute proceedings before the court were discretionary matters which should not be subject to negligence claims.

'The legislative judgment, as we read it, is that the greater good in ensuring so far as possible that children who may be at risk are cared for is to prevail over possible instances of individual injustice.'[20]

Or as Tipping J put it:

'The delicate balance between protecting children and not unnecessarily disrupting family life must always be informed by the need to put the interests of the child first. Negligence proceedings, if allowed, could easily become a wholly inappropriate attack on what are necessarily exercises of discretion and judgment by all concerned.'[21]

Tipping J also took the view that there was no causative link between the actions of the defendants and the harm to the plaintiffs.

Now, the need to act speedily in order to protect children is well recognised. Errors may be made during the course of taking prompt action. Further, where the system provides for judicial officers to play a role in granting warrants and courts to determine whether a child is in need of protection there are good reasons for refusing to impose a common law duty of care. But was this really the situation in *B*, so as to set it so starkly apart from *Prince*? The complaints about the social worker's and psychologist's investigations related surely to the time before there was any judicial determination and indeed before any decision to seek a warrant. Assuming that the allegations of negligence were correct (a matter which would have to be tested at a proper trial), the poor investigations were what set all the subsequent events down an inevitable path. These actions, it is at least arguable,

---

19 [1998] 1 NZLR 262.

20 [1999] 2 NZLR 296, 305 per Blanchard and Keith JJ.

21 [1999] 2 NZLR 296, 310 (failure properly to look after a child once taken into care).

were part of the triggering stage. They were also not so much a matter of discretion as of simply doing a job, not unlike the defendants in the more recent House of Lords judgment in *Barrett v Enfield LBC*.[22]

One other aspect of *B* is worthy of comment. The plaintiffs were both the children and their father. Their respective positions are arguably different. The relevant law at the time, the Children and Young Persons Act 1974 (now replaced by the Children, Young Persons and Their Families Act 1989), was designed to protect children, their welfare being paramount. In the interests of protecting children, an alleged perpetrator of abuse might suffer harm. Yet for policy reasons, perhaps no duty of care should be owed to such a person. State officials should not have to look over their shoulders to the interests of the alleged abuser. But if for this reason the alleged abuser might not be able to sue, why should the children also be unable to do so? They may be harmed by unnecessary intervention just as by a failure to intervene. It is arguable that the imposition of a duty of care on social workers and psychologists in favour of the child conforms with the statutory scheme, not the reverse. State social workers and psychologists should then be expected to maintain standards comparable to those in the private sector.

This leads to the third case, *N v D*.[23] This also involved a false allegation of sexual abuse but the defendant was a child psycho-therapist who was counselling the child concerned on a private basis. The psycho-therapist reached the view that the father had been sexually abusing the child and passed this information on to a report writer who had been instructed by the Family Court in a custody battle between the mother and father. According to the plaintiff father, this action prolonged the custody proceedings and caused the plaintiff to lose contact with the child for 18 months. The abuse allegations were later retracted.

The court refused to strike out the negligence claim. First, it was held that the psycho-therapist ought to have known that her actions, in particular passing her claims on to the person writing a report for the Family Court, would have impacted on the plaintiff. There was therefore sufficient proximity for the purposes of establishing a duty of care. Secondly, an argument based on policy that the psycho-therapist should be immune from liability to the father was rejected. The cases involving experts exercising statutory functions were considered to be different. Here, the defendant was acting in a private capacity and, furthermore, was not dealing with a situation which called for urgent investigation to protect a child. The counselling occurred over a long period of time. While normally a duty of care would be owed only to the client, a wider duty here arose once the psycho-therapist passed her findings on to third parties. In doing this 'she must have intended they be relied upon, and she effectively warranted that she had investigated the matter sufficiently to satisfy herself of those findings'.[24] For this reason, a duty was owed to someone other than her client, ie the father who would have had no other redress.

---

22   [1999] 3 WLR 79.
23   [1999] NZFLR 560.
24   [1999] NZFLR 560, 568.

III *DE FACTO* AND SAME-SEX RELATIONSHIPS

New Zealand has been much slower than a number of other jurisdictions in dealing legislatively with the property rights of unmarried partners. A Bill called the *De Facto* Relationships (Property) Bill, introduced in 1998, has been languishing in a parliamentary select committee. In broad terms, the Bill provides for an equal division of the home and chattels, along lines similar to those which apply to married couples under the Matrimonial Property Act 1976. Unlike matrimonial property however, other 'relationship' property will not normally be divided equally but according to contributions to the relationship (including non-financial contributions). There appear to be two main reasons for the hold-up in the passage of the legislation, one being the opposition of a libertarian right wing party which was supporting the minority government of the day, and the other being uncertainty over what to do with same-sex relationships.

In order to deal with the latter question, the Government arranged for the Ministry of Justice to prepare a booklet and questionnaire for popular consumption.[25] This was issued in August 1999 with responses to be lodged by 31 March 2000. The questions are, however, very open-ended and may be hard to assess properly. For example, people are asked: 'What do you think about there being a law on dividing property when same-sex relationships break down?' which invites virtually any kind of comment. The questionnaire also asks much more wide-ranging questions, such as whether same sex couples ought to be able to marry and whether they ought to be able to adopt children.

In response to the Ministry of Justice's paper, the Law Commission published a short paper of its own entitled 'Recognising Same-Sex Relationships'.[26] The Law Commission recommended that New Zealand follow Scandinavian models and enact legislation for the registration of same-sex partnerships 'such registration to have the same effect as a marriage between opposite-sex parties'. It went on to say:[27]

'There should be no question of registered same-sex partnerships being regarded as in any way inferior to traditional marriage. If it be necessary to afford some hierarchic ranking to the two institutions, they should rank equally.'

For same-sex couples who do not bother to register, the Law Commission recommends that they be treated under the law in the same way as opposite-sex *de facto* couples. The obvious question about the proposal for registration is, if it has exactly the same effect as marriage, why not simply allow such couples to marry? The answer according to the authors is that this option 'would cause unnecessary and understandable offence'. Further:[28]

'Toleration of diversity is a two-way street. If there is available to same-sex couples a system of registered partnerships conferring rights and obligations virtually identical to those resulting from marriage then gays and lesbians should be prepared to

---

25 *Discussion Paper Same-Sex Couples and the Law* (1999, Ministry of Justice, Wellington).
26 Study Paper 4, 1999, Wellington.
27 Ibid, para 33.
28 Ibid, para 28.

acknowledge that they are not harmed by a legal code designed to avoid giving what may be seen as gratuitous offence to those for whom matrimony is a holy estate.'

Of course, those who take the latter view may well be horrified that homosexual partnerships are to receive recognition in any shape or form and homosexuals may be offended that they are still to be treated differently from other groups in society.

In 1999, the Law Commission also produced a much more substantial report on the topic of adoption. While this was a wide-ranging review, the report focused at one point on adoption by same-sex couples and, without making any judgment as to whether homosexuality was in itself undesirable, concluded on the basis of research 'that the homosexuality of the parents makes little difference to the ultimate welfare of the child, as long as parents exercise quality parenting skills'.[29] The Commission's 'preliminary view' is that, rather than creating a blanket prohibition, same-sex couples 'should be assessed on their merits ... The way in which gay or lesbian people plan to take account of their sexual orientation when raising the child – for example, whether they plan to provide appropriate role models – would be an extra element for a social worker and the court to consider'.[30] This proposal will doubtless attract a wide range of responses.

Towards the end of 1999, a general election saw a new centre-left government come into power. This government has far fewer qualms than its predecessor about the State playing an effective role in regulating people's lives. A comprehensive system for such things as division of property is much more attractive to the new government. The principles of the *De Facto* Relationships (Property) Bill are therefore likely to be accepted but indications are that the new statutory régime will be incorporated into the Matrimonial Property Act and extended to include same-sex couples.

IV   CHILD ABDUCTION

The Hague Convention on child abduction was incorporated into domestic New Zealand law by the Guardianship Amendment Act 1991. As in other jurisdictions, international abduction cases have become an increasingly common feature of the law reports. Three 1999 decisions are worth noting briefly.

S v M[31] concerned the fundamental question of 'habitual residence'. A ten-year-old child had lived with his mother in New Zealand, but at a stage when she was having some problems with her new partner the boy went to live with his father in Sydney, Australia. On a visit back to New Zealand, the mother kept him in the country, sparking the father's application for the boy's return to Australia. The Family Court judge acceded to the application on the basis that the boy had lived in Sydney for 13 months and went to school there. The mother argued that the arrangement to let the boy live in Sydney was only a temporary measure, the

---

29   Law Commission *Adoption Options for Reform A Discussion Paper* (Preliminary Paper 38, 1999, Wellington), para 196.

30   Law Commission *Adoption Options for Reform A Discussion Paper* (Preliminary Paper 38, 1999, Wellington), para 197.

31   [1999] NZFLR 337.

boy to be returned to her after a year, but the judge was not convinced that she had proven this.

The mother appealed successfully. Panckhurst J held that the judge was wrong to shift the onus of showing habitual residence on to the mother. He thought that the mother had adduced sufficient evidence to make habitual residence a live issue. In the light of this, Panckhurst J considered the evidence, in particular that of the mother's doctor whom she had consulted before the boy went to Australia and who stated that he had the clear understanding that the arrangement was to last for about one year. As this consultation took place before dissension arose between the parties and when the mother had no reason to misrepresent the position, the judge concluded that habitual residence in Australia had not been proven. An essential prerequisite for the return of the boy to Australia was therefore missing.

The second case was a Court of Appeal decision illustrating the potential strength of the Hague Convention rules. In *S v S*,[32] Fisher J, earlier on appeal, had reversed a Family Court ruling that three children aged 11, 13 and 15 should stay in New Zealand and not be returned to Australia. The Family Court had been influenced by evidence that the mother was a battered wife, and that if the children were returned they might be exposed to physical or psychological harm and be placed in an intolerable situation. Under section 13(1)(c) of the Guardianship Amendment Act 1991, these factors provide grounds for refusing to order a child's return to the country of habitual residence. Fisher J was doubtful whether section 13(1)(c) was satisfied. He thought that '[a]t its highest, the case could have scraped into section 13(1)(c) on only the most marginal of bases',[33] but even so, the Court had an overriding discretion still to order the return of the children. Fisher J thought that the decisive factor was that the children wanted to go back to Australia. In his view 'it would be patronising in the extreme, and contrary to the international Conventions and legislation ..., to fail to give substantial weight to their wishes'.[34] The Court of Appeal held that Fisher J had made no error of law in exercising the discretion and therefore agreed with the return of the children to Australia.

Finally, the case of *Ryan v Phelps*[35] also involved movement between New Zealand and Australia. Following the parents' separation, the children were first in the care of their mother but then it was agreed that this should change and that they should live with their father. The mother went to the United States, apparently for a lengthy period. The father brought the children to New Zealand to live, after which the mother objected and sought their return to Australia. It was accepted that the move to New Zealand was in breach of the mother's rights of custody, a pre-condition for the Hague Convention rules to operate. The dispute, however, was over another pre-condition, *viz* that those rights of custody were actually being exercised by the mother. The High Court judge had found that, by leaving the children with the father and going to the United States, the mother was no longer exercising her custody rights. The Court of Appeal disagreed and held

---

32 [1999] NZFLR 641. Fisher J's judgment is reported at [1999] NZFLR 625.
33 [1999] NZFLR 625, 639.
34 Ibid at 625, 638.
35 [1999] NZFLR 865.

that errors of law had been made. The first error was that regard had not been paid to the relevant Australian law which gave the mother a right in respect to the children's place of residence. This right 'was continuously available to her and always capable of particular actual exercise if the prospect of a change in residence arose ... it is highly likely that she would have exercised her veto over removal to New Zealand had she been asked'.[36] The second error was a failure to distinguish between 'custody' and 'rights of custody':[37]

> 'A breach of any one of the bundle of distinct rights involved with custody may provide a basis for a finding of wrongful removal. The distinct, precisely recognised, right of custody in issue in this case is of course the mother's right to determine her children's place of residence.'

The mother's appeal was therefore allowed but, because of time delays (27 months since the children came to New Zealand), the Court of Appeal remitted the case to the Family Court to see whether in the meantime fresh grounds for refusal to return had arisen.

The Court of Appeal's judgment is another sign of a strengthening stand in favour of the principles of the Hague Convention. Assuming the correctness of a policy of discouraging abduction by immediate return of children to their place of habitual residence, the decision is welcome. But one must have lurking doubts about the construction adopted by the Court. Little attention was given to the phrase 'actually being exercised', which suggests an inherently factual inquiry. Instead, the Court appears to have treated the existence of a say in a child's place of residence and the mere possibility of objecting to a change of residence as an example of actual exercise of the right. If this is so, it is hard to see how a parent, short of formally and explicitly saying so, will ever not be 'actually' exercising a right with respect to residence (or presumably other 'custody' rights).

V CONCLUSION

The examples of medical treatment of children, inquiries into the abuse of children, regulation of *de facto* heterosexual and homosexual relatonships and rules about international child abduction all illustrate how the State maintains vigilance over our private lives. While lawsuits over abuse investigations reveal judicial hesitancy about the extent to which the State ought to be accountable, there can be little doubt that current public policy permits, not without some justification, a considerable degree of intrusion into how we live our lives.

---

36   Ibid at 865, 873.
37   Ibid at 865, 874.

NORTHERN IRELAND

FAMILY LAW: A PROCESS OF REFORM

*Lisa Glennon**

I   INTRODUCTION

Northern Ireland has not been covered in the Survey since 1996[1] and since then there have been several important reforms and proposals which will be considered in this chapter. Before embarking on a discussion of family law in Northern Ireland, however, it is worth noting that constitutionally there have been major developments in Northern Ireland, originating from the Belfast Agreement of April 1998. This agreement has been given legal effect in the Northern Ireland Act 1998 which is the foundation of the new institutions of devolved government in Northern Ireland.[2] From a constitutional perspective, Northern Ireland remains part of the United Kingdom and shall not cease to be so without the consent of a majority of people in Northern Ireland voting in a poll,[3] while the Northern Ireland Assembly is given the power to enact primary legislation by Bill within its legislative competence.[4]

While family law in this jurisdiction broadly resembles the law in England and Wales, consideration of recent developments reveals that there are both substantive and operational differences in Northern Ireland law. This chapter looks at three main areas of reform. First, the Family Homes and Domestic Violence (Northern Ireland) Order 1998 which corresponds, albeit with certain differences, to Part IV of the Family Law Act 1996 in England and Wales, and reforms the law in the context of domestic violence and occupation of the family home. Recent consultation papers illustrate that Northern Ireland family law is undergoing a substantial review process and this chapter looks at two in particular. Secondly, the law relating to matrimonial property has been considered by the Law Reform Advisory Committee and significant proposals have been made. Finally, the Office of Law Reform recently commissioned empirical research into the operation of divorce law in Northern Ireland in order to aid the review process

*   Lecturer in Law, The Queen's University of Belfast.

1   Archbold, 'General Principles and Recent Developments', in *The International Survey of Family Law 1996*, ed A Bainham (Martinus Nijhoff Publishers, 1998) at 297–322.

2   Prior to this Act, Northern Ireland had been governed by direct rule since 1972.

3   Northern Ireland Act 1998, section 1(1).

4   See Northern Ireland Act 1998, sections 5–15. The Assembly can pass legislation dealing with transferred matters which are essentially those matters within the responsibilities of the six Northern Ireland departments before devolution, reflecting paragraph 3 of the Strand One section of the Belfast Agreement. Outside the remit of the devolved Assembly are excepted matters, set out in Schedule 2 to the Act, which largely relate to central government-type functions. The Assembly can make provision dealing with reserved matters, Schedule 3 to the Act, with the Secretary of State's consent and subject to parliamentary control.

on its future legal development. A consultation paper has been issued which suggests reforms which have been tailored specifically to suit divorcing practice in Northern Ireland.

II   DOMESTIC VIOLENCE AND OCCUPATION OF THE FAMILY HOME

A   The Family Homes and Domestic Violence (Northern Ireland) Order 1998

The problem of domestic violence in Northern Ireland is no longer a hidden statistic, largely due to the recent reports which highlight its prevalence.[5] Between 1991 and 1995, 21 women were killed by their partners in Northern Ireland, representing 48% of all women murdered in Northern Ireland during this period. More recent statistics reveal that between 1992 and 1996 the police attended over 15,000 domestic violence incidents and in 90% of cases the victims were women. In 1996, 2,293 interim and 994 full personal protection orders and 2,290 interim and 993 full exclusion orders were made. It is also estimated that in the same year approximately 1,500 women sought emergency accommodation in Women's Aid refuges. Governmental response to the problem includes commitment to an inter-agency approach; taking steps to raise awareness of the damaging nature of domestic violence and its prevalence; and finally, commitment to providing effective and just remedies through the implementation of coherent policies and legislation. The integrated agency approach developed from the Government's policy statement published in June 1995, *Tackling Domestic Violence; A Policy Change for Northern Ireland*. This led to the creation of the Northern Ireland Regional Forum on Domestic Violence in which key professionals and organisations in this field collaborated for the first time at regional level.[6]

The new Family Homes and Domestic Violence (Northern Ireland) Order 1998[7] consolidates the law in this area and provides a single legislative framework to deal with two distinct, but interrelated, areas; protection from domestic violence and occupation of the family home. The provisions of the Order replace Part II of

---

5   See McWilliams and McKiernan, *Bringing it out in the Open: Domestic Violence in Northern Ireland* (HMSO: 1993) and McWilliams and Spence, *Taking Domestic Violence Seriously: Issues for the Civil and Criminal Justice System* (HMSO: 1996).

6   This has been developed further at local level with the establishment of twelve inter-agency fora. Paul Murphy, then Minister of State, Northern Ireland Office stated in January 1998 that '[t]he Government are strongly committed to a multi-agency approach as the best means of creating a structured, integrated and effective response to domestic violence. We congratulate the Northern Ireland regional forum on domestic violence on the important work it has done in the two years since its inception in fostering and developing inter-agency co-operation and information sharing', Eighth Standing Committee on Delegated Legislation, 29 January 1998.

7   This Order came into force on 29 March 1999, except article 35, which will permit third parties to bring court proceedings on someone else's behalf and article 36, which contains an enabling power for the Lord Chancellor to make regulations providing for the separate representation of children in proceedings under the Order. All statutory references in this section of the chapter will be to the 1998 Order, unless otherwise stated.

the Family Law (Miscellaneous Provisions) (Northern Ireland) Order 1984[8] and articles 18, 19 and 21 of the Domestic Proceedings (Northern Ireland) Order 1980.[9] The Order replaces the personal protection order as well as ouster and exclusion orders with a non-molestation order, which can be general or specific, and an occupation order, which can be declaratory or regulatory. The Order was sponsored through Parliament by the Office of Law Reform and, although the provisions implement many of the proposals of the English Law Commission,[10] the legislation is tailored specifically for Northern Ireland and has retained certain features of the previous legislation which were considered beneficial. The Order, therefore, broadly corresponds to Part IV of the Family Law Act 1996,[11] bringing Northern Ireland into line with the position in England and Wales, although there are several important differences which will be highlighted throughout this section.

B   Non-molestation order

Article 20 introduces the new non-molestation order, replacing the personal protection order which was available in the magistrates' court under article 18 of the Domestic Proceedings (Northern Ireland) Order 1980. Article 20 is designed to protect a person who was associated with the respondent, thus ensuring that protection is available to a wider range of applicant.[12] 'Associated persons' are defined by article 3(3) as spouses, former spouses, present or former cohabitees, family members, persons living together other than as lodger and tenant, relatives,[13] those who have agreed to marry one another regardless of whether the agreement has been terminated,[14] parents of a child, or those who have, or have had parental responsibility for the child and parties to the same family proceedings.

A non-molestation order prohibits the respondent from molesting an 'associated person' or a 'relevant child' and it can be worded generally or with reference to particular acts of molestation.[15] In deciding whether to make the order the court shall have regard to all the circumstances of the case, including the need

---

8   Provisions of this Order dealt with the occupation rights of spouses.

9   These provisions gave courts the power to grant personal protection and exclusion orders in cases of domestic violence.

10   *Family Law: Domestic Violence and Occupation of the Family Home*, Law Com. No 207 (1992).

11   For a discussion of the 1996 Act see Douglas, 'Family Values to the Fore?' in *The International Survey of Family Law 1996*, ed A Bainham (Martinus Nijhoff Publishers, 1998) at 157–178.

12   Under the old law only spouses or cohabitees could apply to the court for protection from domestic violence, other parties had to seek an injunction from the High court or county court. While the new legislation addresses this problem, there are those who remain outside its ambit, for example, those sharing accommodation on a commercial basis, relationships which fall outside the definition of relative etc. It is now possible for those who cannot obtain a non-molestation order to obtain a remedy under the Protection from Harassment (Northern Ireland) Order 1997, which corresponds to the Protection from Harassment Act 1997 in England and Wales.

13   See article 2(2).

14   Article 22 states that there must be evidence in writing of the agreement to marry unless this agreement was evidenced by the gift of an engagement ring or a ceremony before witnesses.

15   Article 20(6). The order can be made on application or of the court's own motion in the course of other family proceedings, article 20(2).

to secure the health, safety and well-being of the applicant or any relevant child.[16] One important difference to the old personal protection order is that no specific evidence of violence or threat of violence is required before a non-molestation order can be made. This shifts the focus away from the respondent's behaviour to the action required to secure the applicant's protection. Article 2 of the Order provides that 'molest' includes inciting, procuring or assisting someone else to molest, but beyond this no further definition is given. The intended flexibility of the legislation is also seen in article 20(7) which specifies that the order may be made for a specific period or until further notice. The aim, therefore, is to ensure that the order meets the requirements of each individual case.

C   Occupation Order

The occupation order is the second main order under the new legislation and, although it can be combined with a non-molestation order to protect in situations of domestic violence, it is not limited to this type of case. Instead it is of general application to regulate occupation of the family home. The order replaces the exclusion order under the Domestic Proceedings (Northern Ireland) Order 1980 and the ouster order which was available under the Family Law (Miscellaneous Provisions) (Northern Ireland) Order 1984. While the non-molestation order is available to a wide range of applicant, the availability of the occupation order is limited by comparison. A distinction is drawn between entitled and non-entitled applicants in the manner in which they will be able to seek an occupation order and the nature of the order made.

D   Entitled applicants

Under article 11, entitled applicants are those persons who are entitled to occupy the home by virtue of a beneficial estate or interest or by contract, or by virtue of any entitlement giving them the right to remain in occupation, or having matrimonial home rights. This definition ensures that spouses are entitled applicants as a non-owning spouse gains matrimonial home rights automatically[17] and, as such, can apply for an occupation order against a person with whom he/she was associated, provided that the home in question is, was, or was intended to be their home.[18]

Where an application is made by an entitled applicant the court must have regard to the following general checklist of factors; the housing needs and resources of the parties and any relevant child; the financial resources of each of the parties; the likely effect of any order or failure to make an order on the health, safety or well-being of the parties and any relevant child; and the conduct of the parties in relation to each other and otherwise.[19] An occupation order can be

---

16   Article 20(5).

17   Under article 4 a non-owning spouse will acquire matrimonial home rights provided his/her spouse is entitled in general law to occupy the matrimonial home.

18   Article 11(1)(b).

19   Article 11(6). This is a standard checklist which is applicable to both entitled and non-entitled applicants.

declaratory[20] or regulatory[21] and the court may attach additional conditions on the making of the order or at a later date under article 18.[22] When deciding whether to make a regulatory occupation order the court must have regard to the 'balance of harm test' which specifies that such an order must be made if it appears to the court that the applicant or any relevant child is likely to suffer significant harm attributable to the conduct of the respondent if the order is not made, unless the respondent or any relevant child is likely to suffer greater harm if the order is made.[23] For entitled applicants an occupation order may be made for a specified period, until a specified event occurs, or until further order.[24]

E Non-entitled applicants

A former spouse, cohabitee or former cohabitee, who is not entitled to occupy the property, can apply for an occupation order as a non-entitled applicant under articles 13 and 14 respectively, provided that their former spouse, partner or former partner is entitled to occupy the property which is, was, or was intended, to be their matrimonial home or the home in which they live(d) together as husband and wife.[25] For non-entitled applicants, seeking an occupation order is a two-stage

---

20 For an entitled applicant, under article 11(4), the court can make an order declaring the existence of this entitlement or matrimonial home rights. Additionally, an entitled applicant with matrimonial home rights, may obtain an order during the marriage safeguarding the existence of those rights beyond the death of the other spouse or the termination of the marriage, provided the court considers it just and reasonable to do so. (Article 11(5) and (8)).

21 Article 11(3) sets out the regulatory orders available to entitled applicants. This corresponds to section 33(3) of the English Family Law Act 1996 although the Northern Ireland provisions contain certain regulatory orders, deriving from article 18(4) of the Domestic Proceedings (Northern Ireland) Order 1980, which have no equivalent in the English Act. These are article 11(3)(c), which requires the respondent to permit the applicant to have peaceful use and enjoyment of the property; article 11(3)(h) which provides for the respondent to remove from the property personal effects or any furniture or other contents and article 11(3)(j), which restrains the respondent from disposing of any estate he has in the property. (In relation to the latter, under Schedule 1 an order containing this provision is registrable as a statutory charge and the applicant can apply to the court to have a disposition which contravenes the order set aside). Another difference to the 1996 Act is the power to exclude the respondent from defined areas under article 11(3)(i). This broadly corresponds to section 33(3)(g) of the Family Law Act 1996, although the Northern Ireland provision is wider as it permits the respondent to be excluded from areas outside the home.

22 The order may impose on either party, *inter alia*, obligations as to the repair and maintenance of the dwelling-house, discharge of rent or mortgage repayments or may grant either party possession of furniture or other contents of the home. This corresponds to section 40 of the Family Law Act 1996, however, two additional provisions are included within the Northern Ireland legislation. Article 18(1)(f) prohibits either party from damaging or interfering with services in the dwelling-house or any premises specified in the occupation order and article 18(1)(g) gives the court the power to require either party to repair any damage they have caused to the dwelling-house or its contents or any other premises specified in the order or to restore services with which they have interfered in the dwelling-house or any other premises or to make payment in respect of either. These provisions, which derive from elements which could be included in exclusion orders under article 18(6) and (7) of the Domestic Proceedings (Northern Ireland) Order 1980, are not contained in the corresponding English legislation.

23 Article 11(7).

24 Article 11(10).

25 Article 13(1) and 14(1). A former spouse, cohabitee or former cohabitee, can apply for an occupation order as an entitled applicant provided they can establish that they are entitled to occupy the property which is or was their home, or was intended to be so. However, matrimonial home rights under article 4 are only available to a party to a subsisting marriage which means that

process. The court will first consider whether to make a declaratory order which will give the applicant the right to enter and occupy the property, or the right not to be evicted. If this order has been made the court may then decide whether to add a regulatory provision to the order.[26]

When deciding whether to make a declaratory occupation order the criteria to be applied differ between former spouses and those who are or have been cohabiting. For a former spouse, along with the standard checklist of factors to consider,[27] the court must also consider the following factors: the length of time that has elapsed since the parties ceased to live together; the length of time that has elapsed since the marriage was dissolved or annulled; and the existence of any pending proceedings between the parties.[28]

Under article 14 cohabitees are subject to different criteria. The definition of cohabitee is laid down in article 3(1)(a) as *a man and woman who, although not married, are living together with each other as husband and wife.* On such an application the court must consider the general checklist[29] plus the following factors specific to cohabitees: the nature of the parties' relationship; the length of time they have lived together as husband and wife; whether there are or have been any children who are children of both parties or for whom both parties have or have had parental responsibility; the length of time that has elapsed since the parties ceased to live together; and the existence of pending proceedings between the parties in relation to the property or any financial provision for the children.[30] Significantly, an additional factor to which the court must have regard is the fact that the parties have not given each other the commitment involved in marriage.[31] When deciding whether to make a regulatory occupation order in favour of a former spouse or present or former cohabitee, the court considers all the circumstances of the case, including the general checklist as well as the balance of harm test.[32]

F   Occupation orders: the categories of applicant

While statutory regulation of occupation of the family home covers various forms of domestic relationship, distinctions are made in the criteria to be applied and the nature of the orders made. Non-entitled applicants are treated less favourably in several important respects. The Order ensures that a spouse will usually be able to apply as an entitled applicant who may apply for an occupation order against a

---

unless the former spouse, cohabitee or former cohabitee is joint owner or tenant or has an equitable estate in the property, they will not be able to apply as an entitled applicant, but can apply as a non-entitled applicant under articles 13(1) and 14(1) respectively. In situations where both parties are living in the dwelling-house but neither has a right of occupation, either party may apply to the court for an occupation order under article 15 (present or former spouse) or article 16 (present or former cohabitee).

26   Articles 13(5) and 14(5).
27   Article 13(6)(a)–(d). The same checklist is considered in a claim by an entitled applicant under article 11(6). See the text preceding footnote 19.
28   Article 13(6)(e)–(g).
29   Article 14(6)(a)–(d). *Supra*, note 27.
30   Article 14(6)(e)–(i).
31   Article 19.
32   Articles 13(8) and 14(8).

person with whom he or she is associated.[33] A non-entitled applicant, however, may only apply for an occupation order against his or her spouse, former spouse, cohabitant or former cohabitant.[34] There is also an important distinction made in the duration of the orders for the various categories of applicant. For an entitled applicant, the occupation order may be of unlimited duration,[35] while an order for a non-entitled applicant must not exceed 12 months, although it may be extended for a further period of up to 12 months *on one or more occasions*.[36] This can be contrasted with the position in England and Wales under the Family Law Act 1996 where an occupation order in favour of a former spouse or present/former cohabitant[37] is limited to six months. While a former spouse, under the Act, can apply on one or more occasion for an extension for a further period not exceeding six months,[38] cohabitants can apply on one occasion only for such an extension.[39] This limitation gives cause for concern as the duration of an order is pre-determined by the status of the parties as opposed to the needs of the case. Indeed, one commentator has concluded that such a restriction is an unnecessary inclusion in the provisions and has suggested that the interests of both the applicant and the respondent could be safeguarded within a more flexible legislative framework.[40] While it was not the original aim of the occupation order to provide long-term housing for a cohabitant or former cohabitant, this would not be jeopardised by a provision enabling such a person to apply to the court once the order was extinguished. Indeed, the applicant would have to return to court to justify the extension of the order.[41] The Northern Ireland provisions adopt a more pragmatic approach, allowing a cohabitant or former cohabitant to apply for an extension of the order on more than one occasion.

The Northern Ireland provisions also differ from the Family Law Act 1996 in relation to the application of the 'balance of harm' test. This test, which is common to all applicants, means that in some cases the court is under a duty to make a regulatory occupation order where the consequences of not doing so would result in significant harm to the applicant or a relevant child, unless the respondent or relevant child is likely to suffer greater harm if an order is made. Under the Family Law Act 1996 the test applies with equal force to an entitled applicant[42] and former spouse;[43] however, the court cannot be compelled to make such an order for a non-entitled cohabitant or former cohabitant.[44] For the latter category the 'balance of harm test' merely amounts to a series of factors to be considered as part of the court's overall discretion. However, the original Family

---

33   Article 11.
34   Articles 13 and 14 respectively.
35   Article 11(10).
36   Articles 13(10) and 14(10).
37   The Family Law Act uses the word cohabitant, rather than cohabitee, although their meanings are the same.
38   Section 35(10), Family Law Act 1996.
39   Section 36(10).
40   M Horton, 'The Family Law Bill – Domestic Violence' [1996] *Family Law* 49 at 50.
41   Ibid.
42   Section 33(7), Family Law Act 1996.
43   Ibid, section 35(8).
44   Ibid, section 36(7)–(8).

Homes and Domestic Violence Bill, which was withdrawn due to political pressure, applied the 'balance of harm test' to *all* parties regardless of status. This was amended to satisfy those[45] who suggested that the proposed legislation would give cohabitants the same property rights as married parties. The subsequent failure to apply the 'balance of harm test' in its full rigour places cohabitants at a disadvantage in obtaining regulatory occupation orders. The position in the Northern Ireland legislation is notably different as the 'balance of harm' test applies in its full rigour to non-entitled cohabitees or former cohabitees.[46]

One provision which was not dropped from the Northern Ireland legislation is the requirement that on an application by a cohabitee regard should be had to the fact that the parties have not given each other the 'commitment involved in marriage'.[47] One wonders why this was included as a specific factor for judicial consideration when it is recalled that under article 14(e)–(f) the court is to have regard to 'the nature of the parties' relationship' and 'the length of time during which they have lived together as husband and wife'.[48] Surely the level of commitment demonstrated by the parties during the relationship would be considered at this stage without specific reference to the 'lack of commitment' factor. However, the fact that it was not included in the original Family Homes and Domestic Violence Bill adds weight to the argument that it was a strategic afterthought – indeed, it has been dubbed 'political posturing at its most blatant',[49] indicating the underlying agenda of stressing the importance of marriage. However, the lack of guidance as to the weight to be attached to it makes it unclear to what extent the judiciary will deny an unmarried applicant an occupation order on this footing.

The statutory inclusion of this factor also indicates an assumption that marriage and commitment are contemporaneous, a generalisation that can be refuted by the facts of individual cases. Indeed, it could be asked why former spouses who have broken this commitment are not subject to a comparative consideration. The specific factors considered on an application by a former

---

45   Conservative backbench Members of Parliament and tabloid press, instigated by the *Daily Mail*, 23 October 1995.

46   Article 14(8). It was felt that implementation of the English position would have contravened the Policy Appraisal and Fair Treatment Guidelines (PAFT). The PAFT guidelines, which came into effect in January 1994, are designed to ensure that equality considerations inform policy-making in all areas of Government activity. They apply to all government bodies and non-departmental public bodies and require that in formulating and reviewing policies in Northern Ireland these bodies should assess the potential for unequal treatment in relation to religion and political opinion; gender; race; disability; age; marital status; dependants and sexual orientation. It was stated that 'equality and equity are central issues which must condition and influence policy-making in all spheres and at all levels of Government activity', Central Secretariat Circular, 5/93, Policy Appraisal and Fair Treatment, 22 December 1993. However, although these non-statutory guidelines can highlight factors which might not otherwise have been considered, they can only inform and not determine the final decision. These guidelines have now been replaced with statutory equality provisions under sections 75–76 of the Northern Ireland Act 1998.

47   Article 19.

48   The purpose of these inclusions was voiced by the Lord Chancellor who said that while the courts will have regard to the fact that the parties have not made the same commitment as the parties to a marriage, they will 'also wish to distinguish between a short-lived relationship between cohabitants and a stable and long-term relationship where a couple have lived as man and wife for a number of years …'. *Hansard*, HL Debs, 27 June 1996, Column 1107.

49   *Supra*, note 40.

spouse include the length of time since the parties lived together and the length of time since the marriage was dissolved.[50] Considering that the granting of an occupation order is not exclusive to situations of domestic violence and that there is no statutory time bar restricting the rights of a former spouse to make an application, these are sensible inclusions to safeguard the rights of a respondent from the claims of a far-removed former spouse. However, if it is deemed necessary to include the perceived lack of commitment on the part of cohabitees as a specific factor for consideration in order to stress the importance of marriage, is it difficult to reconcile why the broken commitment in the case of former spouses is not also given express statutory acknowledgement.

G   Enforcement

Under articles 25 and 26, breach of an order made for protective purposes will automatically be an arrestable, criminal offence.[51] The offence will be punishable with a maximum fine of £2,500 and/or a term of imprisonment not exceeding three months.[52] This can be contrasted with the position in England and Wales under the Family Law Act 1996 where breach of the equivalent orders is not an offence. Instead, the court may attach a power of arrest to the order unless it is satisfied that the applicant or child can be adequately protected without it.[53] In Northern Ireland the powers of arrest without warrant have been clarified under article 26, which amends the Police and Criminal Evidence (Northern Ireland) Order 1989[54] to the effect that offences under article 25 are now included in the list of arrestable offences under the 1989 Order. An applicant who wishes to enforce an order otherwise than by way of prosecution under article 25 and those who wish to enforce an occupation order which has been made to regulate the occupation rights of the parties in the absence of domestic violence can make a civil complaint to a magistrates' court.[55]

H   Children and domestic violence

The 1998 Order makes significant changes to the protection given to children in situations of domestic violence. Article 29 inserts new provisions into the Children (Northern Ireland) Order 1995, which permit a court to include an exclusion requirement in an interim care or an emergency protection order. This

---

50   Article 13.

51   Article 25 makes it a criminal offence to breach a non-molestation order; an occupation order or ancillary order made under article 18, where a non-molestation order is in force; an exclusion requirement attached to an interim care order; or an exclusion requirement attached to an emergency protection order.

52   This is the same as the position prior to the 1998 Order where under article 19 of the Domestic Proceedings (Northern Ireland) Order 1980, inserted by article 14 of the Family Law (Northern Ireland) Order 1993, breach of a personal protection order was a criminal offence.

53   Section 47(2), Family Law Act 1996.

54   Arrest without warrant for arrestable offences.

55   Article 27 preserves the procedure set out in article 112(3)–(8) of the Magistrates' Court (Northern Ireland) Order 1981 under which a court of summary jurisdiction may deal with enforcement of court orders other than for payment of money.

means that for the first time a court will have the power to remove a suspected abuser from the family home instead of removing the child. Article 28 contains the second main amendment to the Children Order and provides that when the court is considering whether or not to make a residence or contact order in favour of someone who has a non-molestation order against him (the prohibited person), it will have to consider whether the child has suffered or is at risk of suffering any harm as a result of seeing or hearing ill-treatment of another person by the prohibited person. This provision is not included in the English legislation, but was included in Northern Ireland after consultees felt that such a linkage to the Children Order was beneficial.

I   Conclusion

The purpose of the Family Law Act 1996 and the Family Homes and Domestic Violence (Northern Ireland) Order 1998 is to consolidate the law regulating disputes concerning the occupation of the family home and protection from domestic violence. While a wider category of applicant has been included within the definition of 'associated person' for the non-molestation order, the occupation order is available to a restricted category of applicant. The Order, therefore, tiers the level of regulation depending on the status of the relationship. For example, same-sex cohabitees are included within the definition of 'associated person', but not within the definition of cohabitee, and heterosexual cohabitees are recognised but not fully equated with married parties.[56] Lind and Barlowe assert that the policy of the Family Law Act 1996 illustrates how:

> '[o]nce again the government has sacrificed legal coherence in the resolution of parallel disputes for the sake of maintaining the symbolic and moral superiority of heterosexual relationships over homosexual relationships.'[57]

The tiered nature of the provisions also illustrates the underlying consideration of competing social priorities. There is a distinction between the various potential categories of applicant for an occupation order while no such distinction is made between the applicants for a non-molestation order. The reason for this may be that the non-molestation order is specifically limited to situations of domestic violence, while the availability of the occupation order is extended to all situations depending on the facts and circumstances of the case. While the

---

56   For example, for spouses, the occupation order may be of unlimited duration. However, for cohabitees the occupation order is only designed as a short-term remedy to protect from domestic violence or to satisfy immediate housing needs so it is limited to 12 months initially, although it may be extended for a further period of up to 12 months 'on one or more occasions'. The distinction between spouses and cohabitees is even more marked under the Family Law Act 1996. Horton suggests that a possible side-effect of diluting the protection available to non-entitled cohabitants is that such parties will attempt to establish a right to occupy the family home, thus involving another issue in the proceedings. *Supra*, note 40. The consequence of a successful claim would be to obtain the legislative benefits of being an entitled applicant, significantly, having the potential to gain an occupation order indefinitely. However, the court would still be required to consider the fact that the parties have not given each other the commitment involved in marriage.

57   Lind and Barlowe, 'Family Redefinition under Part IV of the Family Law Act 1996' [1996] 2 Web JCLI (http://webjcli.ncl.ac.uk).

status of the parties is less important when protection from domestic violence is concerned, it is a factor of increased significance when the issue in question is the occupation, use and enjoyment of the family home. Indeed, due to the fact that the occupation order interferes with the property rights of a legal owner/occupier, coupled with the fact that it is applicable in an undefined variety of cases where violence is not a precondition, it seems that the potential consequences of a wider definition of applicant proved too far-reaching. It is interesting to note, once again, that the Bill preceding the Family Law Act 1996 was withdrawn due to the fear that cohabitees with no legal entitlement to the family home would be able to obtain occupation orders interfering with their partners' legal right of occupation. When property issues arise the status of potential applicants becomes more important as the dual aim of upholding the institution of marriage and protecting the rights of the legal owner/occupier take priority. Lind and Barlowe, however, assert that:

'... the need for effective legal remedies is more important than the moral status of particular relationships.'[58]

III OWNERSHIP OF MATRIMONIAL PROPERTY

A Matrimonial property: the issues

The Law Reform Advisory Committee for Northern Ireland has recently published a discussion paper on matrimonial property.[59] This term is used in its broad sense to cover housekeeping money and goods, as well as the matrimonial or quasi-matrimonial home, which is termed the 'joint residence'.[60] Prompted by the unsatisfactory position of the law, the Committee has borrowed and extended the recommendations of an earlier Law Commission Report on matrimonial property.[61] Ownership of matrimonial property, particularly the matrimonial home, remains a live issue despite the fact that Wade stated many years ago that:

'[w]hole forests have been destroyed in the discussion of this question since the Second World War.'[62]

The focus of the debate is usually on the position of cohabitants on the breakdown of their relationship. For married parties the effect of the doctrine of separate property, originating from the Married Women's Property Acts of the 1880s, is

---

58   Ibid.

59   Law Reform Advisory Committee for Northern Ireland, (1999) *Matrimonial Property*, Discussion Paper No 5, Belfast: The Stationery Office.

60   The Committee recommends that the joint residence include such area of land occupied and enjoyed with the dwelling as is required for the reasonable enjoyment of the dwelling having regard to its size and character. Secondary residences are excluded. Ibid, para 6.14.

61   Law Commission, (1988) *Family Law: Matrimonial Property*, Law Commission Report No 175, London: HMSO.

62   Wade, 'Trusts, the Matrimonial Home and *De Facto* Spouses', (1979) *University of Tasmania Law Review* 97–114 at 97.

mitigated on divorce where the court has the power to transfer property between spouses while taking a wide range of factors into account.[63] However, no comparable statutory power is available for cohabitants whose property disputes are determined by the law of trusts, where the existence and quantification of the beneficial interest amounts to calculating the contributions made by the parties to the acquisition of the property. While direct financial contributions to the purchase price will give rise to an interest, the status of indirect contributions has been the subject of academic and judicial debate. In the case of *McFarlane v McFarlane*,[64] which was expressly approved by the House of Lords in *Lloyds Bank v Rosset*,[65] the Northern Ireland Court of Appeal held that an indirect contribution, whether in money or money's worth, could give rise to a beneficial interest, provided this was the subject of an 'agreement, arrangement or understanding' between the parties.[66] The unsatisfactory result is well documented, that traditional trust principles are inappropriate to determine 'domestic' property disputes.[67] The Committee recognise that, while the adjustive powers of the court on divorce reduce the importance of determining the beneficial interest of the property of married couples, it remains an important issue in other contexts, such as bankruptcy and pre-divorce disputes.[68] Recommendations are, therefore, made to determine the ownership of the family home for spouses and qualifying cohabitants during the subsistence of the relationship.

The Committee concomitantly consider the position in relation to housekeeping money and household goods. The Married Women's Property Act 1964, which provides that any allowance made by the husband for the expense of the matrimonial home or for similar purposes, or any property acquired out of such money, shall belong to the husband and wife in equal shares subject to any agreement to the contrary, does not apply in Northern Ireland and no comparable provision has been enacted. The common law rules remain, which means that if a husband provides his wife with an allowance out of his income for housekeeping, any sums saved from it remain his and he is entitled to any property bought with them. Furthermore, when spending such money the wife is deemed to be acting as the husband's agent.[69] The 1964 Act, however, was considered by the Committee to be an inadequate response to the shortcomings of the existing law.[70]

---

63 Matrimonial Causes (Northern Ireland) Order 1978, articles 25–27.

64 [1972] NI 59.

65 [1991] 1 AC 107.

66 Ibid, at 72.

67 See Mee, *The Property Rights of Cohabitees*, (Oxford: Hart Publishing, 1999). Mee's concern lies in the damaging doctrinal effect of applying traditional trust doctrine to domestic disputes.

68 Law Reform Advisory Committee for Northern Ireland, (1999) *Matrimonial Property*, Discussion Paper No 5, para 3.32.

69 See *Hoddinott v Hoddinott* [1949] 2 KB 406.

70 It was felt that the Act contained a number of interpretational difficulties and anomalies (for example, it is unclear what type of payments will be classed as an allowance) as well as perpetuating the stereotype of a breadwinning husband who provides for a housekeeping wife. Law Reform Advisory Committee for Northern Ireland, (1999) *Matrimonial Property*, Discussion Paper No 5, para 6.2. The 1988 Law Commission Report similarly criticised the 1964 Act in having application only where an allowance is made by a husband and not vice versa. Law Commission, (1988) *Family Law: Matrimonial Property*, Law Commission Report No 175, para 2.5.

B   The proposals

The Committee propose a scheme of statutory co-ownership of matrimonial property alongside reform of the law of trusts. It is proposed that beneficial ownership of the joint residence and other property should vest in both spouses and qualifying cohabitants as joint tenants unless the parties expressly agree otherwise. In the case of the joint residence the agreement not to share the beneficial ownership must be in writing.[71] The proposals apply to property acquired or transferred prior to the parties becoming spouses or qualifying cohabitants, provided it was acquired or transferred in the expectation of the marriage or in the context and for the purposes of a relationship of cohabitants.[72] Excluded from the proposed statutory scheme are property purchased or transferred for business purposes, an interest in any life assurance policy, or contracts of deferred annuities. The beneficial ownership of other property of spouses or cohabitants which was purchased by or transferred into the name of a single spouse or cohabitant, will not vest jointly unless the property was wholly or mainly for the use or benefit of both of the parties.[73] This requirement is implied in the case of the joint residence, which is defined as property in which the parties jointly reside as their home.

While the recommendations are broadly similar to the earlier proposals of the Law Commission (1988),[74] they go further in dealing with both real and personal property, while the 1988 Report focused exclusively on the personal property of spouses. Although the majority of the Commission at the time would have supported extending the recommendations to cover land, it was felt that this may have been seen to be controversial, attracting inappropriate opposition, which would have jeopardised the proposals in relation to personal property.[75] It was recognised, however, that:

> '[e]xcluding the matrimonial home may create a new and potentially serious anomaly, in that where one spouse pays for the matrimonial home and the other buys the furniture, the furniture will become jointly owned but the house will not'.[76]

The Northern Ireland Committee were not convinced that there was sufficient justification to treat the joint residence differently from other property and, therefore, recommended statutory co-ownership of the beneficial title of the 'joint residence'.[77] Another recommendation not seen in the earlier report is the

71   Law Reform Advisory Committee for Northern Ireland, (1999) *Matrimonial Property*, Discussion Paper No 5, para 1.5.5.

72   Ibid.

73   Ibid, para 1.5.1.

74   Law Commission, (1988) *Family Law: Matrimonial Property*, Law Commission Report No 175, London: HMSO.

75   Ibid, paras 4.3 and 4.5.

76   Ibid, para 4.4.

77   The Committee also state that consideration must be given to the rights of the parties to realise their respective interests in the property. In Northern Ireland where a joint tenancy or a tenancy in common exists, a joint tenant or tenant in common may apply to the court for an order for sale or partition of lands and where the applicant holds an interest of a half or more in the lands, the court is bound to order a sale rather than partition unless it sees good reason to the contrary (Partition

extension of the proposals to qualifying cohabitants.[78] To qualify, cohabitants must have been living together in the same household, effectively as husband or wife, for at least a total of two years within a period of the last three years, or have had a child by their relationship.

The second main proposal is the reform of the law of trusts in order to accommodate different forms of contributions giving rise to a beneficial interest in situations which will not come under the proposals for statutory co-ownership. Such situations, as envisaged by the Committee, include determining the ownership rights of non-qualifying cohabitants and occasions where the parties have expressly agreed to vest the property in the sole name of one of them but where the other makes contributions to its acquisition or improvement which will not give rise to an interest under existing law. In relation to property which is vested prior to the proposals coming into force, the Committee has not reached a provisional view on this and seeks the views of consultees.[79] If the legislation is not made retrospective such property will not come under the proposals.

In such situations, the Committee recommends that the court should have greater flexibility in determining the availability and quantification of beneficial interests in the joint residence and lists certain factors which the court should be directed to take into account. These include contributions in money and money's worth, direct and indirect, made towards the cost of acquiring, maintaining, repairing and improving the premises as well as towards the cost of discharging any debt secured on the premises and any benefit accruing to the party with legal title from such contributions; and any agreement, understanding or arrangement, express or implied, made by the parties in respect of their beneficial interest, whether prior to the acquisition of the premises or during occupation, or which they might reasonably be expected to have made if they had considered the question of beneficial ownership. The nature of the parties' relationship is also relevant and the court should consider the degree of economic integration of the parties; the reasonable expectations of the parties; and, in the case of unmarried cohabitants, the degree of permanence of the relationship. Any representations, express or implied, made by either party to the other relating to title or beneficial ownership of the premises before acquisition or during occupation should also be taken into account.[80]

The recommendations, therefore, cover the joint residence and other property for both spouses and cohabitants with reformulated trust principles having default

---

Act 1868 and 1876). Article 49 of the Property (Northern Ireland) Order 1997 confers a power on the court to impose a stay, suspension or conditions on the making of an order under the Partition Acts 1868 and 1876. The Committee consider that the legislation should make clear that the court has a general power to decline to make an order under the Partition Acts 1868 and 1876, at least in the case of applications brought by spouses or the mortgagee or chargee of spouses. It is recommended that in the case of such applications the court, in deciding how or if to exercise its powers under the Partition Acts 1868 and 1876, should be directed to have regard to the matters directed to be taken into account under the provisions of the Matrimonial Causes (Northern Ireland) Order 1978.

78   The 1988 Report stated that the position of cohabitants would be a suitable topic for further consideration. Law Commission, (1988) *Family Law: Matrimonial Property*, Law Commission Report No 175, para 4.21.

79   Law Reform Advisory Committee for Northern Ireland, (1999) *Matrimonial Property*, Discussion Paper No 5, para 6.25.1.

80   Ibid, para 6.25.6.

application. However, despite the desire of Northern Ireland policy makers to develop a holistic family law system,[81] the paper does not consider these recommendations in the overall context of relationship breakdown, for example, in relation to the adjustive powers of the court on divorce[82] or situations of third party interests in the joint residence. One commentator speculates that the fact that the Committee was relying upon the Law Commission's 1988 proposals relating to household goods may explain why no attempt was made to consider the effect of the proposals on third parties:

> '[i]n 1988, in the wake of *William's & Glyn's Bank v Boland* [1981] AC 487, it was possible for the Law Commission to assume that section 70(1)(g) of the Land Registration Act 1925 would protect the non-owning party. Following *Abbey National BS v Cann* [1991] 1 AC 56, this is no longer the case. This issue needs to be considered or protection offered by the Committee's proposals may prove illusory in practice.'[83]

One difficulty with these proposals is the Committee's reliance on the 'marriage model' of family form, illustrated by the restricted definition of cohabitation as those who live together 'as husband and wife'. This gender-specific terminology excludes same-sex cohabitants regardless of the duration and nature of their relationship, as well as those who live together platonically and it is unlikely that this term would be judicially interpreted as anything other than a heterosexual conjugal relationship. Indeed, the House of Lords held in *Fitzpatrick v Sterling Housing Association*[84] that a similar term for succession to a private sector tenancy under the Rent Act 1977[85] indicates an intention that there be a biological distinction between the sex of the parties.[86]

Other jurisdictions, however, have adopted a more inclusive approach when determining which familial relationships deserve legislative recognition. In New

---

81   *Divorce in Northern Ireland – A Better Way Forward*, Office of Law Reform (1999), chapter 1.

82   Under the Matrimonial Causes (Northern Ireland) Order 1978. It is interesting that the earlier Law Commission Report (1988) referred to the spouses' rights during marriage only and did not amend the court's power on divorce to vary the spouses' property rights under the Matrimonial Causes Act 1973, sections 23–25. However, it was considered possible that '... altering property rights during marriage will have some effect on divorce proceedings. It may be that knowing who owns what and knowing in particular that most household goods are jointly owned is more likely to lead to an early settlement without the need to go to court'. Law Commission, (1988) *Family Law: Matrimonial Property*, Law Commission Report No 175, para 4.20.

83   'Something old, something new and something borrowed: reform of the law relating to the family home', (2000) 22(1) *Journal of Social Welfare and Family Law* 115 at 118.

84   [1999] 4 All ER 705.

85   The provision in question, which was introduced into Sch 1, para 2(2) to the Rent Act 1977 by the Housing Act 1988, gave succession rights on the death of the original tenant to ... *a person who was living with the original tenant as his or her wife or husband* ... The majority of the Lords held, however, that a same-sex couple were capable of being members of the same family under the legislation.

86   The Lords approved the earlier Court of Appeal decision in *Harrogate Borough Council v Simpson* (1984) 17 HLR 205 which held that the term 'living together as husband and wife', for succession to a public sector tenancy, did not include a lesbian relationship, thus rejecting the argument that the use of the word 'as' meant that '... Parliament was indicating, not only that the provisions were intended to apply to persons who were married in the formal sense, but also to unions which gave the appearance of two people living together in a kind of matrimonial state' at 209.

South Wales the Property (Relationships) Legislation Amendment Act 1999 has amended the *De Facto* Relationships Act 1984[87] to include an extended gender-neutral definition of *de facto* relationships, thus including same-sex couples. Section 4 provides that a *de facto* relationship is a relationship between two adult persons who live together as a couple and who are not married to one another or related by family. In determining the existence of such a relationship all the circumstances of the relationship are to be considered and the court may have regard to the following non-exhaustive factors: the duration of the relationship; the nature and extent of common residence; whether or not a sexual relationship exists; the degree of financial dependence or interdependence, and any arrangements for financial support, between the parties; the ownership, use and acquisition of property; the degree of mutual commitment to a shared life; the care and support of children; the performance of household duties; and the reputation and public aspects of the relationship. The Act also introduces the concept of 'domestic relationships' to include those who are not a couple but who have a cohabiting relationship of interdependence.[88] It is unfortunate that the Northern Ireland proposals do not move beyond assimilation with marriage as a means of extending the remit of the legislation. Similar reasoning can be seen from the dissenting judgment of Lord Hutton in *Fitzpatrick v Sterling Housing Association*,[89] who considered that to be recognised as a 'family' under the Rent Act 1977 a *de facto* relationship must be capable of assimilation with a comparable *de jure* family. The outward appearance of a *de jure* family must be apparent but:

> '... because the essence of marriage is a relationship between a man and a woman there is no de jure family relationship to which a homosexual relationship is equivalent ...'.[90]

On a positive note in relation to qualifying cohabitants the proposals do not appear to 'dilute' the rights of heterosexual cohabitants in order to be seen to prioritise marriage.[91] The only practical difference between spouses and cohabitants is in the requirements to qualify for co-ownership with the intention to include only those cohabitants in a sufficiently permanent relationship. Another difference, however, is in those situations which remain to be determined by the reformed law of trusts. The court must consider, *inter alia*, the degree of permanence of the

---

87 Now called the Property (Relationships) Act 1984.

88 Under section 5, the definition of domestic partners is a *de facto* relationship, or a close personal relationship (other than marriage or a *de facto* relationship) between two adult persons, whether or not related by family, who are living together, one or each of whom provides the other with domestic support or personal care, provided that this is not done for a fee or reward or on behalf of another person or an organisation. This definition of domestic partner is not as extensive, however, as that contained in the Australian Capital Territory's Domestic Relationship Act 1994, which does not require that the parties live together.

89 [1999] 4 All ER 705.

90 Ibid, at 739.

91 This can be seen in other pieces of legislation. For example, the provisions of the Family Homes and Domestic Violence (Northern Ireland) Order 1998 contain certain differences between spouses and cohabitants in the availability of occupation orders and the substance of the orders made.

relationship in cases of unmarried cohabitants, but not when dealing with a claim made by a spouse. This has lead one commentator to conclude that:

> '... since the report is premised on the basis that the relationships of cohabitants are similar to those of married couples, it could be argued that the nature of the relationship should also be taken into account where the couple is married.'[92]

Apart from these qualification differences, the substantive rights of both married couples and unmarried cohabitants are the same.

C   Statutory co-ownership of the joint residence

The proposals have been designed to give effect to the presumed intention of the parties without having to consider any direct or indirect contributions made by the non-legal owner.[93] The fact that the parties can opt out of the statutory scheme would appear, on first view, to avoid imposing rights, duties and obligations which may not have been intended. However, it is open to debate whether the opt-out mechanism is satisfactory in practice. Unless the parties agree otherwise in writing, the beneficial interest of a couple's most significant capital asset will automatically vest in both parties jointly. However, a level of knowledge is required for the parties to rebut the presumption of equal beneficial ownership, alongside a willingness on the part of a legal owner to inform his/her partner or spouse that joint ownership is not intended. As one commentator has noted the proposals place a heavy burden on the legal owner, as only those:

> '... who have full knowledge of the law and are willing to risk the affection of the other party, by indicating that their relationship is not one that is to involve sharing worldly goods, will be able even to raise the topic.'[94]

It has also been suggested that these proposals can work to the disadvantage of a non-owning party who agrees not to share the beneficial ownership but who subsequently regrets this decision.[95] While this may prove to be correct, it should be remembered that an agreement not to share the beneficial ownership can subsequently be overridden by the court on the basis of the contributions made by the non-owning party.[96]

---

92   'Something old, something new and something borrowed: reform of the law relating to the family home', (2000) 22(1) *Journal of Social Welfare and Family Law* 115 at 119.

93   The Law Commission in 1988 based their proposals on co-ownership of matrimonial property, other then real property, on similar grounds. The Report stated that '[w]hilst it will be true that many couples rarely stop to consider questions of property ownership when they are starting out to provide a family home or whilst they are happily married, we consider that if they did the majority of them would expect that much of the property acquired during the marriage would be co-owned'. Law Commission (1988) *Family Law: Matrimonial Property*, Law Commission Report No 175, para 1.5.

94   'Something old, something new and something borrowed: reform of the law relating to the family home', (2000) 22(1) *Journal of Social Welfare and Family Law* 115 at 118.

95   Ibid.

96   Law Reform Advisory Committee for Northern Ireland, (1999) *Matrimonial Property*, Discussion Paper No 5, para 6.25.5.

One factor which has not been made clear, however, is the required timing of the written agreement to opt out of statutory co-ownership. The property covered by the rules is property purchased or transferred during the relationship or prior to marriage or cohabitation provided it was done in consideration of this. However, is it necessary that the written agreement is made at the time of transference or acquisition, or, under the rules, can it be made at any time during the subsistence of the relationship? The committee does not make recommendations on this point.

The justification provided by the committee for interfering with the rights of a legal owner is the need to remedy the current law which is weighted against the wife or female cohabitant. Due to the fact that, statistically, women earn less than men, it is likely that a wife or female cohabitant will have less money to contribute to the acquisition of the property and make indirect contributions. It has been suggested, however, that drafting proposals to remedy this imbalance is unfair to men who suffer the consequences of women's general economic position.[97] It has, therefore, been advocated that a more convincing argument could be based around the financial losses that women experience that are attributable to interruptions due to childcare. This has been deemed preferable as:

> '... the male partner is not required to compensate for abstract discrimination, but rather to share the responsibility for the consequences of the choices that they have made.'[98]

However, both the economic and biological grounds of justification are problematic. The committee's justification is based on the need to remedy the proprietary consequences of women's lower earning capacity. Any proposals drafted on the foot of this sole consideration, however, will be restricted to remedy the economic gender-imbalance in heterosexual relationships. Indeed, this might explain why same-sex couples were not included within the remit of these recommendations. The alternative argument has similar problems, as it is based on giving a non-legal owner a beneficial interest on the ground that financial losses suffered by women are due to the consequences of family life. The problem is that the family life envisaged is that of the traditional family structure which, again, excludes both same-sex relationships and other platonic homesharers. It seems that an inclusive legislative scheme may only become a reality when the policy shifts from solely trying to remedy the economic gender imbalance within the traditional family structure.[99]

---

97   'Something old, something new and something borrowed: reform of the law relating to the family home' (2000) 22(1) *Journal of Social Welfare and Family Law* 115 at 116.

98   Ibid.

99   Focusing on one particular dynamic of familial relations lead Gonthier J to reason, in the dissenting judgment of the Supreme Court of Canada in *M v H* [1999] 171 DLR (4th) 577, that exclusion of same-sex couples from the definition of spouse under section 29 of the Ontario Family Law Act 1990 did not violate section 15(1) of the Canadian Charter of Rights and Freedoms. Section 29 allowed heterosexual cohabiting couples to claim spousal support and, according to Gonthier J, this was designed to remedy gender imbalance in opposite sex relationships caused by the economic, social and biological reality of women's lives, one dynamic of dependency which was not apparent in same-sex relationships. The majority, however, considered that the provision was designed to relieve financial dependency which can arise in an intimate relationship in situations unrelated to biological or other gender-based discrimination. Bastarache J found with the majority that section 29 violated the Canadian

In conclusion, the statutory scheme proposed by the Committee goes some way to improving the position of non-legal owners in both spousal and qualifying cohabitational relationships. It is unfortunate that qualifying cohabitants are restricted to those who satisfy the 'marriage model' and several points require clarification, for example, the timing of the written agreement to opt out of joint beneficial ownership and the effect, if any, on the adjustive powers of the court on divorce. A further point is how the reformed law of trusts would operate in practice in situations not qualifying for statutory co-ownership. A range of factors[100] are to be taken into account when deciding the parties' beneficial interests, factors which are:

> '... closely akin to the matters which the courts take into account in Canada and Australia of unjust enrichment and unconscionability.'[101]

While Mee asserts that the judicial development of the '... Australian unconscionability doctrine ... shares with its Canadian counterpart the absence of a convincing theoretical foundation',[102] the Committee proposes statutory intervention in the determination of equitable ownership. The nature of this recommendation, however, needs to be considered. Initially, it might be thought that the Committee is proposing a scheme comparable to the application of the Matrimonial Causes (Northern Ireland) Order 1978 on divorce.[103] The Committee, however, states that the court's function in determining the equitable interest of the parties would not be the same as the property adjusting power vested in the court in divorce proceedings in which the court can adjust, and thus vary, the parties' beneficial interests.[104] It seems that the Committee is proposing statutory reform of the law of trusts to allow a wider range of contributions to be taken into account when *determining* the beneficial ownership of cohabitants (qualifying or otherwise) and spouses. However, the recommendation, as stated, is made in isolation and unrelated to traditional trust doctrine and its application. It is submitted that the basis of the court's discretion in this instance needs to be clarified. Indeed, one question is whether it is necessary for a claimant to be able to establish, at the outset, an equitable interest under either a resulting or constructive trust, the quantification of which can be determined by the court under the proposed statutory rules. The aim of the recommendation is to give the court greater flexibility in determining 'whether and to what extent a party has an equitable claim'.[105] Although a subtle point, stated in this way, determining 'whether' a party has an equitable interest is declaratory, albeit of a statutory nature, and the subsequent words relate to quantification. A statutory scheme

---

Charter of Rights and Freedoms, but differed in so far as he thought that the legislation dealt with individuals in '"permanent and serious" relationships which cause or enhance economic disparity between the partners'.

100 See text preceding footnote 80.

101 Ibid.

102 Mee, *The Property Rights of Cohabitees*, (Oxford: Hart Publishing, 1999) at 265.

103 See articles 26 and 27.

104 Law Reform Advisory Committee for Northern Ireland, (1999) *Matrimonial Property*, Discussion Paper No 5, para 6.25.7.

105 Ibid, para 6.25.6.

which expressly gives the court the power to *vary* and *transfer* the parties' equitable interests in the matrimonial home would avoid such ambiguity and ensure that the issue was determined without reference to traditional trust doctrine.

IV DIVORCE IN NORTHERN IRELAND

A Introduction

Divorce, from a substantive and procedural perspective, is currently being considered in Northern Ireland as part of the rolling review of family law. The rate of divorce in Northern Ireland is rising and continuing to do so, although it is lower than that in England and Wales. In 1996 the annual rate of divorce in Northern Ireland was 3.4 per 1,000 while the divorce rate in England and Wales in the same year stood at 13.5 per 1,000.[106] Clearly, divorce is an important social issue which requires an efficient and cost-effective governing legal framework. Recently, the Office of Law Reform, the Civil Service Office which has oversight over civil law in Northern Ireland, commissioned empirical research into the operation of divorce law in this jurisdiction. The report, *Divorce in Northern Ireland – Unravelling the System*, was completed in December 1998 and was followed in December 1999 by the publication of a Consultation Paper *Divorce in Northern Ireland – A Better Way Forward*. This chapter will consider many of the proposals of this Paper, which were informed by the interesting trend of the divorce law process in Northern Ireland, identified by the empirical research.

At present divorce in Northern Ireland is governed by the Matrimonial Causes (Northern Ireland) Order 1978 which is modelled on the English Matrimonial Causes Act 1973.[107] The 1978 Order provides for a 'mixed' divorce system containing both fault and no-fault grounds corresponding to the English legislation. The single ground for divorce is irretrievable breakdown of marriage which must be proved in one of the following five ways:

(1)   that the respondent has committed adultery;
(2)   that the respondent has behaved in such a way that the petitioner cannot reasonably be expected to live with them;
(3)   that the respondent has deserted the petitioner for a continuous period of at least two years;
(4)   that the parties have been living separately for two years and the respondent consents to the divorce;
(5)   that the parties have been living separately for five years.[108]

When considering divorce reform, one of the key questions is the desirability of the retention of the fault facts to prove irretrievable breakdown of marriage.

---

106 *Social Trends* 28 (Office of National Statistics, 1998) Table 2.19.

107 Judicial divorce was introduced for the first time in Northern Ireland in 1939 with the passing of the Matrimonial Causes Act (Northern Ireland) 1939 on grounds identical to those contained in the English Matrimonial Causes Act 1937. See Bromley, Passingham and Malcolm, 'Divorce Law Reform in Northern Ireland', *Northern Ireland Legal Quarterly Inc*, 1978.

108 Matrimonial Causes (Northern Ireland) Order 1978, article 3(2).

The operation of divorce in England and Wales under the 1973 Act was criticised in the Law Commission's Report *Family Law – The Ground for Divorce*[109] as being adversarial, confusing and open to abuse. It was felt that insufficient attention was paid to the effect of divorce on children and the possibility of reconciliation. The thrust of the reforms contained in the statutory culmination of the debate, Part II of the Family Law Act 1996,[110] was to remove fault from the divorce process; to encourage couples to consider whether their marriage had irretrievably broken down and, through mediation, to settle post-divorce financial and other arrangements by themselves prior to divorce.[111] Whether similar criticisms can be levelled at the system in Northern Ireland which may justify the introduction of comparable reforms can only be decided once it is clear what the divorcing practice is in Northern Ireland. Of course, the announcement by the Lord Chancellor that the Government does not intend to implement Part II of the Family Law Act in 2000 is significant, and of particular interest is the early indication in the pilot projects being run in England that the information meeting, the compulsory precursor for the initiation of divorce proceedings under the Family Law Act, is not fulfilling its objective to help save saveable marriages and to promote mediation as an alternative to litigation.[112]

B   'The Northern Ireland experience'

Although the 1978 Northern Ireland Order was modelled on the English Act of 1973, there are a number of differences worth noting. First, there is no requirement in Northern Ireland that a solicitor certify that he/she has discussed reconciliation with the petitioner. This is a requirement under the English Act, although in parliamentary debate it was stated that this provision was ineffective.[113] Secondly, article 3(3) of the 1978 Order provides that a court must

---

109   *The Ground for Divorce* Law Com No 192 (1990). This was preceded by the discussion paper *Facing the Future – A Discussion Paper on the Ground for Divorce* Law Com No 170 (1988).

110   Part II of the Act, which will not now be brought into force, treats divorce as a process which is commenced by either spouse attending an information meeting. Pilot projects have been in operation in England to help determine the form this meeting should take. After attending this meeting a cooling off period of three months is invoked before either party can initiate divorce proceedings (section 8(2)). After this period either, or both, parties can file a statement of marital breakdown, which remains the sole ground for divorce established by the passage of a period of time for reflection and consideration. This lasts for nine months, but may be extended, and during this time parties are encouraged to consider reconciliation and, if this is not possible, to resolve post-divorce arrangements. The use of mediation is encouraged; indeed, those couples eligible for legal aid will only be entitled to aid for legal representation after they have attended an information session about mediation. (See section 15 of the Legal Aid Act 1988, as amended by section 29 of the Family Law Act 1996). At the end of this period, either, or both, spouses may apply for a divorce order and, unless there are exceptional circumstances, this must be accompanied by a statement of future financial and child care arrangements (section 9(7) and Schedule 1 para 1–4 of the Family Law Act 1996).

111   For a discussion of the detail of the Family Law Act 1996, see Douglas, 'Family Values to the Fore?' in *The International Survey of Family Law 1996*, ed A Bainham (Martinus Nijhoff Publishers, 1998) at 157–178.

112   The interim results of the pilot testing reveal that only 7% of those attending the pilot exercises had been diverted to mediation and 39% reported that they were more likely than before to go to a solicitor. Lord Chancellor's Department, 17 June 1999, 159/99.

113   *Hansard*, HC Debs 952, Col 320, 1978, per JA Dunn, MP.

hear oral evidence from the petitioner irrespective of whether the divorce is defended or not. This means that the Special Procedure,[114] introduced in England in 1973, is not available in Northern Ireland. While article 15 of the Family Law (Northern Ireland) Order 1993 allows the Family Rules Committee to introduce the Special Procedure, this power has not been exercised. Thirdly, legal aid remains available in Northern Ireland for undefended divorce cases provided that the applicant satisfies the statutory criteria[115] in both divorce and ancillary relief cases. Furthermore, there are more generous exemptions to the statutory charge than are available in England and Wales. Finally, article 44 of the Matrimonial Causes (Northern Ireland) Order 1978, which requires a social worker's report in every divorce case involving children in Northern Ireland, is not contained in the corresponding English legislation. While the rationale of the article 44 report was to protect 'innocent victims' of divorce by giving a social worker the opportunity to discuss custody and access arrangements with parents and assist with conciliation between the parties, in practice it was the main cause of delay in the divorce process and the requirement was abolished when the Children (Northern Ireland) Order 1995 was implemented in November 1996.[116]

While there are a couple of substantive differences between the law in the two jurisdictions, one question which had never been considered in any serious way before was whether divorce law *in practice* operated any differently in Northern Ireland. One would assume that being modelled on the statutory provisions governing England and Wales the 'divorce experience' would be similarly comparable. However, the results of the empirical research, commissioned by the Office of Law Reform, provide very interesting reading.[117] The terms of reference for the multi-disciplinary team conducting the research included evaluating the patterns of the use of divorce and related procedures in Northern Ireland; evaluating attitudes towards the principles, as included within the substantive law, that should govern the availability of divorce in Northern Ireland; identifying the deficiencies within the current law and procedure; and examining the opportunities for the role of mediation in Northern Ireland. The findings of the research team illustrate that there is a clear pattern of divorce procedure unique to Northern Ireland which cannot be fully explained by reference to the few substantive differences in this jurisdiction.

Empirical research reveals that under the 1978 Order divorce in Northern Ireland is the culmination of a lengthy process of marriage breakdown and judicial statistics reveal that around 70% of petitioners use a separation fact as opposed to one of the fault grounds.[118] This is similar to the position in Scotland[119] but can be

---

114 This procedure, commonly known as divorce by post, provides that an undefended divorce can be disposed of on affidavit without the petitioner appearing in court.

115 Legal Aid, Advice and Assistance (Northern Ireland) Order 1981, articles 9 and 10.

116 The Family Proceedings Rules (Northern Ireland) 1996 replace the article 44 report with an amended Statement of Arrangements for Children.

117 The research includes an analysis of existing secondary data, a study of court records, interviews with key practitioners, interviews with divorcees and the analysis of questionnaires issued to those going through the divorce process as well as an audit of the mediation services available in Northern Ireland.

118 *Unravelling the System*, Chapter 3.

119 SLC Discussion Paper No 76, *The Ground for Divorce : Should the Law be Changed?* (1988).

contrasted with the divorce reality in England and Wales where the fault grounds made up 77% of wives' decrees and 61% of husbands' decrees in 1994.[120] In a typical Northern Ireland divorce the petitioner separates from his/her spouse and makes the necessary financial and child-related arrangements through either the magistrates' court or a formal or informal private separation agreement. It is usually only at a later stage that a divorce petition is lodged leading the research team to conclude that in Northern Ireland divorce is '… largely an administrative rather than a judicial affair in that direct judicial involvement is minimal'.[121]

One of the most significant features of divorce in Northern Ireland is the high level of recourse to the magistrates' court. The court record study found that 60% of couples divorcing in 1991 had obtained one or more orders from the Domestic Proceedings Court[122] and judicial statistics reveal that in 1996 over 2,000 orders were made in relation to maintenance and childcare and around 2,000 full and 4,000 interim orders for protection from domestic violence.[123] This can be contrasted with the position in England and Wales where there was only one magistrates' court order for every 30 divorces in 1992.[124] When hypothesising the reasons for this it is interesting to note that the interviews with practitioners and divorcees revealed a common myth in Northern Ireland of the 'separation order'. Although it is not within the jurisdiction of the Domestic Proceedings Court to provide a judicial separation, one of the most commonly cited reasons which solicitors gave for bringing domestic proceedings applications was that their client wanted a 'separation order'. Indeed, some practitioners revealed that clients thought that a separation order was a pre-requisite to divorce. One factor which compounds this misunderstanding is that in many areas the Northern Ireland Housing Executive requires a court order as proof of separation to enable an applicant to obtain housing,[125] although views are now sought as to an alternative cost-effective method to provide proof of separation to public bodies.

It cannot be underestimated, therefore, that in Northern Ireland the magistrates' court plays a useful role in the ultimate resolution of financial and child-related issues. The evidence suggests that there is a negotiation culture in Northern Ireland which leads to early settlement of post-divorce arrangements. Indeed, both divorcees and key practitioners interviewed reveal that couples

---

120 Office of Population Census and Surveys, Update (February 1996).

121 *Unravelling the System*, p 92.

122 The name given to the magistrates' court when it is hearing family law applications. In Northern Ireland a Domestic Proceedings Court consists of a Resident Magistrate sitting alone. See Domestic Proceedings (Northern Ireland) Order 1980, articles 3–5. Prior to the Children (Northern Ireland) Order 1995 which came into effect in November 1996, this court could also make custody and access orders in respect of children. Applications are now made in the Family Proceedings Court, which also sits at magistrates' court level, under the Children (Northern Ireland) Order 1995, article 8.

123 Northern Ireland Judicial Statistics 1996. In recent years applications to the Domestic Proceedings Court have reduced by approximately 25%, largely due to the Family Proceedings Court now having jurisdiction to grant orders regarding contact and residence for children. Furthermore, since 1994 the Child Support Agency has dealt with child maintenance.

124 *Unravelling the System*, at 215.

125 Other practitioners felt that the use of the Domestic Proceedings Court was a useful first step in the divorce process and in financial negotiations with one practitioner revealing the tactical advantage that it is easier to get a respondent to admit to adultery or unreasonable behaviour in the magistrates' court which can later be used in a fault-based divorce.

regularly take steps to resolve issues at an early stage, with a significant number of legally binding private separation agreements negotiated before divorce, which may be attached to an eventual divorce petition or made into a consent order. The research also reveals the low level of ancillary relief orders made on divorce, whether made by consent or otherwise, perhaps due to the high level of magistrates' court orders which remain in force after the divorce. In situations where the couple have property which cannot be dealt with in the magistrates' court,[126] this court can be used as an interim measure with the more significant assets being dealt with at a later stage or by private negotiation.

It is against this background that the Office of Law Reform drafted a Consultation Paper on the future development of divorce law and practice in Northern Ireland. In this Paper the future of divorce law is premised on a distinction being made between the 'divorce law system' and the wider 'matrimonial law system' which covers all aspects of the family law system which are invoked when a marriage breaks down. This is not simply a terminological distinction, but one which ensures distinct objectives for a good divorce law.

Recalling the objectives of divorce law identified by the Law Commission in 1966[127] as saving saveable marriages and ending those which cannot be saved with the minimum of bitterness and humiliation, the Northern Ireland Consultation Paper[128] suggests that these aims may be beyond the function of divorce law and may be better placed within the context of a responsible 'matrimonial law system'. With this in mind, the objectives suggested for a good 'matrimonial law system' in Northern Ireland are the following reformulated objectives the Law Commission identified for a good divorce law (amendments in italics):

(a)   to buttress, rather than to undermine, the stability of marriage;
(b)   *to ensure that appropriate assistance and/or legal remedies are available to all those whose relationships may be in a state of breakdown so that only those relationships which have irretrievably broken down enter the divorce system; and*
(c)   when, regrettably, a marriage has irretrievably broken down, to enable the empty legal shell to be destroyed with the maximum of fairness, and the minimum of bitterness, distress and humiliation.[129]

This shift in emphasis ensures that divorce is not seen in isolation, but is an integral part of the wider 'matrimonial law system', thus encouraging a more holistic approach to family law in Northern Ireland. It is the function of the

---

126 See the Domestic Proceedings (Northern Ireland) Order 1980, articles 4(1) and 4(3).

127 *Reform of the Ground of Divorce – the Field of Choice* (Cmnd 3123) (HMS0 1966).

128 *Divorce in Northern Ireland – A Better Way Forward*, December 1999.

129 A number of additional objectives were outlined. These include the promotion of the best interests of children on the breakdown of the parental relationship; the definition of legal rights with clarity and the making of those rights readily accessible in practice; the recognition of diversity in family patterns; the fair distribution of assets, on the termination of a relationship, taking account of the effects which that relationship had on the parties' economic positions; the promotion of party autonomy; the prevention of exploitation where there is a power imbalance in the relationship; dispute resolution mechanisms which minimise conflict and cost and the promotion of respect for the dignity of the individual. It is suggested that these objectives should underpin the whole matrimonial law system in Northern Ireland, various aspects of which are due to be considered in future consultation papers.

'matrimonial law system' to ensure that only those relationships which have irretrievably broken down enter the divorce system and, although there should be opportunity for reconciliation at all times,[130] it is advocated that the law of divorce should not be primarily dictated with this objective in mind. In general terms, the policy of divorce law should focus on providing an efficient non-adversarial legal mechanism by which marriages can be brought to an end. Indeed, it was stated that:

> '[i]t creates an unnecessary tension in the system if the divorce law itself has as one of its goals the deflection of couples away from it. Rather this objective should be emphasised at earlier stages of the matrimonial law system.'[131]

The objectives advocated by the Office of Law Reform for divorce law in Northern Ireland, therefore, include supporting the family and developing good relationships within marriage and post-divorce, paying particular attention to the relationship between parents and children; encouraging agreement between the parties and the use of mediation alongside the development of less adversarial ways of working. It is important that the divorce process should promote substantive and procedural fairness while minimising unnecessary acrimony at all stages of the process. A further stated objective is the protection of an economically weaker spouse and the protection of children and parties to a marriage from domestic violence. The divorce law should be clear, respected and understood by those using it where parties are made aware at an early stage of the practical consequences of divorce. Furthermore, exit points should be built into the process to facilitate those who realise that divorce is not for them. Finally, it is stated that close working relationships should be developed between legal and other professionals within the system and that ultimately the divorce process needs to be affordable and cost-efficient to the parties and the taxpayer.

C 'Reforming the system'

Subject to the views of the consultees, it is proposed that the desired objectives for divorce law in Northern Ireland can be achieved without adopting the now abandoned 'divorce by process over time' model of the Family Law Act 1996. The procedural distinctions in Northern Ireland, particularly the typical long-drawn out nature of the divorce process and recourse to the no-fault grounds,

---

130 Under article 8 of the Matrimonial Causes (Northern Ireland) Order 1978 the judge can adjourn divorce proceedings if there is a possibility of reconciliation. Due to the fact that divorce in Northern Ireland is a lengthy process with petitions being lodged after a period of separation this provision is used very little in practice. However, it is thought that the provision should be retained along with the current provision that a divorce petition cannot be lodged until two years after the marriage took place. (Article 5 of the Matrimonial Causes (Northern Ireland) Order 1978 as amended by article 3 of the Matrimonial and Family Proceedings (Northern Ireland) Order 1989. In England and Wales there is an absolute bar on divorce within the first year of marriage.)

131 *Divorce in Northern Ireland – A Better Way Forward*, December 1999 at 26. This can be contrasted with Part II of the Family Law Act 1996 which includes within the principles of divorce law supporting the institution of marriage and encouraging the parties to a marriage which may have broken down to take all practicable steps, whether by marriage counselling or otherwise, to save the marriage.

ensure that the criticisms of the English system, which lead to the Family Law Act 1996, are less applicable in Northern Ireland. However, the Paper does not represent the system in Northern Ireland as a perfect model and draws up a charge-sheet of criticisms. One of the main criticisms is the perceived passivity of the current system which is said to 'react' to marriage breakdown without proper consideration of alternative dispute resolutions, such as mediation. Another cause for concern is the fragmentation of the current system, evidenced by the parallel jurisdiction of the Family Proceedings Court and the Domestic Proceedings Court, with child support being dealt with outside the court system altogether.

It is proposed that the ground for divorce in Northern Ireland continues to be irretrievable breakdown of marriage and views are sought as to how this should be proven. The options are a system which is fault-based, not fault-based or a mixture of the two. This debate cannot, however, be seen in isolation, but must be viewed within the backdrop of current Northern Ireland practice, particularly the high use of the separation facts. Indeed, the argument that retention of the fault grounds within a mixed system leads to acrimonious petitions within a fault ethos cannot be sustained in the context of Northern Ireland.[132] It is also recognised that, although in the minority, the number of petitions based on unreasonable behaviour in Northern Ireland is increasing. Indeed, amongst wives petitioning for divorce the unreasonable behaviour fact was the second most popular after two years' separation with consent and more popular than the five years' separation fact.[133] The Research Report suggests several possible reasons for this including the feeling that a petitioner's suffering requires judicial recognition. On this point, one should note that domestic violence is the most commonly cited particular in unreasonable behaviour petitions.[134]

The Government's view, however, is that the ground for divorce in Northern Ireland may be less important in achieving the intended objectives than procedural reform. In this respect, several aspects of the Family Law Act 1996 have been identified for possible inclusion in the Northern Ireland system, notably the provision of information and alternative dispute resolution mechanisms. One of the main proposals, therefore, is the provision of an information service, which would act as a gateway into the matrimonial law system and the availability of both legal and non-legal services. This would help to meet the objective of:

---

132 It is interesting to consider the position in Scotland (the ground for divorce in Scotland under the Divorce (Scotland) Act 1976 is the irretrievable breakdown of marriage proven on one of five facts, similar to England, Wales and Northern Ireland) where 60% of divorce petitions are based on the separation grounds. This was considered by the Scottish Law Commission to be an important factor when reviewing divorce law and lead to the Commission recommending retention of the 'mixed system', but removing desertion and shortening the two and five year separation periods to one and two years respectively. See Scottish Law Commission, *Report on the Reform of the Ground for Divorce*, SLC No 116 (1989).

133 Statistics reveal that 24.2% of High Court and 17% of county court divorces are now based on behaviour. By contrast, in 1984 (when only 18.6% of cases were heard in the county court) only 14.7% of High Court divorces were based on behaviour. See Archbold, 'Divorce – A View from the North' in *The Divorce Act in Practice* (Round Hall Ltd, 1999) at 52.

134 This statistic is compounded by the evidence of a number of those replying to the questionnaire issued by the research team who stated that while they had used a no fault fact for divorce, domestic violence was the main reason for their marriage breakdown. See *Unravelling the System*.

'... locating all the main remedies within a coherent system which can be used as a road to divorce, but which does not inevitably drive parties to that destination.'[135]

Part II of the Family Law Act 1996 provides that an information meeting be the first port of call for anyone who wants to initiate divorce proceedings, although there is evidence from initial pilot exercises that this procedure is not as effective as anticipated.[136] It is not proposed, however, to make the information meeting a compulsory first step in divorce proceedings in Northern Ireland. As the majority of couples who experience marital breakdown in this jurisdiction do not initiate divorce proceedings immediately, it would be too late in the process to have the information meeting at this stage. The provision of information should serve a useful educational role and this would be hampered if the law were to be prescriptive as to the availability of the information. It is not, therefore, intended that obtaining information becomes a compulsory part of the divorce process at all, but that it is a service which is available to anyone experiencing marital breakdown. Establishing a centralised information provision for Northern Ireland is seen as a useful way to integrate legal and non-legal services and to develop a more holistic approach to family law and the assistance available for families in difficulty. It is hoped that the provision of such information will increase the use of mediation as a voluntary alternative dispute resolution mechanism which is recognised as appropriate for some, although not all, couples.[137] Unlike the provision of the Family Law Act 1996, which requires most parties to attend mediation before they are granted legal aid, proposals in Northern Ireland do not make this a compulsory requirement.

D   Streamlining the legal remedies

Another key recommendation of the Consultation Paper is the development of an integrated system of finance, child care and property remedies, with courts at different levels having concurrent jurisdiction to make orders pre-divorce proceedings; during divorce proceedings or after a decree of divorce has been made. It is proposed that such orders become effective when the order is made with a residual judicial discretion to bring into effect only such aspects of the order as are necessary or to adjourn the case until after the divorce. Under the Family Law Act 1996, except in exceptional circumstances, the granting of the divorce decree would have been conditional on the successful resolution of financial and property issues. It is not proposed to enact a comparable provision in Northern Ireland where, under the present system, financial and child care issues are usually resolved before the divorce and, in any event, additional statutory

---

135 *Unravelling the System*, at 224.

136 *Supra*, note 112.

137 The important role that mediation has to play in resolving family disputes was recognised by the Council of Europe in Recommendation R(98)1 which places an obligation on Member States to introduce or promote family mediation and to take, or reinforce, all measures considered necessary for the implementation of family mediation as an appropriate means of resolving family disputes. Mediation in Northern Ireland is currently available through the Family Mediation Service and although there appears to be a high level of satisfaction amongst those who use it, it does not appear to be reaching as many cases in which it might prove useful.

safeguards are built in. The decree of divorce will not be made in Northern Ireland unless arrangements for children have been made to the satisfaction of the court and in a case based on two or five years' separation, proceedings may be stayed if adequate financial provision has not been made for the respondent.[138] Furthermore, the respondent to a divorce based on five years' separation can have the decree denied if he/she shows that they will suffer grave financial or other hardship.[139] It is suggested that these safeguards are adequate and that a provision comparable to that contained in the Family Law Act 1996 regarding the conditional granting of a divorce decree is an unnecessary statutory inclusion. Various other procedural matters are considered, for example, the possibility of introducing an initial directions hearing shortly after proceedings are commenced where the progress of the financial and child care issues are considered. Alternatively, views are sought on whether a summary judgment procedure without the need for either party to attend would be the best way forward in cases in which there were no issues in dispute.

The recent research in Northern Ireland on divorce law reform reveals that the system differs in many practical ways from the system in England and Wales, despite the fact that the substantive legislative provisions are broadly similar. Any future reform, therefore, must bear this in mind and acknowledge that the criticisms which lead to Part II of the Family Law Act 1996 are not applicable to the same extent in Northern Ireland. Although the system appears to be working reasonably well in this jurisdiction, a number of reforms have been suggested and it will be interesting to see the outcome of the consultation process. Although most of the suggested reforms are largely procedural, one of the key themes of the recent Consultation Paper is the re-definition of the purposes of divorce law. The recent work has been useful in attempting to resolve, from a Northern Irish perspective, a number of underlying tensions inherent in divorce law, for example, the role of fault and whether divorce law should aim to save marriages where possible. Taking current practice into account, the fault/no-fault debate may, indeed, prove less influential than the legal and non-legal services which the reformed procedural system intends to promote and incorporate into the legal system at an early stage of family breakdown. It is the underlying purpose of the law in this area which will eventually dictate its future development and the removal of reconciliation as one of the dictating policy objectives of divorce law marks an interesting contrast with the principles governing Part II of the Family Law Act 1996.

V   CONCLUSION

From this discussion, it can be seen that family law in Northern Ireland is a matter of priority and reform. Apart from the subject-specific areas considered, however, one of the most important developments for family law is the Human Rights Act

---

138 Article 12(2) of the Matrimonial Causes (NI) Order 1978. On this point views are sought as to whether there should be an absolute bar in all cases or whether in some cases it may be appropriate to order a stay of proceedings until measures are taken to relieve the hardship.

139 Article 7 of the Matrimonial Causes (NI) Order 1978. Once again, views are sought as to whether this should be extended to all cases.

1998 which incorporates the European Convention on Human Rights into domestic law for the whole of the United Kingdom. Under the Act, Convention jurisprudence must be taken into account by a court when determining any question which has arisen in connection with a Convention right.[140] Under section 3, primary and subordinate legislation must, as far as it is possible, be read and given effect in a way which is compatible with Convention rights and courts can declare that a statute or provision of subordinate legislation is incompatible with a right under the Convention.[141] Under section 6, acts of public authorities[142] which are incompatible with Convention rights are unlawful and any individual who claims that a public authority has acted (or proposes to act) in this way can bring proceedings against the public authority or rely on the Convention right(s) in any legal proceedings.

In Northern Ireland, the Belfast Agreement of 1998 and the Northern Ireland Act 1998 contain human rights safeguards additional to those contained in the Human Rights Act. Under the Northern Ireland Act, the Human Rights Act is an entrenched piece of legislation which cannot be changed by the devolved Northern Ireland Assembly[143] and primary legislation of the Assembly which is not compatible with any of the Convention rights or discriminates against anyone on the grounds of religious belief or political opinion will be outside the Assembly's legislative competence and void.[144] The Northern Ireland Act has established the Northern Ireland Human Rights Commission,[145] whose main functions include keeping under review the adequacy and effectiveness of law and practice relating to the protection of human rights. The Commission may conduct investigations and has the power to advise both the Secretary of State and the Executive Committee of legislative and other measures which should be taken to protect human rights and the Assembly on whether a Bill is compatible with human rights. The Commission may give assistance to individuals in legal proceedings, or more generally bring proceedings involving law and practice relating to the protection of human rights. The Commission also has a statutory obligation to promote understanding and awareness of the importance of human rights in Northern Ireland and may undertake, commission or provide assistance (financial or otherwise) for research and educational activities. One of its most important tasks is to provide advice on a Bill of Rights for Northern Ireland which will be additional to Convention rights.

Equality provisions are also inherent in the Northern Ireland Act. Under section 73, an Equality Commission has been set up and under section 75, statutory duties are imposed on public authorities to have due regard to the need to promote equality of opportunity between persons of different religious belief, political opinion, racial group, age, marital status or sexual orientation and between men and women generally; those with or without a disability and those

---

140 Human Rights Act 1998, section 2.

141 Ibid, section 4.

142 Under section 6(3) of the Human Rights Act 1998 a public authority includes a court or tribunal or any person whose functions are of a public nature, except either House of Parliament or a person exercising functions in connection with proceedings in Parliament.

143 Northern Ireland Act 1998, section 7(1).

144 Ibid, section 6(2).

145 Ibid, sections 68–72 and Schedule 7.

with or without dependants. Public authorities also have a duty to have regard to the desirability of promoting good relations between persons of different religious belief, political opinion or racial group.[146] These equality provisions replace the Policy Appraisal and Fair Treatment Guidelines which were designed to ensure that equality issues played a role in policy making in all spheres and at all levels of Government activity.[147] These developments collectively signify that human rights and equality issues will play an important role in the future development of Northern Ireland family law:

> '[a]ny policies or legislation ... in this jurisdiction will have to undergo a "human rights audit" as part of any new legislative process. It will also be open to scrutiny by the Human Rights Commission, and wider equality issues will also be relevant under the Northern Ireland Act 1998.'[148]

---

146 Schedule 9 to the Northern Ireland Act makes provision for the enforcement of these duties and requires public authorities to submit equality schemes to the Commission specifying how the duties to promote equality of opportunity will be fulfilled.

147 *Supra*, note 46.

148 *Divorce in Northern Ireland – A Better Way Forward*, Office of Law Reform (1999), chapter 4.

SCOTLAND

HOW CHILDREN ARE FARING IN THE 'NEW SCOTLAND'

Elaine E. Sutherland*

I   INTRODUCTION

The Children (Scotland) Act 1995 has been operating for several years and the time is ripe to review its impact.[1] It has long been accepted that 'law', strictly speaking, tells only part of the story in terms of how the legal system addresses children's rights and children's issues. Policy and practice play equally important parts in helping to understand the whole picture. In addition, what is happening in the context of children cannot be understood without placing developments in their wider social and political setting. 1999 saw considerable political change in Scotland, with the creation of the Scottish Parliament and the first effects of the Human Rights Act 1998 being felt, and a few words of explanation may be helpful, particularly for readers outside the United Kingdom.

The Scotland Act 1998 brought a kind of federalism to the United Kingdom by devolving whole areas of legislative competence, including responsibility for most family law issues, to the new Scottish Parliament, sitting in Edinburgh. It has been predicted that this should enable legislators to respond better to local needs and to address concerns more quickly than was possible in a legislature dealing with the whole of the United Kingdom.[2] Certainly, there have been promises of commitment to 'introducing a new style of politics based on partnership and consensus-building' and the undertaking that 'the first priority is to make the Scottish Parliament work for the people of Scotland'.[3] Of course, when such statements come from politicians they are often regarded in Scotland, as elsewhere, with a degree of scepticism. Any meaningful consultation process requires that people are aware of the proposals and have the opportunity to respond. Perhaps inevitably, this has meant that consultation has focused, in the past, on professional organisations and other interested groups. There are

---

*   Reader in Law, School of Law, University of Glasgow and Professor, Lewis and Clark School of Law, Portland, Oregon.

1   While some readers outside the UK will have access to hard copy of the Session Cases (SC – the *Blue Book* citation, Sess Cas, is wrong), Scots Law Times (SLT), Scottish Civil Law Reports (SCLR) and Scottish Criminal Case Reports (SCCR), many will not. Scottish cases can be found through Lexis, which has a separate Scottish library (SCOT), and cases from 1998 onwards can be accessed, free of charge, on the Scottish Courts Website <http://www.scotcourts.gov.uk>. A number of cases discussed below are described as 'unreported'. This means that they are not reported in hard-copy. They will often be available on the Scottish Courts Website or through Lexis.

2   The effect of the Act was described in more detail in Elaine E. Sutherland, 'Consolidation and Anticipation' in *The International Survey of Family Law (2000 Edition)*, ed A Bainham (Family Law, 2000).

3   *The 'Modernising Government' Programme*, DS 1/00, 22 February 2000, at pp 3 and 5.

encouraging signs of more widespread consultation on social and legislative reform, with extensive use of the Internet[4] as a way of disseminating information.

It will be remembered that Article 12 of the United Nations Convention on the Rights of the Child requires States Parties to give children the opportunity to have an input into decisions which affect them. While efforts to comply with this requirement have concentrated on the 'micro' level (ie allowing the child to express views on a specific decision which affects him or her, like future residence), there is scope for its application on the 'macro' level (ie the formulation of policy and legislation). To what extent, then, have children and young people been involved in the consultation process prior to the introduction of new legislation? Anticipating the creation of the Scottish Parliament, the Scottish Office, a department of the UK Government, published *Improving Scottish Family Law*,[5] a consultation document exploring options for reform of various aspects of child and family law. Much of the material contained in the consultation paper revisited proposals of the Scottish Law Commission which had not found their way into legislation,[6] although some of the issues explored were new.[7] No real attempt was made to involve children and young people in the consultation process despite the fact that many of the reforms being considered would affect their lives. There are some encouraging signs that the Scottish Executive is moving towards greater involvement of children and young people than was previously the case. For example, prior to introducing the Standards in Scottish Schools, etc Bill, there was extensive consultation.[8] Concern was expressed at the lack of consultation of children, albeit the Executive was at pains to point out that it had commissioned Save the Children to undertake a series of focus groups with children and young people.[9] Rather more attention was given to feedback from children and young people when the Review of Youth Crime[10] was launched in December 1999. This project is seeking to identify the most effective strategies for preventing youth offending and for dealing with children and young people who offend. Views were sought from the usual range of organisations, but there was a specific focus on input from persons under 18 years old.[11]

Another important development, in the context of children and the legal system, was the appointment of a Minister for Children and Education.[12] While

---

4   While hard copy remains one way of effecting consultation, the Internet has provided an unprecedented opportunity for those with access to it to be aware, if not sometimes overwhelmed, by what is available. The Scottish Parliament site is <http://www.scottish.parliament.uk> and the Scottish Executive can be found on <http://www.scotland.gov.uk>

5   Scottish Office, 1999.

6   For example, parental responsibilities and rights of non-marital fathers, judicial separation, and the grounds for divorce, were revisited.

7   For example, the possibility of giving full parental responsibilities and rights to step-parents by simple agreement between the step-parent and the birth parent, was discussed.

8   The whole process is detailed in *Standards in Scotland's Schools, etc. Bill*, Research Paper 00/02, 15 February 2000, available on <http://www.scotland.gov.uk/library/>.

9   Ibid, at 34.

10 The website for the project is <http://www.scotland.gov.uk/youth/crimereview> and this will be updated as the consultation process progresses.

11 Initial consultation produced 290 responses with 170 of these coming from young people. A significant number of the responses from young people came from residents in young offenders institutions.

12 The current holder of the office, Sam Galbraith, MSP.

this should ensure that the interests and rights of children are represented at the highest level, ministerial representation is only a partial solution. Since such a minister is a member of the government, he or she will, inevitably, be constrained by political considerations and what is needed is the additional provision of an independent Commissioner for Children. Precisely how such a Commissioner would operate requires further exploration, but much can be learned from the experience in Israel, New Zealand and Norway.

The Human Rights Act, which incorporates the substantive provisions of the European Convention on Human Rights into the law of the various parts of the United Kingdom, was passed in 1998 but did not come into force until 2 October 2000. The delay was designed to maximise the opportunity for ensuring compliance with its provisions and, thereby, avoiding embarrassing litigation. However, the Scotland Act brought aspects of the Human Rights Act into effect in Scotland sooner than the general commencement date. All legislation promulgated by the Scottish Parliament is subject to the Act,[13] as are the acts of the Scottish Executive.[14] It would be something of an understatement to say that the results of this early experience of bringing human rights home were not fully anticipated. The sheriff courts[15] were thrown into disarray when a successful challenge to temporary sheriffs (judges) was made on the basis that they were appointed by the Lord Advocate, a member of the Scottish Executive who also heads the prosecution service.[16] The loss of a significant number of judicial personnel caused delays in the courts and, despite the appointment of additional full-time sheriffs, the effects continue to be felt. Other human rights challenges followed.[17] While, undoubtedly, many kites have been flown,[18] it is clear that the Human Rights Act will have considerable impact once it applies more generally.[19]

---

13 Scotland Act 1998, section 29.

14 Scotland Act 1998, section 57.

15 The sheriff courts have enormously wide jurisdiction and can deal with virtually all civil matters, irrespective of the value of any claim involved, and all criminal matters except the Pleas of the Crown (murder, rape and treason). While the sheriff court cannot sentence a person to more than three years imprisonment, it can hear the case and remit to the High Court of Justiciary for sentence upon conviction of the accused. In practice, civil cases involving very large sums of money are dealt with by the Court of Session and prosecutions are brought in the High Court where the Lord Advocate is seeking a sentence substantially in excess of three years.

16 *Starrs and Chalmers v Lord Advocate* 2000 SLT 42. See also, *Gibbs v Ruxton* 2000 SLT 310. The Scottish Executive had been warned of some of these difficulties; see, Robert Black, 'The Scottish Parliament and the Scottish Judiciary' 1998 SLT (News) 321.

17 Mr Ruddle, an inmate at the state mental hospital successfully challenged his continued detention on the basis that, since his condition was untreatable, his detention was no longer justified. The release of an individual who may well pose a danger to the community caused understandable public concern and the Scottish Parliament's first statute, the Mental Health (Public Safety and Appeals) (Scotland) Act 1999, followed. The *Report of the Inquiry into the Care and Treatment of Noel Ruddle*, published on 30 March 2000, suggested that Mr Ruddle was not, in fact, untreatable, and has recommended a number of reforms in the treatment of such patients. Other challenges have centred on the requirement to give information regarding the identity of the driver of a motor vehicle at the time an alleged offence was committed and confiscation of property under the Proceeds of Crime (Scotland) Act 1995.

18 Something in the order of 400 human rights challenges have been mounted, with less than 10 of these being successful.

19 Unsurprisingly, a host of publications on the subject are in preparation. For example, the second edition of Alison Cleland and Elaine E Sutherland (eds), *Children's Rights in Scotland: Scots Law analysed in the light of the UN Convention on the Rights of the Child* (W Green, 1996), to be published in 2001 as, simply, *Children's Rights in Scotland*, will analyse children's rights from

While all of this has been rather embarrassing for the government, there are signs that the 'human rights dimension' is already being taken on board. In the wake of the decision in *T and V v United Kingdom*,[20] where the European Court of Human Rights was critical of the trial of the accused, in England, in the infamous 'Bulger case',[21] Barbara Glover's second application for release on licence came before the Designated Life Tribunal, a sub-committee of the Parole Board for Scotland. Ms Glover had been convicted, in 1991, of the murder of a fellow pupil in a school playground when she was 15 years old and, as with all persons under 18 so convicted at the time, was sentenced to be detained without limit of time. Such persons are entitled to be considered for release on licence after the 'designated part' of their sentence has been completed; the 'designated part' being the period of time judicially determined as the minimum required as a punitive measure.[22] In the event, the Tribunal decided that Ms Glover no longer posed a threat to the public and she was released.[23]

It would be all too easy to allow these general developments to overshadow the everyday operation of the legal system. Undoubtedly, they will have an impact on child and family law. However, for children and their families, it is the day-to-day workings of the legal system, as they impact upon their lives, which matter. The Children (Scotland) Act 1995 provides the framework in this respect, and its provisions, and how they operate, is where we will now focus our attention. *Improving Scottish Family Law*[24] explored options for further reform of the law here and passing reference will be made to them, where relevant.[25]

II   THE CHILDREN (SCOTLAND) ACT 1995

While the Children (Scotland) Act 1995 brings together the bulk of Scottish child law,[26] some issues are still dealt with in other statutes[27] and the long-term goal

---

the perspectives of the European Convention, the United Nations Convention on the Rights of the Child and other international instruments.

20   16 December 1999. The cases are reported on the European Court web site: <http://www.echr.coe.int/>.

21   In particular, the Court found violations of Article 6(1) of the Convention in respect of the accuseds' opportunity to participate in their trials, Article 6(1) in respect of the involvement of the Home Secretary, a member of the government, in setting of the tariff upon conviction, and Article 5(4) in respect of the lack of judicial review of the sentence.

22   The Crime and Punishment (Scotland) Act 1997.

23   The Press Release issued by the Scottish Executive on behalf of the Parole Board for Scotland can be found on <http://www.scotland.gov.uk/news/press2000_01/se0164.asp>.

24   Scottish Office, 1999.

25   A White Paper, detailing proposed changes was due to be published in May 2000, ahead of the anticipated Family Law (Scotland) Bill.

26   A prospective analysis of the Act was provided in Elaine E Sutherland, 'Child Law reform At last!' in *The International Survey of Family Law 1995*, ed A Bainham (Martinus Nijhoff Publishers, 1997) at 435–455. For more recent and detailed analysis of the Act, see, Elaine E Sutherland, *Child and Family Law* (T&T Clark, 1999) and Alexander B Wilkinson and Kenneth McK Norrie, *The Law of Parent and Child in Scotland* (2nd ed, 1999, W Green).

27   For example, financial support for children is governed by the Family Law (Scotland) Act 1985 and the Child Support Acts 1991 and 1995, while adoption is regulated by the Adoption (Scotland) Act 1978. Often, these statutes have been amended by subsequent legislation.

remains the codification of child and family law.[28] Essentially, the Act is in three parts: Part I, dealing with children in the family setting; Part II, addressing child protection and state intervention; and Part III, amending the existing law on adoption. The United Nations Convention on the Rights of the Child was very much in the minds of the drafters of the 1995 Act and, consistent with the Convention, the starting point is that the family setting is generally the best place for the child,[29] although the responsibilities and rights of the various individuals are subject to the paramountcy of the child's welfare.[30] A court will only intervene where such intervention would be better than not intervening and, again, the child's best interests are regarded as paramount.[31] Throughout, there is recognition that the child has a right to express his or her views, and to have them taken into account in the light of that child's age and maturity, when decisions are being taken.[32] Together, these are sometimes described as the 'over-arching principles' and, subject to exceptions,[33] run throughout the 1995 Act.

III   THE CHILD IN THE FAMILY SETTING

For the first time in Scotland, the 1995 Act defines what is meant by parental responsibilities[34] and parental rights.[35] Central to the Act is the emphasis on parental responsibilities, with parental rights existing only in order to enable parents and others to fulfil these responsibilities.[36] It should be noted that, while the Act talks of *parental* responsibilities and *parental* rights, these are simply

---

28   Professor Eric M Clive, of Edinburgh University, is currently working on a project designed to codify various aspects of Scottish law. An earlier blueprint for codification of child and family law can be found in the Scottish Law Commission's *Report on Family Law* (Scot Law Com No 135, 1992).

29   Article 9.

30   Sections 1(1) and 11(7)(a).

31   Section 11(7)(a).

32   Sections 6 and 11(7)(b).

33   Briefly, deviation from these principles is sometimes permitted where public safety requires it and such deviations occur in the context of local authority powers, court decisions on removing a child from the home and, occasionally, in the context of children's hearings.

34   'Parental responsibilities' are defined as the responsibility: to safeguard and promote the child's health, development and welfare; to provide direction and guidance to the child in a manner appropriate to the child's stage of development; where the child is not living with the parent, to maintain personal relations and direct contact with the child on a regular basis; and to act as the child's legal representative; 1995 Act, section 1(1). These parental responsibilities exist only so far as is practicable and in the interests of the child. The child, or anyone acting on the child's behalf, has title to sue or defend in proceedings in respect of parental responsibilities; 1995 Act, section 1(3). Parental responsibilities terminate when the child reaches the age of 16, except the responsibility to provide guidance, which lasts until the child reaches 18; 1995 Act, section 1(2).

35   'Parental rights' are defined as the right: to have the child living with him or her or otherwise to regulate the child's residence; to control, direct or guide the child's upbringing in a manner consistent with the child's stage of development; if the child is not living with the parent, to maintain personal relations and direct contact with the child on a regular basis; and to act as the child's legal representative; 1995 Act, section 2(1). All parental rights give the child or a person acting on his or her behalf title to sue and terminate when the child reaches the age of 16; 1995 Act, section 2(4) and (7).

36   1995 Act, section 2(1).

convenient shorthand terms[37] and each may be owed or held by persons other than parents. Only mothers and married fathers[38] acquire responsibilities and rights automatically[39], although, broadly speaking,[40] 'a person who ... claims an interest', including the child concerned, may apply to the court for an order relating to parental responsibilities or parental rights.[41] In reaching its decision, the court is directed to apply the overarching principles,[42] and the express requirement to take the child's views into account is an innovation of the 1995 Act. So how is the Act working?

At the outset, the invidious position of children of unmarried parents and non-marital fathers should be noted. Unlike all mothers and married fathers, non-marital fathers do not acquire parental responsibilities and rights automatically. The Scottish Law Commission recommended an end to this discrimination, but Westminster chose to reject this rational approach and, instead, threw a sop to non-marital fathers in the form of parental responsibilities and rights agreements.[43] These agreements are only possible between the child's parents and require the consent of each parent. They can be made irrespective of the age of the parents, and only where the mother, herself, has full responsibilities and rights. The agreement must be in a form prescribed by the Secretary of State for Scotland and registered in the Books of Council and Session. Such agreements, once registered, are stated to be 'irrevocable' although, as is always the case with parental responsibilities and rights, the court retains its jurisdiction over the matter.[44] An interesting example of the application of section 4 arose in *J v Aberdeen City Council*,[45] where a married woman executed such an agreement with her child's father who was also her husband's brother. Given that there is a rebuttable presumption that a married woman's husband is the father of her child,[46] this led to some debate over whose consent was required before the child could be freed for adoption.[47]

Comparatively little use has been made of these agreements. In 1998, while 22,319 children were born to unmarried parents, only 230 agreements were

---

37   This point was made in respect of earlier legislation; *F v F* 1991 SLT 357, per Lord Hope at 361.

38   Such fathers are defined as being 'married to the mother at the time of conception or subsequently'; 1995 Act, section 3(1)(b).

39   1995 Act, section 3(1).

40   A person whose parental responsibilities or rights have been extinguished by an adoption order or transferred to an adoption agency or a local authority may not apply for such an order; 1995 Act, section 11(3) and (4). This gives statutory expression to, and widens the scope of, the decision of the House of Lords in *D v Grampian Regional Council* 1995 SLT 519. It should be noted that, where parental responsibilities and rights have been removed in such a way as to prevent the parent from applying under section 11, it remains competent for the child or other interested persons to apply.

41   1995 Act, section 11(3)(a).

42   1995 Act, section 11(7).

43   1995 Act, section 4.

44   1995 Act, section 11.

45   1999 SC 405.

46   Law Reform (Parent and Child) (Scotland) Act 1986, section 5(1)(a).

47   On appeal, the Court of Session accepted that the child's father did have *locus* to contest the freeing order.

registered.[48] It is likely that ignorance of their availability is a partial explanation for the low level of use of parental responsibilities and rights agreements but, very probably, inertia is a greater factor.[49] While all is going well in a relationship, many couples probably feel no need to execute a formal agreement or do not get round to doing so. By the time a dispute arises, it is most unlikely that the mother will agree to endowing the child's father with parental responsibilities and rights. Failing agreement, the only option for a non-marital father is to apply to the court. There is no doubt that the present discrimination is in breach of Articles 2 and 18 of the United Nations Convention on the Rights of the Child and, despite the views of the Lord Chancellor's Department to the contrary,[50] certainly arguably in breach of Articles 8 and 14 of the European Convention.[51] The absurdity of the present position becomes all the clearer when one appreciates that the 22,319 children born to unmarried parents in 1998, represented 39% of total births for the year. The births of 82% of these children were registered by both parents and 72% of these parents were living at the same address.[52] It is encouraging to see concern over the continued discrimination being expressed at judicial level[53] and it is to be hoped that the opportunity is taken to reform the law in forthcoming legislation.

Any person claiming an interest may apply to the court for an order relating to parental responsibilities and rights, unless the person falls within the excluded categories. While section 11 provides the opportunity for the pursuer to seek regulation of another person's parental responsibilities and rights, it is frequently used by pursuers who are asking to be given responsibilities and rights. The very wide ambit of the section does no more than allow a person to get a case into court, but it does ensure the widest opportunity for issues of concern to be raised. The recent controversy in the USA over Washington State's attempt to allow grandparents to apply to a court for visitation rights[54] was thus greeted with some surprise in Scotland, since grandparents are one group of people who make use of the broad provision here.[55] Section 11 provides non-marital fathers with the

48   1999 saw an increase, with 335 agreements being registered. I am grateful to the staff at the Books of Council and Session, Registers for Scotland, for this information. The experience in Scotland mirrors that in England and Wales where such agreements are, again, made in only a small proportion of cases; Children Act 1989, section 4.

49   For a full discussion of these agreements, see, EE Sutherland, 'Parental Responsibilities and Rights Agreements – Better half a loaf than none at all?' 1998 *Scottish Law and Practice Quarterly* 265.

50   In the Consultation Paper, *The Law on Parental Responsibility for Unmarried Fathers* (Lord Chancellor's Department, 1998), at para 62, the view is expressed that 'the current law which does not give responsibility automatically to unmarried fathers on the birth of the child complies with articles 8 and 14 of the Convention'.

51   *Marckx v Belgium* (1979) 2 EHRR 330; *Johnston v Ireland* (1986) 9 EHRR 203; *Kroon v The Netherlands* (1994) 19 EHRR 263; *Soderback v Sweden* [1999] 1 FLR 250.

52   See, Registrar General for Scotland, *Annual Report 1998* (1999), Tables 3.2 and 3.3.

53   In *White v White* 1999 SLT (Sh Ct) 106, at 110H, Sheriff Principal Nicholson expressed the view that it 'appears to be at odds with the United Nations Convention on the Rights of the Child'.

54   *Troxel v Granville* 296 P. 2d 21 (1998). The US Supreme Court decided the case on 5 June 2000, and its decision has attracted great interest, not least because most states allow grandparents to seek visitation in certain circumstances. From a European perspective, arguments around issues of respect for private and family life raise interesting questions when an attempt is made to reconcile the rights of adults with the rights of children.

55   See, for example, *Senna-Cheribbo v Wood* 1999 SC 328, discussed below. The grandparent's right to apply to the court is separate to the situation where the parent, often a young non-marital

opportunity to acquire some or all of the parental responsibilities and rights. It is also used by step-parents[56] and others who have had some involvement with a child. Thus, a woman was able to apply for contact with her former partner's child after the couple's same-sex relationship had come to an end.[57]

It was widely believed, before the 1995 Act, that a child had standing to raise an action in respect of parental responsibilities and rights. However, the Act put the matter beyond doubt.[58] The child's position was strengthened by the fact that a child now has the capacity to instruct a solicitor in a civil matter, provided that he or she has a general understanding of what it means to do so; and a child of 12 or over is presumed to have such understanding.[59] In addition and subject to the general rules on financial eligibility, a child will usually be entitled to legal aid to finance the action. Essentially, actions by children are likely to arise in one of two ways. First, the child may raise an independent action. To date, and contrary to the fears of the anti-children's rights lobby, the Scottish courts have not been inundated by children 'divorcing' their parents,[60] nor by children seeking redress against parental rules requiring the tidying of bedrooms or assistance with the washing-up. A more common way for children to become involved in legal proceedings is where they are separately represented in the action between their, usually divorcing, parents.[61] As we shall see, parents should consult their child over future arrangements for the child's care in the post-separation setting, even where the parents are not in dispute.[62] Where the parents are in dispute, the court is required to take into account any views the child wishes to express.[63]

Where the child does not become a party to proceedings, the question arises of the input a child has in decisions over his or her future care arrangements within the family. Where the parents are in agreement, what attention is given to the child's preferences? Section 6 of the 1995 Act requires any person who is making a *major decision* in the course of fulfilling parental responsibilities or exercising parental rights to give the child the opportunity to express his or her views and to

---

father, applies for a residence order and the fact that his mother will be assisting him in caring for the child is central to his case; *Brixey v Lynas* 1996 SLT 908.

56   See, for example, *Robertson v Robertson*, Outer House, 7 December 1999, unreported, where, in addition to seeking residence of one child and contact with two others, a man sought parental responsibilities and rights in respect of his step-daughter. *Improving Scottish Family Law*, at para 6.1, discusses the possibility of allowing the a step-parent to acquire parental responsibilities and rights through an agreement, along the lines of a section 4 agreement, with the child's parents.

57   The case, *R v F*, which was heard in Dunfermline Sheriff Court is unreported, but an account of it can be found in J Fotheringham, 'Parental Responsibilities and Rights for Homosexual Couples' 1999 SLT (News) 337. Mr Fotheringham acted for the pursuer in the case.

58   1995 Act, section 11(5).

59   Age of Legal Capacity (Scotland) Act 1991, section 2(4A) (added by the Children (Scotland) Act 1995, Schedule 4, paragraph 53(3)).

60   This term was probably borrowed from media reports in the USA surrounding such cases as *Kingsley v Kingsley* 623 So 2d 780 (Fla, 1993) where, in reality, the child was seeking termination of parental rights in order that he could be adopted by the people who had been caring for him for several years. Perhaps a more relevant case is *Re CE (Section 37 Direction)* [1995] FLR 26, where a 14-year-old young woman sought a residence order in England to enable her to continue to live with her boyfriend's parents, in the same home as her boyfriend.

61   In *White v White* 1999 SLT 106, for example, a 14-year-old was separately represented.

62   1995 Act, section 6, discussed below.

63   1995 Act, section 11(7)(b).

take account of them in the light of the child's age and maturity. What constitutes a 'major decision' is not defined, but it seems inconceivable that the future arrangements for a child's care would be outwith the ambit of the provision. However, there are very real doubts that parents and children are aware of the provisions of section 6. Even if they or, at least, the parents know of the provision, one might question the extent to which children are consulted over future arrangements for their care. Where a court is called upon to give effect to a parental agreement by means of a court order, the court ought to ensure that any views the child wishes to express are before it, although it is far from clear in the reported cases that this is always done. In *McAdam v McAdam*,[64] the Lord Ordinary simply expressed the view that, 'I am satisfied that the pursuer should be granted custody of the youngest child, George, as concluded for. The defender did not resist [this] conclusion'. No indication is given of what evidence was before the court regarding the four-year-old's wishes. In *Robertson v Robertson*[65] the parents had eventually agreed that two of the children should reside with the mother while a third should reside with the father, all three children spending alternate weekends together at one or the other parent's home. There, the Lord Ordinary was a little more explicit in stating, 'In the light of the evidence given by the parties and by the defender's aunt, ... I consider that the arrangements for the care and upbringing of the children are satisfactory'. Nonetheless, he made no reference to the views of the children, the eldest of whom was 11 years old.

A further point on facilitating the input of children in decisions which affect them has caused some difficulty. While a child may have views about future arrangements, he or she may prefer that these should not be disclosed to the parents, often to avoid hurting their feelings or, sometimes, due to fear of the parents' reactions. Can a court offer a child confidentiality in these circumstances? The problem is, of course, one of natural justice. How is a parent to present his or her case fully if he or she is being denied access to the full details of something which will feed into the decision? In *Dosoo v Dosoo*,[66] the reporter, who had been appointed by the court, submitted a report indicating that the two boys, aged 12 and 14, had given their views but wished that these be kept confidential due, in part, to what she described as 'a palpable fear of their father'. Accordingly, the boys' views were contained in sealed appendices to the report. The children had obtained separate representation and the father sought to have the appendices opened up. Refusing the father's motion, the sheriff expressed the view that:

'for a child to be able to express his views "freely" he must be able to be confident in privacy if he so wishes and the court should respect that privacy except in very compelling circumstances.'[67]

However, in *McGrath v McGrath*[68] a rather different view was taken. There, a curator *ad litem* had been appointed to a seven-year-old girl in a dispute between

---

64 Outer House, 30 November 1999, unreported.
65 Outer House, 7 December 1999, unreported.
66 1999 SLT 86.
67 Ibid, at 88I.
68 1999 SLT 90.

her parents over her father's contact with her. Again, the child had requested that her views not be disclosed to her parents. The sheriff took account of the child's views and refused the father's request for extended contact. On appeal, rather more weight was attached to the father's arguments on the natural justice point, in general, and his claim that his rights under Article 6(1) of the European Convention had been breached. The case was remitted back for reconsideration with the observation that:

> 'The practicalities involved in reconciling the right to a fair hearing and the child's right to express his views are thus of immense difficulty. They can best be resolved in my view by having regard to the principles set out by Lord Mustill, which involve taking the fundamental principle that a party is entitled to disclosure of all materials as the starting point and next considering whether disclosure of the material would involve a real possibility of significant harm to the child.'[69]

This may, indeed, be the only way to reconcile these two valid, but sometimes competing, rights. However, it is hardly a wholly satisfactory solution for a vulnerable child operating in an adult environment.

In disputed cases, the court must apply the overarching principles. The paramountcy of welfare is a familiar concept in Scots law and, taking a different course of action to that adopted in England and Wales, the Scottish legislation explicitly avoids providing a 'welfare checklist'. Each case will depend on its own facts and circumstances, but courts have considered such matters as physical welfare, who will be looking after the child, role models, emotional welfare, the impact of religion, educational welfare and parental lifestyle. That courts should show an awareness of cultural and racial factors was noted in *Osborne v Matthan (No 2)*,[70] where a foster carer was granted custody, as it then was called, in respect of a child whose racial origins were different to her own. That case also emphasised that it was the welfare of the child before the court that was relevant, rather than the impact the decision might have on another child in the family. It remains the case that each case will turn on its own facts and circumstances, which accords fully with the importance of addressing the individuality of each child. Thus, while as a general rule courts are reluctant to separate the children, they will do so on occasions.[71]

It is a fundamental principle that the decision on welfare is a matter of judgment and, since the judge at first instance has had the opportunity to see witnesses and assess their evidence, his or her decision will only be overturned on appeal where the sheriff has erred in law or where he or she has exercised discretion in an unreasonable manner.[72] In *Senna-Cheribbo v Wood*,[73] a mother

---

69 Ibid at 93B–C. Lord Mustill's three-part test was laid down in *Re D* [1995] 4 All ER 385 at 398.

70 1998 SC 682.

71 In *Robertson v Robertson*, Outer House, 7 December 1999, unreported, it was agreed that two of the children should live with the mother while a third lived with the father. Built into the arrangement was provision for all three children to spend the weekends together.

72 CGB Nicholson and AL Stewart, *I.D. MacPhail's Sheriff Court Practice* (2nd ed, 1998, W Green), para 18.02. In *Sanderson v McManus* 1997 SC (HL) 55, per Lord Hope at 57I–58E, it was observed that the lapse of time inherent in the appeal process may make a fresh application to the court preferable.

73 1999 SCLR 328.

was unsuccessful in regaining residence of her two-year-old who had lived with his paternal grandparents since he was eight months old and was looked after by his grandmother, a 56-year-old diabetic, and the child's father who suffered from multiple sclerosis. The child's mother had been permitted supervised residential contact, but evidence had been led from the social worker involved in the case that there was serious doubt that she could ever look after the child, even with support. This decision was upheld on appeal, not least because the Inner House was satisfied that the sheriff had taken all the relevant circumstances into account, including the long-term effects of the various adults' health problems. In *Pearson v Pearson*,[74] the father had had access (as it then was) to the three children of the marriage, after he and their mother separated, until he was convicted of being drunk in charge of one of the children,[75] when access was terminated. Granting his application for contact with two of the children, the sheriff relied on his own impression of the father in the witness box and the father's claims that he had his drinking under control rather than the, fairly substantial, evidence that the man still had a serious problem with alcohol. The sheriff principal found that the sheriff had erred in failing to take account of this evidence and reversed his decision, a conclusion which was upheld on further appeal to the Inner House.

The requirement that a court should not make an order unless to do so would be better for the child than making no order at all might be seen as reflecting a move away from the notion, prevalent amongst some parents at least in the past, that one should have residence while the other got contact with the child, at best. However, the operation of this principle has been far from unproblematic. Take the case of married parents who are divorcing. They will usually each enter the situation of separation with the full set of parental responsibilities and rights. If they can co-operate, it can be argued that there is no need to remove any of these responsibilities and rights from either of them and, as such, no order is necessary. This accords with Article 19 of the United Nations Convention and recognises the continued involvement of both parents in a child's life even after divorce. If the parents cannot agree and other avenues, like mediation, have failed, then it will be necessary to apply to a court for an order. The House of Lords made it quite clear, in *Sanderson v McManus*,[76] that the onus is on the party seeking the order to demonstrate to the court why the order would serve the child's best interests and ought to be made. That case involved a dispute between unmarried parents and, consequently, the father began from the position of having no responsibilities or rights. However, one might think that, in the case of a married parent the position would be different.[77] In *White v White*,[78] the parents divorced in July 1997 and the mother obtained a residence order in respect of the two children of the marriage.

---

74 1999 SLT 1364.

75 It is an offence to be drunk in charge of a child under ten years of age; Civic Government (Scotland) Act 1982, section 50(2).

76 1997 SC (HL) 55.

77 A parent with full responsibilities and rights would still have to seek a specific issue order in respect of other matters. For example, in *Fourman v Fourman* 1998 Fam LR 98, a mother sought a specific issue order to enable her to take the children to Australia despite the opposition of the children's father. She was unsuccessful since she failed to demonstrate that this was in the children's interests.

78 1999 SLT (Sh Ct) 106.

There was no other order and, in particular, the father's other parental responsibilities and rights were not removed. He did not see either of the children for about 18 months, whereupon he sought an order for contact with the children. He subsequently amended his application to delete reference to the elder child who had indicated that she did not want to have contact with him. At first instance, the sheriff granted the order for contact with the younger child on the basis that, since the father had retained both his responsibility and his right to contact, it was for the mother to demonstrate why this should not take place. That decision was overturned on appeal on the basis that the sheriff had erred in law. The sheriff principal took the view that, since he was seeking an order from the court, the father was obliged to demonstrate why the order would be in the child's interests. In effect, the father was required to prove why he should be allowed to do something which he was already both entitled and obliged to do. At first glance, this seems absurd. The only explanation seems to be that, where the court's authority is sought to make something happen, the rules on onus of proof (and what must be proved) apply. The sheriff principal's concern that any other solution would have the consequence that 'a court will have to apply a different test for determining the welfare of the child depending on whether or not an applicant father was or was not married to the child's mother',[79] is understandable. However, that is precisely the discriminatory approach of the statute as it stands at present.

Without getting bogged down in detail, suffice to say that, in Scotland, family disputes over where the children live and who gets to see them are dealt with by means of a civil, adversarial procedure. Every effort is made to encourage the parties to reach agreement through such methods as mediation and there is even a special step in the court procedure, the child welfare hearing, designed to give additional opportunities for consensus. Inevitably, some disputes are not resolved and work their way through the courts. It has long been recognised that the traditional court system is seriously flawed as a means of helping families to arrive at a workable solution for them. As disputes drag on, families become involved in the myriad of procedural steps and hearings, often involving different judges and support personnel; positions become, if anything, more entrenched; and costs escalate. The Family Court Initiative, being pioneered at Glasgow Sheriff Court by a team of four sheriffs committed to negotiation in a conciliatory environment, is designed to provide a better approach. As soon as an application relating to residence or contact is intimated, the case is allocated to a designated sheriff. He or she will then continue to deal with the case until resolution or until such time as resolution by negotiation seems impossible, in which case the action will go to proof before a different sheriff. The first meeting between the parties and the sheriff takes place in an informal atmosphere and further meetings are scheduled or can be requested as required. At the first meeting, a vigorous attempt is made to encourage parents (and other family members, if involved) to identify the issues of concern and to discuss possible options. While the child is not present at the first meeting, he or she is may see the sheriff separately. If apparent resolution of the dispute is achieved, the parties may return to the same sheriff with any further problems and usually the sheriff will want to monitor the

---

79   Ibid, at 112A.

situation and fine tune it if required. Subsequent hearings are therefore usually fixed at four- to six-week intervals to enable the parties to air any problems and concerns before they become major issues affecting the welfare of the children. The emphasis is on facilitating a non-adversarial approach in a less formal setting, with continuity of judicial involvement. If this pilot project is adjudged a success, it is anticipated that it will be adopted throughout the country.

IV INTERNATIONAL CHILD ABDUCTION

While the number of cases of children being abducted abroad by a parent is relatively small in Scotland, the human misery caused by such action cannot be over-emphasised. As part of the UK, Scotland benefits from being a party to both the Hague Convention on the Civil Aspects of Child Abduction and the European Convention on the Restoration of Custody of Children.[80] Children are regularly returned from Scotland to other party jurisdictions and vice versa.[81] The problems that can occur between jurisdictions which are not both parties to the Hague Convention have been illustrated graphically in the dispute involving the United States and Cuba over Elian Gonzalez. However, that sufficiently determined adults can continue to thwart attempts to counteract international child abduction is illustrated by the ongoing *Cameron* case. The dispute between the parents of two girls, who had been born and raised during their early years in Scotland, began in 1995 when their father took them to France with the permission of their mother. There followed a series of cases in both France and Scotland[82] and, ultimately, the French court awarded custody to the mother in Scotland, subject to the father having access in France. On 10 July 1999, the girls went to France for an arranged visit and should have returned to Scotland on 30 July. Only the elder child returned. In March 2000, a French court convicted the father in his absence of kidnapping his daughter. He has now disappeared with the child and her whereabouts, at the time of writing, remain unknown.

V ADOPTION

Adoption in Scotland, like so many other jurisdictions, has moved a long way from its original purpose of providing new homes for the babies of a single women. It is now used as a means of providing families for older children or of recognising the role of a step-parent.[83] These are very distinct functions and it is

---

80 Both Conventions were given domestic effect in the Child Abduction and Custody Act 1995.

81 In 1999, the Central Authority (the Scottish Courts Administration acting on behalf of the Secretary of State) dealt with a total of 18 cases under the Hague Convention. Of the 12 incoming cases, voluntary return was effected in 7, 1 child was returned by judicial order, 1 case was withdrawn and 2 cases were pending resolution. Of the 5 outgoing cases, voluntary return was effected in 2 cases, 1 case was rejected by the central authority and 2 cases were pending resolution.

82 *Cameron v Cameron* 1996 SLT 306; *Cameron v Cameron* (No 2) 1997 SLT 206.

83 In 1998, over 50% of adoptions were step-parent adoptions. Of the children adopted, 9% were under 2 years old, 60% were aged between 2 and 9, and 30% were aged between 10 and 17. See, Registrar General for Scotland, *Annual Report 1998* (1999), Tables 9.2.

possible for the step-parent to be given parental responsibilities and rights instead,[84] thus acknowledging the step-parent's place in the child's life without terminating the child's legal relationship with the non-resident parent.[85]

Adoption can only take place where either each parent or guardian of the child agrees or where one of a list of grounds for dispensing with parental consent is established and the court decides to dispense with parental consent.[86] There is a procedure whereby a child can be freed for adoption prior to being placed with prospective adopters. Essentially, this amounts to dealing with the consent issue earlier rather than later and, for convenience, the two procedures will be conflated here, since the grounds for dispensing with consent are the same in each case.[87] Dispensing with parental consent to adoption involves a two-stage process.[88] First, it must be established, as a matter of fact, that one of the four grounds for dispensing with parental consent exists.[89] Only then is the court in a position to move to the second stage – deciding whether it *should* make such a dispensation. As with all decisions in the adoption, the court must decide this second stage by applying the welfare test.

The court had a rare opportunity to explore the first ground for dispensing with parental consent, that the parent could not be found, in *S v M*.[90] There, the mother's consent was also dispensed with on the third ground, that she had persistently failed to discharge her parental responsibilities, and the adoption petition by the child's paternal aunt was granted initially. The mother appealed against this decision, alleging that she had been troubled in the past by drug addiction, but was now over the problem. She further claimed that the child's father and the aunt knew how to contact her father and sister and, furthermore,

---

84   1995 Act, section 11. This mechanism can also be used by other persons. In *G and G v M* 1999 SC 439, foster carers sought to adopt a six and a half year-old boy whom they had been looking after. The mother opposed the application and, while one of the grounds for dispensing with her consent was established, the sheriff refused the adoption petition and made orders imposing parental responsibilities on, and granting parental rights to, the foster carers.

85   *Improving Scottish Family Law* raised the possibility of parental responsibilities and rights being extended to step-parents without a court procedure, through the mechanism of an agreement with both birth parents.

86   Adoption (Scotland) Act 1978, section 16.

87   1978 Act, section 18. The main difference between the procedures relates to the position of the non-marital father. It is only if the non-marital father has any of the parental responsibilities or rights, whether by agreement with the child's mother or by court order, that his consent to adoption is required; 1978 Act, section 65(1). Where the child is being freed for adoption, the court must be satisfied: that he does not intend to apply for an order in respect of parental responsibilities or rights; that if he did apply, it is likely that the order would be refused; that he has no intention of entering into a parental responsibilities and rights agreement with the child's mother; and, regardless of his intention, that such an agreement is unlikely to result; 1978 Act, section 18(7).

88   1978 Act, section 16(1)(b). See *P v Lothian Regional Council* 1989 SLT 739 and *L v Central Regional Council* 1990 SLT 818.

89   The grounds for dispensing with parental consent are that the parent or guardian: is not known, cannot be found or is incapable of giving agreement; is withholding agreement unreasonably; has persistently failed, without reasonable cause, to fulfil one of the parental responsibilities to safeguard and promote the child's health, development and welfare; or if the child is not living with him, the responsibility to maintain personal relations and direct contact with the child on a regular basis; has seriously ill-treated the child, whose reintegration into the same household as the parent or guardian is, because of the serious ill-treatment or for other reasons, unlikely; 1978 Act, section 16.

90   1999 SLT 571.

that her solicitor had been in touch with the child's father seeking contact with the child. Granting the appeal, the court stated that, in dealing with allegedly missing parents, 'all reasonable steps must be taken, and if even only one reasonable step is omitted, one cannot say that a person cannot be found'.[91]

The most contentious ground for dispensing with parental consent to adoption is undoubtedly that the parent is withholding consent unreasonably. Since adoption severs the legal link between the child and the birth parent, it can be argued that it would always be reasonable for the parent to want to retain the link. However, the courts take the approach that parents want the best for their children. Thus, a reasonable parent would agree to adoption in certain circumstances and, if those circumstances are present in the instant case, then any parent who withholds agreement is doing so 'unreasonably'. It is not simply the reaction of the parent before the court who is being considered – his or her reaction is judged against that of a hypothetical 'reasonable parent'.[92]

Once it has been established that a ground for dispensing with parental consent exists, the court must apply the welfare test in reaching its final decision. A particularly graphic example of this principle in operation can be found in *Angus Council Social Work Department, Petitioner*.[93] There, the adoption agency applied for an order freeing H, a five-year-old girl, for adoption in the face of opposition from her mother, herself a tragic figure. She had a long history of personality disorders, self-mutilation, suicide attempts and psychiatric care, probably connected to her own disturbed childhood. However, the effect of the mother's problems was that she was frequently unable to provide H with adequate care and, as a result, H had spent large portions of her life being looked after by others, either on a formal or informal basis. While the mother had maintained contact, her visits often disturbed H and, on occasions, she had used contact as an opportunity to abduct the child. In a considered and detailed judgment, granting the order freeing the child for adoption and making no provision for continued contact with the child's mother, the court noted that the decision might have an adverse effect on the mother's fragile mental health. However, the overwhelming evidence supporting adoption as the only course of action which would serve H's welfare left the court no alternative.

A number of cases have arisen where, while finding one or more of the grounds for dispensing with parental consent to be established, the court of first instance has, nonetheless, refused the adoption petition. In *G v M*,[94] for example, the sheriff found that the mother had failed to discharge her parental responsibilities but was not withholding consent to the adoption unreasonably. He noted her continued, albeit minimal, contact with the child and made orders vesting parental responsibilities and rights in the applicants for adoption. In *City of Edinburgh Council v B*,[95] despite finding that the mother had failed to fulfil her parental responsibilities, the sheriff refused an order freeing the child for adoption,

---

91 Ibid, at p 575D. One is left with the impression in this case that the child's father and aunt had been less than wholly honest.

92 *A v B and* C 1971 SC(HL) 129 per Lord Reid at 141; *D and D v F* 1994 SCLR 417; *P v Lothian Regional Council*, above, per Lord Justice-Clerk Ross at 74.

93 1998 GWD 23-1148.

94 1999 SCLR 648.

95 1999 SCLR 694.

in part, because he was not satisfied that there was a likelihood that the child would be adopted. Both cases were overturned on appeal, the Inner House exercising its option to consider the case *de novo*.

A child aged 12 or older has the right to veto or consent to his or her own adoption.[96] In the case of younger children, regard must be had to any views they wish to express in the light of their age and maturity.[97] The report of the curator *ad litem* contains an indication of the child's views and, sometimes, children are also seen by the sheriff. However, it appears that the curator is rarely involved in the appeal process and one wonders whether any real attention is paid to the child's views at that stage. One commentator noted, in respect of *M v S*, *G v M* and *Edinburgh City Council v B*, the three cases discussed above which all went to appeal, 'Why was it that, in all three cases, at the important stage of the appeal, the voices of the children seem to have been unheard?'.[98]

The principle of presumed non-intervention applies in the adoption context and the court is directed not to make an adoption order 'unless it considers that it would be better for the child that it should do so than it should not'.[99] However, the 1995 Act strengthened the whole idea of non-intervention by placing an obligation on adoption agencies to consider whether 'there is some better, practicable, alternative' before making any adoption arrangements.[100] As a result, one finds extensive discussion in the cases of what other options have been explored and why they would or would not work.[101]

Delays continue to plague the adoption process, with a period of years sometimes elapsing between the decision to start adoption proceedings being made and various appeals being concluded. In *G v M*,[102] some five years elapsed between the social work department's initial decision that it should seek a freeing order and the appeal finally being disposed of. Clearly, the decision by an adoption agency that adoption is the best option for a child should not be rushed and it should only be taken after all the other options have been explored fully. Parents must, of course, be given the fullest opportunity to be heard if they oppose the application for adoption. Nonetheless, there is good reason to expedite the court process in order that it can be decided quickly whether or not the adoption is to go ahead.

---

96 Age of Legal Capacity (Scotland) Act 1991, section 2(3).

97 1978 Act, section 6(1)(b)(i).

98 Sheriff David Kelbie, *Commentary* (following the report of *Edinburgh City Council v B*) 1999 SCLR 707.

99 1978 Act, section 24(3).

100 1978 Act, section 6A.

101 See, for example, *Angus Council Social Work Department, Petitioner, supra*.

102 1999 SCLR 648. See also, *Strathclyde Regional Council v F* 1996 SCLR (Notes) 142, where the parallel period was four years. By the time the appeal was heard, the planned adoption placement had broken down and the local authority was forced to abandon its application and place the child in long-term foster care instead.

VI CHILD PROTECTION

Whatever detailed legislation on child protection provides,[103] it is the general climate which can tell us much about how we are protecting children. Sometimes it is specific examples which can throw light on shortcomings. As long as Scots law continues to permit parents the so-called 'right of reasonable chastisement', the legal system is sending out a very mixed message about respect for children's rights and child protection. Granted, the parental right is subject to a 'reasonableness test', but it is clear, and not at all surprising, that this vague standard is not understood by all parents. In 1999, a father, himself a school teacher, was convicted of assaulting his eight-year-old daughter, having slapped her buttocks when she became hysterical in a dentist's waiting room.[104] The point remains, however, that, where the parent's conduct is regarded as reasonable, the legal system is failing to protect the child from what would, in any other circumstances, be regarded as assault.[105] In the light of the decision of the European Court in *A v United Kingdom*,[106] where a step-father's caning of a nine-year-old boy was found to breach the child's rights under Article 3, it is hoped that the Scottish Parliament will take the opportunity, as have so many other legislatures around the world, to wipe out this vestige of Dickensian parenting. At the time of writing, a public consultation process is underway on this issue and the results are awaited.[107]

Bullying in schools remains a problem despite efforts to provide education for teachers, students and parents on the nature of the problem and how to deal with it. One way to ensure that the authorities leave no stone unturned in the fight against bullying is to award damages to the victims. In this respect, the decision in *Scott v Lothian Regional Council*[108] was anxiously awaited by education authorities. There, a young woman who had experienced nasty and sustained bullying at school, resulting in her suffering physical and psychological injuries and attempting suicide, raised an action for damages against the local authority. Ultimately, the case came down to establishing whether the staff at the school, for whom the local authority was liable, had exercised reasonable skill and care. The court concluded on the evidence that they had and, thus, that no liability attached. While one can never be in the position of the court hearing the evidence, it is clear that the staff reactions here were less than rigorous. On the other hand, and as with

---

103 There will not be a review of the details of the legislation on this point here, not least because most of the interesting aspects of it raise European Convention issues and it is intended that they should be considered in this context next year.

104 The father has now been struck off the teaching register by the General Teaching Council for Scotland. This means that he can no longer teach in any public sector school, although he can be employed in a non-teaching capacity. He could also be employed in the private sector. It is understood that he may appeal against this decision, which caused considerable public outcry. While the harm which may result for the family (including the daughter) if this father loses his job is regrettable, it seems perfectly reasonable to conclude that a person convicted of assaulting a child is unsuited to teaching children generally.

105 See, for example, *B v Harris* 1990 SLT 208, where a mother who slapped her nine-year-old and hit her with a belt was ultimately regarded as having exercised her right of reasonable chastisement.

106 (1999) 27 EHRR 611.

107 *The Physical Punishment of Children: A Consultation* (Scottish Executive, 2000).

108 Outer House, 29 September 1999, unreported.

many such victims, the pursuer and her family may not have reported all the incidents as diligently as they probably wished, with the benefit of hindsight, that they had. The case serves a useful function nonetheless. If education authorities see the reality of civil actions relating to bullying, they will have all the more incentive to devote a reasonable part of their limited resources to combatting the problem.

Many children come to be looked after by the State because they have been neglected or abused in the family setting. The prospect of them facing further abuse or neglect in care brings a new layer of suffering. In effect, their self-proclaimed protectors become the abusers. The Kent Report, a broad examination of the arrangements for protecting children who are cared from away from home in Scotland, was published in 1997.[109] In the course of making 62 recommendations, the report left no illusion that all is far from well for many children. While the report noted that there have been positive initiatives[110] and that some of the problems experienced in the past had been eradicated, it saw new problems coming to the fore. It expressed concern over a wide range of dangers facing young people being cared from away from home, including, physical and sexual abuse, bullying, racial issues, drugs and alcohol, running away, self-harm and prostitution. Poor practices in the running of some establishments remained a concern. It recommended that improvements could be made in respect of: recording incidents of abuse; dealing with complaints from children and parents; the selection, recruitment and training of staff; the inspection of facilities; and suggested that a system of independent visitors should be introduced, with every child living away from home being allocated an independent person. In 1998, the Government published its response to the Kent Report,[111] accepting many of the recommendations and detailing the particular steps to be undertaken to implement them.

A reminder of how badly such care can go wrong came in 1997 when two men, who had worked in children's homes, were convicted of a catalogue of sexual offences against children who had lived in the homes in the 1960s and 1970s.[112] It was alleged that there had been a number of complaints about their conduct but, despite internal enquiries and police investigations at the time, no action had been taken. The Marshall Report examined the circumstances of the case and, while it concluded that much had changed in the intervening years in the way complaints were dealt with, it made some 135 recommendations designed to ensure that children are not failed in this way in the future.[113] It may be a

---

109 *Children's Safeguards Review* (Scottish Office, 1997) (the Kent Report). The remit of the Kent Report included young people living away from home in private boarding schools and the army as well as in local authority care.

110 Particular reference is made to *Another Kind of Home* (Scottish Office, 1992) (the Skinner Report), and *Choosing with Care* (Scottish Office, 1992) (the Warner Report).

111 *The Government's Response to Kent Report on Children's Safeguards Review* (Scottish Office, 1998).

112 *HM Advocate v Maclennan, Knott and Cull*, unreported, November 1997. A number of charges were found not proven in respect of the third accused.

113 *Edinburgh's Children* (1999) (the Marshall Report).

reflection of changing attitudes to abuse and neglect that new allegations of long-past abuse are surfacing.[114]

Part II of the 1995 Act, itself largely a product of another inquiry into how the State machinery failed children,[115] sets out, in detail: the responsibilities of local authorities to support children and their families; when intervention is appropriate; the mechanisms for intervention; and the obligations of the local authority to children it is looking after. These statutory provisions are supported by further regulations and guidance,[116] governing their operation, and an extensive training programme has been undertaken in respect of the personnel involved. Central to child protection is the children's hearings system which has been operating with a high degree of success for some 30 years. It is anticipated that some modifications to the system will be required in the light of the Human Rights Act 1998. The reforms of 1995, coupled with the implementation of the recommendations of the Kent and Marshall Reports, should maximise the opportunity for an effective and compassionate approach to the State fulfilling its responsibilities to children.

VII CONCLUSIONS

The 1995 Act appears to be working well, with the courts picking up on the, sometimes subtle, changes it introduced. What that means is that, as far as the Act goes, it has brought about the changes intended. However, the problem was always that the Act itself, while a positive force, did not go far enough. The position of children born to unmarried parents and of non-marital fathers remains iniquitous. That the provision for parental responsibilities and rights agreements is little used is unsurprising. It never was the answer. That parents continue to have the right to perpetrate assaults upon their children is a matter for shame. Speculation is always a risky business, but it is safe to say that the Human Rights Act 1998 will have an enormous impact on future developments in child and family law. Perhaps the recent embarrassing examples of just what an impact the Convention can have – and at a time when it is only partially operative – have been a good thing. Certainly, no one can now fail to understand the importance of the Human Rights Act 1998. Consultation on further reform of the law took place in 1999 and the responses to the consultation document, *Improving Scottish Family Law*, will undoubtedly influence the forthcoming White Paper. It is to be

---

114 Allegations of physical and sexual abuse, dating from the 1930s to the 1970s, in children's homes run by two religious orders, the Poor Sisters of Nazareth and the Daughters of Charity of St Vincent de Paul, have been made by some 400, now-adult, former residents. Legal aid has been granted to enable 11 test cases for damages to be brought. It is understood that the religious orders involved will defend the cases vigorously; *The Scotsman*, Friday, 5 May 2000, page 4.

115 Part II of the Act implements many of the recommendations of the *Inquiry into the Removal of Children from Orkney in February 1991* (1992, Scottish Office) (the Clyde Report), set up in response to *Sloan v B* 1991 SLT 530, which came to be known as 'The Orkney Case'.

116 Three volumes of *Scotland's Children: The Children (Scotland) Act 1995 Regulations and Guidance* were published by the Scottish Office governing, *Support and Protection for Children and their Families, Children Looked After by the Local Authority,* and *Adoption and Parental Responsibilities Orders.* See also, *Protecting Children – A Shared Responsibility: Guidance on Inter-Agency Co-operation* (Scottish Office, 1998). These materials are available on the Internet at <http://www.scotland.gov.uk/library>.

hoped that a keen awareness of the human rights issues will shape the proposed reforms.

Scotland's legal system has long occupied a peculiar legal position. Its integrity was guaranteed by the Treaty of Union of 1707, yet legislation was passed at Westminster, in a Parliament dominated by representatives of the other parts of the United Kingdom. The separate nature of Scots law was reinforced by having a separate law reform body, the Scottish Law Commission, and a distinct court structure. From the outset, economic factors made a degree of assimilation inevitable and, being a small jurisdiction, there has always been a willingness to consider comparative options when approaching law reform. As part of the European Union and the global community, a keen awareness of standards being set internationally is essential, not only because some of them are binding, but because many of them are worth meeting. As an increasingly multi-racial, multi-ethnic and multi-religious society, it is essential that diversity is accommodated. The point is that, at last, we can do this for ourselves in our own Parliament sitting in Edinburgh. The early days of the Scottish Parliament have clarified the point that romantic notions of 'things being different' were, predictably enough, more often than not just that, romantic notions. Politicians remain politicians and the standard of debate is, to put it as generously as possible, mixed. Knee-jerk reactions are still in evidence.[117] The desire to make Scotland a world-leading example of tolerance and inclusion is proving a challenge, as witnessed by the reaction of some sections of the community to the attempt to repeal homophobic legislation.[118] Nonetheless, enlightened proposals for reform of child and family law are being discussed and, while there remains some evidence of intolerance and bigotry, the voice of tolerance and reason is strong. Which prevails is a matter yet to be resolved.

---

117 See, for example, the Mental Health (Public Safety and Appeals) (Scotland) Act 1999 passed in hasty response to the Ruddle case.

118 The Local Government Act 1986, section 2A prohibits the local authority from 'intentionally promoting homosexuality' or the 'acceptability of homosexuality as a pretended family relationship'. Abolition of this section has been proposed and, while there is widespread support for abolition, a campaign under the, somewhat perplexing, banner of 'Keep the Clause' has been funded by a wealthy Scottish businessman. 'Clauses' are parts of a Bill (ie the draft of legislation while it is being proposed), while the parts of an Act of Parliament are 'sections'. Maybe the campaigners meant to use the slogan 'Keep the Closet'.

SLOVENIA

THE INFLUENCE OF VALIDLY ESTABLISHED COHABITATION ON LEGAL RELATIONS BETWEEN COHABITANTS IN SLOVENE LAW

Miroslava Geč-Korošec and Suzana Kraljić*

I   INTRODUCTION

Marriage is a very old legal institution, while legal institutions regulating cohabitation appear later in time. Regulation in national acts is widely conditioned by tradition, history, religion and other factors influencing law in the case of marriage as well as cohabitation. In recent years, more liberal legislation has taken a step forward and cohabitation of homosexual partners has also been regulated.

II   SHORT HISTORICAL OVERVIEW

The oldest Act recognising the legal status of cohabitation was the Yugoslav Workers' Insurance Act of 1992.[1] Following this Act, the female cohabitant of a deceased worker could get material help if she had lived in cohabitation with him for at least one year and if a child had been born to them within this cohabitation. Both of these conditions had to be fulfilled.[2]

The second Act covering the field of cohabitation was the National Liberation Committee of Yugoslavia Decree of 1994, providing for the right to State support for a female cohabitant as for wives, if her cohabitant was taken prisoner, was in the army or if he fell in war, subject to the condition that she had lived with him in a joint household for at least six months before his departure to the army and that he had mainly maintained her.[3]

Other provisions, especially the former Yugoslav Basic Marriage Acts of 1946 and 1965,[4] respectively, did not provide for any legal consequences resulting from cohabitation.[5] But, in practice, disputes occurred, in relation to property

---

*   Faculty of Law, University of Maribor.
1   Published in Ur. l. Kraljevine Jugoslavije, no 117/22.
2   See further Draškić, p 117.
3   See Geč-Korošec/Kraljić, p 121.
4   Published in Ur. l. FLRJ, no 29/46 and Ur. l. SFRJ, no 12/65.
5   In the post-war period cohabitation was treated as something immoral. Court decisions held that cohabitation was prohibited by law, but such interpretation was wrongful. Only cohabitation with a minor as well as cohabitation with members of the same kin and between brothers and sisters was prohibited. These types of cohabitation were prohibited by criminal law provisions. The Supreme Court of Serbia even claimed that relations of partners in cohabitation were immoral. See Draškić, pp 120–121.

earned by work,[6] custody and upbringing of children, maintenance, etc. In these matters, courts took different positions, as a result of which it was completely clear that this state of affairs could not last for much longer. All this was followed by the Supreme Court of Yugoslavia handing down guidelines for the resolution of conflicts connected to cohabitation. Therefore, at the end of the sixties and the beginning of the seventies, the courts began to admit recognised rights for cohabiting partners which formerly applied only to spouses.[7]

The development and change to the position of the family in society itself demanded recognition of cohabitation by society and the law. Marriage itself was no longer a privileged institution. The true meaning of marriage in society is found in family planning, the planning of a community of parents and children. But a family can appear in cohabitation as well. Therefore, the Marriage and Family Relations Act (MFRA)[8] of 1976 provided for recognition of cohabitation in its legal provisions. By the MFRA, Slovenia was alone among the former Yugoslav states in making marriage and cohabitation completely equal in the framework of personal rights and duties and property relations.

III MEANING OF COHABITATION

Under the formulation of article 12 MFRA, cohabitation is a stable living community of a man and woman who have not married. For the cohabiting partners, following the MFRA, such a community has the same legal consequences, as if they married, if there are no reasons by which marriage between them would not be valid. From the wording of the act it is clear that cohabitation arises in a non-formal way, on the basis of an agreement between the cohabiting partners.

Therefore, cohabitation is validly established when the following conditions are fulfilled:

–   *different sexes*: after the MFRA, only a living community between a man and a woman will be legally admitted. In Slovene law, living communities of homosexual partners do not enjoy legal protection.[9]
–   *living community*: the legislator did not specify what a living community is. If we start with the MFRA's formulation, a living community of cohabiting partners must have the same meaning as the living community of spouses. Therefore, it is about a living community in the physical, natural, moral, spiritual, sexual and economic sense. A joint household between

---

6   Property relations arising between cohabitants were governed by Civil Law. So, cohabitants became co-owners of things earned by work, in proportion to the contribution to the joint acquisition. If one of the partners was enriched, the other had the right to readjustment according to the rules of unjust enrichment. See further Popović, p 158.

7   Popović, p 155.

8   Published in Ur. l. SRS, no 15/76 and 1/89.

9   But, it is necessary to mention that in Slovenia there are thoughts about eventual legal recognition of relationships between homosexual partners. The main reason for this special regulation is the protection of the partners' existence. The draft of the Act on homosexual partnerships deals with the registration of these partnerships. See further Geč-Korošec/Kraljić, Vermögensrechtliche Verhältnisse, pp 277–278.

cohabitants is the most visible sign that cohabitation exists between a man and a woman. Therefore, joint living and joint housekeeping are a constitutive element of cohabitation.

−   *duration for a longer time*: the legislator did not specify the duration of the living community except to say it must have been 'lasting for a longer time'. The court will have to decide in every case. Cohabitation has to last for a longer time, ie for a sufficient time that there is similarity between it and the living community we see in the time or duration of marriage.

−   *no reasons, by which an eventual marriage between them would not be valid*: the persons (man and woman) wanting to establish valid cohabitation have to agree freely to its origination; both have to be adults;[10] there must not be any mental disease or incapacity; the relationship must be monogamous;[11] cohabitants must not be related up to the fourth degree; cohabitants must not have the relation of curator and ward; cohabitation must be founded with the intention of joint living.

IV   LEGAL CONSEQUENCES OF ESTABLISHMENT OF COHABITATION

For cohabitants, after the MFRA, a validly established cohabitation has the same legal consequences as if they married.[12] Legal consequences only refer to personal rights and duties of the partners and to property relations.[13]

A   Personal rights and duties of cohabitants

Personal rights and duties of cohabitants represent *ius cogens* after the MFRA. Since cohabitation is equalised with marriage with regard to personal rights and duties, it represents *ius cogens* also for cohabiting partners.

Cohabitants are entitled to mutual respect, trust and mutual help (article 44 MFRA). The duty of mutual respect means that they mutually acknowledge

---

10   'Immaturity alone of one partner living in a living community lasting for a longer time, by itself does not exclude the possibility of equalisation of legal consequences for the partner in such a community with the legal consequences a marriage between them would have (article 12 MFRA).' – legal opinion of the SCS, given on 21 and 22.12.1987 – published in Slovenski pravni register, year IV, pp 130–131.

11   'A living community of a man and a woman lasting for a longer time does not have the same legal consequences as marriage, if one of the partners is still married and thus a new marriage with the cohabitant could not be possible and would be invalid' (article 12 MFRA). – SCS, no Pž 1048/77 from 8.2.1978 – taken from Slovenski pravni register, p 130.

12   Mladenović separates cohabitations into non-free, half-free and free cohabitations. Non-free cohabitation exists where none of the partners meets the conditions. Cohabitation is half-free when one partner meets all conditions, while the other is hindered by not meeting one or more conditions. Free cohabitation occurs where there is no obstacle to an eventual marriage, and only in this case can legal consequences arise. See Mladenović, p 61.

13   Legal consequences of marriage referring to personal status of spouses (citizenship, capacity and family name) do not occur as consequences of validly established cohabitation.

equality, respect the personality of the other, trust each other, help each other in the moral and material sense and are mutually faithful.[14]

Cohabitants freely decide about childbirth. Towards the children, they have the same rights and duties (article 45 MFRA). The cohabitants' right to decide freely about childbirth means that each of them has the right to decide about this issue and the other has the right to veto his or her decision. The right of free decision about childbirth is an individual human right granted by the Constitution of the RS (article 55 section 1) and is not the joint right of both spouses.

Cohabitants are obliged to live together for the duration of cohabitation, since cohabitation is a living community of a man and a woman (article 12 section 1 MFRA). The duty to live together is judged more severely in relation to cohabitation than to marriage since it is the only outward and visible sign of the cohabitation's existence. In certain cases, in spite of separate living, the existence of cohabitation is assumed. The reasons for which the parties live apart have to be well-founded (eg when one of the cohabitants is on work in a foreign country, serving in the army, is in education, etc). Cohabitants have the right to free choice of profession and work (compare article 46 MFRA). That makes it possible for them to be economically autonomous, independent and equal. Cohabitants determine their joint residence by agreement (compare article 47 MFRA). Cohabitants decide on joint matters by agreement (compare article 48 MFRA). Joint matters are those representing the current needs of the living community. It is especially about joint housekeeping.

Cohabitants contribute to maintenance of the family in relation to their capabilities (compare article 49 MFRA). Since they are equal, they are also obliged to contribute to maintenance of their family. The duty of maintenance is measured by their capabilities. The cohabitant without means for living, unemployed without fault or incapable of work is not obliged to maintain the family. In this case, the duty impacts only on the other one. A cohabitant may contribute to maintenance by money, in kind or by work. If one of them avoids providing contributions for maintenance of the family, the other can sue him or her for payment of his/her contribution.

A cohabitant without the means for living, unemployed without fault or incapable of work has the right to be maintained by the other cohabitant, if this is within his or her capability (article 50 MFRA). Therefore, from this provision of the MFRA it can be deduced that the unemployed cohabitant can demand maintenance from the other only in two cases:

(1)   if he or she has no means for living and is unemployed without fault;
(2)   if he or she does not have the means of living and is incapable of work.

In both cases the demand may only be made when the cohabitant is capable of maintaining him or her. If other maintenance obligations, especially to children, would be endangered, then he or she is not obliged to maintain his or her cohabitant. The amount of maintenance is determined by the needs of the person

---

14   Among its provisions, the Slovene MFRA does not contain express provisions demanding spouses and cohabitants, respectively, to be faithful. But, that does not mean it is not their duty. Unfaithfulness means a breach of respect as well as trust of the other spouse.

maintained and the capability of the payor (compare article 129 MFRA). Waiver of the right to maintenance has no legal consequence (compare article 128 MFRA).[15]

B Property relations of cohabitants

The same rules which apply to spouses during the marriage govern the property relations between cohabitants.

1 SPECIAL PROPERTY

Property owned by a cohabitant before cohabitation remains his or her own property and is at his or her independent disposal (compare article 51, section 1 MFRA). Special property also is property acquired by the cohabitant during the period of duration of cohabitation, but not by work. This concerns gratis acquisitions.[16]

Attaching to special property, there are also rights connected with the person of the cohabitant, eg maintenance, disability payments, personal bonds, property benefits a cohabitant has arising from awards, scholarships, etc.

In addition to special property of the cohabitant belong things meant only for personal use by one of the cohabitants, interest from money being the property of one cohabitant and increases in the value of his or her property.[17]

2 JOINTLY OWNED PROPERTY

Jointly owned property is property earned by work during the period of cohabitation (compare article 51, section 2 MFRA). Jointly owned property is in the joint ownership of cohabitants and the shares in jointly owned property are not fixed. Since it is jointly owned property, one cohabitant may not dispose of his undefined share in this property and especially he or she may not sell or burden it (compare article 54 MFRA). The MFRA expressly determines that rights in relation to real property, being jointly owned property, are entered in the land register in the names of both cohabitants as their jointly owned property with undefined shares (compare article 55 MFRA).

---

15 But, in Slovenia there is no agreed view in relation to this. One view is that an adult capable person can waive his/her right to maintenance. The opposite position stresses the social function of maintenance, since nobody can waive a right on which his or her existence depends.

16 Gratis acquisitions are gifts and inheritance. Gifts received by the cohabitant during cohabitation form part of his special property. Therefore, gifts received by cohabitants, eg from friends for moving into a new apartment, are assumed to be their special property. Partners become co-owners of these gifts. There is an exception, when the donor gives the present only to one cohabitant and when it is clear that the present is given to one of the partners (eg a skirt). In those two exceptions, the gift becomes the special property of the cohabitant to whom it was given. See further Kraljić, Premoženjski režim, pp 27–29.

17 It is important that this increase occurs without the investment of work of the cohabitant not being owner of the property. If there is investment of work in special property and if this yields up returns, these returns become the joint property of the cohabitants (eg a cow and her calf). In this case, a property demand is admitted. If investment in special property is disproportionate to the whole value of the original property (eg the building of new windows in a house), the property demand is not admitted, but only the claim based on the specific obligation arising.

Cohabitants dispose of their joint property together and in agreement. But, they can agree on the administration of the whole jointly owned property or just a part of it by only one of them, while he or she always has to respect the other's interest. Each cohabitant may step back from the agreement for single administration of jointly owned property at any time, but not at a disadvantageous time (article 52 MFRA).

Jointly owned property can be divided, when:

– cohabitation ends;
– a creditor demands so – the creditor may demand on the basis of a court's ruling, that the share of the cohabitant/debtor in the joint property is determined. After that he can demand execution in relation to this share. If in the execution procedure, sale of the share the cohabitant has in jointly owned property is admitted, the other cohabitant has the right of pre-emption, which means that he has an option to buy this share in profit to all buyers at a price determined after the execution procedure (compare article 57 MFRA);
– during cohabitation, either on the basis of an agreement between the cohabitants or on the basis of a proposal by one or other cohabitant – if jointly owned property is divided by agreement, cohabitants also determine the shares and the manner of property division.

3 LIABILITY OF COHABITANTS FOR DEBTS

In relation to obligations which the cohabitant had before cohabitation, as well as for obligations which the cohabitant accepts after the start of cohabitation, each cohabitant is liable in relation to all special property and his/her share in the jointly owned property.

For obligations: burdening both cohabitants; arising in connection with joint property;[18] or which one cohabitant accepts for the current needs of the family; *both* cohabitants are jointly liable in relation to jointly owned as well as special property. If in paying-off debts, or burdening both cohabitants, one of them pays more than his share, he or she has the right of recourse against the other (article 56 MFRA).

The creditor of one cohabitant can demand determination of his or her share in jointly owned property and present a motion for execution on this share and so settle his claim from cohabitants' joint property (article 57, section 1 MFRA). If in the execution procedure he is allowed to sell the share which the cohabitant has in jointly owned property, the other cohabitant, before all others, has the right to buy the share for the price determined in accordance with the provisions of execution (article 57, section 2 MFRA).

---

18 Credits and loans separately accepted by spouses for joint construction are treated equally in the determination of shares in jointly earned property, even if on one side there is more than on the other, because paying-off credits and loans means a burden for the joint family assets and by that it is only one way of sharing joint means for construction needs, as long as economic community between the spouses exists. Disproportionality in paying-off credits and loans, appearing later, can be the basis of mutual claims to adjust these burdens to co-owned shares. SC SRS, Pž 1381/72 of 2.3.1973 – report of the VS SRS 1/73 – taken from Geč-Korošec, *Pravna ureditev življenja v dvoje*, p 63.

4   CONCLUSION OF LEGAL TRANSACTIONS BETWEEN COHABITANTS

Cohabitants may mutually conclude all legal transactions which they can conclude with other persons and they may in this way establish among themselves property rights and obligations. For these transactions to be valid, it is necessary to effect a certification by a notary (article 47, point 1 Notary Act). Certification by a notary is not necessary in relation to everyday transactions and smaller presents.

Cohabitants may not conclude any legal transaction which would change the property regime. Thus, they may not agree that property earned by work during cohabitation will be their special property.

C   Other fields

The MFRA admits legal validity to cohabitation only in its own field, while for other fields every act itself has to determine whether cohabitation will be admitted legal validity, under what conditions and with what legal consequences. How single acts regulate cohabitation is visible from following examples:

(1)   The Law of Succession determines, that, in the same way as spouses, a man and woman living in a living community for a substantial time inherit, but only where there are no reasons why marriage between them would be invalid (article 10, section 2 LS). This means that a cohabitant may succeed under the statutory succession in either the first or second succession. If he or she succeeds in first succession, he or she takes together with the children of the deceased cohabitant (biological and adopted) in equal shares (compare article 11 LS). But, if he or she succeeds in second succession (when the deceased cohabitant had no children), usually he or she receives half of the estate and the other half is received by the deceased cohabitant's parents or their children according to the principle of representation (compare articles 14 and 15 LS);

(2)   The Social Security Act determines in article 30 that a person living with the person claiming social help, for at least one year, is assumed to be a family member, since the MFRA equalised the position with marriage;

(3)   The Health Insurance and Protection Act gives an equal right to insurance as between the spouse or cohabitant of an employed person (article 21 HIPA);

(4)   The Annuity and Disablement Insurance Act determines that a person living with the insured in living community for the last three years of his or her life or living with the deceased in such a community for the last year of his or her life and having had a child with him at any time, has the right to a widow's pension when meeting the necessary conditions (article 114 ADIA);

(5)   The Obligations Act determines in article 381, point 4, that expiration of the limitation period does not take place between persons living in cohabitation, as long as this cohabitation exists;

(6)   The Criminal Procedure Act determines that a person living in cohabitation with the accused is not obliged to testify (article 236, section 1, point 1 CPA);

(7)   The Income Act treats a person as a maintained family member if this person has no means of living on his or her own or if his or her means are smaller than the amount required for a maintained family member, if the person was living with the insured in a living community, that is equalised with marriage after the MFRA, for the whole year for which income is measured (article 11);

(8)   The Civil Procedure Act determines in article 233, section 1, that a witness can refuse to answer single questions, if he or she has well-founded reasons, especially if with his or her answer, he or she would put into disrepute, major financial loss or liability to criminal prosecution himself or herself or his or her kinsmen or relatives to the third degree, his or her spouse or the person with whom he or she lives for a substantial time, as the act regulating marriage determines, or relatives in law to the second degree, even if the marriage has already ended, or his or her curator, ward, adopter or adoptee;

(9)   The Private International Law and Procedure Act determines that for property relations between persons living in cohabitation their *lex nationalis* is used and, secondarily, their joint *lex domicilii* (article 41, sections 1 and 2 PILPA).

D   Children born in cohabitation

With a view to the child's benefit, the family enjoys special protection, which derives from numerous international conventions as well as from the Constitution and Acts of Slovenia.

Thus, a validly established cohabitation has legal consequences only regarding the cohabitants but not in relation to them as parents of their common children. For children born or procreated in cohabitation, the legal presumption of fatherhood is not relevant. This is governed instead by acknowledgment of paternity or judicial determination of fatherhood. Only if the children's paternity is established, are those children equal to children born or procreated in marriage regarding the rights and duties towards their parents and relatives.

V   THE END OF COHABITATION

Cohabitation ends by the death of one cohabitant, by marriage, by agreement or by one-sided dissolution of cohabitation. Since the parties established it themselves, they can dissolve it on their own. When cohabitation ends, certain legal consequences arise. Since cohabitation gives rise to the same legal consequences as marriage, the consequences of termination are the same as arise on termination of marriage.

A   Maintenance of dependent cohabitant

When the ending of cohabitation occurs by agreement of both partners or by the will of one of them, the cohabitant having no means of living, being unemployed without fault or being incapable of work, has the right to be maintained by the other cohabitant, to the extent that this is within his or her capability (compare article 50 MFRA). If other maintenance obligations, especially to children, would be endangered, he or she is not obliged to maintain his or her cohabitant.[19] The amount of maintenance is determined in accordance with the needs of the claimant and the capability of the payor (article 129 MFRA). Renunciation of the right to maintenance has no legal consequences (article 128 MFRA).

Cohabitants may reach an agreement on maintenance obligations, their level and adjustment at the Social Care Centre (compare article 130 MFRA). If there is no such agreement, the claimant of maintenance can demand maintenance by suing before a competent court. The court may raise, lower or terminate maintenance determined by agreement or judgment if the circumstances on the basis of which it was determined, later change (article 132, section 5 MFRA). The court may send every ruling on maintenance to the Social Care Centre in the area where the claimant of maintenance has his or her residence (article 132, section 3 MFRA). The Social Care Centre afterwards informs the payor of maintenance and the claimant about every adjustment and new amount of maintenance. The Social Care Centre's notice, together with the court's ruling or the eventual agreement between cohabitants, may be the subject of execution (compare article 132, section 4 MFRA).[20]

In Slovenia, marriage is dissolved when it becomes disrupted for any reason. That means, that the MFRA does not recognise the principle of fault for divorce, since the 'guilty' spouse may also file for divorce. Because this principle would be too severe and unjust in some cases, this is taken into account in cases where the 'innocent' spouse has no means of living and is incapable of work. Where he or she is maintained in that way the court takes into account the reasons leading to the breakdown of marriage. By analogy this also applies to the termination of cohabitation.

B   The return of presents

Presents form part of the special property of cohabitants, since they are gratis. To special property there also belong presents one cohabitant receives from the other. Such presents are separated into *usual presents* and *other presents*. Usual presents are presents in relation to the property status of the donor. Thus, other presents are presents not relating to the donor's financial status.[21] What is treated as a usual and as an other present in a certain case, has to be assessed from case to case, since a present of certain value may be proportional to financial status, while a

---

19   'Obligation to maintenance for a minor child has priority over maintenance for the spouse'. – VSV Rev 850/87 from 7.10.1987 – published in Bilten VSV 6/87 – taken from Rupel, Družinsko pravo, p 95.

20   Valorisation of maintenance is executed by Upravni organ Republike Slovenije, competent for social security, so that it is adjusted to the cost of living and personal incomes in the Republic of Slovenia and published in Uradni list RS (compare article 132, section 1 MFRA).

21   In relation to real estates as presents, they cannot be treated as a usual present. So, it is impossible to treat real estate as relating to the property status of the cohabitant/donor.

present of the same value in another case can obviously be disproportionate to the financial status of the donor.[22]

Separation of usual and other presents is important in the event of returning presents at the dissolution of cohabitation. Usual presents which cohabitants gave each other before or during cohabitation are not returned after dissolution of cohabitation. Presents that cannot be treated as usual are returned. They have to be returned in the state they were in at the moment of the appearance of the reason for dissolution (compare article 84, section 2 MFRA). If it is possible, presents are returned in kind. Otherwise, money or other things received for the present are returned. If over time, a present lost its value, the present's value at the moment of appearance of the reason for dissolution of cohabitation counts. But, since a lot of time can pass between the appearance of the reason and the dissolution itself, it is sometimes very difficult to determine the real value of the present. That is why in determining a present's value another more appropriate time should be considered.

C   Division of jointly owned property

The MFRA states the legal presumption that shares in jointly owned property are equal. Only where cohabitants are not satisfied by this presumption can they establish another proportion of ownership in relation to jointly owned property (article 59, section 1 MFRA). Where there is a dispute regarding joint property, the court does not take into account only the income of each cohabitant, but also other circumstances, for example, help given to the other cohabitant, the custody and upbringing of children, housework, efforts for conservation of property and every other form of work and cooperation in administrating, conserving and increasing jointly owned property (article 59, section 2 MFRA). Before establishing the share of each cohabitant in jointly owned property, debts and claims relating to this property are ascertained (article 61, section 1 MFRA). At the division of jointly owned property, a cohabitant can demand that those things be assigned to his or her share which are relevant to his business or occupation or which have made possible the earning of his salary. In the same way, he or she can demand things to be granted to him or her that are exclusively for his or her personal use (article 61, section 2 MFRA).

At the division of jointly owned property, the rules of division which apply to joint ownership operate (compare article 60 MFRA). The manner of division can be determined by the cohabitants themselves, where they conclude a division contract, certified by a notary (compare article 47, point 1 Notary Act). Division is executed by themselves. Prima facie, they must effect physical division of jointly owned property. Cohabitants must divide property in the way that they would divide single items of jointly owned property or their parts among themselves (*physical division*). When physical division is not possible, because the thing in question cannot be taken apart by its nature or taking it apart would prevent it functioning or devalue it, *civil division* is executed. At civil division, the item of

---

22 So a ring valued at 40.000,00 SIT given by a cohabitant earning 50.000,00 SIT a month to his or her cohabitant as a present, represents an other present. But, if the same ring is given as a present by a cohabitant earning 800.000 SIT, it will be a usual present.

property is sold and the money received is shared by the cohabitants. It is also possible for one cohabitant to pay off the other and keep the object.

If cohabitants cannot agree on the division of jointly owned property on their own, they can refer the matter to court, where in civil procedure the range of jointly owned property, the shares and the manner of division are established. Division itself is executed in non-contentious proceedings. The court primarily uses physical division first and, secondarily, civil division.

D   Succession

If a cohabitant made a will in favour of his or her partner and, afterwards, the cohabitation terminates, the will will be revoked. The surviving cohabitant *ex lege* loses all benefits from the last will which his or her cohabitant made during cohabitation (compare article 100 HA). The right to succession is not lost when a will is made after dissolution of cohabitation.[23]

E   Housing

When cohabitation ends because of death, article 56, section 1 Housing Act (hereafter HA)[24] determines that, in this case, the owner of the apartment is obliged to lease the apartment to the person with whom the tenant lived for a substantial time.

The cessation of cohabitation can also be caused by dissolution. Prima facie, it is left to the cohabitants to agree about who will stay as tenant of the joint apartment. The other partner has to move out (article 57, section 1 HA). If they do not agree, the court rules on this on the application of either cohabitant. Here, the court especially takes into account the needs of both cohabitants, their children (whose interests are primary) and other persons living in the apartment (article 57, section 2 HA). Thus, in deciding about who will stay in the apartment, the court can take into consideration to whom custody of the children will be granted and their upbringing, property relations, prospects of rehousing, etc.[25]

The fact that one of the cohabitants moves out during the proceedings does not mean that he loses the right to be tenant. He or she will not lose this right if he or she moved out because of disrupted relations. This means that the cohabitant who moved out, because of illegal acts by his or her cohabitant interfering with his or her use of the home, does not lose his or her right. In the same way, for as long as the question of who will stay in the apartment is not resolved, the other partner cannot accept any other spouse or partner into the apartment.[26]

As already mentioned, the court determines which cohabitant will be tenant of the apartment, which for the other cohabitant means that he has to move out within the time limit the court sets. The time limit for moving out of the apartment

---

23   See further, Zupančič, Dedno pravo, p 138.

24   Published in Ur. l. RS, no. 18/91-I from 11 October 1991; 21/94; 23/96; 1/2000.

25   Compare Ude, p 73 and Vreš, p 45.

26   Ruling by the SC of Yugoslavia, Už 3097/64 of 17 April 1964 – taken from Ude, p 80.

must not be shorter than 60 and not longer than 90 days. Disputes about who will stay or become tenant of the apartment are urgent (article 59, section 3 HA).[27]

VI CONCLUSION

The number of cohabitations, as everywhere else in the world, is rising in Slovenia. By the same token legal disputes emerge. Before a dispute, which has its roots in cohabitation, can be commenced at all, it is necessary to start the procedure to evaluate whether, in a certain relationship, the conditions for a valid cohabitation are met. Establishment of the existence or non-existence of cohabitation matters only in relation to actual disputes.

The Slovene legislator grants rights and duties to cohabitants equal to those that apply to spouses in many acts and under certain conditions. But, in spite of that, a number of questions connected to cohabitation and its legal consequences remain unanswered.

BIBLIOGRAPHY:

ALINČIĆ Mira; BAKARIĆ-ABRAMOVIĆ Ana; HLAČA Nenad; HRABAR Dubravka. *Obiteljsko pravo,* Birotehnika cdo, Zagreb 1994 (cit. Avtor, V: Obiteljsko pravo).

DRAŠKIĆ Marija. *Vanbračna zajednica,* Naučna knjiga, Beograd 1988 (cit. Draškić).

GEČ-KOROŠEC Miroslava. *Nekatera aktualna vprašanja preživljanja zakoncev in izvenzakonskih partnerjev po pravu jugoslovanskih republik in avtonomnih pokrajin,* Zbornik Višje Pravne šole v Mariboru, 2/1985, str. 223-232 (cit. Geč-Korošec).

GEČ-KOROŠEC Miroslava; KRALJIĆ Suzana. *Družinsko pravo, III. spremenjena in dopolnjena izdaja,* Pravna fakulteta Univerze v Mariboru, Maribor 1999 (cit. Geč-Korošec/Kraljić).

GEČ-KOROŠEC Miroslava; KRALJIĆ Suzana. *Vermögensrechtliche Verhältnisse in der Ehe und der nichtehelichen Lebensgemeinschaft nach slowenischen Recht, V: Eheliche Gemeinschaft, Partnerschaft und Vermögen in europäischen Vergleich, Beiträge zum europäischen Familienrecht,* Verlag Ernst und Werner Giesiking, Bielefeld 1999 (cit. Geč-Korošec/Kraljić, Vermögensrechtliche Verhältnisse).

KOSTANJEVEC Bogomir. *Izvenzakonska življenjska skupnost,* Pravnik 5-7/1987, str. 355-362 (cit. Kostanjevec).

---

27 If regulations of the HA and former Housing Relations Act of 1982 (HRA) are compared, it can be established, that HA did not take over the provisions of HRA, according to which a cohabitant staying in the apartment had to arrange necessary rooms for the cohabitant leaving (compare article 57, section 3 HA and article 17, section 4 HRA).

KRALJIĆ Suzana. *Varstvo otrok, rojenih v zunajzakonski skupnosti, v Republiki Sloveniji in v njenih sosednjih državah, V: Institucionalno varstvo nekaterih človekovih pravic, predvsem s področja družinskih in socialnih razmerij s primerjalnopravnimi vidiki prava Evropska Unije ter njenih članic,* Inštitut za civilno, primerjalno in mednarodno zasebno pravo pri Pravni fakulteti Univerze v Mariboru, Maribor 1998, str. 110-135 (cit. Kraljić).

KRALJIĆ Suzana. *Premoženjski režim zakoncev po pravu Republike Slovenije in pravu držav Evropske unije, s posebnim poudarkom na bodoči ureditvi Republike Slovenije,* magistrska naloga Pravne fakultete Univerze v Mariboru, Maribor 2000 (cit. Kraljić, Premoženjski režim).

KUKOLJAC V. Milorad; RALČIĆ Tomislav. *Priručnik sudske prakse pozitivnih propisa i pravnih instituta iz oblasti građanskog prava sa objašnjenjima, obrascima i registrom pojmova,* Savremena administracija, Beograd (cit. Kukoljac/Ralčić).

LJUJIĆ Borivoj. *Zbirka sodnih odločb- Zakonska zveza in družinska razmerja,* Bonex Založba d.o.o., Ljubljana 1998 (cit. Ljujić).

MITIĆ Mihailo. *Porodično pravo u SFRJ,* Službeni list SFRJ OOUR knjige, Beograd 1980 (cit. Mitić).

MLADENOVIĆ Marko. *Porodično pravo u Jugoslaviji,* Naučna knjiga, Beograd 1989.

POLAJNAR-PAVČNIK Ada. *Kolizijskopravni problemi izvenzakonske skupnosti,* Pravnik 11-12/1987, str. 543-549 (cit. Polajnar-Pavčnik).

POPOVIĆ Milan. *Porodično pravo,* Savremena administracija, Beograd 1982 (cit. Popović).

RIJAVEC Vesna. *Primerjalnopravni prikaz urejanja premoženjskih razmerij izvenzakonskih partnerjev,* Pravnik 11-12/1992, str. 483-495 (cit. Rijavec, Primerjalnopravni prikaz).

RIJAVEC Vesna. *Premoženjska razmerja zunajzakonskih partnerjev v pravdi, V: Institucionalno varstvo nekaterih človekovih pravic, predvsem s področja družinskih in socialnih razmerij s primerjalnopravnimi vidiki prava Evropska Unije ter njenih članic,* Inštitut za civilno, primerjalno in mednarodno zasebno pravo pri Pravni fakulteti Univerze v Mariboru, Maribor 1998, str. 80-109 (cit. Rijavec).

WEDAM-LUKIĆ Dragica. *Procesni problemi ugotavljanja obstoja izvenzakonske skupnosti,* Pravnik 8-10/1987, str. 401-412 (cit. Wedam-Lukić).

ZUPANČIČ Karel. *Izvenzakonska skupnost v pravu Jugoslavije,* Pravnik 5-7/1987, str. 271-289 (cit. Zupančič I).

ZUPANČIČ Karel. *Izvenzakonska skupnost v primerjalnem pravu,* Pravnik 3-4/1987, str. 147-159 (cit. Zupančič II).

SPAIN

THE CATALAN FAMILY CODE OF 1998 AND OTHER AUTONOMOUS REGION LAWS ON *DE FACTO* UNIONS

*Gabriel García Cantero**

I   INTRODUCTION

At the end of the century, Spain has seen interesting innovations in relation to the family, not at the national level, but rather in the autonomous, or territorial, regional law. Constitutional support for this is contained in article 149.1.9 of the Spanish Constitution of 1978, where power is given to legislate in those civil law matters to which the regional (*'foral'*) or special civil law applied at the time when the Constitution was promulgated. In the exercise of this power, Catalonia and Aragon have promulgated laws on family matters in 1998 and 1999.[1]

II   THE CATALAN FAMILY CODE, APPROVED IN LAW 9/1998, OF 15 JULY, BY THE PARLIAMENT OF CATALONIA

Historically, Catalonia has been noted for having certain peculiarities in the matter of family law which were respected in the promulgation of the Civil Code of 1889; mainly this was a matter of the economic regime of the family, whose legislative basis was that of separation of assets, the same as in the Balearic Islands, whereas in the rest of Spain the system is one of a more or less extensive community of assets; also in relation to filiation, it had long favoured the freedom to investigate paternity, whereas severe restrictions were imposed in the Civil Code. The Catalan *Compilación de derecho foral* of 1960 contained about a hundred articles relating to specifically Catalan rules. After the Constitution of 1978, the Parliament of Catalonia has made use of the powers attributed to it in the Constitution over its own laws, promulgating a Code on succession law in 1991. Thereafter, it has promulgated a series of regional laws on family matters (on filiation and tutorship in 1991; on property relations between spouses in 1993; on maintenance between spouses and on their parental authority (*patria potestas*) in 1996) which are now codified in a text of 272 articles. This unique form of legislation (in Europe, the only precedent is that of the Family Codes promulgated

---

*   Emeritus Professor of Civil law at the University of Zaragoza, Spain. Translated by Peter Schofield.

1   A project for legislation on *de facto* couples, presented by the governing Partido Popular was under discussion at State level, But this project fell with the calling of elections. At the time of writing (April 2000), the Partido Popular, which gained an absolute majority, has not yet formed a government. The matter did not figure in its election manifesto.

in the socialist countries after World War II), appears to hold out the prospect of the drawing up of a Catalan Civil Code at a very early date.[2]

Analysing the content of this Family Code: Title I refers to the effects of marriage. Surprisingly, article 1 contains a definition of the latter, since Catalonia does not have competence over this, and it is impossible for the concept of marriage prevailing in the region not to be identical with that operating in the rest of Spain. The constitutional equality of the spouses is found in article 3 on the management of the family. The Catalan Code follows the Civil Code in listing family outgoings, though it extends this to those attributable to other family members who live with the spouses (article 4.2); likewise it regulates the regime of the family home (article 9). On the other hand, aspects such as marriage articles (in Spanish, '*capitulaciones*', in Catalan '*capitols*'), gifts made on account of marriage, and widows' rights (*derechos viduales familiares*), have traditionally been subject to Catalan law and it is logical that they should be conserved.

Also a matter of traditional Catalan law are the matrimonial economic regimes governed by Title II, following the guidelines set out in the Law of 1993.[3] This concerns the regime of separation of assets already mentioned, purchases with a contract of survivorship (*compras con pacto de supervivencia*), the regime of participation in gains (*ganancias*, new to Catalonia and inspired by the reform of the Civil Code in 1981), partnership in purchases and improvements, the '*agermanamente*' or contract of half and half (*mitad por mitad*), the *convivença* or *mitja guadanyeria* peculiar to the Valle de Arán in the Pyrenees and, finally, the regime of community, into which it is possible to contract in Catalonia.

On the other hand, Title III is new and covers the effects of nullity of marriage, divorce and separation and, on these points, it simply reproduces the regime of the Civil Code.

Title IV regulates filiation in its totality, including that which is biological, adoptive, and the result of assisted procreation, substantially reproducing the rules contained in the Law of Filiations of 1991. In contrast to the State legislation, the peculiarities of assisted procreation have been incorporated into the system of filiation. There is no explanation of why so new a matter as this last should differ in an essential point from the State system.[4] The Catalan system of adoption is very similar to the State system, after the reforms of 1987 and 1996. International adoption is featured and, as a novelty – which has given rise to considerable reservations – the adopted person and, while the latter is a minor, the adopters, are accorded an action directed at ascertaining biological paternity, with the sole

---

2   The proposal seems excessive, since Catalonia has never in its history had a complete *Corpus Juris Civilis*. Under the 1978 Constitution, the State has reserved to itself exclusive competence in relation to some civil matters, such as the formalities of marriage, the basis of contractual obligation, the regulation of the Public Registers, and internal conflict of civil laws between regions. The proposed Catalan codification cannot regulate the formalities of marriage, civil or religious, nor the causes of nullity, separation or divorce (though it can regulate the consequences of judgments in matrimonial causes). On the other hand, the traditional matters and some others which are new to Catalonia are complete, such as spousal maintenance and parental authority. Many of these repeat the Civil Code (sometimes slightly modified), duplicating them.

3   On which see García Cantero in Castán Tobeñas, *Derecho civil español, común y foral*, Tomo. V, vol 2, 12th ed (Madrid 1994), pp 787 ff.

4   Posthumous fertilisation is permitted in both systems, but under that of the State there is a time limit of six months from the man's death, and in the Catalan it is nine months, with a power of extension by judicial order.

purpose of claiming from the father or mother in respect of biological damage, and this without prejudice to the duty to preserve minors' rights of action (*deber de reserva de las actuaciones*).[5]

Catalan law never had rules on *patria potestas* prior to the Law of 1996, the text of which is now codified in Title VI. The model which has been adopted is that of the Civil Code after the reform of 1981, with changes in detail; as to terminology, in place of the Roman law term *patria potestas*, it is referred to as the authority (*potestad*) of the father and mother; following the model of Aragon, we find the Family Council (*Junta de Parientes*) as an alternative to judicial intervention in certain cases; judicial authorisation takes the place of the consent of the minor aged over 16 for certain contracts affecting the latter's assets entered into by the parents.

In the matter of tutorship, the model followed in Spain was the judicial one of Roman law origin, but the Civil Code of 1889 substituted the French system of family tutorship. In 1983, this was replaced by a system of tutorship by authorisation, with intervention of the judge; in 1987 there was added a system of administrative tutorship for unprotected minors. Catalonia did not have its own system and the general system of the current Civil Code was applicable. The Parliament of Catalonia, in 1991, laid down rules for the tutorship of minors and persons under incapacity, which now form Title VII. A degree of vacillation can be seen in the basic principles, perhaps because of the lack of a specific Catalan tradition in the matter. Numerous articles are derived from the Civil Code; the Preamble to the Code says the system of family tutorship is applied, but in accordance with the principles of civil liberty; the responsibility of the protutor is suppressed, and, on a facultative basis, provision is made for a Tutorship Council (the old Family Council of the Civil Code), which may take the place of judicial intervention in certain cases. On account of all this, we could characterise the Catalan system of tutorship as a mixed one.

Also an innovation in Catalan law is Title VIII on maintenance between spouses. Its contents coincide with the provisions of the Civil Code.

III CATALAN LAW 10/1998, OF 5 JULY, ON COUPLES IN STABLE UNIONS

On the same day that it approved the Family Code the Catalan Parliament also approved a law on *de facto* unions, thus implying that this was a matter that fell outside family law. A jurist may ask, if not in the classification of family law, to which sector of the civil law does it belong? Is it, perhaps, a purely proprietary or contractual matter – a form of civil partnership?[6]

---

5 It would appear that it is possible to claim from the parents for damages caused by passing on hereditary diseases.

6 Probably this is a systematic vacillation due to doubt as to the competence of the Autonomous Community of Catalonia. As we have seen, the 1978 Constitution gave exclusive competence to the State over forms of marriage, following the wording used in the republican Constitution of 1931. As we have said, doctrinal writers have deduced from this that there should be a uniform regime for marriage, its forms, grounds for nullity, separation and divorce. Although the Constitution has nothing to say on *de facto* unions, there is no doubt that its regulation is fixed by reference to the law of marriage, by emulation or by exclusion. On the other hand, the law itself

The Law contains 35 articles and is very simply constructed, in two chapters, one dedicated to heterosexual and the other to homosexual stable unions; there are no general provisions or rules common to both, so some things are repeated in both chapters.

A **heterosexual stable union** is defined as the stable union of a man and a woman, both being of full age, there being no impediment to their intermarrying, who have cohabited maritally for, at least, an uninterrupted period of two years or have completed a public written declaration of their intention to become subject to this law; further, at least one of them must be subject to Catalan law (ie have his or her *vecindad civil*[7] there).

Where the cohabitants have issue in common, the time element is not necessary. Any evidence which is admissible by law can be called on to prove cohabitation. As a general rule, the law provides that the couple can themselves regulate the personal relationships in their cohabitation as well as their respective rights and duties; each party retains the ownership, enjoyment and administration of his or her own property. The law does lay down an inalienable minimum, as follows:

(1)   the common expenses of the couple, necessary for their own and their children's maintenance;

(2)   they can adopt jointly;

(3)   each has a preferential right to be nominated as the appointed tutor of the other should the latter be declared incapacitated;

(4)   each is obliged to provide for the maintenance of the other in priority to any other person so obliged;

(5)   as against third parties, both are liable *in solidum* for debts contracted for common expenses;

(6)   if either is employed in the public service, the *Generalitad de Cataluña* regards them as entitled to certain benefits;

(7)   neither can dispose of the common dwelling without the other's consent.

The union is terminated as follows:

(1)   by mutual consent;

(2)   unilaterally by authenticated notice from one to the other;

(3)   on the death of either;

(4)   by *de facto* separation for over a year;

(5)   by either marrying a third party.

---

does regulate certain of its effects to the extent that the State legislates on the matter, (to wit the Additional Disposition, in relation to procedure), and on possible registration in the Registro Civil (second Final Disposition).

7   *Vecindad civil* is regulated in article 14 of the Civil Code, in a uniform way for all Spanish citizens. It is the thing that links a person to a particular territory so that the law of that territory or autonomous community is applicable to him or her. Without going into the detail of this, suffice it to say the test is one of *jus sanguinis* (born of Catalan parents), of the choice exercised, in certain cases after the age of 14 years, by a minor born in Catalonia, and of continuous residence for two years in the territory, declared before the Civil Registration Officer, or, in the absence of registration, ten years' residence without contrary indication.

It is evident that the legal force of this union is weaker than that of a contract, since the unilateral will of either party suffices to end it. However, break up can give rise to disadvantageous consequences, consisting of securing economic compensation when the parties are left in an unequal situation with regard to property, which implies unjust enrichment.[8] In addition, when the cohabitation ends, either party can claim periodical alimony from the other if this is necessary for his or her support.[9] If they have children in common, on the ending of the cohabitation the couple may come to an agreement as to their custody and to visitation rights; if there is no agreement, the judge will decide. By way of sanction, and on pain of nullity, a party who has broken off a cohabitation declared in a public written document cannot form a similar union with another person for six months counting from the date of termination.[10]

If the death of a party ends a cohabitation, there are no succession rights either as forced heirs or on by way of intestate succession. All the survivor gets is what is provided for him or her in the will of the deceased partner.[11]

A **homosexual stable union** is defined in the law as the stable union of two persons of the same sex, who live together maritally and declare their willingness to be subject to the law in the manner provided.

The following cannot enter into such a union:

(1)   persons below the age of majority;
(2)   married persons;
(3)   anyone who is already in a stable union with another;
(4)   persons related to each other in direct line by blood or by adoption; and
(5)   persons who do not both possess Catalan *vecindad*.

The only mode of formation is by a joint, notarially attested document, which must state that none of the legal prohibitions applies. There is freedom for the parties to regulate their own personal and proprietary relationships, either in the public writing by which it is formed, or subsequently, by word of mouth, or in a public or private document. But the law establishes an inalienable minimum. Each party retains the ownership, enjoyment and administration of his or her own property.

The minimum legal regime of the homosexual couple is identical to that of the heterosexual, in relation to common expenses, responsibility *vis-à-vis* third parties, tutorship, maintenance, benefits available to Catalan public servants and disposal of the common dwelling. No mention is made of adoption, so the homosexual couple cannot adopt jointly. Also the causes of termination are the

---

8   There is a requirement that the claimant should have worked for the common household or for the other cohabitant without or for inadequate remuneration.

9   But only in the following cases: 1) if the cohabitation has left the claimant in a worse position to obtain an income and 2) if s/he has responsibility for children and has thus less ability to obtain an income.

10   This sanction in the form of a waiting period is more nominal than real. Bear in mind that a new relationship can begin informally and the two year period (unnecessary if there are children of the couple) begins straight away.

11   But the law does allow the survivor the domestic furniture and the benefit of the 'year of mourning' that Catalan law gives a widow (right to reside in the common home and maintenance from the deceased's estate).

same; but, given the formal character of the establishment of the stable homosexual union, it is provided that both the parties are obliged, even if acting separately, on break up to have the instrument of its creation cancelled.[12]

The consequences of the ending of a homosexual union are the same as for a heterosexual one, except in relation to intestate succession. In the case of death intestate of one partner to a heterosexual union the survivor has no succession rights. However, in the case of a homosexual union the law gives the survivor limited rights of succession, which are not the same as those given by Catalan law to a surviving spouse,[13] and which depend on the qualifications of the other heirs who are competing; thus, in competition with ascendants or descendants, the cohabitant who has inadequate economic means of support can claim against the heirs up to a quarter of the estate, subject to the limit of what is needed to ensure adequate maintenance for him or her, whereas the surviving spouse's rights would extend to a share which took into account the standard of living the spouses had enjoyed while both were alive; in competition with brothers and sisters or nephews and nieces, the surviving cohabitant can claim up to half the estate; against more distant relatives, the whole of it.

From the foregoing, it can be seen that Catalan law does not equate the legal effects of the heterosexual union to those of a homosexual one, those of the latter being more extensive, and it is perhaps for this reason that the conditions for its establishment are stricter. Still less are the effects of either form of union equated to those of marriage.[14]

IV ARAGONESE LAW 6/1999, OF 26 MARCH, ON STABLE UNMARRIED COUPLES

Aragon is an Autonomous Community with its own civil law and, since the Constitution of 1978, its Parliament has legislated on this matter also. The law on unmarried couples clearly draws on the Catalan legislation we have just described, with the difference that it does not separate into distinct chapters the rules for the heterosexual and the homosexual couple, and also by taking as its standard of reference – in a positive or in a negative way – the rules of its own civil law.

This law is applicable to persons of full age who, having completed the requirements and formalities which it sets out, form part of a stable, unmarried couple the characteristics of which are analogous to those of marriage.[15] An

---

12 If either fails to collaborate in extinguishing the document, because s/he wants to maintain the union, can the judge make an order to bring it to an end?

13 Articles 379 ff.

14 According to press reports, it was expected that, at the end of a year, about 40,000 *de facto* unions would have been formalised in Catalonia, though there is still some confusion among interested parties as to the rights given them by the law, especially as to the need to agree them in express terms.

15 This description does not coincide with Catalan law; here we see as defining elements, the existence of a couple; that is to say two persons, although not specifically stated, they could be of different or of the same sex; stability is an indeterminate legal concept, which the law clarifies, on the basis of a duration of two years without interruption, although the will of the parties is enough if they express it in a public document; the fact of not being married is a negative element, which refers to any or all of the forms of marriage allowed in Spanish law (which, in any case, excludes homosexual couples); reference to a couple means living in common in a relationship analogous

administrative Registry is set up for this, under the authority of the Aragonese government (*Diputación*) and provision is made for future registration in the national civil register if State law allows this. In dealing with a *de facto* situation, the law regards a couple as stable when conjugal cohabitation has gone on uninterrupted for at least two years, accepting any evidence admissible in law to prove this; it also recognises its existence if it is established in a public written document.[16] The same prohibitions as in Catalonia apply. Also similar, with certain shades of difference, is the regime of cohabitation; first, it can be governed by agreement recorded in a public document, consistent with the autonomy of contracts, provided neither the rights nor the dignity of either party is adversely affected, and that there is no infringement of imperative rules applicable in Aragon; a couple cannot be constituted on a temporary or conditional basis. In the absence of agreement, the law provides a form of agreement, not described, as in Catalonia, as an inalienable minimum, which consists in an obligation to contribute to the maintenance of the common dwelling and the common expenses, each party retaining the ownership, enjoyment and administration of his or her own property. Provision is made that the unmarried couple ceases to exist in the same circumstances as in Catalonia, with the addition – which is obvious – of the death or bankruptcy of either party.[17] Aragonese law declares the principle that either party can unilaterally end the relationship by repudiation authentically notified to the other;[18] accordingly, when they have constituted it by a public document, the law places on each member a duty of cancelling it. The rules of the law of Catalonia and Aragon coincide on the following points: economic compensation in case of unilateral breakup; right to periodical payment of maintenance in certain circumstances; custody and visitation rights in relation to the children of the couple; joint adoption (only for heterosexual couples); nomination as appointed tutor on partner's incapacity; reciprocal rights of maintenance. On other matters the rules differ: in case of absence of a partner, Aragon treats the other party as it would a spouse; Aragonese law explicitly states that being in an unmarried couple gives rise to no family relationship between one party and the relatives of the other (despite silence on this, we must assume the same solution in Catalonia); Aragon allows the couple to make joint wills, contracts for succession rights, and the establishment of a successory trust (*fiducia sucesoria*); public law aspects are formulated differently in Aragon and Catalonia.[19] Finally, the law came into force six months after its publication in the

---

to the conjugal; this concerns another indeterminate legal concept, drawn, this time, from the State law of 1987, on adoption, which raises problems when one comes to apply it to a homosexual relationship (which cannot, by definition, be taken as analogous to the conjugal relationship).

16 Unlike Catalan law, in Aragon a homosexual *de facto* couple can arise by the fact of living together for two years without any written document. To this extent, the treatment is more favourable.

17 Although neither Aragonese nor Catalan law mention this, it must also end if the parties marry each other.

18 There is an apparent contradiction between calling a couple *stable* and this unconditional right of either member to break off the relationship. Would it not be more accurate to call it an *unstable couple*?

19 Aragonese law states that the rights and obligations, of a public law nature, but not related to taxation, established in Aragonese law and applying as between spouses, apply equally to members of a stable union outside marriage; in Catalonia particular benefits are listed, such as the

Official Journal of Aragon, and on the same date the autonomous administrative register of stable unmarried couples came into existence.

V   SOME CONCLUSIONS

The two examples of autonomous legislation have in common a certain degree of imprecision and absence of clarity as to the legal character of an unmarried couple. This is not a case of the coming into existence of a marriage at common law, nor of a union that is equated with marriage *tout court*. It is even doubtful whether the Legislature regards it as a matter of family law. It is highly unstable in that either member has the right to bring it to an end, without showing cause, and without judicial intervention. Over both laws there hovers the doubt as to their constitutional validity, on the ground that they infringe the reservation to the State of legislative competence in the matter of marriage, as we have already indicated. It is likely that the decisions handed down in recent years in Sala 1 of the *Tribunal Supremo*, taken as a whole, offer more appropriate solutions, to the conflicts which present themselves before the courts.

right of voluntary surplus (*excedencia*), that of leave of absence on the death or serious illness of the partner, and that of the reduced working day.

SWEDEN

JOINT CUSTODY, SPECIAL REPRESENTATIVE FOR CHILDREN AND COHABITEES' PROPERTY

*Åke Saldeen**

I   INTRODUCTION

In my report on the development of Swedish Family Law in 1998 I described, *inter alia*, the amended legislation on custody and access, etc which had entered into force on 1 October 1998.[1] In the Government Bill preceding this legislation, the issue was discussed whether or not rules should be introduced concerning automatic joint custody of children of unmarried parents as of the date of determination of paternity. However, the Government considered that, even if joint legal responsibility for the child was also the natural starting point as regards unmarried parents, the issue needed further investigation.[2] This issue was investigated by a sole commissioner during 1999 and the result is presented in a Ministry Memorandum.[3] The proposal from the investigation has recently been the subject of a consultation procedure but has, of course, at the time of writing not yet resulted in any legislation. However, I shall describe here shortly something about the statutory proposal on this matter in Section II.

In 1999, the Riksdag (Swedish Parliament) also adopted an Act providing that a child who is subjected to sexual or other molestation by his/her parents or another closely related person should be able to have a special representative appointed during the preliminary criminal investigation and trial. As the Act has implications regarding the responsibility of custody, I consider that I can report here (in Section III) on this legislation, which entered into force on 1 January 2000.

Finally, I will also describe briefly another statutory proposal submitted during 1999, namely the report from the so-called Cohabitees Commission, which was appointed in 1997. New rules on cohabitation, in which it is proposed, *inter alia*, that the Cohabitees (Joint Homes) Act (1987:232) (The Cohabitees Act) will apply directly not only as regards heterosexual but also as regards homosexual cohabitees are described in Section IV.[4]

By way of introduction I will finally only mention that during 1999 amendments were made to the Act concerning maintenance support, which came

---

* Professor of Private Law, Uppsala University. Translated by James Hurst.
1   See *The International Survey of Family Law (2000 Edition)*, ed A Bainham (Family Law, 2000) at 351–356.
2   Government Bill 1997/98:7, p 52 f.
3   Joint custody for unmarried parents together with a linguistic and editorial review of Chapter 6, Parental Code, Ministry Paper 1999/57, Ministry of Justice.
4   Official Government Report 1999:104.

into force in February 1997, and which applies to social financial support for children whose parents are not cohabiting.[5] Maintenance support of at most SEK 1,173 per month per child is provided. The parent who does not live with the child is liable to repay the maintenance support to the State at a fixed percentage of his/her annual gross income after making certain basic deductions for the liable party's own maintenance. In the rules regarding liability to repay, some amendments have now been made, aimed at providing a better distribution policy profile.[6] The amendments mean in effect that the repayment obligation is reduced for those who have low incomes, yet at the same time increased for those who have high incomes.

II   JOINT CUSTODY FOR UNMARRIED PARENTS

Since about the mid-1970s, a number of amendments have been made to the chapter (Chapter 6) of the Parental Code (formerly known as the Code on Parents, Children and Guardians) that deals with custody, access and also now the residence of children. This legislation has had the effect, *inter alia*, that joint custody is nowadays to prevail as the normal position, even in cases where the parents are not married or are not living together. Since 1977 it has been possible for parents who are not married to have, subject to approval by the court, joint custody. In 1983, it became possible for such parents to obtain joint custody by a simple notification to the Population Registration Authority. In 1991, unmarried parents were afforded an opportunity, by completing a standard form of acknowledgement of paternity (the manner in which the paternity of a child born of an unmarried mother, with the participation of the Social Welfare Committee, is in practice ordinarily determined), to make an application to the Social Welfare Board for joint custody. Since 1 October 1998, the rule is that a court can respectively decide on joint custody, and refuse to dissolve custody, against the wishes of a parent, provided this appears to be in the best interests of the child.

There have been discussions in Sweden for many years concerning the issue of the introduction of a provision whereby unmarried parents (just like married parents) would automatically obtain joint custody as early as the birth of the child or upon the determination of paternity.

However, in 1998 when preparing the legislation (see above) the Government concluded that joint custody should be the main principle even as regards unmarried parents, but that the issue of automatic joint custody for such parents should be investigated further.[7] Such an investigation has now, as mentioned in the introduction, taken place and is reported in a Ministry Memorandum.[8]

The investigation reports, as background to the discussion, adopted certain statistical information regarding the issue in question. This information indicates

---

5   As regards the Act in question see my report in *The International Survey of Family Law 1996*, ed A Bainham (Martinus Nijhoff Publishers, 1998) at 481 ff.

6   Government Bill 1998/99:78, Computation of repayment liability for maintenance support to children with non-cohabiting parents, etc.

7   Government Bill 1997/87:7, p 52.

8   Joint custody for unmarried parents together with a linguistic and editorial review of Chapter 6, Parental Code, Ministry Paper 1999:57.

that, *inter alia*, something over half (54%) of all children who are born in Sweden today have unmarried parents. 95% of unmarried cohabiting parents today give notice of joint custody in conjunction with an acknowledgement of paternity. The corresponding figure is 50% as regards unmarried non-cohabiting parents.

It was also concluded by the investigation that, even if joint custody is almost always the best solution for the child, there are cases where this form of custody is not appropriate, for example when the parents are in serious conflict with each other or one of the parents may perhaps be considered directly unsuitable as custodian as a result of, for example, sexual offences against or molestation of the child. Automatic joint custody is therefore not proposed as of the date of the acknowledgement of paternity. Nor is any rule proposed concerning automatic joint custody for only unmarried *cohabiting* parents. The reason for this is that in Swedish law there is no registration or any definition of the cohabitee relationship which could facilitate a rapid and reliable conclusion as to who was the custodian of the child if the existence of a cohabitee relationship were to be decisive for the custody issue.

What is proposed instead is that upon the birth of the child, unmarried parents should obtain joint custody automatically after three months have elapsed from when paternity was determined by an acknowledgement of paternity that has been approved by the Social Welfare Committee,[9] provided that neither of the parents within this period gives notice to the Social Welfare Committee that he or she objects to joint custody. If there is an objection, the mother will continue to be the sole custodian. A father who has been denied participation in custody will, as is already the case today, be able to institute court proceedings to apply for joint custody or to be awarded sole custody.

III SPECIAL REPRESENTATIVES FOR CHILDREN

When a child is a victim of crime it is normally the custodian/s, that is/are responsible for representing the child, such as for example in relation to deciding whether or not the child should be subjected to a hearing or a physician's examination. However, special problems may arise in such cases where the suspected perpetrator is the custodian of the child or a closely related person. In such cases there may, of course, be a conflict of interest between the child and the custodian which can result in the offence never being investigated or the interests of the child not otherwise being protected. When the custodian of the child is suspected of committing an offence against the child, it may also be inappropriate for the custodian to be contacted at this stage of the preliminary investigation. In such a situation the child has previously not had anyone who was able to represent its interests, even if the problem in some cases could be resolved by the child being put into compulsory care under the provisions of the Care of Young People (Special Provisions) Act (1990:52). However, legislation was introduced in 1999 whereby the court may, at the request of a prosecutor, appoint a special

---

9   If paternity has been determined following a trial and judgment both practical and objective
     reasons suggest, according to the investigation, that joint custody should not arise automatically.
     This also applies if paternity is determined abroad, see Ministry Paper 1999:57, p 67.

representative for a child under the age of 18 who is a victim of a crime for which imprisonment may be imposed, if a custodian is suspected of the offence or if it is feared that a custodian by reason of his/her relationship to the person who is suspected of the offence will not protect the interests of the child.[10] (However, such special representative shall not be appointed if, having regard to the child, it is unnecessary or there are other special reasons for not doing so.[11]) If the child has two custodians who are neither married nor living together under circumstances resembling marriage and if the above circumstances apply only to one of them, the other custodian shall be appointed solely to protect the interests of the child during the preliminary investigation and at the subsequent trial. However, if having regard to the relationship of the custodians to each other or to some other special circumstance, it may be assumed to be in the best interests of the child, a special representative must also be appointed in this kind of case.

The Act of course aims at improving the preconditions for investigating suspected offences against children in those cases where the suspected perpetrator is the custodian or someone who has a close relationship to the child/custodian. An attorney, an assistant lawyer at an attorney's office or another appropriate person will be appointed as special representative. However, a requirement in accordance with the statutory provision is always that the person who is to be appointed as special representative for a child must, by reason of his/her knowledge and experience and also his/her personal qualities, be particularly suitable for the assignment.

The special representative will, in principle, completely take over the rights of the custodian and make decisions for the child as regards the legal proceedings. This assignment includes determining in place of the custodian whether, among other things, the child should undergo questioning or a physician's examination within the framework of the police investigation. The assignment also includes, among other things, a right to pursue an action for damages on the behalf of the child. The special representative should (in accordance with the Minister's explanatory statement preceding the legislation) also be able to take over an action instituted, though later discontinued, by the prosecutor.[12]

IV COHABITEES' PROPERTY

On 1 January 1988, the Cohabitees (Joint Homes) Act (1987:232) (the so-called 'Cohabitees Act'), came into force. The overall purpose of this Act was to afford the weaker party minimum protection on the dissolution of the relationship *inter vivos* or in the event of death. According to the Act it is thus provided, *inter alia*, unless otherwise contracted between the parties, that when a relationship of cohabitation ceases, at the request of one or both partners their joint home and household goods will be distributed between them by a division of property, provided the property was acquired for joint use. At the same time as this Act

---

10   Government Bill 1998/99:133.

11   One cause for it being unnecessary to appoint a special representative may be that the child is of such an age (15 years or thereabouts) that he/she can him/herself protect his/her rights (see Government Bill 1998/99:133, p 27).

12   Government Bill 1998/99:133, p 29.

came into force, the Homosexual Cohabitees Act (1987:813) came into force. According to this Act it is provided that if two persons live together in a homosexual relationship, then the rules applicable to cohabitees of the opposite sex by virtue of certain statutes and provisions specified in the Act, such as for example the above-mentioned Cohabitees (Joint Homes) Act, should also apply to homosexual cohabitees. Thus, homosexual cohabitees were not made equal with heterosexual cohabitees as regards all laws and provisions, but only those specified in the Act.

In June 1997, the Government appointed a Parliamentary Committee (the Cohabitees Committee) with the task of evaluating the Cohabitees Act. This involved deliberating on whether the differences in the legal treatment of homosexual cohabitees compared with heterosexual cohabitees are justified and also surveying whether there is a need for extended legal protection in connection with forms of joint households other than those that are specially governed by statute, particularly if the parties do not have an opportunity to enter into marriage or a so-called registered partnership. The Committee submitted its report in September 1999 ('New Cohabitee Rules', Official Government Report 1999:104). The proposal, which has undergone the consultative procedure but which has not yet resulted in any legislation, means among other things the following.

It is proposed that the Cohabitees (Joint Homes) Act (1987:232) – which it may be mentioned the Committee proposed should be renamed the 'Cohabitees Act' – should be directly applicable also to homosexual cohabitees. For this reason it is also proposed that the definition of the concept of cohabitees be amended. In the current Cohabitees Act, it is stated that the Act applies to 'such cohabitee relationships where an unmarried woman and an unmarried man live together in circumstances resembling marriage'. The Committee proposes that it should be stated instead that cohabitees 'refers to two persons who permanently live together in a relationship as a couple and have a joint household'.

The applicable legislation does not state when a cohabitee relationship should be considered to have ended. As this may create problems in practice, the Committee proposes that the statutory wording should also indicate that a cohabitee relationship ceases when the cohabitees or either of them marry or enter into a registered partnership, when they move apart or when one of them dies. Furthermore, according to the proposal, a cohabitee relationship will be deemed to end in certain specific cases, such as, for example, in the event of one cohabitee's or both cohabitees' applications being submitted to court for the appointment of a division of property administrator or for the right to occupy the home exclusively in the future.

As indicated previously, the joint home and household goods of cohabitees are subject to the Cohabitees Act. The Committee concluded that a car – and in certain parts of Sweden a motorboat or a snow-scooter – which is not primarily used for leisure purposes, but which is mostly operated as a means of transport to and from the workplace or to a children's day home, school, other activities of children or for shopping and other matters that are connected with the household, has a natural link with the basis of the Cohabitees Act. The Committee therefore proposes that all means of transport, which are not primarily used for leisure purposes, should be subject to the Act.

The Committee also, as regards the Cohabitees Act, considers that there should be the opportunity for cohabitees, in the face of an imminent cessation of the cohabitee relationship, to conclude an agreement about the future division of property and matters related thereto. Furthermore, in order to increase certainty, it is also proposed to introduce a rule that a cohabitee who desires to have a division of property must make an application for this to the court not later than one year from the end of the relationship in order not to lose the right to a division of property. Finally, as regards the Cohabitees Act, it may be mentioned that the Committee considers that the information concerning this Act must be improved and that the content of the information should be clear and easily understood and directed to both cohabitees of the same and opposite sexes.

As mentioned above, the Homosexual Cohabitees Act (1987:813) specifies which acts and provisions that are applicable to cohabitees of the opposite sex should apply also to cohabitees of the same sex. As stated, not all acts and provisions that apply to cohabitees of the opposite sex apply also to cohabitees of the same sex. With a starting point of equality prevailing between heterosexual and homosexual cohabitees, just as with lawful spouses and so-called registered partners, the Cohabitees Committee has taken the view that the legal differences that exist between heterosexual and homosexual cohabitees are no longer justified. The Committee has thus considered that the legal differences between heterosexual and homosexual cohabitees are more numerous than the differences between lawful spouses and registered partners. It therefore proposes adjustments whereby the legal differences between cohabitees of the opposite and of the same sex are eliminated in all respects, except as regards the provisions concerning assisted fertilisation and joint custody.

Finally, part of the terms of reference of the Cohabitees Committee was also to examine which other groups of cohabitees, heterosexuals and homosexuals may have a need of increased legal protection and also to clarify what these needs are. The Committee concludes in that connection that those persons who live together with someone other than a spouse/registered partner, cohabitee and/or minor child are a relatively small group. Such cohabitation primarily relates to elderly siblings or adult children and parent/s. The Committee concludes that it is not considered necessary to have any special legal regulation of the mutual relationship between persons in such cohabiting relationships. This is set against the background that, amongst other things, in such cases it is less usual for there to be the intermingling of finances that is commonplace in other cohabitee relationships between spouses or cohabitees of the opposite sex.

TANZANIA

'THIS IS NOT MY CHILD': THE TASK OF INTEGRATING ORPHANS INTO THE MAINSTREAM OF SOCIETY IN TANZANIA

*Bart Rwezaura**

I   INTRODUCTION

The last *Survey* covering the period up to 1997 focused on the proposed reforms of the law of marriage, matrimonial property, succession and child law. I pointed out that the pressure for reform had come mainly from human rights groups and other progressive elements in the community who were anxious to raise the status of women and children. It was further noted that the impetus for reform had also received a boost from Tanzania's ratification of international human rights treaties as well as its enactment of the Bill of Rights. While these progressive reforms remain under active consideration, Tanzania, like many states in the sub-Saharan region, has suffered and continues to suffer gravely from the ravages of the HIV/AIDS epidemic. Indeed, it is now widely recognised that family systems in many parts of the developing world are coming under severe pressure because of changing social structures and demography.[1] Tanzania has yet to grapple with the effects of the HIV/AIDS epidemic on family law, not to mention its detrimental effect on children's rights.

The aim of this *Survey* is to sound an alarm, not only for Tanzania but also for all States in the region, on the plight of orphan children, many of whom continue to suffer from discrimination and neglect. Orphans are defined in this *Survey* as children below the age of 18 years whose parents or parent have died from whatever cause. The *Survey* describes the difficult circumstances faced by orphans in Tanzania and the extent to which economic and cultural considerations contribute to the abuse and neglect of orphans in the region. I argue that although children are by their nature vulnerable, orphans are particularly at risk, given that they lack the protection and support of both parents and are often in need of a family to which they can belong. Although in earlier times orphans were more easily absorbed into the wider family where they grew up with other children, this safety net has almost now disappeared. This reality has not been fully grasped by the State, which continues to assume that the extended family remains as robust as in previous times and is therefore capable of supporting those in crisis.

---

*   Senior Lecturer, Faculty of Law, University of Hong Kong.

1   See UNAIDS Briefing paper on HIV/AIDS: Children and HIV/AIDS, February 1999, cited in G Van Bueren and R Wanduragala, 'Annual Review of International Family Law' in *The International Survey of Family Law (2000 Edition)*, ed A Bainham (Family Law, 2000) at 4.

I begin this essay with an outline of the orphan crisis in Tanzania followed by a discussion of who has responsibility for these children under international law. Next I discuss the field data showing instances of violation of the rights of orphans. I use international norms as the benchmark against which to measure these violations. Then I examine Tanzania's response to the orphan crisis and the extent to which this response is equal to the challenge. The questions how and what can be done to integrate orphans into the mainstream of society are also considered in this section. In conclusion, it is stressed that Tanzania needs to take action now to reverse the process that keeps pushing these vulnerable children to the periphery of society.[2]

II   THE ORPHAN CRISIS IN TANZANIA

Before the outbreak of the HIV/AIDS epidemic in the 1980s, the number of orphaned children in Tanzania was negligible and did not attract much public attention. Today, although figures vary, the number is estimated at one million orphans in a country of nearly 32 million people.[3] With the numbers set to rise as the AIDS epidemic claims more lives, the question of who has legal responsibility for orphans in Tanzania has not been given a clear and firm answer. It seems neither the State nor the community have assumed full responsibility for these children after the death of one or both of their parents. The effect is that for a variety of reasons many orphans have been pushed to the periphery of society. They have become the proverbial second class citizens in their own country. No doubt the extended family in Tanzania has historically played a key role in absorbing, supporting and protecting children in need of families.[4] Even now the wider family continues valiantly to play this role under conditions of diminishing resources and the rapidly rising cost of childcare. Many families accepting responsibility for the care of orphans, unless they are grandparents, have their own children to support. Hence, where resources are scarce and the basic needs greater, families have to make difficult choices of resource allocation, sometimes leading to acts of child discrimination. Furthermore, as the economic squeeze continues to bite and to undermine the capacity of many community-minded individuals and families to assume responsibility for other people's children, the pressure on the State to pick up the tab has increased tremendously.

---

2   This essay is based on research conducted in four regions of Tanzania during the months of July and August 1998 and 1999. Data were collected from Arusha, Dar es Salaam, Mwanza and Kagera. Some of the sources used here were collected in 1995 during an earlier phase of this project. The essay has also drawn from published sources and field studies conducted under the auspices of the Tanzania Aids Project (TAP) and UNICEF in collaboration with various government ministries and institutions. The methodology used in this research includes in-depth interviews with key informants, such as managers of children's homes, officials from local and foreign voluntary agencies, social welfare officers, school teachers, the families caring for orphans, and the orphans themselves. Case studies have also been drawn from the Social Welfare Office at Mwanza and Arusha regional offices.

3   Tanzania, United Republic of, and UNICEF, Programme Plan of Operations: Country Programme of Co-operation 1997–2001, p 101.

4   See Susan Hunter, et al, 'Using rapid research to develop a national strategy to assist families affected by AIDS in Tanzania', *Health Transition Review Supplement* to Vol 7 1997, pp 393–420 at 417.

This *Survey* argues that Tanzania has not discharged its obligations to the orphan child in accordance with international standards. Some orphans have become victims of discrimination, abuse, neglect, and stigmatisation within their own families and in their local communities. Some have suffered property deprivation at the hands of unscrupulous guardians. The State's response to the orphan crisis has been largely mute and ineffectual as it seeks to improve the living condition of all its children.

III WHERE DOES RESPONSIBILITY FOR AN ORPHAN LIE?

Parents have the primary responsibility for the care and upbringing of their child, preferably in a family environment. This is evident not only from the preamble but also from the substantive provisions of the CRC.[5] In order for the child to have a full and harmonious development of his or her personality, the child 'should grow up in a family environment, in an atmosphere of happiness, love and understanding' (Preamble CRC). The African Charter on the Rights and Welfare of the Child (hereafter, ACC) also states that parents have the primary responsibility for their children (Article 20 ACC). In this context the term 'parent' is not confined to the natural or adoptive parents of the child. It includes all legal guardians and other persons responsible for the upbringing of the child.[6] Moreover, the CRC goes further by providing that the members of the extended family or community in accordance with local custom may care for the child (Article 5 CRC). Therefore, an orphan can rely, among others, on certain individuals within the extended family or community for care and protection as if such were that child's legal parents.

The State's obligations under the CRC and the ACC are also spelled out in the two treaties. First, the State has the obligation to assist the parents in the discharge of their obligations to the child (Articles 3(2), 5 and 18 CRC and Article 20(2) ACC). States may provide such assistance in a variety of ways including the provision of free education, medical care and other social services. States may also enact laws or initiate policies conducive to the protection of the family and the proper discharge of its responsibilities. Secondly, the State performs the supervisory role, to ensure that parents perform their obligations to their children in conformity with CRC standards and the domestic law. Where it is shown that the child has suffered or is likely to suffer serious harm, the State has the duty to intervene to protect that child (Article 19 CRC and Articles 16 and 21 ACC). This and other duties of the State are stipulated in the CRC including Article 4 which calls upon States to enact legislation and to set up administrative and other measures 'for the implementation of the rights recognised in the present Convention'.

---

5   See eg Articles 3(2), 5, 9, 10 and 18, all of which recognise the child's family, parents, legal guardians or other individuals legally responsible for the child.

6   Article 20(1) the African Charter; see also to the same effect, Articles 18 and 19 of the African Charter. Note that the African Child's Charter has not yet come into effect as it still lacks five more signatures of the 15 needed to bring it into force under Article 47. It is believed that Tanzania will ratify ACC in the very near future.

In cases where a child has no family, the State shall assume direct responsibility. This could happen where a child is deprived of a family environment following the death of his or her parents or in cases where, in its own best interests, such a child cannot be allowed to remain in that family environment (Article 20 CRC and Article 25 ACC). In such cases the State might initiate placement of the child with foster parents; arrange for that child's adoption; or, as a last resort, initiate placement of that child in a suitable institution for the care of children (Article 20(3) CRC). Finally, it must be stressed that the principles of equality and non-discrimination contained in Articles 2 (CRC) and 3 (ACC) are the pillars supporting the entire structure of children's rights. Thus States are required to ensure that all the rights set forth in the two treaties are available to each child within their jurisdiction without discrimination of any kind whatsoever. As intimated above, the importance of this provision for orphans will become clearer in the next section where cases concerning the violation of orphans' rights are considered.

A   'Not my child': forms and instances of violation

Drawing on their field study of Tanzania Siham Ahmed and her colleagues have developed nine themes representing their major research findings. Two of their themes constitute a good starting point to this discussion. The first theme is that 'the capacity of families to meet the needs and fulfil the rights of children is small'. Secondly, that 'every one is denying or refusing to take care of children ... blaming someone else'.[7] These two themes highlight the key elements of the crisis facing orphans, and indeed, other marginal children in contemporary Tanzania.[8] As some of the case studies in this *Survey* demonstrate, the expression, *not my child* is not just a denial of responsibility. It is also, culturally speaking, an admission of failure to assist a needy child. The speaker appears to be in denial given that according to tradition, 'a child belongs to everyone.[9] Yet as Ahmed, et al found, children were being kicked around like a ball while adults blamed one another, saying, 'this child is not my responsibility'.

This study found that abuse and neglect of orphans takes place mainly at two levels; first, at the level of the family, extended family, and the local community; and secondly, at the State level. This section analyses only the violations occurring at the first level and, by implication, it points at what the State ought to be doing to curb such violations. It must be stressed, however, that my object is not to establish the incidence or magnitude of the problem. Rather, the aim is to establish that these violations are committed and to suggest how they might be addressed. Furthermore, although no statistics exist showing the quality of care

---

7   See Siham Ahmed et al *Children in Need of Special Protection Measures: A Tanzania Study*, UNICEF, Tanzania 1999, p 2.

8   In an earlier paper I described them as 'marginal children' who, for economic and cultural reasons are not as highly valued by their caretakers as other children in the family. Due to their being undervalued there is a tendency on the part of caregivers to expend less time and resources on the child or even to neglect him or her. See B Rwezaura (IJLPF Vol 14, 2000, forthcoming).

9   See A Armstrong, "A child belongs to everyone: law, family and the construction of the 'best interests of the child' in Zimbabwe" *Innocenti Occasional Papers* CRS No 11 Florence, Italy (1995).

given to orphans at national level, it is clear that the majority of foster families do sacrifice a great deal to provide good care to orphans under their charge, often along with their own children.

B Discrimination, abuse, and neglect of orphans

Emotive terms such as child abuse, neglect and discrimination are not particularly controversial when used without reference to a given society. Everyone agrees that it is morally wrong to discriminate against or abuse a child. The difficult question, however, is to determine what constitutes abusive conduct in a given culture at a given historical juncture. As correctly noted by C Henry Kempe, definitions of child abuse vary from culture to culture and evolve over time.[10] It is also agreed that child abuse and neglect occurs often in times of rapid social and economic change when cultural values come under challenge and severe stress. In this period of rapid change child abuse and neglect, according to Kempe, can occur as a concomitant of the disruption in cultural values as society tries to find its balance and to respond to external forces.[11] Le Vine & Le Vine have also argued that it is when the old 'social system starts to fall apart that we begin to come upon instances of abuse and neglect which the old order largely prohibited.'[12] The cases of abuse, neglect and discrimination of orphans examined in this section need to be located and analysed within this wider context of rapid social and economic change in Tanzania. This is also a social context now made more complex by the adverse effects of the HIV/AIDS epidemic.

It is estimated that a total 14.3% of Tanzanian households are living with one or more orphans.[13] The data collected for this study, though by no means representative, show that 55% of the orphans were living with various members of the extended family; 25% were living with the other parent; 15% were living either with an elder sibling or alone; and 5% were residing with a non-relative. In most cases (ie 75%) the foster family was at the same time caring for several of their own minor children. Acts of child abuse, neglect, and discrimination uncovered by this study relate mainly to the differential treatment between the orphan and the caretaker's own children. This was particularly noted in respect of food distribution; allocation of household tasks; denial of the opportunity to attend school or to have adequate school supplies; lack of warmth and effective communication between the child and the caretaker; the harsh punishments meted out to the orphans.

One might ask, why take on additional children when one does not intend to treat them well? This study found, for example, that some relatives accept such responsibility because they are too embarrassed to refuse. Others see it as an opportunity to access the property left behind by the deceased parent. Once the

---

10 C Henry Kempe, 'Foreword' to Jill E Korbin (ed) *Child Abuse and Neglect: Cross-Cultural Perspectives*, University of California Press, Berkeley 1981.

11 See Kempe, op cit, note 11.

12 See Robert Le Vine and Sarah Le Vine 'Child Abuse and Neglect in Sub-Saharan Africa' in Jill E Corbin (ed) *Child Abuse and Neglect: Cross-Cultural Perspectives*, University of California Press, Berkeley 1981, at 38.

13 See Tanzania, The 1991/1992 National Demographic and Health Survey (DHS) at 398.

property is dissipated these orphans may be abandoned or merely neglected until they run away from home to the city. For some, female children are accepted as a potential source of free labour and/or bride-wealth when they get married. Based on the cases examined in the course of this study one would conclude that abuse, neglect, and discrimination of orphans is taking place in Tanzania. Furthermore, that such treatment interferes not only with the child's physical and mental development, but often sets in motion a chain reaction that ultimately leads to the exclusion of the child from the mainstream of society. As will be shown below, misuse or theft of the property of such children often leads to the same effect.

C 'Property grabbing': taking away the orphan's inheritance

The term 'property grabbing' by relatives on the death of a kinsman signifies two elements of the problem. The first, according to Chuma Himonga, is that the relatives seek to inherit the deceased's property without intending to assume full responsibility under customary law; the second describes 'the often disorderly and violent manner in which the relatives conduct themselves when taking away the property'.[14] In Tanzania, as in much of the sub-Saharan region, custom requires the successor to take the property together with the responsibility to protect and support the family of the deceased. In the urban areas where the deceased is likely to own movable property, relatives can literally grab such property from the home of the deceased without waiting for legal procedures to take their course. Such practices, happening as they do at the family's most vulnerable moment, are not only upsetting but also leave the widow and her minor children without the means of support.[15] In an interview with a senior social welfare officer, she revealed that property grabbing was:

> 'common particularly with families affected by the AIDS epidemic, but also in families were the husband dies first leaving behind his widow and minor children. Relatives tend to fight over property left behind by the deceased, often in total disregard of the interests of children and the widow. At the end of the day justice may prevail but it takes a long time for the case to go through the courts and when the widow is ill and without any money, she tends to give up very easily. Often the court's decision may come too late when the property has already been sold or money spent by the culprit.'[16]

---

14 Chuma Himonga, 'Property disputes in law and practice: dissolution of marriage in Zambia' in A Armstrong and W Ncube (eds) *Women and Law in Southern Africa*, Zimbabwe Publishing House, Harare 1987, 56–84 at p 69.

15 The practice of *property grabbing* was also noted at a workshop convened to discuss children's rights. On this occasion participants noted that 'there is an increasing tendency for relatives of the deceased person to interfere with ... the property of the deceased immediately after the death [by taking] the property which could have been used for the maintenance of the surviving spouse, children and other dependants of the deceased ... Participants agreed that this notorious practice (sometimes described as 'grabbing') is a serious violation of the rights of the spouse and children'. See The Morogoro Workshop on the Rights of the Child, Morogoro, June 1989 para 5, p 7.

16 Arusha Case No AR 01/98.

Cases of property grabbing or misappropriation of children's inheritance are also widely reported in the rural areas of Tanzania. Fights over property in mainly agricultural areas tend to focus on arable land, which is the most valuable asset in the community. The Kagera region is particularly well known for practices of land grabbing and land encroachment by relatives. As noted by Frederick Kaijage, 'the most acrimonious claims centre around landed property. In-laws have forcibly evicted widows, along with their children from family homesteads, ostensibly in defence of their clan property interests' (Kaijage 1997:17).

According to the Director of HUYAWA [an NGO working for orphans' rights] Sr Deborah Brycke, a total of 65 cases were received in 1997 where an orphan's landed property had either been encroached upon or illegally grabbed and sold by paternal relatives. Furthermore, during the first five months of 1998 a total of 63 cases involving similar incidents had been lodged, indicating that the numbers were set to double by the end of that year. A survey done in 1997 in the Muleba district of Kagera region of Tanzania by WEVIDHA (a Legal Aid NGO) revealed that dissatisfaction among orphans and widows concerning the distribution of landed property, in cases of inheritance, accounted for 78% of the sample.[17] There were cases also where guardians had sold land belonging to their female wards on various pretexts, including raising money for their school expenses. In some cases these guardians did not give full account for the purchase money.[18] Land disputes became so severe in the region that the Bukoba District Council resolved to enact a piece of subsidiary legislation 'to protect the property of orphans and widows'.[19] It is now provided that all property belonging to the deceased shall belong to his children and his widow unless the deceased has left a valid will. The new subsidiary legislation also provides that any guardian or trustee who mismanages the property of the deceased's children must be replaced with another trustee acceptable to the clan members.

It is sufficient at this stage merely to note here that 'property grabbing' is common in certain parts of Tanzania and it has to be checked in order to protect the property rights of orphans. As will be shown below, encroachment on their property rights has the effect of undermining these children's right to education.

D   Denial of orphan's right to basic education

Articles 28 (CRC) and 11 (ACC) stipulate that states parties are obliged to make basic education free and compulsory for all children in their jurisdiction. They are also to make secondary education available to all children on a progressive basis as each country's resources permit. More specifically, the African Child Charter

---

17   A total of 2,474 people who needed free legal aid to pursue disputes concerning inheritance claims were interviewed. The respondents are drawn from an estimated total population of 33,000 people in the Nshamba and Biirabo wards of Muleba district of Tanzania.

18   In another case, the paternal aunt sold part of the land that she held in trust for her nephew without consulting the clan or her nephew. She was subsequently ordered by the clan to redeem the land she had sold but she could not do so because she had no money. Nothing could be done and the nephew lost his land (Kagera Case, KGR No 01).

19   See By-Law on Orphan and Widows (Protection of Orphans and Widows) of 1997 passed by the Bukoba District Administration. (Translated by Author) (Original title: Sheria Ndogo za Yatima na Wajane (Utunzaji wa Mali za Watoto Yatima na Wajane) za Mwaka 1997 za Halmashauri ya Wilaya ya Bukoba.).

provides that State parties shall take special measures in respect of disadvantaged children in order to ensure equal access to education for all sections of the community (Article 11(3)(e) ACC). The significance of formal education and vocational training to the integration of the orphan into the mainstream of society needs no stressing. It is indeed widely agreed that when a child reaches seven years, which in Tanzania is the age for compulsory primary school enrolment, he or she must begin school at once.[20] Everyone gets concerned if for some reason that child cannot continue with his or her education. Ideally, the path to a stable future for every child is to have good education. With good education, a child has a chance to secure employment and have the means to support his or her family and to contribute to the development of his or her community.

This point came out clearly in the interviews with orphans themselves and their caretakers. As in other studies, a large number of orphans in this study were of school age and the majority had been enrolled in primary school. When asked what concerned them most in their lives, many children cited lack of sufficient money to meet their school needs.[21] They attributed this either to the death of their parent(s) or to their caretakers being too old to work. Hence, of the 16 children interviewed in the Mwanza study, 15 cited shortage of money as their main source of constant worry. For some children their lack of financial support was obvious from their hungry looks and tattered school uniforms. Some admitted that they occasionally engaged in the informal economic sector after school, selling peanuts, pastry and other food items to earn some cash. These findings are confirmed by earlier researchers such as Susan Hunter who notes that school-teachers:

'[r]eported that the standard of living of orphaned children dropped drastically upon the death of their parent, and some come to school dirty, unfed, unable to pay their school contributions, embarrassed by their condition. Many have absentee rates. Most are forced to engage in petty business, selling peanuts, ice cream, and cigarettes to support themselves.' (Hunter, note 4, above.)

Children working in the street to earn money for their school supplies are eventually sucked into full time work. They became part of the ever growing numbers of children working and/or living on the street. Some children drop out of school for reasons ranging from being suspended from school due to non-payment of school fees; teen pregnancy; truancy; neglect and abuse at home or simply because their guardian has also died. As Frederick Kaijage found:

'Orphaned children migrated from one caretaker to another, or drifted onto the streets of Bukoba and Mwanza towns, as foster parents died of AIDS or guardians burned out, forcing the children into situations in which moving out was the preferred alternative.'

---

20 See, Primary Schools (Compulsory Enrolment and Attendance) Rules 1979 (Government Notice No 129 of 1979) which requires a parent or guardian to enrol a child in primary school who has attained the age of seven years.

21 According to Kaijage, the most common needs among families bereaved due to HIV/AIDS related to 'diet, housing, bedding, clothing, health care and opportunities for education and training'. See F Kaijage, 'Social Exclusion and the Social History of Disease: The Impact of HIV/AIDS and the changing Concept of the Family in Northwestern Tanzania', Paper Presented at the History Seminar, 6 February 1997, University of Dar es Salaam, p 16.

It should be noted that lack of formal education has been closely associated with the problem of child workers and children living on the street. A study conducted in Mwanza on the educational background of 122 children on the street found that 93 (ie 76%) children could not read or write and only 32 (ie 26%) had been to primary school. In the case of those who had spent some time at school, the majority had dropped out early.[22] Another study conducted in Dar Es Salaam in 1995 came to a similar conclusion showing that many street children were illiterate. Thus, of the 253 children interviewed, 77% did not have primary school education and only 2.4% had attended a few classes at secondary school level before dropping out. And when asked why they had left home, 51% cited poverty and abuse by parents or guardians as the main reason. To this number one could add 6% who reported that their parents had died.[23] The Dar Es Salaam study also showed that the majority of children came from rural areas and from low income families where the primary occupation of the parent was small scale peasant farming.

In short, as noted by Ahmed et al, the ideal path for every child is through schooling where children can gain 'the requisite education and skills to be able to support themselves and their families through employment in adult life'. But for many orphans 'there are many obstacles that will lead them away from this path and cause them to become children in need of special protection measures'. (Ahmed 1999:14).

E   Neglect of orphan's emotional needs

In the course of interviewing orphaned children, it became clear that many were emotionally disturbed. Some were still grieving the death of their parent(s) while others were worried that the surviving parent would also die and had no idea what might happen next. Those living with their grandparents were insecure and worried about their future source of income. They were worried especially about who would meet their school requirements. Some thought their grandparents might die soon leaving them with no one to support them. One child had dropped out of school for lack of money and in the same week the electricity supply at home had been temporarily disconnected due to unpaid bills. She was living with her maternal aunt who was out of work. One child was angry that his mother died before introducing him to his father. He had been told his father lived in Zanzibar but did not know where and how to find him. Children separated from siblings felt lonely and deeply longed for a reunion. In one case twin sisters had been divided up between their paternal uncles. They met at school during the week days but still they were unhappy about this separation. Another child complained of always being hungry and there being too many other children at their house. In the night they fought over sleeping space and blankets.

Child psychologists have long noted that a sudden change in a child's environment could be stressful and upsetting. If not handled properly and in a

---

22   See Rakesh Rajani & Mustafa Kudrati, *Street Children of Mwanza: A Situation Analysis*, Kuleana Center for Children's Rights, 1994, p 21.

23   See Thea Mulders, *Children en route. A Situation Analysis of Street Children and Street Children's Projects in Dar es Salaam* Dar es Salaam 1995 at 9.

sensitive and timely manner, stress can be a cause of emotional disturbances. Thus children who are not able to cope with changes in their lives exhibit negative symptoms such as fear, anxiety, confusion and frustration. Some become withdrawn unto themselves while others exhibit streaks of violence and are disobedient to authority. As would be expected negative emotional feelings affect the child's academic work sometimes leading to poor performance. Some drop out of school altogether to become child-workers or to be married at a very young age. They end up being child-parents which sets off yet another cycle of vulnerable childhood. Unfortunately, teachers and other adults who are not trained to interpret these symptoms are often unable to respond appropriately. Their gut reaction is to discipline the child who is emotionally disturbed, believing him or her to be mischievous.

In a study on the psychological effect of orphanhood in Uganda, two authors point out three reasons why the emotional needs of orphans in Uganda are not met.[24] First, there is not enough information on the nature and magnitude of this problem. Secondly, there is a cultural belief that children do not have emotional problems. And thirdly, emotional problems are not readily visible to the untrained eye. Even where the child is visibly disturbed, there is a lack of knowledge as to how the problem should be tackled (Sengondo & Nambi 1997: 106). The three factors noted above are not unique to Uganda. According to Mbise 'the child's developmental perspective is not highly valued in Tanzanian society' (1990: 49–51). Mbise argues that children are not normally consulted when crucial decisions affecting their lives are made. An earlier study by this author also confirms that children are rarely consulted when adults make decisions about children's lives.[25] This study has also found that many orphaned children have been divided up among guardians without any real concern as to their preferences.[26] Chuma Himonga, in her study on the child's right to participate in decision making in Zambia, also came to a similar conclusion. She found that children are rarely consulted when crucial decisions are made about matters such as change of schools or residence (1998:110).

Mbise agrees, suggesting that there is often lack of appreciation by adults of a child's mental maturity and capacity at different stages of their development. Consequently, adults do not pay sufficient attention to relationships or activities that are important to a child and appropriate to that child's capabilities or interest. Therefore, a series of factors, including the way childhood is conceptualised in a given community, the lack of a reliable system of orphan care, and the sheer numbers of children per household, lead to the situation where the emotional needs of orphans go unrecognised and often unattended.

---

24   See James Sengondo & Jane Nambi, 'The Psychological effect of orphanhood: a study of orphans in Rakai district', *Health Transition Review, Supplement* to Vol 7, 1997, 105–124 at 115.

25   See B Rwezaura 'The Duty to Hear the Child: A View from Tanzania' in W Ncube (ed) *Law Culture, Tradition, and Children's Rights in Eastern and Southern Africa,* Ashgate, Dartmouth 1998, 57–94.

26   Given that a guardian my be drawn from a pool of available relatives, it is not always possible to tell in advance who will come forward to assume such responsibility for a given child. Such uncertainty makes it difficult to plan ahead for the orphan child.

Both the CRC and the ACC contain general provisions protecting life, health, survival and development of the child.[27] In particular, States are obliged to take all appropriate measures to promote physical and psychological recovery and social reintegration of a child victim of 'any form of neglect, exploitation or abuse' (Article 39 CRC). The process of recovery must take place in 'an environment which fosters the health, self-respect and dignity of the child'. Article 19 CRC requires States to protect the child from all forms of physical and mental violence, injury, or abuse, neglect or negligent treatment and to establish such protective measures including social programmes to provide necessary support to the child and for those who have the care of the child. It is clear that Tanzania has not fully complied with the two treaties. Moreover, the violation of the child's right to health also contributes to other breaches including breach of the child's right to education. For, as may be appreciated, an emotionally disturbed child is unlikely to do well or to complete his or her education successfully.

This *Survey* will now move on to examine Tanzania's response to the orphan crisis and the extent to which its existing legal framework is capable of addressing the situation of children in need of special protection measures.

IV TANZANIA'S RESPONSES TO THE ORPHAN CRISIS

Tanzania's response to the orphan crisis is not easy to pin down to a single action or programme targeting orphans as a group. There are indeed several government ministries, local government institutions and many non-governmental agencies whose activities are in some way directed at or have impact on children's welfare. All these agencies have tended to operate independently until recently when an attempt was made to identify and co-ordinate their activities.[28] Of particular significance here is the project on the rights of children and women that seeks to introduce a children's rights framework into policy-making and planning in all programmes affecting children in Tanzania.[29] In this section, three policy documents are evaluated to determine how they respond to the orphan crisis.[30] But first a short background is given on the growing interest in issues of children's rights in Tanzania.

27　See, eg Articles 23, 24, 6, and 39 of CRC and Articles 13, 14 and 5 of the African Child Charter.

28　See Tanzania, United Republic of; and UNICEF, *Programme Plan of Operations; Country Programme of Co-operation 1997–2001*.

29　See Project No 9 (part of the Programme Plan of Operations) above at pp 203–215. The primary goal of this project is 'to contribute to positive change in society towards realising the rights of children and women' by providing strategic support to the government and civil society, at 207–208.

30　These are (i) a policy document issued by the Social Welfare Department in 1994 spelling out a strategic plan and guidelines on the care and protection of orphans in Tanzania; (ii) the Child Development Policy issued in 1996 by the Ministry of Community Development, Women Affairs and Children outlining its vision and strategy for the welfare of children in Tanzania; and (iii) the Law Reform Commission's Working Group's Report published in 1994 reviewing the law of the child and recommending a number of statutory reforms.

A   Preparing for the Children's Rights Treaty (CRC)

Tanzania has long been active in promoting child survival and development as part of its broader economic and social policy.[31] Its emphasis has always been on raising the health and nutritional status of all children, especially those under five, as part of its social policy and national development strategy. In this sense Tanzania's policy on children was primarily 'welfarist' in that it was not based on the recognition that children have claims or rights against their parents or the State. Furthermore, until the beginning of the 1990s, there was little public discussion of the concept of children's rights and whether children had any rights at all (Ahmed 1999:10; Tanzania/UNICEF 1997:42). During the 1990s, however, following the adoption of the CRC, there was a sudden burst of interest in the status of children and children's rights generally. This was more so in urban areas where the poor living condition of children was more visible. A series of public seminars and workshops were held at which issues of children's rights were raised and discussed (Rwezaura 1999:413). Many senior government officials including the incumbent Chief Justice of Tanzania attended and participated actively in some of these gatherings.

In 1990 Tanzania took part in the World Summit on Children with the incumbent President AH Mwinyi leading the delegation. In June 1991 the Declaration and Plan of Action of the World Summit were unanimously endorsed by the Tanzania Parliament. The Plan of Action became the basis for a National Plan of Action to achieve the goals for Tanzanian children by the year 2000 (NPA: 1993). A new government ministry was established to follow up and co-ordinate the implementation of the blueprint.[32] The implementation of programmes based on the above Plan of Action continues. In May 1991 Tanzania ratified the CRC and also signed the African Charter on the Rights and Welfare of the child (ACC).[33]

In the meantime Tanzania was undergoing economic and social transformation under the influence of the market economy. With the capacity of the family to offer support diminishing, vulnerable family members such as children were gradually being pushed to the margins of society with some of the more prominent victims of this process being the so-called *street children*.[34] Indeed the plight of children living in the street was put more firmly on the national agenda through the tireless work of agencies such as UNICEF, local and

---

31   See *The Situation of Women and Children in Tanzania: An Overview*, Government of the United Republic of Tanzania and United Nations Children Fund, Dar es Salaam, 1990, p 3; *National Programme of Action (NPA) to Achieve the Goals for Tanzanian Children by the Year 2000*, prepared by the National Coordinating Committee for Child Survival, Protection and Development (NCC/CSPD), Dar es Salaam, December 1993.

32   Established in November 1990, the new ministry became known as the Ministry of Community Development, Women's Affairs and Children.

33   As noted above the ACC lacks five more signatures of the fifteen required to bring it into force under Article 47. It is believed that Tanzania will ratify the ACC in the very near future.

34   See Rose Lugembe, 'The Dilemma of Street Children' *The Lawyer, Tanzania* April–August 1994, pp 14–16; JH Mangara, 'Children's Rights in Prison' *The Lawyer, Tanzania,* April–August 1994, pp 9–10.

foreign NGOs and the media.[35] Furthermore, by this time the AIDS epidemic had emerged as the number one cause of death in Tanzania and, inevitably, the number one cause of orphanhood. Hence, by the mid-1990s, orphans had become recognised as *children in need of special protection measures* (Ahmed 1999:5). It is against this backdrop that Tanzania's initial response to the orphan crisis must be located and analysed.

B   The Child Development Policy (CDP)

The publication in 1996 of the *Child Development Policy* (hereafter CDP) is a suitable starting point to analyse Tanzania's response to the orphan crisis. The CDP is the first policy statement by the Tanzania Government on the status of the child. It is the work of the Ministry of Community Development, Women Affairs and Children.[36] It admits having drawn on the CRC as its guide in the design of its ten objectives as well as its recommendations. Perhaps like any policy document, the style of the CDP is not prescriptive. It seeks to provide guidelines to assist the community, the State and voluntary agencies to protect the best interests of all children. Furthermore, the CDP stresses the importance of gaining the co-operation of parents and the wider community in the implementation of children's rights. In short, the CPD aims at mobilising parents and the whole community to become aware of the basic rights of children and the underlying causes of the problems facing Tanzanian children today. As part of the measures to promote child survival, the CDP recommends that the Government should undertake research on the care and protection of orphans and abandoned children and, if appropriate, establish SOS children villages and host families.[37] The latter recommendation reflects one of the main objects of the CDP, namely, 'to provide direction on the upbringing of children in difficult circumstances'.[38] The CDP also articulates the concerns raised during the 1990s at various seminars and in the local media about the deteriorating situation of children in Tanzania. Indeed, as will be shown below, some of the recommendations have now been adopted by the Law Reform Commission and will in time become reflected in new legislation.

In 1994, two years before the publication of the CDP, the Tanzania Law Reform Commission published its *Report on the Law Relating to Children in Tanzania*. For convenience this will be referred to as the child law report (ie CLR). The CLR is a product of years of research and consultation by a panel of experts chaired by a university law professor and seven other members.[39] The CLR was mandated to review the law relating to children in Tanzania. More

---

35   See Save the Children Fund (UK), *Poor Urban Children at Risk, Dar es Salaam. Programme Proposal*, Dar es Salaam, February, 1998.

36   This particular Ministry, as noted above, was established in 1990 to perform the task of implementing and co-ordinating the child development programme throughout Tanzania.

37   See paras 41 and 58 of CDP at p 19 and p 22.

38   This was the terminology used at the time to describe children in need of special protection measures.

39   The other members of the Working Group were from the Social Welfare Department; the Office of the Administrator General; the Faculty of Medicine, Muhimbili University College; the Ministry of Labour; a member of the Tanzania Bar association and a Research Officer from the Law Reform Commission of Tanzania (LRC) who acted as secretary to the panel.

specifically, it was to review childcare, maintenance and custody of children. Furthermore, it was also asked to consider the reform of juvenile justice; child labour and child abuse; child adoption; succession and inheritance. In its recommendations, the CLR like the CDP, took account of the principles of CRC as well as the debates on children's rights that took place during the early 1990s.[40]

About the same time the Family Law Sub-Committee and the Succession Law Sub-Committee, both having been appointed by the Law Reform Commission of Tanzania, also published their recommendations for the reform of family law and the law of succession.[41] The relevant recommendations of the three committees will be examined briefly together. They include the protection of the property rights of the surviving spouse, especially the widow. This recommendation is particularly significant considering the problems faced by orphans and widows especially in relation to property grabbing. It has thus been recommended that criminal sanctions should be imposed upon anyone who engages in acts of 'property grabbing upon death'. Youth centres and other services for abandoned children and orphans are to be expanded and better supported. Parents are to be educated on the psychological needs of children. Here again, this *Survey* has shown how little parents and schools know about the emotional needs of children. Another recommendation was that better policing of child abuse is to be introduced with the support of the social welfare department.

Stiffer sanctions are also recommended against those who hire child labour. As this essay has demonstrated, child labour has become a serious problem in Tanzania. It has been reported that child labour is growing at an alarming rate in Tanzania. According to the Deputy Minister of Labour and Youth Development, there are at least 400,000 children involved in the worst forms of child labour. Other estimates put the figure much higher. Many of these children, as noted by the Chairman of the Federation of Free Trade Unions (TFTU), are 'school age children who have dropped out of studies [and] been absorbed by the informal sector in various areas in the country, mainly in child labour'.[42] The reform and humanisation of the juvenile justice system in Tanzania was also noted by the child law committee (CLR) as a priority area given the rise in the rate of juvenile criminality. This recommendation has great importance to orphans considering that such children are more likely to get into trouble with the law, especially in urban areas.

It should be noted at this juncture that the recommendations of all the three sub-committees of the Law Reform Commission did not specifically target orphans or *children in need of special protection measures* as such. The main reason for this is that the terms of reference of these sub-committees were directed at the problem facing all children rather than focusing on the particular category of

---

40   As the Working Group acknowledges, '[t]o a greater extent, completion of this Report has been facilitated by the recent coming into effect of the UN Convention on the Rights of Children.' LRC Report, p ii. See also several articles on children's rights published in the 1994 issue *The Lawyer, Tanzania*, a Journal of the Tanganyika Law Society (April–August).

41   For a critique of the three LRC's recommendations, see B Rwezaura, 'Gender Justice and Children's Rights: a Banner for Family Law Reform in Tanzania' in *The International Survey of Family Law 1997*, ed A Bainham (Martinus Nijhoff Publishers, 1999) at 413–443.

42   See TOMRIC Agency, 'At Least 400,000 in Dreadful Child Labour in Tanzania' 8 June 2000 (http://www.africanews.org/east/tanzania/stories).

children with special needs. Nonetheless, it is still possible to extract ideas and policies from these recommendations which can form the basis for a programme on the integration of orphans into the mainstream of Tanzanian society. But first an evaluation of the government Guidelines on orphans is offered.

C   The guidelines on orphans

The publication in 1994 of a government policy document spelling out guidelines (hereafter the Guidelines) on the care and protection of orphans in Tanzania is worthy of close attention. The Guidelines were formulated by a working party convened under the auspices of the Ministry of Labour and Youth, with the financial backing of UNICEF. Several government agencies and NGOs participated in this project.[43] First, the working party identified eight key areas of concern affecting orphans that required urgent attention and action.[44] Many of the issues identified by the working party are clear symptoms of the desperate economic status of orphans in Tanzania. They confirm this *Survey*'s argument that orphans have been pushed to the periphery of Tanzanian society. The working party sought to address these problems by spelling out Guidelines whose main object was to introduce a principled and effective structure within which to harness more efficiently much of the existing resources and within which future material support could be channelled and effectively utilised.

The Guidelines aimed at:

(1)   identifying existing participants and their various contributions towards orphans;
(2)   identifying available resources and co-ordinating the various projects and activities at all levels so as to achieve synergy and more effective and sustainable support for orphans;
(3)   setting up organisational structures at all levels to assist the co-ordination process;
(4)   fostering mutual understanding and co-operation between all parties working for orphans at all levels; and
(5)   setting up effective channels as well as to ensure resources reach the target groups.

These Guidelines, it might be noted, are a carefully designed policy document prepared by competent professionals who were familiar with the economic and social problems faced by orphans in Tanzania. The drafters of this policy document were also keenly aware of the need for a clear organisational structure within which assistance to orphans could be undertaken. This *Survey* will now

---

43   They included the Ministry of Community Development, Women Affairs and Children; Ministry of Health; Ministry of Education and Culture; Office of the Regional Development Director, Kagera Region; the National AIDS Control Programme; Tanzania Council of Social Development and Tanzania Non-Governmental Organisations.

44   These are: (i) lack of food/poor nutrition; (ii) poor health care; (iii) lack of schooling; (iv) lack of essential school supplies; (v) lack of care by parent or other adult; (vi) lack of means to generate own income; (vii) rural to urban migration of orphans; (viii) living in harsh environment.

turn to consider whether, and to what extent, these policy initiatives have been implemented.

D   Facing the problem of policy implementation

The transition from policy to action has not been as rapid as the pace of devastation that produces orphans in Tanzania. Thus, despite the good ideas proposed in the Guidelines this policy document has yet to be implemented. Some officials in the Social Welfare Department were convinced that budgetary constraints were the main cause for the six-year delay.[45] Others, however, cited inter-departmental competition over resources, adding that every department craves for access to funding from donor-agencies. Such rivalry is also encouraged by the lack of clear division of responsibility between several government departments. For example, the work of the Department of Social Welfare of the Ministry of Labour and Youth Development currently overlaps with that of the Ministry of Community Development, Women Affairs and Children. According to the Child Development Policy (CDP), the Government created a special Ministry to co-ordinate all activities and programmes relating to child development, including the establishment of centres for children in difficult circumstances, special schools and institutions to cater for children with particular problems. The same Ministry is also planning to set up more juvenile courts and to encourage voluntary organisations to serve and defend children's rights.

At the same time, despite what the CDP says, the Commission for Social Welfare is still the legally designated authority for purposes of licensing and supervising of orphanages and special schools.[46] It advises applicants in cases of child adoption and foster care. The Director acts, as *guardian ad litem,* in cases of child adoption. The Department also provides counselling and probationary services to child offenders. Indeed, the cases cited in this *Survey* also attest to the involvement of this department in the provision of social services. Despite its wide mandate, however, as Susan Hunter and others have noted, the Social Welfare Department plays only a minor role in providing services to families affected by the HIV/AIDS epidemic (Hunter et al 1997:408). Even if the Social Welfare Department had the resources, (which it lacks) it cannot engage in AIDS-related work without inviting friction with the National Aids Control Co-ordinators (ACCs). The ACCs are the official service providers for families affected by the HIV/AIDS epidemic.

In the final analysis whatever may be the real reason why the Guidelines have not yet been implemented; this is very sad because the Guidelines aimed at achieving effective utilisation of scarce resources by eliminating wasteful overlap in service provision. The Guidelines also sought to eliminate competition among service providers and the misuse of resources. These problems remain and continue to slow down the whole process of assisting orphans. For example, in the

---

45   An indication of a similar trend is the Tanzania national HIV/AIDS policy that 'has been in draft since 1995 but there are no indications of its adoption in the near future' see N Othiambo 'Donors Rap Tanzania Over AIDS Scourge' Panafrican News Agency, 31 May 2000 (http://africanews.org.east/tanzania/stories).

46   See The Children's Homes (Regulations) Act 1968 (No 4 of 1968).

Kagera region, this study found some families receiving support from more than one NGO while other families had none. Earlier studies have also reported similar lack of co-operation between various NGOs working for children. Indeed, some NGOs were described as secretive and unwilling to pool resources or share experiences. Such shortcomings in the system have resulted in certain eligible children moving from one project to another trying to get whatever is on offer (Ahmed 1999:271). There were also recurrent complaints against service providers who were reported to have diverted resources for their private use.

It will be recalled that one of the underlying policies of the Guidelines was that any assistance to the orphan (except for emergency relief) must aim at building local capacity to meet basic needs on a sustainable long-term basis. The object was to facilitate empowerment as the primary object of assistance to orphans. Many people interviewed for this study expressed the view that the Government was not doing enough or even interested in assisting families to generate income. Shortage of arable land, especially in the Kagera region, was so acute that alternative means of generating income have to be found in order to break the cycle of poverty in the region. One respondent complained that he lived so close to Lake Victoria but could not exploit the lake's resources, as he did not have money to purchase fishing gear. It is not surprising, therefore, that older orphans, especially the adolescent males, tend to migrate into urban centres in search of education opportunities or paid jobs. As noted by Ahmed et al, a child who runs away from home to the city to become a street child might be looking for 'education opportunities, quite apart from access to other basic needs such as food and shelter' (1999:272). Indeed, studies on children living on the street show that orphans form a significant number of urban working children.[47]

Turning now to the CDP, it should be noted that, as in most policy documents, its style is general and aspirational. It will be necessary to translate it into a programme of action. For example, para 41 of the CDP recommends that *SOS children villages* and host families should be established to provide care for orphans and abandoned children. In para 28, it is stated that the Social Welfare Department 'should ensure that children in difficult circumstances receive their rights and basic services.' And para 69 urges the ministry responsible for community development in collaboration with the Ministry of Education to ensure all children are enrolled in school and 'should develop a system whereby children whose parents or guardians are unable to pay will get an education.' These aspirations may have value in as much as they express what the State wishes to do for its children. Under favourable conditions they could form the basis for programmatic intervention in favour of children. Indeed, it appears the Ministry of Community Development, Women's Affairs and Children has been working closely with the Law Reform Commission of Tanzania, trying to harmonise existing law on children with the principles of the CRC and the UN Convention on the Elimination of Discrimination Against Women (CEDAW). Yet all these policy statements do not appear to bear the stamp of urgency. Considering the findings of this study, it requires no stressing that orphans, and indeed all *children in need of special protection measures* cannot wait and must not wait. As months

---

47   See Thea Mulders, 'Children en Route: A Situation Analysis of Street Children and Street Children Projects in Dar es Salaam', Dar es Salaam, 1995.

and weeks pass, children who have dropped out of school become child workers; those who need emotional support may despair, while those whose property has been 'grabbed' from them may have lost their future.

Yet from the above overview, it is fair to say that despite its ambivalence and inaction, Tanzania is not unaware of the orphan crisis. If the estimated population of orphans, now standing at one million and still rising, is close to the true picture, then there is cause for serious concern. The social and economic consequences of this crisis will be quite significant in a few years to come. It comes as no surprise, therefore, that Tanzania was recently urged to increase its speed in its fight against the HIV/AIDS epidemic. At a recent consultative meeting of bilateral donors, Tanzania was openly criticised for not adopting a coherent national policy on AIDS. Although the said policy appears to have been in draft since 1995, there is no indication as to when it will be adopted or implemented.[48] The final section of this *Survey* offers a few ideas on what could be done to stop the process that keeps pushing the Tanzanian orphan to the fringes of society.

V   TOWARDS THE REINTEGRATION OF ORPHANS INTO SOCIETY

Based on the above discussion it can be argued that Tanzania does not lack good ideas as to how to tackle the orphan crisis. Perhaps what is lacking are the resources, the political will, and possibly, a deeper awareness of how serious the orphan crisis has become in recent years. The Guidelines, in my view, provide an excellent organisational structure for pooling and deploying all the available resources for the benefit of all orphans. The Guidelines also contain four important principles that ought to guide future assistance to orphans.[49] This section will now consider some of the ideas contained in the Child Development Policy (CDP) and some of the recommendations of the Law Reform Commission of Tanzania. This is in order to determine their potential contribution to the reintegration of orphans into the mainstream of Tanzanian society.

A   The duty to assist families in orphan care

The first principle contained in the Guidelines is that the primary responsibility towards orphaned children lies with the surviving parent and the child's extended family. This principle mirrors the CRC (Article 18, among others), the ACC Article 20(1), and the provisions of Tanzanian domestic law. All these require parents and guardians to ensure the child's survival and development.[50] The

---

48   See N Othiambo 'Donors Rap Tanzania Over AIDS Scourge' Panafrican News Agency, 31 May
       2000 (http://africanews.org.east/tanzania/stories).

49   The four underlying principles are: first, the Government recognised that the primary
       responsibility towards orphans lies with the surviving parent and the child's extended family;
       secondly, that the State has the duty to assist families in performing these tasks; thirdly, that any
       assistance for orphans (apart from emergency relief supplies) has to aim at empowering the
       affected community by building the required capacity for meeting basic needs on a sustainable
       long term basis. And finally, that priority should be given to the upbringing of orphans in a family
       environment; and that institutional care should be considered only as the last resort.

50   See, eg Primary Schools (Compulsory Enrolment and Attendance) Rules 1979 (Government
       Notice No 129 of 1979) which requires a parent or guardian to enrol a child in primary school

question as to who has primary responsibility for the orphan is not disputed. As this study found, despite the harsh economic situation faced by families, the extended family has not totally given up on supporting and bringing up the children left behind by a deceased family member. Earlier studies have also made similar findings, noting that in most regions of Tanzania the social norms for fostering relatives' children were still strong. At the same time these studies have also noted that the circle of responsible relatives has began to decrease as the cost of raising children increase. It appears therefore, that economic hardship is the most far-reaching and widely felt constraint on the care and protection of orphans throughout the whole region.[51] Thus Susan Hunter et al are right when they argue that the most important determinant of a family's response to the effect of the AIDS epidemic is its economic status (Hunter 1997:414). The point is not lost to the CDP which also states that parents and guardians have been left on their own to promote their children's welfare at a time when traditional institutions of support have ceased to function properly. This is also the time when the economic capacity of families has sharply declined (CDP 1996: para 64, p 25 and Ahmed et al, 1999:2).

In these circumstances it is imperative to fall back on the principle that the state has the duty to assist families in performing their tasks (CRC Article 18, ACC Article 22(2)). State support for families will ensure that the State will fill the vacuum whenever the family is unable to discharge its responsibility. This understanding has the advantage of providing a form of insurance for the child so that, in theory, there is no moment when a vulnerable child will have no one to turn to when family support fails. By supporting the family, the State obtains a number of advantages. First, the child will remain part of his community, sharing its ethical values and moral standards. Growing up in one's culture is essential for one's identity and emotional health. As noted by the CDP, 'there is a need to strengthen the upbringing and moral guidance of children from an early age so that they can develop in a proper manner' (CDP 1996: para 17). The CDP is particularly keen on the need for children to grow up in a family environment. It urges parents to recognise their joint responsibility in caring for and bringing up their children (para 19(viii)).

The care of orphans within the family or community is also less expensive than care in public institutions such as orphanages and children's homes. As might be expected, the question of availability of resources has to be confronted. At the

---

who has attained the age of seven years. The term 'guardian' includes 'any person having charge of a young person who has no parents or whose parents are unknown and any person to whose care any child or young person has been committed, even temporarily, by a person having authority over him.' Under section 130 of the Law of Marriage Act a court may order a man to pay maintenance for the benefit of the child if he has neglected that child. There are also penal provisions under the criminal law such as section 206 of the Penal Code (Chapter 16) which imposed a duty to care and protect a child upon the guardian or person responsible for the care of that child.

51   According to the CDP, 50% of Tanzanians live in poverty, which is one of the major contributory factors to the poor situation of children. (Para 10) Poverty has been cited as the underlying cause of child discrimination and of children's failure to attend school or to complete their education. Poverty also accounts for the phenomenon of property grabbing, discussed earlier, showing how customs originally aimed at providing care for the orphan are now either ignored or used for personal gain. Poverty is indeed an issue of national significance and has been a subject of a separate policy initiative known as the Poverty Eradication Policy.

moment most of the orphanages and other institutions looking after children are operated by private institutions with minimal State support or involvement. While the State has statutory power to license and oversee their operations, it has been unable to supervise properly the said institutions or to influence their operations.[52] There is evidence, for example, that some orphanages have unwritten policies of excluding children whose parent(s) are known to have died of AIDS.[53] Furthermore, a recent study has found that such institutions are not financially supported. As a result they lack basic facilities and are also not properly managed. All this leads to the view that the state would do much better by relying on relatives and the extended family to look after children who have no parents.

And where the State has no resources, international assistance may be sought within the framework of international co-operation (Article 4 CRC). In this connection, it is heartening to note that foreign governments and international organisations such as the UNICEF, the UNDP, and the ILO, to name just a few, have offered assistance in various areas of child welfare and protection. It should be stressed, however, that the Government should take note of Article 4 CRC which calls upon States Parties to deploy to the maximum their available resources before seeking support from outside. In this connection Tanzania should abandon its current *laissez faire* policy by showing more active involvement in the welfare of its orphans and other children in need of special protection measures. It should provide clear leadership and be proactive by setting up a framework and administrative support structures within which such assistance could be provided by international agencies. Moreover, except for compulsory care provisions, there are at present no statutory provisions empowering the State to intervene directly to provide supportive care to children. Such support would be most desirable where family care fails due to poverty, sickness by the parent or for other unavoidable cause (LRC 1994:15). At the moment there are some informal arrangements, such as the Presidential Bounty, where parents of triplets are given some financial relief. It has been recommended, therefore, that there should be statutory mechanisms enabling State institutions to intervene directly to assist families where it is shown that they are unable to support their children.[54]

Finally it should be stressed that it is not enough merely to enhance the capacity of the family to support its children. It must be remembered that some of the problems facing orphans today arise from a combination of cultural and economic factors. For example, the low status of widows in the community necessarily impacts on their children.[55] Thus, the widow's lack of defined property rights is one of the factors aggravating the economic status of those orphans whose fathers are deceased. It is, therefore, significant that the LRC has finally recommended the enactment of a new law of succession that is intended to protect

---

52   See The Children's Homes (Regulations) Act 1968 (No 4 of 1968).

53   One official in charge of an orphanage in Dar es Salaam, stated that orphans whose parent(s) are known to have died of HIV/AIDS might have to be excluded to avoid putting at risk other children in the orphanage.

54   The Child Law Report (of the LRC) noted that statutory provisions should be enacted to require the State to assist families which are forced to subsist below the poverty line due to circumstances beyond their control (LRC 1994: 15).

55   See A Manji 'The AIDS Epidemic and Women's land Rights in Tanzania' *Law in Africa*, 1(1999) 31–49.

the property rights of widows. The new law will also seek to remove discrimination between children over inheritance. It is in this context also that one must applaud the decision of the Bukoba District Council, noted above, which passed a by-law protecting widows and orphans from property grabbing by relatives.

In sum the programme of family empowerment must also aim at eliminating inequalities within the family and in the wider community. It is important also that the process of enhancing the capacity of families to protect and support children should be sensitive to the fundamental principles of the CRC. In this regard, public awareness campaigns on the rights of the child should be enhanced as suggested by the CDP. Moreover, the involvement of local communities, including children themselves, in the planning and implementation of all programmes beneficial to children should be strengthened.[56]

B   Childcare in the family environment: a priority

It has been proposed that research should be undertaken into 'the possibility of establishing villages for orphans and abandoned children as well as host families system' for children without families to look after them (CDP, para 58, p 22). The principle that institutional care for children should be considered the last resort is contained in Article 20(3) CRC and Articles 25 and 25 ACC. These treaties stress the need to maintain continuity in the child's upbringing and the desirability of retaining the child's cultural roots. Tanzania accepts this principle as reflected in its CDP, the Guidelines, and the various recommendations of the Law Reform Commission. According to the LRC, 'experience has proved that institutional care for children in Tanzania leaves a lot to be desired.' (CLR 1994: xviii). The main reason, according to the LRC, is that Tanzania has failed so far to adopt a proactive strategy for protecting the best interests of disadvantaged children. Many of the State-run institutions are, for various reasons, unfit for accommodating children. As noted by a recent study, 'institutions for children overall seem to lack material resources and the human skills for managing the funds and the infrastructure they do possess' (Ahmed 1999:153). Children living in some of these institutions also complained of poor quality food, abuse from caretakers, unfair treatment, poor health care, lack of educational provision and misuse by institutional staff of funds and other material supplies intended for children (Ahmed 1999: 152–153). Hence, besides the standard objection against placing children in public institutions, in the case of Tanzania, its institutions appear to fall well below the standard expected of such facilities.

Consequently, it has been recommended that community-based support for orphans should be encouraged and supported (Ahmed et al 1999:356). The Law Reform Commission of Tanzania has added its voice suggesting that the foster-care programme ought to be strengthened by giving financial and material assistance to foster parents (CLR 1994: xviii). In this connection, Uganda's experience with family-based care for orphans ought to be carefully considered.

---

56   The idea of building a democracy at the heart of the family is discussed in B Rwezaura et al 'Parting the Long Grass: The African Family' *Journal of Legal Pluralism and Unofficial Law* 35 (1995) 25–73, esp. at 57–72.

Communities in Uganda have been actively involved for over a decade, working with some NGOs such as World Vision, in planning and implementing programmes and support groups such as *orphan-care committees* and the *auntie's* and *uncles* groups and *Munno Mukabi* (UNICEF 1991:22). Uganda's experience has also shown that where a substitute family cannot be found for an orphan, siblings may still be supported within their home environment by a relative or a member of a support group.

Another alternative system of childcare that has not been given adequate attention is child adoption. Although previous studies have shown that Tanzanians are not keen to adopt formally children[57] there is no reason why alternative options should not be studied to determine the community's objection to statutory adoption. In an earlier comment on the recommendations of the Law Reform Committee of Tanzania, I argued that Tanzania may have lost an opportunity to revisit its adoption law with a view to deploying it as a vehicle for the care of orphans (Rwezaura 1999:339). It is submitted that the law of adoption should be reviewed and made more responsive to the problems faced by children in Tanzania. For example, the Resident Magistrates Courts (ie the court immediately below the High Court) could be granted jurisdiction to make adoption orders. This would make the law more accessible to rural communities. The law's procedures could also be reviewed to enable non-lawyers, such as relatives or the Social Welfare Department, to act as legal representatives for the less sophisticated or less affluent applicants. This would remove the problem of having to hire professional lawyers whose high fees are sure to dampen the enthusiasm of many prospective adopters. Furthermore, other possibilities such as international child adoption ought to be carefully considered to determine whether or not such a practice is to be encouraged.

Child adoption law should also be made more child-centred so that it can better serve the best interests of the child. The law should lean toward assisting a child to secure a family and not merely to provide a service to a childless family. In this connection, the law ought to be made more flexible by introducing the notion of 'open adoption'. This concept permits the birth family or extended family of the child to be involved not only in the selection of the prospective adopters but also may be permitted to retain some ties with the child, subject to the best interests of that child. The open adoption model, already tried in jurisdictions such as New Zealand, would be most ideal for Tanzania where parents and relatives might wish to maintain some contact with their child.[58] In some cases the option to maintain contact with the orphan may ease the conscience of the extended family that the child is not simply being abandoned to strangers in breach of traditional African values. Furthermore, in the case of older children, their rights to participate in the process leading to their adoption should be protected and their right to consent to the adoption should also be specifically provided in the law.

---

57   See B Rwezaura & U Wanitzek 'The Law and Practice Relating to the Adoption of Children in Tanzania' *Journal of African Law*, 32, 1, 124–163.

58   See Bridget Lindley, 'Open adoption – Is the door ajar?' *CFLQ*, Vol 9 No 2 (1997) p 115.

D   Assistance to orphans to aim at empowerment

It is provided in the Guidelines that any assistance for orphans (apart from emergency relief supplies) should aim at empowering the affected community by building the required capacity to meet basic needs on a sustainable long-term basis. This approach avoids not only dependence but enables communities to contribute actively and meaningfully to their own economic survival and social development. Thus, capacity building enables the community to prepare itself to take charge of its affairs, particularly when the external assistance is reduced or discontinued.

It has been noted many times in this *Survey* that families looking after orphans are not only exceedingly poor but often have other children to support. The quality of life of their children and that of the orphans they support does not differ. It is estimated that 50% of Tanzanians live in poverty and that each household has an average of six children (CDP 1996:5). Other statistics based on the US1$ per capita poverty line, show that 60% of Tanzania's rural population (ie 85% of the total population) live below the poverty line.[59] The consequence, as this *Survey* has shown, is that no resources are available to meet children's basic needs including their education and healthcare. Thus, where there is mass poverty, as in much of Tanzania, it would be unrealistic to expect those families caring for orphans not to share or even take for themselves some of the resources provided by donor agencies. What is required, therefore, is to provide the means by which the community can improve its standard of living through the enhancement of its productive capacity as well as its organisational skills. We must therefore aim at supporting the entire family rather than merely focusing on the orphans in its care. It is not possible; of course, to state precisely what form of capacity building such assistance should take, as this is likely to vary with time and place.

Another issue connected with capacity building is the need to provide appropriate community education on basic childcare, nutrition and sanitation. It has been reported, for example, that young children die from certain diseases that could be avoided by a timely visit to a local dispensary, proper feeding or by simply avoiding dehydration when a child is ill. For example, the African Medical Research Foundation (AMREF) has reported that children die mostly in the care of the parents, sometimes because parents do not respond adequately to the needs of the child by providing general care.[60] In this connection, capacity building must include improved childcare practices, good understanding of appropriate nutrition, and how to react appropriately and in a timely manner to the needs of children.

Wherever possible, orphans should be given appropriate formal education to facilitate their economic independence. In Tanzania most children completing primary education have to compete for the very few places available in the secondary school system. If they cannot make it to the next academic level, they revert to the subsistence economy, which as we have noted, is largely a life below the poverty line. Where an orphan child cannot move to the next level of

---

59   See 'Norway Challenges Tanzania to Fight Poverty' TOMRIC Agency (www.africanews.org) 17 May 2000.

60   See 'Preventable Diseases Kill 300 Infants Daily in Tanzania' TOMRIC Agency, distributed via Africa News Online (www.africanews.org) 17 May 2000.

education, assistance should be available to enable such a child to continue his or her education.[61] A scholarship to a vocational training school might be one way to deal with such a problem. It is to be hoped that through poverty alleviation projects now underway in Tanzania, orphans and the families that support them will also benefit.[62]

VI CONCLUSION

The main argument of this *Survey* can be briefly restated as follows: there are at least one million orphans in Tanzania today and the number is still rising. It is no exaggeration, therefore, to say that Tanzania has an orphan crisis on its hands. This crisis has not come as a surprise. It was anticipated as early as the 1990s when the Government drew up its policy document spelling out guidelines for the care and support of orphans. Since that time nothing concrete appears to have been done to implement that policy. As the document gathers dust in the files of the relevant ministry, the orphan crisis deepens. Local and foreign NGOs have continued to do their very best to assist vulnerable children, often without a clear national framework or State administrative structure to co-ordinate their efforts. Sadly, it does seem as if orphans are the NGOs' problem rather than the concern of the State. Although Tanzania deserves commendation for its genuine commitment to the general uplifting of the living conditions of all its people, it seems to have been incapable of reacting in a timely manner to a crisis involving a large number of its young and more vulnerable citizens.

This *Survey* has tried to locate the orphan crisis in its historical and socio-economic context, stressing its wider causal links to the economic and social transformations of the previous decades. I have pointed out, echoing previous studies, that many of the problems facing orphans today date back to the early 1970s and beyond. Tanzania is party to the United Nations Convention on the Rights of the Child. It is also a signatory to the African Charter on the Rights and Welfare of the Child. Both instruments place responsibility on the State to provide and protect all children without any discrimination. Indeed, because of their vulnerability, orphans deserve special protection measures to ensure their survival and development. In an effort to bring the orphan question back on the national agenda, this *Survey* has revisited the Government's own policy documents and legal reform proposals to extract what may be termed Tanzania's response to the orphan crisis. An evaluation of these policy documents reveals that Tanzania does not lack good ideas on how to address the problem. What it seems to lack is the steam to drive its own policies towards implementation. In what may be seen as a timely reminder, Tanzania has now been urged by more than 30 foreign governments and international organisations to speed up the implementation of a

---

61 See especially ACC Article 11(3)(e) which calls upon States to take 'special measures in respect of ... disadvantaged children, to ensure equal access to education for all sections of the community'.

62 Some of these include the promotion of small and medium scale enterprises, supported by the United Nations Industrial Development Organisation (UNIDO) and Tanzania Social Action Trust Fund (TASAF) supported largely by the World Bank. UNIDO will also assist Tanzania in addressing the constraints faced by direct investors to Tanzania.

comprehensive and coherent national HIV/AIDS policy as a prerequisite for enhanced bilateral co-operation. As it happens, a draft of the policy actually exists but has been shelved since 1995.[63] Even while conceding that the social and economic problems facing Tanzania are immense and not capable of a quick fix, this does not justify what seems like bureaucratic inaction in the face of a deep crisis.

---

63 See N Othiambo 'Donors Rap Tanzania Over AIDS Scourge' *Panafrican News Agency*, 31 May 2000 (http://africanews.org.east/tanzania/stories).

THE UNITED STATES

CHILD SUPPORT GUIDELINE REVIEW: PROBLEMS AND PROSPECTS

*Marsha Garrison**

Over the past two decades, child support determination in the United States has been revolutionized. Traditional support laws required consideration of the child's needs, prior standard of living, and parental resources, but left to judicial discretion the task of translating these factors into a dollar value.[1] Today, based on directives from Congress, each State has adopted numerical guidelines under which support awards are calculated.[2]

As in other countries that have moved toward support guidelines, the Congressional requirements were adopted with the aim of significantly increasing award levels and decreasing award variability.[3] Under discretionary standards, the average value of child support paid was less than half of what economists estimate as typical child-rearing costs and only 10–12% of average male earnings.[4] Awards appeared to vary dramatically, even among families of similar size and socio-economic characteristics.[5] Moreover, awards were typically set at a level that effected an improvement in the living standard of the child support obligor, while ensuring that the living standard of his child plummeted.[6]

Unfortunately, the available evidence suggests that the new guidelines have not yet significantly altered the results achieved under discretionary standards:

---

*   Professor of Law, Brooklyn Law School.

1   For a description of traditional child support law, see Homer H Clark, Jr, *The Law of Domestic Relations in the United States* 488–498 (1st ed, 1968).

2   Pub. L. No 100-485, § 103(f), 102 Stat. 2343, 2346 (codified as amended at 42 U.S.C. § 667(b)(2) (1991)). For State-by-State guideline descriptions, see G Diane Dodson and Joan Entmacher, *Women's Legal Defense Fund, Report Card on State Child Support Guidelines* (1994).

3   See Irwin Garfinkel and Marygold S Melli, 'The Use of Normative Standards in Family Law Decisions: Developing Mathematical Standards for Child Support', 24 Fam L.Q. 157, 160–162 (1990); Robert G Williams, 'An Overview of Child Support Guidelines in the United States', in *Child Support Guidelines: The Next Generation* 15 (Margaret Campbell Haynes ed, 1994) (hereinafter *Next Generation*).

4   Andrea H Beller and John W Graham, *Small Change: The Economics of Child Support* 34 tbl. 2.7, 38 (1993) (comparing support awards to estimates of child-related expense and average male earnings). Child support obligors reported paying even smaller proportions of their incomes in child support. See Cynthia Needles Fletcher, 'A Comparison of Incomes and Expenditures of Male-Headed Households Paying Child Support and Female-Headed Households Receiving Child Support', 38 Fam. Relations 412, 414 (1989).

5   See Marsha Garrison, 'Autonomy or Community? An Evaluation of Two Models of Parental Obligation', 86 Cal. L. Rev. 41, 43 n. 10 (1998) (summarising reports).

6   For a description of the research findings, see Marsha Garrison, 'Good Intentions Gone Awry: The Impact of New York's Equitable Distribution Law on Divorce Outcomes', 57 *Brooklyn L. Rev.* 621, 633 n. 43 (living standards) and 721 tbl. 56 (per capita income) (1991).

child support awards remain highly variable[7] and, although the introduction of numerical guidelines does appear to have modestly increased the value of new support awards, increases reported to date fall far short of those predicted.[8] In some States, award levels did not increase at all after guidelines were introduced; in others, award levels increased only within one or another income group.[9] Many guidelines also fail to ensure that children are protected from poverty even when parental income is adequate to meet that goal; typically, they continue to produce awards that improve the living standard of the child support obligor, while that of his child declines significantly.[10]

Because federal law requires each State to review its support guideline at least once every four years to ensure that it minimizes award variability and achieves 'appropriate amounts of child support',[11] a mechanism is already in place to improve these results. But in order for that mechanism to be effective, the review

---

7   See David Arnaudo, 'Deviation from State Child Support Guidelines', in *Next Generation, supra* note 3, at 88–94.

8   See Ron Haskins et al, *U.S. Dep't of Health and Human Services, Estimates of National Child Support Collection Potential and the Income Security of Female Headed Families* v, 29 (1985) (predicting that application of either of two guideline models would increase value of average child support 350%); Irwin Garfinkel et al, 'Child Support Guidelines: Will They Make a Difference?', 12 J.Fam.Issues 404 (1991) (predicting that introduction of guidelines would raise award values by 44%). The largest and most detailed study of actual outcomes is described in Nancy Thoennes et al, 'The Impact of Child Support Guidelines on Award Adequacy, Award Variability, and Case Processing Efficiency', 25 Fam.L.Q. 325, 339–40, 343 (in only one (which had the lowest pre-guideline award levels) of three research States did all income groups experience significant increases in the level of child support attributable to the introduction of mandatory guidelines; in one State no income group did). See also Marsha Garrison, 'Child Support and Children's Poverty', 28 Fam.L.Q. 475, 489–490 (1994) (describing and analysing other studies).

9   Thoennes et al, *supra* note 8, at 336 (in Illinois, guidelines did not significantly increase award levels among any income group when differences in employment status of pre and post guideline samples were taken into account). A significant proportion of the increase in average child support values that researchers have noted may also be due to the imposition of token, rather than zero-dollar, awards in cases of unemployed or female noncustodial parents. P Bushard, *Time Series Assessment of Child Support Guidelines: Support Awards in Shared Custody Divorces* (1988) (PhD dissertation, Arizona State University) cited in Thoennes et al at 343 (15% increase in support levels in shared custody cases after adoption of Arizona child support guidelines was entirely due to a reduction in zero-dollar awards).

10   One review, which evaluated all State guidelines in effect in 1989–90, concluded that, on average, awards under the guidelines reviewed caused children's living standards to decline by 26% while non-custodial parents' improved by 34%. None of the guidelines reviewed required lower-income obligors to provide enough child support to ensure a poverty-level or 'minimum decent living' standard for two children; a significant number of States also failed to ensure that children in middle-income families enjoyed a minimum decent living. Dodson and Entmacher, *supra* note 2, at 95, 97–98 (reporting that 18 State guidelines failed to offer a minimum decent living standard in one middle-income scenario, 21 in another, 31 for a third, and 47 for a fourth; 'minimum decent standard of living' was defined as 150% of the federal poverty level). See also Ellen B. Zweibel and Richard Shillington, *Child Support Policy: Income Tax Treatment and Child Support Guidelines* (1994), in Carl E Schneider and Margaret F Brinig, *An Invitation to Family Law: Principles, Process and Perspectives* 972, 978, tbl. 4.1 (1996) (reporting that under both income shares and Melson formulae more than 75% of low-income parents and 31% of middle-income residential parents would have incomes below poverty line); Maureen Pirog-Good, 'Child Support Guidelines and the Economic Well-Being of Children in the United States', 42 Fam. Relations 453, 459 (1993) (using one estimate of family expenditure for a low-income family, guidelines in 14 States failed to produce an adequate award for a low-income family and guidelines in 10 States failed to produce an adequate award for a middle-income family; using another estimate all guidelines fell short).

11   42 U.S.C. § 667(a); 45 C.F.R. § 302.56(e).

process must focus on why current guidelines have had so little effect, and it must produce altered guidelines tailored to remedy current deficiencies. Thus far, the review process has not followed this course: as one expert recently reported, 'guideline reviews fall far short of what is needed to develop a structure that provides appropriate child support awards and limits deviations'.[12]

This chapter assesses the failings of both current guidelines and the federally mandated review process. Because some other nations have adopted guidelines similar to those in the United States, such an assessment has potential relevance for policy-makers outside the United States.

I WHY HAVE CURRENT GUIDELINES HAD SO LITTLE EFFECT?

A The obligor's self-support reserve

One reason why current guidelines have failed to increase significantly award levels is that, in many States, the guideline features a 'self-support reserve' that establishes an income level for the support obligor (typically the federal poverty level for a one-person household) below which a lower award than the guidelines would otherwise require is permitted or presumptively required.[13] When a self-support reserve is available only to the non-resident parent, children of the poor are almost certain to bear the brunt of family dissolution.[14] And because both divorce and non-marital childbearing are disproportionately concentrated at the lower end of the income spectrum,[15] child support proceedings disproportionately involve poor children. Yet only a few States that provide the support obligor with

---

12 Marygold S Melli, 'Guideline Review: The Search for an Equitable Child Support Formula', in *Child Support: The Next Frontier* 113, 114 (J Thomas Oldham and Marygold S Melli eds, 2000).

13 Both the 'income shares' and 'Melson' formulae include a self-support reserve feature. See Robert J Williams, 'Guidelines for Setting Levels of Child Support Orders', 21 Fam. L.Q. 281, 305 tbl. 4. The English and Australian child support formulae also grant the obligor a self-support reserve. See J Thomas Oldham, 'Lessons from the New English and Australian Child Support Systems', 29 Vand. J. Transnat'l L. 691 (1996).

14 Researchers who compared the 'total annual expenditures on two children in a husband–wife family as determined by the U.S. Department of Agriculture with the total annualized support figure determined under the States' child support guidelines' found that '[t]he greatest shortfall is in States that demand a self-support reserve, although this rule is not universal'. Laura W Morgan and Mark C Lino, 'A Comparison of Child Support Awards Calculated Under States' Child Support Guidelines with Expenditures on Children Calculated by the US Department of Agriculture', 33 Fam. L.Q. 191, 215 (1999).

15 Divorce is approximately twice as likely for couples living in poverty as it is for the general population (see US Dep't of Commerce, Bureau of the Census, When Households Continue, Discontinue, and Form 18-21, tbl. I (Current Population Reports, Series P-23, No. 180) (1992)). Non-marital child-bearing is even more strongly associated with low income. See Elizabeth Phillips and Irwin Garfinkel, 'Income Growth Among Nonresidential Fathers: Evidence from Wisconsin', 30 *Demography* 227, 234 tbl.2 (showing that 41% of never married non-resident fathers with tax records were poor in year before support action, as compared to 19% of divorced non-resident fathers). See also US Dep't of Commerce, Bureau of the Census, Family Disruption and Economic Hardship: The Short-Run Picture for Children 2 (Current Population Reports, Series P-70, No. 23 (1991) (reporting that among families with children, 21% of those that experienced the loss of the father from the household during a two-year survey period were already poor, a poverty rate double that of U.S. married-couple households generally).

a self-support reserve provide a comparable support reserve to the child's household.[16]

The self-support reserve concept is hardly a necessary feature of current guidelines. It has no counterpart in traditional support law; empirical research has indeed shown that child support awards under discretionary standards were regressive, with low-income parents typically paying greater proportions of their incomes in child support than high-income parents.[17] Moreover, the concept is inconsistent with the prevailing guideline model, which aims at achieving 'continuity' of parental expenditure. Some studies have found that parents spend approximately the same percentage of household income on their children at all income levels; others have found that poor parents spend more on their children than their wealthier counterparts;[18] but none have reported that poor parents spend less.

B   The guidelines' basic design

Another reason for current guidelines' failure to meet Congressional goals stems from their basic design. All State guidelines now in effect focus on 'continuity' of expenditure by the non-residential parent; only three States utilise guidelines that take poverty prevention as an explicit aim, and none aim at maintaining the child's living standard, or even at equalizing living standard loss.[19] It should hardly be surprising that current guidelines have failed to raise significantly award levels, avert poverty, and minimise children's living standard loss when they were not structured to achieve these goals.

As the name of the continuity-of-expenditure methodology suggests, the goal of such formulae is to replicate typical child-related outlay in an intact two-parent family;[20] support awards are calculated from standardised child-expense

---

16   See Dodson and Entmacher, *supra* note 2, at 49–55 (classifying States).

17   See Lenore J Weitzman, *The Divorce Revolution: The Unexpected Social and Economic Consequences for Women and Children in America* 462–469 (1985) (reporting regressive child support awards in California divorce sample); Garrison, *supra* note 6, at 718 tbl. 53 (reporting significant negative relationship between percentage of obligor income awarded in combined child support and alimony and obligor's income in New York divorce sample); James B McLindon, 'Separate But Unequal: The Economic Disaster of Divorce for Women and Children', 21 Fam. L.Q. 351, 371–372 (1987) (reporting regressive child support awards in Connecticut divorce sample).

18   See Irwin Garfinkel, *Assuring Child Support* 134 (1992) ('No research suggests that … the poor spend a smaller proportion of income on their children than middle-income fathers. Indeed, the evidence suggests either that the proportions are about the same or that the poor actually spend a slightly higher percentage'); Thomas J Espenshad, *Investing in Children: New Estimates of Parental Expenditures* (finding that poor parents spent 26% of their income on one child, while parents with significantly higher incomes spent 15.2%).

19   As of 1999, Delaware, Hawaii, and Montana utilised guidelines based on the 'Melson' formula, developed in Delaware and aimed explicitly at poverty prevention. For a State-by-State comparison of guideline models, see Jane C Venohr and Robert G Williams, 'The Implementation and Periodic Review of State Child Support Guidelines', 33 Fam. L.Q. 7, 11 tbl. 1 (1999).

20   In the three States utilising the 'Melson' formula, guidelines aim at poverty prevention as well as continuity-of-expenditure. In these States, a 'primary support' value, designed to meet the minimum needs of one adult, is first subtracted from each parent's income; the remainder is then applied, in proportion to the parents' relative incomes, to the 'basic child support obligation', designed to meet the minimum needs of one or more children. The basic support obligation equals the sum of the children's primary support needs plus actual, work-related childcare expenses. Extraordinary medical expenses are similarly prorated. If the support obligor still has available income, a fixed percentage of

percentages, derived from one or another consumer expenditure survey, that vary by the number of children in the family.[21] Guidelines of this type are inherently ill-adapted to the task of remedying the problems that led Congress to enact the guideline requirement.

First, the support values such guidelines contain are based on the *marginal*, or extra, costs associated with a new family member, not the per person allocation of family resources. The marginal cost approach makes use of one or another 'household equivalence scale'. These scales were devised by economists to permit living standard comparisons when households are not the same size.[22] Used in this way, the approach has merit; indeed, researchers could not have determined that children typically fare poorly in comparison with their non-residential parents without use of such a scale. But continuity-of-expenditure guidelines make use of household equivalence scales in an unusual way: guideline drafters used them to determine how much more money a couple would need to add a child to their family and maintain their former living standard. This figure – the marginal cost associated with a child – is assumed to be the parent's *total* child-related outlay and is used as a basis for achieving 'continuity' of parental expenditure. But the cost of adding a child to the family and maintaining the family's living standard does not measure the resources available to the child; indeed, more than 90% of typical family expenditure represents goods such as housing, transportation, and utility payments that cannot easily be allocated to specific family members, but which nonetheless benefit each.[23] The child's welfare is thus determined largely by the family's *overall* level of expenditure, not the marginal cost of maintaining that standard when a child joins the family.

Secondly, because the model looks backward at a family situation that no longer exists (or, in the case of non-marital children, that may never have been[24]) it fails to take account of the realities of family dissolution. Two households

---

that income, based on the percentage-of-obligor-income model, is then added to the basic support obligation. See Robert G Williams, 'An Overview of Child Support Guidelines in the United States', in *Next Generation, supra* note 3, at 6.

21 The percentages used in the 'income-shares' model were based on the one study (Espenshade, *supra* note 18) believed to be most reliable. The percentages utilised in the 'percentage-of-obligor income' model were based on a review of the then-current research (Jacques van der Gaag, 'On Measuring the Cost of Children', Children and Youth Services Rev. 4 (1982)) But according to one of the authors of the formula, given the 'enormous' range of estimates, this economic data provided 'only a starting point for determining the percentages.' Garfinkel, *supra* note 18, at 89.

22 For detailed discussions of the limitations of household equivalence scales, see Angus S Deaton and John Muellbauer, 'On Measuring Child Costs: with Applications to Poor Countries', 94 J. Pol. Econ. 720 (1986); Arthur Lewbel, 'Household Equivalence Scales and Welfare Comparisons', 39 J. Pub. Econ. 377 (1989); Julie A Nelson, 'Household Equivalence Scales: Theory versus Policy?', 11 J. Lab. Econ. 471 (1993).

23 See David M Betson, *Alternative Estimates of the Cost of Children from the 1980–86 Consumer Expenditure Survey* 3 (University of Wisconsin Institute for Research on Poverty Special Report No. 51, December 1990) (based on 1980–81 Consumer Expenditure Survey, 90% of total expenditures in families with children represent commodities that could not be assigned to either children or adults based on the nature of the good).

24 In the United States, most mothers of non-marital children do not live with their children's fathers. See Larry L Bumpass and JA Sweet, 'Children's Experience in Single-Parent Families: Implications of Cohabitation and Marital Transitions', 21 Fam. Planning Perspectives 256 (1990) (estimating that in the late 1980s only one quarter of non-marital children were born to cohabiting couples); Andrew J Cherlin, 'The Weakening Link Between Marriage and the Care of Children', 20 Fam. Planning Perspectives 302, 303 (1988) (estimating that 22% of white and 12% of black children under six living with an unmarried mother have mother's cohabitant in the home).

cannot live as cheaply as one; thus the federal poverty level for a family of three is approximately 50% less than that of a family of one plus that of a family of two.[25] Family dissolution therefore assures that, given the same total income, one or both portions of the divided family will experience a living standard decline; for the family that had barely averted poverty when together, dissolution ensures that some, if not all, family members will thereafter be poor.[26] Perhaps because of lost economies of scale, single parents also appear to spend a considerably larger fraction of their incomes on children than do two-parent households.[27]

Continuity-of-expenditure guidelines could be revised to achieve higher awards than they currently produce. For example, one study revealed that nine continuity-of-expenditure guidelines produced awards providing children with less than 60% of what would be needed to achieve a living standard equal to that of the non-residential parent while three – those of Connecticut, Massachusetts, and the District of Columbia – produced awards providing more than 85% of what would be needed.[28] The relative success of the Connecticut, Massachusetts, and District of Columbia guidelines stems, in part, from the fact that they rely on estimates of child-related expenditure higher than those contained in most guidelines; two of the three also provide a fairly generous self-support reserve for the custodial parent.[29]

But because of their exclusive focus on the past, no continuity-of-expenditure guideline is well-adapted to the changed needs of separated families. The States have struggled to adapt continuity-of-expenditure guidelines to typical post-dissolution scenarios such as joint custody or the birth of additional children to the obligor. But because a past-focused methodology provides absolutely no guidance for resolving such cases, it is not surprising that the results are inconsistent and controversial.[30] More important, parents and children typically measure the fairness of a support award in relation to their current rather than prior circumstances; if a support award leaves one segment of the divided family with the lion's share of the income, the other segment is likely to feel aggrieved. Given

---

25   US Dep't of Commerce, Bureau of the Census, *Statistical Abstract of the United States* 1998 478 tbl. 758 (reporting 1996 poverty threshold of $88,163 for one individual under 65 and $10,564 for two persons with a householder under 65).

26   While we lack recent estimates, one expert has estimated that 16% of whites and 28% of blacks who became poor during the early 1980s as a result of movement into a female-headed household did so simply because of the loss of economies of scale. Mary Jo Bane, 'Household Composition and Poverty', in *Fighting Poverty: What Works and What Doesn't* 209, 230 (Sheldon H Danziger and Daniel H Weinberg eds., 1986).

27   See Betson, *supra* note 23, at 55 (based on 1980–86 CPS data, proportion of total expenditure on two children is 35% in a two-parent and 53% in a one-parent family); Edward P Lazear and Robert T Michael, *Allocation of Income within the Household* 90, 98 (1988) (based on 1972–73 data, proportion of income expended on children in a two-child family is 27% in a two-parent and 53% in a one-parent family). But see *U.S. Dep't of Agriculture, Family Economics Research Group, Expenditures of a Child by Families* 10 (1992) (concluding that 'expenses on a child in single-parent households are slightly higher than those in two-parent households, probably because of economies of scale').

28   Dodson and Entmacher, *supra* note 2, at 22 tbl. 3-D.

29   Ibid, at 43, 54.

30   See Robert G Williams, 'An Overview of Child Support Guidelines in the United States', in *Next Generation, supra* note 2, at 1, 12–13 (describing State responses to 'perplexing' and 'emotion-laden' issues of joint custody and additional dependants); Marygold S Melli, 'Guideline Review: Child Support and Time Sharing by Parents', 33 Fam. L.Q. 219, 221 (1999) (finding that 'time sharing beyond traditional visitation is more complex than present guidelines recognize').

the continued dominance of mother custody and disparity in men's and women's wages, the aggrieved segment will most typically be the child and residential parent, at least during the period immediately following a divorce.[31] But in atypical families where the residential parent earns as much or more than the non-residential parent – and in the extremely common case in which the non-residential parent marries a new spouse who does so[32] – continuity-of-expenditure guidelines will comparatively disadvantage the non-residential parent. Because continuity-of-expenditure type guidelines 'severely penalise children for being in the custody of a parent who has less income, and reward them for living with the parent who has more',[33] their results produce cries of unfairness from advocates for both mothers and fathers – and both groups can point to cases in which the charge seems justified.

C   Individualised case processing

The individualised process by which awards are determined also plays a significant role in producing current results; the most frequently stated reason for deviation from the guideline support values is an agreement between the parents themselves.[34] Many parents who negotiate support awards are poorly informed about the relevant legal standards. In a large, and apparently growing, proportion of the cases lawyer representation is available to only one – or neither – parent.[35] Under these circumstances, the resources and attitudes of each parent toward the divorce may play important roles in determining child support outcomes and produce results that bear little relationship to those the lawmakers intended.[36]

---

31   See Laurie J Bassi and Burt S Barnow, 'Expenditures on Children and Child Support Guidelines', 12 J. Pol'y Analysis and Mgmt. 478, 494 (1993) ('Requiring the non-custodial parent to maintain his or her rate of expenditure on the child is likely to result in the child having a lower standard of living and might still leave the non-custodial parent with a higher standard of living than he or she enjoyed prior to dissolution').

32   About five-sixths of divorced men and three-quarters of divorced women remarry; about half of remarriages take place within three years of divorce. See Barbara Foley Wilson and Sally Cunningham Clarke, 'Remarriage: A Demographic Profile', 13 J. Fam. Issues 123, 131 (1992). Younger women – the group most likely to be custodial parents – remarry, on average, more quickly than older women. (reporting that average period between divorce and remarriage was 1.5 years for women aged 20–24 and 2.4 years for women aged 25–29). Yet, although evidence suggests that, on average, the living standard of remarried women is as high after remarriage as it was before divorce (see, eg, Greg Duncan and Saul Hoffman, 'A Reconsideration of the Economic Consequences of Marital Dissolution', 22 *Demography* 485 (1985)), under current guidelines, researchers have reported that neither the father's nor the mother's remarriage is significantly associated with post-divorce modification of the divorce settlement. H Elizabeth Peters et al, 'Enforcing Divorce Settlements: Evidence from Child Support Compliance and Award Modifications', 30 *Demography* 719, 725 tbl. 1 (1993).

33   David Betson et al, 'Trade-offs Implicit in Child-Support Guidelines', 11 J. Pol'y Analysis and Mgmt. 1, 19 (1992).

34   *American Bar Association Center on Children and the Law, Evaluation of Child Support Guidelines: Findings and Conclusion* 2.5, 2.6 (1996) (hereinafter *ABA Report*).

35   See Jessica Pearson, 'Ten Myths About Family Law', 27 Fam. L.Q. 280, 281–282 (1993); Jane C Murphy, 'Access to Legal Remedies: The Crisis in Family Law', 8 B.Y.U.J. Pub. L. 123 (1994).

36   One group of researchers, for example, found that the parties' attitudes toward the divorce was a factor 'of some significance' in determining child support outcomes. Custodial parents who were reluctant to end the marriage and/or whose spouses were impatient to do so obtained significantly better child support awards than the mean of the group; couples also consistently expressed concern about legal fees and sometimes settled in order to avoid additional expense. See Marygold S Melli et al, 'The

The extent of deviation appears to be substantial. Indeed, in some jurisdictions, researchers have reported that the *majority* of support awards deviate significantly from those the guidelines suggest.[37] Unfortunately, the record-keeping requirements of the federal guideline mandate are inadequate to allow determination of the basis for deviation in many cases. Some deviations undoubtedly represent appropriate trade-offs – support-for-property, for example, or extraordinary visitation expenses – but other deviations undoubtedly do not. At this point, we simply do not know how many cases fall into each category.

II   THE FEDERALLY MANDATED REVIEW PROCESS: WHY HAS IT FAILED? CAN IT BE FIXED?

A   The sources of failure

While Congress required the States to conduct guideline reviews every four years to ensure that their guidelines produced 'appropriate amounts of child support', Congress failed to give the States much guidance on how to make such a determination. Federal regulations did mandate two requirements: in conducting a review, States must consider economic data on the cost of raising children; they must also analyse case data to determine the extent of deviation from the guidelines.[38] But Congress did not tell States how they were to develop such data or what they were to do with it.

Perhaps most fundamentally, Congress gave the States no meaningful guidance in determining whether or not their guidelines in fact produce 'appropriate' amounts of support: the term 'appropriate' has no content except in relation to some predetermined goal or value, and Congress offered none. The federal regulation requiring consideration of the cost of raising children suggests that States should measure 'appropriate support' in relation to childcare costs. But as we have seen, childcare costs can be measured on either a marginal or per person basis; they appear to vary significantly for single and dual parent households. To which measures should State policy-makers look? And should childcare costs be the sole value by which 'appropriate support' should be measured, or only one of many? Neither Congress nor the federal Office of Child Support Enforcement has as yet offered States any guidance on these important issues; indeed, Congress did not even require the States to revise their guidelines in response to the review findings.

Compounding the problem of inadequate guidance is the fact that the existing federal mandate subtly encourages State policy-makers not to go beyond the

---

Process of Negotiation: An Exploratory Investigation in the Context of No-Fault Divorce', 40 Rutgers L. Rev. 1133, 1155–1156, 1168–1171 (1988). See also Thoennes et al, *supra* note 8, at 340–341 tbl. 10 (legal representation was significantly correlated with value of child support award at all income levels).

37   See, eg, Marilyn L Ray, *New York State Child Support Standards Act Evaluation Project Report* 1993 54 (1994) (only 22% of sample child support orders followed guidelines). See also *ABA Report*, *supra* note 34 (support award was not within 2% above or below the guideline value in from 10% to 45% of cases across 21 surveyed counties); Amaudo, *supra* note 7 (summarizing State studies).

38   45 CFR §§ 302.56[e] and [h].

prevailing continuity-of-expenditure model in assessing the adequacy of current outcomes. Indeed, during the early days of the guideline movement, the federal Office of Child Support Enforcement commissioned an advisory panel that produced the continuity-of-expenditure approach. Given this history and the continued federal emphasis on child-care costs as part of the review process, it is hardly surprising that State policy-makers would associate such costs with the marginal expenditure approach, and that they would assume evaluation of that approach to be unnecessary and perhaps undesirable. Thus, in the face of accumulating evidence on the deficiencies of current guidelines and despite the fact that the States should by now have completed at least two guideline reviews, only a handful of States have altered their original guideline model.[39]

Finally, the Federal Government does not even require the States to review their guidelines using current data on the cost of raising children. In requiring guidelines, Congress also required the federal Department of Health and Human Services (HHS) to develop data on 'patterns of expenditures on children in two-parent families, [and] in single-parent families ...'.[40] Because this research was not completed until after the federal deadline for guideline adoption, the States typically relied on economic data developed during the early 1970s – data that its developer himself now considers outdated.[41] More recent data, from the HHS study and another study conducted independently by the US Department of Agriculture, are now available. But States need not utilise it in conducting their guideline reviews – and many have chosen not to do so.[42]

Lack of federal guidance means that States are relatively free to conduct the review process as they wish; thus States could, if they so chose, develop goals by which to measure guideline success, conduct research to obtain detailed data on current outcomes, and carefully revise current guidelines in order to ensure that future outcomes met the State's chosen goals. The States have not, however, followed this activist course. As the small number of guideline model changes evidences, very few have attempted to develop goals and values. Indeed, by 1995, only 20 had completed some form of case sampling to determine the extent of deviation from their guidelines,[43] and a large number had not followed the Congressional mandate requiring consideration of child-rearing cost data.[44]

Undoubtedly, one reason for State inertia is the fact that State legislators did not adopt guideline legislation because of a groundswell of enthusiasm at the local level, but because they had to. Indeed, prior to the federal mandate only three States had State-wide guidelines in place.[45] Confronted with a federal mandate and only four years to meet it, State policymakers tended to rely heavily on the federally 'approved' model developed by the Office of Child Support and failed to

---

39 See Venohr and Williams, *supra* note 19, at 26 (reporting that only four States have switched models since first adopting guidelines).

40 Pub. L. No. 100-485 § 128.

41 See Morgan and Lino, *supra* note 14, at 195.

42 See Melli, *supra* note 12, at 115 (reporting that 'none apparently considered the study commissioned under a directive from Congress ...'; Venohr and Williams, *supra* note 19, at 27–28.

43 *ABA Report*, *supra* note 34, at ES-1.

44 Melli, *supra* note 12, at 115.

45 Venohr and Williams, *supra* note 19, at 8.

develop an institutional structure to develop their own data and models.[46] Most States continue to lack agencies and personnel with ongoing responsibility for policy development in the area of child support; the review process is thus conducted on an ad hoc basis, and without ongoing institutional support and expertise. For example, during their first guideline review, some States did update their guidelines in response to the HHS study of childcare costs, which was completed in 1990. But despite the fact that the federal data is now a decade old, 'there has been no study updating the 1990 ... estimates of child-rearing expenditures'.[47]

While State institutions and expertise have been slow to develop, advocacy groups have not. Groups representing parent interests have flourished, and some experts believe that those representing the interests of non-residential parents have deterred guideline reform. These groups typically 'have not been strong enough to reduce guidelines, but they have been strong enough to block action to increase the levels of child support orders based on more recent evidence on child-rearing costs'.[48]

In sum, the federally mandated review process has failed to cure the deficiencies of early guidelines for two reasons: the Federal Government did not require meaningful review; and there are no State-level institutions or advocacy groups with the expertise and power to ensure that such a review takes place.

B   What can be done?

Given that child support guidelines did not emerge without a federal mandate, it seems apparent that guideline reform will also require federal leadership. First, federal regulators must promulgate standards to guide State data collection efforts and ensure that review is based on accurate facts about current outcomes. The best and easiest way to do this would be to require the States to collect non-identifying data as child support orders and modifications are filed. If parties to such an order were required to fill out computer-ready data collection forms as part of the filing process, no review-specific research would be necessary; instead, both federal and State policymakers would routinely have a rich database available to guide policy development on child support, as well as related areas of law such as divorce, paternity, and child custody. Secondly, federal regulators should define and outline the review process; the States need 'guidance on specific issues to be addressed and a recommended process to follow'.[49] Finally, federal regulators should mandate State action in response to review findings. If, for example, review reveals a high level of deviation from the presumptive guideline values, State regulators should be required to determine the causes of such deviation and

---

46   See Nancy D. Polikoff, 'Looking for Policy Choices Within an Economic Methodology: A Critique of the Income Shares Model', in *Women's Legal Defense Fund, Essentials of Child Support Guideline Development: Economic Issues and Policy Considerations* 27–28 (1987) (noting that the economic analysis commissioned by the federal Office of Child Support Enforcement (OCSE) 'creates the appearance of scientific, objective "truth"' and is 'given heightened validity by virtue of OCSE's involvement').

47   Venohr and Williams, *supra* note 19, at 28.

48   Venohr and Williams, *supra* note 19, at 30–31.

49   Melli, *supra* note 12, at 126.

develop an appropriate response. These simple additions to the current review mandate would go a long way toward curing some of the worst deficiencies of the current process.

The Federal Government needs to do more than mandate State action, however. Given the lack of institutional resources and expertise at the State level, it also needs to take a leadership role in formulating policy goals and legislative options. In the early days of the guidelines movement, the Federal Government did just that, commissioning both a study of child-care costs and a guideline development effort that produced the widely-adopted 'income-shares' type guideline. Indeed, it was these efforts that ensured the success of the continuity-of-expenditure model.

It is true that the federal effort is largely responsible for the failure of current guidelines to meet Congressional goals. Federal policy-makers assumed that the continuity-of-expenditure model would significantly raise award levels, without conducting research on current award levels or undertaking a comparison of those levels with the results that the continuity-of-expenditure model would produce. The federal effort was also conducted without addressing the policy basis for guidelines: the goal of raising awards does not provide a means of determining what level of support is adequate; award adequacy cannot be evaluated without a policy yardstick against which to measure results, nor can award fairness.

It is time for the Federal Government to remedy the deficiencies of its initial policy effort: whether measured implicitly or explicitly, the adequacy of child support awards will play a crucial role in determining the current well-being and future prospects of half or more of our children; given current rates of divorce and non-marital childbearing, at least 50% of American children are currently expected to be eligible for child support from a non-resident parent for some portion of their childhood years.[50] Moreover, researchers have found that those who are subject to a law evaluate it normatively, and are more likely to obey those laws that they find fair.[51] These various considerations suggest that a child support guideline should conform to our considered judgments about fairness among family members and the scope of parental obligation. They also suggest that a child support law failing to conform to those judgments will not garner public respect and allegiance.

Current continuity-of-expenditure guidelines do not meet these standards. While research on public attitudes toward child support is sparse, the available data suggests that Americans typically believe that the support obligation should be based on – and updated to take account of – the current incomes and circumstances of family members; that the support calculation should include a comparative element that takes into account the circumstances of both segments of the divided family; and that a parent should contribute something to his child's

---

50 Researchers currently estimate that half to three-quarters of children born in the late 1970s or 1980s will spend some portion of their childhood years in a single-parent household. For a critical review of the estimates, see Donald J Hernandez, *America's Children: Resources from Family, Government and the Economy* 69–71 (1993).

51 See Tom R Tyler, *Why People Obey the Law* 178 (1990) (concluding, based on extensive empirical research, that 'people ... evaluate laws and the decisions of legal authorities in normative terms, obeying the law if it is legitimate and moral and accepting decisions if they are fairly arrived at ...'); Tom Tyler and Robyn M. Dawes, 'Fairness in Groups', in Psychological Perspectives on Justice 87, 89–90 (Barbara A. Mellers and Jonathan Barron eds. 1993) (summarizing research).

support even if he is worse off than the child.[52] While these trends do not definitively point to any particular policy goal, they undeniably fail to support the continuity-of-expenditure approach, which ignores the current circumstances of family members altogether.

If the review process is to succeed, federal policymakers need to turn their attention to the basics: guideline review cannot succeed without good data on current outcomes and a well-defined review process; nor can a meaningful review be conducted without policy goals against which current outcomes can be measured. Americans rank family obligations as the most important of obligations.[53] It is time for federal regulators to address the meaning and scope of the obligation to support one's children.

---

52 See Garrison, *supra* note 5, at 98–101 (describing surveys in detail and assessing what can be learned from them).

53 See Mary Ann Glendon, *Rights Talk: The Impoverishment of Political Discourse* 105 (1991) (describing national survey in which most respondents ranked 'Being responsible for your actions' and 'Being able to provide emotional support to your family', as their most important personal values while 'Being free of obligation so I can do whatever I want to do' came in last).

YUGOSLAVIA

LEGAL STATUS OF THE NON-CUSTODIAL/ NON-RESIDENTIAL PARENT IN YUGOSLAV FAMILY LAW

*Gordana Kovacek Stanic**

I INTRODUCTION

It might be said that the legal relationship between parents and children, viewed from an historical perspective, depended on the married status of parents. It meant that married parents usually had joint custody, but in cases of divorce and children born out of wedlock one parent had sole custody. According to the modern child custody law in a number of countries, married, divorced or never married parents can obtain the same legal status as married parents. Therefore, the married status of the parents seems to be losing priority as the basis for custody and the legal relationship between parents and children seems to be gaining in importance. In Yugoslav family law[1] unmarried parents have an equal legal status to married parents, as long as paternity is established. However, there exists the possibility for divorced parents or parents living apart to exercise parental rights jointly. The legal position of non-residential parents is strengthened in other ways.

In the Yugoslav law on parents and children, terms of importance are: the parental right, the exercise of parental right, entrusting a child to a parent for care and upbringing, etc. It is important to stress that the term 'child custody' does not exist in Yugoslav family law.

II PARENTAL RIGHT

The term 'parental right' includes particular rights and duties of parents and children. One group concerns the personal parent-child relationship (caring for the life and health of a child, looking after a child, upbringing and education; as well as duties and rights in relation to matters of status – determining the name, domicile and citizenship of a child); the other group concerns property relations and maintenance; and as a separate right there is legal representation of a minor

---

* Associate Professor of Law, Law Faculty, University of Novi Sad.

1 There are two family law acts relevant to the legal status of parents in Yugoslavia: The Law on Marriage and Family Relations of Serbia 1980 (*Official Gazette* of Serbia 22/1980, amendments 22/93, 35/94; hereinafter referred to as LMFR) and the Family Law of Montenegro 1989 (*Official Gazette* of Montenegro 7/1989).

child. Particular rights of the child are specified in Family Law Acts and in the UN Convention on the Rights of the Child 1989, which Yugoslavia has ratified.[2]

The parental right is something which parents obtain automatically when a child is born, if parents are married to each other. If parents are not married, the mother obtains the parental right automatically and the father when paternity is established. This might be established by the father's acknowledgement of the child or in court proceedings. If parents live together, they exercise the parental right together and in agreement, in the same way whether they are married or not. If they do not live together, the parent with whom the child lives exercises the parental right *ex lege* (Article 123, 124 LMFR).

In a case of divorce, the court makes a decision as to which parent a child will be entrusted for care and upbringing. This decision is delivered *ex officio*. The court might decide to entrust a child to one of the parents, to a third person, or to an institution (Article 125 LMFR). In deciding to whom the child is to be entrusted for care and upbringing, the main principle in Yugoslav law is the interest of the child – but this principle is not defined. It is stipulated, however, that the court should investigate all circumstances relevant to the proper mental and physical development and upbringing of the child and in decision-making has to follow primarily the interest of the child. The court should consider the emotional needs and wishes of the child in particular, about which the court should ask for a professional opinion, when it is necessary (Article 130 LMFR). In deciding to whom the child is to be entrusted for care and upbringing parents enjoy equal legal status, so there are no automatic preferences *in favour* of either mother or father.[3] The most important criterion is parental consent, both in court practice and in law (Article 125/2 LMFR).

In the case of the parents' separation,[4] parents can make an agreement concerning with whom the child should live. If they cannot reach an agreement, the decision is in the competence of a guardianship authority – the center for social work (Article 124/2 LMFR).

III   COURT PRACTICE ON ENTRUSTING THE CHILD AFTER DIVORCE

In recent years the number of minor children affected by their parents' divorce in Yugoslavia (Republics of Serbia and Montenegro) was: in 1996 – about 4,700 (0.4 per 1000 inhabitants), but in 1986 was about 6,400 (0.6 per 1000 inhabitants). The decrease in the number is due to a decrease in the divorce rate, which is probably the consequence of an unstable economic and political situation. The divorce rate was in 1996 – 0.7; in 1986 – 1.1. The highest divorce rate was in the Province of

---

2   Law on Ratification of the Convention on the Rights of the Child, *Official Gazette* of the Social Federal Republic of Yugoslavia no 15/90.

3   On the other hand, in the Civil Code of the Kingdom of Serbia (1844), Paragraph 118 stipulated that if parents could agree in a case of divorce, boys up to four years and girls up to seven years should be in the mother's care and other children in the father's care, unless special circumstances concerning the child's happiness suggested a different decision.

4   According to Yugoslav law, separation is a *de facto* situation, as judicial separation as an institution does not exist.

Vojvodina (in 1996 – 1.1) and smallest in the Province of Kosovo and Metohia (in 1996 – 0.3).[5]

As an example of court practice on entrusting the child after divorce, the results of my investigation are presented. The investigation was carried out in the Province of Vojvodina, particularly in two courts of first instance, in Novi Sad and Subotica, over a period of three years (1987–1989). These two towns have a very high divorce rate as well as the largest number of new marriages and divorces per year in Vojvodina.[6]

The investigation particularly focused on, first, to whom the children were entrusted after divorce and, second, which criteria the courts used in decision-making. In the majority of cases, the children were entrusted to their mother's care after the divorce (73%–87%). Data from official statistics for Yugoslavia (Serbia and Montenegro) for example in 1986 are: 75% of children entrusted to their mother's care and 20% to their father's care; for Vojvodina: 80% of children to their mother's care and 14% to their father's care.[7] In 1996, for Yugoslavia, statistical data are as follows: 71% of children were entrusted to their mother's care and 23% to their father's care. Other children (to complete the 100%) were divided between mother and father.

Mutual consent of the parents was the most important basis for court decisions according to the study (up to 89% of the sample). The percentage of contested cases was small (6%). The most frequent criterion for entrusting the child to the father was parental consent (65%–90%), as well as in cases of entrusting the child to the mother. The courts accepted parental consent to entrust the child to the mother without special explanation, but parental consent to entrust the child to the father needed to be supported by some other facts. For example, the *status quo* criterion (the child already living with the father), the fact that the mother had abandoned the child and the family, the fact that the father's parents (especially grandmother) took care of the child was of importance. This implies that the courts' view towards women was that women played a more important role than men in the everyday care of children. It is significant that the court of second instance (Supreme Court of Vojvodina) often confirmed the lower court's decisions on the commitment of the child to the mother (about 70%), but not to the father (only about 30%). A frequent criterion for entrusting the child to the mother's care was the tender age of the child.

Furthermore, the investigation focused on the wish of the child as one of the criteria for entrusting the child after divorce. At the time of investigation, Vojvodina had its own family legislation. The relevant article concerning the wish

---

5   Divorce rates per 1,000 inhabitants, *Annual Statistics* of Yugoslavia 1998. In 1999 the divorce rate per 1,000 inhabitants was 0.85 (unofficial data) Federal Statistical Agency, newspaper *Blic* 4 January 2000.

6   For example, in 1987, in Novi Sad there were 2,057 new marriages and 732 divorces (in other words, the number of divorces was 35.6% of the number of new marriages). In Subotica there were 1,111 new marriages and 416 divorces (37.4%); in Vojvodina this percentage was 26.8%; *Annual Statistics* of Yugoslavia, 1988.

7   In Vojvodina the divorce rate is higher and the percentage of children entrusted to the mother's care is higher as compared with the country as a whole. This might be due to the fact that Vojvodina is economically a more developed region and consequently women are probably more emancipated. On the contrary, in the Province of Kosovo, in 1986 a much higher percentage of children are entrusted to the father's care – 71%.

of the child stated that the guardianship authority, when making the decision about with whom the child would live, if parents could not agree, should consider the wish of the child of ten years of age and older.[8] This rule was relevant in court proceedings as well. The results of the investigation showed that the wishes of the child were rarely examined (12%–25% of all children of ten years of age and older). In uncontested cases the court almost never examined the wishes of the child. It could be presumed, however, that the wishes of the child were examined by the guardianship authority, during the process of mediation, in a number of cases, though there was no such evidence in the report. In one of the published court decisions, which is significant for this issue, it is stated that the court in decision-making should start primarily with the wishes of an older minor (14 years of age) as to with whom he/she wishes to live.[9] As mentioned earlier, in the Serbian Act it is stipulated that the court should consider the emotional needs and wishes of the child about which the court should ask for the opinion of professionals when it is necessary. But it is not stipulated at what age the wishes of the child become relevant.

IV THE LEGAL STATUS OF THE NON-CUSTODIAL/NON-RESIDENTIAL PARENT

There are two legal issues relevant to the position of the 'other parent'. One is the decision on entrusting the child to one parent's care and upbringing. This decision may be delivered by the court in divorce proceedings, or by the guardianship authority in the case of parents living apart, if they cannot reach an agreement on the child's residence. In these cases (if there is a decision), it might be said that one parent becomes the custodial and the other non-custodial, again bearing in mind that these terms do not exist as such in Yugoslav law.

The other issue relevant to the status of parents is that of with whom the child lives. This is important if parents do not live together, but are not divorced, or if parents are not married. In these situations the parents have the legal opportunity to agree on the matter with whom the child would live, without asking the help of the court or guardianship authority. It might be said that in this way parents actually decide on the question of which parent is residential and which is non-residential, again bearing in mind that these terms does not exist in Yugoslav law.

It is important to stress that the legal positions of non-custodial or non-residential parents are equal. The parent to whom a child is entrusted, or with whom a child lives, exercises the parental right *ex lege*. The non-custodial or non-residential parent loses the possibility of exercising the parental right, but does not lose the right itself (Article 124 LMFR). He/she has a right to a maintain personal relationship with the child, has a right to object to a decision made by the parent to whom the child is entrusted, the right to ask for modification of the court order on care and upbringing of the child and the obligation to maintain the child.

---

8   Article 9 of the Law of the relationship between parents and children, *Official Gazette* of Vojvodina 2/75.

9   Supreme Court of Vojvodina Rev. 514/81, *Court practice* 1/1982.

As well as the above-mentioned rights and duties the non-custodial or non-residential parent has one specific right, which is a right to make decisions in agreement with the parent to whom the child is entrusted (Article 126, LMFR).[10]

The decision about the arrangements regarding personal relationships with the child is primarily by parents' consent (Article 131/1). There are possibilities, however, that this decision will be made by the court (Article 125/3) or guardianship authority (Article 131/1). The court decides on the personal relationship between parent and child in divorce proceedings or other marital proceedings (annulment of marriage, etc). This decision is delivered only when the particular situation demands it. This is so where the other parent obstructs the maintaining of the personal relationship or if the court determines that this decision is necessary for the child's protection. The guardianship authority decides about the arrangements regarding the personal relationship in other situations where parents can not reach an agreement. The guardianship authority might decide on modification of the order in all situations, whether the order is delivered by the court or by the guardianship authority (Article 131/2). According to Yugoslav law, the primary criterion for maintaining the personal relationship is the interest of the child. Contact might be reduced or forbidden only for protection of the child's health or other important interests of the child (Article 131/3).

The other right of the parent who does not exercise the parental right, is the right to object to a decision made by the other parent (Article 127, LMFR). If he/she does not agree with a step or an action of the other parent, it is possible to inform the guardianship authority about that. The guardianship authority is obliged to decide whether this step or action is in the interest of the child or not.

Parents have the right to ask for modification of the court order on the care and upbringing of the child (Article 125/4, LMFR). The court may change the earlier decision on care and upbringing if circumstances have changed and the order requires modification.

Parents have an obligation to maintain their minor child (Article 298, LMFR). This obligation may continue until the child reaches 26 years of age, if the child attends school or university. If the child is not a minor, but because of illness or physical or mental deficiency is not able to maintain himself/herself, parents are obliged to maintain him/her as well (Article 299, LMFR). In deciding on maintenance the court is obliged to define the needs of a child, particularly bearing in mind his/her age and needs for education (Article 310/2, LMFR). According to the amended LMFR maintenance is determined as a percentage of monthly salary (15%–50%). Where the maintenance provider does not have a regular income, the sum is based on the guaranteed republic payment, without the percentage limit.[11]

---

10   This right was introduced in family law in Serbia in 1980 and in Montenegro in 1989.

11   Amendments in *Official Gazette* of Serbia 22/93, 35/94. For more on the reforms relating to maintenance see: G Kovacek Stanic, 'Legal reforms concerning the family', *The International Survey of Family Law 1995*, ed A Bainham (Martinus Nijhoff Publishers, 1997) at 534–535.

V   CONCEPT OF CONSENSUAL DECISION-MAKING

The concept of consensual decision-making includes the right of the parent to make decisions on matters of great importance for the child's upbringing together with the parent with whom the child lives. For exercising this right there is one condition, which is to fulfil parental obligations towards the child. It is not specified in legislation which obligations must be fulfilled, or what matters are considered as matters of great importance for the child's upbringing.

Concerning obligations, maintenance is primarily implied. It is interesting to analyse whether there is any other obligation which might be relevant to the exercise of the right of consensual decision-making. According to the law, parent and child should maintain a personal relationship. It could be said that in Yugoslav law this personal relationship is considered as the right of the child and the right of the parent, yet even this is not explicitly stated in Yugoslav codes. There is only reference to the future regulation of the personal relationship between child and parent.[12] Yugoslav theory supports the view that maintaining the personal relationship is the right of the child as well as the right of the parent.[13] According to the UN Convention on the Rights of the Child, this right is considered as the right of the child (Article 9, para 3). As Yugoslavia has ratified the Convention, this is true for Yugoslav law, too. But there is the question whether maintaining the personal relationship with the child is an obligation for the parent as well as a right. It might be said that maintaining the personal relationship should be considered as an obligation for both parents. The parent with whom the child lives is obliged to allow contact and the parent who does not live with the child is obliged to maintain a personal relationship with the child. If this approach is right, then the right of the parent to consensual decision-making would also be dependent on whether that parent maintains the personal relationship with the child or not.

Consensual decisions include matters of great importance for a child's upbringing. It could be said that matters on education (eg changing or leaving school), health (eg surgical intervention), residence (eg a move to a different town or country), might be considered as the most relevant.

The question arises as to what would happen in the situation where parents are not able to agree on an important matter. Yugoslav Acts do not give a direct answer to this question. The article which is of help is the article which stipulates that the parent may complain about the decision made by the other parent to the guardianship authority. If this is the case, the guardianship authority will decide if the step which the other parent has taken is in the child's interest or not (Article 127, LMFR). A clearer solution was the one which was stipulated by the former Law of Slovenia, as there was a direct answer to the question of parental conflict. Where this was the case the decision would be one for social protection.[14] This solution seems more adequate to the concept of consensual decision-making. The solution of Serbian law implies that one parent alone makes some step, and the

---

12   Article 125/3,4 and Article 131, LMFR.

13   Olga Cvejic Jancic, *Porodicno pravo II – Roditeljsko i starateljsko pravo*, 1998, p 62; Marija Draskic, *Porodicno pravo*, 1998, p 272, Komar, Korac, Ponjavic, *Porodicno pravo*, 1996, p 179.

14   Law on Marriage and Family Relations, *Official Gazette* of Slovenia 15/76, Article 114/4.

other complains about the existing decision, which the guardianship authority has to re-examine. In a situation of disagreement of parents living together, the decision would be for the guardianship authority (Article 123/1, LMFR). This solution also seems adequate for parents who do not live together.

The right to decision-making depends on whether the parent fulfils his/her obligations towards the child. But, it seems important to consider the interest of the child in relation to consensual decision-making. For instance, if parents cannot agree on important matters, or if they are in constant conflict, it might be in the interest of a child that mutual decision-making should be abandoned. Unfortunately, this solution does not exist in the law. For comparison, the right to a personal relationship might be limited or temporarily abandoned according to the law, if that requires the protection of health or other important matter (Article 131/3, LMFR). Similar provisions might be advisable for the concept of mutual decision-making. If mutual decision-making is not in the interest of the child there might then be an option to restrict or abandon it.

In defining the position of parents who do not live together, it seems important to analyse the relationship between the right to decision-making and the right to represent a child. There is an article which explicitly states that all information and statements which have to be delivered to the minor child, if parents do not live together, should be delivered to the parent with whom the child lives (Article 118, LMFR). Furthermore, in the Yugoslav Citizenship Law there is an article which states that if parents are divorced, the application for release from Yugoslav citizenship for the minor child may be submitted only by the parent to whom the child is entrusted by court decision (Article 21/2).[15] Articles on delivering the information concerning the child to the parent with whom the child lives, and on submitting the application for release from Yugoslav citizenship by the parent to whom the child is entrusted, imply that the parent with whom the child lives, or the parent to whom the child is entrusted by court decision, represents the minor child exclusively.

However, the minor child can not be represented in some family law situations in which the child acts independently. At the earliest, the child of ten years of age gives his/her consent to adoption and to change of his/her name. The child of 16 years of age may seek permission for marriage (Article 49/2, LMFR). The boy of 16 may acknowledge his paternity if he has the ability of judgment (Article 93, LMFR). The child of 16 years of age may give his/her agreement to the acknowledgement of paternity (Article 95/1, LMFR). The girl of 16 years of age may seek an abortion (Article 2 of the Abortion Act).[16]

Theoretically speaking, the right to make decisions in agreement with the parent to whom a child is entrusted causes a dilemma concerning the legal concept of the exercise of the parental right. (There is no dilemma concerning the parental

---

15 The Yugoslav Citizenship Law, *Official Gazette* of Yugoslavia 33/1996. Translation to English in *Odgovor*, Guidebook for refugees, No 2, Belgrade 1997. For this procedure, the consent of the other parent, as well as the opinion of the guardianship authority and the consent of the child over 14 years of age are required (Article 21/1). If the other parent does not agree with the release, or his residence is unknown, or he is deprived of civil capacity or the parental right, the request for release of the child from Yugoslav citizenship must be accepted if, according to the opinion of the guardianship authority, this is in the child s interest (Article 21/3).

16 Abortion Act, *Official Gazette* of Serbia 16/95.

right itself, as it remains *ex lege* with both parents.) According to law, the parent to whom a child is entrusted exercises the parental right. Questions arise as to the character of the right to make decisions in agreement with the parent to whom a child is entrusted: is this right one of the components of the exercise of the parental right or not? If it is, the parent with whom the child does not live exercises the parental right as well, but partially, as he/she has the decision-making right, but not some others which the custodial parent has (to live with a child, day-to-day care, decision-making on not important matters, representation).

VI CONCLUSION

The equal legal status of parents in their relationship with the child seems right and desirable in spite of modified or different circumstances between the parents themselves. The interest of the child in most cases would be to establish or maintain a legal and factual relationship with both parents regardless of different situations: where parents are married, never married, cohabiting, separated or divorced. In this way, the legal position of the non-custodial or non-residential parent is strengthened. In Yugoslavia, the solution which strengths the position of this parent is mutual decision-making on important matters concerning the child.

However, Yugoslav family Acts do not address the possibility of obtaining joint custody after divorce or separation. Bearing in mind the differences in various joint custody concepts, some similarity may be seen when comparing the Yugoslav solution to joint custody concepts. This similarity may be seen in mutual decision-making on important issues concerning the child. The main difference seems to be that physical custody cannot be joint according to the explicit Yugoslav solutions (according to court practice a child is always entrusted to one parent), unlike joint custody concepts which imply the possibility of joint physical custody. The other difference concerns representation of the child. According to the Yugoslav concept, the parent to whom the child is entrusted for care and upbringing represents the child, while according to joint custody concepts both parents have joint legal custody.

The concept of mutual decision-making seems not precise enough. First, the way of resolving problems if parents are not able to make mutual decisions is not clear. Secondly, there is no solution for the situation where mutual decision-making is not in the interest of the child. There is also the theoretical dilemma about the exercise of the parental right. Is it only the parent with whom the child lives who exercises the parental right, or also the parent who has a decision-making right? Consequently, one might suggest that this concept could be improved or even abandoned in future and replaced with the concept of the joint exercise of the parental right (joint custody), as a modern solution for the legal position of divorced or separated parents.

ZAMBIA

PROTECTING THE MINOR CHILD'S INHERITANCE RIGHTS

*Chuma Himonga**

I   INTRODUCTION

The protection of the rights of the child represents one of the most significant developments in Zambian family law in the last decade. This is attested to by the enactment of the laws of succession in 1989, whose primary focus is the inheritance rights of the children of the deceased and their surviving parents;[1] the law on maintenance of children of customary marriages in 1991[2] and the law on affiliation and maintenance of extra-marital children in 1995.[3] No doubt, the impetus for the legislative protection of children partly emanates from the ratification by Zambia of the Convention on the Rights of the Child. In this respect, the latest statute on children, the Affiliation and Maintenance of Children Act, states in its preamble the aim of bringing 'the law of Zambia into conformity with the United Nations Convention on the rights of the child to which Zambia is a State Party'.[4] These developments are furthermore justified by the need to protect children from deprivation in their families in a country where there is a dearth of State social security for the care of its child population.

The aim of this paper is to discuss the protection of minor[5] children's rights in the law of succession enacted in 1989, and to highlight some of the problems and challenges of this endeavour that nearly a decade of the operation of this law has shown.[6] This law consists of the Intestate Succession Act[7] and the Wills and Administration of Testate Estates Act[8] (hereafter referred to as ISA and WATEA respectively). Its importance is marked by the fact that it regulates the inheritance rights of the majority of children in Zambia.[9] Furthermore, in the social and economic contexts of Zambia, inheritance rights may be seen not merely as a

---

*   Associate Professor, University of Cape Town.

1   See especially the Intestate Succession Act, chapter 59 of the Laws of Zambia.

2   See Local Courts Amendment Act no 8 of 1991 (Local Courts Act, chapter 29 of the Laws of Zambia).

3   See the Affiliation and Maintenance of Children Act, chapter 64 of the Laws of Zambia.

4   Ibid.

5   A minor is defined as a person under the age of 18 years. See the Intestate Succession Act, *supra*, section 3 and the Wills and Administration of Testate Estates Act, chapter 60 of the Laws of Zambia section 3.

6   The research on which this paper is based was conducted in 1997 and 1998.

7   *Supra.*

8   *Supra.*

9   The Intestate Succession Act, for example, applies to children of indigenous Zambians (that is, the 73 ethnic groups) who make up the majority of the country's population.

matter of rights that should be protected by the law as such, but also as a way of realising the child's rights to life and survival. This is because in many cases inherited property constitutes a major, if not only, resource for the material support of the deceased person's minor children and other dependant members of his or her nuclear and extended families[10] for two main reasons. First, kinship solidarity and mutual support obligations have increasingly given way to individualism under conditions of social and economic change.[11] The second reason is related to the problems of the impoverishment of most families, the ever rising cost of raising children in modern economic conditions and the lack of state social security and public resources to support indigent children and citizens generally.[12]

II   THE LEGAL FRAMEWORK OF THE CHILD'S INHERITANCE RIGHTS

It is necessary to isolate children's inheritance rights from those of the adult members of their families in Zambia for two reasons. The first reason is that, with the ratification by Zambia of the CRC, the child may be considered to have become a rights bearer. The emphasis can no longer be on the protection of the rights of the child through his or her parents, or guardians, or other adult members of society responsible for him or her. The second reason is the need to minimise the possibility of conflicts between the rights and interests of minor children and those of adult members of the deceased's family. Obviously, children's interests are the most vulnerable in any such conflicts because of the lack of capacity and maturity of children to manage their own interests without assistance by adult family members. The following subsections show how Zambian law has attempted to isolate and protect the inheritance rights of children.

A   Substantive rights

The right of the child to inherit from his or her family member depends on whether the family member made a will or not. A person may make a will disposing of his or her property in favour of his or her minor children. The WATEA[13] regulates the formalities for making wills. This Act applies to all

---

10   Among indigenous Zambians, the extended family may be defined as members of a person's lineage or group of kin who are lineally descended from a common male or female ancestor, and among whom exist recognisable mutual rights and obligations. On the other hand, the nuclear family means a man and his wife (or wives) and their respective children or their children between them, or a man or woman and his or her children in a single-male or single-female headed household.

11   See CN Himonga, *Family and Succession Laws in Zambia: Developments Since Independence*, Munster Lit (1995), 81–109; BA Rwezaura *et al*, 'Parting the Long Grass: Revealing and Reconceptualising the African Family' (1995), *Journal of Legal Pluralism and Unofficial Law*, No 35, 25–73.

12   See Himonga, *supra*, 81–109.

13   *Supra*.

persons in the Republic.[14] However, for various reasons, most Zambians do not make wills.[15] Intestate succession is, therefore, the dominant form of devolution of property after death.

Both the English law and Zambian legislation govern intestate succession. English law, which was in force on 17 August 1911, including the Statutes of Distribution of 1670–85, which govern succession to personal property, forms part of Zambian law.[16] This body of law, however, applies largely to non-Africans (ie whites). The majority of indigenous Zambians (ie Africans) are governed by the Intestate Succession Act of 1989,[17] which has abolished the customary law of succession, apart from a few exceptions.[18] This Act, therefore, governs the inheritance rights of the majority of children in Zambia today, and it is, to all intents and purposes, the most important piece of legislation on the inheritance rights of children.

The main scheme of distribution of the estate under the Intestate Succession Act is governed by section 5, according to which children of the deceased person inherit 50% of his or her estate in such proportions as are commensurate with each child's age, educational needs or both.[19] Children may receive further portions of the estate in the following circumstances.[20] Where the deceased is not survived by a spouse, the children are entitled to 20% of the estate, in proportions commensurate with their respective ages or educational needs or both; where parents do not survive the deceased, the children receive 10% of the estate;[21] and where dependants do not survive the deceased, the children receive 5% of the estate.[22] Additionally, the children (along with their surviving parents) are entitled to personal chattels of the deceased parent. These are defined as clothing, articles of personal use or adornment, furnishings and all other articles of household use or decoration, simple agricultural equipment, hunting equipment, books, and motor vehicles, but excluding chattels used for business purposes, money or securities for money.[23]

---

14 The Act repealed the Wills Act of 1837 of England which applied to Zambia by virtue of the English Law (Extent of Application) Act Cap 4 of the Laws of Zambia.
15 See CN Himonga, 'The law of succession and inheritance in Zambia and the proposed reform' (1989), *International Journal of Law and the Family*, 3, 160–176 at 161–2.
16 See the English Law (Extent of Application) Act, chapter 11 of the Laws of Zambia.
17 See section 2 of the Act.
18 Customary law continues to apply to family property, which is defined as any property which belongs to the members collectively of a particular family of the deceased or is held for the benefit of such members and any receipts or proceeds from such property; land held by the deceased under customary law; and property held by the deceased as part of chieftainship property (See section 2(2) of the Act).
19 See section 5 of the Act.
20 Sections 6 and 7 of the Act.
21 Being half of the parents' share of the estate of 20%.
22 Being half of the dependants' share of the estate of 10%.
23 See section 3. In the case of a monogamous marriage the spouse and children are entitled to this property absolutely in equal shares. In the case of a polygamous marriage, each surviving widow or her children by the deceased, or the widow and her children together, are entitled absolutely to the personal chattels, which were used by the deceased, the widow and children of the particular household. All of the widows and/or their children are then entitled to the deceased's common property, defined as the personal chattels used in common by him and all his wives and children of the polygamous households (see section 10 of the Act).

Perhaps most importantly, children are entitled (together with the surviving spouse(s)) to the house of the deceased, and they have a right to choose a house of their own liking where the estate has more than one house.[24] In the case of the deceased being survived by more than one child, the house is to be held by the children as tenants in common, presumably with each child[25] holding jointly an equal share. Finally, the children (and the surviving spouse) are the sole beneficiaries in the case of small estates, valued at K30,000.[26]

The major criticism that may be made against the rules governing the inheritance of personal chattels and houses is that they aggregate the rights of children with those of their surviving parents. In fact some surviving parents do not seem to treat their own interests in the deceased spouse's estate separately from the interests of their minor children in that estate. The result is that children's interests may be compromised. This is apparent from *Zulu v Zulu*.[27] The deceased was survived by the widow and her minor child. The deceased's father and his family took away all the personal chattels of the deceased before the commencement of the administration of the estate. The widow sued the deceased's father in the High Court for the return of the goods in question. In her submission, she stated that she was prepared to waive her right to the property in question, except a number of specified items. Since the property under negotiation was the entire personal estate of the deceased, it obviously included the share for the minor child. The court granted her application, with the result that the estate to which the child was entitled was negotiated away without proper representation of the child's interests.

Although the mother was entitled as the natural guardian of the minor to administer his personal property as she saw fit, in the interests of the minor, the fact that she made no reference to the minor's share of the estate in her submissions raises the question whether she did not, in fact, identify the minor's interests with her own interests. Furthermore, the law contemplates[28] that the guardian or parent shall have power to hold, and therefore, to manage the minor's share of the estate only after the administration of the estate in which the minor is entitled to inherit. In this case the mother's action was not only taken before the administration of the estate, but it also made such administration unnecessary. This case, obviously, also shows the lack of adequate protection of minor children by the High Court, which is the upper guardian of such children at common law. The High Court could have intervened, in the best interests of the child, to ensure that the deceased's estate was properly administered and not 'distributed' in the manner it was.

To a limited extent, section 42(d) of the ISA addresses the problem of the lack of disaggregation of inherited interests by providing for a mechanism by which the interests of beneficiaries to the estate may be segregated. This section provides that the court has power, upon application by an interested person, to order the

---

24 Section 9 of the Act

25 Or each spouse and her children.

26 See section 11 of the Act. The Minister of Legal Affairs may vary this figure from time to time (see section 12 of the Act).

27 1995/HP/2901.

28 See section 5(2) of the Intestate Succession Act.

sale of the property belonging to the deceased person's estate for the purpose, *inter alia*, of distribution. An application under this section will enable minor children to receive their own share of the estate for which the surviving parent or any other person responsible for the administration of the child's property may be called to account.

Section 42(d) is also of practical importance to the distribution of estates involving potentially conflicting relationships. A typical case is that involving the deceased's extra-marital children or children from his or her earlier dissolved marriage, who are sometimes disinherited by the surviving spouse and his or her children. In cases of this nature, the surviving spouse and his or her children refuse to let the children concerned live in the deceased's house. The sale of the whole estate in terms of section 42(d) and the distribution of the proceeds to beneficiaries would serve the interests of the children excluded from the deceased's immovable property.

With regard to the holding of minors' inherited property, the Act provides that the minor's share of the estate is to be held by the mother, father or guardian in trust for the minor until he or she ceases to be a minor.[29] These persons are, therefore, the recognised 'trustees' for purposes of holding children's inheritances.

Another area of the law of succession important to the protection of children is that of the provision of maintenance for the dependants of the deceased. Both the WATEA and the ISA provide for rights of maintenance of certain family members of the deceased in default of reasonable provision being made for their maintenance by the will or by the intestate succession rules. If the will does not make adequate provision[30] for the testator's dependants (including children), an application may be made to the High Court for reasonable maintenance out of the estate for such dependants.[31] The WATEA defines 'dependant' as 'wife, husband, child or parent' of the deceased. It is noteworthy that of the deceased's extended family, only parents qualify to apply for reasonable maintenance out of the estate of the deceased. This excludes any claims from relatives to whom the deceased may otherwise have owed a duty of support (such as, for example, sisters, brothers, and aunts), based on kinship obligations consistent with African culture. Although decided before the coming into force of the WATEA, the decision of the Supreme Court in *M and Seven Others v H and M*[32] is instructive and persuasive authority on this matter.

The application for maintenance of dependants was brought under the Inheritance (Family Provision) Act 1938 of England which was in force until it was repealed by implication by the WATEA. The applicants for reasonable maintenance out of the deceased's estate included the testator's sisters, brothers and aunt. The beneficiaries of the estate were the testator's wife and children. The 1938 Act empowers the court to make provision for the reasonable maintenance of a dependant (ie a spouse or child) of the testator who was not provided for by the testator either during his or her life or by his or her will. In the court *a quo* (ie the

---

29 Ibid.
30 There is no indication of how the courts will determine what is 'adequate provision' for the purposes of this Act and the Intestate Succession Act.
31 See section 20 of the Act.
32 SCZ/11/1991.

High Court) the applicants referred to section 12 of the High Court Act,[33] which states that all statutes of the Parliament of the United Kingdom in force in the country are to be applied subject to 'local jurisdiction and circumstances'. They argued that on the basis of this provision judges must enlarge the list of dependants in the 1938 Act to include the deceased's brothers, sisters and aunt, taking into account, *inter alia*, the kinship and financial claims made on the deceased by the people concerned when he was still alive. The court *a quo* dismissed the application on the grounds, *inter alia*, that to enlarge the class of potential claimants would amount to a change in the substance of the will which was unwarranted by the language of section 12 of the High Court Act above. The Supreme Court upheld this decision on appeal. It held that the proposed enlargement of the 1938 Act was not envisaged by section 12 of the High Court Act. In its reasoning it states that to add the words sisters, brothers, and aunt to the 1938 Act would result in the alteration or amendment of the Act, and that assistance to relatives during one's life does not necessarily create automatic obligations after one's death. While appellants may have a moral entitlement to the estate, they have no such entitlement in law, let alone in the will.

The effect of a narrow interpretation of dependants in the WATEA as suggested above is that the children of the deceased will have a bigger size of the deceased's estate from which to benefit (if they are beneficiaries) or from which to claim maintenance as dependants by application to the High Court, if necessary.

It is also noteworthy that provision for reasonable maintenance under the WATEA may, in the case of a minor child, continue until the child attains the age of 18 years or until he or she completes school or university, whichever is the later. In the case of a minor under a disability, the provision for maintenance terminates only when the disability ceases.[34]

The provisions of the WATEA for reasonable maintenance apply *mutatis mutandis* to intestate succession.[35] A dependant whose portion of the estate under the inheritance rules would be too small, having regard to the degree of his or her dependence on the deceased, can apply to the court for reasonable maintenance out of the deceased's estate. For this purpose, however, a dependant is defined as '(a) a person who was *maintained by* [the deceased person] immediately prior to his death and who was ... *living with [him]*;[36] or (b) a minor whose education was being provided for by [the] deceased person; and who is incapable ... of maintaining himself'.[37] This definition is wider and more inclusive than the definition of dependant under the WATEA. It is not clear why this term is defined differently for the purposes of testate and intestate succession. From the discussion of the corresponding provision of the WATEA above, the disadvantage of the wider definition of dependant for purposes of intestate succession is obvious. In the context of the African culture and family structure, a much larger group of the deceased's relatives may qualify for reasonable maintenance, thereby reducing the size of the intestate estate from which the minor children of the

---

33   Chapter 27 of the Laws of Zambia.
34   See section 20(2)(ii)(iii).
35   See section 5(1) of the Act and section 20 of the WATEA.
36   The emphasis is my own.
37   See section 3 of the Act.

deceased could benefit. There seems, however, to be no justification for this way of depleting the intestate estate of the deceased to the detriment of his or her minor children. A special consideration in this regard is the economic deprivation and vulnerability of most children after the death of their parent(s). Moreover, not all of the dependants who were *maintained by, and living with*, the deceased before his or her death may be minors who would require support. Such people may have been maintained by, and lived with, the deceased as a matter of family solidarity within the context of the African culture only.

On the other hand, the ambit of the right to reasonable maintenance in respect of intestate succession clearly extends to children other than children of the deceased person. This may be seen as an attempt not to draw distinctions between children who are in need of support by their families, whether these are children of members of the nuclear or extended family.

Finally, it is necessary to point out that legislation does not discriminate against various categories of children for purposes of inheritance. Both the WATEA and the Intestate Succession Act grant equal rights of inheritance to legitimate, illegitimate and adopted children, and to children who are conceived but not yet born at the time of the death of the parent.[38] With regard to a child who is conceived but not yet born, presumably, the child must subsequently be born alive. This appears to be an incorporation of the *nasciturus* fiction originating from Roman Dutch law.[39] The Intestate Succession Act further grants maintenance rights to children, for whom the deceased has assumed legal obligation to maintain, whether they are his children or not, as shown by the definition of dependant above.

B Administration of estates and appointment and responsibilities of guardians

The WATEA and the Intestate Succession Act contain provisions for the protection of minor children's inheritances in relation to probate and administration of estates, and the appointment and responsibilities of guardians of minor children of deceased persons.

Section 30 of the WATEA restricts the grant of probate or letters of administration in respect of estates with minority interests (that is, estates in which there are beneficiaries who are minors) under a will to 'a trust corporation solely or jointly with an individual or to not less than two individuals'.[40] This section seems to override section 29(1), which states that 'probate may be granted by a court only to an executor appointed by a will ...'. Presumably, the court will not appoint as an executor of an estate with a minority interest a person appointed by the will if that person is an individual. Section 30 seems to ensure that estates with minority interests are not administered by one individual. This minimises chances of maladministration and misappropriation of the estates concerned.

---

38 See section 3 of the WATEA and the Intestate Succession Act respectively.

39 *Nasciturus pro iam nato habetur quotiens de commodo eius agitur.* This fiction has been extended to South African law, for example. See Belinda Van Heerden et al *Boberg's Law of Persons and the Family* (second edition), Juta and Co Ltd (1999), 30–41.

40 See section 30(1) of the Act.

The grant of letters of administration of intestate estates is regulated by section 16 of the Intestate Succession Act. It provides that if there is a minority interest in the estate, letters of administration shall be granted to the Administrator-General, to a trust corporation solely or jointly with an individual or to not less than two individuals. In so far as the section talks of the '*grant of letters of administration*', it clearly requires all estates with minority interests to be administered under a court order, and not merely under a family 'order', as happens in many cases in practice. The purpose of this section would appear to be the same as the somewhat similar section of the WATEA,[41] discussed above. However, the courts do not in practice generally follow the provisions for the appointment of administrators or personal representatives in estates with minority interests. In particular, they hardly ever demand the appointment of more than one administrator or personal representative for such estates, thereby undermining the security of minors' inheritances.

With regard to the appointment of guardians, the WATEA empowers the High Court to appoint a guardian for a minor child of the deceased to replace a testamentary guardian who has acted improperly.[42] Presumably, this power includes the replacement of a testamentary guardian who is guilty of maladministration or misappropriation of the estate. The Intestate Succession Act empowers the court to appoint any person as guardian of the minor children of the deceased, and to order the transfer of the minor's inherited property to that guardian.[43] This Act does not, however, empower the court to replace the guardian who acts improperly in the same way as it may replace the guardian of the child of a testator. It is submitted that the court may nevertheless do this in terms of its common law jurisdiction as upper guardian of all minor children, in the interests of the child.

The power of the court to remove and replace the guardian for maladministration and misappropriation of the minor's inheritance is an important protection to minors' inheritance interests, in view of the common problem of misappropriation of deceased estates by administrators and other adult members of the deceased's family.[44] This protection is augmented in both testate and intestate succession by provisions which prohibit a guardian, administrator or personal representative from deriving any pecuniary benefit from his or her office.[45] Furthermore, in both cases the court may set aside any direct or indirect purchase by the guardian, administrator or personal representative of the property of the deceased or of the minor.[46]

The law also creates civil remedies and criminal sanctions to ensure a proper administration of estates and to safeguard the children's interests against misappropriation by trustees and guardians of minor beneficiaries. A personal representative, administrator or guardian who deprives beneficiaries who are minors of their share of the estate or, in the case of intestate estates, any person

---

41   That is, section 30(1).
42   See sections 55(1) and 64(d) of the Act.
43   See section 32(1)(2) of the Act.
44   See generally, Himonga, 1995, *supra* 143–177.
45   See section 57(1) of the WATEA and section 34(1) of the Intestate Succession Act.
46   See section 57(2) of the WATEA and section 34(2) of the Intestate Succession Act.

who meddles with the estate and deprives the beneficiaries of the use of the property, commits an offence, punishable by a fine or imprisonment or both.[47] In addition, the court may order the offender to restore the property connected with the commission of the offence to the minor or order him or her to compensate the minor a sum of money determined by the court for the property concerned.[48] The civil remedies under statutory law, do not, of course, exclude the remedy of restitution that may be obtained under general principles of law.

These statutory and common law protective measures have, however, not completely deterred the misappropriation of children's inherited property by administrators and guardians. In many cases the culprits do not restore the property to the children even when, having squandered the said property, they are ordered by the courts to do so.[49] And there are hardly any cases in which a person who misappropriated the property was sued to compensate the beneficiaries to the estate, presumably because it may not be worthwhile suing such people. Closely related to the problem of misappropriation of children's inherited property by guardians and administrators is the general problem of 'property grabbing', which is still rife in many families. Numerous cases are reported to non-governmental organisations such as the Women's Legal Clinic and the Young Women's Christian Association in Lusaka, as well as to the Administrator-General's Office, in which the property belonging to deceased estates is 'grabbed' unlawfully by members of the deceased's family before the administration of the estate commences or during this process. As a result the beneficiaries, including the minor children of the deceased, lose their inheritances.

Two factors may account for the problems of misappropriation of children's inheritances and meddling with estates. The first is the inherent weakness in the inheritance legislation's protective machinery itself. The penalties for misappropriating estates are insignificant. This was recognised by the High Court in *Gabula v Mwanza*[50] in which it was stated that the law does not provide sufficient protection against the grabbing of deceased persons' property.[51] The court accordingly suggested that the law (in this case the Intestate Succession Act) be amended to provide stiffer punishment of people convicted of the offence associated with property grabbing. The second factor concerns the lack of assistance to minors to protect their inheritance from misappropriation by administrators or personal representatives of estates or by the 'trustees' of their property. In some cases this lack of assistance results from the fact that adult members of the family who would otherwise assist the children are caught between conflicting loyalties and interests within the family. The tension seems to be between respect for the African family and its values and the protection of children's individual inheritance rights in changing conditions. In this regard some adults see and feel the need to protect minor children as individuals with a right to inherit. However, their allegiance to the extended family stops them from assisting

---

47 See sections 14 and 35(1) of the Intestate Succession Act and 58(1) of the WATEA.

48 See sections 35(2) and 58(2) of the Intestate Succession Act and the WATEA respectively. The exception is the offence of meddling with an intestate estate in which the court is, curiously, not empowered to make an order for these alternative civil remedies.

49 Interviews with official at the Women's Legal Clinic. See also Himonga, 1995, *supra*, 170–173.

50 1995/HP/3818.

51 See also Himonga, 1995, *supra*, 174.

minor children to litigate against administrators of their parents' estates or guardians who misappropriate their inheritances. Litigation enforcing children's individual rights against administrators is considered to be detrimental to the cohesion of the family.[52] Some adults who are sympathetic to children's individual rights are furthermore reluctant to take action to protect those rights to avoid alienating themselves from the rest of the family. The existence of this tension can only be because the family is still perceived to perform some important functions for some of its individual members.[53] However, the superior courts and the office of the Administrator-General seem to offer promising prospects for the protection of children's inheritance rights, as shown in the next section.

III PROTECTION OF INHERITANCE RIGHTS BY SUPERIOR COURTS AND ADMINISTRATOR-GENERAL

The disputes commonly taken to court are those of the appropriate person to be appointed as administrator of the estate, the distribution of the estate and property 'grabbing' by the deceased person's relatives. The local courts hear the majority of these disputes.[54] The local courts are the lowest courts in the judiciary. Their primary jurisdiction until 1989 was to apply customary law. Although these courts now have jurisdiction to apply the Intestate Succession Act,[55] their decisions in succession law are still largely influenced by customary law. Children hardly benefit from these decisions[56] because customary law denies children inheritance rights unless they are beneficiaries according to the customary principles of succession. Even when they are beneficiaries, their inheritance interests are sometimes not differentiated from those of the family members responsible for their care, to their detriment.

The property inherited by minor children under customary law is sometimes mixed up with the property of family members entrusted with such property or with the care of the child, with the result that when the initial 'trustees' die, the children's property is inherited as their own estate. This may happen when there is a change of individuals providing care to the child within the customary law framework. This change is hardly ever considered as a change of guardianship (in the western law sense) necessitating the transfer of powers for the administration of the minor's property to the new caregiver. An interview with one orphan, for example, revealed that his inheritance and the inheritances of the other siblings who were minors from their mother were entrusted to their grandmother (the administrator of the estate according to customary law), who had custody of the children after their mother's death. The children were later taken into their father's custody when their grandmother fell ill, but their grandmother remained the

---

52 This obviously ignores the fact that the misappropriation of deceased's estates and the failure of the administrator (or heir) of the estate to discharge his or her duty of support to the deceased's minor children is itself an indication of the disintegration of the family and its traditional values!

53 See Himonga, 1995, *supra*, 265–276; Rwezaura et al, 1995, *supra*.

54 See Himonga, 1995, *supra*, 159.

55 See section 43(2) of the Act.

56 See Himonga, 1995, *supra*, 156–158.

caretaker of their inherited property. The grandmother died three years later and all of her property (and that of the grandchildren) was inherited by her own children, sisters and brothers. The issue of the grandchildren's inherited property did not even arise at the family meeting which decided the question of the inheritance of the estate of the grandmother.

On the other hand, the inheritance disputes taken to the High Court are generally resolved according to the statutory law of succession. A number of cases may be cited to illustrate this. In *Sinkamba v Sinkamba*,[57] the High Court ordered the administrator of the estate to give the widow 50% of the estate representing the interest of three minor children in their deceased father's estate. A similar decision was reached in *Banda v Banda*.[58] In such cases the High Court not only protects the interests of the children against misappropriation by the administrator, but it also indirectly ensures that members of the deceased's family who are not beneficiaries according to statutory law do not inherit the estate under the influences of customary law. The latter is particularly evident from the decision of the High Court in *Gubula v Mwanza*.[59]

The applicant, the widow, sued the respondent, the deceased's brother, for restitution of the deceased's real and personal property and for the same to be given to her and the deceased's nine children, five of whom were minors. In her evidence the applicant alleged that the respondent took over the matrimonial home and chased her and the children out of it. He and his sisters then moved into the house, claiming it to be their own property (according to customary succession law). The respondent rented some of the rooms in the house and used the proceeds for himself and his sisters. He also 'grabbed' a large quantity of the deceased's personal property. The court condemned 'in the strongest terms the conduct of the respondent', which deprived 'the deceased's children their source of livelihood'. It held that the deceased's property belonged to the widow and the children and not to the administrator, and accordingly ordered the respondent to restore to the applicant all the personal chattels and the house.

In *Sibongo v Sibongo and Tembo*,[60] the High Court's supervision and control of the actual process of administration of the estate resulted in the protection of the minor child's interests from the competing interests of older siblings of the half blood. The deceased was survived by eight children from a previous marriage and one minor child from his widow. Both respondents were the deceased's children from a previous marriage, and one of them was the administrator. He had been appointed to this office by the local court. The applicant, the widow, alleged that the respondents had ignored the interests of the minor child. She applied for the revocation of the order of appointment of the administrator and to be appointed administrator of the estate instead. She also claimed, *inter alia*, that the educational needs and age of her child be taken into account in the distribution of the estate (apparently because the other children were all adults). The court rejected the claim for the revocation of the order of appointment of the administrator, but ordered that the administrator render an account in respect of

---

57   1996/HP/116.

58   1995/HP/3819.

59   *Supra*.

60   1995/HP/4432.

his administration of the estate within 30 days, failing which he would be deemed to have failed to administer the estate, and the applicant would then be appointed as joint administrator. The court also ordered that the minor child be given a share of the estate, although it did not make any reference to the applicant's claim for the special consideration of the minor's needs.

In *Sisya v Sisya*,[61] the deceased was survived by the widow and her five children and four adult children from a previous marriage. Three of the widow's children were aged 23 and 21 years,[62] but still at university and college respectively. The other two children were aged 17 and 13 years respectively and still at school. The children from the previous marriage had all lived with the widow and their father before his demise. With the consent of all of the deceased's children, the widow was appointed administrator of the estate by a court order. After her appointment, she completed building the house left by the deceased and moved in with all the children. Three of the children from the previous marriage married and moved out of the house. One of them (the first respondent) married, but brought his wife to live with the family. Otherwise all of the children from the previous marriage were independent and self-supporting. Subsequently, the widow experienced financial difficulties with school fees for children still at school. She proposed to all of the deceased's children that she should rent the house to raise the necessary school fees. The second respondent (one of the children from the previous marriage) objected to this arrangement and instructed the first respondent not to move out of the house. The respondents contended that the house belonged to their father and that it could not be rented, because all the money from the rent would only serve the interests of the youngest children (ie the widow's children). They demanded in addition that the house be registered in the first respondent's name. The widow sued the respondents for an order removing the first respondent from the house, so that she could rent the house to enable her to finance the education of the younger children. In her evidence she stated that she did not dispute the fact that the house belonged to her and all the children, but that she needed to rent it out for the children's education. She also stated that she would give any money from the rent that was not needed for the children's education to the children from the previous marriage as their share of the proceeds of their inheritance in the meantime.

The court ruled in favour of the interests of the minor children. In its judgment, it emphasised the need to protect minor children's interests, in order to secure their future and to advance their welfare. It further held that the actions of the respondents clearly amounted to interference with the administration of the estate by the administrator; the application by the administrator was within the law that required the protection of the younger members of the family, namely, the school-going children; the administrator was entitled to the support of the law through the courts, to ensure that her efforts in advancing the welfare of the young children were not undermined by the unco-operative older members of the deceased's family; the house in question be rented and the proceeds deposited in

---

61   1995/HP/683. In this case the Intestate Succession Act was applied retrospectively to the estate of a man who died before the Act came into force. For this reason, the decision is controversial. The Act has no retrospective application (see section 48 and Himonga, 1995, *supra*, pp 160–161). However, the judgment is relevant with regard to the substantive issues with which it dealt.

62   Two children aged 21 years were twins.

an interest-earning bank account, in the name of the applicant, to assist her with the children's school needs; and that the house be used as such until the youngest child attained the age of 21 years or was at college or university or married. It accordingly ordered any occupant of the house (presumably the first respondent and his family) to vacate the house within about three weeks from the date of the judgment, unless they were tenants paying rent. It also ordered that the police enforce its order in the event of any resistance by the respondents.

This case represents one of the most extensive protections given to children as beneficiaries to an intestate estate on account of their age and needs. It is also noteworthy that the court was concerned about the enforcement of its judgment as it also was in *Kaira v Kaira*.[63] In that case the widow sued the administrator to recover goods being kept by him and not distributed to herself, the children and other beneficiaries of the estate. Two of the children were minors.[64] The court ordered the sharing of the estate to all the beneficiaries according to the law, and issued a warrant of delivery of the goods against the respondent when he failed to deliver them according to the judgment. The High Court's concern about the enforcement of its decisions is commendable; decisions of courts in favour of beneficiaries to the estate are not always enforced in practice nor respected by the deceased person's relatives claiming a right to the estate under customary law.

Finally, in *Silwamba v Nalwamba*,[65] the deceased was survived by two minor children. His sister was appointed administrator of the estate by his family. The widow applied to the High Court for an order, *inter alia*, to be appointed joint administrator with the deceased's sister. The court granted the application. This case also shows that the court is apparently more willing to consider the joint administration of the estate when the applicant is a surviving parent than when he or she is another relative of the deceased. For example, in *M v M*[66] the court refused an application by the deceased's brother for joint administration with the widow. The widow applied for an order of appointment as administrator of her husband's estate. The deceased's brother made a counterclaim to be joined as co-administrator with the widow, so that he could protect the interests of the deceased's extra-marital children. The court refused the counterclaim for the reason, *inter alia*, that the Intestate Succession Act conferred a right on interested parties to apply for a court order, requiring the administrator to render an account of the administration of the estate.[67]

The role of the courts in the enforcement of children's rights is supplemented by that of the Administrator-General. This office administers a considerable number of estates, which are taken there for various reasons.[68] Mostly, however, the estates involve complaints of 'property grabbing'.[69] These estates are generally administered according to the provisions of the succession legislation. The minor children's shares are usually entrusted to surviving parents or other relatives

---

63 1995/HP/2679.
64 Although the paternity of one of them was apparently disputed by the administrator.
65 1995/HP/1816.
66 1990/HN/937.
67 See especially section 19(1)(c).
68 See Himonga 1995, *supra*, 161.
69 Ibid.

caring for the children.[70] The Administrator-General's office has also developed an innovative approach aimed at protecting the interests of minor children in real property. Where the estate includes a house, which devolved upon the minor, the house may be held by the Administrator-General in trust for the minor child until he or she attains majority. If the property is rented, the Administrator-General manages the rental business, and from time to time gives some money to the guardians or custodians for the support of the child if and when necessary. According to the Administrator-General's office, this minimises the possibility of misappropriation of the child's property by the 'trustees' of the property within the family setting. One such case was examined where the deceased man was survived by a widow, who remarried before the administration of the estate was completed, and a minor child aged nine years. The child was in the care of the deceased's brother, who wanted to have the deceased's house transferred to himself and the child. The Administrator-General's office, which administered the estate, transferred the house to itself, to hold it on behalf of the minor until he attained majority.

There are, however, two identifiable problems which threaten the security of children's interests in the estates administered by the Administrator-General. Firstly, like in all other cases, there is no guarantee against misappropriation of the children's property by 'trustees' to whom it is entrusted upon the distribution of the estate.[71] This is because there is no official monitoring of the activities of the 'trustees' of children's interests once the official administration process is over. This was not the position before the Succession Acts came into force because the Administrator-General's office did not consider itself bound to entrust a minor's share of the estate to his or her surviving parent or guardian as is now required by the law.[72] Instead it sent minors' inheritances to the Trust Account of the High Court, which controlled the administration of the proceeds of the minor's trust account *vis-à-vis* the guardians or parents who needed these proceeds for the support of minor children in their care.[73] It is clear from this that a vital mechanism of control against misappropriation of children's inheritances has been lost under the provisions of the new legislation.

Secondly, there is no proper documentation of the real property held by the Administrator-General when it follows the practice of holding property in trust for minor children noted above. This office does not, for instance, maintain a register of such property. Neither is there a way of informing the minors concerned about the property held by the office in trust for them. The lack of documentation of property may result in the internal official abuse of this innovative arrangement. Moreover, the children in whose trust the property is held may never ever get to know about the existence of this property.

---

70   See section 5(2) of the Act.
71   See section 5(2) which provides that the share of the estate of a minor child is to be held by a parent or guardian of the child.
72   See section 5(2).
73   Interviews with officials at the Administrator-General's office.

IV THE INFLUENCE OF CUSTOMARY LAW IN THE FAMILY

As already pointed out, customary law still has a great deal of influence in the administration and distribution of estates in the lower courts. Considerable challenges to the protection of children's statutory inheritance rights also present themselves in the African family where customary law has the most influence. In most cases, the estate of the deceased person is subjected to the application of customary law by the family of the deceased. Some of these estates are administered and distributed entirely by the family of the deceased and never get to be considered under statutory law for various reasons, including the general public's ignorance of the law. Three issues impact on children's inheritance rights in the family under the influence of customary law.

In the first place, members of the extended family, especially in matrilineal societies, still claim the right to inherit from each other according to customary law.[74] In this system of succession, children do not inherit from their fathers. Related to this is the problem that many estates continue to be administered by persons who would have benefited as heirs under customary law had the new legislation not come into force, rather than persons who are entitled to inherit under statutory law.[75] Although statutory law does not provide for this, the family continues to appoint administrators to estates of their members. This is also evident from some of the cases heard by the High Court above. Most of the persons who seek appointment and are actually appointed administrators by the courts in terms of the succession legislation will therefore have been initially appointed by the deceased's family according to customary law.[76] The involvement of the members of the deceased's family who are not beneficiaries of the estate in the administration of the estate creates one of the greatest opportunities for persons who are not entitled to the estate to misappropriate it, to the disadvantage of the beneficiaries, including minor children.[77]

Secondly, according to customary law, the administration of the estate is considered to be a matter for the deceased's kinship group. This means that the person closest to the child, namely, the surviving parent (who is never a member of the deceased's family), may be considered altogether an outsider for the purposes of the administration of the estate. This also denies such parent any power to intervene or have any say on behalf of the child when the family is discussing the distribution of the estate or when the administrator misappropriates the child's inheritance.

Thirdly, administrators of estates do not always distinguish their position of administrator from that of an heir. This is because according to customary law, the heir inherits the property of the deceased and also takes the responsibility of

---

74　This has also been one of the most serious problems experienced in the implementation of the Intestate Succession Law, 1985 of Ghana (PNDCL 111). See EVO Dankwa, 1994, 'The Application of Intestate Succession Law, 1985 (PNDCL) and its Social and Economic Impact' (manuscript). Like the Zambian Intestate Succession Act, the Intestate Succession Law of Ghana now provides for the rights of spouses and children of the deceased to inherit from him or her. Until this statutory reform, among the Akan, about 50% of the population, the matrilineage inherited.

75　See Himonga, 1995, *supra*, 156.

76　Ibid.

77　Ibid.

caring for the minor children of the deceased. There is, therefore, no concept of administrator of the estate under customary law as this is conceived under statutory law. The influence this conceptual muddle seems to have on the protection of children's rights under statutory law is that the administrators of estates consider themselves to be heirs of the estates concerned,[78] and to be entitled to the property of the deceased, subject to the duty to care for the deceased's minor children. They do not perceive their duty as being limited to the distribution of the estate to the beneficiaries as defined by legislation. This is particularly the case where there has been a dual appointment of the same administrator, first, by the family under customary law and, secondly, by a court in terms of statutory law, as stated above. The way these administrators deal with the estates is informed by the expectations of two contradictory systems of law, that is, customary law and statutory law. In most cases this creates opportunities for administrators claiming rights to the estate under customary law to access the estate and to appropriate it with the blessing of the courts that appointed them. Moreover, the courts do not often explain to administrators upon their appointment that they are not heirs but only administrators of the estates. Neither do they require the administrators they appoint to submit accounts for the distribution of the estate during the administration process or at the end of it.[79] Thus in reality some children are systematically excluded from inheritance on grounds of kinship, inheritance rules under customary law and the result of the complex interaction of customary and statutory laws.

V   CONCLUSION

The 1989 succession legislation in Zambia has a great deal of potential for protecting the inheritance rights of minor children. The enforcement by the superior courts and the Administrator-General in particular of these rights enhances their protection. However, much of this potential is not realised mainly because of factors connected with the lack of effective control of the process of administration of estates with minority interests; the lack of the effective representation of children's interests in the process of administration of estates; the absence of proper control of the administration of the inherited property of minors by private individuals and public institutions charged with this responsibility; and the continued influence of customary law on both the administration and distribution of estates. There is therefore a need for the Government to address these problems through appropriate measures to secure effectively children's inheritance rights. In this regard, it seems that there is a need to amend the succession legislation in various respects, as well as a need to review

---

78   See also *Women and Law in Southern Africa Research Project*, Inheritance in Zambia Law and
      Practice (May 1994)(research report) 164–165.

79   The Registrar of the High Court, Mrs Chawatama (personal communication in June 2000) has
      attributed this omission on the part of the courts to the absence of rules for the proper
      administration of the succession laws. These regulations have not been made to date despite the
      statutory provisions empowering the Minister and Chief Justice to make the rules for the
      administration of the WATEA and the Intestate Succession Act respectively.

the whole system of the holding and administration of the inherited property of minors.

ZIMBABWE

INHERITANCE AND MARITAL RAPE

*Fareda Banda**

It would not be an exaggeration to say that Zimbabwe has had a turbulent year. There have been many developments on the political front, not least the rejection of the government-sponsored reform of the constitution in February 2000. More pertinent to the present discussion have been both progressive and retrogressive legal developments that came courtesy of the Supreme Court and High Court of Zimbabwe respectively. This paper considers two cases that have had an important impact on family law in Zimbabwe. The first is a decision[1] of the full bench of the Supreme Court looking at the issue of inheritance whilst the second case[2] concerns the issue of marital rape. Divided into two parts, the paper begins with a consideration of the *Magaya* case.

I   INHERITANCE – THE *MAGAYA* CASE

The *Magaya* case re-opened the debate on inheritance law that many thought had been put to rest with the passing of the Administration of Estates Act of 1997.[3] The issue at hand was whom should be appointed the heir to a man who had died intestate – his eldest child from his first wife who happened to be female or his second son from his second wife, the first son having renounced his interest?[4] Initially the daughter, one Venia Magaya, had been registered as the heir to her father's estate. However, her brother challenged the appointment and the challenge was upheld by the Magistrates' Court. The Magistrates' Court agreed with his contention that, as the eldest male child of the deceased, he was entitled to be appointed heir to his deceased father's estate.

The daughter appealed to the Supreme Court where the appeal was dismissed. The reasons for this are worth exploring in some detail. In coming to its decision the Supreme Court relied on statutory and constitutional principles, a

---

*   Lecturer in Law, School of Oriental and African Studies, University of London.

1   *Magaya v Magaya* 1999 (1) ZLR 100.

2   *H v H* 1999 (2) ZLR 358.

3   See F Banda, 'Inheriting Trouble? Changing the Face of the Law of Succession in Zimbabwe' in *The International Survey of Family Law 1997*, ed A Bainham (Martinus Nijhoff Publishers, 1999) at 525.

4   The facts on which the case was founded arose prior to the promulgation of the Administration of Estates Amendment Act, which contains a formula for the division of property in the event of intestacy. The Supreme Court therefore considered the law as it stood at the time of the deceased's passing.

consideration of anthropological texts and precedents. To start, the court considered the Administration of Estates Act,[5] which provides:

> 'If any African who has contracted a marriage according to African law or custom or, who, being unmarried, is the offspring of parents married according to African law or custom, dies intestate his estate shall be administered and distributed according to the customs and usages of the tribe or people to which he belonged.'[6]

The issue that the court had to decide was whether the customs and usages of the deceased, a Shona male, recognised the right of a daughter to inherit. The court decided that preference was given to the male offspring. In a now famous passage, the Supreme Court compared the status of women under customary law to that of 'junior males'.[7] In reaching the decision that the customs and usages of the deceased pointed towards a male heir, the Supreme Court failed to consider empirical evidence from research conducted by the Women and Law in Southern Africa research trust[8] to the effect that there was no longer a fixed customary position which always privileged the inheritance rights of men. Rather, the evidence suggested that families made practical decisions about who could best take care of the needs of the family left behind and this sometimes pointed to the wife of a deceased or another female relative.[9] The Supreme Court preferred the conclusion of white male anthropologists[10] and a lawyer[11] that inheritance under customary law was done in a representative capacity, a fact also noted by WLSA, and more importantly that in customary law 'it would normally be the oldest son of his first wife who succeeds to the status of the deceased'.[12] In concluding: 'What is common and clear from the above is that under the customary law of succession of the above tribes males are preferred to females as heirs',[13] the Supreme Court seemed to take at face value a view that customary law was static and unchanging.[14] The court appeared unwilling to contemplate that the customs and usages of any group are dynamic and subject to manipulation and change. Moreover, the statement fails to take account of the fact that the preference of men as heirs is situated within a particular historical time where women were

---

5   Chapter 6:01.

6   Section 68(1).

7   *Magaya v Magaya* 1999 (1) ZLR 100, 108.

8   Dengu-Zvobgo *et al* (1994) *Inheritance in Zimbabwe: Law, Customs and Practices* (Women and Law in Southern Africa (WLSA), Harare) 556.

9   Cf J Stewart, 'Untying the Gordian Knot! *Murisa v Murisa* SC 41–92 A Little More Than a Case Note' (1992) *Legal Forum* vol 4 8,10.

10   Goldin and Gelfand (1975) *African Law and Custom in Rhodesia* (Juta, Cape Town) at p 128.

11   Bennett (1995) *Human Rights and African Customary Law Under the South African Constitution* (Juta, Cape Town) at p 126. Interestingly the court also made the point (at p 108) that two of the judges were African and were well acquainted with customary practices. The previous Chief Justice had also been African but had reached a different decision (in *Chihowa v Mangwende* 1987 ZLR 228) highlighting the fact that different interpretations can be made and thus showing that there is more than one construction of what constitutes 'customary law'.

12   Bennett (1995) at p 126.

13   *Magaya v Magaya* 1999 (1) ZLR 100, 109.

14   They did this despite the fact that Mr Ncube, one of the counsel, pointed them (see p 110) to a critique of seeing customary law as static and noted that the version of custom on which the court was relying was in itself ossified and not a true reflection of the way people lived their lives.

themselves regarded as property and where they were not in a social position to take on family responsibility. Also, although women as a group remain economically disadvantaged, they remain the primary caregivers whether in marriage or outside of it. Given that the heirship at customary law is in a representative capacity, there is little to preclude women from being effective administrators. The suggestion[15] that women marry and leave the birth family and would probably use the property for their new marital families is speculative at best and sexist at worst. Men are just as capable of misusing family resources for personal gain. In coming to its decision the Supreme Court relied heavily on the Constitution. At first the court looked at section 23, the non-discrimination provision. Section 23(1) prohibits discrimination, while section 23(2) lists the categories on the basis of which discrimination is outlawed. These include discrimination on the basis of race, tribe, place of origin, political opinions, colour or creed. It is noteworthy that sex is not included.[16] Section 23(3) of the Constitution ring fences aspects of customary law from the non-discrimination section, providing:

'23(3) Nothing contained in any law shall be held to be in contravention of subsection (1)(a) to the extent that the law in question relates to any of the following matters –

(a) adoption, marriage, divorce, burial, *devolution of property on death or other matters of personal law*;
(b) *the application of African customary law in any case involving Africans or an African*[17] and one or more persons who are not Africans where such persons have consented to the application of African customary law in that case …'

The court relied on section 23(3) to rule that the non-discrimination provision of the constitution did not include customary law, hence its discriminatory provisions were 'shielded' from the non-discrimination clause. As the deceased had been married according to African law and custom, his estate was to be dealt with using the customary law of succession (which law gave preference to the inheritance rights of male children over females). Tsanga[18] has criticised the Supreme Court for not taking account of the amendment made[19] to the

---

15 Cf C Masango, '*Chihowa v Mangwende* A Critique' (1993) *Legal Forum* vol 5 55, 56.

16 Interestingly, Chapter 3 of the Constitution which contains the declaration of rights begins with section 11 which states: 'Whereas every person in Zimbabwe is entitled to the fundamental rights and freedoms of the individual, that is to say, the right whatever his race, tribe, place of origin, political opinions, colour, creed *or sex*, but subject to the rights and freedoms of others …' (emphasis added).

Cf J May, (1987) *Changing People, Changing Laws* (Mambo Press, Gweru) at p 42. See also W Ncube, 'Defending and Protecting Gender Equality and the Family Under a Decidedly Undecided Constitution in Zimbabwe' in J Eekelaar and T Nhlapo, (1998) *The Changing Family* (Hart Publishers, Oxford) 510, 512.

17 Emphasis follows that made by the judge on page 5 of the cyclostyled judgment.

18 A Tsanga, 'Criticisms Against the *Magaya* Decision: Much Ado About Something' (1999) *Legal Forum* vol 11 94.

19 The amendment (Constitution of Zimbabwe Amendment Act No 14 of 1996) added gender to the section 23 list of grounds on the basis of which discrimination would not be permissible.

Constitution to the effect that there can be no discrimination on the basis of gender. On the effect of this amendment, the Chief Justice has noted:

> .'The fundamental importance of this provision now being included in the Constitution cannot be over-stressed. It ensures in the most significant way that, in future, discrimination against women by legislation or by official treatment is outlawed and prohibited because the Constitution of Zimbabwe, being the supreme law, prevails over all other laws.'[20]

However, it would seem that as the facts preceded the amendment it did not count.[21] The court was also of the opinion that even if Zimbabwe's adherence to international human rights instruments demanded gender equality, it did not cover customary law, which was protected by section 23(3) of the Constitution.[22] This stance appears to be in direct conflict with the principle of the supremacy of international law over domestic law. Moreover it flies in the face of the Bangalore Principles, which provide that:

> '... when interpreting statutes, including Constitutions, judges should interpret them in such a way that they are consistent with the country's obligations under human rights treaties and Conventions.'[23]

The court then moved on to consider the effect of the Legal Age of Majority Act[24] (LAMA) on the issue. LAMA had three purposes. The first was to bring the age of majority down from 21 to 18. The second was to grant majority status to all people in Zimbabwe over the age of 18. For the first time African women had legal capacity. Finally the Act was said to apply 'for the purposes of any law, including customary law ...'.[25]

The purpose of the inquiry was to ascertain whether the passing of the Act had had any impact upon the issue of rights of succession under the customary law. The court began by considering the case of *Katekwe v Muchabaiwa*,[26] which was the first Supreme Court case to consider the LAMA. The issue was whether a woman who was over the age of 18 and therefore an adult could herself claim seduction damages from her seducer or whether the cause of action lay with her father or legal guardian. The Supreme Court decided in favour of the daughter's right to sue for her own seduction, arguing that the only reason that women had been prevented from bringing actions before was because of their perpetual minority. This disability had been removed by virtue of the LAMA. Subsequent

---

20 A Gubbay, 'International and Regional Standards of Women's Rights: Their Impact and Importance on the Domestic Scene – The Position in Zimbabwe' in K Adams, and A Byrnes (eds) (1999*) Using International Human Rights Standards to Promote the Human Rights of Women and the Girl-Child at the National Level* 112, 114–115.

21 *Magaya v Magaya* 1999 (1) ZLR 100, 101n.

22 Ibid at 105.

23 As quoted by W Ncube, (1998) 509, 513n.

24 Legal Age of Majority Act (formerly Act no 15 of 1982), now section 15 General Law Amendment Act [Chapter 8:07].

25 Section 15(3) LAMA.

26 *Katekwe v Muchabaiwa* 1984 (2) ZLR 112.

cases followed this line of reasoning, not least *Chihowa v Mangwende*.[27] This was a succession case. The deceased, a businessman had two daughters but no sons. On his death, the eldest daughter was appointed heir to her father's estate. The deceased's father contested the appointment arguing that as the closest male relative, he should be appointed the deceased's heir. The Supreme Court found for the daughter on the basis that it was only the legal minority of African women that had barred them from being appointed heirs. This legal disability had been removed with the passing of the LAMA. The *Chihowa* judgment was tempered in the later case of *Vareta v Vareta*[28] where it was held that a daughter's right to be appointed heir was dependent upon the absence of a son/male heir.

In *Magaya*, the court considered the *Katekwe* decision at length and came to the conclusion that in both it and the *Chihowa* case, the Supreme Court had over reached itself and 'defined the provisions of the LAMA too widely',[29] with the result that women had been accorded rights which they had hitherto not had and more importantly, to which they were not entitled. More specifically, the court in *Magaya* was of the view that the LAMA had given women capacity to enforce substantive rights where the law in question (general or customary) already recognised that women could have those rights. Citing Bennett[30] the court noted that customary law did not recognise the right of a woman to sue for her own seduction, nor did it recognise the right of a woman to claim for her own bride-wealth,[31] both these rights being vested in her guardian. The court was particularly concerned with the effect of an overly wide interpretation of the LAMA that 'would give women additional rights which interfered with and distorted some aspects of customary law'.[32] The court went on to note that customary law was already fenced off from the non-discrimination provision in sections 23(1) and (2) of the Constitution. Presumably this meant that, if customary law did not recognise the right of women to inherit and customary law itself was not subject to a non-discrimination check, women could never inherit nor could they complain about their disability. The court further noted the Legislature's disapproval of the *Katekwe* judgment, which had led to calls for the repeal, or amendment of the LAMA, as evidence of the Chief Justice in the *Katekwe* case having overreached himself. Although it is true that the Government came under a lot of pressure to repeal the Act,[33] it is also true that the Government did not yield to this pressure and the Act remains unchanged. Indeed the Minister of Justice at the time of the

---

27 *Chihowa v Mangwende* 1987 (1) ZLR 228.

28 *Vareta v Vareta* SC 126-90.

29 *Magaya v Magaya* 1999 (1) ZLR 100, 111.

30 T Bennett, (1996) *Human Rights and African Customary Law Under the South African Constitution* (Juta, Cape Town) at p 94.

31 In *obiter dicta* in *Katekwe* the court had indicated that a woman could refuse to have bride-wealth paid for her and there would not be anything her guardian could do to demand bride-wealth for her.

32 *Magaya v Magaya* 1999 (1) ZLR 100, 112. The court also cited with approval Bennett (1997) who contends at p 93: 'With the specific aim of empowering women, conditions there for the recognition of customary law were amended to allow the LAMA to apply to persons subject to customary law'.

33 Editorial Comment *The Sunday Mail* 9 September 1984. See also *The Herald* 8 November 1984.

Katekwe case noted, 'Those who harbour the intention of enslaving women can wait until hell freezes'.[34]

Tsanga[35] has challenged the Supreme Court's assertion that the LAMA did not grant women rights under the customary law:

'The argument that customary law does not recognize some of these concepts, far from weakening the application of this provision to include customary law, in fact strengthens it. To have omitted to specifically state so would have meant perpetuating a vicious cycle of subordination, and making the law largely meaningless for the majority of women in the rural areas whose mode of life may be closer to customary than general law but who may equally wish for the protection of the general law ... By passing the Legal Age of Majority Act, the legislature took that initial, most important, step of setting the wheels of change in motion as far as the position of women under customary law is concerned.'[36]

Central to the Supreme Court's concern in the *Magaya* judgment was the sanctity of customary law and the need to preserve it. The court made several assumptions about this law, the first being that it was immutable and timeless. Hence the court noted that whilst acknowledging the need to advance gender equality:

'... great care must be taken when African customary law is under consideration. In the first instance, it must be recognized that customary law has long directed the way African people conducted their lives ... In the circumstances, it will not readily be abandoned, especially by those such as senior males who stand to lose their positions of privilege.'[37]

The court is to be commended for recognising that there are vested interests that are protected by customary law and thus customary law is neither value-neutral nor gender-neutral. However, rather than go on to challenge this privilege, the court decided that 'Matters of reform should be left to the Legislature'.[38] This contrasts sharply with the Supreme Court's previous pronouncements[39] to the effect that:

'Law in a developing country cannot afford to remain static. It must undoubtedly be stable, for otherwise reliance upon it would be rendered impossible. But at the same time if the law is to be a living force it must be dynamic and accommodating to change. It must adapt itself to fluid economic and social norms and values to altering views of justice. If it fails to respond to these needs and is not based on human necessities and experience of the actual affairs of men rather than on philosophical

---

34   *The Herald* 8 November 1984.

35   A Tsanga, (1999).

36   A Tsanga, (1999) 94, 100. This contention finds support in the parliamentary debates that preceded the passing of LAMA with the Minister of Justice noting that the intention of the Bill was to remove 'the disabilities and disadvantages' suffered by African women at customary law. See *Magaya v Magaya* SC-21–98: Parliamentary Debate in (1999) *Legal Forum* vol 11 129.

37   *Magaya v Magaya* 1999 (1) ZLR 100, 113.

38   *Magaya v Magaya* 1999 (1) ZLR 100, 112 Cf Bennett (1996) at pp 94–95 cited with approval by the Supreme Court (at p 114).

39   In *Zimnat Insurance v Chawanda* 1990 (2) ZLR 143.

notions, it will be cast off by the people because it will cease to serve any useful purpose. Therefore, the law must be constantly on the move, vigilant and flexible to current economic and social conditions.'[40]

Given that the Government had already passed a law,[41] albeit after the facts leading up the case had happened, amending the customary position to permit women to inherit, it seems odd that the Supreme Court (while acknowledging this change)[42] still stuck to its position that customary law was immutable and that women could not inherit. It seems therefore that the court was primarily concerned with the preservation of custom at the expense of women's rights. A more purposive approach may well have yielded a different result.

Given that two of the judges[43] in the *Magaya* case were on the original bench that decided *Katekwe v Muchabaiwa* and also *Chihowa v Mangwende*, it seems odd that only one – Justice McNally – saw fit to give reasons for his change of heart. In the light of the Chief Justice's past endorsement of the aforementioned decisions,[44] his silence in the *Magaya* case is puzzling. Of the *Chihowa* case the Chief Justice is on record as saying:

> 'This case constituted a major breakthrough in respect of the right of women to be treated as equal to men within society. In some quarters it caused consternation. It was suggested that there would be a drought of hitherto unknown proportions and terrible calamities would overtake Zimbabwe. But none of these disasters happened. On the contrary, we had the best rainy season for years. Obviously divine authority approved of the judgment.'[45]

Furthermore, his assertion that, in Zimbabwe, the human rights of women are respected seems now to have been at best wishful thinking and at worst misleading.[46] Linked to this issue of judicial commitment to upholding the human rights of women is the existence of many declarations following on from judicial colloquia on the use of human rights instruments in the domestic sphere.[47] The most relevant here would be the Victoria Falls Declaration[48] which provides, *inter alia*:

---

40 Gubbay ACJ in *Zimnat Insurance Co Ltd v Chawanda* 1990 (2) ZLR 143, 153.

41 Administration of Estates Amendment Act 1997.

42 The court acknowledged that, had the facts of the case arisen after the implementation of the Act on 1 November 1997, the result would have been different. *Magaya v Magaya* 1999 (1) ZLR 100, 116.

43 Justice Gubbay, now Chief-Justice and Justice McNally.

44 A Gubbay, 'International and Regional Standards of Women's Rights: Their Importance and Impact on the Domestic Scene – the Position in Zimbabwe' in K Adams, and A Byrnes (eds) (1999) *Using International Human Rights Standards to Promote the Human Rights of Women and the Girl-Child at the National Level* 112 at pp 123–127.

45 A Gubbay, (1999) 112, 126.

46 Ibid at p 128.

47 J Connors, 'General Human Rights Instruments and Their Relevance for Women' in A Byrnes, J Connors, and L Bik (eds) (1997) *Advancing the Human Rights of Women* (Commonwealth Secretariat, London) 27. C Chinkin, 'The Commonwealth and Women's Rights' (1999) *Commonwealth Law Bulletin* 96.

48 Victoria Falls Declaration of Principles for Promoting the Human Rights of Women as agreed by Senior Judges at the African Regional Judicial Colloquium Zimbabwe, 19–20 August 1994.

'The judicial officers in Commonwealth jurisdictions should be guided by the Convention on the Elimination of All Forms of Discrimination Against Women [CEDAW] when interpreting and applying the provisions of the national constitutions and laws, including the common law and customary law, when making decisions.'[49]

Mindful of the old adage, those that can do and those that can't teach, it seems right to suggest ways in which the Supreme Court could have reached a more equitable result. The most obvious would have been to continue interpreting the LAMA in the manner in which it had been in previous decisions.[50] The court could also have taken a more progressive construction of customary law. In this, the court was not without regional precedents to assist it. The Tanzanian case of *Ephraim v Pastory*[51] is an example. The case was about the right of a woman to sell clan land which she had inherited. Her nephew contested saying that whilst women could, in Haya custom, inherit land they could not alienate it having only usufructary rights to it.[52] The Tanzanian Constitution had a non-discrimination provision[53] that, like its Zimbabwean counterpart, did not include sex or gender.[54] Despite this, the court held that the ratification by Tanzania of international human rights instruments such as the African Charter on Human and Peoples' Rights,[55] the International Covenant on Civil and Political Rights[56] and CEDAW[57] should be seen as a commitment to upholding the rights of women even in the face of customary law provisions which may suggest the contrary.[58]

The court could also have made more creative use of international human rights instruments. Although she has signed the CEDAW, Zimbabwe has not yet incorporated it into domestic law as is required by the constitution.[59] However, Zimbabwe has incorporated the African Charter on Human and Peoples' Rights into domestic law. The Charter provides for enjoyment of Charter based rights without distinction on the basis of, *inter alia*, sex,[60] equality before the law and the

---

49 Ibid paragraph 11.

50 This would mean upholding the decision in *Chihowa v Mangwende* 1987 (1) ZLR 228.

51 87 ILR 106, [1990] LRC (Const) 757.

52 His contention appeared to accord with section 20 of the Laws of Inheritance of the Declaration of Customary Law (GN No 436 of 1963) which provided 'women can inherit, except for clan land, which they may receive in usufruct but may not sell. However, if there is not the male of that clan, women may inherit such land in full ownership'.

53 Article 13(5).

54 However, Article 13(1) provides for equality before the law while Article 13(4) provides 'It is forbidden for anyone to be discriminated against by anyone or any authority which is exercising its powers under any law or in carrying out any duty or function of the Authority of the State or the Party and its instruments'.

55 African Charter on Human and Peoples' Rights 1981, reprinted in (1982) 21 ILM 58.

56 International Covenant on Civil and Political Rights 1966, reprinted in (1967) 6 ILM 368.

57 Convention on the Elimination of All Forms of Discrimination Against Women 1981, reprinted in (1980) 19 ILM 33.

58 *Ephraim v Pastory* [1990] LRC 757, 763 UNIFEM (1998). Cf *Bringing Equality Home: Implementing the Convention on the Elimination of all Forms of Discrimination Against Women* (UNIFEM, New York) 21.

59 Constitution of Zimbabwe, section 111B.

60 Article 2.

right to equal protection before the law.[61] Perhaps the most important provision open to the Supreme Court to use is Article 18(3) which provides:

'The State shall ensure the elimination of every discrimination against women and also ensure the protection of the rights of the woman and child as stipulated in international declarations and conventions.'[62]

Arguably the court could have used this provision to hold that succession laws in Zimbabwe discriminated against women and more importantly contravened, not only the African Charter, but also various other international instruments to which Zimbabwe is a signatory. These would include CEDAW and the International Covenant on Civil and Political Rights.[63] CEDAW could have been invoked.[64] Article 1, the equality provision which has as its standard 'sameness with men', would have been a good starting point. The court could also have considered State obligations in Article 2 and particularly Article 2(f) which calls for the State to 'take all appropriate measures, including legislation, to modify or abolish existing laws, regulations, customs and practices which constitute discrimination against women', together with Article 5(a) which demands that States take appropriate measures 'to modify the social and cultural patterns of conduct of men and women, with a view to achieving the elimination of prejudices and customary and all other practices which are based on the idea of the inferiority or the superiority of the sexes or on stereotyped roles for men and women'.

Other courts in the region have shown creativity in making use of international human rights instruments, particularly the African Charter, in the domestic sphere – not least the Botswana courts in the celebrated *Dow* case.[65]

Although some[66] argue that the Zimbabwean Supreme Court is developing a penchant for gender-biased judgments, the court is of course not alone in reaching what many may regard as questionable decisions.[67] There are, of course, those who are of the opinion that the Supreme Court of Zimbabwe was correct in its interpretation of the letter of the law.[68]

---

61 Article 3.

62 Cf penultimate paragraph of the preamble to the African Charter.

63 International Covenant on Civil and Political Rights (1966) Articles 2, 3, 26.

64 In fact the Chief Justice has shown an awareness of the manner in which CEDAW could be used. See A Gubbay, (1999) 112, 114 *et seq.*

65 *Unity Dow v The Attorney General of Botswana* [1991] LRC 574. Cf C Chinkin, (1999) 96, 105; M Freeman, Women, Law, and Land at the Local Level: Claiming Women's Human Rights in Domestic Legal Systems' 16 (1994) *HRQ* 559, 568–570.

66 Feminist Eye 'Continuities and Change: Gender Dimensions in Some Recent Court Judgments' (2000) *Legal Forum* vol 12 44.

67 Fishbayn discusses three South African cases where women were denied rights to property for religious or cultural reasons. L Fishbayn, (1999) 'Litigating the Right to Culture: Family Law in the New South Africa' 13 IJLFP 147, 158 *et seq.* For another view see T Nhlapo, 'African Family Law Under an Undecided Constitution: the Change for Law Reform in South Africa' in J Eekelaar, and T Nhlapo (eds) (1998) *The Changing Family: International Perspectives on the Family and Family Law* 617, 626–630.

68 D Bigge, and A von Briesen, (2000) 'Conflict in the Zimbabwean Courts: Women's Rights and Indigenous Self Determination in *Magaya v Magaya*' 13 *Harvard Human Rights Journal.*

II   RAPE IN MARRIAGE AND *H v H*

After the rather unfortunate result in the *Magaya* case, *H v H* was a welcome boost to the women's movement and marked recognition of the importance of upholding the human rights of women in Zimbabwe. The facts of the case were that the husband and wife, who had a civil marriage under the Marriage Act,[69] had separated but had not yet obtained a judicial divorce. The husband had returned to the former matrimonial home, assaulted his wife and forced her to have intercourse with him against her will. The wife made an *ex parte* application asking that the husband be barred from molesting her and from coming within 200 metres of her or her home.[70] She also asked for an order of judicial separation. The judge granted the interim relief requested. He went on to request that heads of argument be filed[71] on the following points of law:

> 'Whether in law a husband who forcibly has sexual intercourse with his wife without her consent, during the subsistence of the marriage and without any order of judicial separation in force, commits a wrongful act upon his wife?'[72]

Therefore the main issue under consideration was whether the rule that a man could not rape his wife was part of the Roman-Dutch legal tradition. The judge made a thorough investigation of legal authorities. These appeared to be contradictory.[73] Until finally changed by the House of Lords in 1991,[74] the English common law position had been held to be that a married man could not rape his wife,[75] a wife's consent being part of the contract of marriage which consent could only be revoked by divorce, or if an order for judicial separation had been granted.[76]

The judge considered South African case law on the matter and relied heavily on the case of *S v Ncanywa (1)*[77] in which the trial judge had made an exhaustive study of the position of Roman-Dutch law including decided cases. In this case, which was reversed on appeal,[78] Heath J opined: 'The fiction of consent and even irrevocable consent by a wife to intercourse with her husband has no foundation in law and offends against the *boni mores* of any civilized society'.[79] Taking his cue

---

69   Marriage Act Chapter 5:11.

70   Significantly the wife had obtained several peace orders that the Police had failed to enforce. *H v H* 1999 (2) ZLR 358.

71   The Attorney General's office was invited to present the legal argument from the state's perspective which it did. Although the husband (respondent) filed an affidavit conceding that a wife should not be forced to have intercourse against her will, he queried the facts as presented by the wife but did not go on to produce the heads of argument requested. Heads of argument were produced for the wife. *H v H* 1999 (2) ZLR 358, 361.

72   *H v H* 1999 (2) ZLR 358, 361.

73   Ibid 362 *et seq.*

74   *R v R* [1991] 4 All ER 481, [1992] 1 AC 599.

75   1 Hale PC 629.

76   *R v O'Brien* [1974] 3 All ER 663, *R v Clarke* [1949] 2 All ER 448, *R v Roberts* [1986] Crim LR 188.

77   *S v Ncanywa (1)* 1992 (1) SA 182.

78   *S v Ncanywa (2)* 1993 (2) SA 567. Cited in *H v H* 1999 (2) ZLR 359, 363–367.

79   *S v Ncanywa (1)* 1992 (1) SA 182, 211 as cited in *H v H* 1999 (2) ZLR 359, 363.

from Heath J in the first *Ncanywa* case, Justice Bartlett ruled that the marital rape exemption had no place in Zimbabwean law:

'The marital rape exemption, to my mind belongs to the past and not to the present or future of Roman-Dutch law. It would be a sad indictment of Zimbabwe's legal system, if, as it moves into the 21st century, it were to drag with it so outdated a concept as the marital rape exemption.'[80]

CRITIQUE

The first point that must be noted is the willingness of the judge to break away from 'tradition', however interpreted and constructed. He showed himself willing to see law as dynamic and as having to change and adapt to the needs of the people rather than vice versa as was the case in the *Magaya* case.

The second point worth noting was the explicit acknowledgement by the judge of upholding the principle of gender equality. The judge rightly notes that the maintenance of the marital rape exemption would be in 'stark contrast' to the enhancement of gender equality, which according to him has been the 'hallmark of the development of Zimbabwean law since independence'.[81] Although Bartlett J says that he will not consider whether or not the marital rape exemption is in contravention of any of Zimbabwe's international obligations, he does pick up the fact that, at the very least, the marital rape exemption is a violation of the prohibition against degrading treatment, a point made by many before him.[82] This last point is worth exploring further. The issue of sexual violence in the private sphere has been explicitly considered by the Committee which oversees the Convention on the Elimination of All Forms of Discrimination Against Women.[83] Moreover in 1993, the United Nations adopted the General Assembly Declaration on the Elimination of All Forms of Discrimination Against Women,[84] which includes marital rape[85] in its construction of violence against women.

That Justice Bartlett has managed to do by way of judicial enterprise what many other jurisdictions have failed to do is a testament to judicial activism at its best. The only criticism that one can make of the judgment is of the *obiter dicta* urging that rape allegations be treated with caution because 'in some instances wives may convert their grievances against their husbands into allegations of rape'.[86] Given the long and difficult path trodden through medical and legal processes by most rape victims, it is unlikely that wives will be keen to begin malicious prosecutions against their husbands. Indeed the very intimacy and

---

80 *H v H* 1999 (2) ZLR 359, 368.

81 Ibid at p 369.

82 Ibid at p 372 Cf C Mackinnon, (1993) 'On Torture: A Feminist Perspective' in Mahoney and Mahoney (eds) *Human Rights in the 21ˢᵗ Century* 21. See also F Banda, (1999) 'Non Consensual Sex in Marriage: The African Perspective' paper written for CHANGE project on Non Consensual Sex in Marriage, CHANGE, London.

83 Committee on the Elimination of All Forms of Discrimination Against Women, (1992) General Recommendation no 19: Violence against Women, UN Doc. A/47/38.

84 Declaration on the Elimination of Violence Against Women GA Res 48/104, UN Doc A/48/629.

85 Ibid Article 2(a).

86 *H v H* 1999 (2) ZLR 358, 373–4.

privacy of the marital relationship, the impact of 'culture' and social mores and, in some instances, the existence of children will militate against reporting rape in marriage rather than increasing its likelihood.

This paper has considered two important cases, one negating the rights of women and the other advancing them. The decisions show that law can be used as a positive agent for change or as a means to retain and legitimate the continuing subordination of women in the name of custom, culture and continuity.